Research Advances in Cloud Computing

Sanjay Chaudhary · Gaurav Somani
Rajkumar Buyya
Editors

Research Advances in Cloud Computing

 Springer

Editors
Sanjay Chaudhary
School of Engineering and Applied Science
Ahmedabad University
Ahmedabad, Gujarat
India

Rajkumar Buyya
School of Computing and Information
  Systems
The University of Melbourne
Melbourne, VIC
Australia

Gaurav Somani
Department of Computer Science and
  Engineering
Central University of Rajasthan
Ajmer, Rajasthan
India

ISBN 978-981-13-5296-6   ISBN 978-981-10-5026-8   (eBook)
DOI 10.1007/978-981-10-5026-8

Printed on acid-free paper

This Springer imprint is published by Springer Nature
The registered company is Springer Nature Singapore Pte Ltd.
The registered company address is: 152 Beach Road, #21-01/04 Gateway East, Singapore 189721, Singapore

To my wife (Sunita), Son (Mandar) and Daughter (Anuradha)

—Sanjay Chaudhary

To my wife (Priyanka), Daughter (Anaya), and Nephew (Aradhya)

—Gaurav Somani

To my wife (Smrithi) and Daughters (Soumya and Radha)

—Rajkumar Buyya

Foreword

Cloud computing is still growing by leaps and bounds and is likely to be used in all major server centers in future. This will be driven by both the low-cost and rich features of clouds. It is hard to see how traditional institutional data centers can compete except for specialized services such as supercomputing or real-time response to nearby components of the Internet of things. Progress in clouds comes from both the commercial and research communities and their collaboration. This timely book addresses many critical open topics that can be divided into three areas:

1. Programming model, infrastructure, and runtime
2. Resource management
3. Security.

The programming model, infrastructure, and runtime chapters include a futuristic chapter on serverless computing—one of the most promising cloud topics covering micro-services, event-based execution, and the FaaS function as a service model. Other chapters cover high availability, simulation, classification, migration, and virtual network performance. High-performance computing in big data and streaming issues are considered.

The resource management chapters cover resource scheduling including VM placement and use of gaming techniques for pricing and allocation. The important broad topics of auto-scaling and energy management are covered thoroughly.

The security chapters cover broad topics including interoperability, access control, use of trusted computers, and the important special issues raised by containers. A major application focus is health care. Forensic analysis of intrusion events is a fascinating topic.

The value of the book can be measured by the interest of the topics and the quality of the chapter authors. However, a key measure is the credentials of the editors who have put together this magnificent collection. The expertise of the editors covers the three areas as seen in their brief research descriptions below.

Sanjay Chaudhary has made significant contributions in the cloud resource management and allocation methods. Sanjay brings a vast research experience in working on various issues related to cloud infrastructure, performance, SaaS application development, application migration, and workflow scheduling in cloud computing environments. Sanjay also brings a rich experience of working with grid computing systems which have helped him in contributing to various resource management aspects of cloud computing.

Gaurav Somani has worked on multiple aspects of cloud computing domain such as resource management, metering, verification and accounting, and a number of security issues. Gaurav has made a number of significant contributions in the area of attack mitigation and recovery in cloud computing. VM backup, secure deduplication, performance isolation, and DDoS attack prevention are few important research problems he has addressed in the recent past.

Rajkumar Buyya has a very rich experience of developing production-level systems related to cloud computing and grid computing systems. He has made significant contributions in terms of highly cited papers related to the software systems related to overall management of cloud resources. Raj and his group have developed two popular software packages, Aneka and CloudSim, which are for cloud computing research and production usages.

I commend the book "Research Advances in Cloud Computing" to all computing professionals. Read and Enjoy!

Bloomington, USA   Geoffrey Fox
May 2017   Chair, Intelligent Systems Engineering
                                                  School of Informatics and Computing
                                                  Distinguished Professor of Computing
                                              Engineering, and Physics, Director of the
                                            Digital Science Center, Indiana University

Preface

Cloud computing is a novel computing paradigm which has changed the way enterprise or Internet computing is performed. Today, for almost all the sectors in the world, cloud computing is synonym to on-demand provisioning and delivery of IT services in a pay-as-you-go model. The success story of cloud computing as a technology is credited to the long-term efforts of computing research community across the globe. Software as a Service (SaaS), Platform as a Service (PaaS), and Infrastructure as a Service (IaaS) are the three major cloud product sectors. Each one of these product sectors has their effects and reaches to various industries. If forecasts are to be believed, then more than two-third of all the enterprises across the globe will be entirely run in cloud by 2026. These enthusiastic figures have led to huge funding for research and development in cloud computing and related technologies. University researchers, research labs in industry, and scholars across the globe have recreated the whole computing world into a new cloud enabled world. This has been only possible by coordinated efforts into this direction. Today, almost every university across the globe has cloud computing and its related technologies included in their computer science curriculum. Additionally, there are extensive efforts on innovation and technology creation in the direction of cloud computing. These efforts are much visible in the reputed cloud computing research platforms like international conferences and journals.

We feel that there is a significant need to systematically present quality research findings of recent advances in cloud computing for the benefit of community of researchers, educators, practitioners, and industries. Although there are large numbers of journals and conferences available, there is a lack of comprehensive and in-depth tutored analysis on various new developments in the field of cloud computing. This book on "Research Advances in Cloud Computing" discusses various new trends, designs, implementations, outcomes, and directions in the various areas of cloud computing. This book has been organized into three sections:

1. Programming model, infrastructure, and runtime
2. Resource Management
3. Security.

The first chapter on "Serverless Computing: Current Trends and Open Problems" covers various serverless platforms, APIs, their key characteristics, technical challenges, and related open problems. Recently, enterprise application architectures are shifting to containers and micro-services, and it provides enough reasons for serverless computing. The chapter provides detailed requirements of different programming models, platforms, and the need of significant research and development efforts to make it matured enough for widespread adoption.

Cloud providers face the important challenge regarding resource management and aim to provide services with high availability relying on finite computational resources and limited physical infrastructure. Their key challenge is to manage resources in an optimal way and to estimate how physical and logical failures can impact on users' perception. The second chapter on "Highly Available Clouds: System Modeling, Evaluations and Open Challenges", presents literature survey on high availability of cloud and mentions the main approaches for it. It explores computational modeling theories to represent a cloud infrastructure focusing on how to estimate and model cloud availability.

The third chapter on "Big Data Analytics in Cloud—A Streaming Approach" discusses streaming approach for data analytics in cloud. Big data and cloud have become twin words—used sometimes interchangeably. Interpretation of big data brings in idea of mining and analytics. There is significant literature on cloud that discusses infrastructure and architecture but a very little literature for algorithms required for mining and analytics. This chapter focuses on online algorithms that can be used for distributed, unstructured data for learning and analytics over Cloud. It also discusses their time complexity, presents architecture for deploying them over cloud, and concludes with presenting relevant open research directions.

Cloud data centers must be capable to offer scalable software services, which require an infrastructure with a significant amount of resources. Such resources are managed by specific software to ensure service-level agreements based on one or more performance metrics. Within such infrastructure, approaches to meet non-functional requirements can be split into various artifacts, distributed across different operational layers, which operate together with the aim of reaching a specific target. Existing studies classify such approaches using different terms, which usually are used with conflicting meanings by different people. Therefore, it is necessary a common nomenclature defining different artifacts, so they can be organized in a more scientific way. The fourth chapter on "A Terminology to Classify Artifacts for Cloud Infrastructure" proposes a comprehensive bottom-up classification to identify and classify approaches for system artifacts at the infrastructure level, and organize existing literature using the proposed classification.

The fifth chapter focuses on "Virtual Networking with Azure for Hybrid Cloud Computing in Aneka". It provides a discussion on the need of inter-cloud communication in the emerging hybrid, public, or federated clouds. Later, they provide a case of Azure Virtual Private Network (VPN) services to establish such inter-cloud connections using an overlay network for hybrid clouds in Aneka platform. It also presents a functional evaluation of the proposed approach with the help of experiments.

The sixth chapter on "Building Efficient HPC Cloud with SR-IOV Enabled InfiniBand: The MVAPICH2 Approach" presents a detailed case of high-performance computing in cloud. It discusses the single-root I/O virtualization performance in the InfiniBand interconnects and provides locality aware communication designs to optimize the overall performance using MVAPICH2 library. It also proposed advanced designs to support the HPC in cloud computing environments along with open research problems.

To facilitate effective resource allocation, cloud providers should allocate resources ahead of service demands, in a way that does not waste resources. The calculation of optimal allocations requires integer programming, which is computationally difficult to accomplish. The seventh chapter on "Resource Procurement, Allocation, Metering, and Pricing in Cloud Computing" proposes an approach using the uncertainty principle of game theory which achieves close to optimal results. An approach for time-varying tariffs for cloud services, considering varying load levels on the cloud provider's infrastructure, and the time-varying pricing of electricity from a smart grid, is also proposed. The chapter involves the creation of a per-instance power consumption model for VMs on a cloud and a power-aware cloud metering architecture.

Auto-scaling is an important feature of cloud computing which allows flexible just-in-time allocation and release of computational resources in response to dynamic and often unpredictable workloads. The eighth chapter on "Dynamic Selection of Virtual Machines for Application Servers in Cloud Environments" covers the importance of auto-scaling for web applications whose workload is time dependent and prone to flash crowds. Reactive auto-scaling policies are successful, but here the authors are investigating the issue related to which VM type is the most suitable for the specific application and have proposed an approach for dynamic VM-type selection. It uses a combination of online machine learning techniques, works in real time, and adapts to changes in the users' workload patterns, application changes as well as middleware upgrades and reconfigurations. The chapter has described a prototype, which is tested with the CloudStone benchmark deployed on AWS EC2 and it has achieved encouraging results.

One of the current concerns of systems designers is related to the growth of power consumption in cloud computing systems. The techniques to address this problem range from decisions on locations for data centers to techniques that enable efficient resource management. Resource allocation, as a process of resource management, distributes the workload throughout the data center in an efficient manner, minimizing the power consumption and maximizing the system performance. The nineth chapter on "Improving the Energy Efficiency in Cloud Computing Data Centres Through Resource Allocation Techniques" presents an overview of the resource management and resource allocation techniques, which contribute to the reduction of power consumption without compromising the cloud user and provider constraints. It also covers two practical cases to illustrate the theoretical concepts of resource allocation as well as have discussed the open challenges that resource management will face in the coming years.

The tenth chapter on "Recent Developments in Resource Management in Cloud Computing and Large Computing Clusters" provides a comprehensive and detailed overview of overall cloud computing resource allocation framework with a focus on various resource scheduling algorithms. This chapter also provides a definitive direction toward cloud scheduling solutions, architectures, and fairness algorithms.

The eleventh chapter on "Resource Allocation for Cloud Infrastructures: Taxonomies and Research Challenges" provides a classification of VM placements solutions in the form of taxonomies. These taxonomies are prepared for conceptualization of VM placement problem as provider–broker setting, and framing it as an optimization problem. Authors also comment on the formation of cloud markets to provide a basis for multi-objective VM placement algorithms.

The twelth chapter on "Many-Objective Optimization for Virtual Machine Placement in Cloud Computing" presents a comprehensive discussion on virtual machine placement problem and extends the discussion by proposing many objective VM placement algorithms for initial VM placement and reconfiguration. It also gives an overview of open research problems at the end of the chapter to provide the scope of future work toward fully dynamic multi-objective VM placement problems.

The thirteenth chapter on "Performance Modeling and Optimization of Live Migration of Virtual Machines in Cloud Infrastructure" is based on improvement of the pre-copy algorithm for live migration system. The improved pre-copy algorithm is developed by three models: (i) compression model, (ii) prediction model, and (iii) performance model. Each model is used to evaluate downtime and total migration time of different workloads. The first model performs migration of different sizes of VM with three workloads: (i) idle system, (ii) kernel compile, and (iii) static web server. Prediction model works with adaptive dirty rate and adaptive data rate to evaluate complex workloads running in a VM. The performance model is used to find dirty pages using dirty page rate model. It is observed that both prediction model and performance model work efficiently than the existing framework of Xen. It concludes that three proposed models are able to improve pre-copy and the results are tested for the same.

Security and privacy being a very active and hot topic of research and discussion these days, we have five chapters dedicated to the relevant issues associated with cloud computing security. Isolated containers are rapidly becoming a great alternative to traditional virtualized environments. The fourteenth chapter on "Analysis of Security in Modern Container Platforms" makes two important contributions. First, it provides a detailed analysis of current security arrangements in the container platforms. Second, it offers an experimental analysis of containers by providing details on common threat and Vulnerabilities Exposures (CVEs) exploits. This twofold analysis helps in comparing the CVE exploits to be able to compare with the state-of-the-art security requirements by the popular literature.

The fifteenth chapter on "Identifying Evidence for Cloud Forensic Analysis" discusses forensic analysis and post-attack evidence collection on the cloud computing infrastructures. Authors describe the evidence collection activity at three different places which are at Intrusion Detection System (IDS), cloud provider API calls, and VM system calls. It shows a step-by-step attack scenario reconstruction using the proposed prolog-based tool following the proposed evidence collection approach. Forensic analysis of cloud computing infrastructures is still in its infancy and authors provide directions for data collection and forensically capable clouds.

The sixteenth chapter on "An Access Control Framework for Secure and Interoperable Cloud Computing Applied to the Healthcare Domain" addresses various health record security issues and provides an FSICC framework (Framework for Secure and Interoperable Cloud Computing) that provides a mechanism for multiple sources to register cloud, programming, and web services and security requirements for use by applications. Future research directions are provided at the end of this chapter to help the enthusiastic readers about the open areas.

The seventeenth chapter on "Security and Privacy Issues in Outsourced Personal Health Record" provides a detailed survey on existing personal health record management systems (PHRMSs) considering the security and privacy features provided by each one of them. This state-of-the-art survey is extended by giving pointers to multiple open research problems in the healthcare domain.

The last in the series of five chapters dedicated to cloud security is a chapter on "Applications of Trusted Computing in Cloud Context". Trusted computing paradigm has been considered as one of the important security research milestones to leverage various security solutions. This chapter investigates applications of trusted computing in cloud computing areas where security threats exist, namely in live virtual machine migration.

Ahmedabad, India   Sanjay Chaudhary
Ajmer, India   Gaurav Somani
Melbourne, Australia   Rajkumar Buyya

Acknowledgements

We are thankful to

- Contributing authors
- Springer
- Suvira Srivastava
- Ahmedabad University
- Australian Research Council for Future Fellowship
- Prof. M.S. Gaur, MNIT, India
- Central University of Rajasthan
- Antony Raj J.
- Family members

Contents

About the Editors

Dr. Sanjay Chaudhary is a Professor and Associate Dean of the School of Engineering and Applied Science, Ahmedabad University, Ahmedabad, India. His research areas are data analytics, cloud computing, and ICT applications in agriculture and rural development. He has authored four books, six book chapters, and published more than hundred research papers and ten literary articles in international conferences, workshops, and journals. He has served on the program committees of leading international conferences and workshops, and he is also a member of the review committees of leading journals. He holds a doctorate degree in computer science from Gujarat Vidyapeeth, Ahmedabad, India. Earlier, he worked as a Professor and Dean (Academics Programs) at DA-IICT. He has also worked on various large-scale software development projects for the corporate sector, co-operative sector, and government organizations. He is actively involved in various consultancy and enterprise application development projects.

Gaurav Somani is an Assistant Professor at the Department of Computer Science and Engineering at the Central University of Rajasthan (Ajmer), India. He has submitted his PhD in Computer Science and Engineering from MNIT, Jaipur, India. His research interests include distributed systems, network security, cloud computing, and open-source technologies. He has published number of papers in various conferences and journals of international repute and is a reviewer of many top journals. Some of his top papers are published in highly reputed journals such as Computer Networks, Annals of Telecommunications, Computer Communications, IEEE Cloud Computing, Computers and Electrical Engineering, FGCS, and IEEE Cloud. He has written a book on "Scheduling and Isolation in Virtualization" which is published by VDM Verlag Dr. Muller Publishers, Germany. This book is used as a text/reference book in some graduate-level programs across the globe. He is also a part of multiple international conferences across the globe where he has played a role of TPC member, session chair, and invited speaker. He was the keynote and the tutorial chair at the ICISS 2016. He is a member of IEEE and ACM.

Dr. Rajkumar Buyya is a Redmond Barry Distinguished Professor of Computer Science and Software Engineering and Director of the Cloud Computing and Distributed Systems (CLOUDS) Laboratory at the University of Melbourne, Australia. He is also serving as the founding CEO of Manjrasoft, a spin-off company of the university, commercializing its innovations in cloud computing. He served as Future Fellow of the Australian Research Council during 2012–2016. He has authored over 525 publications and seven text books including "Mastering Cloud Computing" published by McGraw Hill, China Machine Press, and Morgan Kaufmann for Indian, Chinese, and international markets, respectively. He has also edited several books including "Cloud Computing: Principles and Paradigms" (Wiley Press, USA, Feb 2011). He is one of the highly cited authors in computer science and software engineering worldwide (h-index=112, g-index=245, 63,900+ citations). Microsoft Academic Search Index ranked Dr. Buyya as #1 author in the world (2005–2016) for both field rating and citations evaluations in the area of Distributed and Parallel Computing. Recently, Dr. Buyya is recognized as "2016 Web of Science Highly Cited Researcher" by Thomson Reuters.

Serverless Computing: Current Trends and Open Problems

**Ioana Baldini, Paul Castro, Kerry Chang, Perry Cheng,
Stephen Fink, Vatche Ishakian, Nick Mitchell, Vinod Muthusamy,
Rodric Rabbah, Aleksander Slominski and Philippe Suter**

Abstract Serverless computing has emerged as a new compelling paradigm for the deployment of applications and services. It represents an evolution of cloud programming models, abstractions, and platforms, and is a testament to the maturity and wide adoption of cloud technologies. In this chapter, we survey existing serverless platforms from industry, academia, and open-source projects, identify key characteristics and use cases, and describe technical challenges and open problems.

I. Baldini · P. Castro (✉) · K. Chang · P. Cheng · S. Fink · N. Mitchell ·
V. Muthusamy · R. Rabbah · A. Slominski
IBM Research, New York, USA
e-mail: ioana@us.ibm.com

P. Castro
e-mail: castrop@us.ibm.com

K. Chang
e-mail: Kerry.Chang@ibm.com

P. Cheng
e-mail: perry@us.ibm.com

S. Fink
e-mail: sjfink@us.ibm.com

N. Mitchell
e-mail: nickm@us.ibm.com

V. Muthusamy (✉)
e-mail: vmuthus@us.ibm.com

R. Rabbah
e-mail: rabbah@us.ibm.com

A. Slominski (✉)
e-mail: aslom@us.ibm.com

V. Ishakian (✉)
Bentley University, Waltham, USA
e-mail: vishakian@bentley.edu

P. Suter
Two Sigma, New York, USA

© Springer Nature Singapore Pte Ltd. 2017
S. Chaudhary et al. (eds.), *Research Advances in Cloud Computing*,
DOI 10.1007/978-981-10-5026-8_1

1

1 Introduction

Serverless computing (or simply serverless) is emerging as a new and compelling paradigm for the deployment of cloud applications, largely due to the recent shift of enterprise application architectures to containers and microservices [21]. Figure 1 shows the increasing popularity of the "serverless" search term over the last 5 years as reported by Google Trends. This is an indication of the increasing attention that serverless computing has garnered in industry trade shows, meetups, blogs, and the development community. By contrast, the attention of the academic community has been limited.

From the perspective of an Infrastructure-as-a-Service (IaaS) customer, this paradigm shift presents both an opportunity and a risk. On the one hand, it provides developers with a simplified programming model for creating cloud applications that abstracts away most, if not all, operational concerns; it lowers the cost of deploying cloud code by charging for execution time rather than resource allocation; and it is a platform for rapidly deploying small pieces of cloud-native code that responds to events, for instance, to coordinate microservice compositions that would otherwise run on the client or on dedicated middleware. On the other hand, deploying such applications in a serverless platform is challenging and requires relinquishing to the platform design decisions that concern, among other things, quality-of-service (QoS) monitoring, scaling, and fault tolerance properties.

From the perspective of a cloud provider, serverless computing provides an additional opportunity to control the entire development stack, reduce operational costs by efficient optimization and management of cloud resources, offer a platform that encourages the use of additional services in their ecosystem, and lower the effort required to author and manage cloud-scale applications.

Serverless computing is a term coined by industry to describe a programming model and architecture where small code snippets are executed in the cloud without any control over the resources on which the code runs. It is by no means an indication that there are no servers, simply that the developer should leave most operational concerns such as resource provisioning, monitoring, maintenance, scalability, and fault tolerance to the cloud provider.

Interest over time

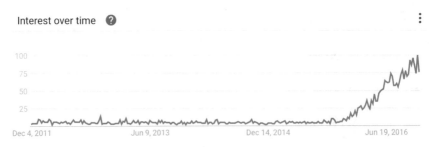

Fig. 1 Popularity of the term "serverless" as reported by Google Trends

The astute reader may ask how this differs from the Platform-as-a-Service (PaaS) model, which also abstracts away the management of servers. A serverless model provides a "stripped down" programming model based on stateless functions. Similar to Paas, developers can write arbitrary code and are not limited to using a prepackaged application. The version of serverless that explicitly uses functions as the deployment unit is also called Function-as-a-Service (FaaS).

Serverless platforms promise new capabilities that make writing scalable microservices easier and cost-effective, positioning themselves as the next step in the evolution of cloud computing architectures. Most of the prominent cloud computing providers including Amazon [1], IBM [24], Microsoft [3], and Google [10] have recently released serverless computing capabilities. There are also several open-source efforts including the OpenLambda project [23].

Serverless computing is in its infancy and the research community has produced only a few citable publications at this time. OpenLambda [23] proposes a reference architecture for serverless platforms and describes challenges in this space (see Sect. 3.1.3) and we have previously published two of our use cases [5, 29] (see Sect. 5.1). There are also several books for practitioners that target developers interested in building applications using serverless platforms [12, 27].

1.1 Defining Serverless

Succinctly defining the term serverless can be difficult as the definition will overlap with other terms such as PaaS and Software-as-a-Service (SaaS). One way to explain serverless is to consider the varying levels of developer control over the cloud infrastructure, as illustrated in Fig. 2. The Infrastructure-as-a-Service (IaaS) model is where the developer has the most control over both the application code and operating infrastructure in the cloud. Here, the developer is responsible for provisioning the hardware or virtual machines, and can customize every aspect of how an application gets deployed and executed. On the opposite extreme are the PaaS and SaaS models, where the developer is unaware of any infrastructure, and consequently no longer has control over the infrastructure. Instead, the developer has

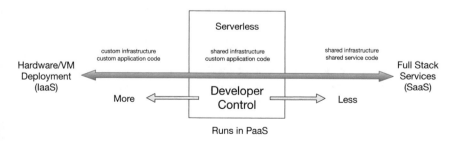

Fig. 2 Developer control and serverless computing

access to prepackaged components or full applications. The developer is allowed to host code here, though that code may be tightly coupled to the platform.

For this chapter, we will focus on the space in the middle of Fig. 2. Here, the developer has control over the code they deploy into the cloud, though that code has to be written in the form of stateless functions. (The reason for this will be explained in Sect. 3.) The developer does not worry about the operational aspects of deployment and maintenance of that code and expects it to be fault-tolerant and auto-scaling. In particular, the code may be scaled to zero where no servers are actually running when the user's function is not used, and there is no cost to the user. This is in contrast to PaaS solutions where the user is often charged even during idle periods.

There are numerous serverless platforms that fall into the above definition. In this chapter, we present the architecture and other relevant features of serverless computing, such as the programming model. We also identify the types of application workloads that are suitable to run on serverless computing platforms. We then conclude with open research problems and future research challenges. Many of these challenges are a pressing need in industry and could benefit from contributions from academia.

2   Evolution

Serverless computing was popularized by Amazon in the re:Invent 2014 session "Getting Started with AWS Lambda" [2]. Other vendors followed in 2016 with the introduction of Google Cloud Functions [10], Microsoft Azure Functions [3], and IBM OpenWhisk [24]. However, the serverless approach to computing is not completely new. It has emerged following recent advancements and adoption of virtual machine (VM) and then container technologies. Each step up the abstraction layers led to more lightweight units of computation in terms of resource consumption, cost, and speed of development and deployment.

Among existing approaches, Mobile Backend as-a-Service (MBaaS) bears a close resemblance to serverless computing. Some of those services even provided "cloud functions", that is, the ability to run some code server-side on behalf of a mobile app without the need to manage the servers. An example of such a service is Facebook's Parse Cloud Code [25]. Such code, however, was typically limited to mobile use cases.

Software-as-a-Service (SaaS) may support the server-side execution of user provided functions but they are executing in the context of an application and hence limited to the application domain. Some SaaS vendors allow the integration of arbitrary code hosted somewhere else and invoked via an API call. For example, this is approach is used by the Google Apps Marketplace in Google Apps for Work [14].

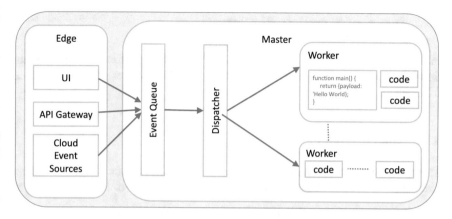

Fig. 3 Serverless platform architecture

3 Architecture

There are a lot of misconceptions surrounding serverless starting with the name. Servers are still needed, but developers need not concern themselves with managing those servers. Decisions such as the number of servers and their capacity are taken care of by the serverless platform, with server capacity automatically provisioned as needed by the workload. This provides an abstraction where computation (in the form of a stateless function) is disconnected from where it is going to run.

The core capability of a serverless platform is that of an event processing system, as depicted in Fig. 3. The service must manage a set of user-defined functions, take an event sent over HTTP or received from an event source, determine which function(s) to which to dispatch the event, find an existing instance of the function or create a new instance, send the event to the function instance, wait for a response, gather execution logs, make the response available to the user, and stop the function when it is no longer needed.

The challenge is to implement such functionality while considering metrics such as cost, scalability, and fault tolerance. The platform must quickly and efficiently start a function and process its input. The platform also needs to queue events, and based on the state of the queues and arrival rate of events, schedule the execution of functions, and manage stopping and deallocating resources for idle function instances. In addition, the platform needs to carefully consider how to scale and manage failures in a cloud environment.

3.1 Survey of Serverless Platforms

In this section, we will compare a number of serverless platform. We first list the dimensions which will be used to characterize the architectures of these platforms, followed by a brief description of each platform.

3.1.1 Characteristics

There are a number of characteristics that help distinguish the various serverless platforms. Developers should be aware of these properties when choosing a platform.

- *Cost*: Typically, the usage is metered and users pay only for the time and resources used when serverless functions are running. This ability to scale to zero instances is one of the key differentiators of a serverless platform. The resources that are metered, such as memory or CPU, and the pricing model, such as off-peak discounts, vary among providers.
- *Performance and limits*: There are a variety of limits set on the runtime resource requirements of serverless code, including the number of concurrent requests, and the maximum memory and CPU resources available to a function invocation. Some limits may be increased when users' needs grow, such as the concurrent request threshold, while others are inherent to the platforms, such as the maximum memory size.
- *Programming languages*: Serverless services support a wide variety of programming languages including Javascript, Java, Python, Go, C#, and Swift. Most platforms support more than one programming language. Some of the platforms also support extensibility mechanisms for code written in any language as long as it is packaged in a Docker image that supports a well-defined API.
- *Programming model*: Currently, serverless platforms typically execute a single `main` function that takes a dictionary (such as a JSON object) as input and produces a dictionary as output.
- *Composability*: The platforms generally offer some way to invoke one serverless function from another, but some platforms provide higher level mechanisms for composing these functions and may make it easier to construct more complex serverless apps.
- *Deployment*: Platforms strive to make deployment as simple as possible. Typically, developers just need to provide a file with the function source code. Beyond that there are many options where code can be packaged as an archive with multiple files inside or as a Docker image with binary code. As well, facilities to version or group functions are useful but rare.
- *Security and accounting*: Serverless platforms are multi-tenant and must isolate the execution of functions between users and provide detailed accounting so users understand how much they need to pay.
- *Monitoring and debugging*: Every platform supports basic debugging by using print statements that are recorded in the execution logs. Additional capabilities may

be provided to help developers find bottlenecks, trace errors, and better understand the circumstances of function execution.

3.1.2 Commercial Platforms

Amazon's AWS Lambda [1] was the first serverless platform and it defined several key dimensions including cost, programming model, deployment, resource limits, security, and monitoring. Supported languages include Node.js, Java, Python, and C#. Initial versions had limited composability but this has been addressed recently. The platform takes advantage of a large AWS ecosystem of services and makes it easy to use Lambda functions as event handlers and to provide glue code when composing services.

Currently available as an Alpha release, Google Cloud Functions [10] provides basic FaaS functionality to run serverless functions written in Node.js in response to HTTP calls or events from some Google Cloud services. The functionality is currently limited but expected to grow in future versions.

Microsoft Azure Functions [3] provides HTTP webhooks and integration with Azure services to run user provided functions. The platform supports C#, F#, Node.js, Python, PHP, bash, or any executable. The runtime code is open-source and available on GitHub under an MIT License. To ease debugging, the Azure Functions CLI provides a local development experience for creating, developing, testing, running, and debugging Azure Functions.

IBM OpenWhisk [24] provides event-based serverless programming with the ability to chain serverless functions to create composite functions. It supports Node.js, Java, Swift, Python, as well as arbitrary binaries embedded in a Docker container. OpenWhisk is available on GitHub under an Apache open-source license. The main architectural components of the OpenWhisk platform are shown in Fig. 4. Compared to the generic architectural diagram in Fig. 3, we can see there are additional components handling important requirements such as security, logging, and monitoring.

3.1.3 New and Upcoming Serverless Platforms

There are several serverless projects ranging from open-source projects to vendors that find serverless a natural fit for their business.

OpenLambda [23] is an open-source serverless computing platform. The source code is available in GitHub under an Apache License. The OpenLambda paper [15] outlines a number of challenges around performance such as supporting faster function startup time for heterogeneous language runtimes and across a load balanced pool of servers, deployment of large amounts of code, supporting stateful interactions (such as HTTP sessions) on top of stateless functions, using serverless functions with databases and data aggregators, legacy decomposition, and cost debugging. We have identified similar challenges in Sect. 6.

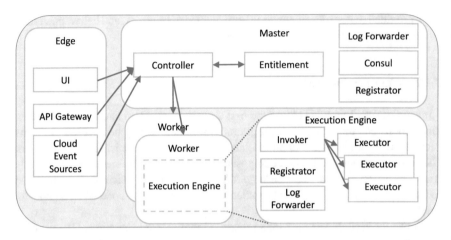

Fig. 4 IBM openWhisk architecture

Some serverless systems are created by companies that see the need for serverless computing in the environments they operate. For example, Galactic Fog [13] added serverless computing to their Gestalt Framework running on top of Mesos D/C. The source code is available under an Apache 2 license. Auth0 has created webtasks [7] that execute serverless functions to support webhook endpoints used in complex security scenarios. This code is also available as open source. Iron.io had a serverless support for tasks since 2012 [28]. Recently, they announced Project Kratos [16] that allows developers to convert AWS Lambda functions into Docker images, and is available under an Apache 2 license. Additionally, they are working with Cloud Foundry to bring multi-cloud serverless support to Cloud Foundry users [9]. LeverOS is an open-source project that uses an RPC model to communicate between services. Computing resources in LeverOS can be tagged, so repeated function invocations can be targeted to a specific container to optimize runtime performance, such as taking advantage of warm caches in a container [20].

3.2 Benefits and Drawbacks

Compared to IaaS platforms, serverless architectures offer different tradeoffs in terms of control, cost, and flexibility. In particular, they force application developers to carefully think about the cost of their code when modularizing their applications, rather than latency, scalability, and elasticity, which is where significant development effort has traditionally been spent.

The serverless paradigm has advantages for both consumers and providers. From the consumer perspective, a cloud developer no longer needs to provision and manage servers, VMs, or containers as the basic computational building block for offering distributed services. Instead the focus is on the business logic, by defining a set of functions whose composition enables the desired application behavior. The stateless programming model gives the provider more control over the software stack, allowing them to, among other things, more transparently deliver security patches and optimize the platform.

There are, however, drawbacks to both consumers and providers. For consumers, the FaaS model offered by the platform may be too constraining for some applications. For example, the platform may not support the latest Python version, or certain libraries may not be available. For the provider, there is now a need to manage issues such as the lifecycle of the user's functions, scalability, and fault tolerance in an application-agnostic manner. This also means that developers have to carefully understand how the platform behaves and design the application around these capabilities.

One property of serverless platforms that may not be evident at the outset is that the provider tends to offer an ecosystem of services that augment the user's functions. For example, there may be services to manage state, record and monitor logs, send alerts, trigger events, or perform authentication and authorization. Such rich ecosystems can be attractive to developers and present another revenue opportunity for the cloud provider. However, the use of such services brings with it a dependence on the provider's ecosystem and a risk of vendor lock-in.

3.3 Current State of Serverless Platforms

There are many commonalities between serverless platforms. They share similar pricing, deployment, and programming models. The main difference among them is the cloud ecosystem: current serverless platforms only make it easy to use the services in their own ecosystem and the choice of platform will likely force developers to use the services native to that platform. That may be changing as open-source solutions may work well across multiple cloud platforms.

4 Programming Model

Serverless functions have limited expressiveness as they are built to scale. Their composition may be also limited and tailored to support cloud elasticity. To maximize scaling, serverless functions do not maintain state between executions. Instead, the developer can write code in the function to retrieve and update any needed state. The function is also able to access a context object that represents the environment in which the function is running (such as a security context). For example, a function written in JavaScript could take the input, as a JSON object, as the first parameter, and context as the second:

```
function main(params, context) {
    return {payload: 'Hello,' + params.name
                    + ' from' + params.place};
}
```

4.1 Ecosystem

Due to the limited and stateless nature of serverless functions, an ecosystem of scalable services that support the different functionalities a developer may require is essential to having a successfully deployed serverless application. For example, many applications will require the serverless function to retrieve state from permanent storage (such as a file server or database). There may be an existing ecosystem of functions that support API calls to various storage systems. While the functions themselves may scale due to the serverless guarantees, the underlying storage system itself must provide reliability and QoS guarantees to ensure smooth operation. Serverless functions can be used to coordinate any number of systems such as identity providers, messaging queues, and cloud-based storage. Dealing with the challenges of scaling of these systems on-demand is as critical but outside the control of the serverless platform. To increase the adoption of serverless computing, there is a need to provide such scalable services. Such an ecosystem enables ease of integration and fast deployment at the expense of vendor lock-in.

4.2 Tools and Frameworks

Creating and managing serverless functions requires several operations. Instead of managing each function independently, it is much more convenient to have a framework that can logically group functions together to deploy and update them as a unit. A framework may also make it easier to create functions that are not bound to one serverless service provider by providing abstractions that hide low-level details of each serverless provider. Other frameworks may take existing popular programming models and adapt them for serverless execution. For example, Zappa [30] and Chalice [8] use an @app.route decorator to make it possible to write python code that looks like a webserver but can be deployed as a serverless function:

```
@app.route("/{name}/{place}")
def index():
    return {"hello": name,"from": place}
```

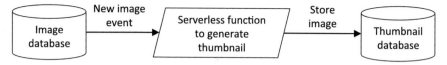

Fig. 5 Image processing

5 Use Cases and Workloads

Serverless computing has been utilized to support a wide range of applications. From a functionality perspective, serverless and more traditional architectures may be used interchangeably. The determination of when to use serverless will likely be influenced by other non-functional requirements such as the amount of control over operations required, cost, as well as application workload characteristics.

From a cost perspective, the benefits of a serverless architecture are most apparent for *bursty, compute-intensive* workloads. Bursty workloads fare well because the developer offloads the elasticity of the function to the platform, and just as important, the function can scale to zero, so there is no cost to the consumer when the system is idle. Compute-intensive workloads are appropriate since in most platforms today, the price of a function invocation is proportional to the running time of the function. Hence, I/O bound functions are paying for compute resources that they are not fully taking advantage of. In this case, a multi-tenant server application that multiplexes requests may be cheaper to operate.

From a programming model perspective, the stateless nature of serverless functions lends themselves to application structure similar to those found in functional reactive programming [4]. This includes applications that exhibit event-driven and flow-like processing patterns.

5.1 Event Processing

One class of applications that are very much suitable for serverless computing is event-based programming [5, 29]. The most basic example, popularized by AWS Lambda, that has become the "Hello World" of serverless computing is a simple image processing event handler function. The function is connected to a data store, such as Amazon S3 [26], that emits change events. Each time a new image file is uploaded to a folder in S3, an event is generated and forwarded to the event handler function that generates a thumbnail image that is stored in another S3 folder. The flow is depicted in Fig. 5. This example works well for serverless demos as the function is completely stateless and idempotent which has the advantage that in the case of failure (such as network problems accessing the S3 folder), the function can be executed again with no side effects. It is also an exemplary use case of a bursty, compute-intensive workload as described above.

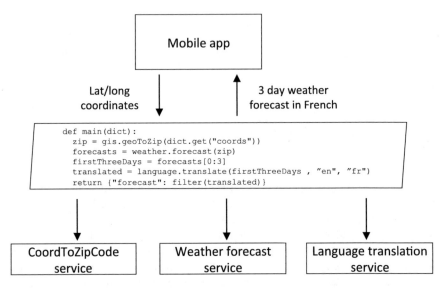

```
def main(dict):
    zip = gis.geoToZip(dict.get("coords"))
    forecasts = weather.forecast(zip)
    firstThreeDays = forecasts[0:3]
    translated = language.translate(firstThreeDays , "en", "fr")
    return {"forecast": filter(translated)}
```

Fig. 6 Offloading API calls and glue logic from mobile app to backend

5.2 API Composition

Another class of applications involves the composition of a number of APIs. In this case, the application logic consists of data filtering and transformation. For example, a mobile app may invoke geolocation, weather, and language translation APIs to render the weather forecast for a user's current location. The glue code to invoke these APIs can be written in a short serverless function, as illustrated by the Python function in Fig. 6. In this way, the mobile app avoids the cost of invoking the multiple APIs over a potentially resource constrained mobile network connection, and offloads the filtering and aggregation logic to the backend.

5.3 API Aggregation to Reduce API Calls

API aggregation can work not only as a composition mechanism, but also as a means to simplify the client-side code that interacts with the aggregated call. For example, consider a mobile application that allows you to administer an Open Stack instance. API calls in Open Stack [18] require the client to first obtain an API token, resolve the URL of the service you need to talk to, then invoke the required API call on that URL with the API token. Ideally, a mobile app would save energy by minimizing the number of required calls needed to issue a command to an Open Stack instance. Figure 7 illustrates an alternative approach where three functions implement the aforementioned flow to allow authenticated backups in an Open Stack instance. The

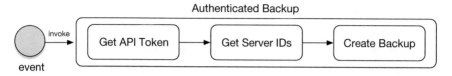

Fig. 7 Reducing the number of API calls required for a mobile client

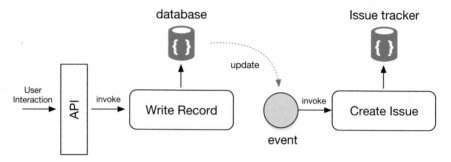

Fig. 8 Batched invocation for issue tracking

mobile client now makes a single call to invoke this aggregate function. The flow itself appears as a single API call. Note that authorization to invoke this call can be handled by an external authorization service, e.g., an API gateway.

5.4 Flow Control for Issue Tracking

Serverless function composition can be used to control the flow of data between two services. For example, imagine an application that allows users to submit feedback to the app developers in the form of annotated screenshots and text. In Fig. 8, the application submits this data to a backend consisting of a scalable database and an on-premise issue tracking system. The latter is mainly used by the development team and is not designed to accept high volume traffic. On the other hand, the former is capable of responding to high volume traffic. We design our system to stage all feedback records in the database using a serverless function which eliminates the need to standup a separate server to handle feedback requests but still allow us a level of indirection between the application and the backend database. Once we collect a sufficient number of updates, we can batch them together into a single update, which invokes a function to submit issues to the issue tracker in a controlled manner. This flow would work for a scalable database system [6] and an issue tracker system that accepts batched inputs [17].

5.5 Discussion

The workload and its relationship to cost can help determine if serverless is appropriate. Infrequent but bursty workloads may be better served by serverless, which provides horizontal scaling without the need for dedicated infrastructure that charges for idle time. For more steady workloads, the frequency at which a function is executed will influence how economical it can be for caching to occur which allows for faster execution on warm containers than executing from a cold container. These performance characteristics can help guide the developer when considering serverless.

Interestingly, the cost considerations may affect how a serverless application is structured. For example, an I/O bound serverless function can be decomposed into multiple compute bound ones. This may be more complex to develop and debug, but cheaper to operate.

6 Challenges and Open Problems

We will list challenges starting with those that are already known based on our experience of using serverless services and then describe open problems.

6.1 System-Level Challenges

Here is a list of challenges at the systems level.

- *Cost*: Cost is a fundamental challenge. This includes minimizing the resource usage of a serverless function, both when it is executing and when idle. Another aspect is the pricing model, including how it compares to other cloud computing approaches. For example, serverless functions are currently most economical for CPU-bound computations, whereas I/O bound functions may be cheaper on dedicated VMs or containers.
- *Cold start*: A key differentiator of serverless is the ability to scale to zero, or not charging customers for idle time. Scaling to zero, however, leads to the problem of cold starts, and paying the penalty of getting serverless code ready to run. Techniques to minimize the cold start problem while still scaling to zero are critical.
- *Resource limits*: Resource limits are needed to ensure that the platform can handle load spikes and manage attacks. Enforceable resource limits on a serverless function include memory, execution time, bandwidth, and CPU usage. In additional, there are aggregate resource limits that can be applied across a number of functions or across the entire platform.
- *Security*: Strong isolation of functions is critical since functions from many users are running on a shared platform.

- *Scaling*: The platform must ensure the scalability and elasticity of users' functions. This includes proactively provisioning resources in response to load, and in anticipation of future load. This is a more challenging problem in serverless because these predictions and provisioning decisions must be made with little or no application-level knowledge. For example, the system can use request queue lengths as an indication of the load, but is blind to the nature of these requests.
- *Hybrid cloud*: As serverless is gaining popularity, there may be more than one serverless platform and multiple serverless services that need to work together. It is unlikely one platform will have all functionality and work for all use cases.
- *Legacy systems*: It should be easy to access older cloud and non-cloud systems from serverless code running in serverless platforms.

6.2   Programming Model and DevOps Challenges

- *Tools*: Traditional tools that assumed access to servers to be able to monitor and debug applications are not applicable in serverless architectures, and new approaches are needed.
- *Deployment*: Developers should be able to use declarative approaches to control what is deployed and tools to support it.
- *Monitoring and debugging*: As developers no longer have servers that they can access, serverless services and tools need to focus on developer productivity. As serverless functions are running for shorter amounts of time, there will be many orders of magnitude more of them running making it harder to identify problems and bottlenecks. When the functions finish the only trace of their execution is what the serverless platform's monitoring infrastructure recorded.
- *IDEs*: Higher level developer capabilities, such as refactoring functions (e.g., splitting and merging functions) and reverting to an older version, etc. will be needed and should be fully integrated with serverless platforms.
- *Composability*: This includes being able to call one function from another, creating functions that call and coordinate a number of other functions, and higher level constructs such as parallel executions and graphs. Tools will be needed to facilitate creation of compositions and their maintenance.
- *Long running*: Currently, serverless functions are often limited in their execution time. There are scenarios that require long running (if intermittent) logic. Programming models and tools may decompose long running tasks into smaller units and provide necessary context to track them as one long running unit of work.
- *State*: Real applications often require state, and it is not clear how to manage state in stateless serverless functions—programing models, tools, and libraries will need to provide the necessary.
- *Concurrency*: Expressing concurrency semantics, such as atomicity (function executions need to be serialized), etc.
- *Recovery semantics*: Such as exactly once, at most once, and at least once semantics.

- *Code granularity*: Currently, serverless platforms encapsulate code at the granularity of functions. It is an open question whether coarser or finer grained modules would be useful.

6.3 Open Research Problems

Now, we will describe a number of open problems. We frame them as questions to emphasize that they are largely unexplored research areas.

What are the boundaries of serverless? A fundamental question about serverless computing is of boundaries: is it restricted to FaaS or is broader in scope? How does it relate to other models such as SaaS and MBaaS?

As serverless is gaining popularity the boundaries between different types of "as-a-Service" may be disappearing (see Fig. 9). One could imagine that developers not only write code but also declare how they want the code to run—as FaaS or MBaaS or PaaS—and can change as needs change. In the future, the main distinction may be between caring about server (server-aware) and not caring about server details (serverless). PaaS is in the middle; it makes it very easy to deploy code but developers still need to know about servers and be aware of scaling strategies, such as how many instances to run.

Can different cloud computing service models be mixed? Can there be more choices for how much memory and CPU can be used by serverless functions? Does

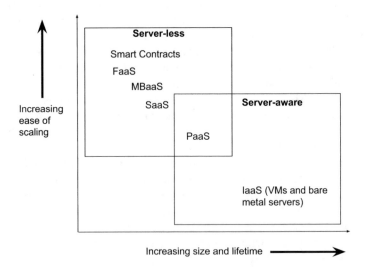

Fig. 9 The figure is showing relation between time to live (x-axis) and ease of scaling (y-axis). Server-aware compute (bare metal, VMs, IaaS) has long time to live and take longer to scale (time to provision new resources); serverless compute (FaaS, MBaaS, PaaS, SaaS) is optimized to work on multiple servers and hide server details

serverless need to have IaaS-like-based pricing? What about spot and dynamic pricing with dynamically changing granularity?

Is tooling for serverless fundamentally different from existing solutions? As the granularity of serverless is much smaller than traditional server-based tools, we may need new tools to deal well with more numerous but much shorter living artifacts. How can we make sure that the important "information needle" is not lost in a haystack? Monitoring and debugging serverless applications will be much more challenging as there are no servers directly accessible to see what went wrong. Instead, serverless platforms need to gather all data when code is running and make it available later. Similarly debugging is much different if instead of having one artifact (a microservice or traditional monolithic app) developers need to deal with a myriad of smaller pieces of code. New approaches may be needed to virtually assemble serverless pieces into larger units that are easier to understand and to reason about.

Can legacy code be made to run serverless? The amount of existing ("legacy") code that must continue running is much larger than the new code created specifically to run in serverless environments. The economic value of existing code represents a huge investment of countless hours of developers coding and fixing software. Therefore, one of the most important problems may be to what degree existing legacy code can be automatically or semi-automatically decomposed into smaller-granularity pieces to take advantage of these new pricing models.

Is serverless fundamentally stateless? As current serverless platforms are stateless will there be stateful serverless services in future? Will there be simple ways to deal with state? More than that is serverless fundamentally stateless? Can there be serverless services that have stateful support built-in with different degrees of quality-of-service?

Will there be patterns for building serverless solutions? How do we combine low granularity "basic" building blocks of serverless into bigger solutions? How are we going to decompose apps into functions so that they optimize resource usage? For example, how do we identify CPU-bound parts of applications built to run in serverless services? Can we use well-defined patterns for composing functions and external APIs? What should be done on the server versus client (e.g., are thicker clients more appropriate here)? Are there lessons learned that can be applied from OOP design patterns, Enterprise Integration Patterns, etc.?

Does serverless extend beyond traditional cloud platforms? Serverless may need to support scenarios where code is executed outside of a traditionally defined data center. This may include efforts where the cloud is extended to include IoT, mobile devices, web browsers, and other computing at the edge. For example "fog" computing [22] has the goal of creating a system-level horizontal architecture that distributes resources and services of computing, storage, control, and networking anywhere along the continuum from Cloud to IoT. The code running in the "fog" and outside the Cloud may not just be embedded but virtualized to allow movement between devices and cloud. That may lead to specific requirements that redefine cost. For example, energy usage may be more important than speed.

Another example is running code that executes "smart contracts" orchestrating transactions in a blockchain. The code that defines the contract may be deployed and running on a network of Hyperledger fabric peer nodes [19], or in Ethereum Virtual Machines [11] on any node of an Ethereum peer-to-peer network. As the system is decentralized, there is no Ethereum service or servers to run serverless code. Instead, to incentivize Ethereum users to run smart contracts they get paid for the "gas" consumed by the code, similar to fuel cost for an automobile but applied to computing.

7 Conclusions

In this chapter, we explored the genesis and history of serverless computing in detail. It is an evolution of the trend toward higher levels of abstractions in cloud programming models, and currently exemplified by the Function-as-a-Service (FaaS) model where developers write small stateless code snippets and allow the platform to manage the complexities of scalably executing the function in a fault-tolerant manner.

This seemingly restrictive model nevertheless lends itself well to a number of common distributed application patterns, including compute-intensive event processing pipelines. Most of the large cloud computing vendors have released their own serverless platforms, and there is a tremendous amount of investment and attention around this space in industry.

Unfortunately, there has not been a corresponding degree of interest in the research community. We feel strongly that there are a wide variety of technically challenging and intellectually deep problems in this space, ranging from infrastructure issues such as optimizations of the cold start to the design of a composable programming model. There are even philosophical questions such as the fundamental nature of state in a distributed application. Many of the open problems identified in this chapter are real problems faced by practitioners of serverless computing today and solutions have the potential for significant impact.

We leave the reader with some ostensibly simple questions that we hope will help stimulate their interest in this area. Why is serverless computing important? Will it change the economy of computing? As developers take advantage of smaller granularities of computational units and pay only for what is actually used will that change how developers think about building solutions? In what ways will serverless extend the original intent of cloud computing of making hardware fungible and shifting the cost of computing from capital to operational expenses?

The serverless paradigm may eventually lead to new kinds of programming models, languages, and platform architectures and that is certainly an exciting area for the research community to participate in and contribute to.

References

1. Aws lambda. Retrieved December 1, 2016, from https://aws.amazon.com/lambda/.

2. Aws re:invent 2014 | (mbl202) new launch: Getting started with aws lambda. Retrieved December 1, 2016, from https://www.youtube.com/watch?v=UFj27laTWQA.
3. Azure functions. Retrieved December 1, 2016, from https://functions.azure.com/.
4. Bainomugisha, E., Carreton, A. L., van Cutsem, T., Mostinckx, S., & de Meuter, W.: A survey on reactive programming. *ACM Computing Surveys, 45*(4), 52:1–52:34 (2013). doi:10.1145/2501654.2501666. http://doi.acm.org/10.1145/2501654.2501666
5. Baldini, I., Castro, P., Cheng, P., Fink, S., Ishakian, V., Mitchell, N., et al. (2016). Cloud-native, event-based programming for mobile applications. In *Proceedings of the International Conference on Mobile Software Engineering and Systems, MOBILESoft '16* (pp. 287–288). New York, NY, USA: ACM. doi:10.1145/2897073.2897713. http://doi.acm.org/10.1145/2897073.2897713
6. Bienko, C. D., Greenstein, M., Holt, S. E., & Phillips, R. T.: *IBM Cloudant: Database as a Service Advanced Topics*. IBM Redbooks (2015)
7. Building Serverless Apps with Webtask.io. Retrieved December 1, 2016, from https://auth0.com/blog/building-serverless-apps-with-webtask/.
8. chalice: Python serverless microframework for aws. Retrieved December 1, 2016, from https://github.com/awslabs/chalice.
9. Cloud Foundry and Iron.io Deliver Serverless. Retrieved December 1, 2016, from https://www.iron.io/cloud-foundry-and-ironio-deliver-serverless/.
10. Cloud functions. Retrieved December 1, 2016, from https://cloud.google.com/functions/.
11. Ethereum. Retrieved December 1, 2016, from http://ethdocs.org/en/latest/introduction/what-is-ethereum.html.
12. Fernandez, O. (2016). *Serverless: Patterns of modern application design using microservices* (Amazon Web Services Edition) (in preparation). https://leanpub.com/serverless.
13. Galactic Fog Gestalt Framework. Retrieved December 1, 2016, from http://www.galacticfog.com/.
14. Google Apps Marketplace. Retrieved December 1, 2016, from https://developers.google.com/apps-marketplace/.
15. Hendrickson, S., Sturdevant, S., Harter, T., Venkataramani, V., Arpaci-Dusseau, A.C., & Arpaci-Dusseau, R. H. (2016). Serverless computation with openlambda. In *8th USENIX Workshop on Hot Topics in Cloud Computing, HotCloud 2016*, Denver, CO, USA, 20–21 June 2016. https://www.usenix.org/conference/hotcloud16/workshop-program/presentation/hendrickson.
16. Introducing Lambda support on Iron.io. Retrieved December 1, 2016, from https://www.iron.io/introducing-aws-lambda-support/.
17. Jira. Retrieved December 5, 2016, from https://www.atlassian.com/software/jira.
18. OpenStack. Retrieved December 5, 2016, from https://www.openstack.org.
19. Learn Chaincode. Retrieved December 1, 2016, from https://github.com/IBM-Blockchain/learn-chaincode.
20. LeverOS. Retrieved December 5, 2016, from https://github.com/leveros/leveros.
21. NGINX Announces Results of 2016 Future of Application Development and Delivery Survey. Retrieved December 5, 2016, from https://www.nginx.com/press/nginx-announces-results-of-2016-future-of-application-development-and-delivery-survey/.
22. OpenFog Consortium. Retrieved December 1, 2016, from http://www.openfogconsortium.org/.
23. Openlambda. Retrieved December 1, 2016, from https://open-lambda.org/.
24. Openwhisk. Retrieved December 1, 2016, from https://github.com/openwhisk/openwhisk.
25. Parse Cloud Code Getting Started. Retrieved December 1, 2016, from https://parseplatform.github.io/docs/cloudcode/guide/.
26. S3 Simple Storage Service. Retrieved December 1, 2016, from https://aws.amazon.com/s3/.
27. Sbarski, P., & Kroonenburg, S. (2016) Serverless architectures on AWS With examples using AWS Lambda (in preparation). https://www.manning.com/books/serverless-architectures-on-aws.
28. Sharable, Open Source Workers for Scalable Processing. Retrieved December 1, 2016, from https://www.iron.io/sharable-open-source-workers-for/.

29. Yan, M., Castro, P., Cheng, P., & Ishakian, V. (2016). Building a chatbot with serverless computing. In *First International Workshop on Mashups of Things, MOTA '16 (colocated with Middleware)*.
30. Zappa: Serverless python web services. Retrieved December 1, 2016, from https://github.com/Miserlou/Zappa.

Highly Available Clouds: System Modeling, Evaluations, and Open Challenges

Patricia Takako Endo, Glauco Estácio Gonçalves, Daniel Rosendo, Demis Gomes, Guto Leoni Santos, André Luis Cavalcanti Moreira, Judith Kelner, Djamel Sadok and Mozhgan Mahloo

Abstract Cloud-based solution adoption is becoming an indispensable strategy for enterprises, since it brings many advantages, such as low cost. On the other hand, to attend this demand, cloud providers are facing a great challenge regarding their resource management: how to provide services with high availability relying on finite computational resources and limited physical infrastructure? Understanding the components and operations of cloud data center is a key point to manage resources in an optimal way and to estimate how physical and logical failures can impact on users' perception. This book chapter aims to explore computational modeling theories in order to represent a cloud infrastructure focusing on how to estimate and model cloud availability.

P.T. Endo (✉)
University of Pernambuco, Recife, Brazil
e-mail: patricia@gprt.br; patricia.endo@upe.br

G.E. Gonçalves
Rural Federal University of Pernambuco, Recife, Brazil
e-mail: glauco@gprt.ufpe.br

D. Rosendo · D. Gomes · G.L. Santos · A.L.C. Moreira · J. Kelner · D. Sadok
Federal University of Pernambuco, Recife, Brazil
e-mail: daniel.rosendo@gprt.ufpe.br

D. Gomes
e-mail: demis.gomes@gprt.ufpe.br

G.L. Santos
e-mail: guto.leoni@gprt.ufpe.br

A.L.C. Moreira
e-mail: andre@gprt.ufpe.br

J. Kelner
e-mail: jk@gprt.ufpe.br

D. Sadok
e-mail: jamel@gprt.ufpe.br

M. Mahloo
Ericsson Research, Recife, Brazil
e-mail: mozhgan.mahloo@ericsson.com

© Springer Nature Singapore Pte Ltd. 2017
S. Chaudhary et al. (eds.), *Research Advances in Cloud Computing*,
DOI 10.1007/978-981-10-5026-8_2

1 Introduction

Cloud providers have gained popularity because they have changed the current and traditional business models, replacing a huge initial investment by a pay-as-you-go model, in which users can deploy their applications with guarantees of high availability, scalability, and security. Currently, one of the biggest challenges cloud providers have facing is to guarantee increasingly stringent availability terms on SLAs (Service-Level Agreements), which is tightly connected to the strategies adopted for the full-stack failure management (from hardware to software) at their data centers. Unforeseen data center failures are expensive (for both sides, providers, and users) and require special attention. The costs of these failures stem from business disruption, lost revenue, diminished end-user productivity in addition to business reputation. To mitigate this issue, a deep understanding of the possible failures as well as the amount of effort and money to spend to fix them is of high interest.

There are some terms commonly used to describe systems performance regarding to their failures handling, such as availability, reliability, MTTF (Mean Time To Failure) and MTBF (Mean Time Between Failures). However, these concepts are frequently used without a precise definition and, in several cases, some of these concepts are used interchangeably. A clear definition of these concepts and how they are related to each other is necessary to understand how cloud services might be impacted in case of failure. Furthermore, a comprehensive modeling of the cloud infrastructure and its performance during runtime is vital towards detecting possible single points of the failure, and calculating the end-to-end availability of the services offered to the customers. A good starting point for reliability assessment of cloud services would be to model the hardware system in the data center in order to estimate the availability of each service, end-to-end, which can be done by defining the involved components related to each service. This helps to have a reliable architecture while modeling the data center infrastructures from the beginning to fulfill service requirements.

Considering aforementioned factors, this chapter will introduce essential concepts about high availability for cloud computing, as well as highlighting some open research questions, via presenting a survey about available modeling theories and how they can be used by cloud providers to handle service reliability issues.

The chapter aims to equip readers with a good insight about high availability challenges and modeling of cloud data centers. Specific competencies to be achieved by the reader at the end of this chapter are:

- To identify the basic principles used for designing and modeling high availability in cloud data centers;
- To identify what research topics should be relevant in high availability in cloud computing area in the coming years. This item is important to guide the future research in this area;
- To know the main available methods proposed by the scientific community on the cloud mechanisms for high availability, as well as understand how they relate to each other; and

- To comprehend the importance of cloud modeling and analysis in high availability area, identifying how one can develop solutions for this aspect.

This chapter is organized as follows: Sect. 2 describes the basic concepts regarding cloud high availability, such as definitions of Service Availability Forum (SAF) models, discussion about reliability *versus* availability, and some techniques for modeling high availability in clouds; Sect. 3 presents an overview of possible impacts of outages in cloud data centers, as well as an overview about data centers infrastructure, and some mechanisms to provide high availability; Sect. 4 shows a systematic literature review about modeling high availability clouds; Sect. 5 presents some open challenges; and finally the Sect. 6 describes our final considerations and future trends.

2 High Availability Concepts

High availability in data centers is of the high importance due to the impact of the failures on service continuity which can be translated into high operational costs for cloud providers and costumers. This Section describes some basic concepts and modeling techniques related to cloud availability.

2.1 SAF Concepts

With emergence of new technologies, several challenges arise for ICT (Information and Communications Technology) companies in regard to fulfilling the quality of their services towards customers. To attend the expectations of users, service providers need to provide high availability and reliability to their customers. On the other hand, they must reduce deployment costs of their services. To achieve these goals, many companies adhere to the open specifications. At this point, the SAF (Service Availability Forum) [43] standardizes interfaces to provide high availability to carrier-grade systems with off-the-shelf hardware platforms, middleware, and applications. The SAF is a consortium of many ICT companies that provides standardized solutions for building high availability services [45]. Using the standard solutions can reduce costs of deployment, human training, and software development, by using compatible and inter-operable solutions from different vendors.

SAF has developed a set of software specifications interfaces to middleware applications and carrier-grade platforms [43]. These specifications are divided into: AIS (Application Interface Specifications) and Hardware Interface Interface Specifications (named HPI (Hardware Platform Interface)). AIS defines standard interfaces to developers for building high availability programs that are portable in multiple platforms. On the other hand, the HPI allows ISVs (independent software vendors) provide COTS (commercial off-the-shelf) components, providing hardware management platform across multiple heterogeneous platforms. Since this paper is treating of high availability on data centers, we described only the AIS components, because its focus is interfaced for providing high availability for services.

2.1.1 Application Interface Specifications

These specifications are formed by 12 services and two frameworks. The services are classified into three functional groups, and frameworks form another functional group [43].

The three services functional groups are: Platform Services, Management Services and Utility services. Platform Services provide abstraction of the hardware and operating system from other applications and services. Their components allow monitoring hardware and software components required for the nodes' operation. These abstractions facilitate the infrastructure management of clusters and can ensure their smooth operation. Management Services provide basic and standard management interfaces that can be used for the implementation and execution of applications and services. They also offer security, log, and notifications services that facilitate the management of applications and services. Finally, Utility Services provide common interfaces in distributed systems with high availability, such as event distribution and checkpointing messages. The implementation of these services are important for the system to provide high availability, due to mechanisms of detection and disaster recovery [15, 16]. Figure 1 shows a general architecture of framework components proposed by SAF.

SAF also standardizes two frameworks: AMF (Availability Management Framework) and SMF (Software Management Framework). AMF provides functions for managing availability of applications and middleware, while monitoring other softwares running on a system. In addition, AMF includes functions for error reports, life cycle management and health monitoring, which provide important information about services availability. The AFM setting allows prioritization of resources and provides many redundancy models [43]. On the other hand, SMF is used to manage the middleware and applications during upgrades. This framework maintains information about the availability and deployment of softwares and allows the system evolution and orchestrating the migration from one configuration to another. The SMF complements AMF providing a reliable and consistent framework that delivers and update the software in a system [15, 16].

2.2 Reliability Versus Availability

The reliability term is frequently used without a precise definition and, in several cases, this concept is used interchangeably with availability. However, these two terms are not conveying the same message [23]. Reliability can be defined as the ability of an item to perform its required functions for a stated time and under

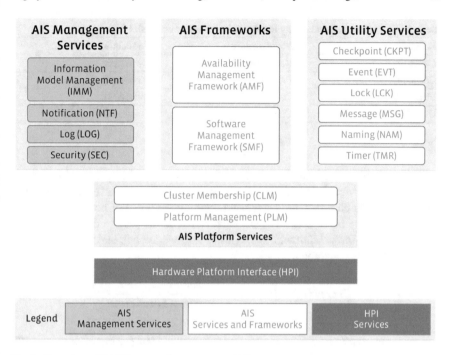

Fig. 1 Overview of SAF Framework components [15]

operational conditions. An item is any component or system, while required functions are the combinations of necessary actions to provide a service.

Reliability denotes the ability of an item to work properly until a failure occurs, independent of downtime and repair time. The ability of an item/system to be restored, using prescribed procedures and resources, to a state that it can perform its required functions is called maintainability [23]. Reliability is not influenced by maintainability and vice-versa because the former one is measured until a failure occur and the later one denotes the recovery rate of an item when it fails. A system can be less reliable and high maintainable or high reliable and less maintainable.

These two concepts (maintainability and reliability) are jointly defining the availability. According to Toeroe and Tam [47], availability is the percentage of time in which the service is up during a given interval. The QuEST Forum[1] describes availability as the probability that a system is running when it is required. More precisely, [23] introduces availability of an item/system as the combination of its reliability and maintainability to perform its required function at a stated instant of time or period.

In other words, availability is a probability of an item is functioning in a time t. This way, an item is more available when it is hard to fail (reliable) and has a high recovery rate (maintainable). The relation between reliability and maintainability to improve availability is shown in Table 1.

---

[1] http://tl9000.org/about/tl9000/overview.html.

Table 1 Dependency of availability in relation to reliability and maintainability [4]

Reliability	Maintainability	Availability
Constant	Decreases	Decreases
Constant	Increases	Increases
Increases	Constant	Increases
Decreases	Constant	Decreases

The availability also can be calculated by service availability, as enlightened in Eq. 1. During service uptime, the service is operational. The service total time denotes the period in which a system is evaluated, being operational or not. Therefore, the service total time is the sum of operational time and the service downtime, as the Eq. 2 shows. In the downtime, the service is not operational, staying in the repair process until it is concluded.

$$serviceAvailability = \frac{serviceUptime}{serviceTotalTime} \qquad (1)$$

$$serviceTotalTime = serviceUpTime + serviceDownTime \qquad (2)$$

2.3 MTBF and MTTR

As discussed in Sect. 2.2, the availability can be defined as service uptime over total service time, where total time is described as the sum of service uptime and service downtime. These concepts can be associated with the average behavior of the system for the purpose of availability calculation. In the following formula, the availability is calculated by division of the MTTF (Mean Time To Failure) and the MTBF (Mean Time Between Failures). The MTBF also is defined as the sum of MTTF and MTTR (Mean Time to Repair), indicating the time between the detection of a failure and the detection of next failure, as showed in Eq. 3.

$$availability = \frac{MTTF}{MTBF} = \frac{MTTF}{MTTF + MTTR} \qquad (3)$$

Figure 2 illustrates the lifecycle of a hypothetical service. The variables d, u, and tt denote service downtime, uptime, and total time, respectively. A service can be either in downtime, defined by variables d_1, d_2, and d_3, or in uptime, with variables u_1, u_2, and u_3. Note that these times can have different values. Denoting n as the number of failures of system, 3 in our example, the MTTF can be calculated by Eq. 4, as well as MTTR is defined by Eq. 5. These equations state MTTF and MTTR as the

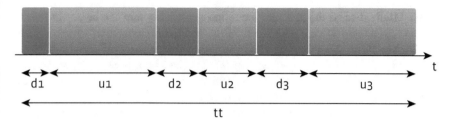

Fig. 2 MTTF, MTTR and MTBF related to service uptime, outage time and total time

averages of uptime and downtime, respectively. MTBF corresponds to mean service total time.

$$MTTF = \frac{\sum_{i=1}^{i} u_i}{n} \tag{4}$$

$$MTTR = \frac{\sum_{i=1}^{i} d_i}{n} \tag{5}$$

Some studies such as [13] and [8] do not employ MTTF metric. They replace the MTTF definition by MTBF, i.e., the authors state MTBF as the mean service uptime, denoted by time after failure recovery until the next failure. In the aforementioned studies, availability is calculated using Eq. 6. The result of this calculus is similar of Eq. 3 because MTBF assumes the same meaning that MTTF in these studies. We recommend the use of Eq. 3.

$$availability = \frac{MTBF}{MTBF + MTTR} \tag{6}$$

2.4 Techniques for High Availability Modeling

In order to avoid service outage and the consequential financial losses in cloud data centers, companies are interested in defining and applying formal models to verify and ensure correctness of hardware and software components to achieve highly available systems [10].

In this section, we describe various models used to solve real-life cloud high availability problems. We will mainly focus on the following three topics: (1) what are the advantages and drawbacks of each approach; (2) which model is better fitted to which scenarios/systems; and (3) how these models can be combined to extract the best of each one when modeling and analyzing cloud systems.

We briefly discuss the different modeling approaches that can be used to evaluate the dependability, availability, reliability, and fault tolerance of systems. These approaches differ according to their modeling power, ease of use, and system complexity [31]. In this way, they can be classified into three cathegories: Non-combinatorial or State-space models; Combinatorial or Non-state-space models; and Hierarchical and Fixed-Point Iterative models.

The Non-Combinatorial or State-Space Models are good for analyzing and verifying system behaviors. These models can be built using approaches like Markov Chains, Semi-Markov processes, Markov Regenerative Processes, Stochastic Petri Nets, or Stochastic Reward Nets. Those strategies make a state space structure that models all states and transitions that a system can reach (e.g., failures and repair operations). They permit the representation of complex systems with resource constraints and dependencies between subsystems [12]. However, those models face the state explosion problem, a problem related to the huge number of states in a system, making the built model difficult to be solved through analytical tools [10].

The Combinatorial or Non-State-Space Models enable a high level and concise representation of the relationship between components of systems and subsystems [48]. In this class, we can find Reliability Block Diagrams, Fault Trees, or Reliability Graphs. Differently from the state space methods, these methods are free of the state-space explosion problem. The main disadvantage of using the Combinatorial models is that they do not enable the representation of system activities and processes, such as rejuvenation, repairs, and failures.

The Hierarchical and Fixed-Point Iterative Models come to mitigate the weaknesses and put together the advantages of the Non-combinatorial and Combinatorial methods to leverage the analysis and modeling of many kinds of systems. This hybrid approach is commonly used to model systems with multiple components. In order to model such systems, it is recommended to use the combination of various simple methods to build multiple simple models, rather than using a single sophisticated model [40].

Some examples of models will be presented in Sect. 4, in which we present the results of a systematic review of the literature on the usage of models to assess high availability on cloud computing data centers.

3   How Do Clouds Achieve High Availability?

According to [8], hardware and software failures are inevitable. Highly available systems are designed so that no single failure causes unacceptable service disruption. Cloud providers have a great challenge to manage the data center infrastructure, considering the continuous need to optimize the resource usage and provide redundancy at the same time. This section presents some examples of how outages in data centers affected the service continuity and business reputation of several large companies, as well as an overview about mechanisms to provide high availability in data centers.

3.1 Outages Examples

The growing number of companies using cloud services brought several new challenges to the cloud providers. Maintaining high availability to meet the demands of these customers is a difficult task for providers. This demand is dynamic, and cloud services must be always available as the service interruption may represent high financial losses for cloud users [20].

Often the root cause of a cloud service unavailability is not completely clear to its customers, but one can point several recent cases which was made public. For instance, on March 13, 2009, during an upgrade operational system, the Deployment Service of Windows Azure began to fail due to network interruption problems. Many applications that running only one instance stopped when the corresponding server went down. On October 3, 2009, BitBucket was unavailable for 16 h. The reason were two DDoS attacks targeted at the network interfaces on Amazon EBS (Elastic Block Store) service for storage used with EC2 instances [41].

On 2012, Salesforce, a cloud company that provides on-demand software service, including CRM (customer relationship management), faced an outage that lasted 7 h. The root cause was a failure in the data center power system which affected several CRM customers. On May 6, 2014, the cloud service provider, Internap, faced three interruptions of services at its New York data centers. The reason was a fault in the power supply system that affected 20 companies, including the online video streaming platform Livestream. Another example of outage occurred in the Joyent data center, a company that provides high performance cloud infrastructures services. The event took place on May 27, 2014, and it was related to a human error that restarted the whole system. On September 3, 2014, the social network Facebook was down during 10 min. Many users realized the unavailability and demonstrated discontent on other social networks [5].

The outages' cost may be high for companies that provide or use cloud services. The Ponemon Institute conducted studies about costs of outages in data centers [2]. The recent study performed in 2016, evaluated 63 data centers of 49 companies in the United States. The survey showed an 7% increase in the average cost of data center outage of $690,204 in 2013 to $740,357 in 2015. Among the types of costs associated with outages, which generate more expenses for companies are business interruptions, something around $256,000. The study also showed that the average outages times, in 12 months, is 95 min, an increase with respect to 2013 average, that was 86 min. The study also showed the maximum cost per minute of an outage is $17,244.

The financial impacts and losses related to service outages can prove the importance of the high availability mechanism in cloud computing area. The best way to avoid breach of contract due the unavailability of service is to assess and measure the availability that data centers are able to deliver.

3.2   Datacenter Overview

In this section, we present the main components of a data center infrastructure that is composed of IT equipment (servers, storage, and network), electrical, and mechanical subsystems. We also present some data center standards that define best practices and recommendations regarding data center design and infrastructure.

3.2.1   Information Technology Infrastructure

Data center IT equipment may be classified as servers, storage, and networking devices. Servers are mounted within racks and consist of hardware resources (such as CPUs, NICs, and RAMs) hosting applications like video streaming and big data. All the data generated by these applications are stored in storage systems.

Data center storage consists of high capacity (around Terabytes) disk drives or flash devices. The storage tiers are connected to the servers either directly or through networking devices (managed by a global distributed file system), forming a NAS (Network Attached Storage) [7]. The RAID (Redundant Array of Independent Disks) storage technology can be used to provide high availability, redundancy, and increase fault tolerance.

Networking equipment manages the internal communication between servers and storage systems as well as all the input/output data flow from/to the data center. Typically, a data center network is designed based on three hierarchical levels: core, distribution, and edge. It is through the core level that all data center traffic (ingress/egress) to the outside world will be managed. Distribution is a level between the edge and core levels which aggregates the edge switches. Its main goal is simply network management and cabling reduction. Finally, the edge level passes data from devices (generating or consuming data) to the distribution or core levels [46].

Manage all these components is a great challenge because hardware clusters have a deep and complex memory/storage hierarchy, the system is composed of heterogeneous components, and there are many failure-prone components. It is necessary to use an additional software layer to provide an abstraction of this variety of components. According to [7], this software layer has three levels: platform level, cluster level, and application level. The platform-level software is composed of firmware, operational system, and kernel that provide an abstraction of hardware of a single machine in the cluster and provide server-level services. The cluster-level software is related to any software that managed resources at cluster level, such as distributed file systems, management resource systems, and monitoring systems. The application-level software is composed of software that implements a particular service. The set of all software used to monitor, measure, manage and control the data center behavior is named DCIM (Data Center Infrastructure Management).

3.2.2 Power Infrastructure

IT infrastructure needs power facilities with enough capacities (generators and UPSs) to operate properly. Hence, faults in power system components directly affect the overall data center availability. The CENELEC EN 50600-2-2 standard defines requirements and recommendations for planning and designing data center power supply facilities. The standard introduces Availability Classes from I to IV for the power supply and distribution systems to address various level of data center availability by including layers of redundancy.

A typical data center power system architecture includes an utility substation, an alternate power supply, a transfer switchgear or an ATS (Automatic Transfer Switch), an UPS (Uninterruptible Power Supply) system, and a PDU (Power Distribution Unit). The main power supply of a data center is the utility substation. Data centers may also contain an alternative power feed like fuel cell and renewable energy sources (such as solar, wind, bioenergy, hydroelectric, and wave) [25]. Both primary and secondary power sources are connected to an ATS. The ATS provides input for the cooling and UPS systems. The UPS system routes power to the PDU (rack socket for cabinets). Finally, a PDU distributes electrical energy to the IT equipment. Figure 5 depicts those components.

3.2.3 Cooling Infrastructure

As the power infrastructure, the cooling (or mechanical) system reliability and maintainability are fundamental to a proper data center operation. The heat dissipation of IT equipment requires the deployment of cooling system design strategies [22, 27]. The ASHRAE TC9.9 standard defines thermal design recommendations regarding data center cooling technologies, air flow rack level design (hot aisle and cold aisle), IT equipment (network, storage, and server), and energy-saving techniques (reducing cooling fans speed).

Data center cooling system equipment can be based on different technologies, such as central cooling, water-cooled, air-cooled, direct expansion, evaporative cooling, water economization, direct economization, indirect economization, and economization options. Each one differs according to the operation mode, energy efficiency, costs, heat exchanger technology, and cooling technology [27].

A typical data center cooling system relies on some cooling components, which includes a CRAC (Computer Room Air Conditioning), chillers, cooling towers, piping, pumps, heat exchanger, and water treatment systems.

3.3 High Availability Mechanisms

Providing redundancy in data centers comes with a price. There is always a trade-off between increasing the availability and the amount of required cost investments to

Fig. 3 Distribution of
service disruption events by
most likely cause at one of
Googles main services,
collected over a period of 6
weeks (adapted from [7])

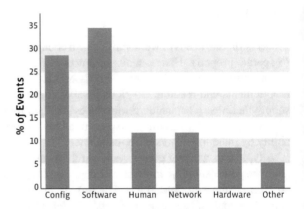

achieve desired level of reliability [7]. Without protection mechanisms, failures can make the data center inaccessible to the users, which might lead to SLA violations and financial losts for the cloud provider. However, having preventive strategies such as planned maintenance of some components in predefined time intervals can reduce service downtime when a failure occur, preventing users to be affected by the failure.

Moreover, it is necessary to discover the main sources and severity of failures which can impact on the data center performance, to offer an uninterrupted service to the users or meet the SLA requirements. Among the data center components, as shown in Fig. 3, the major failures are related to the software (almost 35%) and misconfiguration errors (almost 30%). Hardware components represent between 5% and 8% of failures, whereas network contributes to around 10% of total data center failures. Human errors also cause 10% of failures in data centers. Therefore, high availability mechanisms in a data center must be focused on software failures, so that if a tolerant mechanism at the software level is implemented robustly, it can maintain the service up even if certain hardware failure occur [7].

However, it should be noted that reliable hardware architecture planning and infrastructure design is the basis of any service, meaning that without availability of redundant network paths and hardware resources, it is not possible to implement high availability on the software level. Besides, a failure in a hardware component causes a very high downtime: in network devices, a downtime caused by failures in a device correspond to 78% of total downtime caused by all probable errors [19]. Data centers must implement some mechanisms to mitigate unplanned outages. Distributed storage, health monitoring, and disaster recovery mechanisms are some examples of available methods to achieve highly available cloud services. These strategies are complementary: a disaster recovery requires a monitoring health service to check components and a distributed storage to recovery data in another entity. Distributed storage focuses on errors on application level and must have an easy configuration to avoid misconfiguration problems; health monitoring and disaster recovery provide redundancy in software, but trigger when a failure occurs in the hardware or network.

In a similar way, HDFS (Hadoop Distributed File System) [44] also stores data in geo-diverse nodes. Its architecture is divided into three main nodes: DataNodes, which stores data blocks and can rebalance data distribution among them; NameNode, which manages files information such as namespace, permissions and mapping files to DataNodes; and CheckpointNode, that provides fault tolerance and increases availability saving files and merging it with NameNode.

Regarding to health monitoring, that is related to checking the resources consumption of the application instances running on cloud, we can cite Google System Health, which offers high availability [7]. This solution monitors the configuration, activity, and error data from each server, storing this information in a repository that allows some analytic engine to diagnose and suggests the best approach for repairing or preventing the failure. VMware vSphere² also provides solutions such as the automatic restart of VMs in the servers, instantaneous live migration, and automatic remediation by monitoring at application level. These solutions can be integrated with distributed storage to provide a fast recovery in case of failure.

Disaster recovery has a high adoption rate in data centers. The use of redundant data centers mitigate the service downtime when an active data center turns inaccessible by events such as human errors, fire, terrorist attacks or natural disasters. Huawei provides a disaster recovery solution [3] in three different levels: application level, data level, and media level. These levels have different recovery procedures and times: a failure in application level must be recovered in minutes by replication of virtual machines; in media level, switches and data are mirrored in another data center, with the recovery is established in hours; and media level makes a backup of main data center in others data centers, and its protocol decides which data center will replace the failed one. The recovery is made in one or more days.

VMware offers a Disaster Recovery-as-a-Service called VMware vCloud Air Disaster Recovery. This service avoids the data center to implement your own disaster recovery mechanism using a more consolidated service. The service leverages vSphere Replication, as discussed beforehand, to provide robust, asynchronous replication capabilities at the hypervisor layer. This solution is limited to vSphere environments.

More information about mechanisms used to achieve high availability in clouds can be found in [15].

3.4 Commercial Solutions

This section describes briefly some commercial solutions and shows how they provide high availability.

---

²VMware: Business Continuity and Disaster Recovery— http://www.vmware.com/solutions/business-continuity.html.

Fig. 4 Amazon Availability
Zones (AZ) can be
considered as separate data
centers, with separate power,
cooling, and Internet access.
The elastic load balancing
can be used to balance traffic
between them [9]

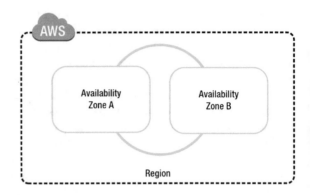

3.4.1   AWS Cloud

The AWS (Amazon Web Services) Cloud provides an elastic load balancing that
automatically distributes incoming application traffic across multiple Amazon EC2
instances, spreaded around the world into multiple regions. Each region is independent of the others in order to design highly available applications with low latency
response time to the customers (Fig. 4).

According to AWS site,[3] the AWS Cloud also supports disaster recovery (DR)
architectures for small customer workload data center failures and for hot standby
environments that enable rapid failover at scale. With data centers in several regions
around the world, AWS provides a set of cloud-based DR services that enable rapid
recovery of the IT infrastructure and data.

3.4.2   Google Cloud Platform

Google Cloud Platform[4] is a platform that provides services such as compute, storage,
machine learning, big data, and more. In general, Google uses its own tools to keep
the services available, such as GFS (Google File System). GFS is one of the most
well-known distributed storage solutions [18], comprised of disk redundancy and
efficient resource allocation. It is designed to provide efficiency, availability, and
scalability to large volumes of data in data centers. GFS distributes files into chunks
of 64 MB that are managed by a master node.

Google Cloud has a service focused on providing high availability in SQL
instances. The developer configures an instance to failover in a failure case or replicates automatically the data in other zones. When a zone comes unavailable, Google
Cloud failover SQL instance in another zone is available.[5]

---

[3]aws.amazon.com.

[4]https://cloud.google.com/.

[5]https://cloud.google.com/sql/faq.

3.4.3   Microsoft Azure

Azure[6] is the Microsoft platform of cloud computing that offers several services for host applications. This platform enables to use other Microsoft solutions for processing data, such as big data and machine learning. Azure has many mechanisms for providing high availability and DR, such as load balancing, replication of data and redundancy of components. Some mechanisms are executed automatically, but in some cases the application developer should have an additional work to configure these mechanisms. For instance, Azure load balancing mechanism uses round-robin to evenly distribute jobs across instances. However, if complexity of jobs varies greatly, it is possible that some instances assigned with a number of complex jobs while other instances remain idle [6].

The structure of Azure is also divided logical and physically into regions, that are composed of data centers. Under some circumstances, it is possible that an entire region become unavailable, for instance due network failures or natural disasters. Azure offers redundancy approach and backup of VMs. Azure provides mechanism that is referred to Geo-Redundant Storage (GRS); GRS replicates storage to a paired data center hundreds of miles apart within a specific geographic region [15].

3.4.4   IBM Cloud

IBM Cloud comprises a set of cloud computing services including IaaS, PaaS and SaaS through public, private, and hybrid delivery models. IBM cloud offers specific products which provide cloud solutions for compute, storage, network, security, management, data and analytics, that can be combined together with other open or third-party solutions. For instance, IBM Bluemix is platform that combines PaaS and IaaS available in local, dedicated, and public and also offers a suite of instant-on services, including Watson,[7] Data Analytics, and Mobile Services.[8] It can deploy a cloud infrastructure using, for instance, OpenStack or CloudFoundry, without loosing integration with other cloud solutions like, for instance, IBM Cloud orchestrator,[9] a cloud management platform for automating provisioning of cloud services.

High availability is mainly provided by IBM cloud services themselves but also by the specific solutions. Also, high availability can be enabled for the cloud service providers and the applications running in the cloud. IBM Bluemix offers a catalog of availability monitoring services that can run synthetic tests to proactively detect and fix performance issues before they impact users. It also has multi-region architectures ans supports different services configuration and data replication.

---

[6]https://azure.microsoft.com/pt-br/overview/what-is-azure/.

[7]https://www.ibm.com/watson/.

[8]https://www.ibm.com/cloud-computing/bluemix.

[9]http://www.ibm.com/software/products/en/ibm-cloud-orchestrator.

3.5   Infrastructure Standards and Tiers

Standards such as TIA-942, Uptime Institute, ANSI/BICSI 002, ASHRAE TC9.9, and CENELEC EN 50600-x define fundamental aspects, best practices, and recommendations regarding data center design and infrastructure. The TIA (Telecommunications Industry Association) covers key topics related to the site space planning, cabling infrastructure, environmental considerations, and tiered reliability. Based on the service requirement and the criticality of applications running on the clouds, data centers can be divided into four tiers with different availability levels.

Uptime Institute consortium provides different recommendations related to the level of redundant components, points of failure, watts per square foot, and availability for each tier. Tier specification goes from Tier 1 to 4, where higher tiers provide greater availability and inherit requirements of lower tiers. Though, increase in the reliability comes in the price of higher costs and operational complexities. The tier classification standards help to compare data centers reliability and design strategies. Table 2 presents some of these recommendations according to tier classification.

The redundant components refer to the number of IT equipment, cooling, and power components that comprises the data center infrastructure. In Tier 1, N means no redundancy indicating that system failures will result in outages. While in Tiers 2, 3, and 4, $N + 1$ means that there is some level of component redundancy. The number of delivery paths refers to the number of distribution paths of the power and

Table 2   Uptime Institutes Tier Classification System for data centers [28]

Tiers	Description	Redundant components	Number of delivery paths	Availability level
Tier 1 Basic	Planned and unplanned activity may cause system disruption	N	Only 1	99.671%
Tier 2 Redundant	Less susceptible to system disruption from planned and unplanned activity	N+1	Only 1	99.741%
Tier 3 Concurrently Maintainable	Equipment replacement and maintenance do not require disrupting computer hardware operation	N+1	1 active and 1 passive	99.982%
Tier 4 Fault Tolerant	Adds fault tolerance to the infrastructure. Sustains a worst case, unplanned event with no critical load impact	2 (N+1)	2 simultaneously active	99.995%

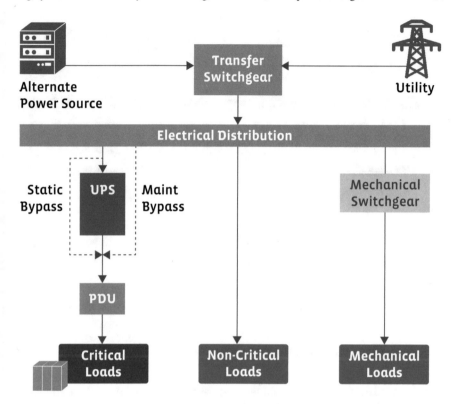

Fig. 5 Example of a power infrastructure—Tier 1 classification (adapted from BICSI [1])

cooling systems serving the IT equipment. That way, more distribution paths result in higher overall system availability [17]. Figures 5 and 6 show examples of a power infrastructure with Tier 1 and 4, respectively.

It is important to highlight that the tier classification relies on the all data center segments (IT equipment, electrical infrastructure, mechanical infrastructure, and facility operations) to deliver the overall availability. Therefore, a data center with a Tier 2 mechanical system and a Tier 4 electrical system will result in a Tier 2 data center availability rating.

Another important note is that the tier selection depends on the business requirements (such as availability, employment costs, and downtime financial consequences), meaning that a Tier 4 selection may not be the best option for a data center running non-critical workloads [49].

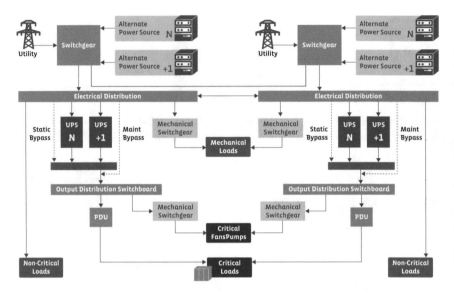

Fig. 6 Example of a power infrastructure—Tier 4 classification (adapted from BICSI [1])

4 Modeling High Availability Clouds

In order to clarify what have been done in the scientific literature about modeling high availability clouds, we performed a systematic review. Using this method, we intend to provide reader with a broad view of the field. The following subsections describe our methodology, results, and some discussions.

The main goal of this systematic review was to answer the following research questions (RQ):

- RQ.1: What is the current state of the art in high availability cloud modeling?
- RQ.2: What are the most common metrics used to measure HA in cloud systems models?
- RQ.3: What are the most common data center subsystems modelled to evaluate high availability in clouds?
- RQ.4: What are the most common approaches used to model high availability for clouds?
- RQ.5: What are the main remaining research challenges in this field?

The initial search returned 8, 20, 110, and 186 articles from ACM Digital Library, IEEE Xplore, Springer, and Science Direct, respectively, totaling 324 works. By reading all abstracts and using the criteria for inclusion or exclusion, we selected 15 papers for data extraction and quality evaluation.

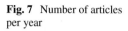

Fig. 7 Number of articles per year

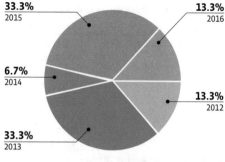

Fig. 8 Number of articles per research source

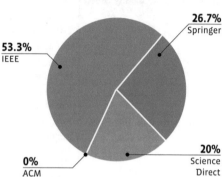

4.1   Overview of High Availability Modeling for Clouds

Considering the RQ.1, Fig. 7 shows the number of published articles per year; while the Fig. 8 shows the number of articles per research source. As one can note, 2013 and 2015 concentrate most of the works done in this research area; and IEEE is the research source with more articles published in this area.

To answer the RQ.2, Table 3 summarizes some metrics and their respective defini-tion presented in various articles addressing highly available cloud solutions. Service availability and SSA (Steady-State Availability) are the most common metrics used by authors [13, 24, 30, 35, 36, 42] and are related directly to the available and operational time of a target service. We also found metrics related to the provider costs due service unavailability, such as downtime cost analysis [38] and number of transactions lost [30]. On the other hand, authors in [37] modeled metrics to a spe-cific application, MMOG (Massively Multiplayer Online Game); these metrics are related to interruptions caused by game unavailability, and two metrics are interesting because analyze the unavailability impact on players, severity of the interruptions and average non-serviced clients.

Answering the RQ.3, the results showed that computing resources are the most focused subsystems (with 93.3%), which are addressed in the literature, reinforcing the crucial role of the IT infrastructure.

Table 3 Main metrics used to evaluate the cloud availability

Metrics	Definitions	References
Service availability	The percentage of served requests in comparison to the total number of received requests	[24]
	The uptime over a year	[35]
	It can be understood as the probability that the system is found operational during a given period of time or has been restored after the occurrence of a failure event	[13]
Steady-state availability (SSA)	Number of nines	[36]
	Represents the long-term probability that the system is operating correctly	[42]
	and available to perform its functions	[30]
Downtime cost analysis	caused by a disaster in a data center per year in minutes	[38]
Number of transactions lost	It is the number of transactions lost due to VMM rejuvenation	[30]
Instantaneous non- interruption ratio	Ratio between the measured state update frequency of the MMOG within one measurement timestep and the required minimal frequency	[37]
Total non-interruption ratio	The percentage of time the MMOG the state update frequency equal or greater than the required frequency, over a given time interval	[37]
Duration of the interruptions	The start of the failure to the moment when all affected clients recover	[37]
Number of interruptions	Number of interruptions in a time interval	[37]
Severity of the interruptions	The percentage of affected players	[37]
Average non-serviced clients	Number of clients who were denied service	[37]

Fig. 9 The most common approaches used to model high availability

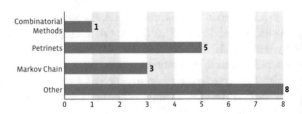

Finally, considering the RQ.4, Fig. 9 shows the most common approaches used to model high availability in cloud data centers. In order to detail these solutions, we will describe them in next subsections.

4.1.1 Markov Chain Solutions

Authors in [13, 26, 36] used Markov chain approach to model cloud availability. In [26], authors proposed three CTMC (Continuous Time Markov Chain) submodels that capture a specific aspect of a cloud data center. These submodels are RASM (Resource Allocation Submodel), VMPSM (Virtual Machine Provisioning Submodel), and Availability Model; and the integration between them is shown in Fig. 10.

While in [36], authors used an extended DTMC (Discrete Time Markov Chain) to model computing resources of a multi-cloud and a controller (dual layer) to guarantee system availability while minimize costs (Fig. 11). The DTMC has physical nodes (that represent concrete elements in the cloud, such as physical server or a pool of VMs offered by a cloud provider) and logic nodes (that represent the success or the failure state of the application). The DTMC has control variables and measured

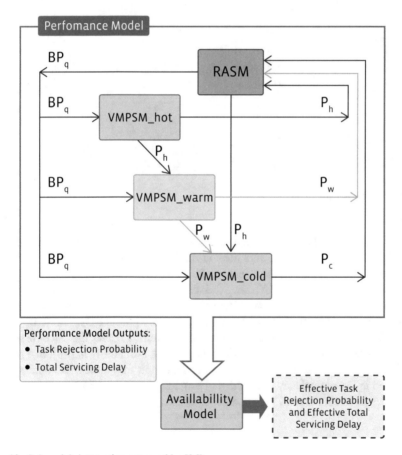

Fig. 10 Submodels integration proposed by [26]

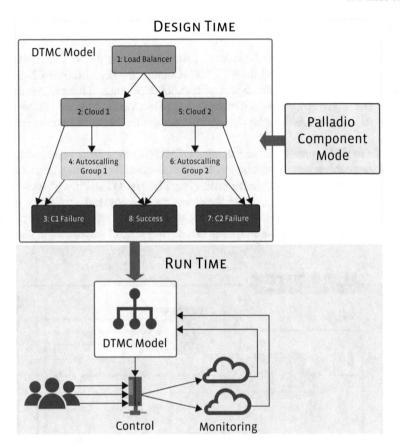

Fig. 11 Approach proposed by [36]

availability as labels to transitions; and rewards or costs can be introduced. The DTMC model is meant to be kept alive at runtime, and the controller is responsible for modifying it, changing the effects on the actual implementation.

Authors in [13] used a different Markov chain, named MRM (Markov Reward Model), in conjunction with RBD (Reliability Block Diagrams) in order to represent the system behavior, that cannot be captured by only pure RBDs. The RBD model (Fig. 12) is used to describe the high-level components, whereas the MRM is used to model the components involved in the evaluation of availability in [13]. In a similar way, in [12], authors also used RBD and MRM, but they model the components involved in the redundancy mechanism. Figure 13 shows the RMR model proposed to represent a redundant system composed of two nodes.

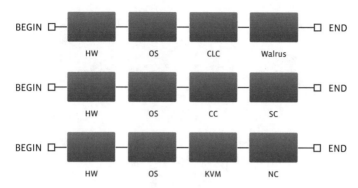

Fig. 12 RBDs that represent cloud, Cluster and Nodes Subsystems (from *top* to *down*) proposed by [13]

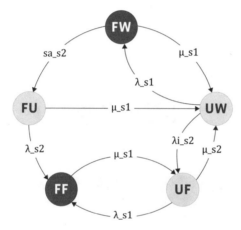

Fig. 13 MRM model that represents a redundant system with two nodes proposed by [12]

4.1.2 Petrinets Solutions

Petrinets are also used to model cloud availability [24, 30, 34, 35, 38, 42]. In [24], authors presented a SCPN (Stochastic Colored Petri Nets) model, which is a class of DSPN (Deterministic Stochastic Petri Nets) models, to evaluate the availability of cloud services and take in consideration the application deployment in geographically distributed data centers. For that, authors propose five different SCPN building blocks, shown in Fig. 14: DC (data center), server, VM (virtual machine), load balancer, and component (multi-tier app).

Petrinets can also be used with others approaches. Still considering the environment with more than one data center, in [38], authors used SRN (Stochastic Reward Nets) to model each component (such as VM, host, storage, data center) as subsystem and the global system is composed of all data centers. Authors consider the disaster

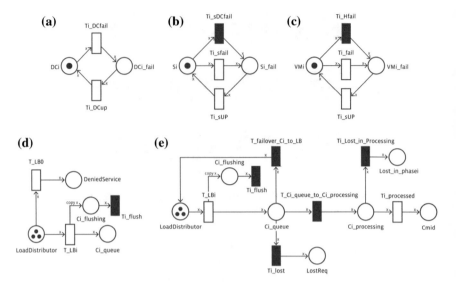

Fig. 14 SCPN models proposed by [24]

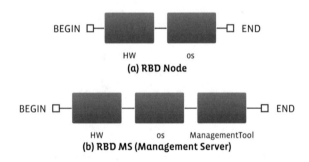

Fig. 15 RBDs that represent Node and Management Server used by [35] and [34]

tolerant scenario, and make a analysis about the trade-off between system availability and downtime cost with infrastructure construction cost.

In [35], SPNs were used to describe low-level modeling and RBD is used again at high-level modeling, forming a hierarchical model to describe system rejuvenation. The RBD models consider only the non-aging failures. Figure 15a shows that a node fails only if both hardware (HW) or operating system (OS) fail; and Fig. 15b shows that a failure in the management tool may provide a fault in the Management Server, independent of hardware and operating system. The proposed SPN model is composed of three submodels: (a) Management Server Model, (b) Clock Model and (c) System Model (Fig. 13).

Following the same combination (including the same RBD models presented in Fig. 15), the same authors evaluated other rejuvenation policies and find steady-state availability and expected annual downtime in [34]. The proposed SPN models were

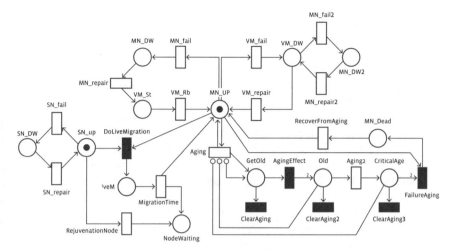

Fig. 16 SPN that represents the system submodel proposed by [34]

based on [35], and they improve the model with a Clock Model with check, that is a enhanced version of Clock Model. The Clock Model with check execute a check on VMM aging status before perform a live migration. Figure 16 shows the SPN that represents the proposed system submodel.

In [30], authors studied the effectiveness of VM migration rejuvenation by modeling it more precisely using CTMC model. However, due to the complexity of construction of CTMC models, the availability models of a server virtualized system is done in an extension of Petrinets, named SRN (Stochastic Reward Net). In [42], authors also used SRN, but they used a SRN hierarchical model for modeling memory virtualization and availability. The proposed SRN is transformed in a MRM to steady state and/or transient analysis.

4.1.3 Other Solutions

Other approaches were used to model cloud availability. In [32], authors used Bayesian networks to allocation of cloud resources in order to maximize the service dependability. Others used mathematical approaches, such as probability distribution [21] to model the accumulated downtime, statistical distribution [37] to model MMOGs (Massively multiplayer online games) as a service-based market, and combinatorial method [39] to define the availability model, considering the operational power and replication mechanism.

4.1.4 Proprietary Tools

There are some commercial tools that simulate a data center infrastructure. 6Sig-maDCX[10] is a commercial simulator that uses CFD (Computational Fluid Dynamics) technique to provide levels of productivity for data center design, troubleshooting and operation. 6SigmaDCX models many data center components, such as cooling, power and IT infrastructures. 6SigmaDCX allows 3D model of data center and configuration of several metrics (such as type of customer, data center floor space and critical IT load). The simulation results are represented by graphs and can be integrated with several DCIM (Data Center Infrastructure Management) solutions.

CoolSim[11] is a tool for performing occasional simulations to determine the best location for cooling and IT equipment. This simulator also uses CFD for modeling the airflow in data centers. An interesting feature of CoolSim is that it allows users to pay as you go for use of the application through a cloud SaaS delivery model.

However, the main disadvantage of these solutions is the price. For instance, the annual license of CoolSim is about $15,000. As an alternative, there is other non-commercial simulators, such as the BigHouse [33], that is a tool focused on infrastructure for data center systems. Instead of simulating servers using detailed micro-architectural models, BigHouse raises the level of abstraction using a combination of queuing theory and stochastic modeling. BigHouse leverages statistical simulation techniques to limit simulation turn around time to the minimum runtime needed for a desired accuracy.

4.2 Discussion

From the review of the literature, we can observe that the cloud availability can be modelled from various perspective based on the goal of the study. However, a holistic view of the all layers are still missing.

We can highlight that each of the presented modeling approaches has its advantages and also disadvantages. For instance, RBDs are commonly used due to their simplicity, but they are not suitable when detail behaviors of systems need to be described. Markov chains can be used with RBDs or separately, but it is not scalable enough for modeling large systems. Hence, to have a comprehensive models and framework addressing all aspects of high availability in data centers, a combination of various models should be considered. Until now, a huge effort was put on modeling the computing resources, while the rest of the subsystems, such as power and cooling systems, are nearly neglected in regarding their availability models.

The RQ.5 that deal with main challenges will be described in next section.

---

[10]http://www.futurefacilities.com/solutions/data-centers/.

[11]http://www.coolsimsoftware.com/Home.aspx.

5 Open Research Challenges

The enterprise applications that rely on data center infrastructure are inherently more available, robust, and scalable. Physical resilience is assured by virtual resource redundancy, and it brings a relatively simple way to deal with a hardware component outage, by migrating the virtual application to other available and healthy physical resource. However, according to [17], *while the spreading of risk across virtual systems reduces the risk of physical outage, complexities of running pools of highly integrated systems have its own challenges.*

These challenges include the need to address the deterioration of physical buildings and systems of the data center, and also have to embrace the degradation of virtual servers, storage, and network components. In this section, we highlight some of the most important challenges in cloud data center availability.

5.1 Cloud Data Center Modeling and Simulation

A comprehensive modeling of the data center system during runtime is the first step towards detecting possible single points of the failure, and calculating the end-to-end availability of the services offered to the customers. A good starting point would be to model the hardware system in the data center in order to calculate the availability of each service, end-to-end, by defining the involved components related to each service.

However, according to [11], *"because of heterogeneous software/hardware components and complicated interactions among them, the probability of failures improves. The services reliability arouses more attention"*. Cloud reliability analysis and modeling are very critical but hard because of the complexity and large scale of the system.

Authors in [29] say that *"a monolithic model may suffer from intractability and poor scalability due to vast parameter space"*. In this way, some authors have proposed separate submodels for different subsystems of a complex cloud center, such as [26]. However, one should integrate these subsystems in a coherent way, considering the general aspect of the model.

Beyond that, there are also some tools that make use of these models to simulate data center behavior under different circumstances, such as hardware failures, resource allocation, and even disasters. However, most of them are focused on physical and logical layers.

5.2 High-Level Metrics

PUE (Power Usage Effectiveness) has been used as a good metric to classify data centers' energy performance. According to [17], PUE determines the energy efficiency of data centers, and has been used worldwide in the technology industry, becoming a mainstream approach to determine data center energy use efficiency. PUE is defined as Eq. 7.

$$PUE = \frac{\sum Power\,Delivered\,To\,DataCenter}{\sum IT\,Equipment\,Power\,Use} = \frac{\sum P_{mechanical} + P_{electrical} + P_{other}}{\sum P_{IT}}$$

(7)

There are many other metrics related to data center performance, such as ERE (Energy Reuse Effectiveness), WUE (Water Usage Effectiveness), Carbon Usage Effectiveness (CUE) and Return Temperature Index (RTI), as shown in Table 4. However, common metrics suffer from lack of relation with user perception. For instance, a system with availability of 0.9999 is down for an of average 52 min during a year. However, if the down time occurs during a peak hour, it has a higher impact than a failure that occurs when the system load is low, and less users will be affected by that failure. It is important to look for other metrics that go beyond the power, mechanical, and IT systems

To address this issue, other high-level metrics can be defined. For instance, we can consider FIF (Failure Impact Factor) proposed by [14]. FIF helps to measure the risk of any single failure for the owner. The definition of this parameter can also help designing a system with improved reliability without investing more than needed. By using FIF it is possible to define the components with high risk in the system, and protect them up to the level that guarantees no more than a given number of

Table 4 Data center performance metrics (from [17])

Metric	Description	Equation
ERE	Recognize that some data centers have the ability to provide energy that can be reused in other parts of the facility or campus	$ERE = \frac{Annual\,Facility\,Energy\,Use - Annual\,Energy\,Reused}{Annual\,IT\,Energy\,Use}$
WUE	Determine the efficacy of water use in the data center, based on the energy used by the IT equipment	$WUE = \frac{Annual\,Site\,Water\,Usage}{Annual\,IT\,Energy\,Use}$
CUE	Judge the amount of carbon that is expended as compared to the annual IT energy used in the data center	$CUE = \frac{Annual\,CO_2\,emissions\,caused\,by\,the\,datacenter}{Annual\,IT\,Energy\,Use}$
RTI	Determine the efficacy of the air management in a data center	$RTI = \frac{Return\,Air\,Temp - Supply\,Air\,Temp}{Rack\,Out\,Mean\,Temp - Rack\,In\,Mean\,Temp} * 100$

customers/services will be affected by a single failure in the system at any given time. Risk is defined by combining the probability of the failure to occur and the severity of the incident (scenario) occurring. So, for calculating FIF, first the system availability should be calculated.

For instance, authors in [14] define a resilience parameter, namely the failure impact (FI) in rational and irrational environments.[12] The FI in a rational environment is proportional to the number of customers disconnected by the failure, N, and the unavailability of the component, U. On the other hand, the FI in an irrational environment, all failures are statistically independent and all failures have a binary consequence: connection is fully disconnected (0) or not (1), no intermediate situations are considered [14]. The FI is given by Eq. 8.

$$FI = N^{\alpha} \times U \tag{8}$$

where $\alpha > 1$ leads to more and more irrationality, and $\alpha = 1$ is the rational environment.

In [37], authors use different metrics in their experiments that reflect the unavailability impact on MMOG players, such as number of interruptions in a time interval, duration of the interruptions (the start of the failure to the moment when all affected players recover), severity of the interruptions (% of affected players), average non-serviced players (# of players who were denied service). These metrics are interesting because relate failures and users interruptions, and were described previously in Table 3.

Another high-level metric is the lost revenue, a simple way of calculating the potential loss in a data center outage [17], as shown in Eq. 9.

$$Lost\,Revenue = \frac{GR}{TH} \times I \times H \tag{9}$$

where GR denotes gross yearly revenue, TH denotes total yearly business hours, I denotes percentage impact, and H denotes number of hours of outage.

According to [17], loss can be viewed in different perspectives, such as monetary loss, reputational loss, employee productivity loss, client loyalty loss, and also combinations of all of these. Every business will suffer different degree of cost and, in the end, must balance against the risk and the cost of a disruption.

According to [17], "*it is important to understand that these metrics should be used together, providing a range of data points to help understand the efficiency and effectiveness of a data center; different combinations of these metrics will produce a synergistic outcome*".

---

[12] According to authors, "*an irrational environment is where a network operator is worried more about a big failure disconnecting all clients for 1 h at the same time than for multiple small failures throughout the year disconnecting every client for 1 h on average [14].*"

6   Final Considerations

According to Gartner, Inc,[13] *"by 2020, a corporate "no-cloud" policy will be as rare as a "no-internet" policy is today"*, in other words, the migration to a cloud-based solution is practically indefeasible. It is interesting to note that it does not means that everyone will be cloud-based; but the scenario with no-cloud will gradually vanish.

Due to a growing number of companies that using services on cloud, many challenges begin to emerge. Serving the demand of many services is a task complicated, due to a limited resources of the data centers. Understanding the cloud data center is a key point to manage resources and to estimate how physical and logical failures occurred on a data center can impact their users' perception.

In this work, we presented basic concepts needed to understand the mechanisms to provide high availability, consequences of outages in cloud data centers and a data center infrastructure overview.

Furthermore, we also presented a systematic literature review about cloud high availability, highlighting the main approaches used to model it. Whereas we have found Markov Chain, RBD, and Petrinets as main approaches, some articles have used hybrid approaches, due limitations of each technique.

The cloud data center is a complex and big system composed of other subsystems, such as power and cooling. Some research questions emerge when we are modeling these subsystems separately: how can they be integrated in order to improve the understanding of overall data center behavior? How does a failure in one of these subsystems affect the overall data center and the cloud users? Which protection strategies can we suggest to mitigate these negative impacts?

Acknowledgements This work was supported by the RLAM Innovation Center, Ericsson Telecomunicações S.A., Brazil.

References

1. Ansi/bicsi 002, data center design and implementation best practices. Retrieved November 2016, from https://www.bicsi.org/uploadedFiles/BICSI_Website/Global_Community/Presentations/CALA/Ciordia_002_Colombia_2016.pdf.
2. Cost of data center outages: Data center performance benchmark series. Retrieved November 2016, from http://www.emersonnetworkpower.com/en-US/Resources/Market/Data-Center/Latest-Thinking/Ponemon/Documents/2016-Cost-of-Data-Center-Outages-FINAL-2.pdf/.
3. Data center disaster recovery and backup solution. enterprise. Retrieved November 2016, from enterprise.huawei.com/ilink/enenterprise/download/HW_322364.
4. Relationship Between Availability and Reliability. Retrieved November 2016, from http://www.weibull.com/hotwire/issue26/relbasics26.htm.
5. Top 4 data center outages of 2014. Retrieved November 2016, from http://www.cyrusone.com/blog/top-5-data-center-outages-of-2014/.
6. Bai, H. (2014). *Zen of cloud: Learning cloud computing by examples on microsoft azure.* CRC Press.

---

[13]http://www.gartner.com/newsroom/id/3354117.

7. Barroso, L. A., Clidaras, J., & Hölzle, U. (2013). The datacenter as a computer: An introduction to the design of warehouse-scale machines. *Synthesis Lectures on Computer Architecture, 8*(3), 1–154.
8. Bauer, E., & Adams, R. (2012). *Reliability and availability of cloud computing.* Wiley.
9. Brian Beach. (2014). *Pro powershell for amazon web services: DevOps for the AWS cloud.* A press.
10. Clarke, E. M., Klieber, W., Nováček, M., & Zuliani, P. (2011). Model checking and the state explosion problem. In *LASER Summer School on Software Engineering*, pp. 1–30. Springer.
11. Chen, J., Liu, Y., Cui, H., & Li, Y. (2013). Methods with low complexity for evaluating cloud service reliability. In *Proceedings 16th International Symposium on Wireless Personal Multimedia Communications*, pp. 1–5. IEEE.
12. Dantas, J., Matos, R., Araujo, J., & Maciel, P. (2012). An availability model for eucalyptus platform: An analysis of warm-standy replication mechanism. In *2012 IEEE International Conference on Systems, Man, and Cybernetics (SMC)*, pp. 1664–1669. IEEE.
13. Dantas, J., Matos, R., Araujo, J., & Maciel, P. (2015). Eucalyptus-based private clouds: availability modeling and comparison to the cost of a public cloud. *Computing, 97*(11), 1121–1140.
14. Dixit, A., Mahloo, M., Lannoo, B., Chen, J., Wosinska, L., Colle, D., & Pickavet, M. (2014). Protection strategies for next generation passive optical networks-2. In *2014 International Conference on Optical Network Design and Modeling*, pp. 13–18. IEEE.
15. Endo, P. T., Rodrigues, M., Gonçalves, G. E., Kelner, J., Sadok, D. H., & Curescu, C. (2016). High availability in clouds: Systematic review and research challenges. *Journal of Cloud Computing, 5*(1), 16.
16. Gailey, G., Taubensee, J., Rabeler, C., Glick, A., & Squillace, R.: Azure resiliency technical guidance: Recovery from a region-wide service disruption. Retrieved December 2016. https://docs.microsoft.com/en-us/azure/resiliency/resiliency-technical-guidance-recovery-loss-azure-region.
17. Geng, H. (2014). *Data center handbook.* Wiley.
18. Ghemawat, S., Gobioff, H., & Leung, S.-T. (2003). The google file system. In *ACM SIGOPS operating systems review*, vol. 37, pp. 29–43. ACM.
19. Gill, P., Jain, N., & Nagappan, N. (2011). Understanding network failures in data centers: Measurement, analysis, and implications. In *ACM SIGCOMM Computer Communication Review*, vol. 41, pp. 350–361. ACM.
20. Gonçalves, G., Endo, P. T., Rodrigues, M., Kelner, J., Sadok, D., & Curescu, C. (2016). Risk-based model for availability estimation of saf redundancy models. In *2016 IEEE Symposium on Computers and Communication (ISCC)*, pp. 886–891. IEEE.
21. Gonzalez, A. J., & Helvik, B. E. (2013). Hybrid cloud management to comply efficiently with sla availability guarantees. In *2013 12th IEEE International Symposium on Network Computing and Applications (NCA)*, pp. 127–134. IEEE.
22. Hoelzle, U., & Barroso, L. (2009). The datacenter as a computer. *Morgan and Claypool.*
23. Høyland, A., & Rausand, M. (2009). *System reliability theory: models and statistical methods*, vol. 420. Wiley.
24. Jammal, M., Kanso, A., Heidari, P., & Shami, A. (2016). A formal model for the availability analysis of cloud deployed multi-tiered applications. pp. 82–87. IEEE.
25. Kao, W., & Geng, H. (2015). Renewable and clean energy for data centers. *Data Center Handbook*, pp. 559–576.
26. Khazaei, H., Mišić, J., Mišić, V .B., & Mohammadi, N. B. (2012). Availability analysis of cloud computing centers. In *Global Communications Conference (GLOBECOM), 2012 IEEE*, pp. 1957–1962. IEEE.
27. Kosik, W. J., & Geng, H. (2014). Energy and sustainability in data centers. *Data Center Handbook*, pp. 15–45.
28. ADC Krone. (2008). Tia-942: Data center standards overview.
29. Longo, F., Ghosh, R., Naik, V.K., & Trivedi, K.S. (2011). A scalable availability model for infrastructure-as-a-service cloud. In *2011 IEEE/IFIP 41st International Conference on Dependable Systems & Networks (DSN)*, pp. 335–346. IEEE.

30. Machida, F., Kim, D. S., & Trivedi, K. S. (2013). Modeling and analysis of software rejuvenation in a server virtualized system with live VM migration. *Performance Evaluation, 70*(3), 212–230.
31. Malhotra, M., & Trivedi, K. S. (1994). Power-hierarchy of dependability-model types. *IEEE Transactions on Reliability, 43*(3), 493–502.
32. Marrone, S. (2015). Using bayesian networks for highly available cloud-based web applications. *Journal of Reliable Intelligent Environments, 1*(2–4), 87–100.
33. Meisner, D., Wu, J., & Wenisch, T. F. (2012). Bighouse: A simulation infrastructure for data center systems. In *2012 IEEE International Symposium on Performance Analysis of Systems and Software (ISPASS)*, pp. 35–45. IEEE.
34. Melo, M., Araujo, J., Matos, R., Menezes, J., & Maciel, P. (2013). Comparative analysis of migration-based rejuvenation schedules on cloud availability. In *2013 IEEE International Conference on Systems, Man, and Cybernetics*, pp. 4110–4115. IEEE.
35. Melo, M., Maciel, P., Araujo, J., Matos, R., & Araújo, C. (2013). Availability study on cloud computing environments: Live migration as a rejuvenation mechanism. In *2013 43rd Annual IEEE/IFIP International Conference on Dependable Systems and Networks (DSN)*, pp. 1–6. IEEE.
36. Miglierina, M., Gibilisco, G. P., Ardagna, G. P., & Di Nitto, E. (2013). Model based control for multi-cloud applications. In *2013 5th International Workshop on Modeling in Software Engineering (MiSE)*, pp. 37–43. IEEE.
37. Nae, V., Prodan, R., & Iosup, A. (2014). Sla-based operations of massively multiplayer online games in clouds. *Multimedia Systems, 20*(5), 521–544.
38. Nguyen, T. A., Kim, D. S., & Park, J. S. (2016). Availability modeling and analysis of a data center for disaster tolerance. *Future Generation Computer Systems, 56*, 27–50.
39. Noor, T. H., Sheng, Q. Z., Yao, L., Dustdar, S., & Anne, H. H. (2016). Ngu. CloudArmor: Supporting reputation-based trust management for cloud services. *IEEE Transactions on Parallel and Distributed Systems, 27*(2), 367–380.
40. Pelánek, R. (2008). Fighting state space explosion: Review and evaluation. In *International Workshop on Formal Methods for Industrial Critical Systems*, pp. 37–52. Springer.
41. Pham, C., Cao, P., Kalbarczyk, Z., & Iyer, R. K. (2012). Toward a high availability cloud: Techniques and challenges. In *IEEE/IFIP International Conference on Dependable Systems and Networks Workshops (DSN 2012)*, pp. 1–6. IEEE.
42. Ro, C. (2015). Modeling and analysis of memory virtualization in cloud computing. *Cluster Computing, 18*(1), 177–185.
43. SAForum. (September, 2011). *Service Availability Forum Service Availability Interface— Overview SAI-Overview-B.05.03*. SAForum.
44. Shvachko, K., Kuang, H., Radia, S., & Chansler, R. (2010). The hadoop distributed file system. In *2010 IEEE 26th symposium on mass storage systems and technologies (MSST)*, pp. 1–10. IEEE.
45. Szatmári, Z., Kövi, A., & Reitenspiess, M. (2008). Applying mda approach for the sa forum platform. In *Proceedings of the 2nd Workshop on Middleware-Application Interaction: Affiliated with the DisCoTec Federated Conferences 2008*, pp. 19–24. ACM.
46. ASHRAE Technical Committee. (2011). Thermal guidelines for data processing environments expanded data center classes and usage guidance.
47. Toeroe, M., & Tam, F. (2012). *Service availability: principles and practice*. Wiley.
48. Trivedi, K., Sathaye, A., & Ramani, S. Availability modeling in practice.
49. Turner, W. P., PE, J. H., Seader, P. E., & Brill, K. J. (2006). Tier classification define site infrastructure performance. *Uptime Institute*, 17.

Author Biographies

Patricia Takako Endo received her PhD of Computer Science from the Federal University of Pernambuco (UFPE) in 2014. She is a professor at University of Pernambuco (UPE) since 2010; and a researcher at Research in Networks and Telecommunication Group (GPRT) since 2009. Her current research interests are: cloud Computing, and resource management.

Glauco Estácio Gonçalves is a professor at Rural Federal University of Pernambuco (UFRPE) since 2013. He received his Ph.D. degree in Computer Science from the UFPE, respectively in 2007 and 2012. His research interests include: Performance Evaluation of Networked Systems; Cloud Computing; and Optimization Algorithms for Resource Allocation.

Daniel Rosendo is a Master Student in Computer Science at UFPE. He is taking part of the GPRT since 2014. His areas of interests are Software-Defined Networking (SDN), Network Management, and Internet of Things (IoT).

Demis Gomes is a student of Information Systems at UFRPE and member of GPRT since 2015. His current research interests are Cloud Computing, Performance Evaluation, Internet of Things, and Fog Computing.

Guto Leoni Santos is a student of Information Systems at UPE. He is taking part of GPRT and his research interests include: Distributed Systems, cloud Computing, Performance Evaluation, Internet of Things, Smart Cities, Neural Networks, and Artificial Intelligence.

André Luis Cavalcanti Moreira received his PhD of Computer Science from the UFPE. His research topic is in self-organization of cloud networks and adaptation of CDN provisioning algorithms. Currently, he is involved in a research project in a platform for clouds at GPRT.

Judith Kelner received her PhD from the Computing Laboratory at the University of Kent at Canterbury, UK in 1993. She is a Full Professor at UFPE, since 1979. Currently she leads the GRVM team as well as coordinates a number of research projects in the areas of multimedia systems, design of virtual and augmented reality applications, and smart communication devices.

Djamel Sadok received his PhD of Computer Science at the University of Kent at Canterbury, UK in 1990. He is a member of staff at UFPE since 1993. His research interests include communication systems, access networks, security, cloud computing and traffic classification. Currently he leads the GPRT team as well coordinates a number of research projects.

Mozhgan Mahloo works as the researcher in cloud technology department of Ericsson. She holds a PhD degree in Communication systems from KTH Royal Institute of Technology, Sweden. Her research interests lie in the general area of cloud computing and networking as well as business and economic evaluation of such technologies. She is author/co-author of over 12 publications in international journals and conferences as well as one patent application. She has been involved in several national projects as well as FP7 European projects.

Big Data Analytics in Cloud—A Streaming Approach

Ratnik Gandhi

Abstract There is a significant interplay between Big Data and Cloud. Data Mining and Data Analytics are required for interpretation of Big Data. The literature on Cloud computing generally discusses infrastructure and architecture, but very little discussion is found on algorithms required for mining and analytics. This chapter focuses on online algorithms for learning and analytics that can be used for distributed and unstructured data over Cloud. It also discusses their time complexity, presents required architecture for deploying them over Cloud and concludes with presenting relevant open research directions.

1 Introduction

Small and medium scale organizations, due to lower operational budgets, and lack of local expertise, are moving rapidly towards cloud based infrastructures. Cloud infrastructure for Big Data processing and Big Data storage is more reliable and these organizations have to only focus on internet connectivity. Large organizations, on the other hand, due to privacy and secrecy issues, are implementing their own cloud solutions. These organizations can be commercial, educational or scientific and might be continuously generating data and storing it over the cloud. These organizations need data analytics over their data for better decision making.

The scientific instrument Large Hadron Collider (LHC) generates 1 TB data per second. The experiments carried out on such instruments require fast computation and high accuracy. Also, for better decision making, some of the experiments carried out needs real-time decision making. Consider a scenario in which people are posting real time information and updates about catastrophic events over social media such as Twitter. Is it possible to mine through volume of terra bytes of data and generate relevant alerts? The scenario requires designing solutions over distributed data and real time data analytics on them.

R. Gandhi (✉)
School of Engineering and Applied Science, Ahmedabad University, Gujarat, India
e-mail: ratnik.gandhi@ahduni.edu.in

© Springer Nature Singapore Pte Ltd. 2017　　　　　　　　　　　　　　55
S. Chaudhary et al. (eds.), *Research Advances in Cloud Computing*,
DOI 10.1007/978-981-10-5026-8_3

Similarly, due to growth of computational power and sensors on mobile and hand held devices Business Intelligence and Analytics (BI&A) is also growing [1]. BI&A requires mobile analytics and visualization of large data. It also needs methods and tools for integrating data from multiple sensors. Results in [2] propose cloud computing infrastructure as an effective means to appreciate analytics and visualization for such large datasets. Further, [2] emphasizes on need of scalable analysis algorithms for producing timely results—pointing out weakness of existing algorithms. In this chapter we attempt to answer these questions by presenting computationally efficient low memory algorithms that can run on data streams and can reuse a bulk of cloud infrastructure.

The applications discussed consider variety of users and applications through which data gets generated. Generally, the nature of the Big Data is either structured or unstructured, i.e., image data, video data, time series data such as temperature or weather parameter or banking or financial data, etc. One of the important parameter for algorithms designed for Big Data analytics over cloud is their ability to work with variety of data. In [3] the definition of Big Data is extended from Volume, Variety, and Velocity (3V model) to a 4 V model—by including a new "V" for Value. The article further discusses many interesting open research problems, including data analytics problems discussed in this chapter. The methods presented in this chapter are not only applicable to structured but unstructured data as well that appreciates 4 V model.

Due to rapid increase in sheer volume of the data and the need of continuous data analytics for better decision making organizations are looking for more real - time or on the fly computations. Such analysis of continuously generated data leads to designing of streaming and online algorithms for data analysis.

In this chapter, we introduce Big Data analytics techniques such as: regression analysis, singular value decomposition and principle component analysis. We also present Big Data analysis architecture for implementing these techniques and present streaming algorithms with complexity analysis.

It must be noted here that the algorithms presented in this chapter do not necessarily need cloud infrastructure. What makes them interesting and relevant for cloud infrastructure is (a) opportunity to distribute data and processing them over streams (b) distributing computation through cloud infrastructure and (c) significant reusability of computational results as well as computing power—offering opportunities to reduce computational cost for the volume of data analyzed.

Structure of the rest of the chapter is as follows. Section 2 introduces Regression Analysis with example and presents a classical (offline) and an online algorithm. Further, it introduces cloud computing architecture for running the online algorithm. Similarly, Sects. 3 and 4 presents offline and online algorithms for computing Singular Value Decomposition (SVD) and Principle Component Analysis (PCA) along with its architecture. Section 5 briefly discusses online algorithms for anomaly detection and k-median clustering. Some implementation aspects on MapReduce-Hadoop type architecture of presented algorithms are discussed in Sect. 6. Before concluding in Sects. 7 and 8 presents important research avenues.

2 Regression Analysis

Consider the scenario in which some industry is monitoring its power consumption data, or some marketing management consultant observing sales data, or meteorological departments are generating weather data. In all these cases some of these data is a simple function of time. And we can think of applying time series analysis. A method used for observing trend lines on such data is called regression.

2.1 Example

Let the following be set of observations of data of some event.

	P1	P2	P3	P4	P5	P6	P7	P8	P9
Time	1	2	3	4	5	6	7	8	9
Observation	2	4	2	9	3	1	6	4	3

These observations can be written as points in $\mathbb{R}^2$ as a set P ={(1, 2), (2, 4), (3, 2), (4, 9), (5, 3), (6, 1), (7, 6), (8, 4), (9, 3)}. A corresponding Fig. 1:

Fig. 1 Event Time series data - X Axis Time vs. Y Axis event outcome

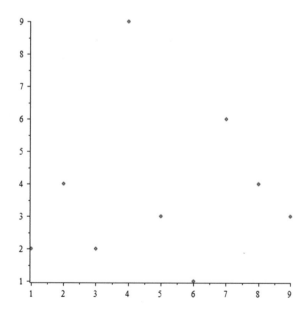

We would like to find out a trend line that passes through these set P of points.

There are various approaches for regression: line or linear regression, curves (using polynomials—non-linear regression) or logistic regression.

2.2 Linear Regression

The idea of linear regression is to pass a candidate line through the data such that it best represents the trend in the data. It is impossible to pass data through all the points in general and thus an aim of drawing a line is via minimizing means squared error (defined below). We show this by following steps (Figs. 2, 3 and 4).

Given data points $P_j = (x_j, y_j)$, $j = 1$ to n, aims is to find a line $y = (\beta_0 + \beta_1 x)$.

So that the mean squared error $MSE = \sum (y_j - (\beta_0 + \beta_1 x_j))^2$ is minimum.

We can do this by writing above system of linear equations in the form of following matrix equation.

$$X\beta = y, \quad \text{where } X = \begin{bmatrix} 1 & x_1 \\ 1 & x_2 \\ \vdots & \vdots \\ 1 & x_n \end{bmatrix}, \quad \beta = \begin{bmatrix} \beta_0 \\ \beta_1 \end{bmatrix}, \quad y = \begin{bmatrix} y_1 \\ y_2 \\ \vdots \\ y_n \end{bmatrix}$$

Fig. 2 Linear regression [4]

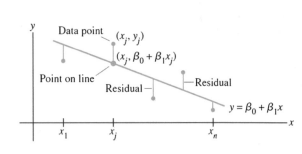

Fig. 3 Linear system for regression

Predicted y-value		Observed y-value
$\beta_0 + \beta_1 x_1$	=	y_1
$\beta_0 + \beta_1 x_2$	=	y_2
$\vdots$		$\vdots$
$\beta_0 + \beta_1 x_n$	=	y_n

Fig. 4 Linear regression of set of input points P

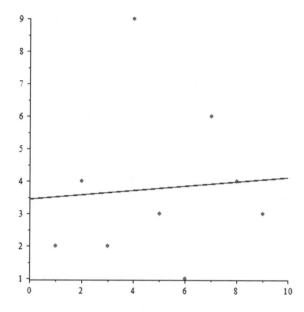

Our aim is to find β and thus we rewrite the above equation as:

$$X^T X \beta = X^T y$$

Further solving it for β, we get:

$$\beta = \left(X^T X\right)^{-1} X^T y$$

The formula above gives us the required line representing given data points—minimizing MSE.

For the example, for the given set of points we get,

$$\beta = \begin{bmatrix} \frac{31}{9} \\ \frac{1}{15} \end{bmatrix}$$

with line equation y = 0.066 x + 3.44.

2.3 Streaming Linear Regression

Next our aim is to design an algorithm that computes the linear regression in an online fashion. We do so by observing the linear regression formula:

$$\beta = \left(X^T X\right)^{-1} X^T y$$

If after computing line for the first set (P1–P9) of points we receive new points (let us say P10, P11) then the new matrices look as follows:

$$\begin{bmatrix} x1 & y1 \\ x2 & y2 \\ xn & yn \\ \hline xp & yp \\ xq & yq \end{bmatrix} \qquad X` = \begin{bmatrix} 1 & x1 \\ 1 & x2 \\ 1 & xn \\ \hline 1 & xp \\ 1 & xq \end{bmatrix} \qquad y` = \begin{bmatrix} y1 \\ y2 \\ yn \\ \hline yp \\ yq \end{bmatrix}$$

Let us denote the new points corresponding part of matrix X' as X_{new} and y' as y_{new}. Then the regression formula can be rewritten as:

$$\beta_{overall} = \left(X^T X + X_{new}^T X_{new}\right)^{-1} \left(X^T y + X_{new}^T y_{new}\right)$$

In other words, if we save $X^T X$ matrix of dimension 2×2 and $X^T y$ of dimension 2×1, we can compute overall new line (old line and new points affecting the old line) by simply applying the formula above. This is a *constant memory polynomial time* algorithm for computing *exact* linear regression in an *online* fashion. Another such algorithm is presented in [5]. Figure 5 gives cloud architecture for the discussed online regression algorithm.

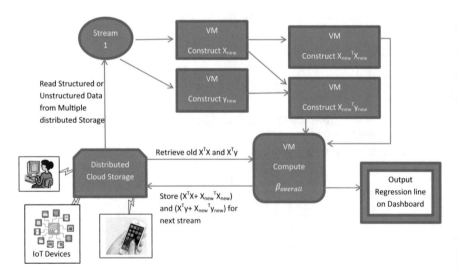

Fig. 5 Cloud architecture for online regression

2.4 Architecture

Algorithm 1 Streaming Linear Regression on Cloud

Input: New Data (x_i, y_i) in streaming fashion and old X^TX and X^Ty

---

Output: Continuously updating Linear Regression on overall (new + old) data

---

1. Read the input (x_i, y_i) from stream collected from distributed cloud storage and build matrix X_{new} and vector y_{new}.
2. Compute Matrix $X_{new}{}^TX_{new}$ and $X_{new}{}^Ty_{new}$.
3. Retrieve old X^TX and X^Ty from cloud storage.
4. Compute

$$\beta_{overall} = \left(X^TX + X_{new}^TX_{new}\right)^{-1}(X^Ty + X_{new}^Ty_{new})$$

5. Store $(X^TX + X_{new}{}^TX_{new})$ and $(X^Ty + X_{new}{}^Ty_{new})$ for next stream computation on cloud storage.
6. Output updated linear regression line on dashboard.

---

3 Singular Value Decomposition (SVD)

Singular Values and Singular Vectors are tools of significant importance for data analytics when the data is represented/representable as a matrix. For eg., low rank approximation of the data, computing principle component analysis, signal processing, pattern recognition, recommendation systems, hotspot detection and computing pseudo-inverse of a matrix are some of the popular use of SVD.

Singular value decomposition of any $m \times n$ matrix A is written as

$$A = U\Lambda V^T$$

where U_{mxm} and V_{nxn} are orthogonal matrices containing left and right singular vectors respectively. Matrix Λ_{mxn} is a diagonal matrix with singular values on the diagonal. A standard algorithm for computing SVD of a given input matrix works by computing $B = AA^T$, let us say.

$$AA^T = \left(U\Lambda V^T\right)\left(U\Lambda V^T\right)^T = U\Lambda\Lambda^TU^T$$

Matrices U and V are orthogonal and thus $U^TU = V^TV = I =$ identity matrix. Further, $\Lambda\Lambda^T$ is a diagonal square matrix with dimension m×m. We can easily compute elements of $\Lambda\Lambda^T$ by computing eigenvalues of matrix AA^T and vectors of U by computing corresponding eigenvectors. A similar computation can lead us to matrix V. It is

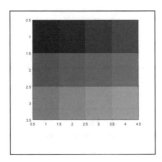

$$A = \begin{bmatrix} 0 & 2 & 4 & 6 \\ 8 & 10 & 12 & 14 \\ 16 & 18 & 20 & 22 \end{bmatrix}$$

$$\begin{bmatrix} -.15 & -.90 & .41 \\ -.50 & -.29 & -.82 \\ -.85 & .32 & .41 \end{bmatrix} \begin{bmatrix} 44.82 & 0 & 0 & 0 \\ 0 & 3.91 & 0 & 0 \\ 0 & 0 & 0 & 0 \end{bmatrix} \begin{bmatrix} -.39 & -.46 & -.53 & -.59 \\ .74 & .30 & -.15 & -.59 \\ -.44 & .34 & .63 & -.54 \\ -.33 & .76 & -.55 & .11 \end{bmatrix}$$

Fig. 6 SVD of the image matrix

important to note that, the algorithm for computing SVD internally uses eigenvalue and eigenvector decomposition—effectively making computational complexity of SVD algorithm to be $O(k^3)$, where k = max(m,n).

3.1 Example

Consider an image given by the following matrix A= (a_{ij}) =[0 2 4 6; 8 10 12 14; 16 18 20 22], where each number a_{ij} indicates colour value. Its singular value decomposition (Fig. 6).

3.2 Incremental SVD

There are multiple algorithms for computing Singular Value Decomposition online [6–9]. In this chapter we discuss a simple algorithm from [9]. First, we define required notations.

For the given input matrix $A \in \mathbb{R}^{m \times n}$ and its SVD defined as earlier, its' best rank –k approximate SVD is given by

$$\hat{A}_{m \times n} = U_k \Lambda_k V_k^T.$$

where U_k and V_k^T are formed by the first k columns of U and V, respectively and Λ_k has the k leading singular values of diagonal matrix Λ.

3.3 Architecture

Algorithm 2 for computing SVD in an online fashion, as a first step, computes SVD of original input matrix $A = U_k \Lambda_k V_k^T$. It is important to note that, if not required, k can be set to rank of the original matrix A and SVD obtained through Algorithm 2

Algorithm 2 Incremental Singular Value Decomposition on Cloud

---

Input: New Data as matrix B and old rank $-$ k SVD $U_k \Lambda_k V_k^T$ of matrix A

Output: Rank $-$k approximate SVD of new matrix [A,B]

---

1. Compute the QR decomposition of matrix $\left(I - U_k U_k^T\right) B = QR$.
2. Compute rank-k SVD of the $(k + r') \times (k + r')$ matrix

$$\begin{bmatrix} \Lambda_k & U_k^T B \\ 0 & R \end{bmatrix} = \widehat{U}\,\widehat{\Lambda}\widehat{V}^T$$

  where r' is the rank of $\left(I - U_k U_k^T\right) B$ matrix.
3. With this computation at hand, best rank-k approximation of new matrix [A,B] is

$$([U_k, Q]\widehat{U})\,\widehat{\Lambda}\left(\begin{bmatrix} V_k & 0 \\ 0 & I \end{bmatrix}\widehat{V}\right)^T$$

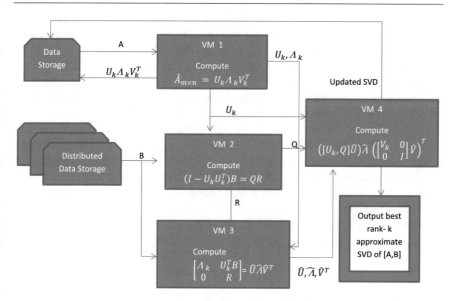

Fig. 7 Cloud srchitecture for computing online SVD update

will be exact, rather than approximate. This first computation is carried out on Virtual Machine 1 and resultant SVD is stored back in local data storage for further use (Fig. 7). This SVD computation runs in $O(n^3)$ time, where $n = max(n, m)$.

On receiving the new data through distributed data storage, in the form of a update matrix B, the matrix with left singular vectors U_k (computed from VM1) is sent to VM2 for computing QR decomposition. The purpose of QR decomposition is to orthogonalize and project new vectors into known singular vector space. QR decomposition over VM2 takes $O(n^3)$ time. Matrix R of QR decomposition, along with B and left singular vectors U_k are further utilized on VM3 and SVD is computed. This computation is exactly same as computing SVD of original input matrix but the matrix on VM3 is upper triangular and thus the SVD computation is much more efficient.

Finally, output of VM3 sends Q matrix from VM2 and left and right singular vectors from VM1 are sent to VM4 for computing rank-k SVD of updated matrix [A,B]. VM4 only does matrix multiplication and thus needs only $O(n^3)$ time. The output from VM4 is sent back to data storage and it awaits new data update for further computing new SVD. Overall complexity of updating SVD in an incremental fashion using Algorithm 2 is $O(n^3)$.

3.4 Efficient Rank-1 Update

For most practical purposes, computing rank-1(or low rank) update of SVD is sufficient. For eg., Rank-1 SVD has been applied for hotspot detection from spatiotemporal data with application to disease outbreak detection in [10]. There are many other results that talks about applications of low rank SVD updates [6, 7, 10–13].

Works in [6, 7] presents algorithms that make sure that only singular values are updated while the left and right singular vector updates are pushed to a later stage for reducing computational complexity. These updates are computed—later—only to reduce growth in approximation due to numeric computational errors.

Works in [11, 12] focus on exploiting matrix structure for efficient computation. The algorithm designed for singular value update models the problem as Chauchy matrix vector product. Algorithm in [11] computes rank-1 exact update in $O(n^2 \log n)$ time while the algorithm in [12] uses approximation scheme and computes rank-1 update in $O(n^2 \log 1/\varepsilon)$ time, where n is the dimension of the matrix and ε is accuracy of computation.

It must be noted that the Algorithm 2 presented in this section is an online constant memory algorithm and it does not require old data for updating SVD.

4 Principle Component Analysis (PCA)

Principle Component Analysis is a method for converting correlated data into linearly uncorrelated form called Principle components. One of the most important uses of PCA is to reduce dimensionality of data. In most real life applications the dimension of the data is very high but information content is low. PCA helps in separating the low content data from high content by projecting the data in space where most of the important content is preserved.

4.1 Example

In Figs. 8 and 9 the Principle Components are obtained such that the first PC is along the direction of maximum variance and the subsequent PCs are along the direction of respective subsequent highest variance—orthogonal to the previously computed PCs. PCA can be used to reduce noise and redundancy in the data [14].

4.2 Model

For computing Principle Component Analysis (PCA) two tools are important—SVD and eigen decomposition. Information about variance and covariance in the data is central for PCA. PCs are constructed by finding eigenvectors of covariance matrix of the data. The diagonal entries in covariance matrix represent autocorrelation while the

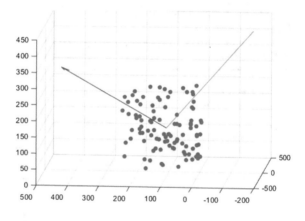

Fig. 8 Three dimensional data, i.e. current feature space is 3. *Green* and *red* are the principle components of this data

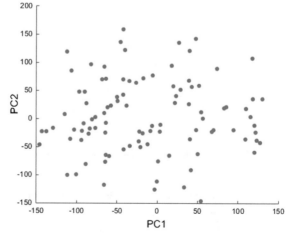

Fig. 9 Data given in Fig. 8 is projected in the space created by principle components PC1 and PC2. This reduces dimension of the data from 3 to 2

off-diagonal entries represent covariance among variables. Zero off-diagonal entries represent data having no redundancy. The diagonalization of the covariance matrix is computed by eigen decomposition. This generates eigenvectors and eigenvalues. The eigenvectors are the PCs (new basis) of the data and eigenvalues represents the variance corresponding to each PC. Variance as eigenvalues can be thought of as a weight/priority assigned to each PC in decreasing order of their importance in retaining information in the data. In case of non-square matrix, PCA can be implemented using SVD.

Let $A \in \mathbb{R}^{m \times n}$ be the data matrix with m being dimension of the data (number of features) and n being number of data/sample points. PCA computes a $k \times k$ projection matrix P such that

$$A_{projected} = P^T A$$

where, columns of matrix $P = [p_1 p_2 \dots p_k]$ are the principal components of matrix A. PCs are the new basis vectors for X.

Algorithm 3 Principle Component Analysis

Input: Input matrix A

Output: Matrix P - Principle Components (PCs) of matrix A.

---

1. Shift the data by subtracting mean from $A_{m \times n}$.
2. Compute covariance matrix
$$S_{n \times n} = AA^T.$$
3. Compute Eigen Vectors of S.
4. Use k – eigenvectors of matrix S for constructing $k \times k$ projection matrix P.
5. Project A on lower dimensional space by computing $P^T A$.

It must be noted that, in practice—while considering dimensionality reduction we have m >> n, i.e., number of samples are significantly less than the feature space (or the dimension of the vectors in matrix A). Computing covariance matrix AA^T is very expensive in this case. Thus, for computing PCs, the algorithm first computes eigenvectors of matrix $A^T A$. These eigenvectors are then pre-multiplied by A—producing PCs of AA^T.

Algorithm 3 computes PCs either by eigen decomposition or SVD (which in effect uses eigen decomposition). This sets the complexity of Algorithm 3 to $O(n^3)$.

4.3 Incremental Principle Component Analysis

In this section, we present an algorithm for computing Principle Component Analysis in an online fashion [15]. The algorithm primarily uses idea of Algorithm 2 for updating SVD, given in Sect. 3.2. It must be noted that for applying this algorithm the data must have low-rank plus shift structure.

Algorithm 4 Incremental Principle Component Analysis on Cloud

Input: Old and new Data matrices A_1 and A_2, where A_1 is $n \times m$ and A_2 is $n \times r$

Output: Rank –k approximate PCs of new matrix $A = [A_1, A_2]_{n \times (m+r)}$

1. Compute the mean shift of matrix A by computing $A - E(A)$.
2. Compute $\Sigma = (A - E(A))^T (A - E(A))$, where

$$\Sigma = \begin{bmatrix} \Sigma_1 & \Sigma_2 \\ \Sigma_2^T & \Sigma_3 \end{bmatrix}.$$

3. Compute eigen decomposition of $\Sigma_1 = U \Lambda U^T$.
4. Compute matrices $P_{l \times m}$, $(Q_1)_{l \times r}$, Q_2 and Q_3 such that

$$\Sigma = \begin{bmatrix} P & Q_1 \\ Q_2 & Q_3 \end{bmatrix}^T \begin{bmatrix} P & Q_1 \\ Q_2 & Q_3 \end{bmatrix}.$$

5. Compute QR decomposition

$$I_{(l+r) \times (l+r)} - \begin{bmatrix} U_k U_k^T \end{bmatrix} \begin{bmatrix} Q_1 \\ Q_3 \end{bmatrix} = JK,$$

where U_k is best rank-k approximation of eigen decomposition of Σ_1.
6. Compute SVD of smaller matrix

$$\begin{bmatrix} \Lambda_k & U_k^T \begin{bmatrix} Q_1 \\ Q_3 \end{bmatrix} \\ 0 & K \end{bmatrix} = \widehat{U} \widehat{\Lambda} \widehat{V}^T,$$

where rank-k approximation of P matrix is $\tilde{P}^{(1)} = \begin{bmatrix} I_k \\ 0 \end{bmatrix}_{l \times k} \Lambda_k V_k^T$.
7. Compute best rank-k approximation of

$$\begin{bmatrix} P & Q_1 \\ Q_2 & Q_3 \end{bmatrix} = ([U_k J] \widehat{U}) \widehat{\Lambda} \left(\begin{bmatrix} V_k & 0 \\ 0 & I_r \end{bmatrix} \widehat{V} \right)^T.$$

Algorithm 4, in Step 1, shifts the data near the origin by subtracting mean E(A) from the data. Computing mean and shifting data to origin requires $O(n^2)$ computation (for simplicity in analysis we assume n ≥ (m+r)). In Step 2, covariance matrix is computed and Step 3 computes eigen decomposition of Σ_1 block of the covariance matrix. This decomposition produces eigenvectors U which are further approximated to rank –k (U_k) and utilized in subsequent computation. These steps require $O(m^3)$ time in worst case. Step 4 offers a different representation of the covariance matrix Σ as set of block matrices $P_{l \times m}$, $(Q_1)_{l \times r}$, Q_2 and Q_3. This representation offers an opportunity to not only update PCs but allows approximation to factor in. As in Algorithm 2, QR decomposition of Step 5 takes $O((l+r)^3)$ time and Step 6 SVD will similarly use an eigen decomposition on upper triangular matrix. These are efficient computation than $O(n^3)$ which give us principle components of required – new

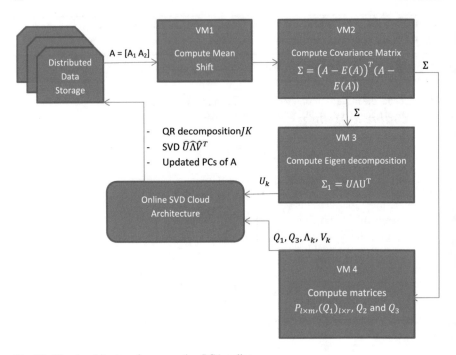

Fig. 10 Cloud architecture for computing PCA online

covariance matrix A. All the parameters, by assumption, are bounded above by n. Thus, overall running time of the online PCA algorithm is $O\left(n^3\right)$. It is important to note that the Algorithm 4 is online PCA update algorithm that uses old data and thus it is memory inefficient.

4.4 Architecture

Figure 10 presents Cloud based architecture for computing PCA in an online fashion. It is worth noting that the online PCA cloud architecture given in Fig. 10 uses online SVD computing architecture shown in Fig. 7. This shows amount of infrastructure *reusability*. A similar exercise can be carried out to unify and define single architecture for library of data analytics algorithms.

There are other variants of online PCA update algorithms [16]. For memory limited online PCA algorithm see [17].

5 Other Algorithms of Interest

In this section we discuss other Big Data analytics related algorithms in brief.

5.1 Online k-Median Clustering

When the data cannot be fitted in memory, the data is generally brought in chunks of manageable size. One of the methods for performing k-median clustering algorithms performs clustering in a hierarchical fashion. The idea is for each chunk D_i find a median. Collect the medians of all D_i till the median bucket (whose size is size of a chunk) is not full. Identify median of collected medians and retain it in the median bucket and for the new chunks start collecting their medians in median bucket again.

When the median of median is found, old data is reassigned their new median and cluster is updated. This process can continue, as the data volume increases the cluster stability increases and number of reassignment decreases. A framework for such k-median clustering is discussed in STREAM framework [18, 19].

5.2 Outlier Analysis

For most time series data, after understanding trends in the data, one of the most important analytics is that of finding anomaly or an outlier. There are many ways in statistics to do outlier analysis, for eg., k-nearest neighbor, support vector machine, neural networks. The area has developed greatly and there is enough literature developed on outlier analysis [20].

6 Implementing Algorithms on Map Reduce and Hadoop

As discussed earlier, for computing PCA we need to subtract the mean of the data and compute it's SVD. Algorithms such as Lanczos and Stochastic SVD can be used from Apache Mahout (MapReduce jobs) after appropriate data preprocessing.

As an alternate, Restricted Boltzmann Machines for deep learning can also be used to achieve dimensionality reduction. The framework allows significant parallelization. Please refer [21] for further discussion on the same.

These implementations allow computation of SVD, online regression and other applications discussed in Sect. 5.

7 Open Research Problems

There are many interesting and relevant research problems related to data analytics on cloud. These research problems can broadly be classified in terms of efficient deployment problems and efficient design problems.

7.1 Efficient Deployment

It is well known that iterative algorithms cannot be efficiently implemented on MapReduce type architecture as these technologies help parallelize computation. The research problems related to efficient deployment would typically ask—how data analytics algorithms can be modified to exploit given cloud infrastructure for efficiency. Can some algorithms be parallelized? Can some algorithms be deployed on Mapper and Reducer like distributed architectures? Algorithms community that is trying to answer these questions is answering it for specific algorithms—there is no generic answer so far. Research contributions in the area of designing schemes that can help convert existing algorithms to algorithms fit for distributed computation or parallel computation will offer an important platform for many algorithms to be deployed on Cloud platform immediately. Further, it will help improve computational efficiency of these analytics.

The scheme should also be able to propose an optimal architecture for deployment of these algorithms (Fig. 11).

7.2 Efficient Design

The algorithms presented in this chapter have use cases in data analytics over Big Data as well as many machine learning algorithms. For instance, online SVD and online PCA algorithms are used for finding variables of importance for data analytics as well as used for clustering and recommendation algorithms. Efficiency of these algorithms in the form of computational time/cost and accuracy are of great relevance.

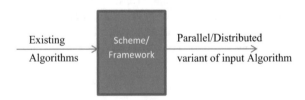

Existing Algorithms → Scheme/Framework → Parallel/Distributed variant of input Algorithm

Fig. 11 Figure shows need to design a scheme/framework for converting existing algorithms to algorithms that can be parallelized or be deployed on distributed architechture

Many of these algorithms cannot have an online version that can compute solutions in an *exact* form (the solutions are approximate). These approximation needs to be improved for better accuracies. In the following we list some of the algorithms that might need immediate answers considering current research scenario (it must be noted that the literature on efficient online algorithm designing for data analytics over cloud is sparse or essentially absent).

Online Linear Discriminant Analysis (LDA): Like PCA, LDAs are useful for dimensionality reduction for Big Data analytics. PCAs are useful for maximizing variance in data, while LDAs are useful for maximizing the inter-class distances. Online algorithm for LDA was first presented in [22] with computational complexity of $O(MCn^3)$, where M is number of classes, C is maximum elements in a class and n is size of the data matrix. There has been many results that attempts to improve complexity of computing LDA in an online fashion (eg. [23–25]). These results are either specific for applications [25] or are not efficient enough [23, 24]. Research in the area of improving complexity and efficiency of online LDA algorithm using cloud computing would be a very important result.

Online SVD: As discussed earlier, one of the first algorithms for computing SVD in an online fashion is given in [6, 7]. For many practical scenario, computing low-rank SVD update is sufficient (for eg., consider the data is coming as one column/row at a time and we have to update the SVD). An efficient method for updating low-rank SVD—that uses structural properties of matrix—is presented in [11]. An approximation based method that improves algorithm in [11] is given in [12]. Recall, the online SVD update is quite useful for computing PCAs and thus improving efficiency of [11] or approximation accuracies in [12] using cloud computing would be an important research contribution.

Online PCA: The presented method of online PCA in Sect. 4.3 makes use of an online SVD algorithm [15]. Further, the algorithm is not truly online as it accesses old data for updating the principle components. This makes the algorithm memory inefficient. Considering the volume of data and purpose of PCA for dimensionality reduction – there is an immediate need to develop a truly online PCA algorithm that does not look up old data for updating PCA.

Similar research questions for efficient implementation of online k-means clustering, Gaussian mixture, online regression, online naïve Bayse classification, online hypothesis testing methods over cloud are unanswered and require immediate attention.

8 Closing Remarks

There is a significant literature related to cloud computing that discuss optimization problems such as resource allocation, its architecture and framework for cloud and related technologies. Literature related to optimization aspects of algorithms designed and deployed for cloud infrastructure is very limited or sparse. In this chapter, we presented set of algorithms that does optimization and are generally deployed for large scale data analytics systems over cloud [26].

One of the most important properties of cloud based systems is the infrastructure to distribute data over many nodes through distributed file systems and allowing local computations. When the data is not available "in-ram" for computation, the algorithm design community for cloud focuses on algorithms that run on stream of data. In this chapter we presented some online algorithms for known static problems and presented architecture though which the algorithms can be deployed over the cloud. We further discussed other research problems of importance.

Acknowledgements Author would like to thank Ms. Amoli Rajgor for helping with Figs. 8 and 9. Author would also like to thank reviewers for constructive comments for improving this chapter.

References

1. Hsinchun, C., Chiang, R. H. L., & Storey, V. C. (2012). Business intelligence and analytics: From big data to big impact. *MIS quarterly, 36*(4), 1165–1188.
2. Talia, D. (2013). Toward cloud-based big-data analytics. *IEEE Computer Science*, 98–101.
3. Kim, T.-K., Stenger, B., Kittler, J., & Cipolla, R. (2015). The rise of "Big Data" on cloud computing: Review and open research issues. *Information Systems, 47*, 98–115.
4. Lay, D. C. (2003). Linear algebra and its applications.
5. Nadungodage, C. H., Xia, Y., Li, F., Lee, J. J., & Ge, J. (2011). Streamffitter: A real time linear regression analysis system for continuous data streams. In *Database Systems for Advanced Applications*, pp. 458–461. Springer.
6. Brand, M. (2002). Incremental singular value decomposition of uncertain data with missing values. In *European Conference on Computer Vision*, pp. 707–720. Springer, Berlin, Heidelberg.
7. Brand, M. (2006). Fast low-rank modifications of the thin singular value decomposition. *Linear algebra and its applications, 415*(1), 20–30.
8. Kwok, J. T., & Zhao, H. (2003). Incremental eigen decomposition. In *Proceedings ICANN*, Istanbul, Turkey, pp. 270–273.
9. Zha, H., & Simon, H. D. (1999). On updating problems in latent semantic indexing. *SIAM Journal on Scientific Computing, 21*(2), 782–791.
10. Fanaee-T, H., & Gama, J. (2015). Eigenspace method for spatiotemporal hotspot detection. *Expert systems, 32*(3), 454–464.
11. Stange, P. (2008). On the efficient update of the singular value decomposition. *PAMM, 8*(1), 10827–10828.
12. Gandhi, R., & Rajgor, A. (2017) Updating singular value decomposition for rank one matrix perturbation. arXiv preprint arXiv:1707.08369.
13. Bunch, J. R., & Nielsen, C. P. (1978). Updating the singular value decomposition. *Numerische Mathematik, 31*(2), 111–129.
14. Feng, J., Xu, H., Mannor, S., & Yan, S. (2013). Online PCA for contaminated data. In *Advances in Neural Information Processing Systems*, pp. 764–772.
15. Zhao, H., Yuen, P. C., & Kwok, J. T. (2006). A novel incremental principal component analysis and its application for face recognition. *IEEE Transactions on Systems, Man, and Cybernetics, Part B (Cybernetics) 36*(4), 873–886.
16. Weng, J., Zhang, Y., & Hwang, W.-S. (2003). Candid covariance-free incremental principal component analysis. *IEEE Transactions on Pattern Analysis and Machine Intelligence, 25*(8), 1034–1040.

17. Mitliagkas, I., Caramanis, C., & Jain, P. (2013). Memory limited, streaming PCA. In *Advances in Neural Information Processing Systems*, pp. 2886–2894.
18. O'callaghan, L., Mishra, N., Meyerson, A., Guha, S., & Motwani, R. (2002). Streaming-data algorithms for high-quality clustering. In *ICDE2*, 685.
19. Guha, S., Mishra, N., Motwani, R., & O'Callaghan, L. (2000). Clustering data streams. In *Proceedings of the 41st Annual Symposium on Foundations of Computer Science*, pp. 359–366. IEEE.
20. Aggarwal, C. C. (2015). Outlier analysis. In *Data Mining*, pp. 237–263. Springer International Publishing.
21. Le, Q. V. (2013). Building high-level features using large scale unsupervised learning. In *2013 IEEE International Conference on Acoustics, Speech and Signal Processing*, pp. 8595–8598. IEEE.
22. Pang, S., Ozawa, S., & Kasabov, N. (2005). Incremental linear discriminant analysis for classification of data streams. In *IEEE Transactions on Systems, Man, and Cybernetics, Part B (Cybernetics)*, 35(5), 905–914.
23. Zhao, H., & Yuen, P. C. (2008). Incremental linear discriminant analysis for face recognition. *IEEE Transactions on Systems, Man, and Cybernetics, Part B (Cybernetics)* 38(1), 210–221.
24. Ye, J., Li, Q., Xiong, H., Park, H., Janardan, R., & Kumar, V. (2005). IDR/QR: An incremental dimension reduction algorithm via QR decomposition. *IEEE Transactions on Knowledge and Data Engineering*, 17(9), 1208–1222.
25. Kim, T.-K., Stenger, B., Kittler, J., & Cipolla, R. (2011). Incremental linear discriminant analysis using sufficient spanning sets and its applications. *International Journal of Computer Vision*, 91(2), 216–232.
26. Aggarwal, C. (2013). A survey of stream clustering algorithms. In C. Aggarwal & C. Reddy (Eds.), *Data Clustering: Algorithms and Applications*, CRC Press.

A Terminology to Classify Artifacts for Cloud Infrastructure

**Fábio Diniz Rossi, Rodrigo Neves Calheiros
and César Augusto Fonticielha De Rose**

Abstract Cloud environments are widely used to offer scalable software services. To support these environments, organizations operating data centers must maintain an infrastructure with a significant amount of resources. Such resources are managed by specific software to ensure service level agreements based on one or more performance metrics. Within such infrastructure, approaches to meet non-functional requirements can be split into various artifacts, distributed across different operational layers, which operate together with the aim of reaching a specific target. Existing studies classify such approaches using different terms, which usually are used with conflicting meanings by different people. Therefore, it is necessary a common nomenclature defining different artifacts, so they can be organized in a more scientific way. To this end, we propose a comprehensive bottom-up classification to identify and classify approaches for system artifacts at the infrastructure level, and organize existing literature using the proposed classification.

1 Introduction

Cloud computing is a large-scale computing paradigm, in which a huge amount of computing resources, usually virtualized, and dynamically scalable in processing power and storage, provides on-demand services to customers over the Internet. The best use of resources provided by cloud environments enables reduction of costs for

F.D. Rossi (✉)
Federal Institute of Education, Science and Technology,
Farroupilha Campus, Alegrete-RS, Brazil
e-mail: fabio.rossi@iffarroupilha.edu.br

R.N. Calheiros
School of Computing, Engineering and Mathematics,
Western Sydney University, Sydney, Australia
e-mail: rnc@unimelb.edu.au

C.A.F. De Rose
Pontifical Catholic University of Rio Grande do Sul (PUCRS),
Porto Alegre, Brazil
e-mail: cesar.derose@pucrs.br

© Springer Nature Singapore Pte Ltd. 2017
S. Chaudhary et al. (eds.), *Research Advances in Cloud Computing*,
DOI 10.1007/978-981-10-5026-8_4

service providers. Several software artifacts supported by these environments work together to meet negotiated Service Level Agreements (SLA).

At infrastructure level, SLAs are translated into non-functional requirements, which describe system attributes that directly affect customer satisfaction (Quality of Experience). From the perspective of the service provider, this can be understood as complying with preestablished service level agreement (SLA), on aspects such as performance, availability, security, interoperability, and so on. The infrastructure layer can offer the artifacts, in different levels of abstraction, either by devices that are part of the physical substrate or by the operating systems, in order to meet such SLAs. Sets of artifacts are generally presented as a solution to meet specific SLA, and are usually split across different layers.

Informally, there are terms that are used to classify each infrastructure-level artifact. Although different, some of these terms are used synonymously, such as technique, mechanism, algorithm, strategy, policy, and architecture. Based on the above, the existing terminology for infrastructure-level artifacts is inconsistent. For example, the energy-efficient cloud literature has Dynamic Voltage and Frequency Scaling (DVFS) sometimes classified as a technique [1], a mechanism [2], a policy [3], a strategy [4], or a module [5]. In the same way, virtual machine migration is referred to as a technique [6], a mechanism [7], or a strategy [8]. Data location, which is a matter of security, can be referred to as a mechanism [9], a policy [10], or architecture [11]. There is no unique, unambiguous, common terminology for the terms used for each whole cloud approach, and this can lead to ambiguity in the description and comparison of approaches.

In order to organize such artifacts, we propose a terminology that allows classification of artifacts at different levels of abstraction. Based on this proposed organization, we classify studies related to each level of abstraction proposed in the terminology, in order to better organize them. Afterwards, we summarize the work, making it possible to view new challenges and trends.

This chapter presents the following contributions:

1. A new comprehensive bottom-up classification of artifacts related to non-functional requirements for cloud environments;
2. The organization of cloud computing-related literature within this new terminology;
3. A discussion about research trends and challenges in the area of cloud computing.

This chapter is organized as follows. In the first section, we proposed a new terminology to classify terms used to represent different artifacts of cloud environments infrastructure layer as well as related work associated to each artifact. In the second section, we present a discussion about future challenges and trends; The chapter ends with our conclusions in the third section.

2 Artifacts Classification Terminology

Cloud computing is widely adopted in the industry of Information Technology (IT), becoming a standard infrastructure for offering services. It is a paradigm that associates the service-oriented model with the flexibility provided by virtualization. Supported by these concepts, cloud computing can be defined as a model that enables on-demand access from customers to a set of configurable computing resources (networks, servers, storage devices, applications, and services) that can be quickly acquired and released with a minimal management effort or service provider interaction. This means that cloud environments consist of a set of services accessed over the network, providing scalability, Quality of Service (QoS), and inexpensive computing infrastructure that can be accessed simply and in a pervasive way.

Cloud environments can be utilized to provide service quality levels and intelligent use of resources through service models. These service models define the architectural standard for the approaches offered in cloud environments. Among these service models, this work is focused on infrastructure. The primary objective of the infrastructure layer (Infrastructure-as-a-Service or IaaS) is to provide on-demand computing resources (such as servers, network, storage, etc.), to meet customers request. The requirements of services are met by infrastructure platforms that manage resources through various components such as load balancers and auto-scalers. As a result, the infrastructure becomes scalable through the use of characteristics such as elasticity. OpenStack [12] and Eucalyptus [13] are examples of infrastructure platforms.

Intelligent approaches should guide the use of these components with the intention of not causing interference on other metrics. Therefore, within the infrastructure, there are several abstraction levels. Aiming to organize such different levels of the same approach, we proposed a bottom-up classification presented in Fig. 1, considering only IaaS level.

A software platform orchestrates components of the infrastructure layer. The infrastructure platform manages and interconnects different modules, each driven by a metric. Each of these modules includes a set of abstractions ranging from strategies to achieve the goal to the hardware support for this strategy to occur. Although the module described in Fig. 1 refers to energy domain, the proposed classification can be used similarly to each of the other modules belonging to an infrastructure platform.

Each of the components of the proposed classification is detailed in the rest of this section.

2.1 Mechanisms

Definition

We define mechanisms as the set of special-purpose tools available in the hardware and operating system levels. Mechanisms are accessed through Application Pro-

Fig. 1 This classification organizes the set of layers of components that meet the requirements of cloud service provider

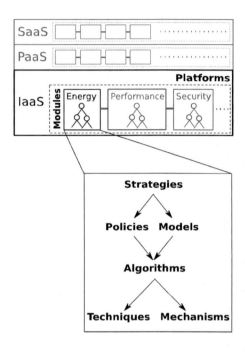

gramming Interfaces (APIs) or programming libraries supported by the operating system to manage hardware features. In this sense, one can say that a mechanism is pre-existing in hardware and software, even if it is not used by higher layers.

Related Work

Wu et al. [14] discusses the Dynamic Voltage and Frequency Scaling (DVFS) mechanism, which is present in modern CPUs to enable changes in their clock frequency by operating system governors, with the objective of reducing processor voltage to save energy.

Sleep states are another mechanism, presented by Min et al. [15] as an energy-efficient option, and it consists of changing the operational state of hardware to states of greater energy efficiency when idleness is detected in the hardware. Such mechanism supports a variety of states with many energy saving levels, each one with specific characteristics, and applied to individual components.

Among works that address mechanism, Lee [16] discusses the new features of a non-bypassable form of hardware access control (ACH) and manycore virtualization security protections.

Guerout et al. [17] present the implementation, simulation, and validation of DVFS support on Cloudsim simulator [18]. Such implementation has shown that there are several cloud scenarios where the use of DVFS can offer energy savings.

Rossi et al. [19] present an analysis of various ACPI states as the DVFS states in addition to sleep states such as standby, hibernate, and soft off, in order to improve the trade-off between performance and energy savings for HPC clusters. The work shows that a smart choice for the states can reduce the energy consumption with a minimum impact on jobs execution time.

2.2 Techniques

Definition

Techniques are a set of hardware-independent procedures abstracted from the operating system. In this event, the system may add capabilities on top of those already supported by hardware and operating system, and enable event handling to meet the goal of a strategy. Accordingly, it can be said that technique is purposely used as a method to achieve a target.

Related Work

Clark et al. [20] present the technique of virtual machine consolidation (VMC) for virtualized environments, such as clouds. This technique regards the transferring of services hosted in virtual machines from one physical server to another. The migration of virtual machines across different physical servers brings several advantages such as load balancing, online maintenance, fault tolerance, and power management. These benefits can increase flexibility and reduce the complexity of managing physical resources in such environments, besides reducing the resources usage.

In the same direction cloud firewalling presented by Lee et al. [21] is a technique that protects cloud hosts from external attacks. Canary presented by Smid et al. [22] also consists of mechanisms that concentrate external attacks to itself, defending the cloud provider's application servers.

Alboaneen et al. [23] present a virtual machine placement technique aimed at saving energy, but also with concern about application performance. In this technique, virtual machine consolidation is based on the utilization rate of the hosts that support applications, in addition to the available bandwidth between these hosts. Based on these values, the authors predict the workload behavior and decide the number of virtual machines that each host must support every moment, guiding the virtual machine placement process.

Ding et al. [24] present a virtual machines allocation technique upon cores using different frequencies. In certain periods, such allocation is performed again, making the environment to adjust itself aiming energy savings. By simulation, the authors claim that their strategy can save up to 20% energy. However, the article assumes that the change in frequency is performed individually on cores where virtual machines are attached, but this operation is not standard on modern processors.

2.3 Algorithms

Definition

Algorithms consist in the translation of an idea, a statement (called strategy in this classification), to a logical implementation, in other words, the realization in code form of policies, models, or both of them. The implementation of such algorithms manages policies and models for the purpose of adapting techniques and mechanisms of the infrastructure to meet a strategy.

Related Work

Han et al. [25] presents allocation algorithms (AA) implemented on a cloud resource management system (RMS), which enables cost-effective elasticity based on utilization rates of the processor, memory, and network, to meet the quality of service requirements.

Yang et al. [26] proposes an algorithm that exploits a limitation of mobile clouds based on usage and battery consumption. Thus, the choice of workload size and time to transmission must be made by an algorithm that controls the mobile device.

Zeng et al. [27] presents an algorithm that receives a request from a cloud customer, and based on metrics such as unit price, distance, responsive team, traffic volume, storage space, chooses which the host will respond to this customer request.

Beloglazov and Buyya [28] presented a virtual machines allocation algorithm for cloud environments to saving power. Such algorithm decides when and what virtual machine should be allocated to available resources, reducing the overhead and avoiding SLA violations through a minimum amount of migration. When virtual machines are moved, idle hosts may enter into a sleep state, reducing thereby the overall power consumption. Results presented energy saving of up to 83% compared to energy-agnostic scenarios, although they showed a minimal SLA violation.

Duy et al. [29] showed a resource allocation algorithm based on a neural network model to optimize the power consumption of servers in a cloud. Such workload prediction model is based on historical usage. In the proposed model, the algorithm turns off unused hosts with the intention of minimizing the number of servers running, thus also reducing their power consumption. Evaluations showed that this model could reduce energy consumption by up to 46% compared to energy-agnostic environments.

Dong et al. [30] stated an algorithm that scales in a multidimensional way the virtual machines on a homogeneous mobile cloud based on two factors: the CPU usage rate and the bandwidth among hosts. Based on previous analysis, the minimum energy consumption and the number of physical machines in operation are derived. The results enabled the development of an algorithm for virtual machines placement in order to save power.

Garg et al. [31] presented an algorithm for reducing the carbon dioxide emissions based on EDF scheduling (Earliest Deadline First). Simulation results showed a reduction in power consumption by 23% and a decrease in carbon dioxide emissions of 25%.

2.4 Models

Definition

A model is a representation or interpretation of reality, or an analysis of a system fragment according to a certain structure. For cloud computing environments, models are mathematical formalisms, deterministic or stochastic, expressing relations, variables, parameters, entities, and relationships between variables and objects or operations, aiding decisions about resource management. Models are often used to estimate what are the actual resource needs, depending on high-level metrics based on the applications or customer behavior.

Related Work

Pietri et al. [32] presented a prediction model (PM) of cloud workloads behavior, based on the relationships among the number of tasks and minimum and maximum acceptable time for their execution and some available slots.

Khomonenko and Gindin [33] proposed a multichannel non-Markovian queue model that analyzes the performance of cloud applications based on many available resources.

Lakew et al. [34] and Sharma et al. [35] present queueing models to estimate the response time in applications, and on that basis, indicate many resources that should be used or released through vertical elasticity.

Niyato et al. [36] stated a Markov model to set the number of active servers for highest performance. Although shutdown can save a considerable amount of power and restart operations on hosts, the main purpose was to perform the configuration of available resources and enable online control according to service behavior, power consumption, and SLA requirements. Results showed an increase in energy efficiency by up to 30%, minimally impacting performance.

Maccio and Down [37] introduce the modeling of some sleep states for servers based on Markov Chains. Such model uses four states: off, setup, busy, and idle. The setup state is the transition time among the other three states. Through incoming jobs guided by Poisson behavior, the model optimizes the states on many hosts to meet SLA constraints.

In the same way, Shen et al. [38] used a Markov model in order to allocate virtual machines on hosts to save energy, aiming to improve the trade-off between performance and energy savings. Compared with state of the art suggested at work, the proposal achieves 23% energy savings.

Guzek et al. [39] presents a Markov model for data centers of cloud computing that can be applied to represent cloud applications, virtual machines, and physical hosts. Several features describe each of these entities: processor, memory, storage, and networking. Results show the DVFS impact on the processing time until the deadline of the applications.

2.5 Policies

Definition

A policy consists of a set of rules and norms that can determine actions through predetermined thresholds, which promotes a dynamic cloud environment through changes in the infrastructure to meet particular strategy. Additionally, policies may limit the decisions on the use of resources, helping to maintain many resources within the acceptable Quality of Service levels.

Related Work

Suleiman and Venugopal [40] analyzed several policies that determine the minimum and maximum (MinMax) use of some resources (processor usage) or high-level metric (response time), aiming to determine when operations of scale-out on cloud resources should be conducted.

Therefore, policies consist of limits imposed by the service provider, and when these limits are exceeded, some action must occur. In terms of security for cloud environments, Felsch et al. [41] present a number of rules (Filter) that must be followed to reduce the chance of an attack, such as using different browsers from frequently used when accessing the cloud, the use of client-side filters, continuous update of environments and services, inspection of the HTTP headers of communication between client and provider, and insertion of security concerns in the development of user interfaces.

2.6 Strategies

Definition

A strategy is part of the realm of ideas, that is, the way the environment or situation will be managed and manipulated to meet objectives. In the context of cloud computing, a strategy is a way in which models and policies are applied to the available computing resources with the intention of improving some aspect of the cloud to better support services.

Related Work

Alvarruiz et al. [42] propose as a strategy, shut down idle hosts in a cluster, in view to save energy. In a layer below, policies and models define when such changes occur, and what limits these changes must obey.

Zhu et al. [43] proposed a strategy that split a cloud into four areas: busy, active idle, sleep, and shutdown. In the busy area, hosts are allocated to running applications. The active idle area maintains a certain number of hosts in the idle state waiting to meet any possible demand. At the sleep state, hosts are kept in a state of suspension; ending with a level in which the hosts are turned off. Such grouping provides an environment that classifies hosts into categories associated with the environment usage. The results show that this method can reduce power consumption up to 84%, with an impact on the runtime of up to 8.85%.

2.7 Modules

Definition

Modules are related to non-functional requirements of the cloud environment [44]. The growing number of customers of cloud services makes non-functional requirements such as portability, performance, security and mobility, essential in most web systems. Furthermore, concerns about interoperability, geographic location, energy saving, and high availability are also part of the mapping and development of non-functional requirements. In this way, modules aim at intelligent management of resources by the service provider, in addition to supporting the offered services to customers with the best Quality of Service. Each module has a particular purpose, and generally, there are several modules managed by the same platform, working concurrently and in some cases complementary to each other.

Related Work

Sequeira et al. [45] presents an architectural environment to reduce energy consumption in big data for enterprise cloud applications. Authors define challenges, implications, benefits, and added value incurred when cloud environments aim at power saving. A conceptual architecture is described, allowing the visualization of components necessary to meet a power management module.

Yu et al. [46] discuss security challenges in cloud environments, such as privacy and data security, external threats, internal threats, and other safety aspects. Also, Yu et al. discuss technologies that can reduce security risks, proposing a safe framework for this kind of computing environment.

Gupta et al. [47] suggest the adoption of high-performance applications for cloud environments. The performance has always been a determining factor in large-scale environments. Even though clouds were not traditionally the target environment for batch processing applications, the advent of the big data paradigm raised the utilization of clouds for such type of applications.

2.8 Platform

Definition

A platform is a software layer that aggregates the management and the interconnection of capacities among cloud infrastructure modules. Each of these modules can be defined as a requirement to meet a high-level metric proposed by the cloud service provider. Therefore, platforms can handle one or more modules to maintain balance among different cloud requirements.

Related Work

An example of infrastructure platform is OpenStack [12], an open source platform for management of public and private clouds. The project aims to provide approaches for all types of clouds, enabling simplified deployment, massive scalability, and easier management of resources. The technology consists of a series of interrelated projects that allow full implementation of a cloud infrastructure approach. The data and virtual machines can be distributed across multiple data centers, being the OpenStack responsible for replication and integrity among clusters.

In the same way, Eucalyptus [13] is an open source cloud platform that enables organizations to create a private cloud environment within its data center using an existing virtualized infrastructure. Eucalyptus enables organizations to build a private cloud compatible with the Amazon Web Service's API, expanding the existing virtualized resources based on on-demand services.

Figure 2 summarizes the studies presented in this section to enable better visualization of the approaches.

Fig. 2 Summary of related work to each component classification

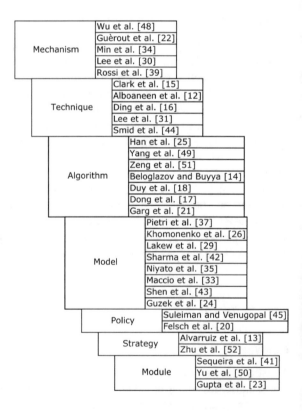

2.9 Hybrid Solutions

Lefèvre and Orgerie [48] showed a cloud strategy that saves power due to many circumstances, such as startup and shutdown hosts mechanism, controls the resources usage rate by policies and uses the virtual machines migration technique. An algorithm to predict, through a model, the behavior of the workload has been proposed. Experimental results showed differences in power consumption among the various scenarios (an algorithm that turns on/off hosts, an algorithm that migrates virtual machines, or a mixed algorithm). In such experiments, energy savings of up to 25% was achieved when compared to an energy-agnostic environment. Moreover, results revealed that, depending on the type of resource, the best alternative might vary.

Min et al. [15] present a strategy that decides the best sleep state based on typical workloads for smartphones. To switch from an idle state to another with lower power consumption, some policies (such as idle time and time in each sleep state) were used along with an algorithm that is applied to different states on the device. Results presented energy savings of up to 50%.

Feller et al. [49] suggested a consolidation model for workloads coupled with an active adjustment of sleep states and changes of processor frequency. The work shows a part of the proposed model, whose purpose was to minimize the number of servers that host applications. For this, a model for adjusting the workload on the servers and setting policies to manage the transitions between idle and off hosts was presented.

Krioukov et al. [50] introduced a strategy for heterogeneous clusters with a focus on saving power and making the smallest likely impact on the tasks response time. Three different architectures were simulated: Nehalem, Atom, and BeagleBoard, and as a workload trace, seven days of HTTP traffic of Wikipedia were used. The DVFS mechanism has been used over underutilized hosts, and sleep states on idle hosts, besides shutdown of part of unused hosts in the cluster. The decision about the fitting number of hosts to meet input tasks is based on combinatorial optimization model (knapsack problem), and the results showed an energy saving of up to 27%, with less than 0.03% of lost requests. In clusters, the use of DVFS is not recommended because when the frequency of the processor is reduced, so is the number of instructions that can be performed.

Kliazovich et al. [51] focuses on communication in cloud computing data centers, presenting a strategy for flow scheduling to provide load balancing of traffic in data center networks, with the goal of optimizing energy consumption. The correct distribution of network flows generated by user applications helps to avoid congestion hotspots and packet loss due to network saturation. As a result, the proposed strategy improves the quality of applications running in the cloud, modeling delays related to communication and packet loss associated with congestion.

Wang et al. [52] investigated approaches to resource allocation and power management through the use of varying workloads and various multi-tier applications. Metrics of interest were throughput, the number of rejected packets, and queuing status, among others. Based on these parameters, authors proposed the design of an adaptive resource allocation algorithm to reduce operating costs.

						Lefèvere and Orgerie [32]	Mechanism
					Min et al. [34]	Technique	Algorithm
				Feller et al. [19]	Mechanism	Model	Model
			Krioukov et al. [28]	Mechanism	Model	Strategy	Policy
		Kliazovich et al. [27]	Algorithm	Policy	Strategy	Module	Strategy
	Wang et al. [47]	Algorithm	Policy	Strategy	Module		Module
Santana et al. [40]	Mechanism	Module	Strategy	Module			
	Model		Module				
	Module						

Fig. 3 Summary of hybrid solutions related to the classification components

Santana et al. [53] stated a model for predicting the application's behavior on web clusters, in order to apply DVFS mechanism and turned idle hosts off, trying to keep up the QoS (Quality of Service). The metric assessed was the processor usage rate. Results presented an energy saving of up to 59%, trying to maintain the quality of service to 95%. On several occasions, this QoS could not be maintained precisely due to the procedure of turning off and restarting hosts.

Figure 3 summarizes the studies presented in this section to enable better visualization of the approaches.

3 Open Research Problems

In an analysis of the work discussed in the previous sections, we can infer certain key points and challenges. We do not expect a practical use of all components of the proposed classification, although several of them could be found during its development. Therefore, few studies use all the mechanisms and techniques available together. Probably this is due to interference that a mechanism or technique can cause over another. For example, an underutilized physical machine may receive a new virtual machine by migration, have a migrated virtual machine to another physical machine and placed in a suspended state, or have reduced the frequency of its processors. However, administration of a cloud environment using all the options together, and the decision of what each physical machine must support to enable energy saving in a given moment is not a trivial task. This is one of the main challenges we identified, namely, how to choose, among all the techniques and mechanisms, which is better suited to each physical machine.

Decisions about what, how, and when to use a mechanism or technique have implications on resource utilization. Even SLAs are set between customer and service provider based on CPU, memory, network, and disk usage. This occurs because the service provider has control only over the over the quality of service of the outer edge of its infrastructure. However, several other external factors can influence a quality of experience (QoE). Therefore, another identified challenge is the translation of low-level metrics such as resources usage to more tangible high-level metric, such as total response time or transactions per second.

Furthermore, there is a paradigm shift in clouds. Initially, the main concern of the research community was about performance, reflecting the main target of HPC environments, where performance is the most important system metric. Currently, there is growing concern about trade-offs, as one particular metric can impact others. The most common of such trade-offs is found in the energy saving area, where power may affect performance. Likewise, trade-offs are identified between scalability and timeliness, security, and encryption on the data, environments, and systems complexity, etc. Another challenge is the understanding of trade-offs and the way that SLAs can be met in view of such trade-offs.

The adoption of network support, new devices, and OS-level virtualization also becomes a challenge. Most of today's data centers have redundant network paths that may support link aggregation mechanisms to increase the communication channel between hosts and enable faster data traffic. Thus, the investigation of how such mechanism may affect decisions to improve trade-offs is an interesting research question. Additionally, OS-level virtualization (such as Linux Containers) consists of virtualized environments that have near-native performance, and they are increasingly present in large-scale environments. Although this new model still has limitations on the isolation capabilities, it has potential applicability on environments where performance is more important, because containers do not incur instantiation delay, unlike traditional virtual machines.

Finally, it can be noticed that few studies were carried out in real cloud environments. Most use simulation to validate their experiments and some use analytics models. Although there are plenty of available cloud environments that can be used to verify studies' results, most of these environments are limited in size or cost. Cloud environments where the researcher has full control of all commonly required parameters are usually small in amount of resources, while large environments such as Amazon have a cost to the researcher, and do not provide infrastructure-level control than most research demands. Thus, simulation has been the most used way to assess research proposals in a large-scale environment. However, simulators may abstract complex low-level operations that may be necessary for the validation of any module in particular, and that can affect the accuracy of results. A new challenge then is to develop more specific simulators to an individual cloud behavior or module, or the adoption of large cloud environment testbeds for research purposes.

4 Conclusion

The cloud infrastructure research community utilizes different terms for the same artifacts. In this way, there is the need for unification of the terms to avoid ambiguity. Therefore, the main objective of this chapter is to propose a comprehensive bottom-up classification to organize the existing terms, classifying the artifacts on different levels of abstraction within the cloud infrastructure layer.

From the creation of this terminology, related work can now be classified by clarifying which technologies are most commonly used to meet certain modules.

This exercise also enabled visualization of new challenges and trends. By analyzing the data presented in the previous sections, we can list issues that can be explored in future research, such as:

- The need for approaches that manage various techniques and mechanisms in harmony on resources based on pre-defined metrics.
- Better tools for evaluation of research outcomes such as simulators for each module type, thereby reducing the level of abstraction.
- Evaluation of new virtualization proposals such as containers, which present better performance issues when compared to traditional virtualization environments.
- The implementation and testing of the approaches in real cloud environments.

Moreover, we also noticed a paradigm shift in the way that cloud environments are evaluated: while earlier studies focused on single metric (typically performance), there is now a strong trend on evaluations that consider trade-offs among two or more metrics. Such studies should be made more frequent, given that there is a need to balance the various metrics composing cloud environments that are expected to reduce costs by the side of the service provider, without impacting on the customer's Quality of Experience (QoE).

References

1. Zhuo, T., Ling, Q., Zhenzhen, C., Kenli, L., Samee, U., & Khan, K. L. (2016). An energy-efficient task scheduling algorithm in DVFS-enabled cloud environment. *Journal of Grid Computing, 14(1)*, 55–74.
2. Silva-Filho, A. G., Bezerra, P. T. L. F., Silva, Q. B., Junior, A. L. O. C., Santos, A. L. M., Costa, P. H. R., et al. (2012). Energy-aware technology-based DVFS mechanism for the android operating system. In *Proceedings of the 2012 Brazilian Symposium on Computing System Engineering (SBESC '12)* (pp. 184–187). Washington, DC, USA: IEEE Computer Society.
3. Stijn, E., & Lieven, E. (2011). Fine-grained DVFS using on-chip regulators. *ACM Transcations Architecture and Code Optimization, 8(1)*, 24.
4. Hafiz, F. S., Hengxing, T., Ishfaq, A., Sanjay, R., & Phanisekhar, B. (2012). Energy-and performance-aware scheduling of tasks on parallel and distributed systems. *Journal on Emerging Technologies in Computing Systems, 8(4)*, 37.
5. Guérout, T., Monteil, T., Da, C. G., Buyya, R., & Alexandru, M. (2013). Rodrigo neves calheiros. Energy-aware simulation with DVFS. *Simulation Modelling Practice and Theory, 39*, 76–91.
6. Isci, C., Liu, J., Abali, B., Kephart, J. O., & Kouloheris, J. (2011). Improving server utilization using fast virtual machine migration. *IBM Journal of Research and Developement, 55(6)*, 365–376.
7. Zhuang, H., Liu, X., Ou, Z., & Aberer, K. (2013). Impact of instance seeking strategies on resource allocation in cloud data centers. In *Proceedings of the 2013 IEEE Sixth International Conference on Cloud Computing (CLOUD '13)* (pp. 27–34). Washington, DC, USA: IEEE Computer Society.
8. Fischer, A., Fessi, A., Carle, G., & de Meer, H. (2011). Wide-area virtual machine migration as resilience mechanism. In: *Proceedings International Workshop on Network Resilience (WNR)*, Madrid, Spain, October 4, 2011.

9. Zhu, Y., Ma, D., Huang, D., & Hu, Ch. (2013). Enabling secure location-based services in mobile cloud computing. In *Proceedings of the second ACM SIGCOMM workshop on Mobile Cloud Computing (MCC '13)*. New York, NY, USA: ACM (pp. 27–32).
10. Adam, A. K., & Lee, J. (2013, June). Combining social authentication and untrusted clouds for private location sharing. In *Proceedings of the 18th ACM Symposium on Access Control Models and Technologies (SACMAT)*.
11. Marc, M. T., & Tobias, C. (2012). SecureSafe: A highly secure online data safe industrial use case. In *Proceedings of the First Workshop on Measurement, Privacy, and Mobility (MPM '12)* (Article 1, 6 pp.). New York, NY, USA: ACM.
12. Rosado, T., & Bernardino, J. (2014). An overview of openstack architecture. In *Proceedings of the 18th International Database Engineering and Applications Symposium, IDEAS '14* (pp. 366–367). New York, NY, USA: ACM.
13. Nurmi, D., Wolski, R., Grzegorczyk, C., Obertelli, G., Soman, S., Youseff, L., et al. (2009). The eucalyptus open-source cloud-computing system. In *Proceedings of the 2009 9th IEEE/ACM International Symposium on Cluster Computing and the Grid, CCGRID '09* (pp. 124–131). Washington, DC, USA: IEEE Computer Society.
14. Wu, C. M., Chang, R. S., & Chan, H. Y. (2014). A green energy-efficient scheduling algorithm using the DVFS technique for cloud datacenters. *Future Generation Computer Systems, 37,* 141–147.
15. Min, A. W., Wang, R., Tsai, J., Ergin, M. A., & Tai, T. Y. C. (2012). Improving energy efficiency for mobile platforms by exploiting low-power sleep states. In *Proceedings of the 9th Conference on Computing Frontiers, CF '12* (pp. 133–142). New York, NY, USA: ACM.
16. Lee, R. B. (2012). Hardware-enhanced access control for cloud computing. In *Proceedings of the 17th ACM Symposium on Access Control Models and Technologies, SACMAT '12* (pp. 1–2). New York, NY, USA: ACM.
17. Guerout, T., Monteil, T., Costa, G. D., Calheiros, R. N., Buyya, R., & Alexandru, M. (2013). Energyaware simulation with DVFS. *Simulation Modelling Practice and Theory, 39,* 76–91.
18. Calheiros, R. N., Ranjan, R., Beloglazov, A., De Rose, C. A. F., & Buyya, R. (2011). CloudSim: A toolkit for modeling and simulation of cloud computing environments and evaluation of resource provisioning algorithms. *Software Practice and Experience, 41*(1), 23–50.
19. Rossi, F., Xavier, M., Monti, Y., & De Rose, C. (2015). On the impact of energy-efficient strategies in HPC clusters. In *Proceedings International Conference on Parallel, Distributed and Network-Based Processing (PDP), 23rd Euromicro* (pp. 17–21).
20. Clark, C., Fraser, K., Hand, S., Hansen, J. G., Jul, E., Limpach, C., et al. (2005). Live migration of virtual machines. In *Proceedings of the 2nd Conference on Symposium on Networked Systems Design and Implementation*, NSDI'05 (Vol. 2, pp. 273–286). Berkeley, CA, USA: USENIX Association.
21. Lee, S., Purohit, M., & Saha, B. (2013). Firewall placement in cloud data centers. In *Proceedings of the 4th Annual Symposium on Cloud Computing, SOCC '13* (pp. 52:1–52:2). New York, NY, USA: ACM.
22. Smid, H., Mast, P., Tromp, M., Winterboer, A., & Evers, V. (2011). Canary in a coal mine: Monitoring air quality and detecting environmental incidents by harvesting twitter. *CHI '11 Extended Abstracts on Human Factors in Computing Systems, CHI EA '11* (pp. 1855–1860). New York, NY, USA: ACM.
23. Alboaneen, D. A., Pranggono, B., & Tianfield, H. (2014). Energy-aware virtual machine consolidation for cloud data centers. In *Proceedings of the 2014 IEEE/ACM 7th International Conference on Utility and Cloud Computing, UCC '14* (pp. 1010–1015). Washinton, DC, USA: IEEE Computer Society.
24. Ding, Y., Qin, X., Liu, L., & Wang, T. (2015). Energy efficient scheduling of virtual machines in cloud with deadline constraint. *Future Generation Computer Systems, 50*(C), 62–74.
25. Han, R., Guo, L., Ghanem, M. M., & Guo, Y. (2012). Lightweight resource scaling for cloud applications. In *Proceedings of the 2012 12th IEEE/ACM International Symposium on Cluster, Cloud and Grid Computing (Ccgrid 2012), CCGRID '12* (pp. 644–651). Washington, DC, USA: IEEE Computer Society.

26. Yang, L., Cao, J., Yuan, Y., Li, T., Han, A., & Chan, A. (2013). A framework for partitioning and execution of data stream applications in mobile cloud computing. *SIGMETRICS Performance Evaluation Reviews*, *40*(4), 23–32.
27. Zeng, W., Zhao, Y., & Zeng, J. (2009). Cloud service and service selection algorithm research. In *Proceedings of the First ACM/SIGEVO Summit on Genetic and Evolutionary Computation, GEC '09* (pp. 1045–1048). New York, NY, USA: ACM.
28. Beloglazov, A., & Buyya, R. (2010). Energy efficient resource management in virtualized cloud datacenters. In *Proceedings of the 2010 10th IEEE/ACM International Conference on Cluster, Cloud and Grid Computing, CCGRID '10* (pp. 826–831). Washington, DC, USA: IEEE Computer Soity.
29. Duy, T. V. T., Sato, Y., & Inoguchi, Y. (2010). Performance evaluation of a green scheduling algorithm for energy savings in cloud computing. In *Proceedings IEEE International Symposium on Parallel Distributed Processing, Workshops and Phd Forum (IPDPSW)* (pp. 1–8).
30. Dong, Y., Zhou, L., Jin, Y., & Wen, Y. (2015). Improving energy efficiency for mobile media cloud via virtual machine consolidation. *Mobile Network Applications*, *20*(3), 370–379.
31. Garg, S. K., Yeo, C. S., & Buyya, R. (2011). Green cloud framework for improving carbon efficiency of clouds. In *Proceedings of the 17th International Conference on Parallel Processing—Volume Part I, Euro-Par'11* (pp. 491–502). Berlin, Heidelberg: Springer.
32. Pietri, I., Juve, G., Deelman, E., & Sakellariou, R. (2014). A performance model to estimate execution time of scientific workflows on the cloud. In *Proceedings of the 9th Workshop on Workflows in Support of Large-Scale Science, WORKS '14* (pp. 11–19). Piscataway, NJ, USA: IEEE Press.
33. Khomonenko, A. D., & Gindin, S. I. (2014). Stochastic models for cloud computing performance evaluation. In *Proceedings of the 10th Central and Eastern European Software Engineering Conference in Russia, CEE-SECR '14* (pp. 20:1–20:6). New York, NY, USA: ACM.
34. Lakew, E. B., Klein, C., Hernandez-Rodriguez, F., Elmroth, E. (2014). Towards faster response time models for vertical elasticity. In *Proceedings of the 2014 IEEE/ACM 7th International Conference on Utility and Cloud Computing, UCC '14* (pp. 560–565). Washington, DC, USA: IEEE Computer Society.
35. Sharma, U., Shenoy, P., & Towsley, D. F. (2012). Provisioning multi-tier cloud applications using statistical bounds on sojourn time. In *Proceedings of the 9th International Conference on Autonomic Computing, ICAC '12* (pp. 43–52). New York, NY, USA: ACM.
36. Niyato, D., Chaisiri, S., & Sung, L. B. (2009). Optimal power management for server farm to support green computing. In *Proceedings of the 2009 9th IEEE/ACM International Symposium on Cluster Computing and the Grid, CCGRID '09* (pp. 84–91). Washington, DC, USA: IEEE Computer Society.
37. Maccio, V., & Down, D. (2015). On optimal policies for energy-aware servers. *Performance Evaluation*, *90*(C), 36–52.
38. Shen, D., Luo, J., Dong, F., Fei, X., Wang, W., Jin, G., et al. (2015). Stochastic modeling of dynamic right-sizing for energy-efficiency in cloud data centers. *Future Generation Computer Systems*, *48*(C), 82–95.
39. Guzek, M., Kliazovich, D., Bouvry, P. (2013). A holistic model for resource representation in virtualized cloud computing data centers. In *Proceedings of the 2013 IEEE International Conference on Cloud Computing Technology and Science—Volume 01, CLOUDCOM '13* (pp. 590–598). Washington, DC, USA: IEEE Computer Society.
40. Suleiman, B., & Venugopal, S. (2013). Modeling performance of elasticity rules for cloud-based applications. In *Proceedings of the 2013 17th IEEE International Enterprise Distributed Object Computing Conference, EDOC '13* (pp. 201–206). Washington, DC, USA: IEEE Computer Society.
41. Felsch, D., Heiderich, M., Schulz, F., & Schwenk, J. (2015). How private is your private cloud?: Security analysis of cloud control interfaces. In *Proceedings of the 2015 ACM Workshop on Cloud Computing Security Workshop, CCSW '15* (pp. 5–16). New York, NY, USA: ACM.
42. Alvarruiz, F., de Alfonso, C., Caballer, M., & Hernandez, V. (2012). An energy manager for high performance computer clusters. In *Proceedings IEEE 10th International Symposium on Parallel and Distributed Processing with Applications (ISPA)* (pp. 231–238).

43. Zhu, H., Liu, Y., Lu, K., & Wang, X. (2012). Self-adaptive management of the sleep depths of idle nodes in large scale systems to balance between energy consumption and response times. In *Proceedings of the 2012 IEEE 4th International Conference on Cloud Computing Technology and Science (CloudCom), CLOUDCOM '12* (pp. 633–639). Washington, DC, USA: IEEE Computer Society.
44. Villegas, D., & Sadjadi, S. M. (2011). Mapping non-functional requirements to cloud applications. In *SEKE* (pp. 527–532). Knowledge Systems Institute Graduate School.
45. Sequeira, H., Carreira, P., Goldschmidt, T., & Vorst, P. (2014). Energy cloud: Real-time cloud-native energy management system to monitor and analyze energy consumption in multiple industrial sites. In *Proceedings of the 2014 IEEE/ACM 7th International Conference on Utility and Cloud Computing, UCC '14* (pp. 529–534). Washington, DC, USA: IEEE Computer Society.
46. Yu, H., Powell, N., Stembridge, D., Yuan, X. (2012). Cloud computing and security challenges. In *Proceedings of the 50th Annual Southeast Regional Conference, ACM-SE '12* (pp. 298–302). New York, NY, USA: ACM.
47. Gupta, A., Kale, L., Gioachin, F., March, V., Suen, C. H., Lee, B. S., et al. (2013). The who, what, why, and how of high performance computing in the cloud. In *IEEE 5th International Conference on Proceedings Cloud Computing Technology and Science (CloudCom)* (Vol. 1, pp. 306–314).
48. Lef'evre, L., & Orgerie, A. C. (2010). Designing and evaluating an energy efficient cloud. *Journal of Supercomputing, 51*(3), 352–373.
49. Feller, E., Rilling, L., Morin, C., Lottiaux, R., & Leprince, D. (2010). Snooze: A scalable, fault-tolerant and distributed consolidation manager for large-scale clusters. In *Proceedings of the 2010 IEEE/ACM International Conference on Green Computing and Communications and International Conference on Cyber, Physical and Social Computing, GREENCOM-CPSCOM '10* (pp. 125–132). Washington, DC, USA: IEEE Computer Society.
50. Krioukov, A., Mohan, P., Alspaugh, S., Keys, L., Culler, D., & Katz, R. H. (2010). Napsac: Design and implementation of a power-proportional web cluster. In *Proceedings of the First ACM SIGCOMM Workshop on Green Networking, Green Networking '10* (pp. 15–22). New York, NY, USA: ACM.
51. Kliazovich, D., Arzo, S. T., Granelli, F., Bouvry, P., & Khan, S. U. (2013). e-stab: Energy-efficient scheduling for cloud computing applications with traffic load balancing. In *Proceedings of the 2013 IEEE International Conference on Green Computing and Communications and IEEE Internet of Things and IEEE Cyber, Physical and Social Computing, GREENCOM-ITHINGSCPSCOM '13* (pp. 7–13). Washington, DC, USA: IEEE Computer Society.
52. Wang, X., Du, Z., & Chen, Y. (2012). An adaptive model-free resource and power management approach for multi-tier cloud environments. *Journal of Systems and Software, 85*(5), 1135–1146.
53. Santana, C., Leite, J. C. B., & Moss'e, D. (2010). Load forecasting applied to soft real-time web clusters. In *Proceedings of the 2010 ACM Symposium on Applied Computing, SAC '10* (pp. 346–350). New York, NY, USA: ACM.

Author Biographies

Fábio Diniz Rossi holds BS degree in Informatics from the University of the Region of Campanha (URCAMP, Brazil, 2000), M.Sc. (2008) and doctoral (2016) degrees in Computer Science from the Pontifical Catholic University of Rio Grande do Sul (PUCRS, Brazil). Since 2008, he is lecturer at Farroupilha Federal Institute (IFFar, Alegrete, RS, Brazil). His primary research interests are cloud computing and energy efficiency.

Rodrigo N. Calheiros is a Lecturer in the School of Computing, Engineering and Mathematics, Western Sydney University, Australia. He works in the field of Cloud computing and related areas since 2008, and since them he carried out R&D supporting research in the area. His research interests also include Big Data, Internet of Things, and their application.

César A. F. De Rose holds BS degree in Computer Science from the Catholic University of Rio Grande do Sul (PUCRS, Porto Alegre, RS, Brazil, 1990), M.Sc. in Computer Science from the Federal University of Rio Grande do Sul (CPGCCUFRGS, Porto Alegre, RS, Brazil, 1993), and a doctoral degree from Karlrsruhe University (Karlsruhe, Germany, 1998). Since 1998, he is a professor at PUCRS and a member of the Parallel and Distributed Processing Group. His research interests include resource management in parallel and distributed architectures and operating systems. Since 2008, he is the lead researcher at the PUCRS High Performance Laboratory (LAD-PUCRS).

Virtual Networking with Azure for Hybrid Cloud Computing in Aneka

Adel Nadjaran Toosi and Rajkumar Buyya

Abstract Hybrid cloud environments are a highly scalable and cost-effective option for enterprises that need to expand their on-premises infrastructure. In every hybrid cloud solutions, the issue of inter-cloud network connectivity has to be overcome to allow communications, possibly secure, between resources scattered over multiple networks. Network visualization provides the right method for addressing this issue. We present how Azure Virtual Private Network (VPN) services are used to establish an overlay network for hybrid clouds in our Aneka platform. First, we explain how Aneka resource provisioning module is extended to support Azure Resource Manger (ARM) application programming interfaces (APIs). Then, we walk through the process of establishment of an Azure Point-to-Site VPN to provide connectivity between Aneka nodes in the hybrid cloud environment. Finally, we present a case study hybrid cloud in Aneka and we experiment with it to demonstrate the functionality of the system.

1 Introduction

Cloud computing is the mainstream paradigm for delivering on-demand and easy-to-use computing services in a pay-as-you-go model. In this paradigm, consumers and organizations adopt cloud-based computational resources and services to deploy their applications and store data. The increasing dependence on information technology (IT) and global explosion of data over the last decade has fostered this adoption more than ever. Moreover, this trend is expected to continue in the upcoming decades as cloud computing becomes the integral and essential part of many emerging IT technologies such as Internet of things [6] and big data applications [1].

A. Nadjaran Toosi (✉) · R. Buyya
Cloud Computing and Distributed Systems (CLOUDS) Laboratory,
School of Computing and Information Systems, The University of Melbourne,
Melbourne, VIC, Australia
e-mail: anadjaran@unimelb.edu.au

R. Buyya
e-mail: rbuyya@unimelb.edu.au

© Springer Nature Singapore Pte Ltd. 2017
S. Chaudhary et al. (eds.), *Research Advances in Cloud Computing*,
DOI 10.1007/978-981-10-5026-8_5

Among the many different forms of cloud computing, hybrid clouds, in which organizations' on-premises infrastructure are expanded by adding third-party public cloud resources, provides one of the best blends for hosting applications. A hybrid cloud allows a seamless integration of an existing on-premises infrastructure (usually a private cloud) and a public cloud, enabling the cloud bursting deployment model. In cloud bursting model, applications run in a private infrastructure and bursts onto a public cloud when the demand for computing capacity spikes. Hybrid cloud delivers the benefits of both the public cloud and in-house cloud computing infrastructures due to its native characteristics such as cost reduction and compliance with the location of sensitive data [18].

In hybrid cloud environments, computational resources are scattered throughout disparate sets of networks (i.e., private and public cloud networks). One of the main issues arises in such a scenario is how nodes (e.g., virtual machines) from multiple sites and clouds are connected together. In other words, there is the issue of managing two separate sets of IP ranges that would have to be combined to enable automated resource provisioning and migration across clouds. Allocation of public IP addresses to nodes requiring communicating with each other provides a viable solution for this issue. However, providing public IP addresses, in particular public IP addresses for private cloud resources in the organizational infrastructure, is not always feasible. Another issue is that in most, if not all, hybrid cloud scenarios, a secure communication channel needs to be built between the private on-premises infrastructure and cloud resources as the public Internet is used to transmit data.

The network virtualization techniques are key enablers to address these issues by constructing of an overlay network over the existing networks such as the Internet. A Virtual Private Network (VPN) is an overlay network that creates a secure network connection to a private network across a public network. As many more cloud providers offering VPN services, enterprises, and organizations looking into hybrid cloud solutions can utilize these VPN services to manage their hybrid cloud platforms. In this book chapter, we go through the process of building a hybrid cloud solution for our Aneka platform using virtual network services of Microsoft Azure.

Aneka [7, 17] is a Platform-as-a-Service (PaaS) solution providing a middleware for the development and deployment of applications in hybrid and multi-clouds. Aneka provides application developers with Application Programming Interfaces (APIs) for transparently harnessing and exploiting the physical and virtual computing resources in heterogeneous networks of workstations, clusters, servers, and data centers. Scheduling and resource provisioning services provided by Aneka allow for dynamic growth and shrinkage of the Aneka cloud to meet Quality of Service (QoS) requirements of deployed applications. This chapter also discusses our extension to Aneka resource provisioning based on Microsoft Azure Resource Manager (ARM) deployment model.

The rest of the chapter is organized as follows: Sect. 2 describes hybrid cloud and its benefits. Section 3 discusses the connectivity issue between clouds in a hybrid cloud environment. Section 4 proposes virtual private networks (VPNs) as a solution for the connectivity issue in hybrid clouds and explores various Azure VPN connections. In Sect. 5, our Aneka Platform-as-a-Service (PaaS) is introduced as a tool for building a hybrid cloud environment. We explain how Azure VPNs can be used to provide inter-cloud connectivity for the establishment of Aneka hybrid cloud in Sect. 6. To demonstrate the effectiveness VPN for hybrid cloud solutions, in Sect. 7, we represent details of a case study on creation of hybrid cloud combining private cloud resource (networked desktop computers) and Azure public cloud resources and the deployment of application on the hybrid cloud infrastructure along with experimental results. Section 8 defines some open research problems and pathways for future work. This chapter is summarized in Sect. 9.

2 Hybrid Clouds

The hybrid cloud, as shown in Fig. 1, is an integration of a public cloud provider such as Microsoft Azure or Amazon Web Services (AWS) with a private cloud platform which is designed to be used within the boundary of a single organization. In a hybrid cloud environment, the organization that owns the private cloud moves part of its operations to the external public cloud provider. In this scenario, the public and private clouds are independent and distinct entities. This allows the organization to perform protected operations and store sensitive or privileged data on its own private infrastructure while retaining the ability to leverage public cloud computational resources when demand for computation exceeds available capacity. This provides the following benefits to the organizations:

- **Cost savings**: Hybrid cloud solutions can increase cost savings. Public clouds' *pay-as-you-go* model give the organization the flexibility of using public cloud resources as much as they require and removes the need for building an internal infrastructure that endures occasional bursts in demand.
- **Security**: Improved security is another main benefit of hybrid clouds. In hybrid cloud model, the organization utilizing hybrid model can run sensitive operations and store sensitive data in the private cloud platform. This helps to protect privacy of data and comply with location and regulatory requirements where it is applicable.

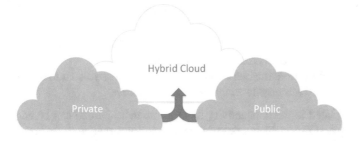

Fig. 1 Schematic view of a hybrid cloud

- **Scalability**: A hybrid cloud environment provides the opportunity to expand capacity by adding external resources to the pool of available resources. This allows for scaling resources up and down as demands change in order to optimize performance and efficiency.
- **Availability and Reliability**: While private clouds do offer a certain level of availability, public cloud services will offer a higher level of availability. By replicating data across hybrid clouds and moving as many non-sensitive tasks as possible to the public cloud, the organization can benefit from higher availability and fewer outages. The hybrid cloud model is also an appealing choice for disaster recovery plans and more reliable systems.

The benefits of hybrid cloud solutions are not limited to the above list. Other benefits such as business agility, more flexibility, and better accessibility can also be resulted from successful application of a hybrid cloud solution.

3   Connectivity Issue in Adoption of Hybrid Clouds

Similar to many other IT examples, even though building hybrid clouds bring many benefits, they still face some challenges that must be addressed before they can be effectively used. Apart from challenges such as portability, compatibility, and needs for middleware supporting hybrid clouds, the connectivity issue is an integral part of every hybrid cloud deployments. Since computational resources in hybrid cloud environments are scattered across multiple administrative domains, needs for reliable, responsive and secure connections between machines (either virtual or physical) residing in separate networks arise.

Even though one might think that the allocation of public IP addresses to these machines resolves the connectivity issue, there are several technical barriers which obstruct such application. They include

1. Assigning public IP addresses to all machines in the hybrid cloud is not feasible in many cases and is a waste of resources. Because IP addresses are limited and many organizations have access to limited range of public IP addresses.
2. Even if organizations can afford to allocate public IP addresses to private cloud machines, this involves security risks outweighing its benefits. Moreover, machines residing in the private infrastructure often located behind organizational firewalls or network address translation (NAT) that protect them from being directly accessed by devices from outside networks.
3. Finally, Public IP addresses do not address the issues related to secure communications between private and public cloud resources.

Issues related to the connectivity issue in the hybrid cloud can be addressed by *network virtualization*. Network virtualization is concerned with the construction of virtual networks over an existing network. In the next section, we discuss how VPN services can resolve the issues related to connectivity and segregated networks in hybrid cloud platforms.

4 Virtual Private Networks

A VPN is a cost-effective and secure way of extending an enterprises private network across a public network such as the Internet. It constructs an overlay network on top of an existing network such as an IP network without changing characteristics of the underlying network. VPNs allow remote resources located outside the local infrastructure for example a public cloud to securely access local network resources and vice versa. This creates a secure communication channel for resources scattered over public and private cloud networks and facilitates automated resource provisioning and migration across them.

Thanks to ongoing advances in *Network Virtualization* solutions and technologies employed by public cloud providers such as Amazon Virtual Private Cloud (Amazon VPC),[1] Google Cloud Virtual Network,[2] and Microsoft Azure Virtual Networks (VNet),[3] building overlay VPNs connecting on-premises networks to public cloud virtual networks becomes more convenient.

4.1 Microsoft Azure VPNs

In this chapter, we present our experience with using Microsoft Azure *Point-to-Site* VPN connections for building a hybrid cloud platform for our Aneka tool (Discussed in Sect. 5). To send network traffic between the on-premises site and Azure Virtual Network (VNet), Azure provides various VPN connectivity options as follows:

1. **Site-to-Site**: A Site-to-Site (S2S) VPN connection is a connection over IPsec (Internet Protocol Security) VPN tunnel. This type of connection requires a VPN device located in on-premises infrastructure with an assigned public IP address not behind a NAT. A virtual private network gateway (VPN gateway) must also be created for the Azure VNet. In Site-to-Site connections, multiple VPN connections from on-premises sites to the VPN gateway can be made which is often called a "multi-site" connection. Figure 2 shows a sample Site-to-Site VPN connections.
2. **Point-to-Site**: A Point-to-Site (P2S) connection allows the creation of secure connections from an individual machine in the on-premises network to the Azure VNet. This VPN connection is built over SSTP (Secure Socket Tunneling Protocol) and does not require a VPN device or a public-facing IP address to work. This solution is used for our case study scenario in Sect. 7 since our hybrid cloud testbed is built on top of multiple desktop machines behind our organizational NAT. Figure 3 shows a sample Point-to-Point VPN in Azure.

---

[1] https://aws.amazon.com/vpc/.

[2] https://cloud.google.com/virtual-network/.

[3] https://azure.microsoft.com/en-us/services/virtual-network/.

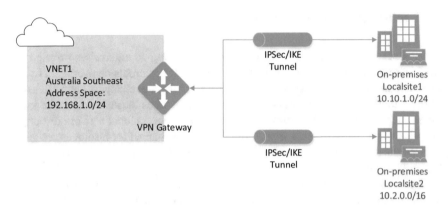

Fig. 2 Azure Site-to-Site VPN connection

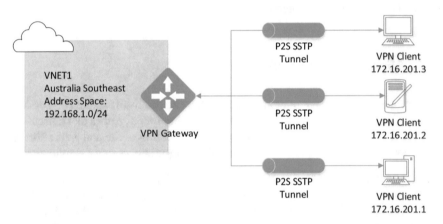

Fig. 3 Azure Point-to-Site VPN connection

3. **VNet-to-VNet**: Connecting an Azure virtual network to another Azure virtual network (VNet-to-VNet) is similar to connecting a VNet to an on-premises site. Both VNets use a VPN gateway to provide a secure tunnel using IPsec/IKE. VNet-to-VNet communication can be combined with multi-site connection configurations. Figure 4 illustrates the schematic view of a sample VNet-to-VNet in Azure.

In addition to above VPN connections, Azure also provides ExpressRoute for those customers in a co-location with Azure cloud exchange to create private connections that directly connects their on-premises infrastructure to Azure data centers.

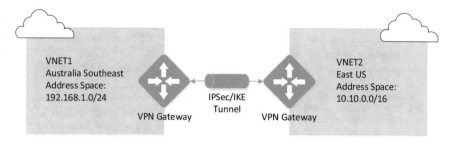

Fig. 4 Azure VNet-to-VNet VPN connection

5 Aneka Cloud Application Platform

Aneka [17] is a *Platform-as-a-Service* framework to facilitate the development and deployment of cloud applications. It offers a collection of tools to build, control, and monitor an Aneka cloud environment. The Aneka cloud can be composed of a collection of heterogeneous resources on the public cloud or the premises of an enterprise, or a combination of both. Aneka provides application developers with *Application Programming Interfaces* (APIs) for transparently exploiting physical and virtual resources in the Aneka cloud. Developers express the logic of applications using programming models and define runtime environments on top of which applications are deployed and executed. Currently the following four different programming models are supported by the Aneka platform [17]:

1. *Bag-of-tasks model*: expressing bag-of-tasks and workflow applications;
2. *Distributed threads model*: allowing for execution of applications composed of independent threads (i.e., threads that do not share data);
3. *MapReduce model*: leveraged for processing of large data sets based on the implementation of Google's MapReduce [10]; and
4. *Parameter sweep model*: designed for execution of the same task over different ranges of values and datasets from a given parameter set.

The Aneka framework has been designed and implemented in a service-oriented fashion. Services are the extension point of the platform allowing for the integration of new functionalities and the replacement of existing ones with different implementations. Brief descriptions of some of these services that are central to hybrid cloud deployment are provided below:

Scheduling: The main role of scheduling service is to assign tasks to available resources. Aneka can be configured to use static resources that are available from the beginning of the scheduling process or dynamic resources that can be provisioned based on the requirements. In a dynamic configuration, the scheduling service communicates with the provisioning service to provision or release resources based on the scheduling algorithm decisions. Scheduling algorithms in Aneka can be developed to fulfill specific Service Level Agreements (SLA) required by users such as the satisfaction of deadline or budget constraints for certain applications.

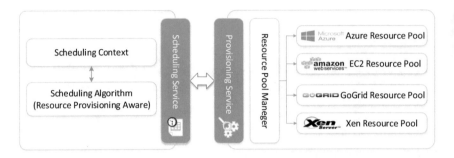

Fig. 5 The interaction between scheduling and provisioning services for dynamic resource provisioning in Aneka

Provisioning: The provisioning service is in charge of acquiring and releasing resources from different cloud providers. To satisfy this requirement, Aneka offers a specialized resource pool connection for each cloud provider that invokes the interface of that specific cloud provider to provision and release resources. These connections are managed by resource pool manager to create a pool of connections that can be invoked any time for the specific cloud provider. Resource pool connections can be created through the *Aneka Management Studio* for adding static resources or as part of dynamic resource provisioning configuration for scheduling algorithms. Figure 5 shows an overview of dynamic resource provisioning and the interaction between scheduling and provisioning services in Aneka. In Sect. 5.2, we present our extension to Aneka to support Microsoft *Azure Resource Manager* (ARM) deployment model for the management of Azure provisioned resources.

Storage: This service is in charge of the management of data and provides an internal storage for applications. It provides applications with basic file transfer facilities and performs data transfers among Aneka nodes. The current release of Aneka provides a storage implementation based on the File Transfer Protocol (FTP) service.

Apart from the above services, Ankea provides other fundamental services such as reservation, licensing, accounting, membership, and execution services as part of its platform services.

5.1 Aneka Architecture

Figure 6 provides the architecture and fundamental services that compose the Aneka platform. The figure shows a layered view of the Aneka components. Aneka provides a runtime environment for executing applications by leveraging heterogeneous resources on the underlying *infrastructure* built on the top of computing nodes employed from network of desktop machines, clusters, and data centers. In other words, the infrastructure layer is a collection of nodes hosting components of Aneka middleware.

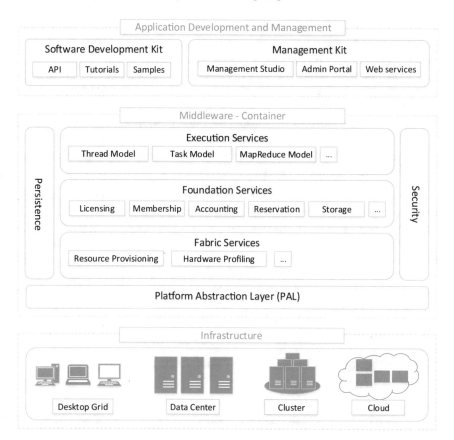

Fig. 6 Aneka framework overview

The *middleware* provides a collection of services for interactions with the Aneka cloud. The container represents the unit of deployment for Aneka clouds and the runtime environment for services. The core functionalities residing in the *Platform Abstraction Layer (PAL)* constitute the basic services that are used to control the infrastructure of Aneka clouds. It provides a uniform interface for management and configuration of nodes and the container instances deployed on them in the infrastructure layer. Middleware is composed of two major components representing the building blocks of Aneka clouds: the *Aneka Daemon* and *Aneka Container*. Each node hosts the Aneka daemon and one or more Aneka container instances. The daemon is a management component controlling the container instances installed on the particular node. A node running the Aneka master container plays the role of resource manager and application scheduler. Nodes running Aneka worker containers are responsible for processing and executing work units of the applications sent from the master node. In addition, each container provides a messaging channel for accessing features of different services provided by the container. There are three classes of services characterizing the container:

1. *Execution services*: are responsible for scheduling and executing applications. Specialized implementations of these services are defined for the execution of work units of each programming model supported by Aneka.
2. *Foundation services*: are in-charge of metering applications, allocating resources, managing the collection of available nodes, and keeping the registry of services updated.
3. *Fabric services*: provide access to the physical and virtualized resources managed by the Aneka cloud. The *Resource Provisioning Service (RPS)* enables horizontal scaling out and allows for elastic and dynamic growth and shrinkage of the Aneka cloud to meet Quality of Service (QoS) requirements of applications.

The services of the middleware are accessible through a set of interfaces and tools in the *development and management* layer. The *Software Development Kit (SDK)* embodies a collection of abstractions and APIs for definition of applications and leveraging existing programming models. The *Management Kit* contains a collection of tools for management, monitoring, and administration of Aneka clouds. All the management functions of the Aneka cloud are made accessible through the *Management Studio*, a comprehensive graphical environment providing a global view of the cloud for administrators.

5.2 Extending Aneka Resource Provisioning with Azure Resource Manager

Aneka resource provisioning service currently supports provisioning requests for cloud providers such as Amazon EC2, GoGrid, and Microsoft Azure. In recent years, Microsoft Azure [4] has undergone a significant transformation and, as a result of that, two different sets of *Azure Resource Manager* (ARM) and *Classic* APIs exist for resource management and deployment in Azure. The ARM and Classic deployment models represent two different ways of managing and deploying Microsoft Azure solutions. Aneka originally supported the Classic deployment model [5] in which each resource (e.g., storage disk, VM, Public IP address, etc.) existed independently and there was no way to group them together. In 2014, Azure offered ARM to simplify the deployment and management of resources by introducing the resource group concept as a container for resources that share a common lifecycle. In order to enable Aneka to use the new Azure APIs for resource provisioning, we extended Aneka by adding an ARM-based resource pool connections.

ARM provides Azure customers with a set of *representational state transfer* (REST) APIs to access Azure IaaS services. These RESTful APIs provide service endpoints that support sets of HTTP operations to access, create, retrieve, update, and delete the Azure cloud resources. This way, resources in Azure can be accessed programmatically. Additionally, ARM supports JSON (JavaScript Object Notation)-based declarative templates to deploy multiple services along with their dependencies. Templates can be used repeatedly to provision resources and deploy applications. In the simplest structure a template contains the following elements:

```json
JSON
{
        "$schema": "",
        "contentVersion": "",
        "parameters": { },
        "variables": { },
        "resources": [ ],
        "outputs": { }
}
```

$schema describes the version of the template language. Any value can be provided for contentVersion and it is used to make sure that the right template is being used for deployments. To customize resource deployment parameters values are set. variables are used to simplify the template language expressions. resources represents resource types that are deployed or updated in a resource group, e.g., VM, VNet or NIC. outputs are returned after deployments.

We added AzureRMResourcePool class in Aneka as the entry point to access Microsoft Azure resources based on ARM interfaces. This class implements the IResourcePool interface of Aneka and in this way, it is transparently included in the design. AzureRMResourcePool implements Provision() and Release() methods of the IResourcePool interface using our Azure template stored in azuretemplate.json. The template is responsible for the creation of a Virtual Machine (VM) and its dependencies such as network interfaces and OS disk based on a given URI of the VM image. The VM image is a VHD (Virtual Hard Disk) file containing a Windows Server 2012 operating system on which Aneka Worker container is configured and installed. In the AzureRMResourcePool class, we pass to Azure APIs the aforementioned template together with a JSON object containing parameters for VM required configurations (e.g., Admin username and password, type of VM, etc.) and references to other already created resources on which creation of a VM is dependent (e.g., virtual network, network security group for the VM, storage account). These parameters are provided to AzureRMResourcePoolConfiguration class and are set by the administrators when they are customizing the Aneka cloud platform. Figure 7 shows a list of these parameters in a screenshot of Resource Pool Manager Editor window in Aneka Management Studio. Whenever, AzureRMResourcePool receives a resource provisioning request, it creates a Resource Group containing the VM and all its dependencies and returns a reference for this deployment to the Aneka Resource pool Manger. Release requests are simply satisfied with deleting the resource group.

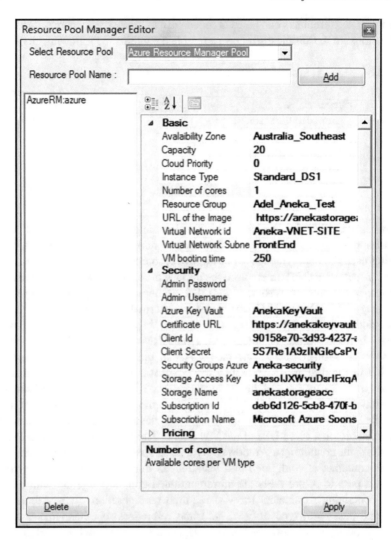

Fig. 7 Azure Resource Manager (ARM) resource pool configuration in Aneka

6 Configuration of Azure Point-to-Site VPN Connection for Aneka Hybrid Cloud

Our aim is to utilize Aneka to expand the computational capacity of a small desktop cloud built on top several desktop machines by adding extra resources from Azure. Since we do not have privileged access to networking devices in our organization, we choose to employ Azure Point-to-Site connection to create our hybrid overlay

VPN. The first step for the establishment of a hybrid cloud network spanning over our on-premises network and the Azure cloud is to create a *VNet* and a *VPN gateway* in Azure.

We created a VNet called `Aneka-VNET-SITE` for our target Azure region which is `Australia Southeast`. The Aneka-VNET-SITE VNet has two subnet address ranges of 192.168.1.0/24 called `FrontEnd` and 192.168.200.0/26 as `GatewaySubnet`. In order to add a VPN gateway to this VPN, a public IP address was created. This IP is used by desktop machines to join the virtual private network. The IP address created this way was configured and connected to the VPN gateway.

We required certificates as VPN clients need to authenticate with Point-to-Site VPNs. For this purpose, a root certificate generated by an enterprise certificate authority (CA), or a self-signed root certificate can be used. We opted to generate a self-signed root certificate. We exported the public certificate data without a private key as a Base-64 encoded X.509. This Root certificate is imported to the Point-to-Site configuration of the Azure Gateway we created earlier. We also used our self-signed root certificate to generate client certificates for our VPN clients. Even though, the same certificate can be used for multiple clients; we exported a unique certificate including the private key for each client. The advantage is that, later on, we can revoke the certificate for each client individually. The last step is to download and install the VPN client configuration package for all clients. For each and every client connecting to the virtual network, we installed both the client certificate and a VPN client configuration package which can be directly downloaded from Azure. At this point, all clients desktop machines were able to connect to our VPN. Figure 8 shows the Azure Point-to-Site virtual network and IP address ranges created for our platform.

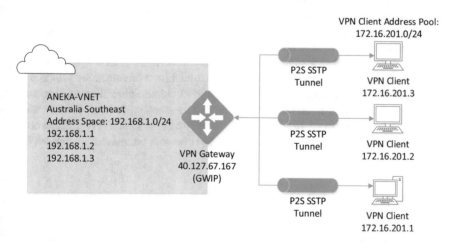

Fig. 8 Azure Point-to-Site VPN for Aneka

7   Case Study: A Hybrid Cloud Using Aneka

In this section, we describe a case study hybrid cloud built on top of Aneka platform and uses Azure virtual networking for connecting computational resources scattered over two separate networks. First, we make a brief review of some related works utilizing hybrid cloud environments for executing applications. Second, we describe the hybrid cloud setup and the established VPN network. Then, we present the parameter sweep application used to be executed on the hybrid cloud environment. Finally, some experimental results are provided to demonstrate the functionality of the design and implementation.

7.1   Related Works

The idea of using public cloud resources to expand the capacity of local infrastructure has been explored by many studies. Mateescu et al. [14] propose an architecture that provides a platform for the execution of High-Performance Computing (HPC) scientific applications. The cornerstone of the proposed architecture is called *Elastic Cluster* which makes an expandable hybrid cloud environment. Assunção et al. [9] analyze the trade-off between performance and usage cost of different provisioning algorithms for use of resources from the cloud to expand a cluster capacity. Javadi et al. [12] propose failure-aware resource provisioning policies for hybrid cloud environments. Xu and Zhao [18] propose a privacy-aware hybrid cloud framework which supports a tagging mechanism for the location of sensitive data. Belgacem and Chopard [2] conduct an experimental study of running a large, tightly coupled, distributed application over a hybrid cloud consisting of resources from Amazon EC2 clusters and an existing HPC infrastructure. Mattess et al. [15] presents a provisioning algorithm for extending cluster capacity with Amazon EC2 *Spot Instances*. Yuan et al. [19] propose a profit maximization model for a private cloud provider by utilizing the temporal variation of prices in hybrid cloud. Scheduling and resource provisioning in hybrid cloud has been researched for many other types of application as well, for example, big data analytics [8], workflows applications [16], online commerce [13], mobile phone applications [11] and compute intensive applications [3].

7.2   Hybrid Cloud Setup

In the hybrid cloud environment, we experiment with two desktop machines (one master and one worker) locating in our CLOUDS laboratory at the University of Melbourne and a number of virtual machines provisioned from Microsoft Azure.

Table 1 Configuration of machines used in the experiments

Machine	Type	CPU	Cores	Memory	OS
Master	Intel Core i7-4790	3.60 CHz	8	16 GB	Windows 7
Worker	Intel Core 2 Duo	3.00 CHz	2	4 GB	Windows 7
Azure instances	Standard DS1	2.4 GHz	1	3.5	Windows Server 2012

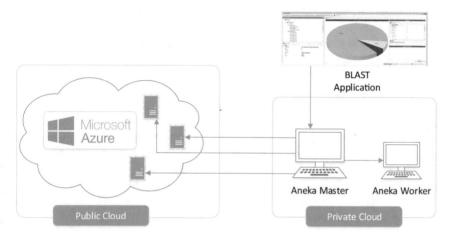

Fig. 9 Hybrid cloud testbed

Table 1 shows the configurations of machines used to setup the hybrid cloud. A schematic view of the hybrid cloud platform used for running the application is also depicted in Fig. 9.

7.3 BLAST Application

To demonstrate the functionality of the virtual network established for supporting connectivity among Aneka hybrid cloud resources, we run a parameter sweep application using Aneka programming APIs. The application, we execute is called BLAST (Basic Local Alignment Search Tool) and is a tool for looking similarities among a given sequence of genes and those stored into classified databases. The BLAST application can be downloaded from the National Centre for Biotechnology Information (NBCI) website.[4] The website also provides a classified repository of all the databases that can be used for similarity searches. We used the database called "ecoli.nt" for our demonstration purpose.

There are many ways of parallelizing a BLAST query against a database. Here, we use the Parameter Sweep Model in order to automatically perform several BLAST queries against the same database. A parameter sweep application is a distributed application that can be defined by a template task characterized by a set of configurable parameters. The template task identifies the set of operations that define the computation. The configurable parameters represent the way in which the template task is specialized.

Aneka provides an integrated tool, called *Design Explorer*, for quickly composing Parameter Sweep applications, controlling and monitoring their execution on Aneka Clouds. Parameter sweep applications in Aneka are expressed by the Parameter Sweep Model (PSM). The Aneka PSM provides the logic for creating the sequence of task instances from a template task and a given set of parameters. The Design Explorer provides a way to serialize its PSM data into an XML.

In our case study, we compose two BLAST-based parameter sweep applications using the Design Explorer tool to run 160 and 320 different queries each has a size of 1 kb over the ecoli.nt database of size 4652 kb. Each query is a sequence of characters representing the target genes and it maps to an Aneka independent task. Figure 10 displays a sample screenshot of the Aneka Design Explorer including a BLAST project with 320 tasks and the below XML shows its related PSM.

```xml
<?xml version="1.0" encoding="Windows-1252"?>
<psm xmlns:xsi="http://www.w3.org/2001/XMLSchema-instance"
xmlns:xsd="http://www.w3.org/2001/XMLSchema">
  <name>Aneka Blast</name>
    <description>BLAST simulation</description>
    <workspace>C:\Projects\Explorer\blast</workspace>
    <parameters>
      <single name="programName" type="String"
       comment="The name of the program" value="blastn" />
      <single name="database" type="String"
       comment="The database file" value="ecoli.nt" />
      <range name="sequenceNumber" type="String"
       comment="The sequence of the input/output"
       from="0" to="319" interval="1" />
    </parameters>
    <sharedFiles>
      <file path="blastall.exe" vpath="blastall.exe" />
      <file path="ecoli.nt.nhr" vpath="ecoli.nt.nhr" />
      <file path="ecoli.nt.nin" vpath="ecoli.nt.nin" />
```

---

[4]https://blast.ncbi.nlm.nih.gov/Blast.cgi.

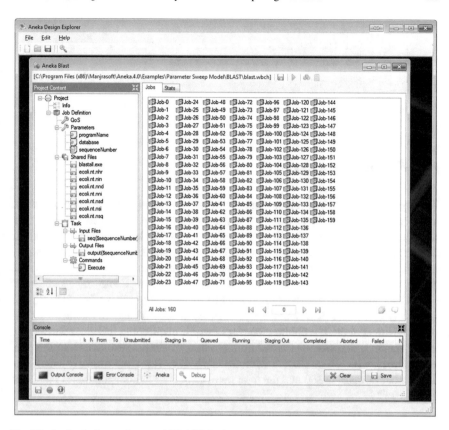

Fig. 10   Aneka design explorer and BLAST Project

```
        <file path="ecoli.nt.nnd" vpath="ecoli.nt.nnd" />
        <file path="ecoli.nt.nni" vpath="ecoli.nt.nni" />
        <file path="ecoli.nt.nsd" vpath="ecoli.nt.nsd" />
        <file path="ecoli.nt.nsi" vpath="ecoli.nt.nsi" />
        <file path="ecoli.nt.nsq" vpath="ecoli.nt.nsq" />
</sharedFiles>
<task>
    <inputs>
        <file path="seq($sequenceNumber).txt"
        vpath="seq($sequenceNumber).txt" />
    </inputs>
    <outputs>
        <file path="output($sequenceNumber).txt"
        vpath="output($sequenceNumber).txt" />
    </outputs>
        <commands>
```

```
    <execute cmd="blastall.exe" args="-p ($programName)
    -d ($database) -i seq($sequenceNumber).txt
    -o output($sequenceNumber).txt" />
  </commands>
 </task>
</psm>
```

7.4 Experimental Results

We expanded our hybrid cloud case study by increasing the number of virtual machines provisioned in Azure. In this scenario, the size of private cloud is constant during the experiments where it remains at two desktop machines and public cloud resources are provisioned as required. Table 2 and Fig. 11 show how the total execution time is reduced when more public cloud resources were added to the Aneka hybrid cloud. When there are no public cloud resources available, the execution of BLAST for 160 and 320 tasks only using private cloud resources takes 215 and 461 s, respectively. These values, respectively, are reduced to 55 and 103 s when 11 VMs are provisioned from the public cloud. It is worth mentioning that the relative gain in performance decreases with adding more computational resources into the pool of resources, which is consistent with *Amdahl's law*. This can be clearly seen when the number of tasks is 160 and the total number of computational cores is increased from 11 to 13.

Table 2 Configuration of machines used in the experiments

Tasks (#)	VMs (#)	Private cloud CPU cores (#)	Total CPU cores (#)	Execution time (mm:ss)
160	0	2	2	03:35
160	1	2	3	02:33
160	3	2	5	02:05
160	5	2	7	01:17
160	7	2	9	01:02
160	9	2	11	00:56
160	11	2	13	00:55
320	0	2	2	07:41
320	1	2	3	05:00
320	3	2	5	03:15
320	5	2	7	02:33
320	7	2	9	02:06
320	9	2	11	01:54
320	11	2	13	01:43

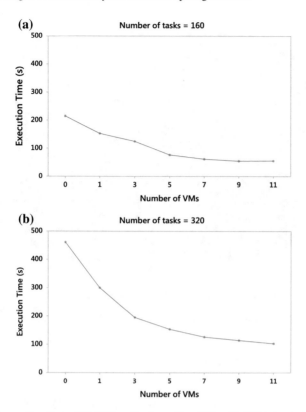

Fig. 11 Total execution time of BLAST application with **a** 160 and **b** 320 tasks on different hybrid cloud size

Figure 12 shows the distribution of tasks among Aneka nodes scattered on private on-premises infrastructure and public cloud resources. Please note that the Aneka master node is also located in the private infrastructure and communicate with all worker nodes (See Fig. 9). Our experiments demonstrate that the established azure VPN provides an appropriate platform for running application over Aneka nodes scattered in multiple separate networks (in different administrative domains) possibly located behind a NAT or firewalls boundary. Moreover, since the VPN encrypts the traffic between its connected nodes, all communications are protected against unauthorized disclosure and confidentiality and privacy of information are enforced.

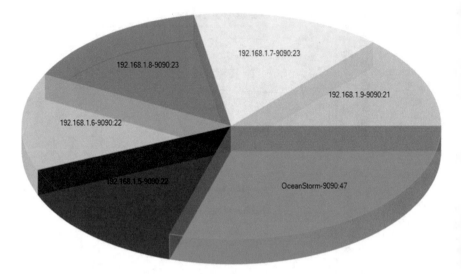

Fig. 12 Distribution of task among Aneka nodes when there are 160 tasks and 7 CPU cores available. Labels in the pie chart shows: address of machine—Aneka worker container port: the number of tasks allocated to that machine. OceanStrom's VNet IP address is 172.16.201.5

8   Open Research Problems

The fundamental idea of uncoupling resource provisioning from vendor-specific dependencies is of a great interest for many application platforms such as Aneka. In this direction, Aneka can be extended to use features of multi-cloud toolkits and libraries such as JClouds.[5] However, to setup the VPN network for the Aneka platform, a great deal of manual work is needed as discussed in this chapter. A promising avenue to advance technologies for building such VPNs is to allow for the network programmability and the network function virtualization. This leads us to more research on software-defined networking (SDN)-assisted techniques in the development of efficient cloud technologies.

In line with our contribution, development of resource provisioning techniques that can acquire resources from multiple clouds can also be explored. In addition, dynamic resource provisioning policies are required for judiciously adding resources to the Aneka cloud based on application requirements such as deadline or budget. Future directions also include new algorithms for innovative provisioning honoring user requirements such as privacy and the location of sensitive data. This can be further extended to support resource allocation techniques in the context of various other programming models such as MapReduce model.

---

[5]JClouds, Available: https://jclouds.apache.org/.

9 Summary and Conclusions

In this chapter, we outlined our experiences of building a virtual private network (VPN) for a hybrid cloud environment in our Aneka platform using Azure VPN services. We described the benefits of a hybrid cloud solution and its connectivity issue for resources residing behind a NAT or firewalls. We discussed how virtual private networks (VPNs) resolve this issue. We presented our Aneka Platform-as-a-Service (PaaS) for building a hybrid cloud environment. We explored through Azure VPN solutions and we presented how Azure point-to-site VPN connection can be used for building an Aneka hybrid cloud. To demonstrate the effectiveness of the VPN for hybrid cloud solutions, we provided details of a case study hybrid cloud for running a parameter sweep application from the biology domain. Our conclusion is that the establishment of VPN overlays over hybrid environments provides a feasible solution for connectivity issue which is more accessible as many more cloud providers offer VPN services. We also identified a number of open issues that form the basis for future research directions.

Acknowledgements We thank Australian Research Council (ARC) Future Fellowship and the Australia-India Strategic Research Fund (AISRF) for their support of our research. We also thank Microsoft for providing access to the Azure IaaS infrastructure.

References

1. Assuno, M. D., Calheiros, R. N., Bianchi, S., Netto, M. A. S., & Buyya, R. (2015). Big data computing and clouds: Trends and future directions. *Journal of Parallel and Distributed Computing, 7980*, 3–15. Special Issue on Scalable Systems for Big Data Management and Analytics.
2. Belgacem, M. B., & Chopard, B. (2015). A hybrid HPC/cloud distributed infrastructure: Coupling EC2 cloud resources with HPC clusters to run large tightly coupled multiscale applications. *Future Generation Computer Systems, 42*, 11–21.
3. Brock, M., & Goscinski, A. (2012, July). Execution of compute intensive applications on hybrid clouds (case study with mpiBLAST). In *Proceedings of the Sixth International Conference on Complex, Intelligent, and Software Intensive Systems* (pp. 995–1000).
4. Brunetti, R. (2011). *Windows Azure Step by Step*. Microsoft Press.
5. Buyya, R., & Barreto, D. (2015, December). Multi-cloud resource provisioning with Aneka: A unified and integrated utilisation of microsoft azure and amazon EC2 instances. In *2015 International Conference on Computing and Network Communications (CoCoNet)* (pp. 216–229).
6. Buyya, R., & Dastjerdi, A. V. (eds.) (2016, May). *Internet of Things: Principles and Paradigms*. Burlington, Massachusetts, USA: Morgan Kaufmann.
7. Calheiros, R. N., Vecchiola, C., Karunamoorthy, D., & Buyya, R. (2012). The Aneka platform and QoS-driven resource provisioning for elastic applications on hybrid clouds. *Future Generation Computer Systems, 28*(6), 861–870.
8. Clemente-Castell, F. J., Nicolae, B., Katrinis, K., Rafique, M. M., Mayo, R., & Fernndez, J. C. (2015, December). Enabling big data analytics in the hybrid cloud using iterative mapreduce. In *Proceedings of the 8th IEEE/ACM International Conference on Utility and Cloud Computing (UCC)* (pp. 290–299).

9. de Assunção, M. D., di Costanzo, A., & Buyya, R. (2010). A cost-benefit analysis of using cloud computing to extend the capacity of clusters. *Cluster Computing, 13*(3), 335–347.
10. Dean, J., & Ghemawat, S. (2008). Mapreduce: Simplified data processing on large clusters. *Communication of the ACM, 51*(1), 107–113.
11. Flores, H., Narayana Srirama, S., & Paniagua, C. (2011). A generic middleware framework for handling process intensive hybrid cloud services from mobiles. In *Proceedings of the 9th International Conference on Advances in Mobile Computing and Multimedia, MoMM '11*, New York, NY, USA (pp. 87–94). ACM.
12. Javadi, B., Abawajy, J., & Buyya, R. (2012). Failure-aware resource provisioning for hybrid cloud infrastructure. *Journal of Parallel and Distributed Computing, 72*(10), 1318–1331.
13. Lackermair, G. (2011). Hybrid cloud architectures for the online commerce. *Procedia Computer Science, World Conference on Information Technology, 3*, 550–555.
14. Mateescu, G., Gentzsch, W., & Ribbens, C. J. (2011). Hybrid computing where HPC meets grid and cloud computing. *Future Generation Computer Systems, 27*(5), 440–453.
15. Mattess, M., Vecchiola, C., & Buyya, R. (2010, September). Managing peak loads by leasing cloud infrastructure services from a spot market. In *Proceedings of the 12th IEEE International Conference on High Performance Computing and Communications (HPCC)* (pp. 180–188).
16. Vasile, M.-A., Pop, F., Tutueanu, R.-I., Cristea, V., & Koodziej, J. (2015). Resource-aware hybrid scheduling algorithm in heterogeneous distributed computing. *Future Generation Computer Systems, 51*, 61–71.
17. Vecchiola, C., Calheiros, R. N., Karunamoorthy, D., & Buyya, R. (2012). Deadline-driven provisioning of resources for scientific applications in hybrid clouds with Aneka. *Future Generation Computer Systems, 28*(1), 58–65.
18. Xu, X., & Zhao, X. (2015, August). A framework for privacy-aware computing on hybrid clouds with mixed-sensitivity data. In *Proceedings of the IEEE International Symposium on Big Data Security on Cloud* (pp. 1344–1349).
19. Yuan, H., Bi, J., Tan, W., & Li, B. H. (2017). Temporal task scheduling with constrained service delay for profit maximization in hybrid clouds. *IEEE Transactions on Automation Science and Engineering, 14*(1), 337–348.

Building Efficient HPC Cloud with SR-IOV-Enabled InfiniBand: The MVAPICH2 Approach

Xiaoyi Lu, Jie Zhang and Dhabaleswar K. Panda

Abstract Single Root I/O Virtualization (SR-IOV) technology has been steadily gaining momentum for high-speed interconnects such as InfiniBand. SR-IOV enabled InfiniBand has been widely used in modern HPC clouds with virtual machines and containers. While SR-IOV can deliver near-native I/O performance, recent studies have shown that locality-aware communication schemes play an important role in achieving high I/O performance on SR-IOV enabled InfiniBand clusters. To discuss how to build efficient HPC clouds, this chapter presents a novel approach using the MVAPICH2 library. We first propose locality-aware designs inside the MVAPICH2 library to achieve near-native performance on HPC clouds with virtual machines and containers. Then, we propose advanced designs with cloud resource managers such as OpenStack and Slurm to make users easier to deploy and run their applications with the MVAPICH2 library on HPC clouds. Performance evaluations with benchmarks and applications on an OpenStack-based HPC cloud (i.e., NSF-supported Chameleon Cloud) show that MPI applications with our designs are able to get near bare-metal performance on HPC clouds with different virtual machine and container deployment scenarios. Compared to running default MPI applications on Amazon EC2, our design can deliver much better performance. The MVAPICH2 over HPC Cloud software package presented in this chapter is publicly available from http://mvapich.cse.ohio-state.edu.

X. Lu (✉) · J. Zhang · D.K. Panda
Department of Computer Science and Engineering, The Ohio State
University Columbus, Columbus, OH, USA
e-mail: luxi@cse.ohio-state.edu; lu.932@osu.edu

J. Zhang
e-mail: zhanjie@cse.ohio-state.edu

D.K. Panda
e-mail: panda@cse.ohio-state.edu

© Springer Nature Singapore Pte Ltd. 2017
S. Chaudhary et al. (eds.), *Research Advances in Cloud Computing*,
DOI 10.1007/978-981-10-5026-8_6

1 Introduction

The last few years have witnessed a rapid increase in the number of processor cores in modern cluster systems and an equally impressive increase in network bandwidth. This growth has been fueled by the current trends in multi-/many-core architectures, and high-performance interconnects such as InfiniBand, Omni-Path, RDMA over Converged-Enhanced Ethernet (RoCE) and 10/40/100-Gigabit Ethernet with Internet Wide Area RDMA Protocol (iWARP). These multi-/many-core architectures and high-performance interconnects are currently gaining momentum for designing clusters (high-end compute clusters, data centers, and cloud computing platforms). Based on the November 2016 TOP500 ranking, 37% clusters in the top 500 supercomputers are using InfiniBand technology and 46% of the Petascale systems on the TOP500 list are connected with InfiniBand.

The deployment of such high-end computing systems is delivering unprecedented performance to HPC and emerging Big Data applications. However, the cost of such high-end clusters with balanced memory and network bandwidth has remained prohibitive for a large number of institutions and users. One method to alleviate the cost bottleneck is to utilize cloud computing model with offering *Infrastructure as a Service* (IaaS). IaaS reduces personnel costs by high degrees of automation and a better overall utilization when compared to dedicated clusters. IaaS provides high-performance resource sharing strategies capable of sharing critical cluster resources efficiently among multiple jobs using the system. *Virtualization* is the classical method for IaaS-based clouds to share such critical resources and it typically refers to the act of creating a virtual (instead of physical) version of computer hardware platforms, storage devices, and computer network resources, and so on [1]. IaaS-based cloud computing platforms with virtualization offer attractive capabilities to consolidate complex IT resources in a scalable manner by providing well-configured virtual machines (VM) or containers. The desirable features of cloud computing solutions include ease of system configuration and management, fast software deployment, performance isolation, security, live migration, etc., and these features meet cloud users' various resource utilization requirements [2].

During the last decade, cloud computing with virtualization technology has been widely used in HPC and distributed computing communities. One of the most successful cloud computing platforms is Amazon's Elastic Compute Cloud (EC2), which utilizes the virtualization technology to consolidate computing, storage, and networking resources for multitenant applications. Although virtualization technology has the potential to dramatically reduce the cost of compute cycles on HPC and Big Data systems, several fundamental challenges need to be addressed for designing virtualized clusters that can deliver the performance of dedicated high-end computing clusters. A big hurdle of using virtualization technology is the unsatisfactory virtualized I/O performance delivered by underlying virtualized environments [3]. For example, native high-performance MPI libraries such as MVAPICH2 [4] and OpenMPI [5] can provide sub-microsecond latencies for point-to-point communication operations. In contrast, recent studies [6] have shown that MPI libraries on virtualization-based environments have not been well designed and such situation incurs significant performance overhead, which limits the adoption of virtualization-based cloud computing platforms for HPC applications.

The main reason of the poor I/O performance with virtualization designs is that they do not provide an efficient mechanism to share the PCI bus which connects the CPU to the network card due to lack of hardware support. Consequently, current generation solutions can only provide *best-effort QoS*, which can have a negative impact on performance. Recently, a new networking virtualization capability, Single Root I/O Virtualization (SR-IOV) [7] is introduced for high-performance interconnects such as InfiniBand and high-speed Ethernet. It specifies native I/O Virtualization (IOV) capabilities and enables us to provision the internal PCI bus interfaces between multiple virtual machines. SR-IOV opens up new opportunities for designers of HPC and Big Data middleware to fundamentally redesign their software to provide true *end-to-end QoS*. The SR-IOV technology also has the potential to enable near-native performance for I/O devices on VMs, by virtue of bypassing the hypervisor and host operating system. With these new capabilities, SR-IOV can significantly reduce the performance gap between MPI point-to-point internode communication on virtual machines and that on physical machines [3]. Due to its high-performance nature, SR-IOV has been emerging as an attractive feature for virtualizing I/O devices on clouds, and it has been widely used in many cloud computing platforms, such as Amazon EC2.

HPC applications can benefit from SR-IOV by improving the inter-node communication performance on virtualized cloud systems. However, purely using SR-IOV in applications will make inter-VM or inter-container communications within the same node (intranode) use the network loopback channel, leading to performance overheads. By contrast, high-performance native MPI and PGAS libraries typically use shared memory-based or kernel-assisted (e.g., Cross Memory Attach (CMA) [8]) techniques to improve intranode communication performance. This motivates us to investigate whether similar communication schemes can be adopted for intranode inter-VM or inter-container communication on SR-IOV-based virtualized environments. On this front, a novel feature, inter-VM shared memory (IVShmem) [9], was proposed to support processes across multiple VMs within the same node to utilize efficient shared memory backed channel to communicate. Using IVShmem can significantly improve the performance of intranode inter-VM communication compared to using SR-IOV-based virtualized network loopback channel [6, 10]. Similarly, for container-based (e.g., Docker) cloud environments, designing high-performance container-aware MPI communication library to take advantage of IPC-based shared memory channel and CMA channel is also crucial to bring more performance benefits to end users [11].

On the other hand, easy and scalable resource allocation and management offered by clouds attract more and more users to migrate their applications to the public clouds or private clouds hosted by their organizations. OpenStack is one of the most popular open-source frameworks to build a cloud and manage vast amounts of resources. Slurm [12] is another very popular resource manager and scheduler in HPC clusters. It has been extended recently to support managing virtual machines [13, 14] and containers [15]. But the open-source versions of OpenStack and Slurm do not have full support for the above features (i.e., SR-IOV and IVShmem) so far. To ensure achieving high performance for applications in HPC clouds, it is necessary to enable SR-IOV and IVShmem when building HPC clouds. Additionally, MPI libraries should be redesigned to adapt to VM or container-based environments so that they can fully take advantage of the novel features provided in the HPC clouds.

To investigate these topics, this chapter first provides an overview of popular virtualization system software on HPC cloud environments, such as hypervisors, containers, OpenStack, Slurm, etc. After that, it provides an overview of high-performance interconnects and communication mechanisms on HPC clouds, such as InfiniBand, RDMA, SR-IOV, IVShmem, etc. We further discuss the opportunities and technical challenges of designing high-performance MPI runtime over these environments. Then, we introduce our proposed novel approaches to enhance MPI library design over SR-IOV enabled InfiniBand clusters with both virtual machines and containers. We also discuss how to further integrate these designs into popular cloud management systems like OpenStack [16] and HPC cluster resource managers like Slurm [13].

Our designs are based on MVAPICH2 [4], which can fully take advantage of the high-performance SR-IOV-based network channel for internode communication as well as IVShmem/IPC-Shm/CMA-based channels for intranode communication. Comprehensive performance evaluations with benchmarks and applications have been conducted on an OpenStack-based HPC cloud (i.e., NSF-supported Chameleon Cloud [17]). We show that our design can deliver near native performance on SR-IOV-based HPC clouds with VMs and containers. Through the performance comparison with Amazon EC2, our design can achieve up to 160X performance improvement on point-to-point communication operations and 65X improvement on collective operations.

2 Overview of Virtualization System Software

2.1 Hypervisor-Based Virtualization

As shown in Fig. 1a, a hypervisor (i.e., virtual machine manager) is a program that allows multiple guests operating systems (OS) in VMs to share a single hardware host. The host's processor, memory, and other resources appear to be occupied by each guest OS itself. The hypervisor interacts with underlying host OS or hardware to manage the host resources and allocates the needed resources to each guest OS. The hypervisor can guarantee that the VMs cannot disrupt each other. We can see that the hypervisor is a powerful tool to consolidate available physical computing resources on multiple servers. These resources can be shared efficiently by applications through hypervisor-based virtualization. However, such type of virtualization incurs additional workload-dependent overhead, since it faithfully replicates true hardware behaviors. The well-known hypervisor-based virtualization solutions

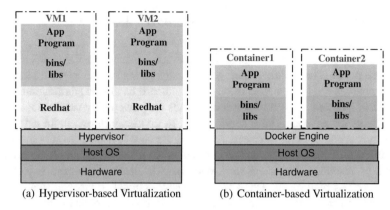

(a) Hypervisor-based Virtualization   (b) Container-based Virtualization

Fig. 1 Hypervisor-based and container-based virtualization

include VMware vSphere ESXi, Citrix XenServer, open-source KVM (Kernel-based Virtual Machine), etc. KVM is a full virtualization solution on Linux, which allows a user space program to utilize the hardware virtualization features (e.g., Intel VT or AMD-V) of various processors. This chapter uses KVM hypervisor to run VMs.

2.2 Container-Based Virtualization

For container-based virtualization, as shown in Fig. 1b, the host allows several iso-lated userspace instances to share the same kernel but possibly run different software stacks (system libraries, services, and applications). Container-based virtualization does not need an extra layer of virtual hardware, while it provides a self-contained execution environment to effectively isolate applications that rely on the same ker-nel in the host OS. Two core mature Linux technologies are widely used to build containers. First, cgroups (control groups) is used to group processes and limit their resources usage. Second, namespace isolation is used to isolate a group of processes at various levels (i.e., networking, filesystem, users, process identifiers, etc.). The popular container-based solutions include LXC, Docker [18], Singularity [19], and Shifter [15]. Docker is one of the most popular open-source container-based virtual-ization solutions to build and execute containers. The Docker platform offers several important features, including portable deployment across machines, reuse of con-tainer image, versioning, and a searchable public registry for images. We use Docker to run containers, as indicated in this chapter.

2.3 OpenStack and Other Cloud Resource Managers

OpenStack is one of the most popular cloud resource management systems that control large pools of computing, storage, and networking resources on a cloud. All these resources can be managed through a dashboard that gives administrative control and web access to users. OpenStack clouds are powered by various OpenStack components or services. These services can be divided into two main categories: core services and optional services. Among these core services, Nova is one of the most important components, which is designed to manage and automate pools of computing resources. Nova can work with many available virtualization technologies, as well as bare metal. There are also many optional services available in the OpenStack project. For example, Horizon is the dashboard service to provide a web-based self-service portal to interact with underlying OpenStack services. Ceilometer is the telemetry service to monitor and meter the OpenStack cloud for billing, benchmarking, and statistical purposes. Similar to OpenStack, Nimbus [20] provides a toolkit for building the IaaS cloud. Nimbus allows deployment of self-configured virtual clusters via hypervisors, VM schedulers, and contextualization. There are other similar systems such as Eucalyptus [21], OpenNebula [22] available in the field. Lu et al. [23, 24] presented Vega LingCloud, which is based on their proposed asset-leasing model to provide a Resource Single Leasing Point System for consolidated leasing physical and virtual machines on shared cloud infrastructure. Crago et al. [25] extended OpenStack to support heterogeneous architectures and accelerators, like GPU. In this chapter, we introduce how to run virtualization aware MPI runtime and applications on OpenStack efficiently.

2.4 Slurm and SPANK

Simple Linux Utility for Resource Management (Slurm) [12] is an open-source resource manager for large scale Linux-based clusters. Slurm provides users with exclusive and/or non-exclusive access to resources. Slurm provides a framework including controller daemons (slurmctld), database daemon (slurmdbd), compute node daemons (slurmd), and a set of user commands (e.g., srun, sbatch, squeue) to start, execute, and monitor jobs on a set of allocated nodes and manages a queue of pending jobs to arbitrate contention. Slurm was originally written only for the Linux operating system, but now supports many other operating systems and many unique computer architectures. It delivers scalability, portability, fault tolerance, and high performance for heterogeneous clusters with up to tens of millions of processors. Slurm has a very modular design with several optional plugins.

Slurm Plug-in Architecture for Node and job (K)control (SPANK) [26] provides a generic interface to be used for dynamically modifying the job launch code. SPANK plugins have the ability to add user options when using srun. SPANK plugins can be loaded in multiple contexts and points during a Slurm job launch. Thus, SPANK provides a low-cost and low-effort mechanism to change runtime behavior of Slurm. In this chapter, we introduce our extensions for Slurm to manage virtual machines efficiently through SPANK.

3 Overview of High-Performance Interconnects and Communication Mechanisms

3.1 InfiniBand

InfiniBand is an industry-level networking communication standard. It leverages the switched fabric topology to provide high bandwidth (up to 200 Gbps for the latest HDR HCA) and low latency($<1\,\mu$s). InfiniBand has been utilized by more than 37% of the supercomputers in TOP500 ranking (November 2016), as well as many cloud computing environments and data centers. InfiniBand provides advanced features, such as Remote Direct Memory Access (RDMA), that enable the design of novel communication protocols and libraries. The RDMA feature allows applications to access the memory of remote processes through "zero-copy" communication semantics and without the involvement at remote side. This is a powerful feature and it can be used to design high-performance communication protocols. The majority of HPC applications and middleware (such as MPI [4]) take advantage of InfiniBand and its associated advanced features either via native IB verbs, RoCE [27], or iWARP [28].

3.2 Overview of High-Performance Communication Mechanisms

PCI Passthrough: This mechanism allows giving access and control of the physical devices to guest VMs. This means users can use the PCI passthrough mechanism to assign a PCI device (e.g., NIC, disk controller, etc.) to a guest domain and give the guest full and direct access to the PCI device. This has two important benefits. The first is using device passthrough can achieve near-native performance, which is perfect for I/O intensive applications. The second is the exclusive use of a device that is not inherently shareable.

Single Root I/O Virtualization (SR-IOV): To leverage InfiniBand in virtualization environment efficiently, PCI Express (PCIe) sharing technology is required. Single Root I/O Virtualization (SR-IOV) [7] is a PCI Express (PCIe) standard which specifies the native I/O virtualization capabilities in PCIe adapters. SR-IOV provides an interface that allows a physical PCIe device, or a Physical Function (PF), offering independent Virtual Functions (VF) to different VMs. As shown in Fig. 2a, a PF can present itself as multiple virtual devices, or Virtual Functions (VFs) through SR-IOV.

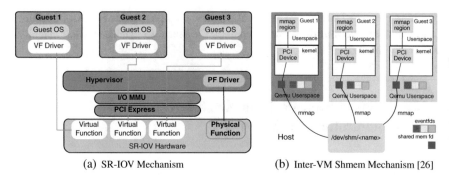

(a) SR-IOV Mechanism   (b) Inter-VM Shmem Mechanism [26]

Fig. 2 Overview of SR-IOV and Inter-VM Shmem communication mechanisms

Each VF can be dedicated to a single VM through the PCI passthrough, which allows each VM to directly access the corresponding VF. Each dedicated VF has isolated context, and all VFs can work concurrently. Hence, SR-IOV is a hardware-based approach to implementing I/O virtualization. Furthermore, VFs are designed based on the existing non-virtualized Physical Functions (PFs); hence, the drivers of the current adapters can also be used to drive the VFs in a portable manner. The virtual InfiniBand device provided by SR-IOV can be accessed through the PCI passthrough mechanism, which allows the networking flows bypassing the software switch layer, to achieve the performance close to physical devices.

Runtime Privilege in Docker: In container context, the runtime privilege mechanism gives Docker containers the access to all devices. For instance, by executing `docker run - -privileged`, Docker will enable access to all devices on the host as well as set some necessary configuration in SELinux to allow processes running inside containers to have nearly the same access to the host as processes running outside containers on the host. This chapter uses this option to give container access to InfiniBand on the host.

Inter-VM Shared Memory (IVShmem): As one implementation of the IVShmem mechanism, Nahanni [9] provides memory backed data access for co-resident VMs through shared memory. IVShmem can be used for guest-to-guest and host-to-guest communications on KVM platform. IVShmem is designed mainly in system calls layer, and its interfaces are also visible to user space processes. As shown in Fig. 2b, IVShmem contains three components: the guest kernel driver, that implements userspace I/O device driver model, the modified QEMU supporting PCI device, and the POSIX shared memory region on the host OS. The shared memory region is allocated by the host POSIX operations and mapped to QEMU process address space. The mapped memory can be used by guest applications by being mapped to guest userspace. Shared Memory Server, a stand-alone host process running outside of QEMU, is used to facilitate inter-VM notification. Evaluation results illustrate that both benchmarks and applications achieve better performance with IVShmem support. However, to fully take advantage of IVShmem support, the existing applications and libraries need to be modified because IVShmem does not support transparent switches between local and remote modes and VM migration is not entirely supported.

IPC-Shared Memory among Docker Containers: Operating systems such as Linux usually provide some tools for sharing memory between processes running on the same host. This mechanism is called Inter-Process Communication (IPC) which performs at the memory speed. It is often used in scientific computing domain such as MPI. By default, Docker creates a unique IPC namespace for each container. The Linux IPC namespace can partition shared memory blocks, semaphores, as well as message queues. The isolated IPC namespace among Docker containers prevents processes in one container from accessing the memory on the host or in other containers. In order to achieve shared memory based high-performance communication across containers, users need to join the containers' IPC namespaces with the '–-ipc' flag. This flag has a container mode that will create a new container in the same IPC namespace as another target container [18].

Cross Memory Attach (CMA): The communication among processes on the same node (i.e., intranode communication) can usually be optimized because they are sharing the same hardware and host operating system. For Linux, CMA [8] is one of the kernel-level mechanism for efficient intranode communication. It allows a destination process to copy data directly from the source process memory into its memory space through a system call. The symmetrical ability to copy from the current process's address space into a destination process's address space is also provided. Efficient intranode communication in applications can be achieved through CMA since it only needs a single copy of the message rather than double copies of the message via traditional shared memory. CMA has been employed by several MPI communication libraries for intranode communication and hierarchical collective communication. Docker provides users the options to share specific namespaces with the host operating system or other containers. This makes it possible to design flexible and efficient interaction mechanisms among containers and host while guaranteeing security. In particular, through enabling sharing namespaces, MPI processes across Docker instances can use CMA for high-performance intranode-inter-container communication [11].

4 Opportunities and Challenges of Building HPC Clouds

As indicated in Sects. 1 and 3, technology advances in multi-/many-core and networking architecture on modern HPC clusters are providing novel features to build high-performance HPC clouds. Especially, SR-IOV has become an attractive hardware-level feature that can enable high-performance communication in virtualized environments. SR-IOV has opened many new opportunities to improve the communication and I/O performance significantly for applications running on HPC clouds. To understand these opportunities in a quantitative manner, we first study

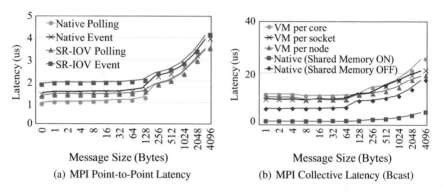

Fig. 3 Performance results of SR-IOV on multicore InfiniBand clusters

the performance characteristics of SR-IOV on InfiniBand clusters. As demonstrated in Fig. 3a, the performance of basic point-to-point inter-VM, inter-node communication operations in both event-based and polling-based modes are similar to that of native InfiniBand, especially for large messages. This stresses the benefits of using SR-IOV to achieve network virtualization when compared to other software-based approaches. However, it is to be noted that there is still a critical performance issue that needs to be carefully addressed to enable the adoption of SR-IOV in HPC clouds. For example, in Fig. 3b, it can be observed that the performance of the collective operation (i.e., MPI_Bcast) with SR-IOV is significantly worse when compared with the case of native InfiniBand with shared memory-based communication enabled. This demonstrates that only using SR-IOV-based communication in applications and runtimes will lead to performance overheads. This is because default MPI library design with SR-IOV will make inter-VM communications within the same node still use network loopback channel. By contrast, high-performance MPI designs which use shared memory or CMA-based techniques can enable fast intranode communication. In this context, another novel feature, IVShmem has been proposed to support shared memory backed intranode-inter-VM communication, which can be used to address this limitation of SR-IOV.

For container-based cloud environments, designing high-performance container-aware MPI communication library to take advantage of the communication mechanisms of IPC-based shared memory and CMA is also crucial to bring more performance benefits to end applications.

To achieve high-performance for MPI applications on HPC clouds, it is necessary to enable virtualized resources as mentioned above (i.e., SR-IOV, IVShmem, IPC-Shared Memory, and CMA) on HPC clouds. For improved flexibility and resource utilization, it is important to manage and isolate these virtualized resources to support running multiple concurrent MPI jobs on different virtual machines and containers. As this requires knowledge of and some level of control over the underlying physical hosts, it is very difficult to achieve this from within the MPI library alone which is only aware of the virtual nodes and resources. In addition, modern multicore architectures allow users to have the flexibility to choose from various VM/container subscription policies, such as one VM/container per node, one VM/container per CPU socket, and one VM/container per CPU core. The choices allow for finer-grained resource management and scheduling, depending on the resource requirements of various applications and workloads. Without adequate support from the resource manager, the user needs to manage various tasks like creating, deploying, initializing, and destroying virtual machines or containers.

Thus, extracting the best performance from virtualized clusters requires support from other middleware like job schedulers and resource managers. Easy and scalable resource management offered by cloud computing systems heavily rely on cloud resource management systems such as OpenStack. Taking into consideration the delivery of high-performance HPC applications in the cloud, it is necessary to enable advanced features such as SR-IOV and IVShmem through OpenStack when building HPC clouds. Besides, Slurm is also a very popular resource manager used by many small and large HPC clusters. However, default Slurm design is not aware of these advanced features, which prevents MPI applications achieving high-performance on HPC clouds.

All these fundamental issues facing the cloud computing community lead to the following broad challenges:

1. How to build efficient HPC Clouds with near-native performance for MPI applications over SR-IOV enabled InfiniBand clusters?
2. How to design a high-performance MPI library to efficiently take advantage of novel features (e.g., SR-IOV, IVShmem, IPC-Shared Memory, and CMA) provided in HPC clouds with virtual machines or containers?
3. How to integrate these advanced designs with HPC cloud resource managers such as OpenStack and Slurm?
4. How much performance improvement can be achieved by our proposed approach on MPI point-to-point operations, collective operations, and applications in HPC clouds?
5. Can HPC clouds built by our proposed approach provide orders of magnitude performance benefits compared with current generation public production clouds, such as Amazon EC2?

Many novel research works and designs have been proposed in the literature recently for addressing these challenges. This chapter will briefly introduce the MVA-PICH2 approach to building efficient HPC clouds in next sections.

5   The MVAPICH2 Approach to Build HPC Clouds

To address the above-mentioned challenges, we propose the MVAPICH2-based approach to build efficient HPC clouds. The MVAPICH2 approach mainly has two steps. We first propose novel designs inside the MVAPICH2 library to achieve near-native performance on the virtual machine-based and container-based environments

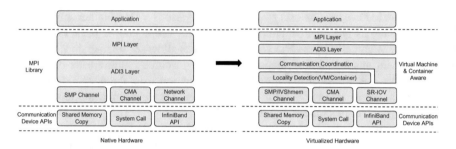

Fig. 4 The MVAPICH2 approach for building HPC clouds

on HPC clouds. Then, we propose more designs with cloud resource managers such as OpenStack and Slurm to make users easier to deploy and run their applications with the MVAPICH2 library on HPC clouds. Through the designs of MVAPICH2 with OpenStack and Slurm, MPI-based applications should be able to get near bare-metal performance on HPC clouds with different VM and container deployment scenarios.

The MVAPICH2 is an open-source MPI library over InfiniBand, Omni-Path, Ethernet/iWARP, and RoCE. MVAPICH2 follows a layered approach, as shown in the left-hand side in Fig. 4. All MPI-level primitives are implemented in the Abstract Device Interface V3 (ADI3) layer. There are multiple communication channels on top of communication device APIs to provide basic message delivery functionalities. Three types of communication channels are available in MVAPICH2: the shared memory (SMP) channel, the CMA channel, and the network channel. The SMP channel enables communication over shared memory to processes running on the same host. The CMA channel can copy the data directly from the source process memory into the destination process address space via a CMA system call. The network channel communicates over InfiniBand user-level APIs to other processes.

As discussed earlier, even though default MPI runtime designed for the native environment can run with SR-IOV enabled virtualized environment, it does not achieve the optimal performance. Alternatively, recent studies [6, 10, 11, 16] have shed light on the significant performance improvements for MPI benchmarks and applications by designing virtual machine and container locality-aware schemes together with SR-IOV-based high-performance interconnects. Such an approach, as shown in the right-hand side in Fig. 4, has been emerging and is seen to be an effective way to design high-performance MPI runtime and applications on modern HPC clouds.

For VM and container-aware MVAPICH2 on HPC clouds, two major components are added, which are 'Communication Coordinator' and 'Locality Detector' between the ADI3 layer and channel layer. In the channel layer, we integrate IVShmem channel into the SMP channel, while maintaining the CMA channel and SR-IOV channel available in VM-based and container-based HPC clouds. The Communication Coordinator is responsible for scheduling communication channel in the lower channel layer, while the Locality Detector maintains the information of co-resident VMs/containers on the same host. The Communication Coordinator makes a decision on going through a channel by utilizing the Locality Detector to identify whether the communicating VMs/containers are co-resident on the same host or not. If they are co-resident on a given host, the Communication Coordinator will select SMP/IVShmem channel or CMA channel for the communication between these co-located VMs/containers depending on the message size. Otherwise, it will go through SR-IOV channel. It is also critical to tune MPI performance for all these channels on top of virtualized architectures. More design details about these components as well as designs with OpenStack and Slurm are provided in the following sections.

6 Designing High-Performance MVAPICH2 on HPC Clouds

6.1 VM-Aware MVAPICH2 on InfiniBand Clusters

As discussed in Sect. 4, a high-performance MPI library on cloud needs to be VM-aware. In the literature, there are several studies have exploited the facility of inter-VM shared memory. For Xen hypervisor, XenSocket [29] is a one-way pipe for high-performance inter-VM communication. It defines a new socket type, and associated system calls to utilize the underlying inter-VM shared memory communication mechanism. Users need to modify their applications and libraries to invoke these calls explicitly. XWay [30] intercepts TCP socket calls to provide transparent and high-performance inter-VM communication for TCP-based applications. XWay only requires modifications to the network protocol stack inside the OS. As a kernel module, XenLoop [31] is designed to intercept every outgoing packet from the network layer. It provides transparency for applications and achieves high communication performance for co-resident VMs by utilizing shared memory channel. IVC [32] is a user-level communication library designed for HPC applications, and it also provides shared memory-based communication for co-resident VMs. MVAPICH2 can take advantage of the proposed IVC mechanism to improve message passing performance on clouds.

Based on the new features provided by both SR-IOV and IVShmem, a redesigned and enhanced MPI library based on KVM hypervisor is proposed [10] to fully exploit the benefits of the features on SR-IOV and IVShmem enabled InfiniBand clusters. Two components are introduced in the enhanced architecture, as shown in Fig. 5, which are VM Locality Detector and VM Communication Coordinator.

VM Locality Detector: To enable VM locality-aware communication, it is required to have an accurate and fast-responsive mechanism to identify co-resident VMs among all VMs. The design in [10] utilizes a locality detector to achieve this goal. Based on IVShmem support, as demonstrated in [9], a VM list structure is created on the IVShmem region of each host, which is visible to all the co-resident VMs.

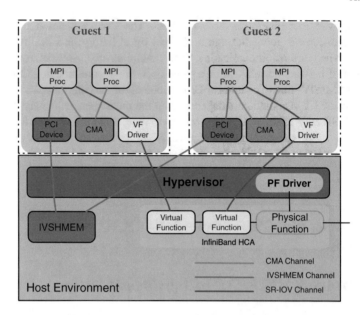

Fig. 5 Architecture of VM-aware MVAPICH2 on SR-IOV enabled InfiniBand clusters

Every MPI process will write its membership information into the shared VM list according to its global rank. In this case, the membership information of the processes is only visible among those co-located VMs on each host. Other positions in the VM list will be left blank, as they are located on different hosts. The local number of processes on one host can be acquired by checking the membership information written in the shared VM list. Similarly, their local ordering will be maintained by their membership information positions in the VM list. The VM locality detector is designed to use multiple bytes, and each byte will be used to save the membership information of each MPI process in the co-resident VMs. Because the byte is the smallest unit for concurrent memory access without a lock, using byte-based storage can guarantee that multiple MPI processes from co-resident VMs can write their membership information on corresponding offsets concurrently in a lock-free manner. This design reduces the locality detection overhead. Moreover, the allocated memory for maintaining the VM list is small. For example, with an MPI job with one million processes, the whole VM list only occupies 1 MB memory space. Thus, it brings excellent scalability on virtualized MPI environments.

VM Communication Coordinator: With the help of VM Locality Detector which is created and maintained in IVShmem region, the co-resident VMs and associated MPI processes can be dynamically identified. Based on the gathered locality information, a Communication Coordinator component is proposed. This component captures the communication requests from the upper layer and selects the best channel for a request by checking the processes' membership information provided by VM Locality Detector. If the communicating processes are co-resident, VM Communication Coordinator will schedule them to communicate through high-performance IVShmem-based channel (from different VMs) or CMA channel (from the same VM). Otherwise, the SR-IOV channel will be selected for communication.

Communication Channel Optimization in VMs: The default environment setting, which is optimized for native environment, may not be able to benefit MPI communication in a virtualized environment to the greatest extent. Therefore, both the IVShmem and SR-IOV channels are further optimized by choosing the optimal protocol switch point, shared buffer size among processes, the number of the shared buffer, etc., on the virtualized environment.

Figure 6a–b show the intranode MPI-level point-to-point performance of VM using SR-IOV on Chameleon cloud. The results indicate that our redesigned MVA-PICH2 library (denoted as 'MV2-Virt-SR-IOV') can achieve up to 160X and 28X performance improvement regarding latency and bandwidth, compared to the performance on Amazon EC2 platform (denoted as 'MV2-EC2'). There is less than 8% overhead, compared to the native performance (denoted as 'MV2-Native'). For the inter-node case, as shown in Fig. 6c–d, the enhanced MVAPICH2 library is able to deliver up to 30X and 16X performance improvement, compared to Amazon EC2, in terms of latency and bandwidth, respectively. Note that Amazon EC2 does not support explicitly VM allocations on one physical node so far. To ensure fair com-

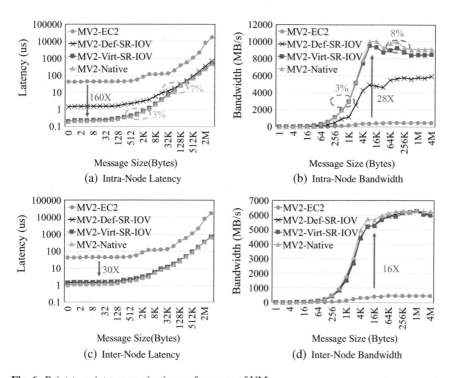

Fig. 6 Point-to-point communication performance of VM

parisons, we allocate multiple VMs in one logical group and take the point-to-point performance numbers for each pair of VMs. The peers with the lowest latency numbers are identified as co-located within one physical node (intranode), otherwise, they are identified as running across two nodes (inter-node).

6.2   Container-Aware MVAPICH2 on InfiniBand Clusters

As a lightweight virtualization alternative, container technology has been becoming popular over the last several years. Many studies focus on comparing the performance of different kinds of hypervisor-based and container-based virtualization technologies for HPC applications. Xavier et al. [33] conducted performance evaluations of hypervisor-based virtualization (Xen) and container-based virtualization (Linux VServer, OpenVZ, and LXC) for HPC regarding computing, memory, disk, network, application overhead and isolation aspects. Wes Felter et al. [34] investigated the performance of VM deployments and compared them with the use of Docker. The results showed that using containers can lead to equal or better performance than using VMs in almost all cases. Cristian et al. [35] conducted the performance evaluation of Linux-based container solutions in various ways of container deployment. The results summarized the limits of using containers, the type of applications that suffer the most, and the impact of container oversubscription on the application performance. Yuyu et al. [36] compared KVM and Docker techniques for HPC regarding features and performance on Chameleon testbed with 10GigE networks.

Although container-based solution reveals less overhead for HPC, compared to hypervisor-based solution, it is still necessary to overcome the performance bottleneck as discussed in Sect. 4. Therefore, a high-performance design of locality-aware MPI library for container-based HPC cloud is proposed in [11], which can dynamically detect co-resident containers and achieve near native performance. The architecture of the proposed container-aware MVAPICH2 on InfiniBand clusters is presented in Fig. 7. The main features of this design are:

Container Locality Detector: Container instances can use the shared memory segments, semaphores, and message queues by sharing IPC namespace with each other. To detect the process locality information, a container locality list structure is created in the shared memory region. During the initialization time, every MPI process writes its locality information into this shared container list according to its global rank. The blank positions in the list structure indicate that the associated MPI processes are on the different hosts. The local number of processes can be acquired by accumulating the written locality information on the shared memory region, and their local order can be identified by the locality information offsets in the container list. Similar to the design of VM locality detector, the container locality list is designed by using multiple bytes to achieve the lock-free design, which can reduce the overhead of concurrent write and read on the container locality list. Once the locality information gets updated after initialization, the actual communication can take place subsequently.

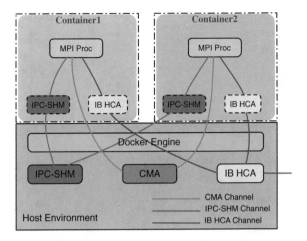

Fig. 7 Architecture of container-aware MVAPICH2 on InfiniBand clusters

Container Communication Coordinator: Similar to VM Communication Coordinator which is discussed in Sect. 6.1, Container Communication Coordinator is responsible for coordinating the communications among containers based on process locality as well as message size. As shown in Fig. 7, if the communicating processes are co-resident, Container Communication Coordinator will schedule them to communicate through the IPC-shared memory-based channel for small messages or CMA channel for large messages. Otherwise, they will go through the HCA channel.

Communication Channel Optimization in Containers: To deliver the optimal MPI communication performance in the container-based HPC clouds, the three types of communication channels, shared memory, CMA, and HCA, are further optimized by choosing the optimal protocol switch point, shared buffer size among processes, etc. on container-based virtualized environment.

Figure 8a and b show the intranode MPI point-to-point performance on the container-based environment on Chameleon cloud. The results indicate that compared to the default performance (denoted as 'MV2-Def-Container'), our optimized MVAPICH2 library (denoted as 'MV2-Virt-Container') can improve up to 81% and 191% regarding latency and bandwidth. On the perspective of the collective operations, the evaluation results, as can be seen in Fig. 8c and d, show that there exists up to 86% and 64% performance improvement for allgather and allreduce operations, respectively. The detailed environment configuration can be found in [11]. Compared to native performance (denoted as 'MV2-Native'), the optimized design can achieve very similar performance.

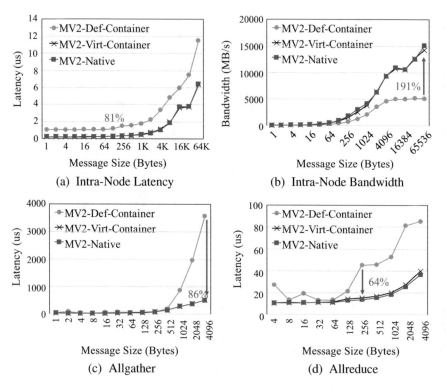

Fig. 8 Point-to-point and collective communication performance of container

7 Integrated Designs with OpenStack and Slurm

7.1 MVAPICH2 over OpenStack with SR-IOV

To deliver high-performance for end applications in the cloud, we can see that it is necessary to enable both SR-IOV and IVShmem when building HPC clouds, as described in Sect. 4. Utilizing MVAPICH2 over OpenStack with SR-IOV to build high-performance HPC clouds is proposed in [16]. The associated designs are described below:

Enable SR-IOV in HPC Cloud over OpenStack: Nova is a core component in OpenStack, which is designed to manage and automate compute resource pools and work with different virtualization technologies, as well as bare metal and HPC configurations. During the configuration phase of Nova system, the PCI passthrough support is enabled by specifying the product ID and the vendor ID of a PCI device (SR-IOV enabled IB HCA). So all the virtual functions of the specified PCI device form a resource pool. A free virtual function will be selected from the pool and passed through to one VM at its launch phase.

Extension to OpenStack: As we have seen above, IVShmem can significantly improve the communication performance across co-resident VMs compared to purely using SR-IOV on virtualized InfiniBand clusters, but the current generation Open-Stack framework does not support it yet. Thus, it is better that OpenStack can be extended to support IVShmem. The study in [16] describes the basic architecture of the OpenStack Nova service. Nova-Compute serves primarily as a worker daemon that takes the charge of creating and terminating VM instances. Nova-Compute accepts instance creation requests from users or other services and converts the requests into XML files. It then invokes the libvirt library to launch the desired VM instances. To enable IVShmem, an IVShmem format function is inserted when Nova generates the VM instance configuration file for libvirt. This function can convert the IVShmem request to the QEMU namespace XML format for the guest VM.

VM Locality-Aware Support: In the HPC cloud deployed by OpenStack with IVSh-mem support, each VM can have both SR-IOV and IVShmem enabled. As we discussed above, we need an effective way to detect co-resident VMs for choosing the optimized communication channel. The OpenStack controller node has a global view of all the resources, so it could help for the detection. However, if a failure or time-out happens during the communication between the controller node and compute node, we can not update the locality information in a timely manner. In addition, the OpenStack controller node may become a bottleneck in HPC clouds, if too many locality information requests come to the control node concurrently. Instead, our VM-aware MVAPICH2 design allows each VM to acquire and maintain the locality information on the IVShmem region, which avoids the unnecessary communication, possible failure issues and bottlenecks.

7.2 Extending Slurm for Building Efficient HPC Clouds

There have been several studies on building cloud computing environments with Slurm, Jacobsen et al. [15] present 'shifter,' which is tightly integrated into Slurm for managing Docker and other user-defined images. Ismael [37] uses VM for dynamic fractional resource management and load balancing in a batch cluster environment. Markwardt et al. [14] propose a solution to run VMs in a Slurm-based batch system. They use a VM scheduler to keep track of the status of Slurm queue on the VMs. Ruivo et al. [38] explore the potential use of SR-IOV on InfiniBand in an OpenNebula cloud toward the efficient support of MPI-based workloads.

As we discussed in Sect. 4, efficient isolation of critical HPC resources, such as SR-IOV enabled virtual functions and IVShmem devices, requires the aid through the middleware like job launchers and resource managers, as they have a global view of the VMs and the underlying physical hosts. To solve such issues, a novel framework, Slurm-V is proposed in [13], which extends Slurm with virtualization-oriented capa-bilities such as job submission to dynamically created VMs with isolated SR-IOV and IVShmem resources. In Slurm-V, three new components are introduced: VM

Configuration Reader, VM Launcher, and VM Reclaimer. Further, three alternative designs are proposed to effectively support these three components.

VM Configuration Reader: It extracts the related parameters for VM configuration. Each time when users request physical resources, they can specify the detailed VM configurations, such as vcpu-per-vm, memory-per-vm, disk-size, vm-per-node, etc. To support high-performance MPI communication, the user can specify SR-IOV devices on those allocated nodes, and the number of IVShmem devices which is the number of concurrent MPI jobs they want to run inside VMs. The VM Configuration Reader will parse this information and set them in the current Slurm job control environment. Thus, the tasks executed on those physical nodes can extract information from job control environment and take proper actions accordingly.

VM Launcher: It is mainly responsible for launching required VMs on each allocated physical node based on user-specified VM configuration. If the user specifies the SR-IOV enabled device, this component detects those occupied VFs and selects a free one for each VM. It also loads user-specified VM image from the publicly accessible storage system, such as NFS or Lustre, to the local node. Then it generates XML file and invokes libvirtd or OpenStack infrastructure to launch VM. During VM boot, the selected VF will be passthroughed to VM. To support IVShmem, it assigns a unique ID for each IVShmem device and sequentially hotplugs them to VMs. In this way, IVShmem devices can be isolated with each other, such that each concurrent MPI job will use a dedicated one for inter-VM shared memory-based communication. Another important functionality is that the VM Launcher records and propagates the mapping records between local VM and its assigned IP address to all other VMs. Other functionalities include mounting global storage systems, etc.

VM Reclaimer: Once the MPI job reaches completion, the VM Reclaimer is executed. Its responsibilities include reclaiming VMs and the critical resources, such as unlocking the passthroughed VFs, returning them to VF pool, detaching IVShmem devices and reclaiming the corresponding host shared memory regions.

Task-based Design: The three new components are treated as three tasks/steps in a Slurm job. Therefore, the end user needs to implement corresponding scripts and explicitly insert them in the job batch file. After the job being submitted, srun will execute these three tasks on allocated nodes.

SPANK Plugin-based Design: In this design, the user can specify all VM configuration options preceded with '#SBATCH' in the batch job file. Once the user submits the job using sbatch command, the SPANK plugin is loaded and the three components are invoked, respectively in different contexts. The snapshot and the multithreading mechanism are utilized to speed up the image transfer and VM launching, respectively. This will further reduce VM deployment time.

SPANK Plugin over OpenStack-based Design: In this design, the VM Launcher and VM Reclaimer components will accomplish their functionalities by offloading the tasks to OpenStack infrastructure. The core component of OpenStack, Nova, is responsible for launching VMs on all allocated compute nodes. For completion, it also takes care of tearing down the VMs and reclaiming the associated resources.

8   The MVAPICH2-Virt Software Distribution and Appliance

We have put together the above-mentioned designs into the MVAPICH2-Virt [4] software distribution. MVAPICH2-Virt, derived from MVAPICH2, is an MPI library to exploit the novel features and mechanisms of high-performance networking technologies with SR-IOV and other virtualization technologies such as IVShmem for VMs and IPC enabled shared memory and CMA for containers. MVAPICH2-Virt can deliver the optimized performance for MPI applications running in both VMs and containers over SR-IOV-enabled InfiniBand clusters.

For processes which are distributed in different VMs/containers, MVAPICH2-Virt can transparently detect the process locality information to automatically choose the optimized channel for high-performance communication. Intranode-intra-VM MPI communication can use CMA channel; Intranode-inter-VM MPI communication can utilize the IVShmem-based channel; Inter-node-inter-VM MPI communication can take advantage of SR-IOV-based channel. For containers, all intranode MPI communication can go through either IPC-based shared memory channel or CMA channel. Inter-node-inter-container MPI communication will go through the InfiniBand channel.

Figure 9a and b show the application's performance with MVAPICH2-Virt (SPEC MPI and Graph500) on VM-based HPC environment. As we can see, compared to the default performance, MVAPICH2-Virt library can significantly improve the application's performance, while introducing less than 9.5% overhead, compared to the native performance.

Similarly, Fig. 10a and b show the performance of Class D NAS and Graph500 on container-based HPC environment. The evaluation results indicate that the MVAPICH2-Virt package is not only able to reduce up to 16% execution time, compared to the default case, but also having minor overhead, compared to the native performance. All these evaluation results are taken on the Chameleon cloud. Please refer to [4] for detailed VM and container environment configuration.

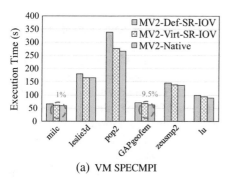

(a) VM SPECMPI

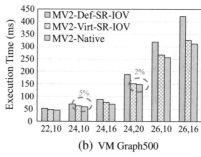

(b) VM Graph500

Fig. 9 Application performance on VM-based HPC environment

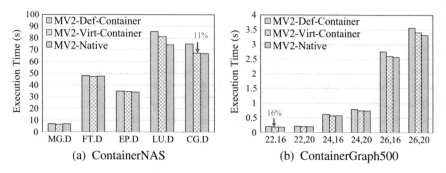

Fig. 10 Application performance on container-based HPC environment

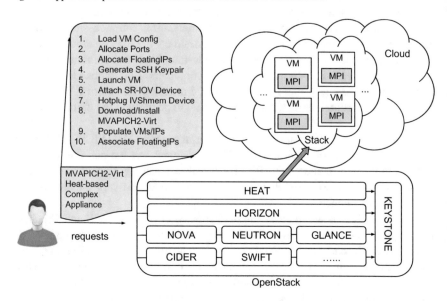

Fig. 11 Overview of OpenStack heat-based complex appliance for MVAPICH2-Virt

To facilitate the end users to quickly deploy a cluster of KVM virtual machines, which uses the MVAPICH2-Virt library and is configured with SR-IOV for high-performance communication over InfiniBand, an OpenStack Heat-based complex appliance for MVAPICH2-Virt is developed and publicly available on Chameleon [39]. Figure 11 illustrates the structure of the appliance. The end user can submit a request of deploying VM cluster with MPI stack through MVAPICH2-Virt Heat-based complex appliance to underlying OpenStack infrastructure. In this complex appliance, the user just needs to provide a few necessary VM configuration parameters. Then, the stack is launched with several procedures executed in the background, which includes load VM config, allocate ports, etc., as shown in the zoom-in box in Fig. 11. Finally, a cluster of KVM virtual machines with MVAPICH2-Virt library is deployed. The end user can log into one of the virtual machines and run MPI jobs in this cluster. Please refer to [39] for more details.

9 Conclusion

Cloud computing with virtualization delivers requested resources by providing a platform for consolidating IT resources in a scalable, flexible, and elastic manner. However, there are still a lot of challenges for efficiently running HPC applications on cloud computing systems. One of the most important hurdles in building efficient HPC clouds is the poor I/O performance offered by underlying virtualized devices. The emerging SR-IOV technology seems a promising approach to solve the performance issues, and it has been supported by modern high-performance interconnects, such as InfiniBand and high-speed Ethernet. Because of its near bare-metal performance for internode communication, many cloud platforms use SR-IOV in their production environments. However, the SR-IOV scheme lacks locality-aware communication support, which causes performance overheads for intranode inter-VM communication.

This chapter presents an overview of popular virtualization system software as well as high-performance interconnects and communication mechanisms available on HPC clouds. Based on these technology advancements, we propose an efficient approach to building HPC clouds based on MVAPICH2 over OpenStack and Slurm with SR-IOV. MVAPICH2 MPI library can fully take advantage of high-performance SR-IOV channel for internode communication as well as IVShmem channel for intranode communication. For the container-based environment, MVAPICH2 MPI library can efficiently utilize the network, shared memory, and CMA channels based on process locality. Performance evaluations with benchmarks and HPC applications on NSF-supported Chameleon Cloud show that our design can deliver near-native performance. Further, compared with the performance on Amazon EC2, HPC clouds built with our approach can exhibit orders of magnitude performance improvement potential. The MVAPICH2 software library over VMs and containers presented in this chapter is publicly available from the MVAPICH2 project site [4].

All of these studies are pushing the envelope of converging HPC and Cloud Computing technologies [40]. By leveraging high-performance interconnects (e.g., InfiniBand) and communication mechanisms (e.g., SR-IOV) available on modern HPC clusters, the novel enhanced designs for MVAPICH2, OpenStack, and Slurm will play an important role in building current and next-generation HPC clouds.

10 Open Research Problems

This chapter has proposed designs to solve several challenges associated with high-performance communication for building efficient HPC clouds. There are still many open research problems, which can be summarized as the following categories.

Virtual Machine Migration with SR-IOV. One of the biggest challenges facing the community is how to efficiently migrate virtual machines with SR-IOV devices. Recent studies [41–43] have shown that SR-IOV-based virtual networks (both Infini-Band and high-performance Ethernet) will prevent VM migration with current generation hypervisors (KVM, Xen, ESXi) and InfiniBand or high-performance Ethernet SR-IOV drivers. Even though these works were proposed, they can only work with specific versions of hypervisors and vendor drivers. So far, there is no out-of-box software solution publicly available to migrate VMs with SR-IOV enabled network interfaces. It may still take a long way to standardize a solution to work with all different hypervisors and hardware devices, by the collaborative effort from researchers, hardware vendors, and hypervisor/driver developers. On this front, we recently proposed a hypervisor independent and adapter driver independent approach [44] for VM migration over SR-IOV enabled InfiniBand clusters. This approach can work efficiently with MPI-based applications, and it can be generalized to other libraries and middleware.

High-Performance Virtualization Support for Accelerators. Another grand challenge in the community is how to provide high-performance virtualization support for accelerators (e.g., GPGPU and Xeon Phi), which are widely used in HPC cloud environments. One possible solution is to enable SR-IOV support for accelerators, which will open up many new research opportunities.

Not only just above-mentioned challenges, a lot of other challenges such as efficient collective algorithms on the cloud, nested virtualization support, cloud-aware elastic communication schemes, etc. are still facing the community today. Researchers need to propose novel solutions to handle these challenges to build efficient HPC clouds with lower cost.

References

1. Virtualization. (2016). https://en.wikipedia.org/wiki/Virtualization.
2. Rosenblum, M., & Garfinkel, T. (2005). Virtual machine monitors: Current technology and future trends. *Computer, 38*(5), 39–47.
3. Jose, J., Li, M., Lu, X., Kandalla, K., Arnold, M., & Panda, D. K. (2013). SR-IOV support for virtualization on InfiniBand clusters: Early experience. In *Proceedings of 13th IEEE/ACM International Symposium Cluster, Cloud and Grid Computing (CCGrid)*, Delft, Netherlands.
4. MVAPICH: MPI over InfiniBand, Omni-Path, Ethernet/iWARP, and RoCE. (2016). http://mvapich.cse.ohio-state.edu/.
5. OpenMPI: Open Source High Performance Computing. (2016). http://www.open-mpi.org/.

6. Zhang, J., Lu, X., Jose, J., Shi, R., & Panda, D. K. (2014). Can inter-VM Shmem benefit MPI applications on SR-IOV based virtualized InfiniBand clusters? In *Proceedings of 20th International Conference Euro-Par 2014 Parallel Processing*, Porto, Portugal.

7. Single Root I/O Virtualization. (2016). http://www.pcisig.com/specifications/iov/single_root.

8. Cross Memory Attach (CMA). (2016). http://kernelnewbies.org/Linuxi_3.2.

9. Macdonell, A. C. (2011). Shared-memory optimizations for virtual machines. Ph.D. Thesis. University of Alberta, Edmonton, Alberta, Fall 2011

10. Zhang, J., Lu, X., Jose, J., Li, M., Shi, R., & Panda, D. K. (2014). High performance MPI library over SR-IOV enabled InfiniBand clusters. In *Proceedings of International Conference on High Performance Computing (HiPC)*, Goa, India.

11. Zhang, J., Lu, X., & Panda, D. K. (2016). High performance MPI library for container-based HPC cloud on InfiniBand clusters. In *Proceedings of the 45th International Conference on Parallel Processing (ICPP)*, Philadelphia, USA.

12. Yoo, A., Jette, M., & Grondona, M. (2003). SLURM: Simple linux utility for resource management. In *Proceedings of 9th International Workshop (JSSPP 2003)*, Seattle, WA, USA

13. Zhang, J., Lu, X., Chakraborty, S., & Panda, D. K. (2016). SLURM-V: Extending SLURM for building efficient HPC cloud with SR-IOV and IVShmem. In *Proceeding of the 22nd International European Conference on Parallel and Distributed Computing (Euro-Par '16)*, Grenoble, France.

14. Markwardt, U., Jurenz, M., Rotscher, D., Muller-Pfefferkorn, R., Jakel, R., & Wesarg, B. (2016). Running virtual machines in a Slurm batch system. http://slurm.schedmd.com/SLUG15/SlurmVM.pdf.

15. Jacobsen, D., Botts, J., & Canon, S. (2016). Never port your code again Docker functionality with Shifter using SLURM. http://slurm.schedmd.com/SLUG15/shifter.pdf.

16. Zhang, J., Lu, X., Arnold, M., & Panda, D. K. (2015). MVAPICH2 over OpenStack with SR-IOV: An efficient approach to build HPC clouds. In *Proceedings of the 15th IEEE/ACM International Symposium on Cluster, Cloud and Grid Computing (CCGrid)*, Shenzhen, China.

17. Chameleon. (2016). http://chameleoncloud.org/.

18. Docker. (2016). https://www.docker.com/.

19. Singularity. (2016). http://singularity.lbl.gov/.

20. Keahey, K., Foster, I., Freeman, T., & Zhang, X. (2005). Virtual workspaces: Achieving quality of service and quality of life in the grid. *Scientific Programming, 13*(4), 265–275.

21. Eucalyptus. (2016). http://eucalyptus.com/.

22. OpenNebula. (2016). http://opennebula.org.

23. Peng, J., Lu, X., Cheng, B., & Zha, L. (2010). JAMILA: A usable batch job management system to coordinate heterogeneous clusters and diverse applications over grid or cloud infrastructure. In *Proceedings of Network and Parallel Computing*, Zhengzhou, China.

24. Lu, X., Lin, J., Zha, L., & Xu, Z. (2011). Vega LingCloud: A resource single leasing point system to support heterogeneous application modes on shared infrastructure. In *Proceedings of IEEE 9th International Symposium on Parallel and Distributed Processing with Applications (ISPA)*, Busan, Korea.

25. Crago, S., Dunn, K., Eads, P., Hochstein, L., Kang, D., Kang, M., et al. (2011). Heterogeneous cloud computing. In *Proceedings of 2011 IEEE International Conference on Cluster Computing (Cluster)*, Austin, TX, USA.

26. SPANK. (2016). https://slurm.schedmd.com/spank.html.

27. Subramoni, H., Lai, P., Luo, M., & Panda, D. K. (2009). RDMA over ethernet—A preliminary study. In *Proceedings of the 2009 Workshop on High Performance Interconnects for Distributed Computing (HPIDC'09)*.

28. Romanow, A., & Bailey, S. (2003). An overview of RDMA over IP. In *Proceedings of International Workshop on Protocols for Long-Distance Networks (PFLDnet2003)*.

29. Zhang, X., McIntosh, S., Rohatgi, P., & Griffin, J. (2007). XenSocket: A high-throughput interdomain transport for virtual machines. In *Proceedings of the ACM/IFIP/USENIX 2007 International Conference on Middleware (Middleware)*, Newport Beach, USA.

30. Kim, K., Kim, C., Jung, S., Shin, H., & Kim, J. (2008). Inter-domain socket communications supporting high performance and full binary compatibility on Xen. In *Proceedings of the 4th ACM SIGPLAN/SIGOPS International Conference on Virtual Execution Environments (VEE '08)*, Seattle, USA.
31. Wang, J., Wright, K., & Gopalan, K. (2008). XenLoop: A transparent high performance inter-vm network loopback. In *Proceedings of the 17th International Symposium on High Performance Distributed Computing (HPDC)*, Boston, USA.
32. Huang, W., Koop, M., Gao, Q., & Panda, D. K. (2007). Virtual machine aware communication libraries for high performance computing. In *Proceedings of the 2007 ACM/IEEE Conference on Supercomputing (SC)*, Reno, USA.
33. Xavier, M., Neves, M., Rossi, F., Ferreto, T., Lange, T., & Rose, C. (2013). Performance evaluation of container-based virtualization for high performance computing environments. *2013 21st Euromicro International Conference on Parallel, Distributed and Network-Based Processing (PDP)* (pp. 233–240). Northern Ireland: Belfast.
34. Felter, W., Ferreira, A., Rajamony, R., & Rubio, J. (2014). An updated performance comparison of virtual machines and Linux containers. Technical Report RC25482 (AUS1407-001).
35. Ruiz, C., Jeanvoine, E., & Nussbaum, L. (2015). Performance evaluation of containers for HPC. In *10th Workshop on Virtualization in High-Performance Cloud Computing (VHPC)*, Vienna, Austria.
36. Zhou, Y., Subramaniam, B., Keahey, K., & Lange, J. (2015). Comparison of virtualization and containerization techniques for high performance computing. In *Proceedings of the 2015 ACM/IEEE Conference on Supercomputing*, Austin, USA.
37. Estrada, I. (2016). Overview of a virtual cluster using OpenNebula and SLURM. https://portal.futuresystems.org/sites/default/files/one-slurm.pdf.
38. Ruivo, T., Altayo, G., Garzoglio, G., Timm, S., Kim, H., Noh, S., et al. (2014). Exploring InfiniBand hardware virtualization in OpenNebula towards efficient high-performance computing. In *Proceedings of 14th IEEE/ACM International Symposium on Cluster, Cloud and Grid Computing (CCGrid)*.
39. MVAPICH2-Virt Heat-based Complex Appliance. (2016). https://www.chameleoncloud.org/appliances/28/.
40. Telfer, S. (2016). *The crossroads of cloud and HPC: OpenStack for scientific research*. OpenStack Foundation.
41. Guay, W., Reinemo, S., Johnsen, B., Yen, C., Skeie, T., Lysne, O., et al. (2015). Early experiences with live migration of SR-IOV enabled InfiniBand. *Journal of Parallel and Distributed Computing (JPDC)*.
42. Xu, X., & Davda, B. (2016). SRVM: Hypervisor support for live migration with passthrough SR-IOV network devices. In *Proceedings of the 12th ACM SIGPLAN/SIGOPS International Conference on Virtual Execution Environments (VEE '16)*, Atlanta, USA.
43. Pan, Z., Dong, Y., Chen, Y., Zhang, L., & Zhang, Z. (2012). CompSC: Live migration with pass-through devices. In *Proceedings of the 8th ACM SIGPLAN/SIGOPS Conference on Virtual Execution Environments (VEE '12)*, London, UK (pp. 109–120).
44. Zhang, J., Lu, X., & Panda, D. K. (2017). High-performance virtual machine migration framework for MPI applications on SR-IOV enabled InfiniBand clusters. In *Proceedings of the 31st IEEE International Parallel and Distributed Processing Symposium (IPDPS '17)*, Orlando, USA.

Resource Procurement, Allocation, Metering, and Pricing in Cloud Computing

Akshay Narayan, Parvathy S. Pillai, Abhinandan S. Prasad
and Shrisha Rao

1 Introduction

Cloud computing is not only a popular paradigm for services offered over the Internet, but has also captured the interest of both academia and industry. The ready possibility of on-demand provisioning of resources is one of the main advantages of cloud computing for its users. These resources are not only limited to classical ones such as computing power and storage, but also encompass a wide variety of services like data analytics, monitoring, etc., that are distributed geographically.

In this chapter, we offer a summarized look at three issues in cloud computing that are doubtless of great importance and call for innovative approaches, yet have not received a great deal of attention in the cloud computing literature:

1. How can cloud resources be procured by cloud users, given a multitude of varied offerings from different cloud vendors, and how should the resources be priced?
2. How can resources be allocated by cloud vendors in preparation for requests from users?
3. How can cloud services be metered in a time-varying way (rather than at a fixed rate that takes no account of changing conditions) to bring advantages to both cloud vendors and cloud users?

A. Narayan · P.S. Pillai
National University of Singapore, Singapore, Singapore
e-mail: anarayan@comp.nus.edu.sg

P.S. Pillai
e-mail: parvathysp@ieee.org

A.S. Prasad
Georg-August-Universität Göttingen, Göttingen, Germany
e-mail: abhinandansp@ieee.org

S. Rao (✉)
International Institute of Information Technology - Bangalore, Bangalore, India
e-mail: shrao@ieee.org

© Springer Nature Singapore Pte Ltd. 2017
S. Chaudhary et al. (eds.), *Research Advances in Cloud Computing*,
DOI 10.1007/978-981-10-5026-8_7

Considering that cloud systems are very large in size (and will probably get only larger over time), serving very large numbers of users and with huge business values, these are not trivial concerns. Answers to these questions are not very simple, and improved answers to them are likely to bring large financial and other benefits to both users and vendors of cloud systems.

Automated resource procurement and resource allocation can be achieved using statistical and other machine-learning techniques that are mostly empirical. In this chapter, we try to address these issues using game theory. As in many other works, we use game theory for a decision model. Our focus in this chapter is primarily on IaaS clouds; however, the methods can be adapted to PaaS or SaaS clouds systems with minimal or no changes.

The structure of this chapter is as follows. We discuss the initial problem of cloud resource procurement in Sect. 2. We present a summary of some recent works [1, 2] that use auctions [3] and mechanism design [4] in the context of cloud resource procurement. Further, we use a game-theoretic approach to solve the problem of resource allocation by cloud vendors. We consider servers owned by a vendor as self-interested agents that need to form coalitions that maximize collective payoffs. We use the recent concept of the uncertainty principle of game theory [5] to solve for fast, near-optimal solutions to the allocation problem that do not require the computationally intensive task of evaluating the payoff matrix [6, 7]. We present our findings in Sect. 4. Finally, for the third problem, it is necessary to note that cloud computing systems increasingly use huge amounts of electrical power (similar to, and often more than, many large industrial systems), and that the cost of electricity used is often the single biggest lifetime cost in a cloud system. With electrical power suppliers increasingly moving to the concept of *smart grids* that supply electrical power at time-varying rates, it follows that cloud vendors may also soon have to think about using power-aware metering. We present our ideas on smart- and power-aware metering of cloud services [8, 9] in Sect. 5.

For the sake of completeness, we present simulation results to show the efficacy of our methods for each of the problems listed in their respective sections.

2 Auction-Based Resource Procurement in Cloud Computing

Currently, cloud users procure resources that are made available at fixed prices. In this manner of procurement, which is also called static pricing, the price of the procured resources does not change either over time or based on other factors. One also cannot enforce service level agreements (SLAs) in this kind of scenario. Hence, recent work [1] has proposed mechanisms and algorithms to implement dynamic pricing in the cloud. Dynamic pricing is very popular in other domains like airlines, etc. In dynamic pricing, the time-varying price can be determined based on the user consumption pattern and demand. This type of pricing is beneficial to both cloud vendors and users. Cloud users can get discounts based on their choices of desirable consumption patterns, and vendors benefit by better (more even) resource utilization of their resources.

The uncertainties in price and lack of knowledge about dynamic pricing of cloud vendors are hurdles for implementing dynamic pricing in the cloud. Auctions are appropriate in this context. Hence, the procurement mechanisms presented in prior work [1, 2] are auction-centric. Prasad and Rao [1] design mechanisms named C-DSIC, C-BIC, and C-OPT. The common thread across the three mechanisms is the incentive payout to the cloud vendors. Incentives are paid to cloud vendors, and the amount of the same depends on the mechanism chosen. In C-DSIC, truthfulness the best strategy for a vendor, irrespective of the strategies of other cloud vendors. In both C-BIC and C-OPT, truthfulness is the best strategy only if other cloud vendors are truthful.

The mechanisms presented by Prasad and Rao [1] cannot be applied in hybrid or federated clouds. In a hybrid cloud, the cloud user should be able to procure a combination of resources from different cloud vendors, so the user has combinatorial choices. Hence a variant of the CABOB algorithm is used [2] to perform a combinatorial auction. Unlike other combinatorial auction algorithms, this algorithm has linear time complexity and is hence suited to practical environments.

2.1 Mechanism Design

Game theory, which is one of the standard paradigms of multiagent systems, can be described as a mathematical abstraction of the conflict and cooperation between intelligent rational agents. Agents have their own preferences, which are kept private (not shared with other agents). To make a collective decision, it is necessary to aggregate these preferences. The goal of mechanism design is to elicit these kind of information so that a global decision can be reached. Mechanism design allows the designer (called the social planner) to design the rules of the game so that the self-interested actions of all agents collectively lead to a desired global system objective. Mechanism design (which thus could be called game design) is used widely in economics. The formal model of mechanism design [10] is as follows:

1. Consider a scenario with N agents and let i denote the ith agent. These agents must make a collective choice from the set of actions or strategies, called the outcome or alternative set denoted by O.
2. Let θ_i be the type of agent i which determine the preference over the outcome set O.
3. Let Θ_i denote all possible types or preferences of an agent i. We denote type profile set by Θ and $\Theta = \Theta_1 \times \Theta_2 \times \cdots \times \Theta_n$. We represent type profile by θ where $\theta = (\theta_1, \theta_2, \ldots, \theta_n)$.
4. Let $\Phi \in \Delta(\Theta)$ be a common prior distribution where the agent's types are drawn. $\Delta(\Theta)$ is the set of all probability distribution functions over the set Θ such that

$\Delta(\Theta) = \{q : \Theta \to \mathbb{R} | \sum_{y \in \Theta} q(y) = 1 \text{ and } q(z) \geq 0, \forall z \in \Theta\}$. Let ϕ be the corresponding probability density function.

5. Since agent i is rational and intelligent, it tries to maximize a Bernoulli utility function $u_i : X \times \Theta_i \to \mathbb{R}$. The Bernoulli utility is a quantitative classification of agents' preferences for outcomes [11] and is denoted by $u_i(x, \theta_i)$ where $x \in X$ and $\theta_i \in \Theta_i$.

6. We assume that type sets $\Theta_1, \ldots, \Theta_n$, utility functions $u_i(.)$ and the probability density $\phi(.)$ are common knowledge among all agents, but the specific instance value is private to each agent.

The social planner faces two challenges in such a situation, these being:

1. Preference aggregation: Given a type profile $\theta = (\theta_1, \ldots, \theta_n)$, which outcome $o \in O$ should be chosen?

2. Truth elicitation: How to extract the true value of θ_i of an agent i?

The work of the social planner is encapsulated in the "social choice function," defined as follows:

Definition 1 A social choice function $f : \Theta_1 \times \cdots \times \Theta_n \to O$ has the property that for each possible type profile θ, it assigns a collective choice $f(\theta_1, \ldots, \theta_n) \in O$.

We illustrate the mechanism design problem in the cloud computing scenario, giving a social choice function that can be used in the cloud scenario by a social planner.

Consider a set of cloud service providers who are able to provide resources. Assume that there is a cloud user who wants to procure a resource. We formulate this scenario as a mechanism design problem as follows:

1. Outcome set O: Let o be the outcome such that
   $o = (a_1, \ldots, a_n, p_1, \ldots, p_n)$ where $a_i = 1$ if the cloud service provider is selected and p_i is the payment received by the cloud service provider i. The set of feasible alternatives is $O = \left\{(a_1, a_2, \ldots, a_n, p_1, p_2, \ldots, p_n) | a_i \in 0, 1, p_i \in \mathbb{R}, \forall i \sum_{i=1}^{n} p_i \leq 0\right\}$

2. Type set Θ_i: This can be interpreted as the cost incurred by the cloud service provider to provide the resources. Θ_i is the possible cost incurred by the cloud service provider i.

3. Utility function $u_i(.)$: Utility of the cloud service provider is the difference between payment received and resource cost. Informally, utility is profit. The utility is given by $u_i(o_i, \theta_i) = u_i(a_1, a_2, \ldots, a_n, p_1, p_2, \ldots, p_n, \theta_i) = \theta_i a_i + p_i$

4. Social choice function f: in this scenario, it is

$$f(\theta) = (a_1(\theta), a_2(\theta), \ldots, a_n(\theta), p_1(\theta), p_2(\theta), \ldots, p_n(\theta)), \forall \theta \in \Theta$$

A fundamental concept in mechanism design is incentive compatibility. Incentives are offered so that agents reveal their true types. Incentive compatibility thus refers to the offering of appropriate incentive to induce truth revelation.

The two classical variants of incentive compatibility are:

1. Dominant strategy incentive compatibility (DSIC): in this case, truth revelation is the best strategy for each user, irrespective of other users' strategies.
2. Bayesian Nash incentive compatibility (BIC): In this case, truth revelation is the best response for an agent only if other agents are also truthful about their types.

Incentive compatibility can be applied only to the direct mechanisms, because truthfulness is always with respect to types. We provide definitions of incentive compatibility for the sake of completeness [10].

Definition 2 A social choice function $f : \Theta_1 \times \cdots \times \Theta_n \rightarrow O$ is said to be incentive compatible if the Bayesian game induced by the direct revelation mechanism $D = ((\Theta_i)_{i \in N}, f(.))$ has a pure strategy equilibrium $s^*(.) = (s_1^*(.), \ldots, s_n^*(.))$ in which $s_i^*(\theta_i) = \theta_i, \forall \theta_i \in \Theta_i, \forall i \in N$.

The dominant strategy incentive compatibility (DSIC) is defined as follows:

Definition 3 A social choice function $f : \Theta_1 \times \cdots \times \Theta_n \rightarrow O$ is said to be dominant strategy incentive compatible if the Bayesian game induced by the direct revelation mechanism $D = ((\Theta_i)_{i \in N}, f(.))$ has a weak dominant strategy equilibrium $s^*(.) = (s_1^*(.), \ldots, s_n^*(.))$ in which $s_i^*(\theta_i) = \theta_i, \forall \theta_i \in \Theta_i, \forall i \in N$.

Formally, Bayesian incentive compatibility (BIC) is defined as:

Definition 4 A social choice function $f : \Theta_1 \times \cdots \times \Theta_n \rightarrow O$ is Bayesian incentive compatible if the Bayesian game induced by the direct revelation mechanism $D = ((\Theta_i)_{i \in N}, f(.))$ has a Bayesian Nash equilibrium $s^*(.) = (s_1^*(.), \ldots, s_n^*(.))$ in which $s_i^*(\theta_i) = \theta_i, \forall \theta_i \in \Theta_i, \forall i \in N$.

2.2 Resource Procurement in Cloud

Resource procurement is a vital and interesting problem in cloud computing. Let us consider a scenario: a user is interested in virtualized computing resources. There are many cloud vendors who provide such resources, but at varying prices and quality of service (QoS) metrics. The user has to mull over each vendor specification and select the best cloud vendor who satisfies both budget and quality requirements. This approach is quite complex and challenging for an enterprise [12]. Also, the cloud vendors update their offerings based on market demand. Hence, in presence of large numbers of diverse cloud vendors, manual selection is complicated at best.

In fixed pricing, there is no provision for negotiation. Also, consumption patterns are not considered and accounted for. These issues are addressed in dynamic pricing. Dynamic pricing favors the cloud vendor. During peak-use hours, the resource utilization is high and the vendor does not desire further load; on the other hand, during off-peak hours the load on the infrastructure is lower but the vendor would like more. If cloud vendors provide some sort of incentives or discounts to cloud users to modify their consumption patterns, this would lead to higher but more uniform overall cloud infrastructure utilization.

In cloud computing, there are uncertainties about the resource prices and cloud vendor. These are obstacles for implementing dynamic pricing in the cloud. Auctions are appropriate in this scenario [3, 13, 14]. In reverse auctions, in particular, the customer is an auctioneer and the sellers are bidders. Reverse auctions are very popular and are known in different names like procurement auction, B2B auctions. These are widely used to procure resources across prominent industries like software licensing, health care, manufacturing, etc. Reverse auctions are preferred due to procurement cost reduction; using such also prevents the unwanted effects of personal bias and political ties [15].

We need to identify a suitable component where we can automate our resource procurement solution. In cloud computing, a cloud broker is an intermediary between cloud vendors and users. Further, it automates most of the tasks like negotiation, etc. Hence, we can deploy our approach using cloud broker.

There are two ways to procure resources; using

(i) conventional models; and
(ii) economic models.

The fundamental difference between these models lies in their assumption about the resource providers. In conventional models, the goal is to maximize overall system usage, while economic models seek to maximize overall utility. In conventional models, a user pays at an agreed rate for the quantum of service received. Economic models require a user to pay not by the quantum of service, but on the value derived thereby [16]. We may therefore accept that, as in other domains, economic models are more suited to the context of cloud services.

Incentive distribution to bidders to act truthfully is one of the key features of economic models. In our case, cloud vendors are bidders, and can be expected to maximize their incentives using strategic behavior, which can include not act truthfully.

Narahari et al. [17] propose a theoretical framework of mechanisms based on dominant strategy and Bayesian incentive compatibility. Mingbiao et al. [18] address the sharing inefficiency in economic models. Subramoniam et al. [19] suggest the use of commodity market models in a different domain, viz., for the purpose of resource allocation in Grid computing. Parsa et al. [20] suggest the use of a double auction for resource allocation.

Lin et al. [21] use dynamic auctions (Vickrey auctions) to perform resource allocation. They assume as a given that all users are honest and reveal their types truthfully, which of course is hardly realistic. They also do not discuss issues with the enforcement of truthfulness. Narahari et al. [17] propose mechanisms for procurement of resources for sweep-type jobs in Grid, which cannot be applied directly to the cloud. In cloud, resources are not limited to sweep-type jobs.

Consider another scenario: a cloud user may require a combination of resources which a single vendor may be unable to provide—this issue is not considered in the classic work [1], which does not address the questions of how a user may require several resources together (rather than a single one at a time), and how a vendor may bid with a combination of resources rather than offering a single one.

To address these matters, we have to take multiple resources and their various combinations into account during the auction. Multiple resource allocation is a combinatorial auction problem which has particular relevance in hybrid cloud computing which is little explored as of now, but is considered to be of importance in the future [22].

Cloud vendors do not yet offer uniform services (which are needed for such services to be interchangeable and not subject to vendor lock-in). Rochwerger et al. [22] suggest that this will happen, and that the "federated cloud has huge potential." When standardized cloud offerings by multiple vendors become a reality, it will certainly become quite possible to mix and interchangeably use offerings from different cloud vendors, and to automate the procurement of the same.

3 Cloud Resource Procurement

Cloud vendors presently have a fixed pricing, pay-as-you-go approach for their resources. (Such pay-as-you-go approaches are also seen elsewhere, e.g., being popular with calling plans and such offered by telecom providers.) On the flip side, such an approach does not allow the vendor to influence usage patterns (e.g., to discourage peak-time demand and encourage slack-time demand, or the avoidance of steep peaks and troughs in demand by load leveling). A fixed price gives no incentive to influence the pattern of consumption by users.

C-DSIC, C-BIC, and C-OPT are proposed [1] for automating resource procurement. C-DSIC is a low-bid Vickrey auction. C-BIC is weaker compared to C-DSIC but is Bayesian incentive compatible. C-OPT achieves both Bayesian incentive compatibility and individual rationality, which the other two mechanisms cannot achieve. Further, it is immune to both overbidding and underbidding since it reduces the incentive and chances of winning, respectively. C-OPT can be applied even if cloud vendors use different distributions for cost and QoS, unlike both C-DSIC and C-BI. Hence, C-OPT may be preferred over the other two mechanisms.

If multiple resources are requested by the user, and the user may procure different resources from different cloud vendors, then a combinatorial algorithm [2] is more appropriate. In hybrid cloud computing, this scenario is valid.

We denote cloud vendors by $N = \{1, 2, \ldots, n\}$. In this reverse auction, each cloud vendor submits a bid with cost c_i and promised QoS parameters. The QoS parameters vary across both cloud vendors and resources. Also, we cannot interpret the QoS parameters uniformly. There is no guarantee that a high number indicates a better quality. There are exceptions like network latency, where smaller numbers indicate better quality. In multiple criteria decision, QoS parameter comparison is a well-known problem. In the earlier work [1], Simple Additive Weighting (SAW) [23] and the Analytic Hierarchy Process (AHP) [24] are used to perform QoS scaling. The QoS scaling approach is summarized below.

1. The cloud user assign AHP scores to QoS parameters based on his criteria.
2. The QoS parameters can be either positive or negative. Hence, they are scaled differently.
3. The final score is calculated based the user-given weights for QoS parameters. These weights are entirely user dependent, and indicate the user's needs or values.

Let $c_i > 0$, and QoS $q_i > 0$ be the execution cost and QoS of cloud vendor i. This information is private. Let $\underline{c}$ be the lowest cost valuation and $\bar{c}$ be the highest cost valuation. Hence, $\underline{c} \le c_i \le \bar{c}$. Similarly, let $\underline{q}$ be the lowest QoS value and $\bar{q}$ be the highest QoS value. Hence, $\underline{q} \le q_i \le \bar{q}$.

Let Θ_i be the set of all possible true types of the cloud vendor and $\Theta_i = [\underline{c}, \bar{c}] \times [\underline{q}, \bar{q}]$. Let $\Theta = \Theta_1 \times \Theta_2 \times \cdots \times \Theta_n$.

We assume that cost and QoS are correlated, albeit not necessarily perfectly. Let Φ be the joint distribution function of cost and QoS. We assume that the joint distribution function Φ is same $\forall n$ cloud vendors, i.e., $\Phi_1 = \Phi_2 = \cdots = \Phi_n$. Hence, all cloud vendors are symmetric. This assumption does hold only for C-DSIC and C-BIC. We assume that a cloud vendor's aim is to maximize utility. Hence, cloud vendors are <u>risk neutral</u>, which implies quasilinearity [25, p. 269].

In this mechanism, the true bid of each cloud vendor is represented by $b_i = (c_i, q_i)$, and reported bid is represented by $\hat{b}_i = (\hat{c}_i, \hat{q}_i)$. Let $b = (b_1, b_2, \ldots, b_n)$ be bid vector, called the bid profile. Let b_{-i} be the cloud vendor bid vector without i, i.e., $b_{-i} = (b_1, b_2, \ldots, b_{i-1}, b_{i+1}, \ldots, b_n)$. Also $b = (b_{-i}, b_i)$. The goal of a mechanism is to design the following functions.

- Allocation function $a : \Theta \to \{0, 1\}$ specifies the winner.
- Payment function $p : \Theta \to \mathbb{R}$ determines the payment to the cloud vendor.

The goal of the cloud user is to minimize the procurement cost. This can be achieved only if all the cloud vendors quote true costs (bid truthfully). This is also called truth elicitation. Truth elicitation can be done in two ways:

- Dominant Strategy Incentive Compatibility (DSIC): This corresponds to dominant strategy equilibrium.
- Bayesian Incentive Compatibility (BIC): This corresponds to Bayesian Nash equilibrium.

Table 1 summarizes the notations of our model.

3.1 Cloud-Dominant Strategy Incentive Compatible (C-DSIC) Mechanism

In DSIC, truth revelation is the best response to the agents, irrespective of other agents' strategies [10]. Let $f(\hat{b}) = (a(\hat{b}), p_1(\hat{b}), \ldots, p_n(\hat{b}))$ be the social choice

Table 1 Notation

Symbol	Description
n	Total number of cloud vendors
N	Cloud vendor set, $\{1, 2, ..., n\}$
O	Set of outcomes
θ_i	Type of i
b_i	True bid of i
$\hat{b}_i$	Reported bid of i
c_i	True resource cost of i
$\hat{c}_i$	Reported resource cost of i
q_i	True QoS provided by i
$\hat{q}_i$	Reported QoS by i
Θ_i	Type set of i
u_i	i's utility function
Φ_i	i's joint distribution of cost and QoS
v_i	i's valuation
b	Bid vector $b = (b_1, b_1, \ldots, b_n)$
o	Outcome and $o \in O$
$f(b)$	Social choice function
a	Allocation function
p	Payment function
a_i	Payment received by i
ξ_i	i's expected social welfare
T_i	i's expected payment
ρ_i	i's offered expected surplus
π_i	i's expected surplus

function in the C-DSIC mechanism which implements dominant strategy incentive compatibility. $a(\hat{b})$ is the allocation rule that represents the winner. $p_i(\hat{b})$ is the payment received by the cloud vendor i. If $p_i(\hat{b}) > 0$, then payment is received by the cloud vendor i, otherwise i pays money to the user.

The allocation rule is given by:

$$a_i(\hat{b}) = \begin{cases} 1 & \text{if} \frac{\hat{c}_i}{\hat{q}_i} = \min(\frac{\hat{c}_1}{\hat{q}_1}, \frac{\hat{c}_2}{\hat{q}_2}, \ldots, \frac{\hat{c}_n}{\hat{q}_n}) \\ 0 & \text{otherwise} \end{cases} \tag{1}$$

In the above allocation rule, the winner is the cloud vendor whose ratio of cost over QoS is minimum. The payment function—which is also called the pivot rule or "Clarke's mechanism" [17]—is given by (2).

$$p_i(\hat{b}) = a_i(\hat{b})\hat{c}_i + \sum_{j \neq i} \hat{c}_j a_j^{-i}(\hat{b}) - \sum_{j \neq i} \hat{c}_j a_j(\hat{b}) \tag{2}$$

The payment received by cloud vendor i is the sum of quoted cost and the difference between optimal cost in the absence of cloud vendor i and optimal cost in presence of cloud vendor i. In this mechanism, only the winner receives payment, and the price is the second lowest bid.

Algorithm 1 gives pseudocode of C-DISC mechanism.

Algorithm 1: C-DSIC

Input : Reported bids $\hat{b}_1, \hat{b}_2, \ldots, \hat{b}_n$
Output: Winner and payments for participants $(p_1, p_2, \ldots, p_n)$

1 $min \leftarrow \infty$;
2 $winner \leftarrow 0$;
3 **for** $i \leftarrow 1$ **to** n **do**
4   **if** $(\frac{\hat{c}_i}{q_i}) < min$ **then** $min \leftarrow \frac{\hat{c}_i}{q_i}$;
5      $winner \leftarrow i$;
6 **end**
7 **for** $i \leftarrow 1$ **to** n **do**
8   // The payment for each cloud vendor
9   // i as per (2)
10     $p_i(\hat{b}) \leftarrow a_i(\hat{b})\hat{c}_i + \sum_{j \neq i} \hat{c}_j a_j^{-i}(\hat{b}) - \sum_{j \neq i} \hat{c}_j a_j(\hat{b})$;
11 **end**

The properties satisfied by C-DSIC are:

- Dominant strategy incentive compatibility: The C-DSIC mechanism is based on the VCG mechanism, which is DSIC, and hence the C-DSIC mechanism is DSIC.
- Individual rationality: The payments received by the cloud vendors are greater than or equal to zero. In this mechanism, cloud vendors never pay the user, and have a non-negative payoff.
- Allocative efficiency: The winner is the cloud vendor with lowest cost over QoS. Hence, C-DSIC is allocative efficient.

3.2 Cloud-Bayesian Incentive Compatible (C-BIC) Mechanism

Since VCG mechanism is not budget balanced [10], C-DISC is also not budget balanced. Non-budget balanced mechanisms require external funding for performing auction. C-BIC is designed to overcome this limitation.

According to the Gibbard-Satterthwaite impossibility theorem [26], only dictatorial social choice functions are individually rational, budgent balanced, and allocative efficient. Non-dictatorial social choice functions can be designed in two scenarios: we can restrict to quasilinear utility, or design Bayesian incentive compatibility which is weaker than VCG. The dAGVA mechanism [27] is Bayesian incentive compatible. In the dAGVA mechanism, each agent contributes money, and a payment is made to the agents using the contributed money [25, p. 289].

Let $f(\hat{b}) = (a(\hat{b}), p_1(\hat{b}), \ldots, p_n(\hat{b}))$ be the social choice function in the C-BIC mechanism. Let $a_i(\hat{b})$ be the allocation rule and $p_i(\hat{b})$ be the payment received by cloud vendor i. If $p_i(\hat{b}) > 0$ then payment is received by i, otherwise i pays the cloud user.

The allocation rule is the same as C-DSIC but the payment function is different from C-DSIC. The allocation rule is given by the following:

$$a_i(\hat{b}) = \begin{cases} 1 & \text{if} \frac{\hat{c}_i}{\hat{q}_i} = \min(\frac{\hat{c}_1}{\hat{q}_1}, \frac{\hat{c}_2}{\hat{q}_2}, \ldots, \frac{\hat{c}_n}{\hat{q}_n}) \\ 0 & \text{otherwise} \end{cases} \tag{3}$$

The payment rule is based on the dAGVA mechanism. The contributed money of cloud vendors is used for paying all the cloud vendors. In other words, cloud vendors pay a participation fee. Let ξ_i be the expected social welfare [25] of agent i and is calculated using the following:

$$\xi_i(\hat{b}_i) = \mathbb{E}_{\hat{b}_{-i}}[\sum_{i \neq j} c_j(a_j(\hat{b}_i, b_j))] \tag{4}$$

The payment rule [27] is given by

$$p_i(\hat{b}_i) = \xi_i(\hat{b}_i) - \left(\frac{1}{n-1} \sum_{j \neq i} \xi_j(\hat{b}_j)\right) \tag{5}$$

The cloud vendor i receives payment $\xi(\hat{b}_i)$ and each contributes an equal $\frac{1}{n-1}$ of its share. Hence, cloud vendor i's net transfer is $\xi_i(\hat{b}_i) - (\frac{1}{n-1}) \sum_{j \neq i} \xi_j(\hat{b}_i)$.

Algorithm 2 gives pseudocode of C-BIC mechanism.

In C-BIC, each cloud vendor pays a participation fee, but only the winner gets payment. Hence, the procurement cost is less than C-DSIC. However, the other cloud vendors suffer a loss merely by paying participation fee. Since the allocation rules of C-DSIC and C-BIC are the same, C-BIC is also allocative efficient. The C-BIC mechanism cannot guarantee individual rationality. This is an important property— even though ex ante individual rationality is preserved, interim individual rationality is not preserved. This implies that the cloud vendors suffer a loss if they withdraw from the auction after they submit bids.

Algorithm 2: C-BIC

Input : Reported bids $\hat{b}_1, \hat{b}_2, \ldots, \hat{b}_n$
Output: Winner and payments for participants $(p_1, p_2, \ldots, p_n)$

1 $min \leftarrow \infty$;
2 $winner \leftarrow 0$;
3 **for** $i \leftarrow 1$ **to** n **do**
4 $\quad$ **if** $(\frac{\hat{c}_i}{\hat{q}_i}) < min$ **then** $min \leftarrow \frac{\hat{c}_i}{\hat{q}_i}$;
5 $\quad$ $winner \leftarrow i$;
6 **end**
7 **for** $i \leftarrow 1$ **to** n **do**
8 $\quad$ // Pay each cloud vendor i
9 $\quad$ // based on (4)   and (5)
10 $\quad$ $\xi_i(\hat{b}_i) \leftarrow \mathbb{E}_{\hat{b}_{-i}} [\sum_{i \neq j} c_j(a_j(\hat{b}_i, b_j))]$;
11 $\quad$ $p_i(\hat{b}_i) \leftarrow \xi_i(\hat{b}_j) - \left(\frac{1}{n-1} \sum_{j \neq i} \xi_j(\hat{b}_j)\right)$;
12 **end**

3.3 Cloud-Optimal Mechanism (C-OPT)

The C-DSIC mechanism is not budget balanced. On the other hand, even though the C-BSIC overcomes this limitation, it is not <u>interim</u> individual rational. Hence, we propose the C-OPT mechanism to address limitation of both mechanisms. The design of an optimal auction is not trivial.

Iyengar and Kumar [15] propose an optimal mechanism for procurement auctions for suppliers who have finite production capacity (capacitated suppliers). Let X_i and T_i be the expected allocation and payment, respectively. Iyengar and Kumar [15] give the following definitions:

Definition 5 The offered expected surplus for a procurement mechanism (a,p) is defined as $\rho_i(\hat{c}_i, \hat{q}_i) = T_i(\hat{c}_i, \hat{q}_i) - \hat{c}_i X_i(\hat{c}_i, \hat{q}_i)$. It is the expected transfer payment when the vendor i bids $(\hat{c}_i, \hat{q}_i)$.

Definition 6 The <u>expected surplus</u> of a vendor i when the bid is $\hat{b}_i = (\hat{c}_i, \hat{q}_i)$ is defined as $\pi_i(\hat{c}_i, \hat{q}_i) = T_i(\hat{c}_i, \hat{q}_i) - c_i X_i(\hat{c}_i, \hat{q}_i)$.
Also,
$$\pi_i(\hat{c}_i, \hat{q}_i) = \pi_i(\hat{c}_i, \hat{q}_i) + (c_i - \hat{c}_i)X_i(\hat{c}_i, \hat{q}_i)$$
In an incentive compatible mechanism, the <u>true surplus</u> π_i is equal to offered surplus.

In simple terms, the <u>expected surplus</u> is the difference between what the cloud vendor willing to get and what it actually gets. Myerson [11] defines a virtual parameter for ranking the buyers, called <u>virtual cost</u>.

Definition 7 The <u>virtual cost</u> is defined as $H_i(c_i, q_i) = c_i + \frac{F_i(\frac{c_i}{q_i})}{f_i(\frac{c_i}{q_i})}$

In order to develop an optimal mechanism, we assume the following [15]:

- the joint distribution function $\Phi_i(c_i, q_i)$ is completely defined; and
- the virtual cost function H_i is non-decreasing in both c_i and q_i.

Let $\pi(g, h)$ be the total expected profit of the user. The goal of an optimal mechanism is to maximize $\pi(g, h) = \mathbb{E}[\mathbb{R} - \sum_{i=1}^{n} h_i(b)]$, subject to

1. individual rationality: the expected interim surplus for each cloud vendor is nonnegative, i.e., $\pi_i(b_i) \geq 0$; and
2. bayesian incentive compatibility: the truth elicitation should be weakly dominant strategy for all cloud vendors, i.e., $\mathbb{E}_{b_{-i}}[h_i(b_i, b_{-i}) - c_i g_i(b_i, b_{-i})] \geq \mathbb{E}_{b_{-i}}[h_i(\hat{b}_i, b_{-i}) - c_i g_i(\hat{b}_i, b_{-i})]$, $\forall i \in N, \forall b_i, \hat{b}_i \in \Theta_i$.

By Myerson [11, 15], a mechanism that satisfies the above constraints and maximizes cloud user profit is optimal. Also, Myerson assumes unit demand. In our model, the cloud user has QoS requirement, and QoS plays important role in the selection of cloud vendor. This multidimensional attribute of cloud vendors makes this a non-trivial problem.

The properties of an optimal procurement mechanism [15] with capacitated suppliers are:

1. The expected allocation $X_i(c_i, q_i)$ is non-increasing in the cost parameter $c_i \forall$ suppliers.
2. The offered surplus $\rho_i(\hat{c}_i, \hat{q}_i)$ is of the form

$$\rho_i(\hat{c}_i, \hat{q}_i) = \rho_i(\bar{c}, \hat{q}) + \int_{\hat{c}_i}^{\bar{c}} X_i(y, \hat{q}_i).$$

The proofs of the above properties are given by Iyengar and Kumar [15].
The C-OPT mechanism satisfies the above properties [1].

The expected surplus of the winning vendor is called the information rent of the vendor [28]. Classically, surpluses like supplier surplus and consumer surplus are examples of information rent.

Lemma 1 *The offered surplus $\rho_i(\hat{c}_i, \hat{q}_i)$ in C-OPT mechanism is of the form*
$$\rho_i(\hat{c}_i, \hat{q}_i) = \rho_i(\bar{c}, \hat{q}) + \int_{\hat{c}_i}^{\bar{c}} X_i(y, \hat{q}_i)$$

The allocation rule is given by (6).

$$a_i(\hat{b}) = \begin{cases} 1 & \text{if } H_i = \min(H_1, H_2, \ldots, H_n) \\ 0 & \text{otherwise} \end{cases} \tag{6}$$

By (6), the cloud vendor i whose virtual cost H is minimum is declared the winner. The payment rule is given by the following.

$$p_i(\hat{b}_i) = c_i a_i(\hat{b}) + \int_{c_i}^{\bar{c}} X_i(y, \hat{q}_i) dy \tag{7}$$

Algorithm 3 gives pseudocode of C-OPT mechanism.

Algorithm 3: C-OPT

Input : Reported bids $\hat{b}_1, \hat{b}_2, \ldots, \hat{b}_n$
Output: Winner and payments for participants $(p_1, p_2, \ldots, p_n)$

1 $min \leftarrow \infty$;
2 $winner \leftarrow 0$;
3 **for** $i \leftarrow 1$ **to** n **do**
4 　 Compute H_i;
5 　 **if** $(H_i < min)$ **then** $min \leftarrow H_i$;
6 　 $winner \leftarrow i$;
7 **end**
8 **for** $i \leftarrow 1$ **to** n **do**
9 　 // Pay each cloud vendor i
10 　 // based on (7)
11 　 $p_i(\hat{b}_i) \leftarrow c_i a_i(\hat{b}) + \int_{c_i}^{\bar{c}} X_i(y, \hat{q}_i) dy$
12 **end**

Theorem 1 *The C-OPT mechanism with allocation rule (6) and payment rule (7) is Bayesian incentive compatible, individually rational and revenue maximizing.*

C-OPT is an optimal mechanism and is more generic due to the ability to handle asymmetric cloud vendors. Also, in realistic scenarios, different cloud vendors may have different price distributions. C-OPT reduces to C-DSIC under the following conditions:

- Cloud vendors are symmetric.
- The joint distribution function Φ is regular.

C-DSIC is susceptible to bidder collusion. On the other hand, non-winners lose money in C-BIC. C-OPT not only overcomes limitation but also implements strengths of other mechanisms (budget balance and BIC). Hence, C-OPT is suitable in a larger set of real world contexts than C-DSIC and C-BIC.

These mechanisms have linear time complexities. Hence, can be applied in real time.

3.4 Combinatorial Auctions in Cloud

In a federated or hybrid cloud [22], the cloud user has the option of procuring resources from different cloud vendors. Hence, combinatorial auctions are appropriate [2]. In combinatorial auctions, the winner determination is a non-trivial task [29]. In reality, there are a large number of cloud vendors. Hence, a scalable solution for performing combinatorial auctions in a cloud is non-trivial.

Bids are normalized to have integer values. In the initial step, the set of resources is divided such that no bid includes resources from more than one subset. The set of bids is represented as tree nodes. The tree nodes are labeled as either winning or losing. The tree is searched using depth-first search, and this is performed on each subset to speedup search. $\mathcal{CA}$ uses an upper threshold on the revenue the unallocated resources can contribute. If the current solution is not better than the optimal solution, $\mathcal{CA}$ prunes the search path. An LP formulation can be used for estimating the upper threshold. After estimating the upper threshold, an integer relaxation is applied where we can either accept the bid completely, or reject the bid completely.

Algorithm 4 gives the detailed pseudocode [2].

This algorithm does not make copies of the LP table, but incrementally adds (or: deletes) rows from the LP table as bids are removed (or: re-inserted) into G as the search proceeds down a path (or: backtracks). Hence, it has linear time complexity. The proof is given by Sandholm and Suri [30]. Therefore, our algorithm can run in real time.

3.5 Experimental Results

As far we know, there is a lack of tools for automating cloud vendor selection. Usually, the cloud vendor with low cost is selected. Hence, we performed simulation with our in-house tool. Our simulation approach is as follows:

1. The resource pricing of cloud vendors is different. We performed distribution fitting on popular webservice and result revealed that prices are lognormally distributed.
2. QoS is an emanating concept in cloud. There is yet a lack of standard models about the QoS and its properties in the context of cloud. Hence, we perform simulations with different distributions of QoS. We have considered both uniform and normal distribution.
3. In our simulation, we do not take the cloud resource type (SaaS, IaaS, etc.) into account, since our aim is to evaluate the proposed mechanism.
4. Currently, there is a lack of any standard toolkit for evaluating mechanisms in cloud. Hence, we implemented our simulation using Java based on the equations presented in this work, without compromising on cloud properties.

The results of earlier work [1] (where a graphical representation may also be seen) are summarized here. Table 2 shows the procurement cost to the user in C-DSIC, C-BIC and C-OPT for a different number of cloud vendors in the scenario 1. In this scenario, QoS is uniformly distributed. Table 3 shows the procurement cost in scenario 2 where QoS is normally distributed.

The observations made in respect of auction-based allocation [1, 2] are summarized below:

1. The payment made is inversely proportional to a number of cloud vendors, irrespective of the mechanism implemented.
2. The nature of the procurement costs is similar in both scenarios.

Algorithm 4: $\mathcal{CA}\,(G, g, min)$

Input : Bid Graph G, revenue generated from winning bids g, minimum revenue min per $\mathcal{CA}$
Output: Set of winning bids F_{opt_solved}

1 **if** $|E| = \frac{n(n-1)}{2}$ **then**
2 $\quad$ $f_{opt} \leftarrow \max B$;
3 $\quad$ return f_{opt} ;
4 **end**
5 **if** $|E| = 0$ **then**
6 $\quad$ Accept all the remaining bids;
7 $\quad$ update f_{opt} and return f_{opt};
8 **end**
9 FindConnectedComponents$(\underline{G, C})$;
10 $\alpha \leftarrow |C|$;
11 // ϵ is the number of components
12 **for** $i \leftarrow 1$ **to** ϵ **do**
13 $\quad$ calculate an upper threshold $(UT)_i$;
14 **end**
15 **if** $\sum_{i=1}^{\epsilon} (UT)_i \leq min$ **then**
16 $\quad$ return 0;
17 **end**
18 Apply *Integer Relaxation*;
19 **for** $i \leftarrow 1$ **to** ϵ **do**
20 $\quad$ calculate lower threshold $(LT)_i$;
21 **end**
22 $\triangle \leftarrow g + \sum_{i=1}^{\epsilon} (LT)_i - f_{opt}$;
23 **if** $\triangle > 0$ **then**
24 $\quad$ $f_{opt} \leftarrow f_{opt} + \triangle; min \leftarrow min + \triangle$;
25 **end**
26 **if** $n < 1$ **then**
27 $\quad$ Choose next bid B_k to branch on ;
28 $\quad$ $f_{opt\_old} \leftarrow f_{opt}; f_{in} \leftarrow \mathcal{CA}(G, g + p_k, min - p_k)$;
29 $\quad$ $min \leftarrow min + (f_{in} - f_{opt\_old})$;
30 $\quad$ $\forall B_j$ s.t. $B_j \neq B_k$ and $S_j \cap S_k \neq \emptyset, G \leftarrow G \cup B_k$;
31 $\quad$ $f_{opt\_old} \leftarrow f_{opt}; f_{out} \leftarrow \mathcal{CA}(G, g, min)$;
32 $\quad$ $min \leftarrow min + (f_{in} - f_{opt\_old})$;
33 $\quad$ Return $max(f_{in}, fout)$;
34 **end**
35 $F_{opt\_solved} \leftarrow 0; H_{unsloved} \leftarrow \sum_{i=1}^{c} (UT)_i$;
36 $L_{unsloved} \leftarrow \sum_{i=1}^{c} (LT)_i$;
37 **for** each component $c_i \in C$ **do**
38 $\quad$ **if** $F_{opt\_solved} + H_{unsloved} \leq min$ **then**
39 $\quad\quad$ return 0;
40 $\quad$ **end**
41 $\quad$ $t_i' \leftarrow F_{opt\_solved} + (L_{unsloved} - (LT)_i)$;
42 $\quad$ $f_{opt\_old} \leftarrow f_{opt}$;
43 $\quad$ $f_{opt\_i} \leftarrow \mathcal{CA}(G_i, g + t_i', min - t_i')$;
44 $\quad$ $min \leftarrow min + (f_{opt\_old} - f_{opt})$;
45 $\quad$ $F_{opt\_solved} \leftarrow F_{opt\_solved} + f_{opt\_i}; H_{unsloved} \leftarrow H_{unsloved} - H_i$;
46 $\quad$ $H_{unsloved} \leftarrow H_{unsloved} - H_i$;
47 **end**
48 return F_{opt_solved}

Algorithm 5: FindConnectedComponents(G, C)

Input : Bid Graph G
Output: Set of components $C = \{c_1, c_2, \ldots, c_n\}$

```
1 // DFS annotates each vertex with discover and finishing time
2 DFS(G);
3 // In undirected graph G, G^T = G
4 // Consider vertices in decreasing finishing time
5 DFS(G);
6 Vertices in each tree of the depth-first forest is a separate component;
```

Table 2 Procurement costs in scenario 1

Cloud vendors	Procurement cost ($)		
	C-DSIC	C-BIC	C-OPT
10	289.62	225.12	1005.16
20	243.32	107.02	616.56
30	475.42	67.65	487.03
40	254.71	57.44	272.45
50	165.87	46.97	232.82
100	91.95	26.27	123.71
200	54.79	16.36	54.16
300	28.65	10.29	40.85
400	28.67	7.35	34.19
500	44.16	6.17	30.2

Table 3 Procurement costs in scenario 2

Cloud vendors	Procurement cost ($)		
	C-DSIC	C-BIC	C-OPT
10	243.32	225.12	1005.17
20	227.96	107.03	616.57
30	227.96	68.86	487.03
40	272.39	52.82	272.45
50	165.87	46.47	232.82
100	57.59	26.16	123.71
200	36.51	16.36	54.16
300	14.23	10.24	40.85
400	28.65	7.3	34.19
500	36.77	4.16	30.12

3. The payment in C-BIC decreases more rapidly compared to other methods with an increase in the number of cloud vendors, in both the scenarios. As the number of cloud vendors increases, C-BIC outperforms both C-DSIC and C-OPT.
4. In C-DSIC, the marginal contribution is the difference between the lowest and second lowest costs. If the marginal contribution is low, then the procurement cost becomes high. In C-OPT, incentive is calculated as the difference between quoted cost and highest valuation. Hence, the incentive decreases as the quoted cost approaches highest cost valuation. Therefore the procurement cost in C-DSIC is greater than C-OPT. This is the case where marginal contribution is less but the quoted cost nears the highest cost valuation.
5. The C-OPT procurement cost depends on the interval of the cost.
6. In sequential auctions, the cost per resource increases sequentially with the number of resources to. But that is not the case in combinatorial auctions.
7. The CABOB algorithm is scalable and was tested using various distributions like random, uniform, decay and CATS (Combinatorial Auction Test Suite) [31].

3.6 Cloud Broker Procurement Module

The cloud broker is an intermediary between cloud user and cloud vendor. The resource procurement mechanism is presented elsewhere [1, 2].

Consider a use case of cloud application hosting. There are a lot of cloud vendors, with non-uniform specifications; comparing these specifications manually is very complex. So it is very challenging for an organization to select an appropriate cloud vendor. This is especially true in case of a large number of cloud vendors. Hence, the selection of cloud vendors must be automated. Figure 1 is the activity diagram of the procurement module of a cloud broker proposed in [1].

The main components of the procurement module are:

- User interface: The cloud vendor presents the requirements to the cloud broker.
- Authentication Manager: This authenticates the cloud user using security methods like Radius, etc.
- Resource requirement manager: This component performs initial screening of the cloud user requirements. After validation, the requirements are broadcasted to the cloud vendors.
- Auction Manager: This is the core component of the procurement module to implement the procurement mechanisms [1, 2]. The winner is determined and the payment is calculated based on the implemented mechanism. Finally, both the user and winner are notified.

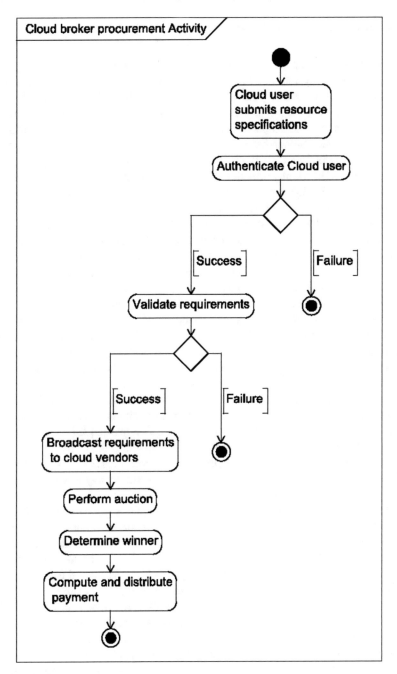

Fig. 1 Flow of cloud broker procurement

4 Cloud Resource Allocation Using Game Theory

Under-utilization of resources in server farms and on the cloud leads to heavy monetary losses. These systems are huge and cost billions, and manage commerce worth even more. The uncertainty principle of game theory is useful to model coalitions of resources in such large distributed systems profitably. Coalitions are formed to satisfy requests that need capabilities than what a single resource host can provide. We devise a resource allocation mechanism for tasks with unknown arrival patterns. Coalition formation modeled as a two-player zero-sum game and solving the payoff matrix using the uncertainty principle of game theory avoids the application of integer programming which has higher computational complexity. This resource allocation mechanism, has better performance in our experiments requiring lesser time for task allocation, reduced wastage of unused resources, and better satisfaction of requests.

Resource allocation [32] in a distributed computing environment such as server farms and clouds which offer infrastructure as a service (IaaS), aims at mapping the client resource requirements for processors, memory, storage, etc., with the provider's infrastructure, while ensuring minimum wastage and complete task performance. Service requirements may not always be limited to the capacity of a single machine, and thus may need multitude of machines to cooperate to provide the needed service. Coalitions of servers in a server farm, and virtualization of resources on the cloud, are means to ensure scalable and economic resource allocation and management. As we speak of server farms and clouds which consist of tens of thousands of machines (or even more), collating resources to service tasks is a complex optimization problem.

Traditional approaches to solve optimization problems such as using integer programming have a higher complexity computationally and are untractable if we increase the number of host machines and (or) task requests [33]. Game-theoretic approaches simplify optimization problems by modeling the scenario as a game between two or more players. Solving the game's payoff matrix provides the respective strategies to be taken by the players to ensure maximum payoff which translates to the solution to the optimization problem.

Székely and Rizzo proposed the uncertainty principle of game theory [5] to obtain near-to-optimal solutions of two-player zero-sum games without actually solving the payoff matrix. It is possible to model server coalition formation as multiple two-player zero-sum games, each involving the central authority (to which the task requests arrive from users) and a particular agent (which possesses the resources) [6, 7, 33] and use the uncertainty principle of game theory to find coalitions providing benefits in terms of less wastage of resources. In this section the applications of this theory to two scenarios, in which each agent can participate in a *i*. single coalition, and *ii*. more than one coalition, are described. The two scenarios are applied on a server farm and the cloud, respectively. Results [7] suggest the efficacy of the approach in terms of **task allocation time, wastage of resources, and request satisfaction**.

4.1 Modeling Multiagent Coalition Formation Using Game Theory

Coalition formation among multiple agents has to occur when a requested task requires capabilities beyond those of a single agent. Agents have to cooperate and share resources within their coalition/group, which then is able to address the resource requirements. A typical multiagent system which we consider for coalition formation is described below.

- **Agents**, S_i form a set of n agents, host the resources. The resource capacity of an agent is denoted by its capability vector, B_{S_i}. The capability vector defines the quantity of each resource the agent holds. These resources in a distributed computing environment could be compute power, memory, storage etc.
- **Tasks**, T_j form a set of m tasks. Each task has a resource requirement vector, which we call the necessities vector, N_{T_j}. The quantity of minimum resources required to complete a task is defined by the necessity vector.
- **Coalitions**, C_l, are formed by agent combination. The resource capability of a coalition, D_{C_l}, is defined by the combined capability of its member agents, i.e., $D_{C_l} = \sum_{\forall H_i \in C_l} B_{S_i}$. If all the member agents are interested and agree to form it, we say that the coalition becomes feasible.
- **Payoff Matrix**, A is a table which depicts the payoff which the opponent player/agent has to pay to the winner, in case he/she loses. Each task/request is associated with a payoff, P_{T_k} which is proportional to its resource requirements ($P_{T_k} \propto N_{T_k}$). This payoff is rewarded to the coalition which services the task T_k. Each member agent of the coalition receives a part of P_{T_k} depending on its resource contribution to the coalition (($\mathbb{P}_{S_i}, C_l, T_j) \propto (B_{S_i}, P_{T_j})$). Higher an agent's contribution, higher is its payoff share.

The tasks as mentioned above may require numerous of such resources. Coalitions of agents could satisfy such requests if their combined capability exceeds the task requirements (i.e., $N_{G_k} \sqsubseteq D_{C_l}$). If coalitions are formed prior to the task request arrival, the scalability concerns of a large distributed system can be addressed, while continuing to serve requests in a timely fashion. In order to accomplish this, we assume that while the exact task is unknown until it arrives, the set of tasks that can be possibly allotted to and satisfied by the agents are known. From the task list available to the agents, they could compute the payoff they could expect for being part of a coalition. Comparing the expected payoffs across coalitions and the tasks that they serve, the agents could derive a preference list. A coalition offering higher payoff to an agent features higher up in its preference list.

This scenario can be viewed as each agent playing a game with task coordinator (the central authority) for choosing its optimal strategy, i.e., its <u>favored coalition</u>. The coordinator, in turn, has to find its optimal strategy, i.e., has to ensure that the largest possible number of requests can be serviced. The game formulation involves two players (agent and task coordinator), and is a zero-sum game as the payoff gained by one player is lost by the opponent. Each agent-coordinator combination has a payoff matrix. The optimal strategies of the players are computed by solving the payoff matrix. As each agent is selfish, it tries to forms its preferred coalition and makes the task coordinator pay. Through iterative dominance (removal of the dominated strategies), a list of favored coalitions can be computed. Though each agent computes its coalition list, a coalition materializes only after a feasibility check to ensure that all other members are interested in forming the coalition. We call the coalitions that have passed the feasibility test but have not yet assigned to service a task as open coalitions. Once the task arrives, an open coalition may easily be allocated to service the task, whereby it becomes a servicing coalition.

Since agents do not have prior knowledge of the exact task specifications, and are restricted to a possible task list, the computation of the preference list is not straightforward. The task coordinator of the multiagent system would want that the maximum requests be serviced, in contrast to the agents which would want merely to be part of such coalitions that maximize their own payoffs. The pure strategies of the agents correspond to the possible coalitions they can be part of and that of the coordinator are the tasks that can be serviced. In the absence of exact task specifications prior to request arrival, agents and the coordinator are ignorant of each other's pure strategies. This results in a situation where a mixed strategy is favorable. Each player uses a mixed strategy. A mixed strategy is a probability distribution assumed by the player to choose randomly among its available pure strategies to avoid predictability. However, obtaining optimal mixed strategies for players is computationally hard and becomes intractable as the number of players and their strategies increase [5, 33].

4.2 Solving Multiagent Coalition Formation Using the Uncertainty Principle of Game Theory

Heisenberg's uncertainty principle [34] is a well-known result in physics. Its analog in game theory gives a lower bound on the entropy of optimal strategies of zero-sum games [5, 7]. The randomness of the optimal strategies in zero-sum games is given in terms of δ, the commutator, of maximum and minimum of the payoff matrix A (whose entries are identified as $a_{w,z}$). The min and max operators are nonlinear and the commutator is the extent of commutativity between them. The commutator is defined as

$$\delta = \left(\min_z \max_w - \max_w \min_z \right) a_{w,z}. \tag{8}$$

Theorem 2 (Székely and Rizzo [5]) *If $G(\delta)$ denotes the class of two-player, finite, zero-sum games with commutator coefficient δ and $h(\delta)$ is the entropy of the two-*

point distribution $(\frac{1}{1+\delta}, \frac{\delta}{1+\delta})$, *then a lower bound for entropies of optimal solutions* (x^*, y^*) *of games in* $G(\delta)$ *is given by*

$$\min(H(x*), H(y*)) \geq h(\delta) \tag{9}$$

Moreover, $h(\delta)$ *is the greatest lower bound.*   □

We apply the uncertainty principle of game theory for zero-sum games to prioritize coalitions for agents. When $(\delta = 0)$, a saddle point exists, the optimal strategy for each player can be obtained via iterative removal of dominated strategies. The optimal strategy in this case is a pure strategy. When the commutator is positive $(\delta > 0)$, a mixed strategy is optimal, but each player is unsure of the other player's optimal mixed strategy. The probability mass when concentrated on fewer mixed strategies results in a smaller entropy. The easiest mixed strategies to analyze are of two-point distributions. The minimum entropy $h(\delta)$ occurs for the particular two-point distribution $\left(\frac{1}{1+\delta}, \frac{\delta}{1+\delta}\right)$. This means that the optimal mixed strategy is least random when it is supported on two points with probabilities $\left(\frac{1}{1+\delta} \text{ and } \frac{\delta}{1+\delta}\right)$ [5] exactly. The uncertainty principle of game theory offers a way to find a near-optimal mixed strategy without actually solving the payoff matrix. Each player obtains a close to optimal solution using this approach because it is guaranteed of an expected payoff above a well-defined lower bound (see Theorem 2).

In each agent-coordinator game, when the value of the commutator is greater than 0, two coalitions having probabilities, $\frac{\delta}{1+\delta}$ and $\frac{1}{1+\delta}$ are added the preference list of an agent. The game is repeated with the rest of the coalitions in the next iteration to find the next best coalitions. This process is repeated for adding all the possible coalitions featuring that agent in the order of preference. We form preference lists for individual agents, rather than single near-optimal coalitions, because an agent's most preferred coalition may not be preferred by the other members. The rationale behind creating a preference list is to manage with a lookup of the list to check for the feasibility of the next coalition and to avoid full computation yet again. Ranking coalitions is akin to the ordering the candidates in the Gale-Shapley algorithm for stable marriage [35]. Due to the non-deterministic nature and type of task requests, we may assume that saddle points rarely occur without loss of generality with random payoff matrices [5]. Applying the uncertainty principle of game theory results in errors as low as 0.1 in 98 percent of the games with random matrices [5].

4.3 Applications

The coalition formation problem is solved using the uncertainty principle of game theory for resource allocation in server farms [6]. This in turn leads to work for virtual machine allocation on the cloud [7]. The descriptions of the two problems (refer Table 4) and their solutions are given below.

Table 4 Example applications

Specifications	One fixed size open coalition	Multiple flexible size open coalitions
Agents	The n servers of the data center act as the n agents. Each server agent has a capability in terms of the resources they host; their number of processor cores, physical memory and storage. The agents could be in any of the four states, i. available (not yet in a coalition) ii. open coalition (not yet assigned a task) iii. servicing coalition (servicing a request) iv) unavailable	The n host machines on the cloud act as the n agents. Each host machine has a capability in terms of their number of processor cores, physical memory and storage. The agents could be in any of the four states, i) available (not yet in a coalition) ii) open coalition (not yet assigned a task) iii) servicing coalition (servicing a request) iv) unavailable. The host machines form coalitions to cater the VM requests
Opponent	We assume that the task scheduler of the data center is the other player in the game of coalition formation	We assume that the task allocator of the cloud is the other player in the game of coalition formation for VM allocation
Tasks	The m tasks that the data center is capable of handling is specified by the quantity of resources they require. A typical request would look like $\mathcal{R} = \langle cores, memory, storage \rangle$ describing the number of cores, quantity of memory and storage required to carry out the task	The m tasks that the cloud is capable of handling is specified by the number of VMs of a particular configuration that they require. It is common practice in clouds that the available VM configurations are previously defined. The clients may then request for the number of VMs of the respective configurations. A typical request would look like $\mathcal{R} = \langle no_{VM1}, no_{VM2}, \dots no_{VMs} \rangle$ where the components are the number of VMs of each available configuration required to service the request
Coalitions	The server agents which may be incapable of serving a specific request on their own, form coalitions so that their combined capabilities could serve the request. The servers would prefer to be in coalitions that would give them higher payoffs as they are monitored by agents	Coalitions of host machines are formed so that the number of VMs required for a task could be collectively hosted on them. The host machines prefer coalition offering higher payoffs and that require lesser communication cost, i.e, closely placed VMs are better
Payoff Matrix	Each server agent-task scheduler combination forms a payoff matrix. The strategies for the server agents are the coalitions and that of the task scheduler are the tasks. The solution of the payoff matrix gives the optimal coalition rewarding the highest payoff to the agent	Each host machine-task allocator combination forms a payoff matrix. The strategies for each of the players are the same as the other application. In payoff calculation, we also consider the nearness of the machines hosting the VMs. Higher payoffs are rewarded to the host machine coalitions that are closer to each other

One Agent In A Fixed Size Open Coalition

In the problem of resource allocation for requests that come to a server farm, the coalition formation game happens between the task scheduler at the data center and the individual servers. It is assumed that each server acts as an agent for playing the two-player zero-sum game against the task scheduler.

It is assumed that each agent can be part of only a single open coalition and that each coalition could only be of a fixed size, k. This means that after forming the preferred coalition which is feasible, the agent is not available to form further coalitions. Once a coalition is assigned a task to be served, it is dispersed only after completion of that task.

One Agent In Flexibly Sized Multiple Open Coalitions

In the problem of virtual machine (VM) allocation for VM requests that come to a cloud, the coalition formation game happens between the task allocator at the cloud, and each individual host machine. It is assumed that each host machine acts as an agent for playing the two-player zero-sum game with the task allocator. An example of this set up is described for the Windows Azure [36] cloud is described in our paper [7] on resource allocation for the cloud.

The virtual machine allocation proposed using this approach has the benefit of topology awareness, as closely placed VMs can be preferred for coalitions. This approach is also demand-aware, in the sense that since we know the configurations of VMs that can be requested, coalitions to host VMs can be formed even before the actual request is available. We define a number for each of the host machines called the <u>maximum number of simultaneous coalitions</u>, defining the upper limit of the concurrent coalitions that it can be part of. Unlike the other applications, an agent is still available to form coalitions when it is servicing a request or in an open coalition, provided the number of coalitions does not exceed the maximum. Also, the restriction we placed on the number of agents that could be part of a coalition is lifted. This allows host machines to be in coalitions with varied number of members. However, in practice, it is always observed that the sizes remain within a specified bound. This ensures that different coalition sizes are possible, while remaining within pre-specified limits.

4.4   Algorithms

There are two major steps in the formation of open coalitions [6].

1. **Calculate coalition preference**: Let t denote the number of ready agents. An agent can choose its coalition partners from $\binom{t-1}{r-1}$ possibilities to form a coalition of size r. Next, we calculate the expected payoff. The expected payoffs are arranged in a matrix against the tasks from the opponent. The resulting two-player zero-sum games are solved using the uncertainty principle of game theory. We build the preference list that indicates an agent's favored order to form the coalitions. Two high-payoff coalitions with least entropy as specified by Theorem 2

are added to the preference list in each iteration of the game between the agent and the central authority.

2. **Negotiation step**: In this step, the agents check if their coalitions are feasible according to the order in their preference list. All agents of a coalition, C_l agree to be part of it for the coalition to become feasible. If an agent's preferred coalition is not agreeable to others in it, the next one from its preference list is tried. C_l becomes an open coalition, on passing the feasibility check. In the server farm scenario, an agent is removed from the set of available agents on forming an open coalition. However, in the cloud scenario, after a machine participates in the maximum permissible number of open coalitions, it ceases to be available and is cleared from the list of ready machines. Once an agent is removed from the set of available agents, the other available agents remove those coalitions involving the not-ready agents.

Once a task is assigned to an open coalition, the agents cannot leave the coalition until the task completion. Once formed, coalitions remain fixed in size. If none of the existing open coalitions are capable of serving a task request when it arrives, the central authority allocates an agent or group of ready agents. It has to ensure that the necessary requirements of a task are met for this sudden demand. A coalition is dissolved after task completion, and agents in that coalition update their coalitions list. All constituent agents become available after the coalition dissolution.

Detailed descriptions of the algorithms, their proofs of correctness, and message complexity analyses may be found elsewhere [6, 7].

4.5 Open Coalition Formation

The Open Coalition Formation Algorithm (Algorithm 6) computes the set of available agents, in lines 2 to 4. In line 6, For each available agent, a set of coalitions that are feasible is computed. Payoff computation for a particular coalition happens in line 9. Based on the payoffs calculated in line 9, each agent computes a preference list of coalitions in line 10. The negotiation step to check a coalition's feasibility among the member agents happens in line 18. Lines 19–27 carry out the coalition formation. On reaching the maximum list of participatable open coalitions, it is removed in lines 31–36. If the agent can participate in only one open coalition, its number of simultaneous coalitions is 1. The preference lists are updated for each agent in lines 37–39. The coalitions involving unavailable agents are removed here.

4.6 Coalition Dissolution

Before dissolving a coalition, the task that it is being serviced by it needs to be completed (line 2). We need the coalition and its assigned task as inputs to Algorithm 7. Once the algorithm verifies that the assigned task is complete, the coalition is dis-

---

Algorithm 6: Open Coalition Formation Algorithm

Data: available_agents
Data: total_agents
Result: set_coalitions

1 **begin** openCoalitionFormationAlgorithm
2   **foreach** agent in total_agents **do**
3   **if** agent.agentstatus=available **then**
4   add(available_agents, agent)
5   **end**
6   **end**
7   **foreach** agent in available_agents **do**
8   agent.list_potential_coalitions ← computeCoalitions(agent)
9   agent.payoff_matrix ← computePayoffMatrix(agent.list_potential_coalitions)
10   agent.list_preference ← computePrefernceList(agent.payoff_matrix)
11   **end**
12   **while** available_agents ≠ NULL **do**
13   Counter ← 0
14   **foreach** agent in available_agents **do**
15   Counter ← Counter+1
16   agent.bestpossible ← agent.list_preference[1:Counter]
17   **foreach** coalition in agent.bestpossible **do**
18   **if** isfeasible(coalition) **then**
19   **if** agent.cur_no_coalitions < agent.max_no_coalitions **then**
20   joinCoalition(coalition, agent)
21   coalition.status ← OPEN
22   **if** agent.agentstatus=available **then**
23   changeStatus(agent, open_coalition)
24   **end**
25   agent.cur_no_coalitions ← agent.cur_no_coalitions + 1
26   add(set_coalitions,coalition)
27   **end**
28   **end**
29   **end**
30   **end**
31   **foreach** agent in available_agents **do**
32   **if** agent.cur_no_coalitions = agent.max_no_coalitions **then**
33   available_agents ← remove(available_agents, agent)
34   changeStatus(agent, max_coalition)
35   **end**
36   **end**
37   **foreach** agent in available_agents **do**
38   update(agent.list_preference)
39   **end**
40   **end**
41 **end**

---

solved and its members become available to participate in other open coalitions. This is effected by adding the dissolved coalition's member agents to the set of available agents (line 4). The capabilities of the agent that were used by the coalition to be dissolved are released (line 5). If the agent is part of no other current coalition, its status is updated to be available. Otherwise, the number of current coalitions of the agent is decremented by 1 (lines 6-12). The coalition is removed from the set of coalitions (line 14) and is dissolved finally (line 15).

Algorithm 7: Coalition Dissolving Algorithm

    Data: set_coalitions
    Data: coalition
    Data: available_agents
    Data: task
1 **begin** coalitionDissolvingAlgorithm
2   **if** task.taskstatus=COMPLETE and task.id=coalition.task_id and coalition.ID = task.coalition_id **then**
3   **foreach** agent in coalition **do**
4   add(available_agents, agent)
5   update agent.vector_capability
6   **if** agent.cur_no_coalitions = 1 **then**
7   changeStatus(agent, available)
8   **end**
9   **else**
10   changeStatus(agent, open_coalition)
11   **end**
12   agent.cur_no_coalitions ← agent.cur_no_coalitions - 1
13   **end**
14   remove(set_coalitions,coalition)
15   coalition ← NULL
16   **end**
17 **end**

4.7 Task Allocation Algorithm

In order to allocate a task to an open coalition, Algorithm 8 requires as input, the task to be allocated, G_j and the set of coalitions, $set\_coalitions$. We need to check if the necessities of the task are satisfiable by the of the capability vector of an OPEN coalition C_l. This is done by checking if $N_{G_j} \sqsubseteq D_{C_l}$ (line 3). If there is a match, the algorithm ensures that the task has not been assigned to any other coalition, before allocating the task to the matched coalition (lines 5–7). Further, the algorithm updates the coalition's status is updated to ENGAGED (line 8) and the capability vectors of the member agents (lines 9–10). If none of the open coalitions is a match, then the task allocator is asked to do a forced allocation of the task to a group of available agents (lines 16–17).

4.8 Experiments

We compare our cloud resource allocation mechanism with existing approaches such as:

  (i) RR-R: Round robin allocation, (RR), across the racks of servers, (R);
  (ii) RR-S: Round robin allocation, (RR), across the host machines, (S). Eucalyptus [37], (cf. [38]) cloud uses this method as its default policy.
 (iii) H-1: Hybrid policy of RR-S and RR-R. It prefers host machines from the same rack, but limits only to select 20 host machines from the same rack.
 (iv) H-2: Similar to H-1; only 10 servers from the same rack may be selected.

Algorithm 8: Task Allocation Algorithm

Data: task
Data: set_coalitions
1 **begin** taskallocate
2 | **foreach** coalition in coalitions_set **do**
3 | | **if** task.vector_necessity ⊑ coalition.vector_capability **then**
4 | | | **if** task.taskstatus ≠ COMPLETE **then**
5 | | | | **if** task.coalition_id=NULL and coalition.status=OPEN **then**
6 | | | | | coalition.task_id ← task.id
7 | | | | | task.coalition_id ← coalition_id
8 | | | | | coalition.coalitionstatus ← ENGAGED
9 | | | | | **foreach** agent in coalition **do**
10 | | | | | | update(host_machine.vector_capability)
11 | | | | | **end**
12 | | | | **end**
13 | | | **end**
14 | | **end**
15 | **end**
16 | **if** task.coalition_id=NULL **then**
17 | | forceallocate(task)
18 | **end**
19 **end**

We assume a virtual topology of 400 machines, with 100 machines of each configuration in our experiments [7]. The host machines with identical configurations are assumed to be placed adjacently. Their configurations are specified in terms of i. number of cores (n_{cores}) and ii. hard-disk storage (hd). The following configurations are considered: (a) n_{cores} = 1 core, hd = 125 GB disk storage; (b) n_{cores} = 2 cores, hd = 250 GB storage; (c) n_{cores} = 4 cores, hd = 500 GB storage; and (d) n_{cores} = 8 cores, hd = 1000 GB storage. The VM configurations are specified in terms of i. number of cores ($n_{vmcores}$) ii. main memory capacity (mm_{vm}) and iii. hard-disk storage (hd_{vm}). considered are: (i) Small ($n_{vmcores}$ = 1 core, mm_{vm} = 1.75 GB Memory, hd_{vm} = 0.22 TB Storage); (ii) Medium ($n_{vmcores}$ = 2 cores, mm_{vm} = 3.5 GB Memory, hd_{vm} = 0.48 TB Storage); (iii) Large ($n_{vmcores}$ = 4 cores, mm_{vm} = 7 GB Memory, hd_{vm} = 0.98 TB Storage); and (iv) Extra Large ($n_{vmcores}$ = 8 cores, mm_{vm} = 14 GB Memory, hd_{vm} = 1.99 TB Storage). The four types of task requests considered are represented as: (10, 0, 0, 0), (10, 10, 0, 0), (10, 10, 10, 0), and (10, 10, 10, 10); the first number indicates the number of small VMs needed, the second indicates the number of medium VMs needed, and so on. The three task sets considered are: (a) Task set 1: 4 task requests—one each of the four types of requests (b) Task set 2: 8 task requests—two each of the four types of requests and (c) Task set 3: 12 task requests—three instances each of the four types of requests (Figs. 2, 3, 4, 5 and 6).

Results for resource allocation on the cloud [7] suggest that this approach performs better in terms of the task allocation time, which is the time elapsed between the time a request is submitted to the cloud service provider, and the time of the resource allocation (of one or more machines to host the necessary VMs) is made.

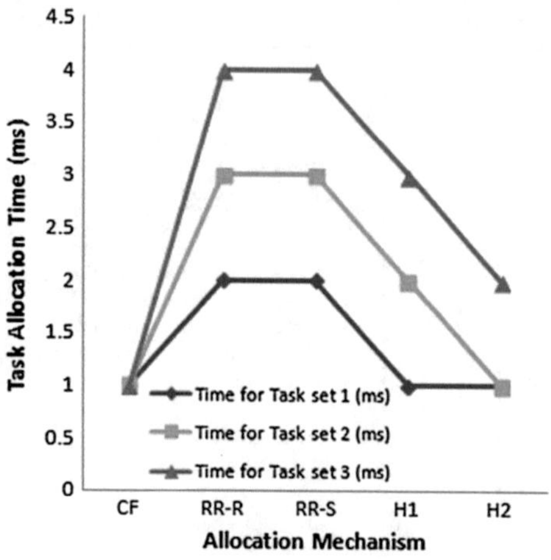

Fig. 2 Time for task allocation for the different strategies

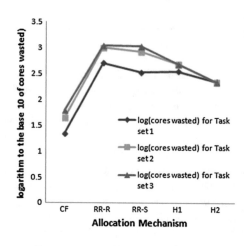

Fig. 3 Core wastage for the different strategies

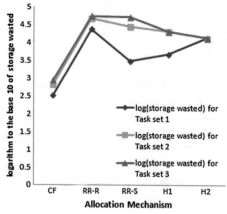

Fig. 4 Storage wastage for the different strategies

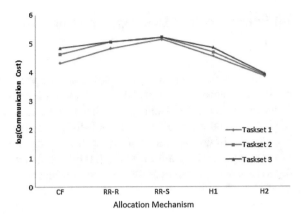

Fig. 5 Communication cost for the different strategies

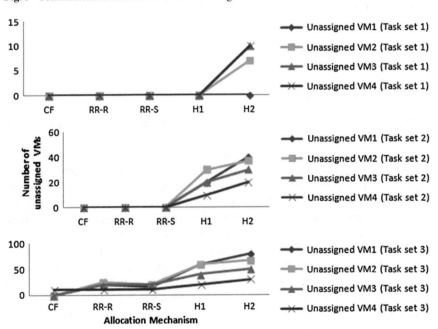

Fig. 6 Number of unassigned VMs for the different strategies

It also outperforms the other allocation mechanisms as far as the resource wastage is concerned, i.e., resources (like the number of cores and the amount of storage) wasted are far less when this approach is used. It provides good results in the experiments for comparing the number of requests satisfied (experiment details, graphs, and comparison to other approaches are given elsewhere [7]).

5   Smart and Power-Aware Metering: An Opportunity for Green IT

Cloud computing provides for ubiquitous access to shared computing resources including processor cores, network, storage, GPUs and application on demand [39]. These resources can be provisioned and managed with reduced user effort. Enterprise consumers and end users can use compute clouds for their IT needs in lieu of hosting their own servers, thereby minimizing their in-house capital expenditure (CapEx). Not only does cloud computing help minimize the CapEx but also it provides enormous opportunity to consolidate resources and maximize utilization.

Development of virtualization as the enabling technology has resulted in cloud computing gain momentum. At the core of the cloud computing paradigm are virtual machines (VMs). These virtual machines are deployed on servers hosted in data centers. Organizations typically provision multiple VM on a single bare metal server and consolidate workloads using these VMs. Doing so has multiple advantages:

   (i)   compute resource utilization is maximized;
  (ii)   server idle time is reduced;
 (iii)   power and space utilization is reduced [40]; and
  (iv)   cooling requirements are reduced.

These characteristics/advantages of cloud computing provides opportunity for Green IT.

Adopting cloud platforms in enterprise environments has its own set of challenges. These include making decisions related to resource provisioning, virtual machine migration, monitoring, metering, quality of service guarantees, workload placement and consolidation, etc. Each of these aspects have been in some way addressed by the research community. A typical cloud service management setup is shown in Fig. 7. We provide a brief introduction to each of them in the following.

VM provisioning for reduced the power consumption is discussed by Kansal et al. [41]. Workload placement strategy to achieve optimal energy consumption has been discussed by Verma et al. [42] and Uddin et al. [43]. Workload consolidation using statistical analysis has been discussed by Ganesan et al. [44]. Interested readers can refer to these to get different perspectives of the opportunity cloud computing provides to power researchers. The above works can be considered as solving the problem from end user perspective (workload consolidation and placement).

In this section, we concentrate on metering mechanisms for cloud deployments. This problem can be thought of from the service provider point of view. We like to make a note here that the resource utilization needs of consumers are dynamic (time-varying), which poses a challenge for metering resource consumption. This has an implication on the service provider, in the sense that as demand increases, the physical compute resources requirements to serve consumers also increase. As more and more physical servers are commissioned, the power consumptions in data centers increase.

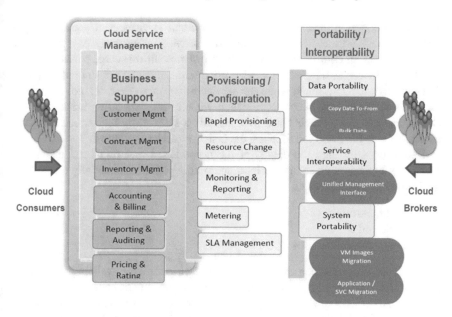

Fig. 7 Typical steps in cloud service management. Image courtesy [39]

We are thus interested in identifying a metering mechanism which considers resource utilization and power consumption. To this end, we consider two separate but related problems here. First, the different metering mechanisms in the market and their short comings. We then describe a "smart metering" mechanism akin to smart meters for electricity consumption. Second, given an input of electricity pricing from power companies, we look at the possibility of pricing cloud services based on this input.

5.1 Metering Cloud Services

On-demand resource acquisition and time-varying resource consumption are characteristics of cloud resource utilization. This, coupled with multi-tenancy [45], where multiple clients (or tenants) use resources from the same resource pool, make it extremely important that the metering mechanism for cloud services should be robust. Such metering mechanisms must consider resource utilization and appropriately bill consumers for their respective utilization. In this section, we describe a model for billing and pricing cloud services or cloud instances based on resource usage.

Prevalent mechanisms for metering and billing cloud services can be categorized as fixed-cost pay-per-use models, or spot pricing models. The former is based mostly on service level agreements (SLAs). Consumers are promised predefined service up-time and availability, and billing is based on a predefined tariff plans [46, 47]. This is the most common metering mechanism for cloud services used presently. Spot pricing models, on the other hand, are those in which consumers pay upfront or bid the highest amount payable for a cloud instance. In this case, consumers can use their instances as long as the service price remains below the amount they bid. The instances are shut down when the service price surpasses their bid. Such spot instances are useful for batch jobs, which are not time-critical and risk tolerant. Consumers can spawn their batch jobs and bid a sufficiently high amount for the instance. Once the batch job finishes, the instance can be shut down.

Before dwelling into the details of the usage-based metering mechanism, we describe a typical cloud setup. A cloud computing platform essentially consists of the following components,

  (i) cloud controller;
 (ii) nodes; and a
(iii) storage controller.

The cloud controller is responsible for monitoring resource availability, resource arbitration and deploying cloud instance in the platform. Nodes in the cloud platform are physical servers on which instances are deployed. Storage controller provides as the data store for the platform on which virtual machine images and (optionally) local storage is provided. It is possible to deploy storage controller service on the cloud controller. A typical cloud setup looks similar to Fig. 8. Cloud controller collects and maintains useful information regarding the resource usage of cloud instances. Hence, it is appropriate to place the metering module in the cloud controller.

Pricing

We propose pricing the cloud service based on the operational cost at that time instance. The base cost incurred to host the cloud service include fixed costs such as hardware, software licenses etc. We denote it by C_{base}.

The cost of running the service is a function of the load ratio (l) at time t. This is denoted as $\beta(l, t)$. Load ratio is defined as the current load against the system capacity. Using the above, we can derive the price of the cloud service at t as

$$P_t = C_{base} \times \beta(l, t) \tag{10}$$

Once the current price is determined as above, consumers are billed based on their resource utilization. We denote resource utilization at time t by u_t. Hence, the amount billed to the consumer at time t is given by $P_t \times u_t$. For n time intervals, the bill amount is given by:

$$\mathcal{B} = \sum_{t=1}^{n} P_t \times u_t \tag{11}$$

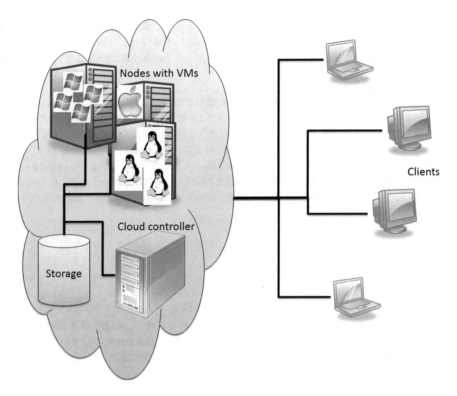

Fig. 8 A typical cloud setup

Load Prediction

Service pricing is one of the determining factors for service utilization [48]. To mimic smart meters in electricity, we provide an indicative price for cloud service based on the predicted load for the next m time intervals. We use historical monitoring data and an ARIMA model [49] for this purpose. We use p coefficients estimated from the past data and p historical data points to obtain one-step-ahead prediction. Mathematically this is given by

$$\hat{x}_t = \varphi_1 x_{t-1} + \varphi_2 x_{t-2} + L + \varphi px + t - p \tag{12}$$

where x_i are the historical utilization data points, $\hat{x}$ is the one-step-ahead prediction and φ_i are the estimated coefficients. In our implementation, we use past four hours of data (collected at 15 min intervals) to predict load at the next time instance. The empirically determined differencing order of eight gives prediction accuracy of 96%. Thus in our implementation ARIMA model reduces to AR(8). We use ARIMA implementation in the **R** statistical tool [50] for the prediction.

The predicted load from (12) is used in (11) to get the indicative resource pricing for the next time instance. This indicative price is made available to consumers to choose between continuing the service usage or terminating the instance.

Resource Monitoring

Resource monitoring is an essential component of smart metering. We can make use of data center monitoring frameworks like Nagios[1] or Hyperic SIGAR[2] to obtain resource utilization. We need utilization data for (i) the individual cloud instances, and (ii) the hosting servers. We store the monitored resource utilization and predicted price. Resource utilization is then used to bill consumers at the end of the instance lifetime or at fixed intervals (like monthly bills). Implementation details and experimental evidence of the hitherto described metering mechanism can be found in [8].

5.2 Power-Aware Metering

In the previous section, we considered the problem of metering the cloud service based on resource usage. Maintaining our focus on green IT, we discuss a metering mechanism that prices cloud services based on the input electricity cost (hence, making it power-aware) in what follows. From a service provider point of view, the operational expense (OpEx), majority of which is electricity cost, is much larger than the CapEx [51–53]. Hence, it is important to consider the input cost of electricity while pricing cloud services. With the advent and wide spread use of electricity smart meters, and time-varying electricity costs this problem is of particular interest in moving toward green IT. Power-aware metering mechanism enables compute infrastructure and smart grid managers to work together and help enforce policies to charge consumers based on the power consumed by their instances.

In order to price cloud services based on input electricity cost, we need to calculate the power consumed by each cloud instance. To this end, we describe a model for power consumption of cloud instances. Next, we describe a cost model which is aligned with the dynamic electricity price provided by a smart grid. Using these two, we generate a price model for cloud service based on the input electricity cost. A schematic representation of the power-aware cloud metering architecture is as shown in Fig. 9.

Cloud Instance Power Consumption Model

We first introduce power consumption models for servers and then follow up the discussion with power consumption models for cloud instances. Power models for servers can be categorized as (i) server component's power model and (ii) full system power model.

---

[1]http://www.nagios.org/.

[2]http://www.hyperic.com/products/sigar.

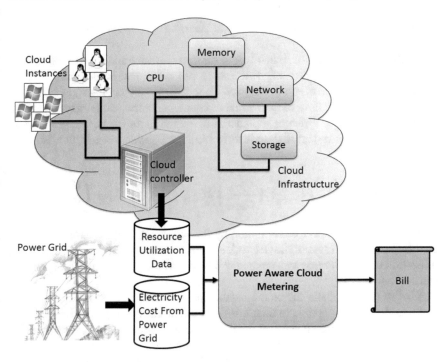

Fig. 9 Power-Aware cloud metering architecture

Researchers have obtained accurate power consumption characterization of CPU and memory subsystems using component specific power models like [54, 55]. Though accurate, these power models fall short in characterizing full system power consumption in the sense that, (i) they introduce extreme levels of approximation, and/or (ii) using different models for different subsystems increases the metering complexity. Hence we need to look at the system as a whole and determine the power consumption.

The underlying idea of full system power models is that the total power consumption is a linear sum of individual components in the system, i.e.,

$$P_{total} = P_{idle} + \alpha_1 P_{cpu} + \alpha_2 P_{mem} + \alpha_3 P_{io} + \alpha_5 P_{net} \tag{13}$$

where α_i is an appropriately selected scaling factor for each component.

Full system power modeling can be achieved by various methods which can be categorized as (i) experimental analysis and power characterization, and (ii) analytically determining power consumption.

In the first case, determining power consumption of every component individually and then obtaining the system level power consumption as a weighted sum of these components are common [56, 57]. These methods usually need an offline calibration run before it can be used in enterprise cloud metering and are specific to a particular class of systems.

Analytic models on the other hand use system power rating and resource utilization to determine the power consumed. Resource utilization can be determined using processor performance events and corresponding CPU performance counters [58]. However, in reality, polling for performance counter data frequently may reduce the system efficiency. In a different approach, the weight factor (α_i in (13)) is the ratio $\frac{resource\ utilization}{rated\ capacity}$. This model is described in [59]. The power consumption is hence given by,

$$
P_{total} = B + \left(\frac{U_{cpu}}{C_{cpu}}\right) M_{cpu} + \left(\frac{U_{mem}}{C_{mem}}\right) M_{mem} + \left(\frac{U_{io}}{C_{io}}\right) M_{io} + \left(\frac{U_{net}}{C_{net}}\right) M_{net}
$$
(14)

where B is the idle power consumption by the server, M_i is the measure of power consumption of cpu/memory/io/network subsystem when at full capacity; U is the utilization and C the capacity. A more detailed description of various power models can be found in [9].

We use (14) to obtain the cloud instance power consumption. It is to be noted that thus far it is impossible to obtain VM (or cloud instance) power consumption. Secondly, research has shown that when there is a one-to-one mapping between a virtual CPU and a physical CPU via threads, power consumption of VM follows the hosting hardware's power consumption [60]. Virtualization technologies such as kvm [61], which are commonly used in cloud computing, normally spawn VMs as independent threads on hosting hardware. The instance power model below is based on these observations.

Consider the clould instance j; let the resource utilization be u_i for some resource i. From (14), we get the cloud instance power consumption model as follows.

$$
p_j = \left(\frac{u_{cpu}}{C_{cpu}}\right) M_{cpu} + \left(\frac{u_{mem}}{C_{mem}}\right) M_{mem} + \left(\frac{u_{io}}{C_{io}}\right) M_{io} + \left(\frac{u_{net}}{C_{net}}\right) M_{net}
$$
(15)

where M_i and C_i have the same meaning as in (14). It has been shown that the network and i/o components consume negligible power [62]. Hence, they can be ignored in (15). Findings in [62] also show that processor subsystem accounts for 85% and memory accounts for $\sim$ 10% of the total system power consumption. Hence, we arrive at the following relation between memory and processor power consumption: $P_{mem} = 0.11 P_{cpu}$. Thus, (16) gives the power consumed by cloud instance j.

$$
p_j = \left(\frac{u_{cpu}}{C_{cpu}}\right) M_{cpu} + \left(\frac{u_{mem}}{C_{mem}}\right) M_{mem} = 1.11 \left(\left(\frac{u_{cpu}}{C_{cpu}}\right) M_{cpu}\right)
$$
(16)

We can arrive at the power consumed by the cloud hosting data center as, $P_{cloud} = B + \sum_j p_j$, where B is the idle power consumption of the hosting infrastructure.

Economic Model

We first derive the operating cost as a function of the electricity price (input from the power grid) and resource utilization. Let ξ be the electricity cost given by the power grid, and $\mathfrak{B}$ denote the base cost incurred, which includes license, hardware and maintenance costs. The cost of cloud service at time t (C_t) is given by (17)

$$C_t = \mathfrak{B} + \xi \cdot P_{cloud} \tag{17}$$

When we know the infrastructure capacity, we can divide the base cost of hosting the service ($\mathfrak{B}$) among the cloud instances hosted. This forms the fixed price (ϕ) consumers pay. A component of the price varies based on the utilization and we include a balance factor to reduce the separation between resource demand and availability. The price per cloud instance at time t is given in (18).

$$\mathfrak{p}(j, t) = \phi + k \left(u_j \times \frac{C_t}{\mathbb{C}} - \alpha \left(\mathbb{C} - \sum_j u_j \right) \right) \tag{18}$$

where $\mathbb{C}$ is the total resource capacity; scale factor, k and penalty multiplier, α are constants that depend on market economics. Equation (18) ensures:

- Service provider is not burdened by various fee like license, maintenance etc., via the term ϕ.
- ($\mathbb{C} - \sum_j u_j$) is high when the utilization is low. Hence the instance price is reduced, encouraging consumers to avail additional services.
- Conversely, when the resource utilization is high, the balance factor is low. Hence instance price increases. This discourages consumers from deploying more instances or requesting additional capacity.
- The cost of electricity is considered (via C_t) and customers are charged based on their resource utilization.

Equation (18) captures the price at any time interval t, hence the total bill for instance j (B) is given by,

$$B = \sum_t \mathfrak{p}(j, t) \tag{19}$$

Experimental Evidence

We deployed a Eucalyptus[3] cloud running Ubuntu Linux[4] similar to the one shown in Fig. 8. Ubuntu server was deployed on the instances. Resource utilization was monitored using Hyperic SIGAR framework. As a part of the experiment, real time

---

[3]https://www.eucalyptus.com/.
[4]https://www.ubuntu.com/cloud.

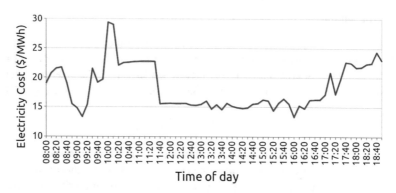

Fig. 10 Variation of electricity cost. Image courtesy [9]

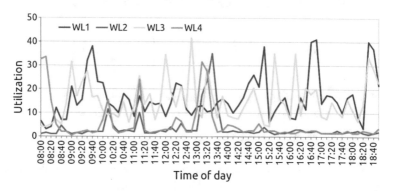

Fig. 11 Resource utilization pattern. Image courtesy [9]

electricity cost from PJM Interconnect[5] was supplied as input to the metering application. Variation of the cost of electricity is as shown in Fig. 10.

We deployed four workloads $WL1$, $WL2$, $WL3$, and $WL4$ on four cloud instances. These represent typical workload on the cloud with a good mix of compute intensive ($WL1$ and $WL3$) and moderate ($WL2$ and $WL4$) workloads. Workload characteristics are shown in Fig. 11. Notice that $WL1$ and $WL3$ reach peak utilization frequently.

We deployed the metering mechanism described above and provided as input the data presented in Figs. 10 and 11. Resource utilization and corresponding cloud service price were calculated as per Eqs. (16) and (18). The output (for a subset of the input data) is observed in Fig. 12. A more detailed description of the experiments and results can be found in earlier work [9].

---

[5]https://www.edata.pjm.com/eData/index.html.

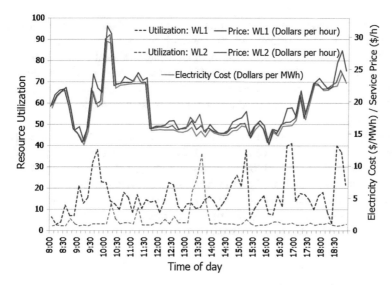

Fig. 12 Service price varies according to resource utilization and electricity cost. Image courtesy [9]

6 Conclusion

Currently, cloud users pay a fixed price for resources or services. This type of pricing is called fixed pricing. Fixed pricing is very popular with telecom providers as it does not require any complex models and is easy to implement. On the flip side, it does not allow for any provision for incentives for users (as might be desirable for load leveling, better utilization, etc.). Resource procurement, being presently done manually, is slow, inefficient, and error-prone. It needs to be automated and to incorporate models that permit dynamic pricing. Resource procurement with dynamic pricing is not only an important problem in cloud computing but is also an unexplored area. The models and approaches suggested here thus permit cloud vendors and brokers to meet an important need, while improving the speed and efficiency of resource procurement. Cloud users will also benefit, as they will be able to procure their requested combinations of resources at an economical price, compared to procuring the same sequentially. Thus, our work has value for both the service provider and the cloud user with a win-win situation for both parties in a system using our approach.

Resource allocation is another problem yet to be fully addressed in cloud systems, as existing approaches do not do well enough at avoiding under-utilization of the allocated resources. In order to satisfy task requests needing more than a single machine's resource capability, multiple machines have to collaborate. Through virtualization, we propose an approach that configures VMs on the cloud that are actually coalitions of the underlying host machines. We present an approach to model coalition formation among machines on the cloud. In our approach, we solve the optimization problem of forming the best coalitions using the uncertainty principle of game theory. Our mechanism is suitable for the resource allocation of tasks with unknown arrival patterns. The advantage of our approach is that we avoid the complexities of integer programming to solve our optimal resource allocation problem, but find mixed strategies that are close to optimal in most cases. We experimentally verified our approach and it performed better with lesser task allocation time, lower resource wastage and higher request satisfaction compared to exisiting allocation strategies on the cloud.

Finally, we also address the problem of considering electrical power costs in cloud usage and metering. To this end, we use the input cost of electricity from smart gird, cloud service utilization, and consumer resource utilization to develop a power-aware cloud metering mechanism. We show how to use this relation to achieve a dynamic tariff model for cloud services. This work is relevant particularly in IaaS clouds, which can operate in the presence of smart grids for electricity distribution, and new/forthcoming green power technologies.

7 Open Research Problems

The following are some of the important problems we consider as being worthy of attention.

In Cloud Resource Procurement:

Most works on cloud computing auction make some assumptions about the probability distributions of user bids, which at best is an oversimplification and at worst is grossly erroneous. In reality, each user can bid from a different distribution, and existing mechanisms are not optimal when the distribution used is different from that which was assumed. It is very important to develop mechanisms which retain optimality despite the change in probability distribution.

In federated or hybrid cloud computing, service providers will collude among themselves for providing cloud services and resources. It is extremely important to devise fair profit sharing mechanisms for service providers. Unfairness not only affects the profits but also the coalitions of service providers. We believe that these problems are really important for the successful deployment of cloud services, besides offering fertile ground for theoretical development.

In Cloud Resource Allocation:

There are other open challenges in the area of optimal cloud resource allocation. In this chapter, we primarily focused on the IaaS cloud model, but the same can be extended to incorporate a unifying approach that works for other cloud models such as PaaS, SaaS and the like. Another direction to extend the work is to include a mechanism that could predict the kind of task requests based on a history of such requests. We could involve a more active learning approach, that constantly updates the allocation strategy while keeping in view the task arrival patterns.

In Cloud Metering and Pricing Based on Power and Usage:

As future work, the power-aware metering mechanism proposed here can be enhanced to incorporate predictive pricing for cloud services.

On the basis of the mechanisms developed in this work, we can build systems that achieve power-aware scheduling of cloud instances. This is one of the directly added advantages of having a power consumption model in place. We can enhance the proposed cloud pricing mechanisms by incorporating information on incoming request volume. One of the ways this can be achieved is by modeling user request as a stochastic process. The current metering mechanism we proposed does not consider any specific SLA requirements, but is based on current utilization and the electricity cost. One of the directions to extend this work would, therefore, be to include SLA requirements and generate pricing based on different service levels desirable for both providers and consumers.

References

1. Prasad, A. S., & Rao, S. (2014). A mechanism design approach to resource procurement in cloud computing. *IEEE Transactions on Computers, 63*(1), 17–30. https://doi.org/10.1109/TC. 2013.106.
2. Prasad, G. V., Prasad, A. S., & Rao, S. (2017). A combinatorial auction mechanism for multiple resource procurement in cloud computing. *IEEE Transactions on Cloud Computing*. https://doi.org/10.1109/TCC.2016.2541150, supersedes https://doi.org/10.1109/10.1109/ISDA.2012.6416561.
3. S. Parsons, J. A. Rodriguez-Aguilar, & Klein, M. (2011, January). Auctions and bidding: A guide for computer scientists. *ACM Computing Surveys, 43*(2). https://doi.org/10.1145/1883612.1883617.
4. Nisan, N., & Ronen, A. (2001). Algorithmic mechanism design. *Games and Economic Behavior, 35*(1–2), 166–196.
5. Székely, G., & Rizzo, M. L. (2007). The uncertainty principle of game theory. *The American Mathematical Monthly, 114*, 688–702.
6. Pillai, P. S., & Rao, S. (2013). A resource allocation mechanism using coalition formation and the uncertainty principle of game theory. In *7th annual IEEE international systems conference (IEEE SysCon 2013)*, (pp. 178–184). Orlando, FL, April 2013. https://doi.org/10.1109/SysCon. 2013.6549878.
7. Pillai, P. S., & Rao, S. (2016). Resource allocation in cloud computing using the uncertainty principle of game theory. *The IEEE Systems Journal, 10*(2), 637–648. https://doi.org/10.1109/JSYST.2014.2314861.
8. Narayan, A., Rao, S., Ranjan, G., & Dheenadayalan, K. (2012, March). Smart metering of cloud services. In *6th annual IEEE international systems conference (IEEE SysCon. 2012)*. BC, Canada: Vancouver. https://doi.org/10.1109/SysCon.2012.6189462.
9. Narayan, A., & Rao, S. (2014, September). Power-aware cloud metering. *IEEE Transactions on Services Computing* 440–451. https://doi.org/10.1109/TSC.2013.22.
10. Mas-Colell, A., Whinston, M. D., Green, J. R. (1995, June). *Microeconomic theory*. Oxford University Press.
11. Myerson, R. B. (1981). Optimal auction design. *Mathematics of Operations Research, 6*(1), 58–73.
12. Mithani, M. F., Salsburg, M., & Rao, S. (2010). A decision support system for moving workloads to public clouds. *GSTF International Journal on Computing, 1*(1), 150–157. https://doi.org/10.5176_2010-2283_1.1.25.

13. Bichler, M., Kalagnanam, J., Katircioglu, K., King, A. J., Lawrence, R. D., & Lee, H. S., et al. (2002). Applications of flexible pricing in business-to-business electronic commerce. *IBM System Journal, 41*(2), 287–302.
14. Narahari, Y., Raju, C., Ravikumar, K., & Shah, S. (2005). Dynamic pricing models for electronic business. *Sadhana, 30,* 231–256.
15. Iyengar, G., & Kumar, A. (2008). Optimal procurement mechanisms for divisible goods with capacitated suppliers. *Review of Economic Design, 12*(2), 129–154.
16. Buyya, R., Abramson, D., Giddy, J., & Stockinger, H. (2002). Economic models for resource management and scheduling in Grid computing. *Concurrency and Computation: Practice and Experience, 14*(13–15), 1507–1542.
17. Narahari, Y., Garg, D., Narayanam, R., & Prakash, H. (2009). *Game theoretic problems in network economics and mechanism design solutions.* Springer.
18. Li Mingbiao, L. J., & Shengli, X. (2007). Posted price model based on grs and its optimization using in grid resource allocation. In *International conference on wireless communications, networking and mobile computing, 2007. WiCom 2007,* September 2007 (pp. 3172–3175).
19. Subramoniam, K., Maheswaran, M., & Toulouse, M. (2000). Towards a micro-economic model for resource allocation in grid computing systems. In *Canadian conference on electrical and computer engineering, 2002. IEEE CCECE 2002* (Vol. 2, 2002, pp. 782–785).
20. Parsa, S., Shokri, A., & Nourossana, S. (2009). A novel market based grid resource allocation algorithm. In *First international conference on networked digital technologies, 2009. NDT '09,* July 2009 (pp. 146–152).
21. Lin, W.-Y., Lin, G.-Y., & Wei, H.-Y. (2010). Dynamic auction mechanism for cloud resource allocation. In *CCGRID '10: Proceedings of the 2010 10th IEEE/ACM international conference on cluster, cloud and grid computing* (pp. 591–592). Washington, DC, USA: IEEE Computer Society.
22. Rochwerger, B., Tordsson, J., Ragusa, C., Breitgand, D., Clayman, S., & Epstein, A., et al. (2011, March). RESERVOIR—when one cloud is not enough. *IEEE Computer.*
23. Hwang, C., & Yoon, K. (1981). *Multiple attribute decision making: Methods and applications.* Springer.
24. Saaty, T. (1980). *The analytic hierarchy process, planning, piority setting, resource allocation.* New York: McGraw-Hill.
25. Shoham, Y., & Leyton-Brown, K. (2008, December). *Multiagent systems: Algorithmic, game-theoretic, and logical foundations.* Cambridge University Press.
26. Gibbard, A. (1973). Manipulation of voting schemes: A general result. *Econometrica, 41*(4), 587–601. https://doi.org/10.2307/1914083.
27. d'Aspremont, C., & Gérard-Varet, L.-A. (1979). Incentives and incomplete information. *Journal of Public Economics, 11*(1), 25–45.
28. Katzman, B., Reif, J., & Schwartz, J. A. (2010). The relation between variance and information rent in auctions. *International Journal of Industrial Organization, 28*(2), 127–130.
29. Vries, S. D., & Vohra, R. (2000). Combinatorial auctions: A survey, Northwestern University, Center for Mathematical Studies in Economics and Management Science, Discussion Papers, 2000. http://EconPapers.repec.org/RePEc:nwu:cmsems:1296
30. Sandholm, T., & Suri, S. (2000). Improved algorithms for optimal winner determination in combinatorial auctions and generalizations. In *Proceedings of the seventeenth national conference on artificial intelligence and twelfth conference on innovative applications of artificial intelligence* (pp. 90–97). AAAI Press.
31. Sandholm, T. (2002). Algorithm for optimal winner determination in combinatorial auctions. *Artificial Intelligence, 135*(12), 1–54.
32. Goncalves, G. E., Endo, P. T., & Damasceno, T. (2011). Resource allocation in clouds: Concepts, tools and research challenges. In *29th Simpósio Brasileiro de Redes de Computadores.*
33. Enumula, P. K. (2008, June). *Coalition formation in multi-agent systems with uncertain task information.* Master's thesis, International Institute of Information Technology—Bangalore.
34. Heisenberg, W. (1927). Über den anschaulichen Inhalt der quantentheoretischen Kinematik und Mechanik. *Zeitschrift für Physik, 43*(3–4), 172–198. https://doi.org/10.1007/BF01397280.

35. Gale, D., & Shapley, L. S. (1962). College admissions and the stability of marriage. *The American Mathematical Monthly, 69*(1), 9–15.
36. Windows Azure. Retrieved June, 2013, from http://www.windowsazure.com.
37. Nurmi, D., Wolski, R., Grzegorczyk, C., Obertelli, G., Soman, S., Youseff, L., & Zagorodnov, D. (2009). The Eucalyptus open-source cloud-computing system. In *Ninth IEEE/ACM international symposium on cluster computing and the grid (CCGrid 2009)* (pp. 124–131). https://doi.org/10.1109/CCGRID.2009.93.
38. Ristenpart, T., Tromer, E., Shacham, H., & Savage, S. (2009). Hey, you, get off of my cloud: exploring information leakage in third-party compute clouds. In *Sixteenth ACM conference on computer and communications security (CCS '09)* (pp. 199–212). https://doi.org/10.1145/1653662.1653687.
39. Pritzker, P., & Gallagher, P. (2013, July). *NIST cloud computing standards roadmap* (pp. 500–291). NIST Special Publication.
40. Abood, D., Murdoch, R., N'Diay, S., Albano, D., Kofmehl, A., & Tung, T. (2010). Cloud computing and sustainability: The environmental benefits of moving to the cloud. *Accenture in Collaboration with WSP Environment and Energy*, Technical report. Retrieved from http://www.goo.gl/4QNigm.
41. Kansal, A., Zhao, F., Liu, J., Kothari, N., & Bhattacharya, A.A. (2010). Virtual machine power metering and provisioning. In *Proceedings of the first ACM symposium on cloud computing*, ser. SoCC '10 (pp. 39–50). ACM. https://doi.org/10.1145/1807128.1807136.
42. Verma, A., Dasgupta, G., Nayak, T. K., De, P., & Kothari, R. (2009). Server workload analysis for power minimization using consolidation. In *Proceedings of the 2009 USENIX annual technical conference*, ser. USENIX'09 (p. 28). USENIX Association.
43. Uddin, M., & Rahman, A. A. (2010). Server consolidation: An approach to make data centers energy efficient and green. *CoRR*. arXiv:1010.5037.
44. Ganesan, R., Sarkar, S., & Narayan, A. (2012). Analysis of SAAS business platform workloads for sizing and collocation. In *2012 IEEE 5th international conference on cloud computing (CLOUD)* (pp. 868–875). IEEE.
45. Bezemer, C.-P., Zaidman, A., Platzbeecker, B., Hurkmans, T., & Hart, A. (2010). Enabling multi-tenancy: An industrial experience report. In *2010 IEEE international conference on software maintenance (ICSM)* pp. 1–8. IEEE.
46. Amazon EC2 pricing. Retrieved from http://www.goo.gl/ysnIAf.
47. Rackspace cloud servers: Pricing. Retrieved from http://www.goo.gl/6wMnvg.
48. CSC Cloud Usage Index (2011, December). CSC, Technical report. Retrieved from http://www.goo.gl/SAoUq4.
49. Box, G. E., Jenkins, G. M., & Reinsel, G. C. (2013). *Time series analysis: Forecasting and control*. Wiley.
50. The R Project for Statistical Computing. Retrieved from http://www.r-project.org/.
51. Barroso, L. A. (2005). The price of performance. *ACM Queue, 3*(7), 48–53.
52. Curtis, P. M. (2007). *Maintaining mission critical systems in a 24/7 environment*. Wiley-IEEE Press. ISBN: 978-0471683742.
53. Brill, K. (2008, November). *Understanding the true cost of operating a server*. Facilitiesnet. Retrieved from http://www.facilitiesnet.com/datacenters/article/Understanding-the-True-Cost-of-Operating-a-Server--10063
54. Ranganathan, P., Leech, P., Irwin, D., & Chase, J. (2006). Ensemble-level power management for dense blade servers. *SIGARCH Computer Architecture News, 34*(2), 66–77. https://doi.org/10.1145/1150019.1136492.
55. Deng, Q., Meisner, D., Ramos, L., Wenisch, T. F., & Bianchini, R. (2011). Memscale: active low-power modes for main memory. *SIGARCH Computer Architecture News, 39*(1), 225–238. https://doi.org/10.1145/1961295.1950392.
56. Economou, D., Rivoire, S., & Kozyrakis, C. (2006). Full-system power analysis and modeling for server environments. In *In workshop on modeling benchmarking and simulation (MOBS)*.
57. Krishnan, B., Amur, H., Gavrilovska, A., & Schwan, K. (2011). Vm power metering: Feasibility and challenges. *SIGMETRICS Performance Evaluation Review, 38*(3), 56–60. https://doi.org/10.1145/1925019.1925031.

58. Bircher, W., & John, L. (2012). Complete system power estimation using processor performance events. *IEEE Transactions on Computers*, *61*(4), 563–577. https://doi.org/10.1109/TC.2011. 47.

59. Heath, T., Diniz, B., Carrera, E. V., Meira, W., Jr., & Bianchini, R. (2005). Energy conservation in heterogeneous server clusters. In *Proceedings of the tenth ACM SIGPLAN symposium on principles and practice of parallel programming*, ser. PPoPP '05 (pp. 186–195). ACM. https:// doi.org/10.1145/1065944.1065969.

60. Chen, Q., Grosso, P., van der Veldt, K., de Laat, C., Hofman, R., & Bal, H. (2011, December). Profiling energy consumption of VMS for green cloud computing. In *2011 IEEE Ninth International Conference on Dependable, Autonomic and Secure Computing (DASC)* (pp. 768–775). https://doi.org/10.1109/DASC.2011.131.

61. Kivity, A., Kamay, Y., Laor, D., Lublin, U., & Liguori, A. (2007). KVM: The linux virtual machine monitor. Technical report. Retrieved from http://www.goo.gl/P20ueu.

62. McCullough, J. C., Agarwal, Y., Chandrashekar, J., Kuppuswamy, S., Snoeren, A. C., & Gupta, R. K. (2011). Evaluating the effectiveness of model-based power characterization. In *Proceedings of the 2011 USENIX conference on USENIX annual technical conference*, ser. USENIX-ATC'11 (pp. 12–12). USENIX Association.

Dynamic Selection of Virtual Machines for Application Servers in Cloud Environments

Nikolay Grozev and Rajkumar Buyya

Abstract Autoscaling is a hallmark of cloud computing as it allows flexible just-in-time allocation and release of computational resources in response to dynamic and often unpredictable workloads. This is especially important for web applications, whose workload is time dependent and prone to flash crowds. Most of them follow the 3-tier architectural pattern, and are divided into presentation, application/domain and data layers. In this work, we focus on the application layer. Reactive autoscaling policies of the type "*Instantiate a new Virtual Machine (VM) when the average server CPU utilisation reaches X%*" have been used successfully since the dawn of cloud computing. But which VM type is the most suitable for the specific application at the moment remains an open question. In this work, we propose an approach for dynamic VM type selection. It uses a combination of online machine learning techniques, works in real time and adapts to changes in the users' workload patterns, application changes as well as middleware upgrades and reconfigurations. We have developed a prototype, which we tested with the CloudStone benchmark deployed on AWS EC2. Results show that our method quickly adapts to workload changes and reduces the total cost compared to the industry standard approach.

1 Introduction

Cloud computing is a disruptive IT model allowing enterprises to focus on their core business activities. Instead of investing in their own IT infrastructures, they can now rent ready-to-use preconfigured virtual resources from cloud providers in a "pay-as-you-go" manner. Organisations relying on fixed size private infrastructures often realise it can not match their dynamic needs, thus frequently being either

N. Grozev · R. Buyya (✉)
Cloud Computing and Distributed Systems (CLOUDS) Laboratory,
School of Computing and Inforamtion Systems, The University of Melbourne,
Melbourne, VIC, Australia
e-mail: rbuyya@unimelb.edu.au

N. Grozev
e-mail: anadjaran@unimelb.edu.au

© Springer Nature Singapore Pte Ltd. 2017
S. Chaudhary et al. (eds.), *Research Advances in Cloud Computing*,
DOI 10.1007/978-981-10-5026-8_8

under or overutilised. In contrast, in a cloud environment one can automatically acquire or release resources as they are needed—a distinctive characteristic known as *autoscaling*.

This is especially important for large-scale web applications, since the number of users fluctuates over time and is prone to flash crowds as a result of marketing campaigns and product releases. Most such applications follow the 3-tier architectural pattern and are divided in three standard layers/tiers [1, 18, 32]:

- **Presentation Layer**—the end user interface.
- **Business/Domain Layer**—implements the business logic. Hosted in one or several Application Servers (AS).
- **Data Layer**—manages the persistent data. Deployed in one or several Database (DB) servers.

A user interacts with the presentation layer, which redirects the requests to an AS which in turn can access the data layer. The presentation layer is executed on the client's side (e.g. in a browser) and thus scalability is not an issue. Scaling the DB layer is a notorious challenge, since system architects have to balance between consistency, availability and partition tolerance following the results of the CAP theorem [5, 6]. This field has already been well explored (Cattel surveys more than 20 related projects [8]). Furthermore, Google has published about their new database which scales within and across data centres without violating transaction consistency [13]. Hence data layer scaling is beyond the scope of our work.

In general, autoscaling the Application Servers (AS) is comparatively straightforward. In an Infrastructure as a Service (IaaS) cloud environment, the AS VMs are deployed "behind" a load balancer which redirects the incoming requests among them. Whenever the servers' capacity is insufficient, one or several new AS VMs are provisioned and associated with the load balancer and the DB layer—see Fig. 1.

But what should be the type of the new AS VM? Most major cloud providers like Amazon EC2 and Google Compute Engine offer a predefined set of VM types with different performance capacities and prices. Currently, system engineers "hardcode" preselected VM types in the autoscaling rules based on their intuition or at best on historical performance observations. However, user workload characteristics vary over time leading to constantly evolving AS capacity requirements. For example, the proportion of browsing, bidding and buying requests in an e-commerce system can change significantly during a holiday season, which can change the server utilisation patterns. Middleware and operating system updates and reconfigurations can lead to changes in the utilisation patterns as well [9]. This can also happen as a result of releasing new application features or updates.

Moreover, VM performance can vary significantly over time because of other VMs collocated on the same physical host causing resource contentions [14, 34, 39]. Hence even VM instances of the same type can perform very differently. From the viewpoint of the cloud's client, this cannot be predicted.

To illustrate better, let us consider a large-scale web application with hundreds of dedicated AS VMs. Its engineers can analyse historical performance data to specify the most appropriate VM type in the autoscaling rules. However, they will have to

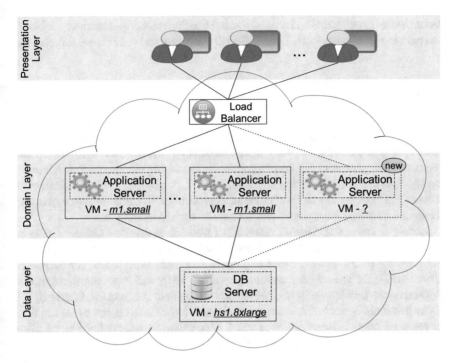

Fig. 1 A 3-tier application in Cloud. Whenever the autoscaling conditions are activated, a new application server should be provisioned. In this work, we select the optimal VM type for the purpose

reconsider their choice every time a new feature or a system upgrade is deployed. They will also have to constantly monitor for workload pattern changes and to react by adjusting the austoscaling rules. Given that VM performance capacities also vary over time, the job of selecting the most suitable VM type becomes practically unmanageable. This can result in significant financial losses, because of using suboptimal VMs.

To address this, the key **contributions** of our work are (i) a machine learning approach which continuously learns the application's resource requirements and (ii) a dynamic VM type selection (DVTS) algorithm, which selects a VM type for new AS VMs. Since both workload specifics and VM performance vary over time, we propose an online approach, which learns the application's behaviour and the typical VM performance capacities in real time. It relieves system maintainers from having to manually reconfigure the autoscaling rules.

The rest of the chapter is organised as follows: In Sect. 2 we describe the related works. Section 3 provides a succinct overview of our approach. Section 4 discusses the machine learning approaches we employ to "learn" the application's requirements in real time. Section 5 describes how to select an optimal VM type. Section 6 details the architecture of our prototype and the benchmark we use for evaluation. Section 7 describes our experiments and results. Section 8 defines some open research problems and pathways for future work. Finally, Sect. 9 concludes and summarises this chapter.

2 Related Work

The area of static computing resource management has been well studied in the context of grids, clouds, and even multi-clouds [41]. However, the field of dynamic resource management in response to continuously varying workloads, which is especially important for web facing applications [41], is still in its infancy. Horizontal autoscaling policies are the predominant approach for dynamic resource management, and thus they have gained significant attention in recent years.

Lorido-Botran et al. classify autoscaling policies as *reactive* and *predictive* or *proactive* [26]. The most widely adopted *reactive* approaches are based on threshold rules for performance metrics (e.g. CPU and RAM utilisation). For each such characteristic the system administrator provides a lower and upper threshold values. Resources are provisioned whenever an upper threshold is exceeded. Similarly, if a lower threshold is reached resources are released. How much resources are acquired or released when a threshold is reached is specified in user defined autoscaling rules. There are different "flavours" of threshold based approaches. For example, in Amazon Auto Scaling [3] one would typically use the average metrics from the virtual server farm, while RightScale [33] provides a voting scheme, where thresholds are considered per VM and an autoscaling action is taken if the majority of the VMs "agree" on it. Combinations and extensions of both of these techniques have also been proposed [10, 11, 35]. *Predictive* or *proactive* approaches try to predict demand changes in order to allocate or deallocate resources. Multiple methods using approaches like reinforcement learning [4, 15], queuing theory [2] and Kalman filters [19] to name a few have been proposed.

Our work is complementary to all these approaches. They indicate at what time resources should be provisioned, but do not select the resource type. Our approach selects the best resource (i.e. VM type) once it has been decided that the system should scale up horizontally.

Fernandez et al. propose a system for autoscaling web applications in clouds [17]. They monitor the performance of different VM types to infer their capacities. Our approach to this is different, as we inspect the available to each VM CPU capacity and measure the amount of "stolen" CPU instructions by the hypervisor from within the VM itself. This allows us to normalise the VMs' resource capacities to a common scale, which we use to compare them and for further analysis. Furthermore, their approach relies on a workload predictor, while ours is usable even in the case of purely reactive autoscaling.

Singh et al. use k-means clustering to analyse the workload mix (i.e. the different type of sessions) and then use a queueing model to determine each server's suitability [36]. However, they do not consider the performance variability of virtual machines, which we take into account. Also, they do not select the type of resource (e.g. VM) to provision and assume there is only one type, while this is precisely the focus of our work.

A part of our work is concerned with automated detection of application behaviour changes through a Hierarchical Temporal Memory (HTM) model. Similar work has been carried out by Cherkasova et al. [9], who propose a regression based anomaly detection approach. However, they analyse only the CPU utilisation. Moreover, they consider that a set of user transactions' types is known beforehand. In contrast, our approach considers RAM as well and does not require application specific information like transaction types. Tan et al. propose the PREPARE performance anomaly detection system [38]. However, their approach can not be used by a cloud client, as it is built on top of the Xen virtual machine manager to which external clients have no access.

Another part of our method is concerned with automatic selection of the *learning rate* and *momentum* of an artificial neural network (ANN). There is a significant amount of literature in this area as surveyed by Moreira and Fiesler [27]. However, the works they overview are applicable for static data sets and have not been applied to learning from streaming online data whose patterns can vary over time. Moreover, they only consider how the intermediate parameters of the backpropagation algorithm vary and do not use additional domain specific logic. Although our approach is inspired by the work of Vogl et al. [42] as it modifies the *learning rate* and *momentum* based on the prediction error, we go further and we modify them also based on the *anomaly score* as reported by the Hierarchical Temporal Memory (HTM) models.

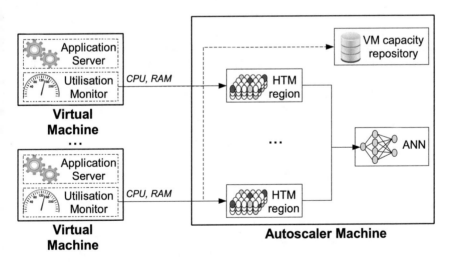

Fig. 2 System components and their interaction

3   Method Overview

Figure 2 depicts an overview of our machine learning approach and how the system components interact. Within each AS VM we install a monitoring program which periodically records utilisation metrics. These measurements are transferred to an *autoscaling component*, which can be hosted either in a cloud VM or on-premises. It is responsible for (i) monitoring AS VMs' performance (ii) updating machine learning models of the application behaviour and (iii) autoscaling.

Within each AS VM the *utilisation monitors* report statistics about the CPU, RAM, disk and network card utilisations and the number of currently served users. These records are transferred every 5 s to the *autoscaling* component, where they are normalised, as different VMs have different de facto resource capacities. In the machine learning approaches we only consider the CPU and RAM utilisations, as disk and network utilisations of AS VMs are typically small [21, 25].

For each AS VM the *autoscaler* maintains a separate single-region Hierarchical Temporal Memory (HTM) model [22], which is overviewed in a later section. In essence we use HTMs to detect changes in the application behaviour of each AS VM. We prefer HTM to other regression based anomaly detection approaches, as it can detect anomalies on a stream of multiple parameters (e.g. CPU and RAM). Whenever monitoring data is retrieved from an AS VM, the *autoscaler* trains its HTM with the received number of users, CPU and RAM utilisations and outputs an *anomaly score* defining how "unexpected" the data is.

As a next step we use these utilisation measurements to train a 3-tier artificial neural network (ANN) about the relationship between the number of served users and resource consumptions. We choose to use an ANN because of its suitability for online data streams. Other "sliding window" approaches operate only on a portion of the data stream. As a system's utilisation patterns can remain the same for long time intervals, the window sizes may need to become impractically large or even be dynamically adjusted. On the contrary, an ANN does not operate on a fixed time window and is more adept with changes in the incoming data stream, as we will detail in a later section.

There is only one ANN and training samples from all AS VMs are used to train it. In essence the ANN represents a continuously updated regression model, which given a number of users predicts the needed resources to serve them within a single VM without causing resource contentions. Thus, we need to filter all training samples, which were taken during anomalous conditions (e.g. insufficient CPU or RAM capacity causing intensive context switching or disk swapping respectively). Such samples are not indicative of the relationship between number of users and the resource requirements in the absence of resource contentions. Furthermore, we use the *anomaly score* of each training sample (extracted from HTM) to determine the respective *learning speed* and *momentum* parameters of the back propagation algorithm so that the ANN adapts quickly to changes in the utilisation patterns.

Training the ANN and the HTMs happens online from the stream of VM measurements in parallel with the running application. Simultaneously we also maintain a *VM capacity repository* of the latest VM capacity measurements. When a new VM is needed by the autoscaling component, we use this repository to infer the potential performance capacity of all VM types. At that time the ANN is already trained adequately and given the predicted performance capacities can be used to infer how many users each VM type could serve simultaneously. Based on that we select the VM type, with minimal cost to number of users ratio.

4 Learning Application Behaviour

4.1 Utilisation Monitoring

To measure VM performance utilisation, we use the *SAR*, *mpstat*, *vmstat* and *netstat* Linux monitoring tools. We use the mpstat *%idle* metric to measure the percentage of time during which the CPU was idle. The *%steal* metric describes the percentage of "stolen" CPU cycles by a hypervisor (i.e. the proportion of time the CPU was not available to the VM) and can be used to evaluate the actual VM CPU capacity. Similarly, SAR provides the *%util* and *%ifutil* metrics as indicative of the disk's and network card's utilisations.

Measuring the RAM utilisation is more complex as operating systems keep in memory cached copies of recently accessed disk sectors in order to reduce disk access [21]. Although in general this optimisation is essential for VM performance, web application servers (AS) are not usually I/O bound, as most of the application persistence is delegated to the data base layer. Hence, using the *vmstat* RAM utilisation metrics can be an overestimation of the actual memory consumption as it includes rarely accessed disk caches. Thus, we use the *"active memory" vmstat* metric to measure memory consumption instead. It denotes the amount of recently used memory, which is unlikely to be claimed for other purposes.

Lastly, we need to evaluate the number of concurrently served users in an AS VM. This could be extracted from the AS middleware, but that would mean writing specific code for each type of middleware. Moreover, some proprietary solutions may not expose this information. Therefore, we use the number of distinct IP addresses with which the server has an active TCP socket, which can be obtained through the *netstat* command. Typically, the AS VM is dedicated to running the AS and does not have other outgoing connections except for the connection to the persistence layer. Therefore, the number of addresses with active TCP sockets is a good measure of the number of currently served users.

4.2 Normalisation and Capacity Estimation

Before proceeding to train the machine learning approaches, we need to normalise the measurements which have different "scales", as the VMs have different RAM sizes and CPUs with different frequencies. Moreover, the actual CPU capacities within a single VM vary over time as a result of the dynamic collocation of other VMs on the same host.

As a first step in normalising the CPU load, we need to evaluate the actual CPU capacity available to each VM. This can be extracted from the */proc/cpuinfo* Linux kernel file. If the VM has n cores, */proc/cpuinfo* will list meta information about the physical CPU cores serving the VM including their frequencies $fr_1, \ldots fr_n$. The sum of these frequencies is the maximal processing capacity the VM can get, provided the hypervisor does not "steal" any processing time. Using the *%steal* mpstat parameter we can actually see what percentage of CPU operations have been taken away by the hypervisor. Subtracting this percentage from the sum of frequencies gives us the actual VM CPU capacity at the time of measurement. To normalise we further divide by the maximal CPU core frequency fr_{max} multiplied by the maximal number of cores n_{max_cores} of all considered VMs in the cloud provider. This is a measure of the maximal VM CPU capacity one can obtain from the considered VM types. As clouds are made of commodity hardware, we will consider $fr_{max} = 3.5$ GHz. This ensures that all values are in the range (0, 1], although for some cloud providers all values may be much lower than 1, depending on the underlying hardware they use. This is formalised in Eq. 1.

$$cpuCapacityNorm = \frac{(100 - \%steal) \sum_{i=0}^{n} fr_i}{100 \, n_{max\_cores} \, fr_{max}} \tag{1}$$

Having computed the VM CPU capacity, we store it into the *VM capacity repository*, so we can use it later on to infer the capacities of future VMs. Each repository record has the following fields:

- *time*—a time stamp of the capacity estimation;
- *vm type*—an identifier of the VM type—e.g. "m1.small";
- *vm-id*—a unique identifier of the VM instance—e.g. its IP or elastic DNS address;
- *cpuCapacityNorm*—the computed CPU capacity.

If we further subtract the *%idle* percentage from the capacity we will get the actual CPU load given in Eq. 2.

$$cpuLoadNorm = \frac{(100 - \%idle - \%steal) \sum_{i=0}^{n} fr_i}{100 \, n_{max\_cores} \, fr_{max}} \tag{2}$$

Normalising the RAM load and capacity is easier, as they do not fluctuate like the CPU capacity. We divide the *active memory* by the maximal amount of memory RAM_{max} in all considered virtual machine types in the cloud—see Eq. 3.

$$ramLoadNorm = \frac{active_memory}{RAM_{max}} \tag{3}$$

Whenever a new AS VM is needed, we have to estimate the CPU and RAM capacities of all available VM types based on the *capacity repository* and their performance definitions provided by the provider. The normalised RAM capacity of a VM type is straightforward to estimate as we just need to divide the capacity in the provider's specification by RAM_{max}. To estimate the CPU capacity of a VM type we use the mean of the last 10 entries' capacities for this type in the *capacity repository*. If there are no entries for this VM type in the repository (i.e. no VM of this type has been instantiated) we can heuristically extrapolate the CPU capacity from the capacities of the other VM types. Typically IaaS providers specify an estimation of each VM type's CPU capacity—e.g. Google Compute Engine Units (GCEU) in Google Compute Engine or Elastic Compute Units (ECU) in AWS. Hence given an unknown VM type vmt we can extrapolate its normalised CPU capacity as:

$$cpuCapacity(vmt) = \tag{4}$$
$$\frac{1}{|V|} \sum_{vmt_i \in V} \frac{cpuCapacity(vmt_i) \times cpuSpec(vmt_i)}{cpuSpec(vmt)}$$

Where V is the set of VM types present in the *capacity repository* and whose CPU capacity can be determined from previous measurements, $|V|$ is its cardinality, and $cpuSpec(vmt_i)$ defines the cloud provider's estimation of a VM type's capacity— e.g. number of GCEUs or ECUs.

4.3 Anomaly Detection Through HTM

The Hierarchical Temporal Memory (HTM) model is inspired by the structure and organisation of the neocortex. It has been developed and commercialised by the Grok company [20] (formerly Numenta [29]), and follows the concepts from Jeff Hawkins' book "On Intelligence" [23]. The model creators build upon the seminal work of Mountcastle [28] that the neocortex is predominantly uniform in structure and function even in regions handling different sensory inputs—e.g. visual, auditory, and touch. The HTM model tries to mimic this structure in a computational model. There are several differences compared to the biological structure of the neocortex in order to be computationally viable as described in the implementation white paper [22]. Grok's implementation is available as an open source project called NuPIC [30]. In this section, we provide only a brief overview of HTM to introduce the reader to this concept. The interested reader is referred to the official documentation [22].

Fig. 3 HTM region structure

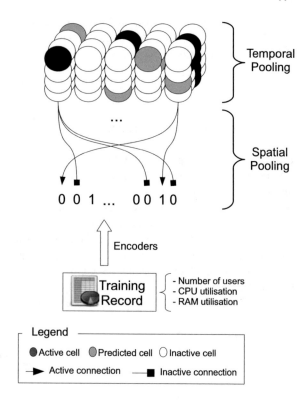

HTMs consist of one or several stacked regions. During inference, input arrives into the lowest region, whose output serves as input to the successive one and so forth until the topmost region outputs the final result. The purpose of a region is to convert noisy input sequences to more stable abstract representations. Conceptually, the different regions represent different levels of abstraction in the learning process— i.e. the lowest level recognises low-level patterns, while each higher level layer recognises more complex ones based on the result of the previous one. In this work, we use single-region HTMs and we will focus on them in the rest of the section.

A HTM region consists of columns of cells, which are most often arranged in a three dimensional grid—see Fig. 3. Each cell can be in one of three possible states: (i) active form feed forward input, (ii) active from lateral input (i.e. predicted), or (iii) inactive. Conceptually, active cells represent the state of the last input and predicted cells represent the likely state after future inputs. A HTM region receives as input a bit sequence. Special *encoders* are used to convert input objects into bitwise representations, so that objects which are "close" in the sense of the target domain have similar bit representations. Upon receiving new binary input the HTM changes the states of the columns based on several rules summarised below.

As a first step, the HTM has to decide which columns' cells will be activated for a given input—an algorithm known as *Spatial Pooling*. It nullifies most of the 1 bits, so that only a small percentage (by default 2%) are active. Each column is connected with a fixed sized (by default 50% of the input length) random subset of input bits called the *potential pool*. Each column's connection to an input bit has a ratio number in the range [0, 1] associated with it known as the *permanence*. HTM automatically adjusts the *permanence* value of a connection after a new input record arrives, so that input positions whose value have been 0 or 1 and are members of the *potential pool* of a selected column are decreased or increased respectively. Connections with *permanences* above a predefined thresholds are considered active. Given an input, for each column the HTM defines its *overlap score* as the number of active bits with active connections. Having computed this for every column, HTM selects a fixed sized (by default 2%) set of columns with the highest *overlap score*, so that no two columns within a predefined radius are active.

As a second step, HTM decides which cells within these columns to activate. This is called *Temporal Pooling*. Within each of the selected columns the HTM activates only the cells which are in *predicted* state. If there are no cells in predicted state within a column, then all of its cells are activated, which is also known as *bursting*.

Next, the HTM makes a prediction of what its future state will be—i.e. which cells should be in predicted state. The main idea is that when a cell activates it establishes connections to the cells which were previously active. Each such connection is assigned a weight number. Over time if the two nodes of a connection become active in sequence again, this connection is strengthened, i.e. the weight is increased. Otherwise, the connection slowly decays, i.e. the weight is gradually decreased. Once a cell becomes active, all non-active cells having connections to it with weights above a certain threshold are assigned the predicted state. This is analogous to how synapses form and decay between neurons' dendrites in the neocortex in response to learning patterns.

The presence of predicted cell columns allows a HTM to predict what will be its likely state in terms of active cells after the next input. However, it also allows for the detection of anomalies. For example, if just a few predicted states become active this is a sign that the current input has not been expected. Thus the *anomaly_score* is defined as the proportion of active spatial pooler columns that were incorrectly predicted and is in the range [0, 1].

In our environment for every 5 s, we feed each HTM with a time stamp, the number of users and the CPU and RAM utilisations of the respective VM. We use the standard NuPIC scalar and date encoders to convert the input to binary input. As a result we get an *anomaly score* denoting how expected the input is, in the light of the previously described algorithms.

4.4 ANN Training

Figure 4 depicts the topology of the artificial neural network (ANN). It has one input—the number of users. The hidden layer has 250 neurons with the sigmoid activation function. The output layer has two output nodes with linear activation functions, which predict the normalised CPU and RAM utilisations within an AS VM.

Once a VM's measurements are received and normalised and the *anomaly score* is computed by the respective HTM region, the ANN can be trained. As discussed, we need to filter out the VM measurements which are not representative of normal, contention free application execution, in order to "learn" the "right" relationship between number of users and resource utilisations. We filter all VM measurements in which the CPU, RAM, hard disk or network card utilisations are above a certain threshold (e.g. 70%). Similarly, we filter measurements with negligible load—i.e. less than 25 users or less than 10% CPU utilisation. We also ignore measurements from periods during which the number of users has changed significantly—e.g. in the beginning of the period there were 100 users and at the end there were 200. Such performance observations are not indicative of an actual relationship between number of users and resource utilisations. Thus, we ignore measurements for which the number of users is less than 50% or more than 150% of the average of the previous 3 measured numbers of users from the same VM.

Since we are training the ANN with streaming data, we need to make sure it is not overfitted to the latest training samples. For example if we have constant workload for a few hours we will be receiving very similar training samples in the ANN during this period. Hence the ANN can become overfitted for such samples and lose its fitness for the previous ones. To avoid this problem, we filter out measurements/training samples, which are already well predicted. More specifically, if a VM measurement is already predicted with a *root mean square error* (RMSE) less than 0.01 it is filtered out and the ANN is not trained with it. We call this value $rmse^{pre}$ because it is obtained for each training sample before the ANN is trained with it. It is computed as per Eq. 5, where $output_i$ and $expected_i$ are the values of the output neurons and the expected values respectively.

$$rmse^{pre} = \sqrt{\sum (output_i - expected_i)^2} \qquad (5)$$

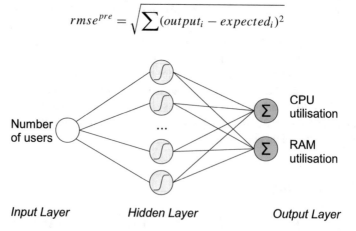

Fig. 4 ANN topology

With each measurement, which is not filtered out, we perform one or several itera-tions/epochs of the backpropagation algorithm with the number of users as input and the normalised CPU and RAM utilisations as expected output. The backpropagation algorithm has two important parameters—the *learning rate* and the *momentum*. In essence, the *learning rate* is a ratio number in the interval (0, 1) which defines the amount of weight update in the direction of the gradient descent for each training sample [27]. For each weight update, the *momentum* term defines what proportion of the previous weight update should be added to it. It is also a ratio number in the interval (0, 1). Using a *momentum* the neural network becomes more resilient to oscillations in the training data by "damping" the optimisation procedure [27].

For our training environment, we need a low *learning rate* and a high *momentum*, as there are a lot of oscillations in the incoming VM measurements. We select the *learning rate* to be $lr = 0.001$ and the *momentum* $m = 0.9$. We call these values the *ideal parameters*, as these are the values we would like to use once the ANN is close to convergence. However, the low *learning rate* and high *momentum* result in slow convergence in the initial stages, meaning that the ANN may not be well trained before it is used. Furthermore, if the workload pattern changes, the ANN may need a large number of training samples and thus time until it is tuned appropriately. Hence, the actual *learning rate* and *momentum* must be defined dynamically.

One approach to resolve this is to start with a high *learning rate* and low *momen-tum* and then respectively decrease/increase them to the desired values [27, 42]. This allows the backpropagation algorithm to converge more rapidly during the ini-tial steps of the training. We define these parameters in the initial stages using the asymptotic properties of the sigmoid function, given in Eq. 6.

$$s(x) = \frac{1}{1 - e^{-x}} \tag{6}$$

As we need to start with a high *learning rate* and then decrease it gradually to lr, we could define the learning rate lr_k for the k-th training sample as $s(-k)$. However, the sigmoid function decreases too steeply for negative integer parameters and as a result the learning rate is higher than lr for just a few training samples. To solve this, we use the square root of k instead and thus our first approximation of the *learning rate* is

$$lr_k^{(1)} = max(lr, s(-\sqrt{k})) \tag{7}$$

As a result, $lr_k^{(1)}$ gradually decreases as more training samples arrive. Figure 5 depicts how it changes over time.

We also need to ensure that it increases in case unusual training data signalling a workload change arrives and thus we need to elaborate $lr_k^{(1)}$. For this we keep a record of the last 10 samples' *anomaly scores* and errors (i.e. $rmse^{pre}$). The higher the latest anomaly scores, the more "unexpected" the samples are and therefore the *learning rate* must be increased. Similarly, the higher the sample's $rmse^{pre}$ compared to the previous errors, the less fit for it the ANN is and thus the *learning rate* must be

Fig. 5 The $lr_k^{(1)}$
approximation of the
learning rate and the
respective momentum during
the initial ANN training
stages

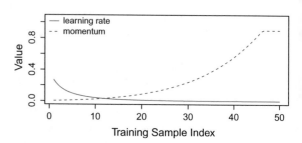

increased as well. Thus, our second elaborated approximation of the *learning rate*
is:

$$lr_k^{(2)} = lr_k^{(1)} \, max(1, \frac{rmse_k^{pre}}{\overline{rmse}}) \prod_{i=0}^{9} 2s(an_{k-i}) \qquad (8)$$

where an_k and $rmse_k^{pre}$ are the *anomaly score* and the error of the k-th sample and
$\overline{rmse}$ is the average error of the last 10 samples. Note that we use the sigmoid function
for the anomaly scores in order to diminish the effect of low values.

In some cases, the *learning rate* can become too big in the initial training iterations,
which will in fact hamper the convergence. To overcome this problem, for each
sample k we run a training iteration with $lr_k^{(2)}$, compute its RMSE $rmse_k^{post}$ and then
revert the results of this iteration. By comparing $rmse_k^{pre}$ and $rmse_k^{post}$ we can see
if training with this $lr_k^{(2)}$ will contribute to the convergence [42]. If not, we use the
ideal parameter lr instead. Thus, we finally define the *learning rate* parameter lr_k in
Eq. 9:

$$lr_k = \begin{cases} lr_k^{(2)} & \text{if } rmse_k^{pre} > rmse_k^{post} \\ lr & \text{otherwise} \end{cases} \qquad (9)$$

Similarly, we have to gradually increase the *momentum* as we decrease the *learning rate* until the ideal *momentum* is reached. If a workload change is present we
need to decrease the *momentum* in order to increase the learning speed. Hence, we
can just use the ratio of the ideal learning rate lr to the current one as shown in Eq. 10.

$$m_k = min(m, \frac{lr}{lr_k^{(2)}}) \qquad (10)$$

Figure 5 depicts how the *learning rate* and *momentum* change during the initial
training stages, given there are no anomalies, accuracy losses and $\forall k : rmse_k^{pre} >
rmse_k^{post}$—i.e. when $\forall k : lr_k^{(1)} = lr_k^{(2)} = lr_k$. Figure 7 shows the actual lr_k given real-
istic workload.

Furthermore, to speed up convergence it is beneficial to run multiple *epochs*
(i.e. repeated training iterations) with the first incoming samples and with samples

---

Algorithm 1: Dynamic VM Type Selection (DVTS)

---

input : $VT, ann, \Delta, minU, maxU$

1 $bestVmt \longleftarrow$ null;
2 $bestCost \longleftarrow 0$;

3 **for** $vmt \in VT$;   // Inspect all VM types
4 **do**
5     $cpuCapacity \longleftarrow vmt$'s norm. CPU capacity ;
6     $ramCapacity \longleftarrow vmt$'s norm. RAM capacity;
7     $vmtCost \longleftarrow vmt$'s cost per time unit;

8     $userCapacity \longleftarrow 0$;
9     $n \longleftarrow minU$;
10   **while** *True* ;   // Find how many users it can take
11   **do**
12       $cpu, ram \longleftarrow predict(ann, n, minU, maxU)$;
13   **if** $cpu < cpuCapacity$ and $ram < ramCapacity$ **then**
14          $userCapacity \longleftarrow n$;
15   **else**
16   break;
17   **end**
18       $n \longleftarrow n + \Delta$;
19   **end**

   // Approximate the cost for a user per time unit
20    $userCost \longleftarrow \frac{vmtCost}{userCapacity}$;

   // Find the cheapest VM type
21   **if** $userCost < bestCost$ **then**
22       $bestCost \longleftarrow userCost$;
23       $bestVmt \longleftarrow vmt$;
24   **end**
25 **end**
26 **return** $bestVmt$;

---

taken after a workload change. The ideal *learning rate lr* and its approximation $lr_k^{(2)}$ already embody this information and we could simply use their ratio. However, $\frac{lr_k^{(2)}}{lr}$ can easily exceed 300 given $lr = 0.001$, resulting in over-training with particular samples. Hence, we take the logarithm of it as in Eq. 11:

$$e_k = \left\lfloor 1 + ln(\frac{lr_k^{(2)}}{lr}) \right\rfloor \qquad (11)$$

5 Virtual Machine Type Selection

When a new VM has to be provisioned the ANN should be already trained so that we can estimate the relationship between number of users and CPU and RAM requirements. The procedure is formalised in Algorithm 1. We loop over all VM types VT

Algorithm 2: Resource Utilisation Estimation

---

   input : $ann, n, minU, maxU$

1 $cpu \longleftarrow 0$;
2 $ram \longleftarrow 0$;

3 **if** $n < maxUsers$;   // If within range - use ANN
4 **then**
5 | $cpu, ram \longleftarrow ann.run(n)$;
6 **else**
       | // If outside range - extrapolate
7 | $minRam, minCPU \longleftarrow ann.run(minU)$;
8 | $maxRam, maxCPU \longleftarrow ann.run(maxU)$;
9 | $cpuPerUser \longleftarrow \frac{(maxCPU - minCPU)}{(maxU - minU)}$;
10 | $ramPerUser \longleftarrow \frac{(maxRam - minRam)}{(maxU - minU)}$;
11 | $cpu \longleftarrow maxCPU + cpuPerUser(n - maxU)$
       | $ram \longleftarrow maxCPU + ramPerUser(n - maxU)$
12 **end**
13 return cpu, ram;

(line 3) and for each one we estimate its normalised CPU and RAM capacity based on the *capacity repository* as explained earlier (lines 5–6). The VM cost per time unit (e.g. hour in AWS or minute in Google Compute Engine) is obtained from the provider's specification (line 7).

Next, we approximate the number of users that a VM of this type is expected to be able to serve (lines 10–18). We iteratively increase n by Δ starting from $minU$, which is the minimal number of users we have encountered while training the neural network. We use the procedure *predict* (defined separately in Algorithm 2) to estimate the normalised CPU and RAM demands that each of these values of n would cause. We do so until the CPU or RAM demands exceed the capacity of the inspected VM type. Hence, we use the previous value of n as an estimation of the number of users a VM of that type can accommodate. Finally, we select the VM type with the lowest cost to number of users ratio (lines 20–23).

Algorithm 2 describes how to predict the normalised utilisations caused by n concurrent users. If n is less than the maximum number of users $maxU$ we trained the ANN with, then we can just use the ANN's prediction (line 5). However, if n is greater than $maxU$ the ANN may not predict accurately. For example if we have used a single *small* VM to train the ANN, and then we try to predict the capacity of a *large* VM, n can become much larger than the entries of the training data and the regression model may be inaccurate. Thus, we extrapolate the CPU and RAM requirements (lines 7–11) based on the range of values we trained the ANN with and the performance model we have proposed in a previous work [21].

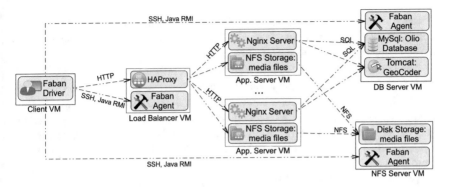

Fig. 6 CloudStone benchmark's extended topology

6 Benchmark and Prototype

There are two main approaches for experimental validation of a distributed system's performance—through a simulation or a prototype. Discrete event simulators like CloudSim [7] have been used throughout industry and academia to quickly evaluate scheduling and provisioning approaches for large- scale cloud infrastructure without having to pay for expensive test beds. Unfortunately, such simulators work on a simplified cloud performance model and do not represent realistic VM performance variability, which is essential for testing our system. Moreover, simulations can be quite inaccurate when the simulated system serves resource demanding workloads, as they do not consider aspects like CPU caching, disk data caching in RAM and garbage collection [21]. Therefore, we test our method through a prototype and a standard benchmark deployed in a public cloud environment.

We validate our approach with the CloudStone [12, 37] web benchmark deployed in Amazon AWS. It follows the standard 3-tier architecture. By default CloudStone is not scalable, meaning that it can only use a single AS. Thus, we had to extend it to accommodate multiple servers. Our installation scripts and configurations are available as open-source code. For space considerations, we will not discuss these technical details and will only provide an overview. The interested readers can refer to our online documentation and installation instructions.[1]

The benchmark deployment topology is depicted in Fig. 6. CloudStone uses the *Faban* harness to manage the runs and to emulate users. The *faban driver*, which is deployed in the client VM communicates with the *faban agents* deployed in other VMs to start or stop tests. It also emulates the incoming user requests to the application. These requests arrive at a HAProxy *load balancer* which distributes them across one or many application servers (AS). CloudStone is based on the Olio application, which is a PHP social network website deployed in a Nginx server. In the beginning we start with a single AS "behind" the *load balancer*. When a new AS VM is pro-

---

[1]http://nikolaygrozev.wordpress.com/2014/06/02/advanced-automated-cloudstone-setup-in-ubuntu-vms-part-2/.

visioned we associate it with the *load balancer*. We update its weighted round robin policy, so that incoming request are distributed among the AS VMs proportionally to their declared CPU capacity (i.e. ECU).

The persistent layer is hosted in a MySql server deployed within a separate DB VM. CloudStone has two additional components—(i) a geocoding service called *GeoCoder*, hosted in an Apache Tomcat server and (ii) a shared *file storage* hosting media files. They are both required by all application servers. We have deployed the geocoding service in the DB VM. The file storage is deployed in a Network File System (NFS) server on a separate VM with 1TB EBS storage, which is mounted from each AS VM.

We use "m3.medium" VMs for the client, load balancer and DB server and "m1.small" for the NFS server. The types of the AS VMs are defined differently for each experiment. All VMs run 64bit Ubuntu Linux 14.04.

Our prototype of an autoscaling component is hosted on an on-premises physical machine and implements the previously discussed algorithms and approaches. It uses the JClouds [24] multi-cloud library to provision resources, and thus can be used in other clouds as well. We use the NuPIC [30] and FANN [16] libraries to implement HTM and ANN respectively. We ignore the first 110 *anomaly scores* reported from the HTM, as we observed that these results are inaccurate (i.e. always 1 or 0) until it receives initial training. Whenever a new AS VM is provisioned we initialise it with a deep copy of the HTM of the first AS VM, which is the most trained one. The monitoring programs deployed within each VM are implemented as bash scripts, and are accessed by the autoscaling component through SSH. Our implementation of Algorithm 2 uses $\Delta = 5$.

Previously, we discussed that the number of current users could be approximated by counting the number of distinct IP addresses to which there is an active TCP session. However, in CloudStone all users are emulated from the same client VM and thus have the same source IP address. Thus, we use the number of recently modified web server session files instead.

Our autoscaling component implementation follows the Amazon Auto Scaling [3] approach and provisions a new AS VM once the average utilisation of the server form reaches 70% for more than 10 s. Hence, we ensure that in all experiments the AS VMs are not overloaded. Thus, even if there are SLA violations, they are caused either by the network or the DB layer, and the AS layer does not contribute to them. We also implement a *cool down* period of 10 min.

7 Validation

In our experiments, we consider three VM types: *m1.small, m1.medium,* and *m3.medium*. Table 1 summarises their cost and declared capacities in the Sydney AWS region which we use.

In all experiments we use the same workload. We start by emulating 30 users and each 6 min we increase the total number of users with 10 until 400 users are reached. To achieve this, we run a sequence of CloudStone benchmarks, each having 1 min ramp-up and 5 min steady state execution time. Given CloudStone's start-up and shut-down times, this amounts to more than 5 h per experiment. The goal is to gradually increase the number of users, thus causing the system to scale up multiple times.

To test our approach in the case of a workload characteristic change we "inject" such a change 3.5 h after each experiment's start. To do so we manipulate the *utilisation monitors* to report higher values. More specifically they increase the reported CPU utilisations with 10% and the reported RAM utilisation with 1 GB plus 2 MB for every currently served user.

We implement one experiment, which is initialised with a *m1.small* AS VM and each new VM's type is chosen based on our method (DVTS). We also execute 3 baseline experiments, each of which statically selects the same VM type whenever a new VM is needed, analogously to the standard AWS Auto Scaling rules.

First, we investigate the behaviour of DVTS before the workload change. It continuously trains one HTM for the first AS VM and the ANN. In the initial stages, the ANN *learning rate* and *momentum* decrease and increase, respectively, to facilitate faster training. For example, the *learning rate* lr_k (defined in Eq. 9) during the initial stages is depicted in Fig. 7. It shows how lr_k drastically reduces as the ANN improves its accuracy after only a few tens of training samples. Once the AS VM gets overloaded we select a new VM type. At this point we only have information about *m1.small* in the *capacity repository* and therefore we infer the other CPU capacities based on Eq. 4. Finally using Algorithm 1 we select *m3.medium* as the type for the second VM.

After the new VM is instantiated, the autoscaling component starts its monitoring. It trains the ANN and a new dedicated HTM with its measurements. It also updates the *capacity repository* with the CPU capacity of the new VM. Surprisingly, we observe that on average its CPU capacity is about 35% better than the one of the *m1.small* VM, even though according to the specification *m3.medium* has 3 ECUs and *m1.small* has 1. Therefore, the previous extrapolation of *m3.medium*'s capacity has been an overestimation. Hence, when a new VM is needed again, the algorithm selects *m1.small* again.

3.5 h after the start of the experiment the workload change is injected. This is reflected in the HTMs' anomaly scores an_k and the ANN's errors. Consequently, the *learning rate* lr_k, the *momentum* m_k and the *epochs* e_k also change to speed up the learning process as per Eqs. 9–11 and as a result the ANN adapts quickly to the

Table 1 AWS VM type definitions

VM type	ECU	RAM (GB)	Cost per hour
m1.small	1	1.7	$0.058
m1.medium	2	3.75	$0.117
m3.medium	3	3.75	$0.098

Fig. 7 Learning rate lr_k during initial stages of training the ANN

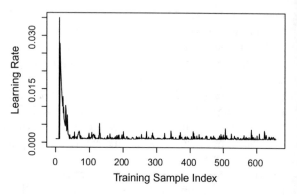

Fig. 8 RMSE-pre in the presence of a workload change. The 0 index corresponds to the first sample after the workload change

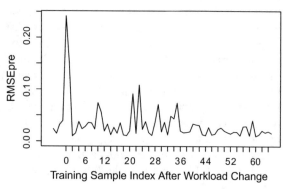

workload change. As discussed, for each sample we compute its error (RMSE-pre) before updating the ANN. Figure 8 depicts how these errors increase when the change is injected and decrease afterwards as the ANN adapts timely.

Eventually, the load increases enough so the system needs to scale up again. Due to the injected change, the workload has become much more memory intensive, which is reflected in the ANN's prediction. Hence *m1.small* can serve just a few users, given it has only 1.7 GB RAM. At that point the CPU capacity of *m1.medium* is inferred from the capacities of *m1.small* and *m3.medium* as per Eq. 4, since it has not been used before. Consequently Algorithm 1 selects *m1.medium* for the 4th VM just before the experiment completes.

For each experiment, Fig. 9 depicts the timelines of the allocated VMs and the total experiment costs. For each VM the type and cost are specified to the right. Our selection policy is listed as *DVTS*. The baseline policy which statically selects *m1.small* allocates 8 new VMs after the workload change as *m1.small* can serve just a few users under the new workload. In fact, if there was no *cool down* period in the autoscaling, this baseline would have exceeded the AWS limit of allowed number of VM instances before the end of the experiment. The baselines which select *m1.medium* and *m3.medium* fail to make use of *m1.small* instances before the change injection, which offers better performance for money.

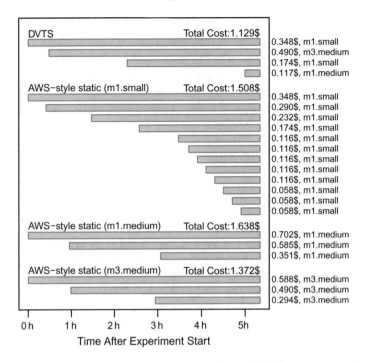

Fig. 9 Timelines and costs of all VMs grouped by experiments. DVTS is our approach. The AWS-style policies are the baselines, which statically select a predefined VM type

Admittedly, in the beginning DVTS did a misstep with the selection of *m3.medium*, because it started with an empty *capacity repository* and had to populate it and infer CPU capacities "on the go". This could have been avoided by prepopulating the *capacity repository* with test or historical data. We could expect that such inaccuracies are avoided at later stages, once more capacity and training data are present. Still, our approach outperformed all baselines in terms of incurred costs with more than 20% even though its effectiveness was hampered by the lack of contextual data in the initial stages.

Our experiments tested DVTS and the baselines with a workload, which is lower than what is observed in some applications. While our tests did not allocate more than 12 VMs (in the baseline experiment, which statically allocates *m1.small*) many real-world systems allocate hundreds or even thousands of servers. We argue that in such cases, DVTS will perform better than demonstrated, as there will be much more training data and thus the VM types' capacity estimations will be determined more accurately and the machine learning approaches will converge faster. As discussed, that would allow some of the initial missteps of DVTS to be avoided. Moreover, as the number of AS VMs grows, so does the cost inefficiency caused by the wastage of allocated resources, which can be reduced by DVTS.

Finally, the response times in the DVTS experiment and all baseline experiments were equivalent. All experiments scale up once the AS VMs' utilisations exceed the predefined thresholds, and thus never become overloaded enough to cause response delays. The load balancer is equally utilised in all experiments, as it serves the same number of users, although it redirects them differently among the AS VMs. Similarly, the DB layer is equally utilised, as it always serves all users from all AS VMs.

8 Open Research Problems

Our approach can achieve even greater efficiency, if it periodically replaces the already running VMs with more suitable ones in terms of cost and performance, once there is a workload change. New load balancing policies, which take into account the actual VM capacities can also be explored. Another promising avenue is optimising the scaling down mechanisms—i.e. selecting which VMs to terminate when the load decreases. Our approach, which currently optimises cost, can be extended to also consider other factors like energy efficiency. This would be important when executing application servers in private clouds. One can incorporate historical data about VM types' resource capacity and workload characteristics in our proposed algorithms.

To enhance *reliability*, autoscaling systems in clouds need to consider failures of services and resources within and across one or more cloud service providers [31]. To enhance *sustainability* of clouds, autoscaling systems need to manage multiple types of resources (i.e. compute, storage, network and cooling systems) within cloud data centres in a seamless manner to reduce overall energy consumption. Furthermore, they can also scale across multiple clouds to harness renewable energy-powered cloud data centres to minimise their carbon footprint on the environment [40].

9 Summary and Conclusions

In this work, we have introduced an approach for VM type selection when autoscaling application servers. It uses a combination of heuristics and machine learning approaches to "learn" the application's performance characteristics and to adapt to workload changes in real time. To validate our work, we have developed a prototype, extended the CloudStone benchmark and executed experiments in AWS EC2. We have made improvements to ensure our machine learning techniques train quickly and are usable in real time. Also, we have introduced heuristics to approximate VM resource capacities and workload resource requirements even if there is no readily usable data, thus making our approach useful given only partial knowledge. Results show that our approach can adapt timely to workload changes and can decrease the cost compared to typical static selection policies. We identified a number of open issues that form the basis for future research directions.

Acknowledgements We thank Rodrigo Calheiros, Amir Vahid Dastjerdi, Adel Nadjaran Toosi, and Simone Romano for their comments on improving this work. We also thank Amazon.com, Inc for their support through the AWS in Education Research Grant.

References

1. Aarsten, A., Brugali, D., & Menga, G. (1996). Patterns for three-tier client/server applications. In *Proceedings of Pattern Languages of Programs (PLoP '96)*.
2. Ali-Eldin, A., Tordsson, J., & Elmroth, E. (2012). An adaptive hybrid elasticity controller for cloud infrastructures. In *Network Operations and Management Symposium (NOMS), 2012 IEEE* (pp. 204–212).
3. Amazon. Amazon Auto Scaling, January 14 2016.
4. Barrett, E., Howley, E., & Duggan, J. (2013). Applying reinforcement learning towards automating resource allocation and application scalability in the cloud. *Concurrency and Computation: Practice and Experience, 25*(12), 1656–1674.
5. Brewer, E. A. (2000). Towards Robust Distributed Systems. In *Proceedings of the Annual ACM Symposium on Principles of Distributed Computing*, New York (Vol. 19, pp. 7–10). ACM.
6. Brewer, E. (2012). CAP twelve years later: How the "rules" have changed. *Computer, 45*(2), 23.
7. Calheiros, R. N., Ranjan, R., Beloglazov, A., De Rose, C. A. F., & Buyya, R. (2011). CloudSim: A toolkit for modeling and simulation of cloud computing environments and evaluation of resource provisioning algorithms. *Software: Practice and Experience, 41*(1), 23–50.
8. Cattell, R. (2010). Scalable SQL and NoSQL data stores. *SIGMOD Record, 39*(4), 12–27.
9. Cherkasova, L., Ozonat, K., Mi, N., Symons, J., & Smirni, E. (2009). Automated anomaly detection and performance modeling of enterprise applications. *ACM Transactions on Computer Systems, 27*(3), 1–32.
10. Chieu, T. C., Mohindra, A., & Karve, A. A. (2011). Scalability and Performance of Web Applications in a Compute Cloud. In *Proceedings of the IEEE International Conference on e-Business Engineering* (pp. 317–323).
11. Chieu, T. C., Mohindra, A., Karve, A. A., & Segal, A. (2009). Dynamic Scaling of Web Applications in a Virtualized Cloud Computing Environment. In *Proceedings of the IEEE International Conference on e-Business Engineering (ICEBE 2009)* (pp. 281–286).
12. CloudSuite. CloudSuite's CloudStone, January 14 2016.
13. Corbett, J. C., Dean, J., Epstein, M., Fikes, A., Frost, C., Furman, J. J., et al. (2013). Spanner: Google's globally distributed database. *ACM Transactions on Computing Systems, 31*(3), 8:1–8:22.
14. Dejun, J., Pierre, G., & Chi, C.-H. (2009). EC2 performance analysis for resource provisioning of service-oriented applications. In *Proceedings of the International Conference on Service-Oriented Computing (ICSOC 2009), ICSOC/ServiceWave'09* (pp. 197–207). Heidelberg: Springer.
15. Dutreilh, X., Kirgizov, S., Melekhova, O., Malenfant, J., Rivierre, N., & Truck, I. (2011). Using reinforcement learning for autonomic resource allocation in clouds: Towards a fully automated workflow. In *Proceedings of the 7th International Conference on Autonomic and Autonomous Systems (ICAS 2011)* (pp. 67–74).
16. FANN. FANN, January 13 2016.
17. Fernandez, H. et al. (2014). Autoscaling web applications in heterogeneous cloud infrastructures. In *Proceedings of the IEEE International Conference on Cloud Engineering* (pp. 195–204).
18. Fowler, M. (2003). *Patterns of enterprise application architecture*. Addison-Wesley Professional.

19. Gandhi, A., Dube, P., Karve, A., Kochut, A., & Zhang, L. (2014). Adaptive, model-driven autoscaling for cloud applications. In *11th International Conference on Autonomic Computing, ICAC '14* (pp. 57–64).
20. Grok. Grok, January 13 2016.
21. Grozev, N., & Buyya, R. (2013). Performance modelling and simulation of three-tier applications in cloud and multi-cloud environments. *The Computer Journal.*
22. Hawkins, J., Ahmad, S., & Dubinsky, D. (2011). Hierarchical temporal memory including HTM cortical learning algorithm. Technical report, Numenta Inc.
23. Hawkins, J., & Blakeslee, S. (2004). *On intelligence.* New York: Times Books.
24. JClouds. JClouds, January 14 2016.
25. Lloyd, W., Pallickara, S., David, O., Lyon, J., Arabi, M., & Rojas, K. (2013). Performance implications of multi-tier application deployments on infrastructure-as-a-service clouds: Towards performance modeling. *Future Generation Computer Systems, 29*(5), 1254–1264.
26. Lorido-Botrán, T., Miguel-Alonso, J., & Lozano, J. A. (2012). Auto-scaling techniques for elastic applications in cloud environments. Technical Report EHU-KAT-IK-09-12, Department of Computer Architecture and Technology, University of the Basque Country.
27. Moreira, M., & Fiesler, E. (1995). Neural networks with adaptive learning rate and momentum terms. Technical Report 95-04, IDIAP, Martigny, Switzerland.
28. Mountcastle, V. (1978). An organizing principle for cerebral function: the unit model and the distributed system. In G. Edelman & V. Mountcastle (Eds.), *The mindful brain.* Cambridge: MIT Press.
29. Numenta. Numenta, February 13 2014.
30. Numenta. Numenta Platform for Intelligent Computing (NuPIC), February 13 2014.
31. Qu, C., Calheiros, R. N., & Buyya, R. (2016). A reliable and cost-efficient auto-scaling system for web applications using heterogeneous spot instances. *Journal of Network and Computer Applications, 65,* 167–180.
32. Ramirez, A. O. (2000). Three-tier architecture. *Linux Journal, 2000*(75) (2000).
33. RightScale. RightScale, January 14 2016.
34. Schad, J., Dittrich, J., & Quiané-Ruiz, J.-A. (2010). Runtime measurements in the cloud: Observing, analyzing, and reducing variance. *The Proceedings of the VLDB Endowment (PVLDB), 3*(1–2), 460–471.
35. Simmons, B., Ghanbari, H., Litoiu, M., & Iszlai, G. (2011). Managing a saas application in the cloud using paas policy sets and a strategy-tree. In *Proceedings of the 7th International Conference on Network and Services Management, CNSM '11* (pp. 343–347), Laxenburg, Austria, Austria, 2011. International Federation for Information Processing.
36. Singh, R., Sharma, U., Cecchet, E., & Shenoy, P. (2010). Autonomic mix-aware provisioning for non-stationary data center workloads. In *Proceedings of the 7th International Conference on Autonomic Computing, ICAC '10,* New York, NY, USA, 2010 (pp. 21–30). ACM.
37. Sobel, W., Subramanyam, S., Sucharitakul, A., Nguyen, J., Wong, H., Klepchukov, A., et al. (2008). Cloudstone: MultiPlatform, multi-language benchmark and measurement tools for web 2.0. In *Proceedings of Cloud Computing and Its Applications (CCA '08), CCA '08.*
38. Tan, Y., Nguyen, H., Shen, Z., Gu, X., Venkatramani, C., & Rajan. D. (2012). Prepare: Predictive performance anomaly prevention for virtualized cloud systems. In *Proceedings of the 32nd International Conference on Distributed Computing Systems (ICDCS)* (pp. 285–294).
39. Tickoo, O., Iyer, R., Illikkal, R., & Newell, D. (2010). Modeling virtual machine performance: Challenges and approaches. *ACM SIGMETRICS Performance Evaluation Review, 37*(3), 55–60.
40. Toosi, A. N., Qu, C., de Assunção, M. D., & Buyya, R. (2017). Renewable-aware geographical load balancing of web applications for sustainable data centers. *Journal of Network and Computer Applications, 83,* 155–168.
41. Tordsson, J., Montero, R. S., Moreno-Vozmediano, R., & Llorente, I. M. (2012). Cloud brokering mechanisms for optimized placement of virtual machines across multiple providers. *Future Generation Computer Systems, 28*(2), 358–367.
42. Vogl, T. P., Mangis, J. K., Rigler, A. K., Zink, W. T., & Alkon, D. L. (1988). Accelerating the convergence of the back-propagation method. *Biological Cybernetics, 59*(4–5), 257–263.

Improving the Energy Efficiency in Cloud Computing Data Centres Through Resource Allocation Techniques

Belén Bermejo, Sonja Filiposka, Carlos Juiz, Beatriz Gómez
and Carlos Guerrero

Abstract The growth of power consumption in Cloud Computing systems is one of the current concerns of systems designers. In previous years, several studies have been carried out in order to find new techniques to decrease the cloud power consumption. These techniques range from decisions on locations for data centres to techniques that enable efficient resource management. Resource Allocation, as a process of Resource Management, assigns available resources throughout the data centre in an efficient manner, minimizing the power consumption and maximizing the system performance. The contribution presented in this chapter is an overview of the Resource Management and Resource Allocation techniques, which contribute to the reduction of energy consumption without compromising the cloud user and provider constraints. We will present key concepts regarding energy consumption optimization in cloud data centres. Moreover, two practical cases are presented to illustrate the theoretical concepts of Resource Allocation. Finally, we discuss the open challenges that Resource Management must face in the coming years.

B. Bermejo (✉) · C. Juiz · B. Gómez · C. Guerrero
Computer Science Department, University of the Balearic Islands, Palma, Spain
e-mail: belen.bermejo@uib.es

C. Juiz
e-mail: cjuiz@uib.es

B. Gómez
e-mail: b.gomez@uib.es

C. Guerrero
e-mail: carlos.guerrero@uib.es

S. Filiposka
Faculty of Computer Science and Engineering, University Ss.
Cyril and Methodius, Skopje, Macedonia
e-mail: sonja.filiposka@finki.ukim.mk

© Springer Nature Singapore Pte Ltd. 2017
S. Chaudhary et al. (eds.), *Research Advances in Cloud Computing*,
DOI 10.1007/978-981-10-5026-8_9

1   Introduction

Computing has traditionally been based in a local environment using our own computer and other specific hardware to process and store information. However, this vision is increasingly changing as computing is becoming a global phenomenon, becoming a set of centralized facilities offered as a utility, similar to water, gas or telephony. This is possible thanks to the *dynamic provisioning* concept, which allows on-demand access to services in a transparent user-friendly way. In such a model, users fulfil their needs by hiring facilities based on their requirements regardless of the hosting location [16].

This way of processing information is already supported and boosted by several computing paradigms, such as Grid Computing and Cloud Computing. Lately, centralized information processing has proved to be more efficient, on large farms of computing and storage systems accessible via the Internet [39]. Thus, Information Technology (IT), in general, becomes a synonym for different resources available through the Internet provided by cloud providers on a pay-per-use basis according to the amount of resources utilization [16]. In fact, John McCarthy predicted this idea in 1961, remarking that "computation may someday be organized as a public utility" [64].

Since the early days of mainframes in the early 1950s, the evolution of distributed computing technologies has created favourable conditions for the realization of Cloud Computing; currently, it embodies aspects of all distributed technologies [16]. Cluster-based technology enables machines connected by a high-bandwidth network and managed by specific software to be viewed as a single system. Grid Computing is a dynamic aggregation of geographically dispersed clusters by means of Internet connections. It proposed a new approach to access through the Internet to a set of large computational power resources, huge storage facilities and a variety of services. In contrast, the virtualization technology allows different applications to be allocated on a single Physical Machine (PM) in logically scheduled Virtual Machines (VMs) using virtualization functions such as: VM migration, VM creation, VM modification and VM destruction. Web 2.0 facilitates the creation of web pages which are more interactive and flexible, improving the user experience by allowing web-based access to all functions that traditionally was deployed only in desktop environments. Service-Oriented Computing (SOC) is the core reference model for cloud systems [43]. The SOC approach is based on a development pattern of building services as the man system. It supports the development of brisk, low-cost, flexible, interoperable, and evolvable applications and systems. The intrinsic design of service computing is based on a service delivery model, in which users pay providers for using on-demand computing power [15].

Cloud and Grid Computing have common objectives: reducing the cost of processing the information and power/energy consumption and harnessing the opportunities that are offered by centralization to improve scalability, reliability, and availability, among others; all of these are transparent to final users and are managed by a third party [64]. Cloud Computing is deployed in large data centres hosted by a single organization, which provide virtually infinite capacity while being tolerant to failures and always on, delivering more abstract resources and services, which are consumed on a pay-per-use basis.

The definition of Cloud Computing that has achieved commonly accepted status was created by NIST [41]: "Cloud Computing is a model for enabling ubiquitous, convenient, on-demand network access to a shared pool of configurable computing resources (e.g. networks, servers, storage, applications and services) that can be rapidly provisioned and released with minimal management effort or services provider interaction". The management and the maintenance costs are in charged by cloud providers [64].

The combination of the previously mentioned technologies generates different deployment models and provides useful information regarding the nature and services offered by the cloud. One useful classification, given according to the administrative domain of a Cloud Computing, differentiates four possible types of clouds according to the deployment model [49]:

- *Private cloud*: the cloud infrastructure is operated internally by the organization itself or by a single third party that acts only on behalf of the organization. This cloud-based in-house solution is usually used by those who store and manipulate highly confidential information with a critical level of security, privacy and regulatory concerns. The adoption of private clouds by SMBs (Small and Medium Business) and enterprises has increased by 14% in recent years.
- *Community cloud*: an interest-specific community of organizations that share similar concerns (as mentioned above) operates over the pool of shared infrastructure.
- *Public cloud*: a third-party service provider sells cloud services to any consumer on a subscription basis. The adoption of public clouds has been increased by 1% in recent years by SMBs and enterprises.
- *Hybrid cloud:* a composition of public and private cloud resources is used when the private-only resources are unable to meet the users' Quality of Service (QoS) requirements. Although clouds are linked by standardized or proprietary technology that allows data and application portability, each of them remains as an individual entity. The adoption of hybrid clouds by SMBs and enterprises has increased by 13% in recent years.

In [39], these types of clouds are classified as deployment models depending on their characteristics and user requirements. However, clouds can also be classified based on its capability to deliver a variety of IT services on demand, thus taking a user point of view. According to the NIST reference architecture (see Fig. 1), cloud delivery models and services are presented in a service layer and described by the Cloud Security Alliance [7] as follows:

- *Infrastructure-as-a-Service* (IaaS) delivers infrastructure such as processing, storage, networks, and other resources on demand mostly in the form of virtual interfaces. This provides computing on demand in the form of VM instances. In this model, customers cannot manage the cloud infrastructure although may run software in the VMs, for example the AWS (Amazon Web Service).

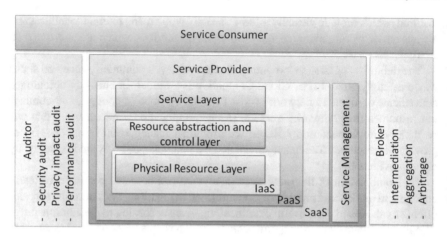

Fig. 1 Cloud computing reference model based on [41]

- *Platform-as-a-Service* (PaaS) provides scalable and elastic runtime environments on demand and hosts the execution of applications. The cloud provider enables users to use programming languages and tools by controlling their deployed applications as well as the configurations of hosting environment. The responsibility of the service provider, among others, is to provide scalability and to manage fault tolerance, e.g. Google App Engine.
- *Software-as-a-Service* (SaaS) delivers applications and services on demand. The applications are accessible from client device interfaces, as simple as a browser. The user does not manage the platform or the infrastructure as these are the provider's responsibility, e.g. Google Drive or Dropbox.

Beloglazov and Buyya [11] defined the main challenges for cloud providers, namely, performance, availability and dependability. All of these challenges impact on the design and the operation of cloud services in which energy efficiency is crucial factor due to the increasing of power consumed by PM. In fact, up to 40% of current IT budget is directly related to energy cost [49].

Cloud Computing is based on the dynamic provisioning concept, thanks to the Resource Management process and how it performs in the virtual interface. This process affects performance, functionality and cost, three criteria for system evaluation. An inefficient Resource Management inherently produces a direct negative effect on performance, cost and ulterior defect on the functionality of the system, and the power consumption. There are many techniques for performing an efficient Resource Management process that incorporates energy consumption awareness. The greatest challenge is achieving the minimum energy consumption without compromising the Service-Level Agreement (SLA) and the Service Level Objective (SLO) established between the customer and the cloud provider.

The aim of this chapter is to provide an overview of the Cloud Computing concepts and data centres that support cloud services and to discuss Resource Management techniques that can be performed in an IaaS environment. Particularly, we focus on Resource Allocation techniques that aim to reduce the energy consumption, taking into account the customer and provider constraints.

The remainder of this chapter is organized as follows: in Sect. 1, we introduce key concepts of Cloud Computing underlying technologies and virtualized data centres. Additionally, we introduce issues related to the power and energy consumption, as well as the power proportionality. In Sect. 2, we explain the Resource Management concept, its implementation process and the most important techniques involved. In Sect. 3, we discuss the details of the Resource Allocation concept being an essential part of the Resource Management process. Particularly, we focus on Resource Allocation techniques that incorporate energy efficiency. In Sects. 4 and 5, we present the conclusions and future challenges of Cloud Computing.

1.1 Data Centres in Cloud Computing

Although cloud offers are generally marketed as IaaS, PaaS and SaaS, this chapter is devoted to the IaaS model. Thus, the focus of this section is on the features that cloud data centres have in an IaaS environment.

As already discussed, Cloud Computing shares some common characteristics with Cluster and Grid Computing but differs in that Cloud Computing adds a virtualization layer over the infrastructure, which enables the Resource Management process [64]. Figure 2 shows the conceptual difference between traditional computing and virtualized environment. In the former, applications interact directly with the Operating System (OS). In the latter, multiple OS images share the same hardware resources (CPU, RAM, storage and networking). A virtualization layer, commonly called hypervisor or Virtual Machine Monitor (VMM), is in charge of managing these multiple OSs.

In this context, a resource is any physical or logical component with a limited availability within a computer system. Due to the use of virtualization, it is necessary to classify the resources (see Fig. 3) that are involved in Resource Management [33]:

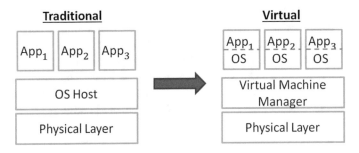

Fig. 2 Transition from traditional computing to virtualized computing based on [39]

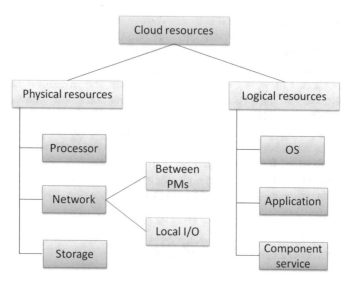

Fig. 3 Cloud resources taxonomy based on [33, 38]

- Physical Resources: these include all the tangible resources that compose a PM. The typical physical resources are: (a) the PMs, each comprised of one or more CPUs, memory, network interfaces and local I/O; virtualization software is deployed to host a number of VMs; (b) networking resources (i.e. switches) enabling connections between the PMs via a high-bandwidth network; (c) the storage resources that usually are, between others types, disks, databases, etc. The level of data consistency and reliability vary among the types of storage.
- Logical/Virtual Resources: a system abstraction that has temporary control over the physical resources. They can support development of applications and efficient communication protocols. The main logical resources are the host OS, component services such as VMs and VMMs.

From the Cloud Computing reference model point of view (see Fig. 1), there are three actors interacting with the cloud stack services (see Fig. 4) in IaaS [5]: the cloud provider, the cloud user and the end user. The cloud provider manages the physical and logical resources of the data centre, providing an abstraction of these resources to cloud users. Cloud users host applications offered to their end users. Providers' objectives are in charge of meet the user SLA and get economical profits. They have to guarantee that the dedicated resources are scaled as the end users' demand is increased. The workload processed by these resources is generated by the end users. Their behaviour influences in the Resource Management process.

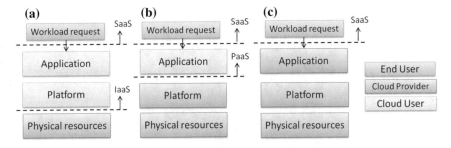

Fig. 4 Cloud models for provisioning: **a** IaaS, **b** PaaS and **c** SaaS. Own design based on [5]

1.2 Energy, Energy Efficiency and Power-Proportional Systems

As Cloud Computing adoption has been increasing by 2% per year, the power consumption has also been increasing. Moreover, 26% of enterprises are becoming more concerned with managing cloud costs that become a big challenge for them. Improvement in power consumption means a significant opportunity for reducing cloud costs, no matter if it is done by powering down unused workloads or by selecting lower cost clouds or regions [49].

As [23] indicates, the projected energy consumption grows of data centres is around 1000 billion kWh by 2020. For example, since 2000 to 2007, it increased from 70 to 330 billion. This grow is also expected in the resources of the data centres. The power density of a single rack will be around 30 kW by 2020, in comparison to the range of 250 W–1.5 kW they were at 2003. Another important factor is that PMs consume 50% of energy while they are in idle state, moreover if we consider that their average utilization is around 10–50%. For a 20% of use of the resources, the power consumption is around 80% of power consumption of the same infrastructure at 100% of use. Thus, improving the energy efficiency of PM is a key factor for data centre deployment. Moreover, the distribution of the power consumption in a data centre is as follows: 10% corresponds to power distribution, 12% corresponds to air movement, 25% corresponds to the cooling system, 50% corresponds to IT equipment and the last 3% is related to auxiliary issues [32]. Also, as [32] describe, the Power Usage Effectiveness (PUE) is a measure of how efficiently a data centre uses energy in computing tasks. PUE is defined as the ratio between the total amounts of energy used by a data centre as a whole and the energy delivered to PM. Elements such as lighting and cooling, fall into the category of facility energy consumption because they are not considered computing devices. While an ideal PUE has a value of 1.0, the global average of respondents' largest data centres is approximately 1.7.[1]

There are two main metrics related to power consumption in cloud data centres: Energy Efficiency and Power Proportionality. In [40], the Energy Efficiency is defined

---

[1] https://www.google.com/about/datacenters/efficiency/internal/.

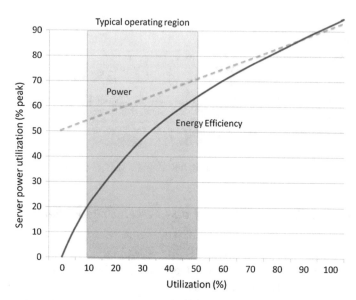

Fig. 5 Server power usage as a function of utilization in an energy-proportional system as it appears in [9, 32]

as a reduction of used energy to develop a service. It is also defined as the ratio of system's performance and its power consumption. Therefore, [32] defines the Power Proportionality as the ideal property of a system that consumes power in proportion to the amount of work performed. The power proportionality is not a requirement for a system to be an energy efficiency, however, proportional energy consumption is not a definitive solution since the workload variation of real systems demands not only proportional energy but also power proportional, too (see Fig. 5). The variation of power consumption in function of system utilization is represented by dotted line. It represents how the system when is being completely idle consumes half of the peak power. The system shows poor power proportionality because the energy efficiency increases from a very low value as the utilization growths. An ideal proportional system is also included in Fig. 5, where the energy efficiency keeps a constant level starting at 0 when the system is idle.

Thus, it is important to highlight the difference between power and energy. Power reduction can be achieved by lowering the CPU performance, but if an application has a longer execution time, it may consume the same or an extra amount of energy. The reduction of peak power consumption minimizes infrastructure provisioning costs, but diminished energy consumption cuts the electricity cost [1].

1.3 Energy Efficiency in Cloud Computing Data Centres

Power consumption is limited by high frequencies in computer systems. That involves the minimization of the power consumption of each computation device of the system. Power-supply sizing, cooling/heatsink requirements and criteria for device selection are determined by power consumption calculations. It can also determine the maximum reliable operating frequency. The static and dynamic power determine the power consumption in a CMOS circuit [14].

Current leakage that are present in any active circuit cause static power consumption, independently of clock rates and usages scenarios and are mainly determined by the type of transistors and process technology. Dynamic power consumption is created by circuit activity and depends mainly on a specific usage scenario. Static power management is not the aim of this chapter because this implies the improvement of the low-level system design. The fact that the dynamic power value depends on the component usage implies that this value can be managed in a cloud data centre [14].

As Fig. 6 shows, the dynamic power can be managed in two layers: hardware and software. The former includes all techniques related to the low-level design, e.g. transistors (circuit level), the physical location of the data centre, switching on/off techniques, Dynamic Voltage and Dynamic Performance Scaling techniques, such as DVFS (Dynamic Voltage Frequency Scaling) and DPS (Dynamic Power Switching) at PM level, and network topology that connect the data centre (network architecture). The latter includes all techniques related to the logical resources (workload, VM, etc.). The VMM level applies techniques related to the virtual resources, the VMs, performing any operations on them (consolidation, migration, etc.). The OS level includes techniques that perform traditional OS operations, such as workload scheduling and resource sharing (workload management) and network latency and network protocols (network management).

Table 1 shows some relevant works in the presented areas. For example, [22, 45] illustrated the improvement of energy efficiency in cloud data centres through low-level techniques, network architecture and network management.

In this chapter, we are particularly interested in the software level, where resource management techniques and policies can be applied (see Fig. 6). Throughout the chapter, we will show the techniques and the mechanism used to implement resource management policies. Then, the techniques used to implement the resource scheduling process (as a part of resource management) and the resource allocation (as a part of resource scheduling) for energy-aware techniques will be discussed (Fig. 7).

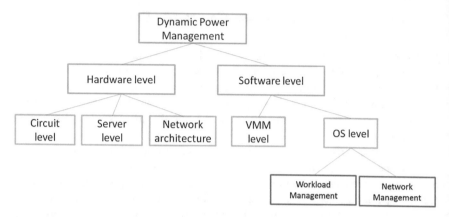

Fig. 6 Taxonomy of dynamic power management areas in a cloud data centre based on [14]

Table 1 Dynamic power management relevant works by areas

Dynamic power management area	Reference
Circuit level	[6, 18, 22, 63]
Server level	[34]
Network architecture	[45]
VMM level	[27, 30, 35, 61]
Workload management	[4, 18, 48, 60]
Network management	[26, 45]

Fig. 7 Resource management taxonomy based on [1, 2]

DYNAMIC POWER MANAGEMENT THROUGH RESOURCE MANAGEMENT

POLICIES
Admission control, Capacity allocation, Load balancing, Energy consumption optimization and QoS guarantee

MECHANISMS
Control theory, Machine learning, Utility-based techniques and Market-oriented

RESOURCE SCHEDULLING PROCESS
Virtualization-based, energy conservation-based, SLA-based and cost-effectiveness-based

2 Resource Management in Cloud Computing

Resource Management is a general process covering different stages ranging from the request submission to the request execution for different workloads [54]. Resource Management is used also to meet end users' requirements in terms of performance through allocating information technology hardware, namely, network, servers, etc. Consequently, other resources are indirectly managed, e.g. power consumption. The Resource Management is a complex problem in cloud environments due to heterogeneous nature of PMs and then their scalability problem in data centres. Moreover, the high variation of unpredicted workload [33] causes new interdependent problems in managing the cloud resources.

The different ways to solve Resource Management problems are connected with the cloud models—IaaS, PaaS and SaaS—even though may be delivered in different ways [39]. Nevertheless, there are common policies that guide the Resource Management decisions. The mechanisms represent the means to implement the policies, and these differ between delivery models. Depending on the system objective, the cloud Resource Management policies can be grouped into five classes: admission control, capacity allocation, load balancing, energy consumption optimization and QoS guarantee.

Marinescu [39] explains that the admission control policy should prevent the cloud system from workload harming higher level control policies. Additionally, capacity allocation means to assign resources for end users requests, but balancing the workload, whereas trying to optimize the energy consumption at PMs. Thus, all these policies are correlated and affected by the cost of providing the services. Load balancing and energy optimization policy are probably the most difficult to address in Resource Management. Simultaneously, it is possibly one of the most important issues for the future of Cloud Computing and the main topic of this chapter.

Regarding the mechanism needed to implement these policies at different layers of the cloud stack, four different techniques can be employed; first, control theory that uses the feedback of the system to guarantee system stability and predict future behaviour; second, machine learning that uses the information of the system performance over time to not use a system model; third, utility-based techniques, which require a performance model of the system and correlation of the user-level performance with cost. Thus, all of these techniques need a model of the system. The last, market-oriented and economic mechanisms use approaches based on Game Theory, e.g. combinatorial auction for bundles of resources and heuristics. In this last case, these techniques do not require a model of the system to make a decision.

Moreover, the main objective of the Resource Management process is the efficient and effective cloud provider resource usage within the constraints of SLA and SLO. Moreover, each actor has a specific objective in Resource Management. On the one hand, the cloud provider seeks sticking to the SLA (and SLO) with the cloud user regarding the provision of virtual interfaces over its physical resources. The provider also needs to multiplex the end users depending on the SLA. It should offer different service levels to the end users and may choose to prioritize the use of resources to different end users. Regarding the Resource Management, the cloud provider objectives are related to the balanced workload, fault tolerance and usage of physical resources. The aim is to optimize metrics depending on criteria, e.g. optimize the energy efficiency rather than physical resources utilization, etc. On the other hand, the cloud user seeks to exploit the elasticity property of cloud environments, making available additional resources to accommodate new demands or release according to the requests arrival rate. Moreover, the cloud user may formulate Resource Management objectives that reflect its approach to resource reservation, aiming to accommodate demand waves.

The main technologies that are directly or indirectly associated with cloud Resource Management processes are another important aspect to consider, as detailed below:

- Infrastructure scaling: hosting services can be offered at a low cost by cloud providers by concentrating large numbers of connected PMs, i.e. economies of scale.
- Virtualization: the hosting of multiple VMs into a PM is the most important benefit from the resource management perspective, together with the capability to configure VMs to utilize different PM resources [11, 17].
- VM migration: VMs allocation in a smaller number of PMs can be performed dynamically impacting on the energy efficiency of the data centre. This example of allocation strategy is well known as consolidation.
- Equipment power state adjustment: power management to minimize the energy consumption have been developed by equipment vendors and processor manufacturers, i.e. DVFS Marinescu [39].

The Resource Management in cloud systems consists of three main functions [38, 54]: Resource Provisioning, Resource Scheduling and Resource Monitoring (see Fig. 6). Taking into account the QoS requirements of end user, it submits its workload to the cloud provider platform for it execution. Based on QoS requirements and these constraints, the resources are provisioned as $\{r_1, r_2, r_3, \ldots, r_n\}$ for the end user's workloads $\{w_1, w_2, w_3, \ldots, w_m\}$ with maximum resource utilization and end user satisfaction.

In the next subsections, different parts of the resource management process are explained, as well as each subprocess. We will also explain in more detail some techniques to achieve the objective of each process.

2.1 Resource Provisioning

Manvi and Shyam [38] defined the Resource Provisioning as the distribution of services from the cloud provider to end users. To consider this problem, let $R = \{r_k, 1 \leq k \leq n\}$ be the collection of resources and n is the total number of resources; and $w = \{w_i | 1 \leq i \leq m\}$ as the collection of cloud workloads and m is the total number of cloud workloads. The set of independent workloads has to be mapped on a set of dynamic and heterogeneous resources.

The development of an efficient service provisioning policy is among the major issues in cloud research. The issue here is to provide better QoS in the IaaS model by provisioning the resources to the end users or applications via load balancing mechanisms and high availability mechanisms.

The Resource Provisioning process is composed of two functions: Resource Discovery and Resource Selection. The former is the identification of the available resources. The latter is the selection of the best workload resource, from the available ones, based on QoS requirements described by the cloud user in the terms of SLA (Fig. 8).

2.2 Resource Monitoring

Cloud resource utilization needs an efficient monitoring process in order to optimize data centre performance. Hence, cloud providers should control cloud user deviations from SLA in order to maintain QoS [38].

Resource Monitoring has three functions: Resource Usage, Resource Modelling and Resource Estimation. The Resource Monitoring system compiles the physical

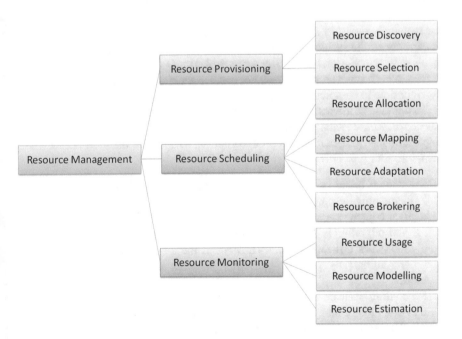

Fig. 8 Resource management processes, based on [33, 55]

resource usages by measuring performance through CPU and main memory utilization. Resource Modelling is based on the detailed information provided by transmission network elements regarding the resources. Current resources required for an application needs the computation of the Resource Estimation. In [47], a framework that illustrates the most important attributes of resources monitoring is provided: state, transitions, inputs and outputs within a given environment. It also helps in predicting the resource requirements in subsequent time intervals.

2.3 Resource Scheduling

Resource Scheduling in the cloud environment is always a complex task due to the geographical distribution of resources having varying load conditions, different user requirements and price models [37].

Open challenges in Resource Scheduling are still unresolved by traditional algorithms because of the dispersion, heterogeneity and uncertainty of the resources. The properties of cloud environment need to be considered to make cloud services and cloud-oriented applications more efficient.

Resource Scheduling is composed of four functions: Resource Allocation, Resource Mapping, Resource Adaptation and Resource Brokering. Resource Allocation is the distribution of resources economically among cloud users. Resource Mapping manages the correspondence between resources required by the cloud users and resources available within the cloud provider. Resource Adaptation is the ability or capacity of the system to adjust the resources dynamically to fulfil the requirements of the cloud user. Finally, Resource Brokering is the negotiation of the amount of resources through an agent to ensure that the necessary resources are available at the right time to complete the SLA objectives.

To implement the resource scheduling process, a series of techniques have been developed. These techniques consider variables related to cloud environments, such as performance and energy/power consumption, to optimize them. We can classify them into four types [37]:

1. Scheduling based on virtualization: VM migration is of higher importance in implementing Resource Management strategies for the optimization performance metrics, e.g. power consumption, utilization of PMs and QoS. The main challenge for VM migration is the minimization of service downtime and minimization of high network utilization [10, 44]. Most of the algorithms are based on linear programming [24], genetic algorithms [46], and machine learning techniques bib61.

2. Scheduling based on energy conservation: the current literature is indicative of the fact that PMs in many data centres usually operate at 30% of their full capacity [9]. The energy-oriented Resource Allocation policies consider two important characteristics: QoS expectations and PM power consumption. Most of these techniques are based on VM migration based on heuristics to consolidate the

maximum of VMs in the minimum of PMs [37]. The optimized metrics are energy efficiency [2, 11], execution time of a workload [3, 53], the cost of migration, the SLA violation rate, the PM utilization and the VM migration rate.

3. Scheduling based on SLA: as already discussed, the cloud provider and the cloud user have to negotiate a SLA, which basically outlines the service requirements and the certainty of service delivery. Violation of the SLA is a key issue, because it tends to make cloud users disaffected and eventually their level of satisfaction declines. Three metrics are optimized though many techniques: SLA violation rate, the service ranking and the cloud user satisfaction. These techniques [17, 52] are related to admission control algorithms, a general control-theoretic approach and the formulation of the resource scheduling programming based on mixed Integer Linear Programming (ILP).

4. Scheduling based on cost-effectiveness: in cloud environments, cloud providers want to minimize resource rental costs as they continue to meet workload demands, while cloud users look forward to the lowest possible prices for the resources they lease. The variables to optimize are usually the monetary cost, the PM utilization, the execution time, the SLA violation rate and the energy efficiency. In order to achieve that, the most used techniques are related to VM placement and migration [51], the reduction total execution time [50] and the dynamic resource renting schemes [42].

This chapter is devoted to Resource Allocation techniques because they have a significant impact in cloud environments, especially in pay-per-use deployments, where the numbers of resources are charged by cloud providers. The question here is how to allocate suitable resources to perform a task with minimal time and infrastructure cost. Suitable resources need to be selected for specific applications in IaaS, and instances of these resources are allocated to execute the task.

3 Resource Allocation for Energy-Awareness in Cloud Computing Data Centres

From the Resource Allocation techniques, we are interested in techniques that improve the energy efficiency taking into account the cloud user and provider constraints. Of particular interest are those techniques that are performed in the virtual interface layer. A vast number of works related to Resource Allocation techniques have been published in recent years. In Table 2, the most relevant techniques to achieve energy efficiency are shown. All these techniques are performed in the virtual layer.

Through these schemes, there are many implemented techniques that act at the virtual interface layer based on the VM consolidation and the VM migration. In [27], several heuristics are described; aiming to evaluate their capabilities, with special attention paid to balanced resource usage versus total number of used PMs. In their work, a community-based framework is shown for VM placement indoors a cloud

Table 2 Resource allocation for energy-aware techniques

Technique	Goal	Reference
Machine learning	Reduce the temperature and minimize the power consumption	[34]
VM migration	Minimize the energy cost	[30]
	Minimize energy consumption	[63]
Load prediction	Minimize the power consumption	[60]
VM clustering	Minimize the energy consumption and maximize the VM allocation quality	[61]
Sleep PM, considering VM usage	Reduce the energy consumption of data centre	[22]

data centre. The approach uses complex networks and it is based on the process of grouping the nodes that are tightly coupled and the mapping of VM communities to PM communities. The solution is addresses to optimize the energy consumption and the system performance.

Beloglazov and Buyya [13] proposed an efficient adaptive heuristic for dynamic allocation of VM in order to minimize the energy consumption while ensuring a high level of adherence to the SLA. They took into account the current utilization of resources, and by applying live migration, switching idle nodes to sleep mode, the energy consumption minimization can be achieved.

The VM allocation process may be divided in two different parts as [12] proposed: first, how to allocate VMs on PM (VM placement) and the VM provisioning when newer requests are admitted; second, how to optimize current VM allocation. Additionally, they proposed a general algorithm for VM allocation based on PM overloading detection and VM migration to available resources in PM. Cao et al. [19], proposed a VM allocation solution based on forecasting the power demand, reducing the total processor's frequency by switching on/off the PM. Moreover, [48], proposed diverse cloud resource allocation policies: Round Robin, Packing, Striping, Load Balancing (free CPU ratio), Load Balancing (free CPU count), and Cost per Core and Watts per Core, real cases. In [56], the energy metric presented establishes the relationship between the QoS obtained and the power consumed by the PM in web server clusters.

Furthermore, there are recent studies gather other energy-aware techniques, such as [58]. These newer strategies include resource requirements prediction and the Resource Allocation algorithms. In this work, they studied several Resource Allocation techniques used in cloud systems through a comparison between the benefits and drawbacks of these techniques.

Regarding the VM operations, [29] proposed a technique to minimize the impact of VM migration due to the cost of this operation in terms of power consumption and QoS violation during the downtime [59]. In [57], the current approaches with respect to costs of VM migration were summarized, classified and evaluated.

Of all the presented approaches, the Market-Oriented Resource Allocation and the dynamic Resource Allocation and consolidation mechanisms are mostly used to reduce energy consumption in cloud environments, especially in the VM layer. Moreover, there are architectures for implementing these techniques. Each architecture defines its own entities and Resource Management functions based on three main blocks: Resource Provisioning, Resource Scheduling and Resource Monitoring. The interest in managing the virtual interface layer is because 48% of the companies that manage a virtualized data centre have more than 1000 VMs running in its data centre [49].

In the next subsections, we will discuss two case studies of architectures to reduce the power consumption, using intelligent management in the VM layer. For each architecture, we will explain the objective, the involved entities and their interrelationship, and the Resource Management theory uncovered in the previous sections.

3.1   A case study of an architecture for dynamic Resource Allocation and Consolidation mechanism

The Green Cloud Architecture [12] aims to lead the design of the next generation of data centres by designing them as networks of virtual services. Consequently, users can access and deploy applications on demand from anywhere via the Internet depending on their QoS requirements.

In this case, the authors propose an efficient heuristic for dynamic adaptation of VM allocation according to the current utilization of resources applying live migration by switching idle PM to sleep mode in order to minimize the energy consumption.

Figure 9 shows the high-level architecture used to support energy-aware service allocation in green cloud infrastructures. This architecture comprises four entities:

- End users: they submit service requests wherever they are to the cloud provider.
- Green Service Allocator: performs interface functions to communicate the cloud provider with end users. In order to support the energy-efficient Resource Management is necessary the interaction of following entities.

    - Green Negotiator: mediates the prices and pain (for violations of the SLAs with the end users and the clouds provider), depending on its QoS and energy saving requirements.
    - Service analyser: determines if the cloud provider can accept the service requirements of a request. The decision is based on the history of the power consumption and VM Manager information.
    - Consumer profiler: collects specific features of end users to prioritize them and determine the special privileges depending on the agreed SLA.

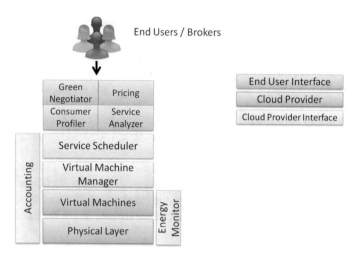

Fig. 9 Green cloud architecture for resource allocation based on [12]

- Pricing: decides is the price of the request to manage the supply and demand of computing resources and facilitate the priority of services allocation, taking into account the price.
- Energy monitor: gathers data related to the energy consumption from VMs and PMs. The VM manager uses this data to optimize the Resource Allocation addresses to maximize the energy efficiency.
- Service scheduler: subscribe service requests to VMs and determines corresponding resources for the allocated VMs. The service scheduler has to decide when VMs will be submitted again with the new features or removed if the self-scaling functionality has been requested by end user.
- VM Manager: monitors the availability and utilization of VMs resources. Its functions are the provisioning of new VMs, as well as the migration of VMs to other PMs in order to adapt the placement.
- Accounting: monitors the current VMs resources utilization and accounts for its cost (in terms of power consumption and performance). Historical data of the resources utilization can be used to improve future Resource Allocation decisions.

• VMs: providing the flexibility of configuring various portions of resources on the same PM to different requirements of service requests is possible to VM operations. These operations are start and stop a VM on a single PM according to incoming request requirements. Multiple VMs are allowed to used and run applications from different OS. Consolidation allows reducing the power consumption of unused resources by switching them off or reconfiguring them to operate at low-performance levels (e.g. using DVFS).
• PMs: hardware infrastructure.

References [30, 31] presented other green-based architectures and frameworks: the GreenSlot and the Order@Cloud. The former is a scheduler based on parallel batch job for a virtualized data centre which is powered by a photovoltaic solar array. The workload balancing is performed trying to minimize energy consumption before the deadline of jobs. The work also contains a comparison with other convectional scheduler and their proposal. The latter is a flexible and extensible framework to improve the VM assignments of a cloud environment. The requested VMs on the cloud are reallocated by multi-objectives-based techniques. These objectives are defined by rules, quantifiers and costs, evolutionary and avid searches. The Order@Cloud framework is able to guarantees the best set of placements theoretically.

3.2 A Case Study of Market-Oriented Architecture for Resource Allocation

Cloud providers have to know the requirements and objectives of end users in order to help their computing operations. Therefore, cloud providers have to consider and respect the QoS requirements by SLA negotiation. Thus, market-oriented Resource Management is useful to balance the supply and demand of cloud resources to share resources but not distinguishing end users by its QoS requirements in order to achieve equilibrium. The Resource Management process is providing feedback based on economic-incentives for both end user and cloud user. Also, QoS-based Resource Allocation techniques end users can obtain some cost reductions from cloud providers, which could start to a more competitive market with lower costs [17].

In Fig. 10, the high-level architecture for supporting market-Oriented Resource Allocation in cloud data centres is shown. There are essentially four main entities (or mechanisms) involved:

- End users/Brokers: end users or brokers submit service requests from anywhere to the cloud provider for processing.
- SLA Resource Allocator: it is the interface between providers and users/brokers. The SLA management is based on the following elements:

  - Service Request Examiner and Admission Control: this mechanism determines whether to accept or reject the submitted request, ensuring that PM's resources are not overloaded by analyzing the submitted requests. To determine the future requests, it is needed the information of VM Monitor about resource availability and workload processing from the Service Request Monitor. Then, it places end users' requests to VMs and determines the most suitable resources to allocate VMs.
  - Pricing: the pricing mechanism determines the cost of service requests depending on peak, pricing rates and resources' availability. Similar to the previous

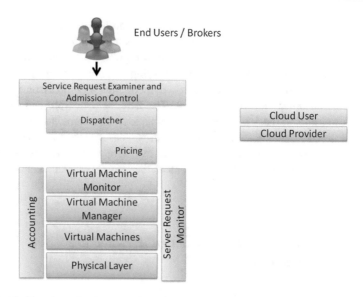

Fig. 10 Market-oriented architecture for resource allocation based on [17]

example, pricing can be used as a basis for managing the resources' supply and demand and facilitates its resources allocation prioritization effectively.

- Accounting: this mechanism monitors the current resource utilization for each request. Hence, the final cost can be computed and charged to the end users. Furthermore, the use of historic usage data can improve the Resource Allocation.
- VM Monitor: the VM Monitor mechanism takes care of the VMs' availability and their resource requests.
- Dispatcher: it is in charge of starting the execution of the services once they are accepted.
- Service Request Monitor: this mechanism monitors the progress of service requests' execution.

- VMs: multiple VMs can be dynamically started and stopped on a single PM according to incoming requests.
- PM: the data centre comprises many PMs providing resources to meet service demands.

The commercial offers of the Market-Oriented approach should be able to support the end user-driven service management based on end user profiles and SLA type. Additionally, the management of the computational risk (penalties) involved in the execution of an application with SLA limitations is necessary.

There are many techniques based on the presented architecture, such as the Combinatorial Auctions, the Pricing and Allocation Algorithms and the ASCA Combinatorial Auction Algorithm [39]. All of these techniques have common entities (see Fig. 9): auctioneers, the banking system, brokers, consumers and providers. In this example, market participants' bids are cleared by auctioneers periodically and the bank industry ensures transaction agreements between end users and cloud providers. There are brokers acting as intermediaries between end users and cloud brokers, as in share store market. The end users, brokers and cloud providers have to fulfil with their requirements and associated compensations through SLAs [17].

Reference [39] defined the combinatorial auction as a technique consisting of getting a bid on items' combinations, which are called combinatorial auctions. They propose a solution for cloud Resource Management that is scalable, and computable. The Pricing and Allocation Algorithms consist of partitioning the set of users into winners and losers, which are two disjoint sets. These algorithms have to satisfy some requirements. They should be computationally tractable as well as scaled in terms of number of service requests. Also, they have to be objective using a rule together with be fairing by making sure that the prices are uniform. To claim the uniformity is necessary to describe the prices of the resource pool at the end of the auction. The ASCA Combinatorial Auction Algorithm allows users to define a resource vector with its quantities and how much they want to pay for it. The auctioneer determines is the existence of an excess demand and, if so, the price of more demanded resources is hiked and new bids are requested.

Moreover, in the Market-Oriented approach, the Game Theory techniques are gaining strength. Recent works manage the QoS, the energy consumption and the cloud security through game theory through Nash equilibrium based algorithms [20]. In [28], the authors proposed a scalable risk assessment model using Game Theory. In [25], a meta-heuristic approach was also proposed for cloud resource allocation, based on the bio-inspired coral-reefs optimization paradigm to model cloud elasticity and on game theory to optimize the resource allocation focussing on the optimization objectives of the SLA.

Moreover, [8] presented three algorithms to solve the problem of Spot Price Prediction (SPP), against a state-of-the-art Three-Layer Perceptron (TLP) algorithm. The experimental results demonstrate that the behaviour of Support Vector Poly Kernel Regression (SMOReg) algorithm was the more suitable for this type of problems.

4 Conclusions

This chapter summarizes the main concepts of Cloud Computing technology and the Resource Management and Resource Allocation processes, focusing on the reduction of the energy consumption of cloud data centres in an IaaS environment.

Due to the increase of IT usage in general and cloud services in particular, the utilization of the resources of the data centres that support these services has increased; consequently, the energy consumption of these data centres also grows. Thus, many techniques have been developed with the aim of reducing the energy consumption without harming QoS and SLA. These techniques range from the improvement of cooling systems to the management of physical and logical resources of data centres.

Resource Management is a key factor in improving the efficiency and reducing the energy consumption of cloud systems. Thanks to the virtualization technology, the migration of logical resources through a data centre allows for the optimization of Resource Allocation, taking into account its current and future state. Among the different Resource Management techniques, in this chapter, we focused on the Resource Allocation techniques because they are in charge of mapping the logical resources to the physical ones in an optimal manner.

In particular, in this chapter, Resource Allocation techniques focusing on the reduction of energy consumption by improving the management of the virtualization layer have been described. Moreover, we depicted some practical cases of the most popular architectures based on the dynamic allocation and consolidation and the Market-Oriented approach.

The future research lines are open to overcoming the proposed challenges that this research area faces, along with the desire to achieve more efficient cloud systems, reduce the CO_2 footprint and use IT in a more sustainable manner.

5 Open Research Problems

Open challenges that are in general and, especially, energy-aware Resource Management which will be faced in the coming years are introduced in [2, 55].

In the Resource Provisioning area, the main challenges are related to achieving application hosting on the cloud in an elastic manner without compromising the SLA. Additionally, it is necessary to develop prediction models to aid proactive scaling in the cloud so that allocated applications can support the workload variations with the least impact in performance and availability. Moreover, the design of clustered applications to support *n-tier* architecture needs to be considered. Currently, the prediction models are only used to retract over-provisioned resources, but they also need to make bottleneck prediction in advance to overcome the VM boot-up latency problem [38].

In Resource Scheduling, open issues are related with the dispersion, heterogeneity and uncertainty of the features of the resources, not solved with traditional approaches. The development of service cloud-oriented applications in an efficient manner is also necessary.

Regarding the QoS and SLAs, it is necessary to fulfil the QoS with the resources provisioned by the provider. Based on these QoS requirements, techniques for SLA design and violation detection are needed to determine the penalties.

The VM migration is one of the crucial activities to work balancing in virtualization, since it allows responsive provisioning in data centres. However, workload peak detection and agile reaction to workload variation are important parts of the migration process. VM migration supports PM consolidation methodologies for improving resource utilization. Thus, VM migration may save data centre energy by consolidation of VM allocated into a reduced number of PMs [55]. To perform a better VM allocation optimization it is necessary that the VMs being reallocated in function of the current multiple system resources utilization of. The problem arises when trying to provide strict SLAs ensuring no performance degradation. The prediction of performance peaks is necessary in order select the candidate VM to be migrated. Fast and more effective VM placement approaches are needed to prevent degradation of the performance [17].

As we know, a massive volume of data has been produced and cloud technologies help to process and store this data volume. Cloud Computing provides end users, data analysts and data mining programmers the possibility to use data analytics in different service models. The challenges faced in this area are the data staging, the distributed storage systems, the data analysis and the data security [21].

Considering power management, the current limitation is that optimization algorithms need to deal with large-scale scenarios where the complexity of the computation and the machine learning requirements and their speed to find solutions is not able to quickly respond to changes in the system and in the workload. The research challenge is effectively combining optimization techniques and ensuring that the found solution is near the global optimum.

References

1. Akhter, N., & Othman, M. (2002). Energy aware resource allocation of cloud data center: Review and open issues. *Cluster Computing, 19*(3), 1163–1182. https://doi.org/10.1007/s10586-016-0579-4.
2. Akhter, N., & Othman, M. (2016). Energy aware resource allocation of cloud data center: Review and open issues. *Cluster Computing, 19*(3), 1163–1182. https://doi.org/10.1007/s10586-016-0579-4.
3. Al-Qawasmeh, A. M., Pasricha, S., Maciejewski, A. A., & Siegel, H. J. (2015). Power and thermal-aware workload allocation in heterogeneous data centers. *IEEE Transactions on Computers, 64*(2), 477–491. https://doi.org/10.1109/TC.2013.116.
4. Arjona Aroca, J., et al. (2015). Power-efficient assignment of virtual machines to physical machines. *Future Generation Computer Systems, 54*, pp.82–94. https://doi.org/10.1016/j.future.2015.01.006.
5. Armbrust, M., Fox, A., Griffth, R., Joseph, A. D., Katz, R., Konwinski, A., et al. (2010). A view of cloud computing. *Communications of the ACM, 53*(4), 50–58. https://doi.org/10.1145/1721654.1721672.
6. Arroba, P., et al. (2016). DVFS-Aware consolidation for energy-efficient clouds. Parallel Architectures and Compilation Techniques - In *Conference Proceedings* (pp. 494–495) PACT.
7. Archer, J., Boehm, A. (2009). Security guidance for critical areas of focus in cloud computing, *Cloud Security Alliance 2, 1*(76). Retrieved from https://downloads.cloudsecurityalliance.org/initiatives/guidance/csaguide.v3.0.pdf.
8. Arévalos, S., López-Pires, F., & Barán, B. (2016). A comparative evaluation of algorithms for auction-based cloud pricing prediction. In *IEEE International Conference on Cloud Engineering* (pp. 99–108).
9. Barroso, L. A., & Hölzle, U. (2007). The case of energy-proportional computing. *Computer, 40*(12), 33–37. https://doi.org/10.1109/MC.2007.443.
10. Baruchi, A., Toshimi Midorikawa, E., & Netto, M. A. (2014). Improving virtual machine live migration via application-level workload analysis. In: *10th International Conference on Network and Service Management (CNSM) and Workshop*. https://doi.org/10.1109/CNSM.2014.7014153.

11. Beloglazov, A., & Buyya, R. (2010). Energy efficient resource management in virtualized cloud data centers. In: *Proceedings of the 2010 10th IEEE/ACM International Conference on Cluster, Cloud and Grid Computing CCGRID '10*. Melbourne. https://doi.org/10.1109/CCGRID. 2010.46.

12. Beloglazov, A., Abawajy, J., & Buyya, R. (2012). Energy-aware resource allocation heuristics for efficient management of data centers for cloud computing. *Future Generation Computer Systems, 28*(5), 755–768. https://doi.org/10.1016/j.future.2011.04.017.

13. Beloglazov, A., & Buyya, R. (2012). Optimal online deterministic algorithms and adaptive heuristics for energy and performance efficient dynamic consolidation of virtual machines in Cloud data centers. *Concurrency Computation Practice and Experience, 24*(13), 1397–1420.

14. Beloglazov, A., Buyya, R., Choon Lee, Y., & Zomaya, A. (2011). A taxonomy and survey of energy-efficient data centers and cloud computing systems. *Advances in Computers, 82*, pp. 47–111. Retrieved from http://beloglazov.info/papers/2011-advances-in-computers-taxonomy.pdf.

15. Buyya, R., & Sulistio, A. (2008). Service and utility oriented distributed computing systems: Challenges and opportunities for modeling and simulation communities. In 41st Annual Simulation Symposium. Retrieved from http://ieeexplore.ieee.org/stamp/stamp.jsp?arnumber= 4494407.

16. Buyya, R., Vecchiola, C., & Selvi, S. T. (2013). Mastering cloud computing: Foundations and applications programming. Retrieved from http://store.elsevier.com/Mastering-Cloud-Computing/Rajkumar-Buyya/isbn-9780124095397/. ISBN:9780124095397

17. Buyya, R., Yeo, C. S., Venugopal, S., Broberg, J., & Brandic, I. (2009). Cloud computing and emerging IT platforms: Vision, hype, and reality for delivering computing as the 5th utility. *Future Generation computer systems, 25*(6), 599–616. https://doi.org/10.1016/j.future.2008. 12.001.

18. Calheiros, R.N., & Buyya, R. (2015). Energy-efficient scheduling of urgent bag-of-tasks applications in clouds through DVFS. In *Proceedings of the International Conference on Cloud Computing Technology and Science, Cloud Com.* pp. 342–349.

19. Cao, J., Wi, Y. and Li, M. (2012). Energy efficient allocation of virtual machines in cloud computing environments based on demand forecast. In *International Conference on Grid and Pervasive Computing*. https://doi.org/10.1007/978-3-642-30767-6_12.

20. Chen, H., Liu, X., Xu, H., & Wang, C. (2016). Cloud service broker based on dynamic game theory for bilateral SLA negotiation in cloud environment. *International Journal of Grid and Distributed Computing, 9*(9), 251–268. Retrieved from http://www.sersc.org/journals/IJGDC/ vol9_no9/22.pdf.

21. Chen, H., Chiang, R.H.L. & Storey, V.C. (2012). Business intelligence and analytics: From big data to big impact. *MIS Quarterly, 36*(4), pp. 1165–1188. Retrieved from http://dl.acm.org/citation.cfm?id=2481683.

22. Dabbagh, M., et al. (2015). Energy-efficient resource allocation and provisioning framework for cloud data centers. *IEEE Transactions on Network and Service Management, 12*(3), 377–391.

23. Emerson Network Power. (2014). *New strategies for cutting data center energy costs and boosting capacity.* Retrieved from http://www.emersonnetworkpower.com/documentation/en-us/latest-thinking/edc/documents/white

24. Ferreto, T. C., Netto, M. A., Calheiros, R. N., & De Rose, C. A. (2011). Server consolidation with migration control for virtualized data centers. *Future Generation Computer Systems, 27*(8), 1027–1034.

25. Ficco, M., Esposito, C., Palmieri, F., & Castiglione, A. (2016). A coral-reefs and Game Theory-based approach for optimizing elastic cloud resource allocation. *Future Generation Computer Systems.* https://doi.org/10.1016/j.future.2016.05.025.

26. Filiposka, S., Mishev, A., & Juiz, C. (2015). Community-based VM placement framework. *The Journal of Supercomputing, 71*(12), 4504–4528. https://doi.org/10.1007/s11227-015-1546-1.

27. Filiposka, S., Mishev, A., & Juiz, C. (2016). *Balancing performances in online VM placement in ICT Innovations 2015.* (pp. 153–162). Springer International Publishing.

28. Furuncu, E., & Sogukpinar, I. (2015). Scalable risk assessment method for cloud computing using game theory (CCRAM). *Computer Standards & Interfaces, 38*, 44–50. https://doi.org/10.1016/j.csi.2014.08.007.
29. Gerardus, J. (2011). Inter-cloud live migration of virtualization systems. U.S. Patent patent no. US20120311568 A1. Retrieved from https://www.google.ch/patents/US20120311568.
30. Geronimo, A., Brundo, R., & Becker, C. (2016). Order@Cloud: AVM organisation framework based on multi-objectives placement ranking. In *Network Operations and Management Symposium NOMS, 2016 IEEE/IFIP*. pp. 529–535. IEEE.
31. Goiri, I., Le, K., Beauchea, R., Nguyen, T., Haque, M., Guitart, J., et al. (2011). GreenSlot: Scheduling energy consumption in green datacenters. In: *24th ACM/IEEE International Supercomputing Conference for High Performance Computing, Networking, Storage and Analysis (SC'11)*. WA, USA: Seattle.
32. Hoelzle, U., & Barroso, L.A. (2009). The datacenter as a computer: An introduction to the design of warehouse-scale machines. Retrieved from http://dl.acm.org/citation.cfm?id=1643608.
33. Jennings, B., & Stadler, R. (2015). Resource Management in Clouds: Survey and Research Challenges. *Journal of Network and Systems Management, 23*(3), 567–619. https://doi.org/10.1007/s10922-014-9307-7.
34. Kitada, K., et al. (2016). Dynamic Power simulator utilizing computational fluid dynamics and machine learning for proposing task allocation in a data center. In pp. 87–94.
35. Khosravi, A., Garg, S. K., & Buyya, R. (2013). Energy and carbon efficient placement of virtual machines in distributed cloud data centers. pp. 317–328.
36. Mcbay, C., Parr, G., & Mcclean, S (2016). Energy saving in data center servers using optimal scheduling to ensure QoS. In pp. 57–60.
37. Mangla, N., Singh, M., & Rana, S. K. (2016). Resource scheduling in cloud environment: A Survey. *Advances in Science and Technology Research Journal, 10*(30), 38–50. https://doi.org/10.12913/22998624/62746.
38. Manvi, S. S., & Shyam, G. K. (2014). Resource management for Infrastructure as a Service (IaaS) in cloud computing: A survey. *Journal of Network and Computer Applications, 41*. https://doi.org/10.1016/j.jnca.2013.10.004.
39. Marinescu, D. C. (2013) Cloud computing: Theory and practice. Retrieved from http://www.sciencedirect.com/science/book/9780124046276.
40. Mastelic, T., & Brandic, I. (2015). Recent trends in energy-efficient cloud computing. *IEEE Cloud Computing, 2*(1), 40–47.
41. Mell, P., & Grance, T. (2011). 800-145: The NIST Definition of Cloud Computing. Gaithersburg.
42. Palanisamy, B., Singh, A., & Liu, L. (2015). Cost-effective resource provisioning for mapreduce in a cloud. *IEEE Transaction on Parallel and Distributed Systems, 26*(5), 1265–1279.
43. Papazoglou, M. P., Traveso, P., Dustdar, S., & Leymann, F. (2007). Service-oriented computing: State of the art and research challenges. *IEEE Computer, 40*(11), 38–45. https://doi.org/10.1109/MC.2007.400.
44. Park, J. G., Kim, J. M., Choi, H. & Woo, Y. C. (2009). Virtual machine migration in self-managing virtualized server environments. In *11th International Conference on Advanced Communication Technology 2009*. Retrieved from http://ieeexplore.ieee.org/document/4809490/.
45. Peng, M. et al. (2015). Energy-efficient resource assignment and power allocation in heterogeneous cloud radio access networks. In *IEEE Transactions on Vehicular Technology*. pp. 5275–5287.
46. Quang-Hung, N., Nien, P. D., Nam, N. H., Tuong, N. H., & Thoai, N. A. (2013). A genetic algorithm for power-aware virtual machine allocation in private cloud, In Information and Communication Technology-EurAsia Conference. Yogyakarta, Indonesia. https://doi.org/10.1007/978-3-642-36818-9_19.
47. Rak, M., Venticinque, S., & Mahr, T. (2011). Cloud application monitoring: The mOSAIC approach. In *1 Third IEEE International Conference on Cloud Computing Technology and Science*. https://doi.org/10.1109/CloudCom.2011.117.

48. Raycroft, P., Jansen, R., Jarus, M., & Brenner, P. R. (2014). Performance bounded energy efficient virtual machine allocation in the global cloud. *Sustainable Computing: Informatics and Systems, 4*(1), 1–9. https://doi.org/10.1016/j.suscom.2013.07.001.

49. RightScale (2016). Cloud Computing Trends: 2016 State of the Cloud Survey. Retrieved from http://www.rightscale.com/blog/cloud-industry-insights/cloud-computing-trends-2016-state-cloud-survey.

50. Rodriguez, M. A., & Buyya, R. (2014). Deadline based resource provisioning and scheduling algorithm for scientific workflows on clouds. In *IEEE Transactions on Cloud Computing, 2*(2), pp. 222–235. Retrieved from http://doi.ieeecomputersociety.org/.

51. Sahal, R. & Omara, F. A. (2014). Effective virtual machine configuration for cloud environment. In *9th International Conference on Informatics and Systems*. https://doi.org/10.1109/INFOS. 2014.7036720.

52. Serrano, D., Bouchenak, S., Kouki, Y., de Oliveira, F. A., Ledoux, T., Sopena, J., et al. (2016). SLA guarantees for cloud services. *Future Generation Computer Systems, 54*, 233–246. https://doi.org/10.1016/j.future.2015.03.018.

53. Sharifil, M., Salimi, H., & Najafzadeh, M. (2011). Power-efficient distributed scheduling of virtual machines using workload-aware consolidation techniques. *The Journal of Supercomputing, 61*(1), 46–66. https://doi.org/10.1007/s11227-011-0658-5.

54. Singh, S., & Chana, I. (2016). A survey on resource scheduling in cloud computing: Issues and challenges. *Journal of Grid Computing, 14*(2), 217–264. https://doi.org/10.1007/s10723-015-9359-2.

55. Singh, S., & Chana, I. (2016). Cloud resource provisioning: survey, status and future research directions. *Knowledge and Information Systems, 49*(3), 1005–1069. https://doi.org/10.1007/s10115-016-0922-3.

56. Sola-Morena, J. M., Gilly, K., & Juiz, C. (2014). Sustainability in web server systems. *Computers in Industry, 65*(3), 401–407. https://doi.org/10.1016/j.compind.2013.11.009.

57. Strunk, A. (2012). Costs of virtual machine live migration: A survey. In *IEEE Eighth World Congress on Services*. Retrieved from http://ieeexplore.ieee.org/stamp/stamp.jsp?arnumber=6274069.

58. Vinothina, V., Dean, R. S., & Ganapathi, P. (2014). A survey on resource allocation strategies in cloud computing. *International Journal of Advanced Computer Science and Applications, 3*(6), pp. 97–104. Retrieved from http://thesai.org/Downloads/Volume3No6/Paper%2016-A%20Survey%20on%20Resource%20Allocation%20Strategies%20in%20Cloud%20Computing.pdf.

59. Voorsluys, W., Broberg, J., Venugopal, S., & Buyya, R. (2009). Cost of virtual machine live migration in clouds: A performance evaluation. In *1st International Conference on Cloud Computing*. Retrieved from http://dl.acm.org/citation.cfm?id=1695684.

60. von Kistowski, J., Schreck, M., & Kounev, S., (2016). Predicting power consumption in virtualized environments. In *Lecture Notes in Computer Science (including subseries Lecture Notes in Artificial Intelligence and Lecture Notes in Bioinformatics)*. pp. 79–93.

61. Wood, T. et al. (2009). Sandpiper: Black-box and gray-box resource management for virtual machines. *Computer Networks, 53*(17), pp. 2923–2938. https://doi.org/10.1016/j.comnet. 2009.04.014.

62. Xu, X., Hu, H., Hu, N., & Ying, W. (2012). Cloud Task and Virtual Machine Allocation Strategy in Cloud Computing Environment. *Network Computing and Information Security* (pp. 113–120). Berlin Heidelberg: Springer.

63. Xu, M., Dastjerdi, A. V., & Buyya, R. (2016). Energy efficient scheduling of cloud application components with brownout. CoRR, (August), pp. 1–12.

64. Zhan, Z.-H., Liu, X.-F., Gong, Y.-J., Zhang, J., Chung, H. S.-H., & Li, Y. (2015). Cloud computing resource scheduling and a survey of its evolutionary approaches. *ACM Computing Surveys (CSUR), 47*(4). https://doi.org/10.1145/2788397.

Recent Developments in Resource Management in Cloud Computing and Large Computing Clusters

Richard Olaniyan and Muthucumaru Maheswaran

Abstract Cloud computing and large computing clusters consist of a large number of computing resources of different types ranging from storage, CPU, memory, I/O to network bandwidth. Cloud computing exposes resources as a single access point to end users through the use of virtualization technologies. A major issue in cloud computing is how to properly allocate cloud resources to different users or frameworks accessing the cloud. There are a lot of complex, diverse, and heterogeneous workloads that need to coexist in the cloud and large-scale compute clusters, thus the need for finding efficient means of assigning resources to the different users or workloads. Millions of jobs need to be scheduled in a small amount of time, so there is a need for a resource management and scheduling mechanism that can minimize latency and maximize efficiency. Cloud resource management involves allocating computing, processing, storage, and networking resources to cloud users, in such a way that their demands and performance objectives are met. Cloud providers need to ensure efficient and effective resource provisioning while being constrained by Service Level Agreements (SLAs). This chapter gives the differences and similarities between resource management in cloud computing and cluster computing, and provide detailed information about different types of scheduling approaches and open research issues.

1 Introduction

Modern data centers and clusters allow multiple workloads and frameworks with thousands of jobs to run on them which necessitates the need for a mechanism to manage cloud and cluster-wide resources while ensuring efficient allocation of resources, minimizing latency, satisfying specific framework constraints and ensuring fairness. Due to an increase in size data centers and clusters (thousands/millions

R. Olaniyan (✉) · M. Maheswaran
McGill University, Montreal, QC, Canada
e-mail: richard.olaniyan@mail.mcgill.ca

M. Maheswaran
e-mail: maheswar@cs.mcgill.ca

© Springer Nature Singapore Pte Ltd. 2017
S. Chaudhary et al. (eds.), *Research Advances in Cloud Computing*,
DOI 10.1007/978-981-10-5026-8_10

of processing cores), advancement in cloud and cluster computing techniques and the complexity of modern-day applications and frameworks, there is a need for more robust resource management frameworks that can handle scheduling a large number of jobs (both homogeneous and heterogeneous) onto a cloud or large computing cluster while ensuring that scheduling goals are met.

Cloud resource management involves matching processing, storage, and networking resources to cloud users workloads, in such a way that their demands and performance objectives are met [53]. Cloud providers need to ensure efficient and effective resource provisioning while being constrained by Service Level Agreements (SLAs). Cloud resource management is motivated by the following factors (i) the need for a mechanism to handle a non-perfect global state information in the cloud, (ii) the handling of unexpected activities within the cloud such as failures and attacks, (iii) the handling of varying and heterogeneous workloads while ensuring scalability, (iv) the large scale of modern data centers, and (v) the unpredictability of different workloads within the cloud. Cloud resource management policies are designed bearing the following in mind:

- Distributing the workload evenly among the servers within the cloud or cluster thereby ensuring load balancing.
- Minimizing the cost and energy usage within the cloud.
- Ensuring that the desired Quality of Service (QoS) is achieved.
- Ensuring that workload-specific constraints are satisfied.

Resource management in large computing clusters involves matching the requests for cluster resources to the corresponding cluster resources in a way that the desired resource management goals are achieved. Modern data centers and clusters allow multiple workloads and frameworks with thousands of jobs to run on them. Thus, there is a need for a mechanism to schedule cluster-wide resources to these differing frameworks while ensuring efficient allocation of resources, minimizing latency, satisfying specific framework constraints, and ensuring fairness. Design goals of a good and efficient resource scheduler are [4, 60]:

1. High cluster utilization: Scheduling decisions must be made in such a way that the cluster is load balanced. That is, parts of the cluster are not overloaded while others are underloaded. Jobs must be evenly distributed within the cluster taking into consideration the runtime of tasks.
2. Low latency: This attribute is particularly important when running jobs that take a very short amount of time to execute. The scheduler must make scheduling decisions as fast and efficient as possible. A scheduler must be able to make rapid scheduling decisions so that it does not become the bottleneck in the scheduling process.
3. Strict enforcement of scheduling invariants: There are frameworks that have job-specific constraints such as the kind of processor they can run on (e.g., only GPUs), minimum memory and storage requirement or data locality.
4. Diverse application framework support: A scheduler must be able to support multiple heterogeneous frameworks that run within the cluster.

5. Fairness and fine-grained resource sharing: In a cluster with diverse framework, the scheduler must ensure that resources are allocated to the different frameworks in a fair way such that no framework is starved of resources or given a very small share of the resources. There should be a fair sharing of resources among different resource users and groups.
6. Fault tolerant: A scheduler must be fault tolerant such that a failure or crash of some nodes in the system does not lead to a total failure of the scheduling process.
7. Highly scalable: A scheduler must be able to effectively scale up and down depending on the operating conditions (cluster size and workload size) without affecting its scheduling efficiency.

This remainder of this book chapter is structured as follows. Section 2 provides a background on resource scheduling, stating the different types of scheduling, scheduling solutions, scheduling architectures, and also the fairness algorithms used to achieve fairness in resource scheduling. Section 3 focuses on resource scheduling frameworks and algorithms that have been proposed for the cloud computing environments and large computing clusters. In Sect. 4, research challenges and issues in resource management and scheduling are discussed. The conclusion of the survey is presented in Sect. 5.

2 Resource Management and Scheduling

This section presents various categories of resource management and scheduling in the cloud and in large computing clusters. Different types of scheduling are also discussed, ranging from batch scheduling, coscheduling, gang scheduling, Directed Acyclic Graph (DAG) scheduling to fair scheduling. The centralized, distributed and hybrid (a combination of centralized and distributed) scheduling solutions are also explained. Scheduling architectures and fairness algorithms are discussed later in this section.

2.1 Resource Management in Cloud Computing and Large Computing Clusters

Resource management in the cloud computing environment involves allocating and scheduling cloud resources to cloud workloads from cloud users. Various policies that have been proposed and developed for resource management in cloud computing focus mainly on admission control, energy usage minimization, load balancing across servers, ensuring QoS agreements are guaranteed, and resource allocation for various services. Most resource management schemes in the cloud tend to maximize the utilization of cloud resources (servers) allocated to cloud users workloads, minimize the completion time of such workloads and also minimize the waiting time for jobs before they are run.

Trade-offs have to be made among parameters governing resource management in the cloud, these parameters include resource utilization, job makespan, energy consumption, job deadline, job constraints, load balancing, scalability, and cost effectiveness [41, 60]. All these factors cannot be guaranteed by any cloud resource manager, but these decisions on which parameters to guarantee are determined by the SLA between the cloud user and cloud provider. Resource management in large computing clusters mostly considers all the parameters governing resource management in the cloud, but are not out to maximize profit, rather they focus on performance and efficiency.

2.2 Types of Scheduling

Earlier scheduling types include First-In-First-Out(FIFO) [5], Earliest Deadline First (EDF) [25], Shortest Job First (SJF) [34], and priority scheduling [59]. The different types of scheduling are given as follows.

Batch Scheduling: In batch scheduling, jobs are not scheduled as single entities, rather, jobs are combined into batches and scheduled together. It is mostly employed in clusters that are dedicated for running non-interactive jobs. Batch schedulers are used in applications to avoid memory swapping and they are characterized by high utilization and high latency. Jobs are grouped into predetermined batch sizes and scheduled together [1]. In [40], they identified that large batches are characterized by high machine utilization, but processing a large batch may lead to a bottleneck as more important jobs belonging to a different batch or family could be delayed.

Coscheduling: This involves scheduling related processes or tasks to run in parallel. There are frameworks consisting of dependent tasks or tasks that need to communicate with one other for successful completion, and thus, must be scheduled together [39]. There are distributed applications that require that subtasks should be coordinated and synchronized, thereby bringing about the need for a scheduling mechanism to guarantee this synchronization. Coscheduling solves this problem by ensuring that communicating subtasks are available for interaction when needed. For example, consider an application where a running task needs to send a message to a task that has not been scheduled, the task will keep waiting for a reply that is not forthcoming, which will cause blocking in the execution of the application.

In coscheduling, all tasks or processes from an intra-task dependent framework must be scheduled together so that there can be efficient communication among the tasks. There are two variations of coscheduling namely implicit coscheduling and explicit coscheduling [48]. In explicit coscheduling, all dependent tasks are scheduled at the same time, that is, it is either all the tasks are scheduled together or none of the tasks is scheduled. A global scheduling mechanism is employed in explicit coscheduling. In implicit coscheduling, there is no strict enforcement of the rule that all tasks must be scheduled together, rather, tasks can be scheduled independently using local scheduling but scheduling decisions are made in cooperation.

Gang Scheduling: It is a stricter form of coscheduling where dependent tasks are scheduled simultaneously. The tasks are usually from the same job or framework. Gang scheduling ensures that tasks can communicate with one another at any point in time and are thus scheduled concurrently. In [24], they examined and identified optimal performance conditions and efficient mean response time of jobs while ensuring fairness to different categories of gangs (small and large gangs). The main challenge of gang scheduling is how to achieve high cluster utilization, this is because all the tasks in a gang have to wait till enough machines are available to run all the tasks at once. Resource sharing among running tasks also incurs some overhead in gang scheduling [17]. To solve the inherent problem of the neglect of memory considerations in gang scheduling, a gang scheduling algorithm with memory considerations was proposed in [3]. They argued that running a subset of jobs and delaying other jobs and putting them in a queue till memory becomes available. They found that their system produced better performance than when all jobs are either scheduled together or not scheduled at all.

A paired gang scheduling algorithm was proposed in [56] where they looked to solve the basic problem of gang scheduling which is resource idleness that occurs when all the tasks in a gang cannot be scheduled at once. They matched gangs with high CPU use with gangs with low CPU use as pairs and schedule them together, the local scheduler is thus allowed to pick either of the two gangs depending on the availability of resources thus reducing the probability that the resources will be idle at any point in time.

DAG Scheduling: Directed Acyclic Graph (DAG) scheduling is used mostly in cases where there are a number of interacting jobs running in parallel in a dynamic environment [42]. The interdependence among the interacting jobs is generally modeled as a DAG where the nodes represent the tasks themselves and the directed edges are used to represent the dependencies as well as communication among tasks. In DAG scheduling, a task is not scheduled until all its parents have finished executing and all necessary messages have been sent. It is generally assumed that DAGs have a single entry (root) node and a single exit (end) node. The scheduling problem in DAG is how to assign cluster resources such that precedence constraints are met and ensuring that there is load balancing and the total execution time is minimized [43]. Most DAG scheduling algorithms try to achieve load balancing and have minimized total runtime depending on the type of job being scheduled and the scheduling goals. Later research [9] in DAG scheduling looked at ways to also minimize cost of scheduling DAGs as well as reducing execution time in the cloud. They proposed a DAG scheduling algorithm that is cost-optimal using the VM cost model.

Fair Scheduling: In fair scheduling, cluster-wide resources are evenly shared among all jobs or frameworks running in the cluster over time regardless of their resource demands. For a single running job the entire cluster is used, but when there are multiple jobs running, the cluster resources are freed up so that other jobs can get almost the same amount of resources [6]. Jobs are usually organized into pools by the fair scheduler and it divides the cluster resources among the pools. If two jobs are running together, they each get 50% of the cluster resources, but when two more jobs are added to the system, the cluster resources are shared evenly (25%) among the four jobs.

2.3   Resource Scheduling Solutions

Resource scheduling solutions can be divided into the centralized, distributed, and hybrid (a combination of centralized and distributed) solutions. Each of the solutions is explained in more details.

Centralized schedulers: In centralized scheduling, all jobs that are to be executed must pass through a single scheduler (central controller). Centralized schedulers are always on the critical path of all scheduling decisions and as such they are responsible for all scheduling activities within the system. Centralized schedulers are built such that they usually have an accurate view of the cluster state at every point in time and for this reason they make very good scheduling decisions [12]. Due to this global cluster view of the centralized scheduling solution, they are more effective for scheduling jobs that require strict and secure enforcement of constraints and invariants (memory constraints, I/O constraint, storage constraints among others) [23]. Centralized schedulers are therefore efficient for scheduling long running and batch jobs because of their ability to make good scheduling decisions. Wrongly or inefficiently scheduling a long running job can lead to a very low system performance as long jobs can easily become bottlenecks in the system, especially in cases where there are a number of short jobs that need to be scheduled. These short running jobs can be starved of cluster resources if the long running jobs are not carefully scheduled. The general architecture of the centralized scheduler is shown in Fig. 1.

A centralized scheduler can be a bottleneck by itself because it has to constantly update information about the cluster state which can be expensive in cases where the cluster is of a large size [12]. To make a good scheduling decision, the centralized scheduler has to scan through the entire cluster to pick the best machine for a particular task, this can be time-consuming and can prove to be ineffective in situations where

Fig. 1 Overview of a centralized scheduler

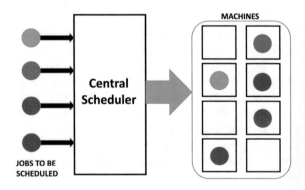

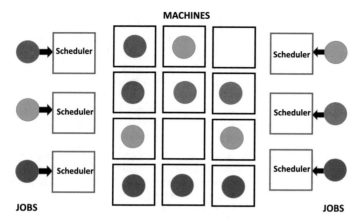

Fig. 2 Overview of a fully distributed scheduler

jobs to be run on the cluster are time-sensitive and need to be scheduled as early and fast as possible.

Distributed schedulers: In distributed scheduling, schedulers are wide spread over the entire cluster and there is no global view of the entire cluster state. Rather, scheduling decisions are made locally by the distributed schedulers. Distributed schedulers achieve high scheduling throughput and low latency for short running jobs because they only need local information to make scheduling decisions [23, 37]. Distributed schedulers therefore trade good scheduling decisions for high throughput and scalability. They are inefficient for scheduling long running jobs because of their poor scheduling decisions which can lead to an overall poor scheduling performance. Figure 2 shows an overview of the distributed scheduling architecture.

The distributed schedulers schedules jobs to machines that are within their scope (local to the distributed scheduler) in the cluster of machines or data centers. They have information about only these machines. A detailed comparison of centralized and distributed scheduling is presented in Table 1.

Hybrid schedulers: Hybrid scheduling consists of a combination of centralized and distributed scheduling. It leverages the strengths of both centralized schedulers and distributed schedulers. Hybrid schedulers are useful when there is a small number of long running (batch) jobs and a very large number of short running (low-latency) jobs [12]. The long jobs are scheduled by the centralized scheduler (for good scheduling decisions to avoid head of the line blocking as much as possible). Since long jobs can tend to be bottlenecks in the system when they are not effectively scheduled, the centralized scheduler is used because it has a global view of the cluster state and can make more effective scheduling decisions based on this knowledge. Short jobs, on the other hand, are scheduled by distributed schedulers (to achieve high system through-put and scalability) because they make fast scheduling decisions without requiring all the information about the cluster state, they only need partial information about their locality. In general, the centralized scheduler helps to make better scheduling

Table 1 Comparison of centralized and distributed scheduling [12, 23, 37]

Metric	Centralized scheduling	Distributed scheduling
Cluster state	Have an accurate view of the entire cluster at all times and thus have an updated cluster state information	Only have an updated local state information and have an inaccurate global cluster state information
Scheduling decision	Make very good scheduling decisions because they have an accurate view of the cluster	Sometimes make inferior scheduling decisions due to partial cluster state information
Scheduling latency	Relatively high scheduling latency since the cluster state information has to be updated everything a scheduling decision is to be made	Low scheduling latency as jobs/tasks are scheduled almost immediately they are submitted for execution
Scalability	Not highly scalable especially for heterogeneous workloads. Does not scale well as the number of jobs rapidly increases	Highly scalable for heterogeneous workloads and scales well for rapidly increasing number of jobs
Job runtime	Very suitable for long running jobs as it makes good and optimal scheduling decision	More suitable for a large number of short jobs that require very little start-up time
Job constraints	Efficient for ensuring that job-specific constraints are met	Not very efficient for jobs with specific constraints
Scheduler location	Centrally located and is on the critical path of all scheduling decisions made	Located locally close to the machines running the jobs

decisions and to enforce invariants and constraints, while the distributed schedulers help to improve scalability and reduce latency. Examples of hybrid schedulers are Hawk [12] and Mercury [23].

2.4 Resource Scheduling Architectures in Cloud Computing and Large Computing Clusters

The four major classifications of resource scheduling architectures are the monolithic schedulers, the two-level schedulers, the shared-state schedulers, and the fully distributed schedulers. More detailed information about these architectures are presented next.

Monolithic schedulers: They consist of a single centralized scheduling algorithm that schedules all jobs and frameworks within the cluster. The scheduler runs on a single machine and schedules jobs to other machines. It is difficult to add new implementations and policies to monolithic schedulers and therefore do not scale up well especially in heterogeneous environments where there are different frameworks.

This is because whenever a new framework is added, the entire scheduling policy of the monolithic scheduler has to be modified. Issues such as head-of-line blocking are quite common in monolithic schedulers as in centralized schedulers. Jobs waiting to be scheduled are from different frameworks as depicted by different colors. Examples of monolithic schedulers are Google's Borg [52], early Hadoop schedulers, Paragon scheduler [13] and Quasar scheduler [14].

Two-level schedulers: There is a single and active resource manager which offers computing and processing resources to independent and parallel application-specific scheduling frameworks. The process of resource allocation and task placement are separated in two-level schedulers. Examples include Apache Mesos [20] and Hadoop-on-Demand. In a system such as Mesos, resource offers are used to implement the two-level scheduling. The Mesos master offers resources to the different framework schedulers in the cluster while the framework schedulers decide whether to accept or reject the offers and also decide what tasks to run on what machine. One of the major disadvantages of the Mesos two-level scheduling is that the framework schedulers do not have enough information about the cluster and have to depend on the Mesos master for necessary information. This makes priority preemption difficult and makes it hard to detect interference from workloads that are running that might affect the quality of resources. The application-specific schedulers totally depend on the information (resource offers) provided by the resource manager and thus are limited in the decisions they can make.

Shared-state schedulers: These consist of multiple schedulers that have access to all cluster-wide resources. The shared-state model is a semi-distributed model that allows the different schedulers to update the "cluster state". An optimistic concurrency control is employed to update the shared cluster state, multiple replicas of the cluster state are updated by application-specific schedulers. These transactional updates are expected to fail sometimes in shared-state schedulers. Two major drawbacks of the shared-state architecture are i) that occasionally the system must work with stale or not yet updated cluster state information and under high load queues and resource contention, and ii) the shared-state architecture may experience reduced scheduling performance when the rate of contention by application-specific schedulers for cluster resources is high. Examples of shared-state scheduling architecture include Apollo [4] and Omega [44].

Fully distributed scheduling architectures: In the fully distributed architecture, there is no coordination between the schedulers, different schedulers can be used to serve incoming workloads. Each scheduler uses its own local copy of the "cluster view or state" which is partial and often outdated to make scheduling decisions. There is no central controller as in the shared-state schedulers. The distributed scheduling architecture is based on a "slot" concept where each machine is splitted into a number of uniform slots and a worker side queue is maintained. There is difficulty in enforcing constraints and invariants due to the absence of a central controller. They make rapid decisions with minimal cluster-based information and as such can make bad scheduling decisions. An example of a distributed scheduler is Sparrow [37].

A detailed comparison of the different scheduling architectures and solutions is provided in Table 2.

Table 2 Comparison of large cluster scheduling architectures and frameworks

Metric	Centralized/monolithic schedulers	Two-level schedulers	Shared-state schedulers	Hybrid schedulers	Fully distributed schedulers
Cluster state information	Accurate	Accurate	Accurate	Partial	Partial
Scheduling accuracy	High	Moderate	Optimistic	Mixed	Traded off for speed
Scheduling speed	Moderate	Dependent on application schedulers	High	Mixed	Very high
Job length suitability	Long	Dependent on application schedulers	Short	Long and short	Short
Cluster utilization	Moderate	Moderate	High	High	High
Scalability	Not very scalable	Moderately scalable	Highly scalable	Highly scalable	Highly scalable
Constraints	Easily satisfied	Moderately satisfied	Moderately satisfied	Moderately satisfied	Hard to satisfy
Support for gang scheduling and coscheduling	Yes	Yes	Yes	Partial	No

The efficient functioning of a cloud or cluster is largely dependent on the resource management and scheduling system. Data centers and large computing clusters are built to support different workload environments (homogeneous or heterogeneous), and the resource scheduling approach implemented depends on such environment. Other factors determining the resource scheduling solution and architecture chosen are the types of job (dependent or independent, long running or short running) that are expected to be run by the scheduling framework. The presence of constraints or invariants that need to be satisfied for jobs that will run on the cluster machines and more generally the desired scheduling goals are determinants factors of the scheduling approach used.

Centralized schedulers have been found to be more suitable for jobs that are not so time-sensitive and jobs that require good scheduling decisions. Due to the availability of the global view of the cluster to centralized schedulers, applications where scheduling accuracy, task dependency, coscheduling and gang scheduling are required tend to favor the use of the centralized scheduling solution. Centralized schedulers can sometimes be slow in making scheduling decisions because the global view of the cluster has to be updated regularly and can lead to the centralized scheduler being the bottleneck in the scheduling process. Distributed schedulers, on the other hand, are more suitable for time-sensitive jobs in massive quantity. This is because distributed schedulers trade-off accuracy for speed since they only need partial local information about the cluster state. Hybrid schedulers act as a bridge between centralized and distributed schedulers. They are suitable for cases where there are heterogeneous workloads running within the cluster with varying job parameters (running time, constraints, resource requirements, and time-sensitivity).

The monolithic scheduling architecture employs the centralized scheduling solution. The pros and cons of the monolithic scheduling architecture are similar to those of centralized scheduling. Two-level scheduling architecture decouples the scheduling process by having a central resource manager offer resources to application schedulers which they can decide to accept or reject. This scheduling architecture causes a high between of the application schedulers on the central resource manager since they have very little or no information about the state of the cluster. The shared-state scheduling architecture uses a free-for-all approach where individual application schedulers compete for resources. This scheduling architecture is not suitable for jobs with high dependency and constraints. Fully distributed schedulers employ the distributed scheduling solution and thus have similar pros and cons.

2.5 Fairness Algorithms

Achieving fairness is one of the scheduling goals of a large computing cluster resource scheduler. Most scheduling frameworks in large computing clusters employ the use of fairness algorithms to achieve this goal. In this section, the most common and frequently used fairness algorithms are presented.

Max-Min Fairness (MMF): MMF [10, 29] is achieved when an increase or decrease in the cluster resource allocation of any job/framework results in a corresponding decrease or increase in the cluster resource allocation of another job/framework with an equal or almost equal amount. The basic concepts of MMF are that (i) resource allocation is dependent on resource demand, that is, resources are allocated in order of increasing demand, (ii) a job does not get cluster resources more than what it has demanded for and finally, (iii) jobs that have pending demands receive an equal share of the remaining cluster resources.

Take for example three frameworks A, B, and C having resource demands 1, 4, and 3 with the cluster having a total resource capacity of 6. The resources are initially evenly divided among the frameworks giving them 2 resource capacities each. Since framework's A resource demand is 1, there is a leftover of 1 which makes a total of 5 available resource capacity. This is then evenly divided between frameworks B and C, giving them 2.5 resource capacities each.

Dominant Resource Fairness (DRF): It is a more general case of the max-min fairness applied to multiple resource types rather than a single resource type. The idea behind DRF is that resource allocation is dependent on the dominant share of a job or framework (this is the largest share of any of the resource type that has been given to a particular job or framework). It is used in heterogeneous environments where there are multidimensional resources. The key idea in DRF is to maximize the minimum dominant share across all frameworks within the cluster [54]. The dominant share of a user is the maximum of all its resource shares and the corresponding resource is called the dominant resource [18].

For example, take a case where two users A and B are running tasks within a cluster. Suppose user A is running a memory-intensive task and user B is running a CPU-intensive task, user A is allocated more memory and less CPU while user B is assigned more CPU and less memory thus equalizing the memory share of user A with the CPU share of user B.

3 Resource Scheduling Frameworks and Algorithms

In this section, we present the recent resource scheduling frameworks and algorithms that have been proposed and developed for cloud computing and large computing clusters. The first part shows resource scheduling algorithms in the cloud, the second part gives detailed explanation of the most common large computing cluster scheduling frameworks, while other related scheduling frameworks and algorithms for both cloud computing and large computing clusters are presented last.

3.1 Resource Scheduling Frameworks and Algorithms in Cloud Computing

A largely significant amount of algorithms have been proposed for scheduling in the cloud. Likewise, a lot of reviews and surveys [26, 36, 41, 46, 47, 51, 61] have also been conducted to compare and contrast these algorithms. These algorithms can be classified (but not limited) into the following categories; cost-based [33, 45], QoS-based [57, 58], Ant Colony Optimization (ACO) based [30], Particle Swarm Optimization (PSO) based [38], Min-Min algorithm based [8, 32], Genetic Algorithm Based [11, 27], and Round-Robin Based [22]. Next, we present more recent scheduling algorithms that have been proposed and developed for cloud computing.

A bin-balancing algorithm was proposed in [49], it combines the pros of bin packing and polygons correlation calculations. The resource scheduling algorithm was designed mainly to minimize energy usage while putting into consideration deadlines of jobs and also other factors such as processing element, bandwidth, and memory usage. A number of assumptions were made in developing the bin-balancing model, they include: (i) A virtual machine (VM) has a processing element which is controlled by a single host. (ii) VMs are independent of each other once they are bound with specific jobs. (iii) All jobs to be scheduled are independent of each other. (iv) Jobs are allocated to VMs that executes a single job, that is, a VM is occupied by a single task. (v) Data transmission time and memory usage do not affect the network bandwidth (assumed to be large enough).

The bin-balancing algorithm checks for jobs that are not currently assigned to any VM and bounds them with available VMs. The necessary parameters for VMs and jobs are calculated and the bound VMs are sorted in ascending order of time allowance (time allowed between a job deadline and VM starting execution time). A check is also done to decide whether or not a host has enough resources for a VM. The polygon combination method is used to update hosts by tracking the usage of resources in the host. If all *on* hosts are unavailable, an *off* host is found which consumes the minimum amount of energy among all *off* hosts. A VM is assigned to a host with the minimum processing element usage rate and the VM powers *off* when it has executed all allocated jobs, this is done to avoid overloading and under loading among hosts and also to prevent frequent host switching and VM migration.

A greedy resource scheduler was developed in [16] aimed at minimizing energy usage of servers in cloud computing data centers. The approach taken in [16] requires minimizing active servers in use thereby minimizing energy usage. In the proposed algorithm, servers with the most computational and processing power and capacity are given priority while allocating jobs. A central scheduling approach is adopted that sorts servers based on energy usage and allocates jobs to the most efficient server in terms of energy usage and follows the sorted list thereafter. For the case of a data center with only one server type, the central scheduler keeps and updates a sorted list of active and non-overloaded servers according to their energy profiles sorting them in descending order of their energy efficiency. The server assigns jobs to servers following this list, once a server is found to be overloaded, task allocation goes to the next server in the list, and the overloaded server is removed from the list until it becomes free. This resource scheduling scheme assumes that the energy profiles of servers are known aforehand.

In [50], a credit-based task scheduling algorithm was proposed considering two parameters namely: task length and task priority. Thus, two types of credit systems were considered. In the **task length credit system**, tasks are sorted in increasing order of execution time, with the shorter tasks at the top of the list and the longer tasks being put at the bottom of the list. Next, the average task length is calculated and the absolute difference between all tasks and this average is also calculated. After the absolute difference is gotten, each task is assigned a credit (divided into 5 categories) based on the where they are in the list. Basically, length credits are attached to all tasks based on their execution length.

In the task priority credit system, there are as many credits as there are tasks and task priority are assigned by the user. It is worthy to note that two tasks can have the same priority number. The system finds the highest priority value and a division factor based on the number of digits of the value, i.e., (a single digit highest value has a division factor 10, 100 for two digits, 1000 for the digits and so on). Therefore, a priority credit is assigned to each task by dividing the priority value of each task by the division factor. Finally, the total credit for each task is gotten by multiplying the length credit by the priority credit of each task. The tasks are then sorted based on their total credit score and scheduled in descending order of total credit score.

More recent resource scheduling algorithms have been proposed by using the PSO-based approach. In [7], the PSO approach was employed, but the optimized objectives included deadline and load balancing, rather than only cost and makespan which are considered in earlier PSO scheduling algorithms. Similarly, a resource scheduling algorithm for cloud computing was proposed in [2] where they developed a load balanced mutation model using PSO, taking into account reliability and availability of cloud resources. Reliability is achieved by taking into account available resources and rescheduling tasks that failed to execute initially.

An improved ACO based scheduling was proposed in [63], job makespan and user budget costs are considered as constraints of the optimization problem, while achieving an optimization boost on cost and performance. The algorithm uses the two constraints parameters to adjust and modify the scheduling quality on time based on a feedback approach to achieve an optimal solution. In [31], the proposed algorithm combined the strong positive feedback and efficiency of ACO and the global search ability of GA to come up with an optimal scheduling solution as quickly as possible.

3.2 Resource Scheduling Frameworks in Large Computing Clusters

The most common and recent resource scheduling frameworks for large computing clusters with heterogeneous workloads are shown next. These frameworks are designed to handle large amount (in millions) of jobs. Here are the frameworks.

Apache YARN: The Apache YARN (Yet Another Resource Negotiator) [55, Chap. 4] is used by Hadoop for its cluster resource management. YARN comprises of two main components namely the resource manager and the node managers. The resource manager manages resource use and allocation within the cluster and there is only one resource manager per cluster. Node managers are run on all nodes in

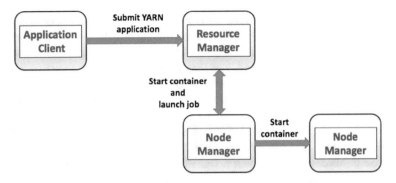

Fig. 3 Work flow of YARN [19]

the cluster and are used to monitor containers. Both the resource manager and node managers are long running daemons in YARN. The work flow of YARN is shown in Fig. 3.

An application running on YARN contacts the resource manager through the application client. The resource manager has a global view of all node managers and thus pools the node managers to find one that can launch the application master in a container. The application master can then decide to run computations in the container in which it is running or request more containers from the resource manager.

Three basic schedulers are provided with YARN, they are FIFO, capacity and fair schedulers. FIFO places applications in a queue as they arrive and are scheduled and executed in the order of their arrival. Capacity schedulers allow cluster resources to shared by different entities within the cluster such that each entity is assigned a particular quantity of the overall cluster resources. Fair schedulers ensure that all running applications get the same share of cluster resources.

Mesos: Apache Mesos [20] is a resource management platform for sharing cluster resources among different frameworks. Mesos uses resource offers which are a two-level and distributed scheduling scheme. In the resource offer mechanism, the amount of resources to offer the different frameworks is decided by Mesos while the different frameworks choose which of the resources to accept and the corresponding computations to run on the resources. Mesos provides frameworks within the system with an interface for gaining access to the resources within the cluster. Frameworks do not need to specify their respective resource requirements in Mesos, rather it gives frameworks the ability to reject offers. Constraints and invariants are satisfied using filters, filters are just a way of optimizing performance, the frameworks still have control on whether to accept or reject resource offers.

Mesos revokes tasks that are running for too long but offers a grace period to frameworks to cleanup. The allocation module decides the policy for revoking tasks and ensures that the guaranteed allocation (the amount of resources a framework may hold without the risk of losing any jobs or tasks) can be met. There are times when a framework makes take time to respond to a resource offer, resources offered by Mesos to frameworks count towards their allocation of cluster resources, this is an incentive mechanism to make frameworks give fast response to resource offers [20]. To achieve fault tolerance, the Mesos master is built to be soft state, the only states of the master are a list of slaves that are currently active, frameworks within the system and tasks that are running. This ensures that the internal state of a former master can be reconstructed by a new master from information extracted from frameworks and the Mesos slave. Zookeeper [21] is used to handle the master selection, failure and leader election.

Resources in Mesos are divided into *mandatory* and *preferred*. The mandatory resources are those that must be acquired by a framework before it can run while preferred resources are those that a framework needs in order to perform better. Mesos assumes that a framework cannot have its mandatory resources greater than its guaranteed share of cluster resources. This assumption is necessary for deadlock prevention. Two allocation modules were implemented in Mesos, the first uses fair sharing based on max-min fairness and second implements strict priorities (where tasks are scheduled based on some assigned priority).

Limitations of Mesos are that it will not perform as well as a centralized scheduler when there is a high level of interdependency between frameworks. In the two-level scheduling approach used by Mesos, application schedulers do not have enough information about the cluster and have to depend on the Mesos master for all needed information. This makes priority preemption difficult and makes it hard to detect interference from workloads that are running that might affect the quality of resources. The application-specific schedulers totally depend on the information (resource offers) provided by the resource manager and thus are limited in the decisions they can make. Likewise, using resource offers introduces more complexity into the scheduling process.

Sparrow: Sparrow [37] is a stateless distributed scheduling solution that uses randomized sampling approach. It is specifically designed and targeted at scheduling a very large number low latency tasks (short tasks) in a very short time. Sparrow exploits the power of two choices load balancing technique [35] to task scheduling. The key concepts in Sparrow include:

- Batch sampling: Rather than using per-task sampling, batch sampling sends probes for all of a job's tasks and gets load information, it then places the job?s m tasks on the worker machines that are least loaded. The number of probes is chosen as d.m (where d = 2), that is, for 1000 tasks, 2000 machines are probed.
- Late binding: This helps to solve race condition. Probed workers do not reply to probes immediately, rather they place a reservation for the task in their internal work queue. A RPC is sent to the scheduler by the worker whenever the reservation of a task gets to the head of the internal work queue and requests for job associated with the reservation.
- Proactive Cancelation: Probes that are remaining after the corresponding tasks have been launched are handled in two ways, first, the scheduler can send a cancelation RPC to all workers or the scheduler waits for workers to send requests for tasks and responds with a "no more un-launched task message".

- Handling placement constraints: In Sparrow, per-job constraints are not well handled, they are enforced trivially by randomly selecting a subset of workers that satisfy the stated constraint. Whereas, per-task constraint is handled by per-task sampling and it is optimized in Sparrow by sharing information across tasks rather than doing individual task probing.
- Resource allocation policies: Sparrow provides support for two resource allocation policies namely strict priority and weighted fair sharing.

Identified downsides of the techniques employed by Sparrow are that for late binding, worker machines are idle during the period when they are sending an RPC to the scheduler to request for tasks. Proactive cancelation can also lead to extra RPCs being sent. For example, a case where a worker gets a cancelation RPC after it has initially sent a request for the task with the reservation. Gang scheduling is not supported by Sparrow because tasks are queued plenty machines and lack a central controller.

Omega: Omega [44] is a shared-state parallel scheduler architecture that uses a lock-free and optimistic concurrency control. Omega looks to solve the shortcomings of monolithic and two-level schedulers. All schedulers are granted access to the entire cluster, and they compete equally for cluster resources, optimistic control is used to mitigate the effect of clashes when the cluster state is being updated. All resource allocation and scheduling decisions take place in schedulers since there is no centralized control. Each scheduler stores a copy of the cell state (resource allocations in the cluster) and updates this shared copy of the cell state immediately a placement decision is made by the scheduler in an atomic commit (all-or-nothing transaction). This shared cell state update is done whether or not the transaction is successful.

In order to achieve gang scheduling in Omega, schedulers use an all-or-nothing transaction, that is, either all tasks are scheduled together or none of them is scheduled. The shared-state's performance is dependent on the number of failed transactions and the cost of the failures. All schedulers must agree upon the permitted resource allocations and a mechanism for deciding job priority (precedence) while implementing their own separate policies. Omega's performance is totally dependent on the ratio of transaction failure and the cost of those failures. Omega however does not guarantee fairness in the resource allocation process because of the free-for-all approach employed [44].

Apollo: Apollo [4] is a distributed and coordinated scheduling framework that uses the shared-state concept. Independent scheduling decisions are made opportunistically and are coordinated using a synchronized cluster utilization information. Schedulers perform weighted decisions while scheduling in order to reduce the execution time of tasks. Tasks in Apollo are divided into regular tasks and opportunistic tasks. Low latency is maintained for regular tasks and is scheduled as soon as possible whereas, opportunistic tasks are used to drive up the utilization of the cluster, that is, when there are idle cluster resources, opportunistic tasks are scheduled to fill up the idle resources thus maintaining a high cluster utilization. The architecture of Apollo is shown in Fig. 4.

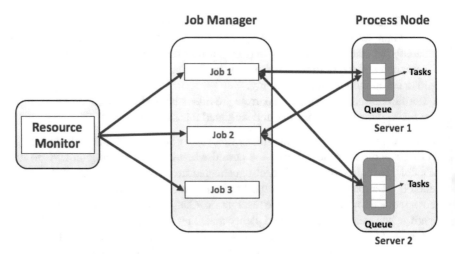

Fig. 4 Apollo architecture [4]

The scheduler also called the Job Manager manages the life cycle of each job. Each cluster has a Resource Monitor and each server has a Process Node. The global load information of the cluster is supplied by combining the information from the Resource Monitor and the Process Node. The Process Node is run on each server and manages the local resources and performs local scheduling. A local queue is maintained at each Process Node. The Resource monitor pools load information from the Process Nodes and aggregates it to provide a global cluster view. The Resource Manager is implemented using Paxos [28] in a master–slave architecture.

Hawk: Hawk [12] is a hybrid scheduler for scheduling heterogeneous (many of short running jobs and a few long running jobs) workloads. It attempts to strike a balance between centralized and distributed schedulers. It exploits the scalability and fast decision-making of distributed schedulers and the efficient scheduling decisions of centralized schedulers. The centralized scheduler handles scheduling long running jobs while a distributed approach is employed in scheduling short running jobs. Hawk dedicates a portion of the cluster resources to serve short running tasks only while the remaining part of the cluster resources are decided to long running tasks. This is to ensure that long running jobs do not negatively impact short jobs. An estimated runtime for all tasks that comprise a job is computed and this value is taken as the average runtime for all tasks within the job. The average task runtime is compared against a threshold to differentiate a job as either long or short.

In order to ensure high cluster utilization, randomized task stealing is used to reduce the delays caused by occasional poor scheduling decisions made by distributed schedulers due to the limited cluster information they have. Idle servers are allowed to steal tasks from heavily loaded servers.

Mercury: Mercury [23] is a hybrid resource management framework that supports both centralized and distributed scheduling. Mercury was implemented as an extension of Apache YARN. Mercury comprises of two subsystems, the *mercury runtime* that runs on all worker nodes, manages all system-wide interactions, and enforces each node's execution policy and the *resource management framework* which is the central scheduler in mercury and runs on a single node reserved for the reason, it consists of distributed schedulers that run on the worker nodes. A loose coordination of the worker nodes is done by the *Mercury Coordinator*.

Mercury uses containers for execution. There are two basic types of containers, the GUARANTEED (containers that incur no queuing delay) and the QUEUEABLE (containers that allow a task queue). The central scheduler controls the allocation of the GUARANTEED containers while the distributed controllers handle the allocation of QUEUEABLE containers [23]. Tasks in Mercury are executed in the order in which they are submitted to the framework. To mitigate the effect of occasional poor placement decisions for QUEUEABLE containers by the distributed schedulers, load shedding is used to dynamically rebalance the queues across machines.

3.3   Other Related Work

Borg [52] is a large cluster management system was developed at Google. Borg consists of two main components, the Borgmaster which has the main Borgmaster process and a scheduler and Borglets that run on each cell machine. The Borgmaster records jobs that are submitted persistently using Paxos and the job's tasks are added to the existing queue. The pending queue is asynchronously scanned by the scheduler in order of task priority (high to low) and uses a round-robin mechanism to ensure fairness and prevent head-of-line blocking. The scheduler assigns tasks to machines that have enough resources and that can satisfy the job's constraints. Borg's scheduling algorithm is divided into two phases, the feasibility-checking phase and the scoring phase. During feasibility checking, machines with the right amount of resources and that can satisfy the constraints posed by tasks are found. Scoring involves determining the suitability of each feasible machine. Scoring is mostly driven by built-in criteria and sometimes by user-defined preferences. In order to reduce task start-up latency, Borg scheduler gives preference to tasks that already have the necessary packages to run installed on a machine it is to be scheduled.

A fault-tolerant resource management and scheduling framework was developed in [62] (Fuxi). Fuxi uses a master–slave architecture and has three components: the FuxiMaster, FuxiAgent, and application masters. The FuxiMaster acts as a bridge between available resources and resource requests. The FuxiAgent runs on each cluster machine collection local state information and sending it to the FuxiMaster. The application masters are the different computation frameworks running on the cluster. Fuxi employs incremental scheduling and incremental communication to cater for the dynamism (rapidly changing number of tasks) in the cluster and the massive message communication among components within the system. The FuxiMaster maintains two data structures which are the available resource pool (free resources) and the locality tree (queues). The Fuxi framework uses DAG to represent the general user workflow because it is easily configurable. To ensure that the system is fault-tolerant, two FuxiMaster processes are started and are mutually excluded using a distributed lock. The system state is separated into soft state (collected from FuxiAgents) and hard state (retrieved from checkpoints). Fault tolerance is achieved for FuxiAgent by rebuilding the complete states initially collected by the Fuxi Agent before it failed.

In [15], Tarcil, a scheduling scheme for optimizing scheduling speed and quality was proposed. Tarcil adopts a distributed and shared-state architecture where multiple schedulers compete for shared cluster resources. Tarcil uses sampling-based techniques to provide guarantees on the quality of resources allocated to scheduled jobs, and uses batch sampling when a job requires multiple cores to run. Tarcil follows two major steps in processing submitted jobs from different workloads. (i) It checks for the job's preferences (resources and interference sensitivity), that is, it gets an estimate of the job's performance on different resource platforms and also the tolerated and generated interference of the job in the shared cluster resources. (ii) It decides whether the scheduler will find resources that meets the quality requirements of the job and then further determines whether the job should be scheduled immediately or queued. Tarcil also measures job's performance while running to ensure that it is not running below a specified threshold, else, the scheduling decisions are changed by the scheduler to improve the job's running performance.

4 Research Challenges and Future Research Directions in Resource Scheduling in Clouds and Large Clusters

Cloud users are increasing daily, and as such, more applications are been deployed in the cloud. Finding an efficient way to schedule those differing and heterogeneous tasks in the cloud while ensuring high performance and efficiency and also guaranteeing a good QoS still remains an open research issue. Likewise, managing and scheduling resources in large computing clusters with heterogeneous workloads is still a major research topic. Next, we present issues in resource scheduling both in cloud computing and large computing clusters, and propose possible future research directions.

1. **Trade-offs**: There are a number of trade-offs that need to be made in resource scheduling.In cloud computing, several factors need to be considered (resource utilization, job makespan, energy consumption, job deadline, job constraints, load balancing, scalability, and cost-effectiveness) to make good scheduling decisions. All these constraints cannot be met, thus, a scheduling algorithm for cloud computing must make a trade-off between the aforementioned parameters based on the goal of the scheduling algorithm. In the case of scheduling in large computing clusters, one of the trade-offs that needs to be made is between making a good scheduling decision and reducing latency. Both are goals of a scheduler, but there has to be a trade-off between them as evident in centralized schedulers and also

distributed schedulers. Another major trade-off made in resource scheduling is between providing execution guarantees and maintaining scheduling efficiency, this is particularly related to hybrid scheduling. Looking at ways to minimize the impact of these trade-offs while maintaining a high scheduling efficiency and performance is an open research issue in resource management and scheduling.

2. **Enforcing invariants and constraints**: Most user tasks that are run in the cloud have constraint that needs to be satisfied. These constraints (memory, dependency etc.) vary depending on the type of job to be run. This is typically an issue for most cloud computing resource schedulers as they have to find a balance between guaranteeing high performance and efficiency while guaranteeing such constraints. For large computing clusters, resource schedulers have to make guarantees to frameworks running within the cluster that their framework-specific, job-specific, or task-specific constraints and requirements will be met. Most of the proposed and developed scheduling frameworks do not totally guarantee that all invariants and constraints will be met while still guaranteeing an overall high scheduling performance. However, enforcing invariants such as I/O and network resource constraints in resource management and scheduling are possible research directions.

3. **Global guarantees**: Providing and ensuring global guarantees in distributed schedulers for large computing clusters is a major research issue. Global guarantees such as fairness and starvation avoidance need to be ensured in distributed scheduling. This is particularly a challenging problem because distributed schedulers do not have a global view of the cluster and as such it is difficult for them to ensure global guarantees. A possible research direction is to look at ways in which distributed schedulers can be extended to have a more detailed view of the cluster in order to ensure global guarantees.

4. **Coexistence**: In an hybrid system such as Hawk, the centralized component has no idea of where the short jobs are scheduled and assumes that the centralized component will not be a bottleneck. Looking at ways of efficiently improving the coexistence of centralized and distributed scheduling is a possible research direction.

5. **Communication and data dependency**: Coscheduling and gang scheduling involve scheduling a group of tasks when there is a strong data dependency and high communication between the group of tasks and the tasks need to all be scheduled together at the same time or none of them is scheduled at all. Most large cluster and cloud computing scheduling frameworks and algorithms do not consider either coscheduling or gang scheduling. Integrating coscheduling and gang scheduling into existing cloud computing and large computing cluster resource management and scheduling frameworks is a research challenge and an area for further research.

5 Conclusion

Resource scheduling is a major part in the operations of cloud computing and large computing clusters since they receive very large number of jobs. With the increasing rate in data generated and processed daily, there is a need for better and optimized scheduling algorithms that will make efficient scheduling decisions. Recent applications (mobile, web, etc.) are mostly time-sensitive and thus need data processing as fast as possible and thus scheduling algorithms have to come up with better ways of ensuring that scheduling goals are achieved.

In this chapter, we discussed the resource management in cloud computing and large computing clusters. We presented different types of scheduling and the different scheduling solutions, architectures, and fairness algorithms used to achieve fairness in large computing clusters. The current and state-of-the-art scheduling frameworks and algorithms were also presented, explaining their architecture, mode of operation, technologies, schemes adopted and also their strengths, and weaknesses. Finally, we identified open issues in scheduling in large clusters and laid out areas of possible future research in resource management and scheduling.

References

1. Amatriain, X., & Griffiths, D. (2004). Free software in education is it a viable alternative? In *Proceedings of 7th IMAC Conference on Localization and Globalization in Technology Design Use and Transfer as a Subject of Engineering* (Vol. 7(1)).
2. Awad, A., El-Hefnawy, N., & Abdel_kader, H. (2015). Enhanced particle swarm optimization for task scheduling in cloud computing environments. *Procedia Computer Science, 65*, 920–929.
3. Batat, A., & Feitelson, D. G. (2000). Gang scheduling with memory considerations. In *Proceedings 14th International Parallel and Distributed Processing Symposium, IPDPS* (pp. 109–114).
4. Boutin, E., Ekanayake, J., Lin, W., Shi, B., Zhou, J., Qian, Z., Wu, M., & Zhou, L. (2014). Apollo: Scalable and coordinated scheduling for cloud-scale computing. In *11th USENIX Symposium on Operating Systems Design and Implementation (OSDI 14)*, Broomfield, CO (pp. 285–300). USENIX Association.
5. Chang, G., & Su, H. (2003). Fifo scheduling time sharing. US Patent App. 10/163,047.
6. Chaskar, H. M., & Madhow, U. (2003). Fair scheduling with tunable latency: A round-robin approach. *IEEE/ACM Transactions on Networking, 11*(4), 592–601.
7. Chen, H., & Guo, W. (2015). *Real-Time Task Scheduling Algorithm for Cloud Computing Based on Particle Swarm Optimization* (pp. 141–152). Cham: Springer International Publishing.
8. Chen, H., Wang, F., Helian, N., & Akanmu, G. (2013). User-priority guided min-min scheduling algorithm for load balancing in cloud computing. In *2013 National Conference on Parallel Computing Technologies (PARCOMPTECH)* (pp. 1–8).
9. Convolbo, M. W., & Chou, J. (2016). Cost-aware dag scheduling algorithms for minimizing execution cost on cloud resources. *The Journal of Supercomputing, 72*(3), 985–1012.
10. Danna, E., Hassidim, A., Kaplan, H., Kumar, A., Mansour, Y., Raz, D., et al. (2012). Upward max min fairness. In *INFOCOM, 2012 Proceedings IEEE* (pp. 837–845).
11. Dasgupta, K., Mandal, B., Dutta, P., Mandal, J. K., & Dam, S. (2013). A genetic algorithm (ga) based load balancing strategy for cloud computing. *Procedia Technology, 10*(Complete), 340–347.

12. Delgado, P., Dinu, F., Kermarrec, A.-M., & Zwaenepoel, W. (2015). Hawk: Hybrid datacenter scheduling. In *Proceedings of the 2015 USENIX Annual Technical Conference* (pp. 499–510).
13. Delimitrou, C., & Kozyrakis, C. (2013). Paragon: Qos-aware scheduling for heterogeneous datacenters. In *Proceedings of the Eighteenth International Conference on Architectural Support for Programming Languages and Operating Systems, ASPLOS '13*, New York, NY, USA (pp. 77–88). ACM.
14. Delimitrou, C., & Kozyrakis, C. (2014). Quasar: Resource-efficient and qos-aware cluster management. In *Proceedings of the 19th International Conference on Architectural Support for Programming Languages and Operating Systems, ASPLOS '14*, New York, NY, USA (pp. 127–144). ACM.
15. Delimitrou, C., Sanchez, D., & Kozyrakis, C. (2015). Tarcil: Reconciling scheduling speed and quality in large shared clusters. In *Proceedings of the Sixth ACM Symposium on Cloud Computing* (pp. 97–110).
16. Dong, Z., Liu, N., & Rojas-Cessa, R. (2015). Greedy scheduling of tasks with time constraints for energy-efficient cloud-computing data centers. *Journal of Cloud Computing: Advances, Systems and Applications, 4*(1), 5.
17. Frachtenberg, E., Petrini, F., Coll, S., Feng, W., Modeling, C., & Group, I. *Gang scheduling with lightweight user-level communication.*
18. Ghodsi, A., Zaharia, M., Hindman, B., Konwinski, A., Shenker, S., & Stoica, I. (2011). Dominant resource fairness: Fair allocation of multiple resource types. In *Proceedings of the 8th USENIX Conference on Networked Systems Design and Implementation, NSDI'11*, Berkeley, CA, USA (pp. 323–336). USENIX Association.
19. Grandl, R., Ananthanarayanan, G., Kandula, S., Rao, S., & Akella, A. (2014). Multi-resource packing for cluster schedulers. *ACM SIGCOMM Computer Communication Review, 44*(4), 455–466.
20. Hindman, B., Konwinski, A., Zaharia, M., Ghodsi, A., Joseph, A. D., Katz, R., et al. (2011). Mesos: A platform for fine-grained resource sharing in the data center. In *Proceedings of the 8th USENIX Conference on Networked Systems Design and Implementation, NSDI'11*, Berkeley, CA, USA (pp. 295–308). USENIX Association.
21. Hunt, P., Konar, M., Junqueira, F. P., & Reed, B. (2010). Zookeeper: Wait-free coordination for internet-scale systems. In *Proceedings of the 2010 USENIX Conference on USENIX Annual Technical Conference, USENIXATC'10*, Berkeley, CA, USA (pp. 11–11). USENIX Association.
22. Kapgate, D. (2014). Improved round robin algorithm for data center selection in cloud computing. *International Journal of Engineering Sciences and Research Technology, 3*(2), 686–691.
23. Karanasos, K., Rao, S., Curino, C., Douglas, C., Chaliparambil, K., Fumarola, G. M., et al. (2015). Mercury: Hybrid centralized and distributed scheduling in large shared clusters. In *Usenix-Atc* (pp. 485–497).
24. Karatza, H. D. (2006). Scheduling gangs in a distributed system. *International Journal of Simulation: Systems, Science and Technology, 7*(1), 15–22.
25. Kargahi, M., & Movaghar, A. (2006). A method for performance analysis of earliest-deadline-first scheduling policy. *The Journal of Supercomputing, 37*(2), 197–222.
26. Kaur, R., Kaur, G., & Scholar, R. (2016). A review on efficient hybrid framework for scheduling in cloud computing. *International Journal of Engineering Science and Computing, 6*(7), 8698–8700.
27. Kaur, R., & Kinger, S. (2014). Article: Enhanced genetic algorithm based task scheduling in cloud computing. *International Journal of Computer Applications, 101*(14), 1–6.
28. Lamport, L., et al. (2001). *Paxos made simple. ACM Sigact News, 32*(4), 18–25.
29. Leith, D. J., Cao, Q., & Subramanian, V. G. (2012). Max-min fairness in 802.11 mesh networks. *IEEE/ACM Transactions on Networking, 20*(3), 756–769.
30. Li, K., Xu, G., Zhao, G., Dong, Y., & Wang, D. (2011). Cloud task scheduling based on load balancing ant colony optimization. In *2011 Sixth Annual ChinaGrid Conference* (pp. 3–9). IEEE.

31. Liu, C. Y., Zou, C. M., & Wu, P. (2014). A task scheduling algorithm based on genetic algorithm and ant colony optimization in cloud computing. In *2014 13th International Symposium on Distributed Computing and Applications to Business, Engineering and Science (DCABES)* (pp. 68–72).

32. Liu, G., Li, J., & Xu, J. (2013). *An improved min-min algorithm in cloud computing* (pp. 47–52). Berlin: Springer.

33. Liu, K., Jin, H., Chen, J., Liu, X., Yuan, D., & Yang, Y. (2010). A compromised-time-cost scheduling algorithm in swindew-c for instance-intensive cost-constrained workflows on a cloud computing platform. *International Journal of High Performance Computer Application, 24*(4), 445–456.

34. Lupetti, S., & Zagorodnov, D. (2006). Data popularity and shortest-job-first scheduling of network transfers. In *International Conference on Digital Telecommunications (ICDT'06)* (pp. 26–26).

35. Mitzenmacher, M. (2001). The power of two choices in randomized load balancing. *IEEE Transactions on Parallel and Distributed Systems, 12*(10), 1094–1104.

36. Mohammadi, F., Jamali, S., & Bekravi, M. (2014). Survey on job scheduling algorithms in cloud computing. *International Journal of Emerging Trends & Technology in Computer Science (IJETTCS), 3*(2), 151–154.

37. Ousterhout, K., Wendell, P., Zaharia, M., & Stoica, I. (2013). Sparrow: Distributed, low latency scheduling. In *Proceedings of the Twenty-Fourth ACM Symposium on Operating Systems Principles, SOSP '13*, New York, NY, USA (69–84). ACM.

38. Pandey, S., Wu, L., Guru, S. M., & Buyya, R. (2010). A particle swarm optimization-based heuristic for scheduling workflow applications in cloud computing environments. In *2010 24th IEEE International Conference on Advanced Information Networking and Applications* (pp. 400–407).

39. Petrini, F., & Feng, W.-C. (2000). Improved resource utilization with buffered coscheduling. *Journal of Parallel Algorithms and Applications (Special Issue), 16*(2–3),

40. Potts, C. N., & Kovalyov, M. Y. (2000). Scheduling with batching: A review. *European Journal of Operational Research, 120*(2), 228–249.

41. Ruchita, P., & Moni, C. (2016). Analysis of various task scheduling algorithms in cloud computing. *International Research Journal of Engineering and Technology (IRJET), 3*(3), 493–496.

42. Saifullah, A., Ferry, D., Li, J., Agrawal, K., Lu, C., & Gill, C. D. (2014). Parallel real-time scheduling of dags. *IEEE Transactions on Parallel and Distributed Systems, 25*(12), 3242–3252.

43. Sakellariou, R., & Zhao, H. (2004). A hybrid heuristic for DAG scheduling on heterogeneous systems. In *Parallel and Distributed Processing Symposium, 2004. Proceedings. 18th International* (pp. 111–123).

44. Schwarzkopf, M., & Konwinski, A. (2013). Omega: Flexible, scalable schedulers for large compute clusters. In *EuroSys '13 Proceedings of the 8th ACM European Conference on Computer Systems* (pp. 351–364).

45. Selvarani, S., & Sadhasivam, G. S. (2010). Improved cost-based algorithm for task scheduling in cloud computing. In *2010 IEEE International Conference on Computational Intelligence and Computing Research (ICCIC)* (pp. 1–5).

46. Shimpy, E., & Sidhu, J. (2014). Different scheduling algorithms in different cloud environment. *International Journal of Advanced Research in Computer and Communication Engineering, 3*(9), 2278–1021.

47. Singh, S., & Chana, I. (2016). A survey on resource scheduling in cloud computing: Issues and challenges. *Journal of Grid Computing* (pp. 1–48).

48. Sobalvarro, P., Pakin, S., Weihl, W. E., & Chien, A. A. (1998). Dynamic coscheduling on workstation clusters. In *Proceedings of the Workshop on Job Scheduling Strategies for Parallel Processing, IPPS/SPDP '98*, London, UK (pp. 231–256). Springer.

49. Tang, J. M., Luo, L., Wei, K. M., Guo, X., & Ji, X. Y. (2015). A heuristic resource scheduling algorithm of cloud computing based on polygons correlation calculation. In *Proceedings—12th IEEE International Conference on E-Business Engineering, ICEBE 2015* (pp. 365–370).

50. Thomas, A., Krishnalal, G., & Jagathy Raj, V. P. (2015). Credit based scheduling algorithm in cloud computing environment. *Procedia Computer Science, 46*(Icict 2014), 913–920.
51. Tilak, S., & Patil, P. D. (2012). A survey of various scheduling algorithms in cloud environment. *International Journal of Engineering Inventions, 1*(2), 36–39.
52. Verma, A., Pedrosa, L., Korupolu, M., Oppenheimer, D., Tune, E., & Wilkes, J. (2015). Large-scale cluster management at Google with Borg. In *Proceedings of the Tenth European Conference on Computer Systems—EuroSys '15* (pp. 1–17).
53. Vignesh, V., Kumarand, S., & Jaisankar, N. (2013). Resource management and scheduling in cloud environment. *International Journal of Scientific and Research Publications, 3*(6), 1–6.
54. Wang, W., Li, B., & Liang, B. (2013). Dominant resource fairness in cloud computing systems with heterogeneous servers. *CoRR.* arXiv:abs/1308.0083.
55. White, T. (2012). *Hadoop: The definitive guide.* O'Reilly Media, Inc.
56. Wiseman, Y., & Feitelson, D. G. (2003). Paired gang scheduling. *IEEE Transactions on Parallel and Distributed Systems, 14*(6), 581–592.
57. Wu, X., Deng, M., Zhang, R., Zeng, B., & Zhou, S. (2013). *A task scheduling algorithm based on qos-driven in cloud computing* (Vol. 17, pp. 1162–1169).
58. Xu, M., Cui, L., Wang, H., & Bi, Y. (2009). A multiple qos constrained scheduling strategy of multiple workflows for cloud computing. In *2009 IEEE International Symposium on Parallel and Distributed Processing with Applications* (pp. 629–634). IEEE.
59. Yang, X., & Vaidya, N. H. (2002). Priority scheduling in wireless ad hoc networks. In *Proceedings of the 3rd ACM International Symposium on Mobile Ad Hoc Networking & Amp; Computing, MobiHoc '02*, New York, NY, USA (pp. 71–79). ACM.
60. Zhan, Z.-H., Liu, X.-F., Gong, Y.-J., Zhang, J., Chung, H. S.-H., & Li, Y. (2015a). Cloud computing resource scheduling and a survey of its evolutionary approaches. *ACM Computing Survey, 47*(4), 63:1–63:33.
61. Zhan, Z.-H., Liu, X.-F., Gong, Y.-J., Zhang, J., Chung, H. S.-H., & Li, Y. (2015b). Cloud computing resource scheduling and a survey of its evolutionary approaches. *ACM Computing Surveys, 47*(4), 1–33.
62. Zhang, Z., Li, C., Tao, Y., Yang, R., Tang, H., & Xu, J. (2014). Fuxi: A fault-tolerant resource management and job scheduling system at internet scale. *Proceedings of VLDB Endowment, 7*(13), 1393–1404.
63. Zuo, L., Shu, L., Dong, S., Zhu, C., & Hara, T. (2015). A multi-objective optimization scheduling method based on the ant colony algorithm in cloud computing. *IEEE Access, 3,* 2687–2699.

Resource Allocation for Cloud Infrastructures: Taxonomies and Research Challenges

Benjamín Barán and Fabio López-Pires

Abstract Cloud computing datacenters dynamically provide millions of virtual machines in real-world cloud computing environments. A large number of research challenges have to be addressed toward an efficient resource management of these cloud computing infrastructures. In the resource allocation field, Virtual Machine Placement (VMP) is one of the most studied problems with several possible formulations and a large number of existing optimization criteria, considering solutions with high economical and ecological impact. Based on systematic reviews of the VMP literature, a taxonomy of VMP problem environments is presented to understand different possible environments where a VMP problem could be considered, from both provider and broker perspectives in different deployment architectures. Additionally, another taxonomy for VMP problems is presented to identify existing approaches for the formulation and resolution of the VMP as an optimization problem. Finally a detailed view of the VMP problem is presented, identifying research opportunities to further advance in cloud computing resource allocation areas.

1 Introduction

Cloud computing datacenters deliver infrastructure (IaaS), platform (PaaS), and software (SaaS) as a service, provided to customers in a pay-as-you-go basis [1]. Several studies in this emergent field already identified a significant number of research challenges for delivering computational resources as an utility [2]. Achieving an efficient resource management in cloud computing datacenters could be considered one of the most relevant challenges, including important topics such as: resource allocation, resource provisioning, resource mapping, and resource adaptation [3, 4].

B. Barán (✉)
National University of Asunción, San Lorenzo, Paraguay
e-mail: bbaran@pol.una.py

F. López-Pires
Itaipu Technological Park, Hernandarias, Paraguay
e-mail: fabio.lopez@pti.org.py

© Springer Nature Singapore Pte Ltd. 2017
S. Chaudhary et al. (eds.), *Research Advances in Cloud Computing*,
DOI 10.1007/978-981-10-5026-8_11

1.1 Background

The present chapter studies the Virtual Machine Placement (VMP), recognized as one of the most relevant resource allocation problems [5]. At the Infrastructure as a Service (IaaS) model, provider-oriented VMP problems can be enunciated as the process of assigning physical machines (PMs) to host requested virtual machines (VMs) in multi-tenant environments. Several research articles demonstrated that solving the VMP problem as an optimization problem for efficient allocation of cloud resources could significantly improve several different objective functions; all of them with significant impact in several fields [6–8].

Some of the most studied problems for resource allocation in cloud computing are presented in [3], to propose a conceptual cloud architecture showing interactions between key management issues for predictive elasticity, admission control, and placement (or scheduling) of VMs. In the architecture presented in [3], the VMP problem is one of the most relevant ones, considering that it can be formulated considering different approaches and criteria for optimization. Beloglazov et al. studied in [9] the problem of dynamic resource allocation in cloud computing infrastructures, defining four different subproblems: (1) host overload detection, to migrate VMs from an overloaded PM; (2) host underload detection, to migrate all VMs from an underloaded PM to change it to sleep mode; (3) VM selection, for migration of these VMs from an overloaded PM; and (4) selecting a new placement of selected VMs, optimizing different objective functions.

The specialized VMP literature includes several presented surveys, where most of the existing works only studied particular issues of the problem, such as: (1) energy-efficient techniques applied to the resolution of VMP problems [7, 10], (2) federated-clouds as deployment architectures where the VMP problem is studied [11], and (3) methods for comparing performance of algorithms for VMP problems in on-demand cloud computing infrastructures [12].

1.2 Motivation

The abovementioned surveys and research articles focused into very specific issues related to the VMP problem and do not summarize the literature considering a general vision, identifying research opportunities for the VMP problem. Consequently, López-Pires and Barán proposed in [5] a general and extensive study of a large part of the VMP literature including more than 80 studied articles systematically selected [13], presenting a wide analysis of the existing approaches for the formulation and resolution of the VMP as an optimization problem. The analysis was summarized as a novel taxonomy for the classification of the studied articles by the main following criteria: (1) optimization approach, (2) objective function, and (3) solution technique. Next, the authors extended their previous work in [5] with novel taxonomies, to present a detailed view of the existing approaches as well as several possible research opportunities to further advance in this research area. The taxonomies presented in [14] could guide interested readers to: (1) understand different possible environments where a VMP problem could be studied, considering both provider and broker perspectives in different deployment architectures (see Sect. 2), (2) identify existing approaches for the formulation and resolution of the VMP as an optimization problem (see Sect. 3), and (3) present a detailed view of the VMP problem, identifying research opportunities to further advance in cloud computing resource allocation areas (see Sect. 4).

Based on the taxonomies presented in [5, 14], this chapter summarizes relevant concepts related to the VMP problem, including formal definitions that could help the research community to avoid terminological ambiguity as well as to follow common terminology and concepts. The remainder of this chapter is organized in the following way: Sect. 2 presents a VMP problem environment taxonomy for the classification of related articles by: (1) orientation, (2) deployment architecture, and (3) types of formulation. Section 3 presents a VMP problem formulation and resolution taxonomy considering the following criteria: (1) optimization approach, (2) objective function, and (3) solution technique. Section 4 details identified research opportunities on this research area, while conclusions are left to Sect. 5.

2 VMP Problem Environment Taxonomy

Different possible VMP environments could be identified by classifying research works in the VMP literature by: (1) orientation, (2) deployment architecture, and (3) type of formulation. Depending on the particular environment where a VMP problem will be studied, several different considerations should be taken into account before proposing a particular formulation or technique for the resolution of the considered VMP problem. For a complete understanding of the possible environments where a VMP problem could be studied, considering both provider and broker orientations in four different deployment architectures for online and offline formulations, Fig. 1 presents the taxonomy proposed in [14] described in this section, including relevant references from the studied VMP literature [13].

Two main perspectives could be considered when studying a VMP problem: provider-oriented or broker-oriented (see Sect. 2.1). In this context, provider-oriented VMP problems may consider one of the following deployment architectures: single-cloud, distributed-cloud, or federated-cloud, while broker-oriented VMP problems may be studied taking into account a multi-cloud deployment architecture (see Sect. 2.2). Provider-oriented and broker-oriented VMP problems could be formulated as offline or online optimization problems (see Sect. 2.3).

The following subsections present a detailed description of the mentioned classification criteria, including definitions for a complete understanding of the problem.

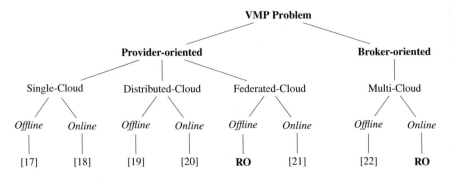

Fig. 1 VMP Problem Environment Taxonomy. Relevant references for each environment are presented. Unexplored environments are considered Research Opportunities (RO)

2.1 Orientation: Provider-Oriented or Broker-Oriented

Definition 1 A provider-oriented VMP problem is the process of selecting which VMs should be hosted at each PM of a cloud computing infrastructure.

Resource allocation in cloud computing datacenters is a main concern for Cloud Service Providers (CSPs). According to [5], the VMP problem is mainly formulated from this perspective. It should be mentioned that in a provider-oriented VMP problem, a Cloud Service Tenant (CST) cannot decide which PMs will host the requested VMs. In the specialized literature, this particular problem is also known as Virtual Machine Allocation (VMA) problem [15].

Definition 2 A broker-oriented VMP problem is the process of selecting which VMs should be hosted at each Cloud Service Provider of a cloud computing market.

Considering that the number of CSPs has been rapidly increased and nowadays there are different pricing schemes as well as VM offers, it is difficult for CSTs to search for a correct option in cloud computing markets and decide which CSP is the most convenient to host requested VM resources. Consequently, a VMP problem can also be formulated from a broker perspective, who is responsible of helping CSTs to find good allocation deals. In the specialized literature, this particular problem is also known as Cloud Resource Brokerage (CRB) problem [16].

2.2 Deployment Architectures

Different deployment architectures can be considered for VMP problems, depending on the type of cloud computing infrastructure associated to the problem and the interconnection mechanism of the datacenters, as well as the considered perspective (see Sect. 2.1). A provider-oriented VMP problem could be studied considering one of the following deployment architectures: single-cloud, distributed-cloud, or federated-cloud (see Definitions 3–5), while a broker-oriented VMP problem could be studied in a multi-cloud deployment architecture (see Definition 6).

Definition 3 A provider-oriented VMP problem in a single-cloud deployment architecture is the process of selecting which VMs should be hosted at each PMs of a single-cloud computing datacenter.

In scenarios considering a single-cloud computing datacenter, a CSP could formulate a VMP problem subject to commonly studied constraints such as: unique placement of VMs [17], maximum capacity of resources [18], or Service Level Agreement (SLA) compliance [6, 19]. According to [5], the single-cloud deployment architecture is the most studied scenario in the considered VMP literature.

Definition 4 A provider-oriented VMP problem in a distributed-cloud deployment is the process of selecting which VMs should be hosted at each PMs of more than one cloud computing datacenter owned by the same Cloud Service Provider.

For CSPs with a global infrastructure (e.g., Amazon Web Services), a single-cloud deployment architecture could be extended to several geographically distributed cloud computing datacenters, where the formulation of a VMP problem may include particular constraints and considerations. CSPs with geo-distributed cloud computing datacenters may be interested in studying a VMP problem for the provisioning of differentiated services to world-wide CSTs, such as fault-tolerance for services (placement of VMs in different cloud datacenters) [20] or response time of services (placement of VMs in datacenters near to customers) [21], increasing the complexity of the VMP problem formulation.

Definition 5 A provider-oriented VMP problem in a federated-cloud deployment architecture is the process of selecting which VMs should be hosted at each PMs of more than one cloud computing datacenter owned by different Cloud Service Providers in a cloud computing federation.

In federated clouds, CSPs with idle capacity lease resources to other CSPs in need of additional resources on workload peaks; consequently, particular considerations associated to a VMP problem in this deployment architecture have to be studied [11]. For example, trading policies are generally not the same for CSPs that form part of the same cloud federation, so a VMP problem could be studied for cost-effective selection of CSPs for workload peaks, just to cite a simple example.

Definition 6 A broker-oriented VMP problem in a multi-cloud deployment is the process of selecting which VMs should be hosted at each Cloud Service Provider of a cloud computing market composed by more than one CSP.

Cloud Service Brokers (CSBs) or CSTs can require VMs to be deployed in cloud computing datacenters owned by different CSPs, according to particular requirements such as disaster recovery reasons or due to legislation [22], just to cite a few.

2.3 Types of Formulation: Offline or Online

VMP problems could be studied considering both offline (static or semi-dynamic) or online (dynamic) formulations. An online problem formulation is considered when an algorithm makes decisions on-the-fly without knowing upcoming events (e.g., online heuristics for dynamic VMP problems) [9]. If an algorithm has complete knowledge of future events of a problem instance, the formulation is called offline (e.g., Memetic Algorithms (MAs) for static [17] or semi-dynamic [23] VMP problems). Combining online and offline formulations is a relevant research topic [24].

A VMP problem could be formulated as an offline problem considering the placement of VMs into PMs (for provider-oriented VMP) or VMs into CSPs (for broker-oriented VMP) for a static or semi-dynamic virtual service deployment.

Definition 7 An offline formulation of a provider-oriented VMP problem in any possible deployment architecture could be understood as the process of selecting which VMs should be hosted at each PMs of the considered cloud computing datacenters for a given (static or semi-dynamic) virtual service deployment.

For a static provider-oriented VMP problem, an offline formulation does not consider possible relocation of VMs; therefore, there is no need for migration techniques. It should be noted that this type of offline formulation is mostly appropriate in VMP for initial placement of VMs or for virtualized datacenters with deployments of VMs that rarely change its configuration over time.

For a semi-dynamic provider-oriented VMP problem [23], some considerations of dynamic environments are taken into account (e.g., the set of requested VMs changes dynamically over time) but there are also limitations of a static alternative (e.g., there is no short time decision constraints), been mostly appropriate in VMP with reconfigurations of VMs through migration of VMs between PMs.

Definition 8 An offline formulation of a broker-oriented VMP problem could be understood as the process of selecting which VMs should be hosted at each CSP of the considered cloud computing market for a given (static) service deployment.

The broker-oriented VMP problem is mostly formulated as an offline problem, where possible relocation of VMs between different CSPs are not considered taking into account cloud computing interoperability issues in actual markets.

A VMP problem could also be formulated as an online problem considering the placement of VMs into PMs (provider-oriented VMP) or VMs into CSPs (broker-oriented VMP) for a cloud service deployment with dynamic demand or parameters.

Definition 9 An online formulation of a provider-oriented VMP problem in any possible deployment architecture could be understood as the process of selecting which VMs should be hosted at each PMs of a cloud computing infrastructure considering dynamic demand or resource parameters that change over time.

It should be noted that an online formulation for a provider-oriented VMP problem could be the most appropriate approach for resource allocation in cloud computing datacenters, considering the dynamic model of cloud computing with on-demand resource provisioning and dynamic workloads of cloud applications [9].

Ortigoza et al. [25] extended the taxonomy presented in [14], identifying more detailed VMP environments for online formulations of provider-oriented VMP problems. In real-world environments, cloud computing providers dynamically receive requests for the placement of cloud services with different characteristics, according to different dynamic parameters such as [25]: (1) resource capacities of VMs (associated to vertical elasticity) [26], (2) number of VMs of a cloud service (associated to horizontal elasticity) [27], and (3) utilization of resources of VMs (relevant for overbooking) [6]. Taking into account the mentioned dynamic parameters, environments for online formulations of provider-oriented VMP problems could be classified by one or more of the following classification criteria: (1) service elasticity and (2) overbooking of physical resources [25].

A cloud service could request additional resources to scale (up/down/out/in) the application resources to be able to efficiently attend current demand, where cloud computing providers should model these requirements accordingly. Different VMP environments could be formulated considering one of the following service elasticity values: no elasticity, horizontal elasticity, vertical elasticity, or both horizontal and vertical elasticity [25]. Additionally, resources of VMs are dynamically used, giving space to re-utilization of idle resources that were already reserved. In this context, cloud computing environments identified in [25] may also consider one of the following overbooking values: no overbooking, server resources overbooking, network resources overbooking, or both server and network overbooking.

Definition 10 An online formulation of a broker-oriented VMP problem in any possible deployment architecture could be understood as the process of selecting which VMs should be hosted at each CSP of a given cloud computing market considering dynamic demand or parameters that change over time.

Considering that the number of CSPs has increased rapidly, nowadays several dynamic parameters could be considered for the broker-oriented VMP problem such as: dynamic pricing schemes, dynamic VM offers, or dynamic requirements. Research on online formulations of the broker-oriented VMP problem should advance to address existing opportunities in emerging cloud computing markets [28–30].

2.4 Conceptual Example

This subsection presents a conceptual example in order to better understand VMP environments above described and its considered terminology (see Fig. 2).

Considering the life-cycle of a cloud infrastructure [3], the first decision that a CST should perform is to decide which VMs should be hosted at each CSP of a cloud computing market. In case only one CSP is selected by the CST (e.g., host all

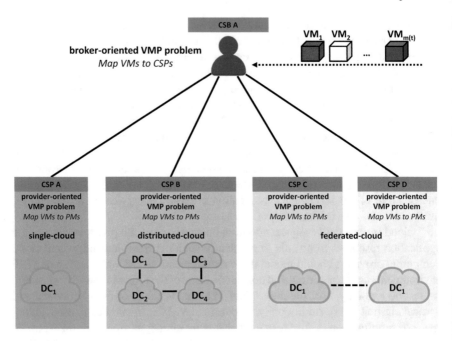

Fig. 2 Summary of possible VMP environments presented in this chapter

requested VMs V_j in CSP A), a trivial broker-oriented VMP problem is solved. On the other hand, a multi-cloud deployment architecture could be considered for the broker-oriented VMP problem if different CSPs are selected (e.g., CSP A and B).

Once each requested VM V_j have been assigned to be hosted in a particular CSP, each CSP have to decide which VMs should be hosted at each available PM, defined as a provider-oriented VMP problem.

CSPs could own cloud infrastructures with different deployment architectures, where the most basic one is a single-cloud deployment, as presented in Fig. 2 for CSP A. In single-cloud deployments requested VMs V_j could be located on PMs H_i available on cloud datacenter DC_1. No other available PMs could be considered.

Additionally, a CSP could own a distributed-cloud deployment, considering more than one cloud computing datacenter, where requested VMs V_j could be located on any PM available on any available cloud computing datacenter (e.g., requested VMs V_j could be located on PMs H_i available on DC_1 to DC_4 at CSP B).

Finally, a federated-cloud deployment could be considered to host requested VMs. In Fig. 2, CSPs C and D are members of a cloud federation and; consequently, idle resources from CSP C (or CSP D) are available for CSP D (or CSP C) in demand peaks transparently to CSTs.

3   VMP Problem Formulation and Resolution Taxonomy

Taking into account each possible environment where a VMP problem can be studied (see Fig. 1), several different VMP problem formulations could be considered. In this context, formulations of a VMP problem may be classified by the: (1) optimization approach, (2) objective function, and (3) solution technique [5].

First, a VMP problem could be formulated considering one of the following approaches for optimization: (1) mono-objective (MOP), (2) multi-objective solved as mono-objective (MAM), or (3) pure multi-objective (PMO). Once a particular approach is selected, formulations may be classified by the considered objective function(s), for its minimization and/or maximization. These objective functions could be optimized separately or simultaneously, depending on the selected optimization approach. Finally, a third classification criterion can be defined considering solution techniques for solving a VMP problem [5] (see Table 1).

For a complete understanding of possible approaches for the formulation and resolution of a VMP problem, Table 1 presents the taxonomy described in this section, including example references from the studied VMP literature [13]. The following subsections present a detailed description of the classification criteria defined above as well as special considerations for each particular formulation.

Table 1 VMP Formulation and Resolution Taxonomy. Example references for each environment are presented. Unexplored environments are considered Research Opportunities (RO)

Technique	Approach	Objective functions				
		$f_1(x)$	$f_2(x)$	$f_3(x)$	$f_4(x)$	$f_5(x)$
Deterministic algorithms	MOP	[36]	[37]	[31]	[38]	[39]
	MAM	[6, 40]	[6, 41]	**RO**	**RO**	[40, 41]
	PMO	**RO**	**RO**	**RO**	**RO**	**RO**
Heuristics	MOP	[42]	[43]	[33]	[44]	[39]
	MAM	[45, 46]	[46, 47]	[47, 48]	[27, 45]	[49, 50]
	PMO	**RO**	**RO**	**RO**	**RO**	**RO**
Metaheuristics	MOP	[51]	**RO**	[52]	[53]	**RO**
	MAM	[54, 55]	[54, 56]	[55, 57]	[56]	[55, 57]
	PMO	[18, 58]	[18, 59]	[18, 59]	**RO**	[58]
Approximation algorithms	MOP	[60]	**RO**	**RO**	**RO**	**RO**
	MAM	[61]	**RO**	**RO**	**RO**	**RO**
	PMO	**RO**	**RO**	**RO**	**RO**	**RO**

3.1 Optimization Approaches

This section presents a classification of optimization approaches identified in research works studied in [13]. The identified optimization approaches may be classified as: (1) mono-objective (MOP), (2) multi-objective solved as mono-objective (MAM), and (3) pure multi-objective (PMO), which are detailed in as follows.

3.1.1 Mono-objective (MOP)

A mono-objective optimization approach (MOP) considers the optimization of one objective function or the optimization of more than one objective function, one at a time. Research on the VMP problem has been mainly guided by this MOP approach, identifying almost 40 different objective functions already proposed considering this optimization approach [5]. It should be noted that an objective function could be studied taking into account different approaches for modeling (e.g., economical revenue maximization could be achieved by minimizing the total economical penalties for SLA violations [31], by minimizing operational costs [19, 32], or even by maximizing the total profit for leasing resources [33]).

3.1.2 Multi-objective Solved as Mono-objective (MAM)

The optimization of multiple objective functions scalarized into one objective function is considered in this chapter as a multi-objective problem solved using a mono-objective approach (MAM). This hybrid approach enables the optimization of multiple objectives functions with the disadvantage that it requires a complete knowledge of the decision space of the problem domain in order to effectively combine the objective functions, which in most cases is not possible [34].

In the last years, a growing number of articles have proposed formulations of the VMP problem with this hybrid optimization approach [13]. Different methods could be considered for a formulation of a VMP problem with a MAM approach such as: weighted sum, solving the problem as mono-objective while considering the other objective functions as constraints or even proposing fuzzy logic to provide an efficient way for combining conflicting objectives and expert knowledge [13].

3.1.3 Pure Multi-objective (PMO)

Pure Multi-Objective Optimization (PMO) problems may be defined by a set of p decision variables and q objective functions, as well as r constraints. Both objectives and constraints are functions of the decision variables. In a PMO problem formulation, the decision vector is represented as x, while the objective vector is represented as y. The decision space is denoted by X and its corresponding objective space is denoted as Y. A PMO problem formulation may be formalized as [35]:

Optimize:

$$y = f(x) = [f_1(x), f_2(x), \ldots, f_q(x)] \tag{1}$$

subject to:

$$e(x) = [e_1(x), e_2(x), \ldots, e_r(x)] \geq 0 \tag{2}$$

where:

$$x = [x_1, x_2, \ldots, x_p] \in X \tag{3}$$

$$y = [y_1, y_2, \ldots, y_q] \in Y \tag{4}$$

The set of constrains $e(x) \geq 0$ defines the set of feasible solutions $X_f \subset X$ and its corresponding set of feasible objective vectors $Y_f \subset Y$. The feasible decision space X_f is the set of all decision vectors x in the decision space X satisfying constraints defined in $e(x)$. The feasible objective space Y_f is the set of the objective vectors y that represents the image of X_f onto Y. These feasible spaces are defined as follows:

$$X_f = \{x \mid x \in X \wedge e(x) \geq 0\} \tag{5}$$

$$Y_f = \{y \mid y = f(x) \quad \forall x \in X_f\} \tag{6}$$

Comparing solutions for a PMO problem requires the consideration of Pareto dominance concepts. To compare two feasible solutions $u, v \in X$, if $f(u)$ is better or equal to $f(v)$ in every objective function and strictly better in at least one objective function it could be said that u dominates v, denoted as $u \succ v$. If neither u dominates v, nor v dominates u, u and v are said to be non-comparable, denoted as $u \sim v$.

A decision vector (or possible solution) x is non-dominated with respect to a set U, if there is no solution in U dominating x. The set of all the non-dominated solutions from X_f is commonly known as optimal Pareto set P^* and its corresponding image is denoted as PF^* [35].

Considering the large number of existing objective functions and possible approaches for objective function modeling identified in [5], PMO approaches could result in more realistic formulations of a VMP problem, optimizing several objective function at a time (e.g., achieve economical revenue maximization by simultaneously minimizing at least the total economical penalties for SLA violations, minimizing operational costs, and maximizing the profit for leasing resources). In this context, PMOs optimizing more than three objective functions are specifically known as Many-Objective Optimization Problems (MaOPs), as defined in [62].

MaOPs differ significantly from PMOs because several issues should be considered when solving optimization problems with more than three objective functions [63]. In case of Pareto-based algorithms, these issues are intrinsically related to the fact that as the number of objective functions increases, the proportion of non-dominated solutions grows, being increasingly difficult to discriminate among solutions using only the Pareto dominance relation [64]. Additionally, determining which solution to keep and which to discard in order to converge toward the Pareto set is still a relevant issue to be addressed [63]. As the number of objective functions grows, the proportion of non-dominated solutions to the total number of solutions tends to one [65], making more difficult to solve a MaOP.

3.2   Objective Function Groups

In cloud computing datacenters, several criteria can be considered when selecting a possible solution for a VMP problem, depending on resource management techniques and optimization objectives. These criteria can even change from one period of time to another, which implies a variety of possible formulations of the problem and different objectives to be optimized. According to [5], the VMP literature mainly focuses on the optimization of objective functions that specifically concerns CSPs (provider-oriented VMP). Objective functions may also be studied considering the requirements of CSTs for allocation of particular services or applications, often composed by more than one VM (broker-oriented VMP).

It should be mentioned that in [5], nearly 60 different objective functions were identified for the three optimization approaches presented in Sect. 3.1. Considering the large number of proposed objective functions, identified objective functions with similar characteristics and goals were classified into five objective function groups that are presented in the following subsections. Considering that MAM and PMO optimization approaches may take into account any combination of each objective function group or even different objective functions from the same objective function group, a simplified classification is presented in Tables 1 and 2 [14].

3.2.1 $f_1(x)$—Energy Consumption

Energy consumption management is a relevant studied objective in the provider-oriented VMP literature, with high impact in operational costs and carbon dioxide emissions for cloud datacenter operations. According to [66], most of the time, servers operate in a very low energy-efficiency possible region (i.e., between 10 and 50% of resource utilization), even though energy efficiency is a very important issue to address, considering its economical and ecological impact in modern datacenters. Energy consumption is the most studied objective function for a VMP problem including different modeling approaches [5].

The most studied alternatives for modeling energy consumption include [5]: consolidating VMs on the minimum number of PMs [67] and considering a linear relationship between power consumption and Central Process Unit (CPU) utilization [7]. Joint optimization of energy consumption and network traffic is also studied very well in the VMP literature, considering that network communication equipment represents between 10 and 20% of the total datacenter energy consumption [61].

3.2.2 $f_2(x)$—Network Traffic

Network traffic could also be considered as a relevant objective function for cloud datacenters supporting provider-oriented VMP decisions, as proposed in [7].

The main approaches for modeling network traffic include the optimization of: network communication between VMs, overhead of VM live migration, and network metrics such as: delay, data access and data transfer time, link congestion, network performance, service response time as well as average latency, and Wide Area Network (WAN) communication when considering distributed-cloud architectures.

Avoiding the placement of VMs with high network communication rate in different PMs when possible is the most studied approach, in order to minimize the network traffic between VMs. If VMs should not be allocated in the same PM for fault-tolerance purposes, VMs could be allocated at least in the same rack to avoid the utilization of core network equipment. Considering this approach, traffic characterization are studied as well as machine learning techniques for clustering VMs with a similarity based on network behavior. Finally, effectively quantifying network traffic overhead due to VM live migration could also be considered a relevant research challenge for provider-oriented VMP network traffic optimization [5].

Considering cloud computing environments where VMs are dynamically created and destroyed, a consolidation process should present high level of flexibility where traditional routing protocols have limitations to adjust flow paths. In [68], the authors proposed network traffic load balancing to improve QoS in a VMP context considering Software Defined Networks (SDN) [69], where flow paths are determined based on network status metrics such as low delay, low packet loss, or high security, just to cite a few.

3.2.3 $f_3(x)$—Economical Costs

Economical cost optimization is an important studied issue in both provider-oriented and broker-oriented VMP literature.

For a provider-oriented VMP, economical costs optimization is a key objective to be optimized and could be achieved by reducing operational costs. These operational costs could be mainly related to energy consumption minimization but additional formulations could also be considered, such as thermal dissipation costs [55]. Reducing penalty costs of SLA violations is another relevant approach in order to maximize economical revenue of CSPs. Finally, CSPs may maximize its economical revenue by leasing all its available resources or at least the maximum possible [13]. In this context, VMP could be studied jointly with admission control problems [3] and two possible scenarios could be identified: (1) if demand for resources exceeds the current available resources, overbooking techniques, or cloud federation [3] can help CSPs support requirements of the CSTs; or, (2) idle resources could be offered in an auction-based scheme such as Amazon's Spot Instances [70], where both scenarios represent open challenges for the VMP problem in cloud computing.

For a broker-oriented VMP, economical costs optimization is a key issue in actual cloud markets where CSTs try to find CSPs that meet the particular requirements of a cloud service, preferably with the lowest economical costs for the required cloud infrastructure. The most studied pricing scheme in the considered VMP literature is fixed price. However, the recent trend of dynamic pricing of cloud resources introduces the idea that prices of resources can vary depending on the free capacity and load of the CSP and a few articles have recently proposed formulations of a VMP problem considering dynamic prices schemes [71].

3.2.4 $f_4(x)$—Performance

Performance optimization is an important studied issue in both provider-oriented and broker-oriented VMP literature. Performance modeling includes the optimization of: availability, CPU demand satisfaction, deployment time, QoS, resource interference, security metrics, Shared Last Level Cache (SLLC) contention, and total job completion time [13]. Most of these performance metrics may be considered for CSPs to improve the QoS in a provider-oriented VMP or for CSTs in order to select an appropriate CSP to host their services in a broker-oriented VMP.

3.2.5 $f_5(x)$—Resource Utilization

Cloud computing datacenters are commonly composed by different types of physical and virtual resources such as CPU, RAM, storage, network bandwidth, and even Graphical Process Unit (GPU) in some cases. The main approaches include the maximization of resource utilization, but performing a balanced utilization of each resource [13] is also an important issue to consider. Li et al. studied the concept of elasticity, referring to how well a datacenter may satisfy the input VMs resource demands under limitations of PMs and network link capacities [26].

Considering the relevance of the efficient utilization of resources, an interesting analysis of the main anomalies and drawbacks in a few existing techniques for efficient resource utilization is presented in [72], introducing a novel vector-based technique that addresses the considered anomalies.

3.3 Solution Techniques

In the VMP literature considered in [13], different techniques were considered for solving a VMP problem. The main solution techniques include: (1) deterministic algorithms (optimal), (2) heuristic algorithms, (3) metaheuristic algorithms, and (4) approximation algorithms. The four mentioned solution techniques are detailed in the following subsections.

3.3.1 Deterministic Algorithms (Optimal)

Classical deterministic techniques were considered for a VMP problem, including Constraint Programming (CP), Linear Programming (LP), Integer Linear Programming (ILP), Mixed Integer Linear Programming (MILP), Pseudo-Boolean Optimization (PBO), and Dynamic Programming (DP) [5]. Most of these approaches are considered for introducing novel mathematical formulations of a VMP problem with no practical intention, considering that obtaining the optimal solution implies a search in a universe of N possible solutions [18]:

$$N = (n + 1)^m \tag{7}$$

where:

N Size of the searching universe
n Number of physical machines
m Number of virtual machines.

3.3.2 Heuristics

Considering that VMP is a combinatorial NP-hard problem [40], it is impracticable to optimally solve instances of the problem for large number of PMs and VMs. Commonly, CSPs are composed by thousands to millions of PMs and VMs, a scenario where optimal solutions with exhaustive search algorithms can result extremely expensive. Therefore, a trade-off between quality of solutions and computational cost has to be considered for real-world cloud management systems.

Heuristics have already been extensively studied in the literature for exponential complexity problems. Several articles proposed heuristic-based solution techniques for a VMP problem. Most of the studied articles have proposed heuristics based on well-known algorithms such as: First-Fit, First-Fit Decreasing, Best-Fit, Best-Fit Decreasing, Worst-Fit, and Heaviest-Fit. Other greedy algorithms were also proposed in addition to novel heuristics for the resolution of the VMP problem [13].

3.3.3 Metaheuristics

As previously mentioned, approximations to optimal solutions are sufficient in most of cloud infrastructure environments. Metaheuristics are also very useful in order to obtain good solutions in practical time. Metaheuristics include [5]: Memetic Algorithms (MA), Particle Swarm Optimization (PSO), Ant Colony Optimization (ACO), Genetic Algorithm (GA), Neighborhood Search (NS), Cut-and-Search, Simulated Annealing (SA), and Tabu Search (TS). According to the proposed taxonomy, metaheuristics are mainly studied with multi-objective approaches (MAM and PMO) for solving VMP problems (see Table 1).

3.3.4 Approximation Algorithms

Heuristics and metaheuristics provide good quality solutions, but the quality of the expected solutions is hardly measurable. In a p-approximation algorithm, the value of a solution will not be more (or less) than a factor p times the optimal solution. A small number of articles proposed approximation algorithms for solving a VMP problem [5]. It is worth noting that for cloud infrastructures, solutions obtained using heuristics or metaheuristics techniques are sufficiently good for most cases.

4 VMP Taxonomy: Research Opportunities

Based on a universe of 84 studied publications systematically chosen [13], Table 2 summarizes the taxonomies presented in this chapter (see Fig. 1 and Table 1). Considering that five studied articles [6, 39, 60, 61, 73] proposed two different solution techniques for the same VMP formulation, presented statistics are based on 89 different VMP formulations (see Table 2).

Taking into account a detailed analysis of the information provided by Table 2, this section summarizes research opportunities as well as ongoing research work by the authors in order to further advance in this very active research area. It should be noted that statistics presented in the following subsections are defined following the studied VMP literature (of 89 different VMP formulations) and considered only as a simple reference, given that more articles may be considered in this rapidly growing research area. Additionally, different systematic reviews of the VMP literature (e.g., considering different keywords) or extended systematic reviews (e.g., considering additional keywords) could result in different numbers.

Considering the diversity of existing environments, formulations and solution techniques for the VMP problem (see Table 2), it is important to provide a general vision on the main approaches for the mentioned problem, enabling interested readers to define specific research alternatives.

Table 2 Virtual Machine Placement Taxonomy. Elements of column % represent the percentage of articles in the studied universe [13]. For simplicity, MAM and PMO consider only the number of considered objectives in column $f(x)$. See Sect. 3.2 for $f(x)$ details

Oriented	Deployment architecture	Formulation	Optimization approach	$f(x)$	Solution technique	%
Provider	Single-cloud	Offline	MOP	$f_1(x)$	Heuristic	3.37
					Metaheuristic	2.25
				$f_2(x)$	Heuristic	2.25
				$f_4(x)$	Heuristic	1.12
			MAM	3	Heuristic	2.25
					Metaheuristic	3.37
				2	Deterministic	1.12
			PMO	3	Metaheuristic	2.25
				2	Metaheuristic	1.12
		Online	MOP	$f_1(x)$	Deterministic	4.49
					Heuristic	6.74
					Metaheuristic	1.12
					Approximation	1.12
				$f_2(x)$	Deterministic	2.25
					Heuristic	5.62
				$f_3(x)$	Deterministic	1.12
					Heuristic	5.62
				$f_4(x)$	Heuristic	7.87
					Metaheuristic	1.12
				$f_5(x)$	Deterministic	1.12
					Heuristic	4.49
			MAM	3	Heuristic	3.37
					Metaheuristic	1.12
				2	Deterministic	3.37
					Heuristic	16.85
					Metaheuristic	1.12
					Approximation	1.12
	Distributed-cloud	Offline	MOP	$f_4(x)$	Deterministic	1.12
		Online	MOP	$f_2(x)$	Heuristic	1.12
					Deterministic	1.12
				$f_3(x)$	Heuristic	1.12
				$f_5(x)$	Heuristic	1.12
			MAM	3	Deterministic	1.12
				2	Metaheuristic	1.12
	Federated-cloud	Online	MOP	$f_1(x)$	Heuristic	1.12
Broker	Multi-cloud	Offline	MOP	$f_3(x)$	Deterministic	1.12
					Metaheuristic	1.12
Total						**100**

The following subsections describe research opportunities identified in [14] and presented in this chapter as a main result of the general research vision and the proposed VMP taxonomies (see Fig. 1 and Tables 1 and 2).

4.1 Unexplored Environments, Formulations, and Solution Techniques

Considering the studied VMP literature [13], unexplored VMP environments were identified in [14] and presented in this chapter (see Research Opportunities in Fig. 1). First, provider-oriented VMP problems in federated-cloud deployments were not considered with offline formulations. Second, broker-oriented VMP problems in multi-cloud deployments were not considered with online formulations. No formulation or solution technique was studied for the mentioned VMP environments.

Additionally, unexplored formulations and solutions techniques were also identified in [5] (see Research Opportunities in Table 1). For a MOP optimization approach, $f_2(x)$ (network traffic) and $f_5(x)$ (resource utilization) were not studied considering metaheuristics as solution technique. Approximation algorithms were studied as a solution technique only for $f_1(x)$ (energy consumption), representing unexplored alternatives for the remaining studied objective function groups.

For MAM optimization approach, the resolution of VMP formulations considering $f_3(x)$ (economical revenue) and $f_4(x)$ (performance) with deterministic algorithms were not studied. Similar to the MOP approach, approximation algorithms were studied as a solution technique only for $f_1(x)$ (energy consumption), representing unexplored alternatives for the remaining studied objective functions (see Research Opportunities in Table 1). For PMO optimization approach, $f_4(x)$ (performance) was not studied considering metaheuristics as solution technique, while neither deterministic algorithms, heuristics nor approximation algorithms studied PMO formulations of the VMP problem, representing unexplored alternatives.

Taking into account a complete understanding of the VMP problem composed by VMP environments and VMP formulations as well as solution techniques (see Table 2), several unexplored VMP problems could also be identified. In this context, Table 2 could guide interested readers to identify existing research on VMP problems according to the studied VMP literature [13]. It should be noted that all possible VMP problems that are not presented in Table 2 could also be considered as a research opportunity. As an example, MAM and PMO optimization approaches are not presented in Table 2 for the following VMP environments: (1) provider-oriented VMP in distributed-clouds with offline formulations, (2) provider-oriented VMP in federated clouds with online formulations, and (3) broker-oriented VMP in multi-clouds with offline formulations.

4.2 Broker-Oriented VMP Considering Online Formulations

According to the proposed VMP Environment Taxonomy (see Fig. 1), a broker-oriented VMP problem could be studied in a multi-cloud deployment architecture considering offline or online formulations. A broker-oriented VMP problem could also be studied considering a mono-objective approach (MOP) or multi-objective approaches (MAM or PMO), optimizing different objective functions (see Table 1).

Considering that only 2.24% of the considered VMP literature studied a broker-oriented VMP problem as an offline optimization problem (see Table 2), on going research by the authors focus on exploring broker-oriented VMP formulations. In this context, an extended systematic review of research articles demonstrate that broker-oriented VMP includes several research opportunities, mainly novel multi-objective formulations for online broker-oriented VMP problems.

Several dynamic parameters could be studied for online broker-oriented VMP problems such as: (1) pricing schemes, (2) VM offers, or (3) user requirements, but a detailed survey on these parameters and formulations is still needed (research opportunity). It should be noted that the implementation of possible migrations of VMs across different CSPs is limited by cloud interoperability factors, and it is out of the scope of the VMP problem.

4.3 Provider-Oriented VMP Considering Online Formulations

Considering the on-demand model of cloud computing, a provider-oriented VMP problem should be solved dynamically to efficiently attend typical workload of modern applications. According to the studied articles, 77.53% considered this particular type of VMP problem with several different formulations and dynamic parameters.

Ortigoza et al. [25] studied a large part of the online provider-oriented VMP literature to be able to identify most relevant dynamic parameters that could be considered for modeling different IaaS environments where CSPs should address several challenges. In this context, dynamic environments for online formulations of the provider-oriented VMP problem could be classified by one or more of the following classification criteria: (1) elasticity and (2) overbooking [25]. Both classification criteria are mainly related to the identified dynamic parameters, as: resource capacities of VMs (vertical elasticity), number of VMs of a cloud service (horizontal elasticity), and utilization of resources of VMs (overbooking).

According to [25], dynamic VMP environments for cloud computing could be formulated considering one of the following elasticity values: no elasticity, horizontal elasticity, vertical elasticity, or both horizontal and vertical elasticity. Additionally, identified dynamic VMP environments may also consider one of the following overbooking values: no overbooking, server resources overbooking, network resources overbooking, or both server and network overbooking.

Research opportunities for online formulations of a provider-oriented VMP problem include detailed studies on complex dynamic environments (e.g., VMP considering both types of elasticity and both types of overbooking) in order to enable CSPs to efficiently support modern cloud applications and services. Considering that modern cloud services are often composed by several inter-related VMs, the authors of this chapter presented in [25], modeling techniques for these complex cloud services to consider any type of deployment architecture (i.e., single-cloud, distributed-cloud, federated-cloud, or multi-cloud).

4.4 Provider-Oriented VMP Considering PMO Optimization

According to the studied articles, only 3.37% considered a PMO approach for an offline formulation of provider-oriented VMP problems simultaneously optimizing two or three objective functions. PMO approaches could result in more realistic formulations of a VMP problem, optimizing more than one objective function at a time.

Taking into account that existing PMO formulations of a provider-oriented VMP problem consider at most three objective functions and more than 60 different objective functions were identified in [5], several formulations could still be considered, specially for PMO approaches. In this context, it is important to remember that PMOs optimizing more than three objective functions are known as MaOPs. As described in Sect. 3.1.3, several issues should be considered when solving optimization problems with more than three objective functions [63]. Considering the mentioned challenges for solving MaOPs, López-Pires and Barán have proposed in [17] a general many-objective optimization framework that is able to consider as many objective functions as needed when solving an offline VMP problem in a PMO context. In order to converge to a treatable number of non-dominated solutions, the authors proposed the utilization of interactive lower and upper bounds associated to each objective function to reduce the number of possible solutions of the Pareto set approximation P_{known}, following a decision maker needs.

Additionally, online formulations of a provider-oriented VMP considering a PMO approach should be explored. For this particular type of VMP problem, PMO approaches should include strategies for an appropriate solution selection from the Pareto set approximation P_{known}, composed by non-dominated solutions. In this context, Ihara et al. already proposed a first formulation of a Many-Objective VMP problem (MaVMP) for semi-dynamic environments, presenting studies on the evaluation of several strategies for VMP problems formulated as MaOPs [23].

4.5 Provider-Oriented VMP in Distributed and Federated Clouds

According to the studied articles, only 7.87% proposed a provider-oriented VMP problem in a distributed-cloud deployment architecture, while only [42] studied the provider-oriented VMP problem considering a federated-cloud deployment architecture (see Table 2). Resource allocation in distributed and federated cloud environments is an active research area [74]. In a provider-oriented VMP context, several particular constraints and objective functions may still be studied and evaluated in order to fulfill the requirements of a CSP with geo-distributed cloud computing datacenters or different CSPs in a cloud federation.

It should be noted that a broker-oriented VMP in a distributed-cloud deployment architecture may be adapted as a multi-cloud deployment architecture by considering each datacenter as a different CSP in order to fulfill requirements of high-availability or legal issues (e.g., Amazon's us-east-1 or eu-west-1 datacenters).[1]

For a VMP problem in a distributed or federated-cloud deployment architecture, several research opportunities may be still proposed considering unexplored objective functions, novel formulations in MOP, MAM or PMO approaches or even experimental evaluation of different solution techniques.

5 Conclusions and Future Directions

Based on a universe of 84 studied articles with 89 different VMP formulations [13], this work presented general taxonomies of the VMP problem (see Table 2) considering possible environments where the VMP problem could be studied (see Research Opportunities in Fig. 1) as well as different possible formulations and techniques for the resolution of the VMP problem (see Table 1).

Depending on the particular environment where a VMP problem will be studied, several different considerations should be taken into account before considering a particular formulation or technique for a VMP problem resolution. Different possible environments were identified by classifying research articles in the VMP literature by: (1) orientation, (2) deployment architecture, and (3) type of formulation.

Provider or broker perspectives could be considered when studying a VMP problem (see Sect. 2.1). For provider-oriented VMP problems, different architectures could be considered for deployments: single-cloud, distributed-cloud, or federated-cloud. For broker-oriented VMP problems only multi-cloud architectures could be considered (see Sect. 2.2). Both provider-oriented and a broker-oriented VMP problems, considering any of the mentioned architectures for deployment, may be formulated as both offline or online optimization problems (see Sect. 2.3).

---

[1]https://aws.amazon.com/about-aws/global-infrastructure.

Different formulations of the VMP problem were considered, mainly taking into account the identified VMP environments (see Fig. 1). In this context, each VMP problem formulation was characterized considering: (1) optimization approach and (2) objective functions as well as (3) solution technique. Initially, a VMP problem was formulated considering any of the following approaches for optimization: (1) mono-objective (MOP), (2) multi-objective solved as mono-objective (MAM), or (3) pure multi-objective (PMO). According to the considered optimization approach, VMP formulations were classified by the studied objective function(s) group(s), taking into account maximization and minimization scenarios. Depending on the optimization approach, considered objectives could be optimized simultaneously or not. Finally, techniques for solving a VMP problem were considered as a third classification criterion [5].

According to Table 2, the VMP problem have been mostly studied as an online problem from the provider perspective, considering a single-cloud deployment architecture, representing 69.66% of the studied articles. For this particular VMP environment, 42,70% considered a MOP approach. It could be said that online formulations of provider-oriented VMP problems in single-cloud deployment architecture is a well-studied problem and existing literature should guide CSPs to solve VMP problems with these considerations.

Based on the proposed taxonomies, several research opportunities were identified in the following research directions (see Sect. 4): (1) unexplored environments, formulations and solution techniques, (2) broker-oriented VMP considering online formulations, (3) provider-oriented VMP considering online formulations, (4) provider-oriented VMP considering PMO optimization, and (5) provider-oriented VMP in distributed and federated clouds. It should be mentioned that other relevant research opportunities could also be identified with the proposed taxonomies.

Focusing on the large number of identified objective functions [5], the following questions still have no answer considering the studied VMP literature [13]:

1. can CSPs efficiently optimize more than three objective functions for the VMP problem in a reasonable time?
2. which solution technique is the most appropriate for solving VMP problems considering PMO approaches for real scenarios?
3. are PMO approaches the best alternative for online formulations or MAM approaches have the potential of performing even better?

Additionally, the following questions focus on the variety of possible deployment architectures where the VMP problem could be studied:

1. how can CSPs model, formulate and solve VMP problems in distributed or federated clouds?
2. which solution technique is the most appropriate for broker-oriented VMP for large scale customers?
3. which objective functions should a CSP consider in different deployment architectures?

In order to answer the abovementioned relevant questions, research should focus on unexplored formulations of the VMP problem, developing novel techniques, and providing methods and accepted benchmarks to compare and evaluate different approaches. Addressing this unexplored formulations may start applying an extended review, considering that this work studied a relevant subset of the existing VMP literature in order to guide interested readers, providing a general vision on this research area. Additionally, remembering the high complexity of the VMP problem as a NP-hard combinatorial optimization problem, novel approaches to reduce possible combinations for placement of VMs should be developed [56].

Studying dynamic schemes for resource pricing in cloud computing in the context of the VMP problem may also be considered a relevant future direction to further advance this research area, taking into account open challenges for both CSPs and CSBs in highly dynamic markets of cloud computing.

It is important to mention that actual cloud markets are mostly composed by thousands to millions of VMs which are dynamically created and destroyed, so experimental tests for VMP problem should consider: (1) large number of VMs and PMs, (2) heterogeneity in PMs and VMs configurations, (3) diverse types and workload distribution, and (4) trending dynamic parameters. As a general conclusion, it could be said that different methods and algorithms should be still evaluated before a real good tool is ready for massive use in commercial cloud computing datacenters.

References

1. Mell, P., & Grance, T. (2009). The nist definition of cloud computing. *National Institute of Standards and Technology, 53*(6), 50.
2. Buyya, R., Yeo, C. S., Venugopal, S., Broberg, J., & Brandic, I. (2009). Cloud computing and emerging it platforms: Vision, hype, and reality for delivering computing as the 5th utility. *Future Generation Computer Systems, 25*(6), 599–616.
3. Elmroth, E., Tordsson, J., Hernández, F., Ali-Eldin, A., Svärd, P., Sedaghat, M., et al. (2011). Self-management challenges for multi-cloud architectures. In *Towards a Service-Based Internet* (pp. 38–49). Springer.
4. Manvi, S. S., & Shyam, G. S. (2014). Resource management for infrastructure as a service (iaas) in cloud computing: A survey. *Journal of Network and Computer Applications, 41*, 424–440.
5. López-Pires, F., & Barán, B. (2015). A virtual machine placement taxonomy. In *Proceedings of the 2015 IEEE/ACM 15th International Symposium on Cluster, Cloud and Grid Computing.* IEEE Computer Society.
6. Anand, A., Lakshmi, J., & Nandy, S. K. (2013). Virtual machine placement optimization supporting performance SLAs. In *2013 IEEE 5th International Conference on Cloud Computing Technology and Science (CloudCom)* (Vol. 1, pp. 298–305). IEEE.
7. Beloglazov, A., Abawajy, J., & Buyya, R. (2012). Energy-aware resource allocation heuristics for efficient management of data centers for cloud computing. *Future Generation Computer Systems, 28*(5), 755–768.
8. Buyya, R., Yeo, C. S., & Venugopal, S. (2008). Market-oriented cloud computing: Vision, hype, and reality for delivering it services as computing utilities. In *10th IEEE International Conference on High Performance Computing and Communications, 2008. HPCC'08.* (pp. 5–13). IEEE.

9. Beloglazov, A., & Buyya, R. (2012). Optimal online deterministic algorithms and adaptive heuristics for energy and performance efficient dynamic consolidation of virtual machines in cloud data centers. *Concurrency and Computation: Practice and Experience, 24*(13), 1397–1420.
10. Salimian, L., & Safi, F. (2013). Survey of energy efficient data centers in cloud computing. In *Proceedings of the 2013 IEEE/ACM 6th International Conference on Utility and Cloud Computing* (pp. 369–374). IEEE Computer Society.
11. Gahlawat, M., & Sharma, P. (2014). Survey of virtual machine placement in federated clouds. In *Advance Computing Conference (IACC), 2014 IEEE International* (pp. 735–738). IEEE.
12. Mills, K., Filliben, J., & Dabrowski, C. (2011). Comparing vm-placement algorithms for on-demand clouds. In *2011 IEEE Third International Conference on Cloud Computing Technology and Science (CloudCom)* (pp. 91–98). IEEE.
13. López-Pires, F., & Barán, B. (2015). Virtual machine placement literature review. arXiv:abs/1506.01509.
14. López-Pires, F., & Barán, B. (2016). Cloud computing resource allocation taxonomies. *International Journal of Cloud Computing*.
15. Jansen, R., & Brenner, P. R. (2011). Energy efficient virtual machine allocation in the cloud. In *Green Computing Conference and Workshops (IGCC), 2011 International* (pp. 1–8). IEEE.
16. Tordsson, J., Montero, R. S., Moreno-Vozmediano, R., & Llorente, I. M. (2012). Cloud brokering mechanisms for optimized placement of virtual machines across multiple providers. *Future Generation Computer Systems, 28*(2), 358–367.
17. López-Pires, F., & Barán, B. (2015). A many-objective optimization framework for virtualized datacenters. In *Proceedings of the 2015 5th International Conference on Cloud Computing and Service Science* (pp. 439–450).
18. López-Pires, F., & Barán, B. (2013). Multi-objective virtual machine placement with service level agreement: A memetic algorithm approach. In *Proceedings of the 2013 IEEE/ACM 6th International Conference on Utility and Cloud Computing* (pp. 203–210). IEEE Computer Society.
19. Huang, Z., & Tsang, D. H. K. (2012). Sla guaranteed virtual machine consolidation for computing clouds. In *2012 IEEE International Conference on Communications (ICC)* (pp. 1314–1319). IEEE.
20. Lu, K., Yahyapour, R., Wieder, P., Kotsokalis, C., Yaqub, E., & Jehangiri, A. I. (2013). Qos-aware vm placement in multi-domain service level agreements scenarios. In *2013 IEEE Sixth International Conference on Cloud Computing (CLOUD)* (pp. 661–668). IEEE.
21. Bouyoucef, K., Limam-Bedhiaf, I., & Cherkaoui, O. (2010). Optimal allocation approach of virtual servers in cloud computing. In *2010 6th EURO-NF Conference on Next Generation Internet (NGI)* (pp. 1–6). IEEE.
22. Espling, D., Larsson, L., Li, W., Tordsson, J., & Elmroth, E. (2014). Modeling and placement of cloud services with internal structure. *IEEE Transactions on Cloud Computing* (Vol. 99, pp. 1–1).
23. Ihara, D., López-Pires, F., & Barán, B. (2015). Many-objective virtual machine placement for dynamic environments. In *Proceedings of the 2015 IEEE/ACM 8th International Conference on Utility and Cloud Computing*. IEEE Computer Society.
24. López-Pires, F., Barán, B., Amarilla, A., Benítez, L., Ferreira, R., & Zalimben, S. (2016). An experimental comparison of algorithms for virtual machine placement considering many objectives. In *9th Latin America Networking Conference (LANC)* (pp. 75–79).
25. Ortigoza, J., Lpez-Pires, F., & Barn, B. (2016). A taxonomy on dynamic environments for provider-oriented virtual machine placement. In *2016 IEEE International Conference on Cloud Engineering (IC2E)* (pp. 214–215).
26. Li, K., Wu, J., & Blaisse, A. (2013). Elasticity-aware virtual machine placement for cloud datacenters. In *2013 IEEE 2nd International Conference on Cloud Networking (CloudNet)* (pp. 99–107). IEEE.
27. Wang, W., Chen, H., & Chen, X. (2012). An availability-aware virtual machine placement approach for dynamic scaling of cloud applications. In *2012 9th International Conference*

on *Ubiquitous Intelligence & Computing and 9th International Conference on Autonomic & Trusted Computing (UIC/ATC)* (pp. 509–516). IEEE.

28. Chamorro, L., López-Pires, F., & Baran, B. (2016). A genetic algorithm for dynamic cloud application brokerage. *IEEE International Conference on Cloud Engineering.*

29. Li, W., Tordsson, J., & Elmroth, E. (2011). Modeling for dynamic cloud scheduling via migration of virtual machines. In *2011 IEEE Third International Conference on Cloud Computing Technology and Science (CloudCom)* (pp. 163–171). IEEE.

30. Simarro, J. L. L., Moreno-Vozmediano, R., Montero, R. S., & Llorente, I. M. (2011). Dynamic placement of virtual machines for cost optimization in multi-cloud environments. In *2011 International Conference on High Performance Computing and Simulation (HPCS)* (pp. 1–7). IEEE.

31. Dang, H. T., & Hermenier, F. (2013). Higher SLA satisfaction in datacenters with continuous VM placement constraints. In *Proceedings of the 9th Workshop on Hot Topics in Dependable Systems* (p. 1). ACM.

32. Huang, Z., Tsang, D. H. K., & She, J. (2012). A virtual machine consolidation framework for mapreduce enabled computing clouds. In *Proceedings of the 24th International Teletraffic Congress, International Teletraffic Congress* (p. 26).

33. Shi, W., & Hong, B. (2011). Towards profitable virtual machine placement in the data center. In *2011 Fourth IEEE International Conference on Utility and Cloud Computing (UCC)* (pp. 138–145). IEEE.

34. Barán, B., von Lücken, C., & Sotelo, A. (2005). Multi-objective pump scheduling optimisation using evolutionary strategies. *Advances in Engineering Software, 36*(1), 39–47.

35. Coello, C. A. C., Lamont, G. B., & Van Veldhuizen, D. A. (2007). *Evolutionary algorithms for solving multi-objective problems.* Springer.

36. Goudarzi, H., & Pedram, M. (2012). Energy-efficient virtual machine replication and placement in a cloud computing system. In *2012 IEEE 5th International Conference on Cloud Computing (CLOUD)* (pp. 750–757). IEEE.

37. Piao, J. T., & Yan, J. (2010). A network-aware virtual machine placement and migration approach in cloud computing. In *2010 9th International Conference on Grid and Cooperative Computing (GCC)* (pp. 87–92). IEEE.

38. Bin, E., Biran, O., Boni, O., Hadad, E., Kolodner, E. K., Moatti, Y., & Lorenz, D. H. (2011). Guaranteeing high availability goals for virtual machine placement. In *2011 31st International Conference on Distributed Computing Systems (ICDCS)* (pp. 700–709). IEEE.

39. Li, W., Tordsson, J., & Elmroth, E. (2012). Virtual machine placement for predictable and time-constrained peak loads. In *Economics of grids, clouds, systems, and services* (pp. 120–134). Springer.

40. Sun, M., Gu, W., Zhang, X., Shi, H., & Zhang, W. (2013). A matrix transformation algorithm for virtual machine placement in cloud. In *2013 12th IEEE International Conference on Trust, Security and Privacy in Computing and Communications (TrustCom)* (pp. 1778–1783). IEEE.

41. Song, F., Huang, D., Zhou, H., Zhang, H., & You, I. (2014). An optimization-based scheme for efficient virtual machine placement. *International Journal of Parallel Programming, 42*(5), 853–872.

42. Dupont, C., Giuliani, G., Hermenier, F., Schulze, T., & Somov, A. (2012). An energy aware framework for virtual machine placement in cloud federated data centres. In *2012 Third International Conference on Future Energy Systems: Where Energy, Computing and Communication Meet (e-Energy)* (pp. 1–10). IEEE.

43. Dias, D. S., & Costa, L. H. M. K. (2012). Online traffic-aware virtual machine placement in data center networks. In *Global Information Infrastructure and Networking Symposium (GIIS), 2012* (pp. 1–8). IEEE.

44. Gupta, A., Kalé, L. V., Milojicic, D., Faraboschi, P., & Balle, S. M. (2013). Hpc-aware vm placement in infrastructure clouds. In *2013 IEEE International Conference on Cloud Engineering (IC2E)* (pp. 11–20). IEEE.

45. Sato, K., Samejima, M., & Komoda, N. (2013). Dynamic optimization of virtual machine placement by resource usage prediction. In *2013 11th IEEE International Conference on Industrial Informatics (INDIN)* (pp. 86–91). IEEE.

46. Dong, J., Wang, H., Jin, X., Li, Y., Zhang, P., & Cheng, S. (2013). Virtual machine placement for improving energy efficiency and network performance in IaaS cloud. In *2013 IEEE 33rd International Conference on Distributed Computing Systems Workshops (ICDCSW)* (pp. 238–243). IEEE.
47. Hong, H.-J., Chen, D.-Y., Huang, C.-Y., Chen, K.-T., & Hsu, C.-H. (2013). Qoe-aware virtual machine placement for cloud games. In *2013 12th Annual Workshop on Network and Systems Support for Games (NetGames)* (pp. 1–2). IEEE.
48. Dalvandi, A., Gurusamy, M., & Chua, K. C. (2013). Time-aware vm-placement and routing with bandwidth guarantees in green cloud data centers. In *2013 IEEE 5th International Conference on Cloud Computing Technology and Science (CloudCom)* (Vol. 1, pp. 212–217). IEEE.
49. Calcavecchia, N. M., Biran, O., Hadad, E., & Moatti, Y. (2012). Vm placement strategies for cloud scenarios. In *2012 IEEE 5th International Conference on Cloud Computing (CLOUD)* (pp. 852–859). IEEE.
50. Cao, Z., & Dong, S. (2014). An energy-aware heuristic framework for virtual machine consolidation in cloud computing. *The Journal of Supercomputing* (pp. 1–23).
51. Tang, M., & Pan, S. (2014). A hybrid genetic algorithm for the energy-efficient virtual machine placement problem in data centers. *Neural processing letters* (pp. 1–11).
52. Mark, C. C. T., Niyato, D., & Chen-Khong, T. (2011). Evolutionary optimal virtual machine placement and demand forecaster for cloud computing. In *2011 IEEE International Conference on Advanced Information Networking and Applications (AINA)* (pp. 348–355). IEEE.
53. Tsakalozos, K., Roussopoulos, M., & Delis, A. (2011). Vm placement in non-homogeneous iaas-clouds. In *Service-oriented computing* (pp. 172–187). Springer.
54. Chen, K.-Y., Xu, Y., Xi, K., & Chao, H. J. (2013). Intelligent virtual machine placement for cost efficiency in geo-distributed cloud systems. In *2013 IEEE International Conference on Communications (ICC)* (pp. 3498–3503). IEEE.
55. Xu, J., & Fortes, J. A. B. (2010). Multi-objective virtual machine placement in virtualized data center environments. In *2010 IEEE/ACM Int'l Conference on & Int'l Conference on Cyber, Physical and Social Computing (CPSCom) Green Computing and Communications (GreenCom)* (pp. 179–188). IEEE.
56. Shigeta, S., Yamashima, H., Doi, T., Kawai, T., & Fukui, K. (2013). Design and implementation of a multi-objective optimization mechanism for virtual machine placement in cloud computing data center. In *Cloud computing* (pp. 21–31). Springer.
57. Adamuthe, A. C., Pandharpatte, R. M., & Thampi, G. T. (2013). Multiobjective virtual machine placement in cloud environment. In *2013 International Conference on Cloud & Ubiquitous Computing & Emerging Technologies (CUBE)* (pp. 8–13). IEEE.
58. Gao, Y., Guan, H., Qi, Z., Hou, Y., & Liu, L. (2013). A multi-objective ant colony system algorithm for virtual machine placement in cloud computing. *Journal of Computer and System Sciences, 79*(8), 1230–1242.
59. López-Pires, F., Melgarejo, E., & Barán, B. (2013). Virtual machine placement. A multiobjective approach. In *Computing Conference (CLEI), 2013 XXXIX Latin American* (pp. 1–8). IEEE.
60. Wu, J.-J., Liu, P., & Yang, J.-S. (2012). Workload characteristics-aware virtual machine consolidation algorithms. In *Proceedings of the 2012 IEEE 4th International Conference on Cloud Computing Technology and Science (CloudCom)* (pp. 42–49). IEEE Computer Society.
61. Fang, W., Liang, X., Li, S., Chiaraviglio, L., & Xiong, N. (2013). Vmplanner: Optimizing virtual machine placement and traffic flow routing to reduce network power costs in cloud data centers. *Computer Networks, 57*(1), 179–196.
62. Cheng, J., Yen, G. G., & Zhang, G. (2014). A many-objective evolutionary algorithm based on directional diversity and favorable convergence. In *2014 IEEE International Conference on Systems, Man and Cybernetics (SMC)* (pp. 2415–2420).
63. Farina, M., & Amato, P. (2002). On the optimal solution definition for many-criteria optimization problems. In *Proceedings of the NAFIPS-FLINT International Conference* (pp. 233–238).
64. Deb, K., Sinha, A., & Kukkonen, S. (2006). Multi-objective test problems, linkages, and evolutionary methodologies. In *Proceedings of the 8th Annual Conference on Genetic and Evolutionary Computation* (pp. 1141–1148). ACM.

65. von Lücken, C., Barán, B., & Brizuela, C. (2014). A survey on multi-objective evolutionary algorithms for many-objective problems. *Computational optimization and applications* (pp. 1–50).
66. Barroso, L. A., & Hölzle, U. (2007). The case for energy-proportional computing. *IEEE Computer, 40*(12), 33–37.
67. Dong, J., Jin, X., Wang, H., Li, Y., Zhang, P., & Cheng, S. (2013). Energy-saving virtual machine placement in cloud data centers. In *2013 13th IEEE/ACM International Symposium on Cluster, Cloud and Grid Computing (CCGrid)* (pp. 618–624). IEEE.
68. Wang, S.-H., Huang, P. P.-W., Wen, C. H.-P., & Wang, L.-C. (2014). Eqvmp: Energy-efficient and qos-aware virtual machine placement for software defined datacenter networks. In *2014 International Conference on Information Networking (ICOIN)* (pp. 220–225). IEEE.
69. McKeown, N., Anderson, T., Balakrishnan, H., Parulkar, G., Peterson, L., Rexford, J., et al. (2008). Openflow: Enabling innovation in campus networks. *ACM SIGCOMM Computer Communication Review, 38*(2), 69–74.
70. Ben-Yehuda, O. A., Ben-Yehuda, M., Schuster, A., & Tsafrir, D. (2013). Deconstructing Amazon EC2 spot instance pricing. *ACM Transactions on Economics and Computation, 1*(3), 16.
71. Li, W., Svärd, P., Tordsson, J., & Elmroth, E. (2013). Cost-optimal cloud service placement under dynamic pricing schemes. In *Proceedings of the 2013 IEEE/ACM 6th International Conference on Utility and Cloud Computing* (pp. 187–194). IEEE Computer Society.
72. Mishra. M., & Sahoo, A. (2011). On theory of vm placement: Anomalies in existing methodologies and their mitigation using a novel vector based approach. In *2011 IEEE International Conference on Cloud Computing (CLOUD)* (pp. 275–282). IEEE.
73. Ferreto, T., De Rose, C. A. F., & Heiss, H.-U. (2011). Maximum migration time guarantees in dynamic server consolidation for virtualized data centers. In *Euro-Par 2011 Parallel Processing* (pp. 443–454). Springer.
74. Hassan, M. M., Hossain, M. S., Sarkar, A. M. J., & Huh, E.-N. (2014). Cooperative game-based distributed resource allocation in horizontal dynamic cloud federation platform. *Information Systems Frontiers, 16*(4), 523–542.

Many-Objective Optimization for Virtual Machine Placement in Cloud Computing

Fabio López-Pires and Benjamín Barán

Abstract Resource allocation in cloud computing datacenters presents several research challenges, where the Virtual Machine Placement (VMP) is one of the most studied problems with several possible formulations considering a large number of existing optimization criteria. This chapter presents the main contributions that studied for the first time Many-Objective VMP (MaVMP) problems for cloud computing environments. In this context, two variants of MaVMP problems were formulated and different algorithms were designed to effectively address existing research challenges associated to the resolution of Many-Objective Optimization Problems (MaOPs). Experimental results proved the correctness of the presented algorithms, its effectiveness in solving particular associated challenges and its capabilities to solve problem instances with large numbers of physical and virtual machines for: (1) MaVMP for initial placement of VMs (static) and (2) MaVMP with reconfiguration of VMs (semi-dynamic). Finally, open research problems for the formulation and resolution of MaVMP problems for cloud computing (dynamic) are discussed.

1 Introduction

This chapter presents contributions related to the Virtual Machine Placement (VMP) problem from a Many-Objective Optimization perspective. Provider-oriented VMP problems can be enunciated as the process of assigning physical machines (PMs) to host requested virtual machines (VMs) in multi-tenant environments. Depending on particular requirements of a cloud computing infrastructure, the VMP problem could be formulated as several different optimization problems, considering several different objective functions. It is important to notice that these requirements may change over time and be defined as dynamic resource management policies. These

F. López-Pires (✉)
Itaipu Technological Park, Hernandarias, Paraguay
e-mail: fabio.lopez@pti.org.py

B. Barán
National University of Asunción, San Lorenzo, Paraguay
e-mail: bbaran@pol.una.py

© Springer Nature Singapore Pte Ltd. 2017
S. Chaudhary et al. (eds.), *Research Advances in Cloud Computing*,
DOI 10.1007/978-981-10-5026-8_12

particular considerations open different possible environments and formulations for the VMP problem. As a previous work by the authors, more than 60 different objective functions were identified in the specialized VMP literature [1, 2].

In real-world cloud computing infrastructures, the resolution of VMP problems could require the optimization of several objective functions in practical cases. This particular requirement could be clearly noted taking into account the large number of already studied objective functions, which could be formulated considering different possible approaches for modeling each objective function. In this context, Cloud Service Providers (CSPs) might be faced with the need to simultaneously optimize several conflicting objective functions when solving VMP problems.

It is important to consider that optimization problems simultaneously optimizing more than three objective functions are commonly known as Many-Objective Optimization Problems (MaOPs), as defined in [3]. In this context, there are several current research challenges for the resolution of MaOPs [4, 5].

Many-Objective Optimization is still considered an unexplored domain in resource management of cloud computing infrastructures [6], although there are already a few many-objective formulations proposed for the VMP problem in the specialized literature [7–9], as presented in this chapter.

The following sections present contributions and research challenges for different variants of Many-Objective VMP (MaVMP) problems, such as: (1) MaVMP for initial placement of VMs (static), (2) MaVMP with reconfiguration of VMs (semi-dynamic) and (3) MaVMP for cloud computing environments (dynamic).

2 Many-Objective VMP for Initial Placement of VMs

Considering that no many-objective formulation for the VMP problem was presented in the literature [2, 9], basic static environments such as initial placement of VMs were first studied [8]. This section presents a general many-objective optimization framework which is able to consider as many objective functions as needed when solving a MaVMP problem for initial placement of VMs (see Sect. 2.1). As an example of utilization of the presented framework, a first formulation of a MaVMP problem is presented, considering the simultaneous optimization of the following five objective functions: (1) power consumption, (2) network traffic, (3) economical revenue, (4) quality of service (QoS) and (5) network load balancing.

In the formulation of the MaVMP for initial placement of VMs to be presented in Sect. 2.2, a multilevel priority is associated to each VM, representing a Service Level Agreement (SLA) considered in the placement process, in order to effectively prioritize important VMs (e.g., in peaks situations where the total requested VMs resources are higher than available PMs resources). To solve the formulated MaVMP for initial placement of VMs, an interactive Memetic Algorithm (MA) was proposed (see Sect. 2.3) considering particular challenges associated to the resolution of a MaVMP problem, as the potentially unmanageable number of non-dominated solutions that compose a Pareto set approximation P_{known}.

2.1 Many-Objective Optimization Framework

The general many-objective optimization framework for the VMP problem proposed in [8] considers that as the number of conflicting objectives of a MaVMP problem formulation increases, the total number of non-dominated solutions normally increases (even exponentially in some cases), being increasingly difficult to discriminate among solutions using only the dominance relation [4]. For this reason, it is recommended the utilization of lower and upper bounds associated to each objective function $f_z(x)$, where $z \in \{1, \ldots, q\}$ ($L_z \leq f_z(x) \leq U_z$), to be able to iteratively reduce the number of possible non-dominated solutions of P_{known}.

A formulation of a MaVMP for initial placement of VMs, based on many objective functions and constraints to be detailed in Sect. 2.2, may be written as:

Optimize:

$$y = f(x) = [f_1(x), f_2(x), f_3(x), \ldots, f_q(x)] \quad \text{typically with } q > 3, \tag{1}$$

where for example:

$$
\begin{aligned}
&f_1(x) = \text{power consumption;} \\
&f_2(x) = \text{inter-VM network traffic;} \\
&f_3(x) = \text{economical revenue;} \\
&f_4(x) = \text{quality of service;} \\
&f_5(x) = \text{network load balancing;} \\
&\quad \vdots \\
&f_q(x) = \text{any other considered objective function.}
\end{aligned}
\tag{2}
$$

subject to constraints as:

$$
\begin{aligned}
&e_1(x) : \text{unique placement of VMs;} \\
&e_2(x) : \text{assure provisioning of highest SLA;} \\
&e_3(x) : \text{processing resource capacity of PMs;} \\
&e_4(x) : \text{memory resource capacity of PMs;} \\
&e_5(x) : \text{storage resource capacity of PMs;} \\
&e_6(x) : f_1(x) \in [L_1, U_1]; \\
&e_7(x) : f_2(x) \in [L_2, U_2]; \\
&e_8(x) : f_3(x) \in [L_3, U_3]; \\
&e_9(x) : f_4(x) \in [L_4, U_4]; \\
&e_{10}(x) : f_5(x) \in [L_5, U_5]; \\
&\quad \vdots \\
&e_r(x) : \text{any other considered constraint.}
\end{aligned}
\tag{3}
$$

2.2   Problem Formulation

A few articles have already proposed formulations of a pure multi-objective VMP problem (MVMP), considering the simultaneous optimization of at most three objective functions [10, 11]. A previous work of the authors proposed for the first time a MaVMP formulation [8]. This section presents a formulation of a MaVMP problem considering the following five objective functions to be simultaneously optimized: (1) power consumption, (2) network traffic, (3) economical revenue, (4) quality of service and (5) network load balancing. In the presented MaVMP formulation, a multilevel priority is associated to each VM considered in the placement process in order to effectively prioritize VMs. Formally, the presented offline (static) MaVMP problem for initial placement of VMs can be enunciated as [8]:

Given a set of PMs, $H = \{H_1, H_2, ..., H_n\}$, a network topology G (as illustrated in Figure 1) and a set of VMs, $V = \{V_1, V_2, ..., V_m\}$, it is sought a correct placement of the set of VMs V into the set of PMs H satisfying the r constraints of the problem and simultaneously optimizing all q objective functions defined in this formulation (as energy consumption, network traffic, economical revenue, QoS and load balancing in the network), in a pure many-objective context.

2.2.1   Input Data

The presented formulation of the MaVMP problem for initial placement of VMs models a virtualized datacenter infrastructure, composed by PMs, VMs and a network topology that interconnects PMs.

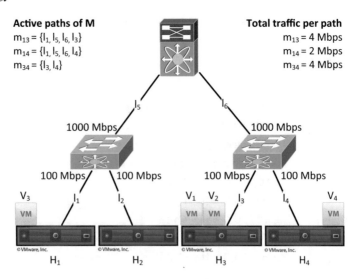

Fig. 1 Example of placement in a virtualized datacenter infrastructure, composed by PMs, a network topology and VMs

The set of PMs is represented as a matrix $H \in \mathbb{R}^{n \times 4}$. Each PM H_i is represented by processing resources of CPU (as ECU),[1] RAM [GB], storage [GB], and a maximum power consumption [W] as:

$$H_i = [Hcpu_i, Hram_i, Hhdd_i, pmax_i], \quad \forall i \in \{1, ..., n\} \tag{4}$$

where

$Hcpu_i$:   Processing resources of H_i;
$Hram_i$:   RAM memory resources of H_i;
$Hhdd_i$:   Storage resources of H_i;
$pmax_i$:   Maximum power consumption of H_i;
n: Number of PMs.

It should be mentioned that the proposed notation is general enough to include additional characteristics associated to each PM such as Graphic Processing Units (GPUs) or Network Interface Cards (NICs) just to cite a few.

As shown in the example of Fig. 1, a network topology of a virtualized datacenter is represented as:

G: Network topology;
L: Set of links l_a in G. For simplicity, links are assumed as semi-duplex in what follows;
M: Set of paths for all-to-all PM network interconnections;
K: Capacity set of the communication channels, typically in [Mbps].

The set of VMs requested by customers is represented as a matrix $V \in \mathbb{R}^{m \times 5}$. Each VM V_j requires processing resources of CPU (as ECU) (see Footnote 1), RAM [GB], and storage [GB], providing an economical revenue R_j [$] to the provider.

A SLA is also assigned to each VM to indicate its priority level. Consequently, a V_j is represented as:

$$V_j = [Vcpu_j, Vram_j, Vhdd_j, R_j, SLA_j], \quad \forall j \in \{1, ..., m\} \tag{5}$$

where

$Vcpu_j$:   Processing requirements of V_j;
$Vram_j$:   Memory requirements of V_j;
$Vhdd_j$:   Storage requirements of V_j;
R_j: Economical revenue for locating V_j;
SLA_j: Service Level Agreement SLA_j of a V_j. If the highest priority level is s, then $SLA_j \in \{1, \ldots, s\}$;
m: Number of VMs.

---

[1]http://aws.amazon.com/ec2/faqs.

The traffic between VMs is represented as a matrix $T \in \mathbb{R}^{m \times m}$. Each V_j requires network communication resources [Mbps] to communicate with other VMs. The network traffic between requested VMs is represented as:

$$T_j = [T_{j1}, T_{j2}, ..., T_{jm}], \quad \forall j \in \{1, ..., m\} \tag{6}$$

where

T_{jk}:   Average network traffic between V_j and V_k [Mbps]. Note that it is considered that $T_{jj} = 0$.

Figure 1 presents an example of a virtualized datacenter, composed by 4 PMs ($H = \{H_1, H_2, H_3, H_4\}$) and a network topology considering six physical network links ($L = \{l_1, l_2, l_3, l_4, l_5, l_6\}$). In this example, the set of capacity for each communication channel is $K = \{100, 100, 100, 100, 1000, 1000\}$ [Mbps]. Using shortest path, a path m_{12} between H_1 and H_2 uses links $\{l_1, l_2\}$, i.e., $m_{12} = \{l_1, l_2\}$. Analogously, $m_{13} = \{l_1, l_5, l_6, l_3\}$ and $m_{14} = \{l_1, l_5, l_6, l_4\}$, as shown in Fig. 1. All four requested VMs of Fig. 1 are correctly located into one of the available PMs.

2.2.2 Output Data

A possible solution x indicates a complete placement of each VM V_j into the necessary PMs H_i, considering the many-objective optimization criteria applied. A placement (or solution x to the proposed VMP problem) is represented as a matrix $P = \{P_{ji}\}$ of dimension ($m \times n$), where $P_{ji} \in \{0, 1\}$ indicates if V_j is located ($P_{ji} = 1$) or not ($P_{ji} = 0$) for execution on a PM H_i (i.e., $P_{ji} : V_j \rightarrow H_i$).

2.2.3 Constraint 1: Unique Placement of VMs

A VM V_j should be executed on a single PM H_i or alternatively, it could be not located into any PM if the associated SLA is not the highest level of priority s (i.e., $SLA_j < s$). This constraint is mathematically formulated as:

$$\sum_{i=1}^{n} P_{ji} \leq 1 \quad \forall j \in \{1, ..., m\} \tag{7}$$

where

P_{ji}:   Binary variable equals 1 if V_j is located on H_i; otherwise, it is 0.

2.2.4 Constraint 2: Assure SLA Provisioning

A VM V_j with the highest level of SLA (i.e., $SLA_j = s$) must be mandatorily located to run on a PM H_i. Consequently, this constraint is expressed as:

$$\sum_{i=1}^{n} P_{ji} = 1 \quad \forall j \text{ such that } SLA_j = s \tag{8}$$

2.2.5 Constraints 3–5: Physical Resources Capacities of PMs

A PM H_i must be able to meet the requirements of all VMs V_j that are located to run on H_i. In this chapter, it is not considered the overbooking of resources [12]. Consequently, these constraints can be mathematically formulated as:

$$\sum_{j=1}^{m} Vcpu_j \times P_{ji} \leq Hcpu_i \tag{9}$$

$$\sum_{j=1}^{m} Vram_j \times P_{ji} \leq Hram_i \tag{10}$$

$$\sum_{j=1}^{m} Vhdd_j \times P_{ji} \leq Hhdd_i \tag{11}$$

$\forall i \in \{1, \ldots, n\}$, i.e., for all physical machine H_i.

2.2.6 Adjustable Constraints

The work presented in [8] proposed the utilization of lower and upper bounds associated to each objective function to reduce the number of possible solutions of the Pareto set approximation P_{known}, when needed by a decision-maker. Consequently, this set of adjustable bounds can be formulated as the following constraints:

$$f_z(x) \in [L_z, U_z], \quad \forall z \in \{1, \ldots, q\} \tag{12}$$

A VMP problem can be defined as a many-objective optimization problem, when considering the simultaneous optimization of more than three objective functions. As a concrete example, this chapter proposes the simultaneous optimization of the following five objective functions.

2.2.7 Objective Function 1: Power Consumption Minimization

Based on [13] formulation, the work presented in [8] also proposes the minimization of power consumption, represented by the sum of the power consumption of each PM H_i:

$$f_1(x) = \sum_{i=1}^{n} ((pmax_i - pmin_i) \times Ucpu_i + pmin_i) \times Y_i \qquad (13)$$

where

$f_1(x)$:   Total power consumption of the PMs;
$pmin_i$:   Minimum power consumption of H_i. It should be noted that $pmin_i \approx pmax_i \times 0.6$ according to [13];
$Ucpu_i$:   Utilization ratio of processing resources used by H_i;
Y_i: Binary variable that equals 1 if H_i is turned on; otherwise, it is 0.

2.2.8 Objective Function 2: Inter-VM Network Traffic Minimization

Shrivastava et al. proposed in [14] the minimization of network traffic among VMs by maximizing locality. Based on this approach, the work presented in [8] proposes Eq. (14) to estimate network traffic represented by the sum of average network traffic generated by each VM V_j, that is located to run on any PM, with other VMs V_k that are located to run on different PMs.

$$f_2(x) = \sum_{j=1}^{m} \sum_{k=1}^{m} (T_{jk} \times D_{jk}) \qquad (14)$$

where

$f_2(x)$:   Total network traffic among VMs;
T_{jk}:   Average network traffic between V_j and V_k [Mbps]. Note that it is considered that $T_{jj} = 0$.
D_{jk}:   Binary variable that equals 1 if V_j and V_k are located in different PMs; otherwise, it is 0.

The traffic between two VMs V_j and V_k which are located on the same PM H_i does not contribute to increase the total network traffic given by Eq. (14); therefore, $D_{jk} = 0$ if $P_{ji} = P_{ki} = 1$.

2.2.9 Objective Function 3: Economical Revenue Minimization

Based on [11], the work presented in [8] proposes Eq. (15) for the estimation of the total economical revenue that a datacenter receives when supporting the requested resources of its customers, represented by the sum of the obtained revenue of each VM V_j that is located for execution on any PM.

$$f_3(x) = \sum_{j=1}^{m} (R_j \times X_j) \tag{15}$$

where

$f_3(x)$: Total economical revenue for placing VMs;
X_j: Binary variable that equals 1 if V_j is located for execution on any PM; otherwise, it is 0.

2.2.10 Objective Function 4: QoS Maximization

In the work presented in [8], the QoS maximization proposes to locate the maximum number of VMs with the highest level of priority associated to the SLA. This objective function is formulated in Eq. (16).

$$f_4(x) = \sum_{j=1}^{m} (\hat{C}^{SLA_j} \times SLA_j \times X_j) \tag{16}$$

where

$f_4(x)$: Total QoS figure for a given placement;
$\hat{C}$: Constant, large enough to prioritize services with a larger *SLA* over the ones with a lower *SLA*.

2.2.11 Objective Function 5: Network Load Balancing Optimization

The work presented in [8] calculates the total amount of network traffic going through a semi-duplex link l_a as:

$$T_{l_a} = \sum_{i=1}^{n} \sum_{i'=1}^{n} F_{aii'} \times \left(\sum_{j=1}^{m} \sum_{j'=1}^{m} P_{ji} \times P_{j'i'} \times D_{jj'} \times T_{jj'} \right) \tag{17}$$

where:

Tl_a: Total amount of traffic going through link l_a [Mbps];
$m_{ii'}$: Network path between H_i and H'_i;
$F_{aii'}$: Binary variable that equals 1 if $l_a \in m_{ii'}$; otherwise, it is 0.

Inspired in the formulation presented in [15], the work presented in [8] calculates the Maximum Link Utilization (MLU) as:

$$MLU = \max_{\forall l_a \in L} \left(\frac{Tl_a}{Cl_a} \right) \tag{18}$$

where:

MLU: Maximum Link Utilization;
Cl_a: Channel capacity of link l_a [Mbps].

In [8], the load balancing optimization of the network is formulated as the minimization of the MLU, denoted as:

$$f_5(x) = MLU \tag{19}$$

2.3   Interactive Memetic Algorithm for MaVMP

A Memetic Algorithm (MA) could be understood as an Evolutionary Algorithm (EA) that in addition to the standard selection, crossover, and mutation operators of most Genetic Algorithms (GAs) includes a local optimization operator to obtain good solutions even at early generations of an EA [16]. In the VMP context, it is valuable to obtain good quality of solutions in short time. Consequently, a MA could be considered as a promising solution technique for VMP problems.

The work presented in [8] proposes an interactive MA for solving the VMP problem in a many-objective context, considering the proposed formulation presented in Sect. 2.2 to simultaneously optimize the five objective functions presented in the previous section. The proposed algorithm is extensible to consider as many objective functions as needed while only minor modifications may be needed if the number of objective functions changes.

It was shown in [5] that many-objective optimization using Multi-Objective Evolutionary Algorithms (MOEAs) is an active research area, having multiple challenges that need to be addressed. The interactive MA presented in this section is a viable way to solve a MaVMP problem, including desirable ranges of values for the objective functions in order to interactively control the possible huge number of feasible non-dominated solution. The interactive MA presented in Algorithm 1 is based on the MA proposed in [11] and works as described next:

At step 1, the algorithm verifies that the problem is solvable (considering only VMs with $SLA_j = s$) to continue its execution. If the problem could not be solved, the algorithm returns an appropriate error message. If the problem is solvable, the algorithm continues with step 2, generating a set of aleatory population P_0, whose candidate solutions are repaired at step 3 to ensure that P_0 contains feasible solutions only. Then, the algorithm tries to improve solutions at step 4 using a local search. With the obtained non-comparable solutions, the first Pareto set approximation P_{known} is

---

Algorithm 1: Interactive Memetic Algorithm

Data: datacenter infrastructure (see Section 2.2.1)

Result: Pareto set approximation P_{known}

1 check if the problem has a solution
2 initialize set of solutions P_0
3 P'_0 = repair infeasible solutions of P_0
4 P''_0 = apply local search to solutions of P'_0
5 update set of solutions P_{known} from P''_0
6 $t = 0; P_t = P''_0$
7 **while** *stopping criterion is not met* **do**
8   Q_t = selection of solutions from $P_t \cup P_{known}$
9   Q'_t = crossover and mutation of solutions of Q_t
10   Q''_t = repair infeasible solutions of Q'_t
11   Q'''_t = apply local search to solutions of Q''_t
12   update set of solutions P_{known} from Q'''_t
13   increment t
14   **if** *interaction is needed* **then**
15 | ask for decision-maker modification of (L_z and U_z)
16   **end**
17   P_t = non-dominated sorting from $P_t \cup Q'''_t$
18 **end**
19 **return** Pareto set approximation P_{known}

---

generated at step 5. After initialization at step 6, evolution begins (iterations between steps 7 and 18). The evolutionary process follows the same behavior: solutions are selected considering the union of P_{known} with the evolutionary set of solutions (or population) also known as P_t (step 8), crossover and mutation operators are applied as usual (step 9), and solutions are eventually repaired, as there may be infeasible solutions (step 10). Improvements of solutions may be generated at step 11 using local search in the evolutionary population P_t (local optimization operators). At step 12, the Pareto set approximation P_{known} is updated (if applicable); while at step 13 the generation counter is updated. At step 15, the decision-maker adjusts the lower and upper bounds if it is necessary, while at step 17 a new evolutionary population P_t is selected. The evolutionary process stops according to defined stopping criterion (as maximum number of generations), returning at the end the set of found non-dominated solutions P_{known} at step 19.

2.3.1 Population Initialization

Initially, a set of solutions P_0 is randomly generated. Each possible solution (or individual) x is represented as a chromosome $C = [C_1, C_2, \ldots, C_m]$ (matrix P in Sect. 2.2.2). The possible values that can take each C_k for VMs with the highest value of SLA_j ($SLA_j = s$) are in the range [1, n]. On the other hand, for VMs V_j with $SLA_j < s$, C_k can take values in the range [0, n]. Within these ranges defined by the SLA_j of each V_j, the algorithm ensures that all VMs V_j with the highest level of priority will be located for execution on a PM H_i, while for a VM V_j with lower levels of priority SLA_j, there is always a probability larger than 0 that it may not be located for execution in any PM.

2.3.2 Infeasible Solution Reparation

With a random generation at the initialization phase (step 2 of Algorithm 1) and/or solutions generated by genetic operators (step 9 of Algorithm 1), infeasible solutions may appear, i.e., the resources required by the VMs allocated on particular PMs could exceed available resources, or at least one objective function may not meet adjustable constraints.

Repairing infeasible solutions (steps 3 and 10 of Algorithm 1) may be done in two stages: first, in the feasibility verification process, the population is classified in two classes: feasible or infeasible (Algorithm 2). Next, in the process of repairing infeasible solutions (Algorithm 3), the infeasible solutions are repaired in three ways: (1) migrating some VMs to an available hardware, (2) turning on some PMs and then migrating VMs to them, or (3) turning off some VMs with $SLA_j < s$.

2.3.3 Local Search

With a population composed by feasible solutions only, a local search is performed (steps 4 and 11 of Algorithm 1) improving solutions found until then in the evolutionary population. The local search pseudocode is presented in Algorithm 4.

For each individual in the evolutionary population P_t, the interactive MA proposed in [8] attempts to optimize a solution with a local search (step 2 of Algorithm 4).

Algorithm 2: Feasibility Verification

Data: set of solutions P_t
Result: set of feasible solutions P'_t
1 **while** *there are solutions not verified* **do**
2   feasible = true ; i = 1
3   **while** $i \leq n$ *and feasible = true* **do**
4   **if** *solution does not satisfy constraints (3-5)* **then**
5   feasible = false ; break
6   **else**
7   increment i
8   **end**
9   **end**
10   **if** *feasible = false* **then**
11   call Algorithm 3 (repair solution)
12   **end**
13 **end**
14 **return** set of feasible solutions P'_t

Algorithm 3: Infeasible Solutions Reparation

Data: infeasible solution
Result: feasible solution
1 feasible = false ; j = 1
2 **while** $j \leq m$ *and feasible = false* **do**
3   **if** *it is possible* **then**
4 | migrate V_j to H'_i $(i' \neq i)$
5   **else**
6   **if** $SLA_j \neq s$ **then**
7 | turn off V_j on H_i
8   **else**
9 | replace solution with another solution from P_{known}
10   **end**
11   **end**
12 **end**
13 **return** feasible solution

Algorithm 4: Local Search

Data: set of feasible solutions P'_t
Result: set of feasible optimized solutions P''_t
1 probability = random number between 0 and 1
2 **while** *there are solutions not verified* **do**
3   **if** *probability* < 0.5 **then**
4   Try to turn off all the possible H_i by migrating all the V_j assigned to H'_i with available resources $(i' \neq i)$ and then try to turn on all the possible V_j (using SLA_j priority order) assigning them to a H_i with available resources
5   **else**
6   Try to turn on all the possible V_j (using SLA_j priority order) assigning them to a H_i with available resources and then try to turn off all the possible H_i by migrating all the V_j assigned to H'_i with available resources $(i' \neq i)$
7   **end**
8 **end**
9 **return** set of feasible optimized solutions P''_t

For this, with probability $\frac{1}{2}$, the algorithm tries maximizing the number of allocated VMs with higher level of priority, locating all possible VMs that were not located so far, increasing $f_3(x)$ (total economical revenue) and $f_4(x)$ (total quality of service) (steps 3 to 5 of Algorithm 4). Additionally, also with probability $\frac{1}{2}$, the algorithm tries minimizing the number of PMs turned on, directly reducing $f_1(x)$ (total power consumption) (steps 6 to 8 of Algorithm 4). With the proposed probabilistic local search method, a balanced exploitation of objective functions (economical revenue, quality of service and power consumption) is achieved, as experimentally verified with results presented in next section.

2.3.4 Fitness Function

The fitness function considered in the proposed algorithm is the one proposed in [17]. This fitness defines a non-domination rank in which a value equal to its Pareto dominance level (1 is the highest level of dominance) is assigned to each individual of the population. Between two solutions with different non-domination rank, the individual with lower value (higher level of dominance) is considered better.

To compare solutions with the same non-domination rank, a crowding distance is used. Basically, a crowding distance finds the Euclidean distance (properly normalized when the objectives have different measure units) between each pair of solutions, based on the q objectives, in a hyper-dimensional space [17]. The solution with higher crowding distance is considered better.

2.3.5 Variation Operators

The proposed interactive MA considers a Binary Tournament approach for selecting individuals for crossover and mutation [18]. The crossover operator used in the presented work is the single point cross-cut [18]. The selected individuals in the ascending population are replaced by descendants individuals.

The work presented in [8] uses a mutation method in which each gene is mutated with a probability $\frac{1}{m}$, where m represents the number of VMs. This method offers the possibility of full uniform gene mutation, with a very low probability (but larger than zero), which is beneficial to the exploration of the search space, reducing the probability of stagnation in a local optimum. The population evolution in the proposed interactive MA is based on the population evolution proposed in [17]. A population P_{t+1} is formed from the union of the best known population P_t and offspring population Q_t, applying non-domination rank and crowding distance.

2.3.6 Many-Objective Considerations

Given that the number of non-dominated solutions may rapidly increase, an interactive approach is recommended. That way, a decision-maker can introduce new constraints or adjust existing ones, while the execution continues learning about the shape of the Pareto front in the process. For simplicity, the present work considers lower and upper bounds associated to each objective function in order to help the decision-maker to reduce interactively the potential huge number of solutions in the Pareto set approximation P_{known}, while observing the evolution of its corresponding Pareto front PF_{known} to the region of his preference.

Table 1 Types of PMs considered in experiments. For notation see Eq. (4)

PM type	Hcpu [ECU]	Hram [GB]	Hhdd [GB]	pmax [W]
h1.small	4	16	150	440
h1.medium	180	512	10000	1000
h1.large	350	1024	10000	1300

2.4 Experimental Results

This section summarizes experimental results obtained by the proposed algorithm [8] in carefully designed experiments to validate its effectiveness considering challenges associated to the resolution of a MaVMP problem previously introduced.

First, Experiment 1 performed a quality evaluation of the solutions obtained by the proposed algorithm against optimal solutions obtained with an exhaustive search algorithm in two different scenarios. Next, Experiment 2 performed an evaluation using lower and upper bounds associated to each objective function $f(z)$ ($L_z \leq f_z(x) \leq U_z$) to be able to converge to a manageable number of solutions in the Pareto set approximation. Finally, Experiment 3 evaluates the proposed algorithm solving instances of the problem with large numbers of PMs and VMs. For simplicity, all experiments considered a datacenter infrastructure composed by PMs interconnected in a simple two-tier network topology.

2.4.1 Experimental Environment

Different problem instances were proposed for the above-mentioned experiments considering both homogeneous and heterogeneous hardware configurations of PMs, as well as homogeneous and heterogeneous VMs instance types offered by Amazon Elastic Compute Cloud (EC2).[2] A detailed description of the hardware configuration of the PMs and VMs instance types considered for the experiments is presented in Tables 1 and 2 respectively. Additionally, a general description of the considered problem instances including its decision space size is presented in Table 3.

The complete set of datacenter infrastructure input files used for the experiments with the corresponding experimental results are available online.[3]

Algorithms considered in the experiments were implemented using ANSI C programming language (gcc) and the source code is available online[3]. All the presented experiments were executed on a CentOS 6.5 Linux Operating System, with an Intel(R) Xeon(R) CPU E5530 at 2.40 GHz processor and 8 GB of RAM.

---

[2]http://aws.amazon.com/ec2/instance-types.
[3]https://github.com/flopezpires/iMaVMP.

Table 2 Instance types of VMs considered in experiments. For notation see Eq. (5)

Instance type	Vcpu [ECU]	Vram [GB]	Vhdd [GB]	R [$]
t2.micro	1	1	0	9
t2.small	1	2	0	18
t2.medium	2	4	0	37
m3.medium	1	4	4	50
m3.large	2	8	32	100
m3. × large	4	15	80	201
m3.2 × large	8	30	160	403
c3.large	2	4	32	75
c3. × large	4	8	80	151
c3.2 × large	8	15	160	302
c3.4 × large	16	30	320	604
c3.8 × large	32	60	640	1209
r3.large	2	15	32	126
r3. × large	4	30	80	252
r3.2 × large	8	61	160	504
r3.4 × large	16	122	0	320
r3.8 × large	32	244	0	320

Table 3 Problem instances considered in experiments, all with 50% of VMs with SLA $s = 2$

Experiment	Input	# PMs	# VMs	PMs and VMs	$(n + 1)^m$
1	3×5.vmp	3	5	Homogeneous	1024
1	4×8.vmp	4	8	Heterogeneous	390625
2	12×50.vmp	12	50	Heterogeneous	$\sim 5 \times 10^{55}$
3	100×1000.vmp	100	1000	Heterogeneous	$\sim 2 \times 10^{2004}$

2.4.2 Experiment 1: Quality of Solutions

To compare the results obtained by the proposed interactive MA and to validate its proper operation, an Exhaustive Search Algorithm (ESA) was also implemented for finding all $(n + 1)^m$ possible solutions of a given instance of the VMP problem, when this alternative is computationally possible for the authors. These results were compared to the results obtained by the proposed interactive MA.

Considering that this particular experiment aims to validate the good level of exploration in the set of feasible solutions X_f, the local search of the algorithm was disabled, strengthening its capability of exploration rather than the rapid convergence to good solutions even in early generations of the population.

Table 4 Summary of results obtained by the proposed algorithm in Experiment 1

Input	P^* size	P_{known} size	Execution time (ESA) (s)	Execution time (MA) (s)
3×5.vmp	51	51	~1	~12
4×8.vmp	30	30	~720	~29

For each problem instance considered in this experiment (see Table 3), one run of the exhaustive search algorithm was completed, obtaining the optimal Pareto set P^* and its corresponding Pareto front PF^*.

Furthermore, 10 runs of the proposed algorithm were completed, after evolving populations composed by 100 individuals for 100 generations at each run. The results obtained by the proposed algorithm for each run were combined to obtain the Pareto set approximation P_{known} and its corresponding Pareto front PF_{known}.

For both considered problem instances, the proposed algorithm obtained 100% of the solutions of P^* and its corresponding PF^*. Additionally, the proposed algorithm performed well in execution time against the ESA, even obtaining the same optimal results in less execution time for the 4×8.vmp scenario. A summary of the number of elements in the corresponding Pareto sets obtained and the execution time of both algorithms is presented in Table 4.

2.4.3 Experiment 2: Interactive Bounds

For the problem instance considered in this experiment (12×50.vmp), one run of the proposed algorithm was completed, after evolving populations of 100 individuals for 300 generations. The number of generations was incremented for this experiment from 100 to 300, taking into account the large number of possible solutions for the particular considered problem (see Table 3). An interactive adjustment of the lower or upper bounds associated to each objective function was performed after every 100 generations in order to converge to a treatable number of solutions. It is important to remark that the interactive adjustment used in this experiment is only one of several possible ones. As an example, we may consider: (1) automatically adjusting a % of the lower bounds associated to maximization objective functions when the Pareto front has a defined number of elements or (2) manually adjusting upper bounds associated to minimization objective functions until the Pareto front does not have more than 20 elements, just to cite a pair of alternatives.

The Pareto front approximation PF_{known} represents the complete set of Pareto solutions considering unrestricted bounds ($L_z = -\infty$ and $U_z = \infty$). On the other hand, Pareto front approximation $PF_{reduced}$ represents the reduced set of Pareto solutions obtained by interactively adjusting bounds L_z and U_z. In the first 100 generations, the proposed algorithm obtained 251 solutions with unrestricted bounds. A decision-maker evaluated the bounds associated to $f_1(x)$ (power consumption) and adjusted the upper bound U_1 to $U_1' = 9000$ [W], selecting only 35 out of the 251 solu-

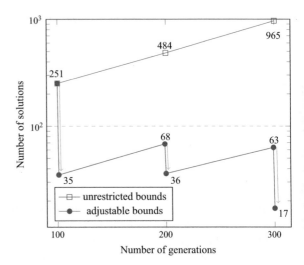

Fig. 2 Summary of results obtained in Experiment 2 using adjusted lower and upper bounds

tions (not considering 216 otherwise feasible solutions) for the $PF_{reduced}$ as shown in Fig. 2. After 200 generations, the algorithm obtained a total of 484 solutions with unrestricted bounds. Considering instead $U_1' = 9000$ [W], the algorithm only found 68 solutions. The decision-maker evaluated the bounds associated to $f_2(x)$ (network traffic) and adjusted the upper bound U_2 to $U_2' = 115$ [Mbps], selecting only 36 out of the 68 solutions (not considering 32 otherwise feasible solutions) for the $PF_{reduced}$. Finally, after 300 generations, the algorithm obtained a total of 965 solutions with unrestricted bounds. Considering $U_1' = 9000$ [W] and $U_2' = 115$ [Mbps], the algorithm found 63 solutions. The decision-maker evaluated the bounds associated to $f_3(x)$ (economical revenue) and adjusted the lower bound L_3 to $L_3' = 13500$ [\$], selecting only 17 out of the 63 solutions (not considering 46 feasible solutions) for the final $PF_{reduced}$ as shown in Fig. 2. Clearly, at the end of the iterative process, the decision-maker found 17 solutions according to his preferences instead of the unmanageable number of 965 candidate solutions.

2.4.4 Experiment 3: Algorithm Scalability

It should be noted that increasing the number of PMs and VMs in a VMP problem could result in extremely large decision spaces, considering all $(n + 1)^m$ possible solutions (see Table 3). Consequently, algorithms designed for the resolution of VMP problems should be able to effectively solve VMP problem instances composed by large numbers of VMs and PMs in a reasonable time.

For the problem instance considered in this experiment (100×1000.vmp), one run of the proposed algorithm was completed, after evolving populations composed by 100, 200, and 300 individuals for 500 generations. For this particular experiment, the Pareto front approximation PF_{known} represents the complete set of Pareto solu-

Table 5 Summary of results obtained by the proposed algorithm in Experiment 3

Input	# of individuals	P_{known} size	# of generations
100 × 1000.vmp	100	397	100
100 × 1000.vmp	200	399	100
100 × 1000.vmp	300	509	100
100 × 1000.vmp	100	769	200
100 × 1000.vmp	200	811	200
100 × 1000.vmp	300	1087	200
100 × 1000.vmp	100	1103	300
100 × 1000.vmp	200	1329	300
100 × 1000.vmp	300	1641	300
100 × 1000.vmp	100	1434	400
100 × 1000.vmp	200	1791	400
100 × 1000.vmp	300	2178	400
100 × 1000.vmp	100	1742	500
100 × 1000.vmp	200	2192	500
100 × 1000.vmp	300	2719	500

tions considering unrestricted bounds for each $f_z(x)$ ($L_z = -\infty$ and $U_z = \infty$) in order to experimentally demonstrate that large instances of the formulated MaVMP problem could result in unmanageable number of solutions. A summary of the results obtained by the proposed algorithm is presented in Table 5. The obtained results prove the capabilities of the proposed algorithm to effectively solve instances of the proposed MaVMP problem with large numbers of PMs and VMs, as considered in real-world scenarios. Additionally, it could be observed that increasing the number of individuals on populations or the number of generations, the algorithm obtained larger numbers of non-dominated solutions with unrestricted bounds. Considering that the proposed algorithm could find more non-dominated solutions than the obtained in this particular experiment if more computational resources for calculation are considered (or increasing the number of individuals or the number of generations), it could be noted the importance of including additional methods to the Pareto dominance relation (e.g., adjustable bounds) for the selection of a manageable subset of P_{known} in MaVMP problems for initial placement of VMs.

3 Many-Objective VMP with Reconfiguration of VMs

Once an initial placement of VMs has been performed (as presented in Sect. 2), a virtualized datacenter could be reconfigured through live migration in order to maintain efficiency in operations, considering that the set of requested VMs changes over time (i.e., the set V presented in Sect. 2.2.1 is a function of time). Studying this particular semi-dynamic formulation of a MaVMP with reconfiguration of VMs represents a first approximation to dynamic formulations in real-world cloud computing environments, where several dynamic parameters should also be considered.

According to [2, 9], the optimization of the power consumption is the most studied objective function in VMP literature [13, 19]. Furthermore, network traffic [20] and economical revenue [21, 22] are also very much studied as objective functions for the VMP problem. For a VMP problem formulation with reconfiguration of VMs, two additional objective functions associated to migration of VMs represent challenges for CSPs: minimizing the total number of VM migrations [23] as well as the total network traffic overhead due to VM migrations [24].

Considering the large number of existing objective functions for the VMP problem identified in [2, 9], López-Pires and Barán have proposed in [8, 25] a many-objective optimization framework in order to consider as many objective functions as needed when solving a MaVMP problem for initial placement of VMs in virtualized datacenters (see Sect. 2). To the best of the authors' knowledge, there was no published work presenting a formulation of a MaVMP problem with reconfiguration of VMs. Consequently, this section extends the formulations presented in Sect. 2 [8, 25] presenting the first MaVMP with reconfiguration of VMs, considering this time the simultaneous optimization of the following five objective functions: (1) power consumption, (2) inter-VM network traffic, (3) economical revenue, (4) number of VM migrations, and (5) network traffic overhead for VM migrations [7].

To solve the formulated MaVMP problem, the interactive MA presented in Sect. 2.3 was extended to consider particular challenges associated to the resolution of a MaVMP problem with reconfigurations of VMs, as next introduced.

Several challenges need to be addressed for MaVMP formulations with reconfiguration of VMs. In Pareto-based algorithms, the Pareto set approximation can include a large number of non-dominated solutions. Selecting one of the non-dominated solutions can be considered a problem for a MaVMP problem. In consequence, the work presented in [7] evaluates the following five selection strategies: (1) random, (2) preferred solution, (3) minimum distance to origin, (4) lexicographic order (provider preference), and (5) lexicographic order (service preference) to identify convenient strategies for automatic selection of a non-dominated solution.

3.1   Problem Formulation

This chapter presents the formulation of a MaVMP with reconfiguration of VMs [7], considering this time the simultaneous optimization of the following five objective functions: (1) power consumption, (2) inter-VM network traffic, (3) economical revenue, (4) number of VM migrations and (5) network traffic overhead for VM migrations. Formally, the presented offline (semi-dynamic) MaVMP problem with reconfiguration of VMs can be enunciated as:

Given the available PMs and their specifications, the requested VMs and their speci-
fications, the network traffic between VMs and the current placement of the VMs, it is
sought a new placement of the set of VMs in the set of PMs, satisfying the constraints
of the problem while simultaneously optimizing all defined objective functions (as
power consumption, inter-VM network traffic, economical revenue, number of VM
migrations and network traffic overhead for VM migration), in a pure many-objective
context, before selecting a specific solution for a given time instant t.

3.1.1   Input Data

The set of available PMs is represented as a matrix $H \in \mathbb{R}^{n \times 4}$, previously introduced
in Sect. 2.2.1 (see Eq. (4)). Accordingly, the set of VMs at instant t is now represented
as a matrix $V(t) \in \mathbb{R}^{m \times 5}$:

$$V(t) = \begin{bmatrix} Vcpu_1 & Vram_1 & Vhdd_1 & SLA_1 & R_1 \\ \ldots & \ldots & \ldots & \ldots & \ldots \\ Vcpu_{m(t)} & Vram_{m(t)} & Vhdd_{m(t)} & SLA_{m(t)} & R_{m(t)} \end{bmatrix} \qquad (20)$$

Each V_j represents the required processing resources of CPU [ECU], RAM memory [GB], storage [GB], SLA, and revenue [$]:

$$V_j = [Vcpu_j, Vram_j, Vhdd_j, SLA_j, R_j], \quad \forall j \in \{1, \ldots, m(t)\} \qquad (21)$$

where

$Vcpu_j$:   Processing requirements of V_j;
$Vram_j$:   Memory requirements of V_j;
$Vhdd_j$:   Storage requirements of V_j;
R_j: Economical revenue for placing V_j;
SLA_j: Service Level Agreement SLA_j of a V_j, where $SLA_j \in \{0, 1, \ldots, s\}$ being s
     the highest priority level;
$m(t)$:   Number of VMs at instant t, then $m(t) \in \{1, \ldots, m_{max}\}$;
m_{max}:   Maximum number of VMs.

Once a V_j is powered off by the tenant, its resources are released, so the physical
resources can be reused. For simplicity, the index j is not considered to be reused;
therefore, for the work presented in [7] V_j is not a function of time.
   The traffic between VMs at instant t is represented as a matrix $T(t) \in \mathbb{R}^{m(t) \times m(t)}$:

$$T(t) = \begin{bmatrix} T_{1,1}(t) & \ldots & T_{1,m(t)}(t) \\ \ldots & \ldots & \ldots \\ T_{m(t),1}(t) & \ldots & T_{m(t),m(t)}(t) \end{bmatrix} \qquad (22)$$

   In Eq. (22), $T_{jk}(t)$ represents the average communication rate in [Mbps], between
VM V_j and VM V_k at instant t. Note that we can consider $T_{jj}(t) = 0$.
   The placement at instant t is represented as a matrix $P(t) \in \mathbb{R}^{m(t) \times n}$:

$$P(t) = \begin{bmatrix} P_{1,1}(t) & \cdots & P_{1,n}(t) \\ \cdots & \cdots & \cdots \\ P_{m(t),1}(t) & \cdots & P_{m(t),n}(t) \end{bmatrix} \tag{23}$$

where:

$P_{ji}(t) \in \{0, 1\}$ indicates if V_j is located ($P_{ji} = 1$) or not ($P_{ji} = 0$) for execution on a PM H_i (i.e., $P_{ji}(t) : V_j \rightarrow H_i$) at instant t.

3.1.2 Output Data

A solution of the problem at each instant is a new VM placement $P(t + 1)$. In order to accommodate a new placement, a series of management actions (MAc) (i.e., VM migrations, creation or destruction) must be performed. These are presented by the following output data: (1) the new VM placement and (2) the list of required management actions.

The new placement at instant $(t + 1)$ is represented as a matrix $P(t + 1)$ of dimension $m(t + 1) \times n$:

$$P(t + 1) = \begin{bmatrix} P_{1,1} & \cdots & P_{1,n} \\ \cdots & \cdots & \cdots \\ P_{m(t+1),1} & \cdots & P_{m(t+1),n} \end{bmatrix} \tag{24}$$

where $P_{ji}(t+1) \in \{0, 1\}$ indicates if V_j is located ($P_{ji}(t+1) = 1$) or not ($P_{ji}(t+1) = 0$) for execution on a PM H_i at instant t (i.e., $P_{ji}(t + 1) : V_j \rightarrow H_i$).

The set of necessary management actions in order to evolve from $P(t)$ to $P(t+1)$ is represented by:

$$MAc_{t \rightarrow t+1} = \left[MAc(V_1), \ldots, MAc(V_{m(t+1)}) \right] \tag{25}$$

where $MAc(V_j) \in \{0, 1, 2, 3\}$ which represents the management actions that a hypervisor must execute in order to accommodate $P(t + 1)$ corresponding to V_j. Values returned by the $MAc(V_j)$ function should be interpreted as follows:

$MAc(V_j) = 0$: no management action is necessary, i.e., $P_{ji}(t + 1) = P_{ji}(t)$, $\forall i$;
$MAc(V_j) = 1$: a new VM V_j is placed on a PM H_i, i.e., $P_{ji}(t + 1) = 1$;
$MAc(V_j) = 2$: an existing VM V_j is migrated from $H_{i'}$ to another H_i, i.e., $P_{ji'}(t) = 1$ and $P_{ji}(t + 1) = 1$;
$MAc(V_j) = 3$: a VM V_j is shutdown, i.e., $P_{ji}(t) = 1$ but $P_{ji}(t + 1) = 0$.

3.1.3 Constraint 1: Unique Placement of VMs

A VM V_j should be located to run on a single PM H_i or alternatively, it could be not located in any PM if the associated SLA_j is not the highest level of priority (in [7] $s = 2$). Consequently, this constraint is expressed as:

$$\sum_{i=1}^{n} P_{ji}(t) \leq 1 \quad \forall j \in \{1, ..., m(t)\}, \quad \forall t \tag{26}$$

where

$P_{ji}(t)$: Binary variable equals 1 if V_j is located to run on H_i at instant t; otherwise, it is 0.

3.1.4 Constraint 2: Assure SLA Provisioning

A VM V_j with the highest level of SLA ($s = 2$) must necessarily be located to run on a PM H_i. Consequently, this constraint is expressed as:

$$\sum_{i=1}^{n} P_{ji}(t) = 1 \quad \forall j \text{ such that } SLA_j = s \tag{27}$$

$$\forall t \text{ where } V_j \text{ should be active.}$$

It should be remarked that different levels of SLA can be considered, as presented in [8].

3.1.5 Constraints 3–5: Physical Resources Capacities of PMs

A PM H_i must have sufficient available resources to meet the requirements of all VMs V_j that are located to run on H_i at instant t. In the work presented in [7], the overbooking of resources [26] is not considered; consequently, the set of constraints can be mathematically formulated as:

$$\sum_{j=1}^{m(t)} Vcpu_j \times P_{ji}(t) \leq Hcpu_i \tag{28}$$

$$\sum_{j=1}^{m(t)} Vram_j \times P_{ji}(t) \leq Hram_i \tag{29}$$

$$\sum_{j=1}^{m(t)} Vhdd_j \times P_{ji}(t) \leq Hhdd_i \tag{30}$$

$\forall i \in \{1, ..., n\}$, i.e., for all physical machines H_i and $\forall t$.

Next section presents five objective functions that are simultaneously optimized in the presented MaVMP formulation with reconfiguration of VMs. These objective functions are mathematically formulated as follows.

3.1.6 Objective Function 1: Power Consumption Minimization

Based on Eq. (13), the power consumption at each discrete time t can be represented by the sum of the power consumption of each PM H_i:

$$f_1(x, t) = \sum_{i=1}^{n} ((pmax_i - pmin_i) \times Ucpu_i(t) + pmin_i) \times Y_i(t) \tag{31}$$

where

$f_1(x, t)$:   Total power consumption of the PMs at each discrete time t;
$Ucpu_i(t)$:   Utilization ratio of processing resources used by H_i at instant t;
$Y_i(t)$:   Binary variable equals 1 if H_i is turned on; otherwise, it is 0.

3.1.7 Objective Function 2: Inter-VM Network Traffic Minimization

A very much studied approach for inter-VM network traffic minimization is the placement of VMs with high communication rate in the same PM (or at least in the same rack) to avoid the utilization of network resources (or at least core network equipment).

The minimization of network traffic among VMs, by maximizing locality, was proposed in [14]. Based on Eq. (14), Eq. (32) represents the sum of average network traffic between VM V_j and VM V_k when located on different PMs.

$$f_2(x, t) = \sum_{j=1}^{m(t)} \sum_{k=1}^{m(t)} (T_{jk}(t) \times D_{jk}(t)) \tag{32}$$

where

$f_2(x, t)$:   Total inter-VM network traffic at each discrete time t;
$D_{jk}(t)$:   Binary variable that equals 1 if V_j and V_k are located in different PMs at instant t; otherwise, it is 0.

The traffic between two VMs V_j and V_k located on the same PM H_i does not contribute to increase the total network traffic given by Eq. (32); therefore, $D_{jk}(t) = 0$ if $P_{ji}(t) = P_{ki}(t) = 1$.

3.1.8 Objective Function 3: Economical Revenue Maximization

Based on Eq. (15), Eq. (33) is presented to estimate the total economical revenue that a datacenter receives for meeting the requirements of its customers, represented by the sum of the economical revenue obtainable by each VM V_j that is effectively located for execution on any PM at instant t.

$$f_3(x, t) = \sum_{j=1}^{m(t)} (R_j \times X_j(t)) \tag{33}$$

where

$f_3(x, t)$: Total economical revenue for placing VMs at each discrete time t;
$X_j(t)$: Binary variable that equals 1 if V_j is located for execution on any PM at instant t; otherwise, it is 0.

3.1.9 Objective Function 4: Number of VM Migrations Minimization

Performance degradation may occur when migrating VMs from one PM to another [24]. Logically, it is desirable that the number of migrated VMs is kept to a minimum for better quality of service (QoS). Therefore, Eq. (34) represents the number of VM migrations at time instant t:

$$f_4(x, t) = \sum_{j=1}^{m(t)} Z_j(t) \tag{34}$$

where

$f_4(x, t)$: Number of VM migrations at instant t;
$Z_j(t)$: Binary variable that equals 1 if $MA(V_j) = 2$, i.e., V_j is migrated, see (25); otherwise, it is 0 (V_j is not migrated).

3.1.10 Objective Function 5: Network Traffic Overhead for VM Migrations Minimization

As explained in [24], the overhead of VM migrations on network resources is proportional to the memory size of the migrated VM. In the work presented in [7], (35) is proposed to minimize the amount of RAM memory that must be copied between PMs at instant t.

$$f_5(x, t) = \sum_{j=1}^{m(t)} V\,ram_j \times Z_j(t) \tag{35}$$

where

$f_5(x, t)$:   Network traffic overhead for VM migrations at instant t;

It should be mentioned that there are other possible modeling approaches to estimate the migration overhead, as presented in [27].

Finally, it should be noted that the main difference between the above-described objective functions for the MaVMP with reconfiguration of VMs (see Eqs. (31)–(35)) with the ones previously presented in Sect. 2 for the MaVMP for initial placement of VMs (see Eqs. (13)–(18)) is that Eqs. (31)–(35) are calculated at each discrete time t.

3.2   Extended Memetic Algorithm for MaVMP

The work presented in [7] extends the interactive MA proposed in [8, 25] for solving the MaVMP problem with reconfiguration of VMs, as the one formulated in Sect. 3.1. The proposed algorithm simultaneously optimizes the five objective functions presented in the previous sections.

Many-objective optimization using Multi-Objective Evolutionary Algorithms (MOEAs) is an active research area, with multiple challenges that need to be addressed regarding scalability analysis, solutions visualization, algorithm design, and experimental algorithm evaluation as shown in [5]. At each time instant, the set of feasible placement solutions can be composed by a large number of non-dominated solutions. Therefore, the algorithm proposed in [7] automatically selects one of the possible placements after each time instant according to one of the considered selection strategies (see Sect. 3.3). The proposed algorithm is based on the one proposed in Sect. 2 [8] and it works as follows (see Algorithm 5):

The algorithm iterates over each set of requested VMs received at each instant t. At step 3, the algorithm verifies if the problem has at least one solution to continue with next steps. If there is no possible solution to the problem, the algorithm returns an appropriate error message. If the problem has at least one solution, the algorithm proceeds to step 4 in order to determine the current placement. After the first iteration, the current placement is the one selected from the previous iteration.

At step 5, a set P_0 of candidates is randomly generated. These candidates are repaired at step 6 to ensure that P_0 contains only feasible solutions. Then, the algorithm tries to improve candidates at step 7 using local search. With the obtained non-dominated solutions, the first set P_{known} (Pareto set approximation) is generated at step 8. After initialization in step 9, evolution begins (between steps 10 and 18).

The evolutionary process basically follows the same behavior: solutions are selected from the union of P_{known} with the evolutionary set of solutions (or population) also known as P_u (step 11), crossover and mutation operators are applied as usual (step 12), and eventually solutions are repaired, as there may be infeasible solutions (step 13). Improvements of solutions of the evolutionary population P_u may be generated at step 14 using local search (local optimization operators).

At step 15, the Pareto set approximation P_{known} is updated (if applicable); while at step 16 the generation (or iteration) counter is updated. At step 17 a new evolutionary population P_u is selected. The evolutionary process is repeated until the algorithm meets a stopping criterion (such as a maximum number of generations), returning one solution $P_{selected}$ from the set of non-dominated solutions P_{known} in step 20, using one of the selection strategies presented in Sect. 3.3.

It should be mentioned that the main phases of Algorithm 5 are based on the ones previously presented in Sect. 2 (see Sects. 2.3.1–2.3.5 for details).

3.3   Solution Selection Strategies

Several challenges need to be addressed for a MaVMP problem with reconfiguration of VMs. In Pareto-based algorithms, the Pareto set approximation can include a large number of non-dominated solutions; therefore, selecting one of the non-dominated solutions (step 19 of Algorithm 5) can be considered as a new difficulty for MaVMP problems with reconfiguration of VMs.

The work presented in [7] performed an experimental evaluation of the following five selection strategies: (1) random, (2) preferred solution, (3) minimum distance

---

Algorithm 5: Extended Memetic Algorithm

Data: datacenter infrastructure (see Section 3.1.1) and solution selection strategy parameter
Result: solution $P_{selected}$ for instant t

1 $t = 0$
2 **while** *there are VM requests to process* **do**
3 | check if the problem has a solution
4 | $P_{previous} = P_{selected}$
5 | initialize set of solutions P_0
6 | $P_0' =$ repair infeasible solutions of P_0
7 | $P_0'' =$ apply local search to solutions of P_0'
8 | update set of solutions P_{known} from P_0''
9 | $u = 0; P_u = P_0''$
10 | **while** *is not stopping criterion* **do**
11 | | $Q_u =$ selection of solutions from $P_u \cup P_{known}$
12 | | $Q_u' =$ crossover and mutation of solutions of Q_u
13 | | $Q_u'' =$ repair infeasible solutions of Q_u'
14 | | $Q_u''' =$ apply local search to solutions of Q_u''
15 | | update set of solutions P_{known} from Q_u'''
16 | | increment number of generations u
17 | | $P_u =$ non-dominated sorting from $P_u \cup Q_u'''$
18 | **end**
19 | $P_{selected} =$ selected solution (selection strategy parameter)
20 | **return** $P_{selected}$
21 | increment instant t; reset P_{known}
22 **end**

to origin, (4) lexicographic order (provider preference), and (5) lexicographic order (service preference), as next explained.

3.3.1   Random (S1)

Considering that the Pareto set approximation is composed by non-dominated solutions, randomly selecting one of the solutions could be an acceptable strategy.

3.3.2   Preferred Solution (S2)

A solution is defined as preferred to another non-comparable solution when it is better in more objective functions [28]. When several solutions can be considered as preferred ones (there is a tie), only one of these solutions is randomly selected.

3.3.3   Minimum Distance to Origin (S3)

The solution with the minimum Euclidean distance to the origin is selected, considering all normalized objective functions in a minimization context. For this purpose, $f_3(x, t)$ is redefined as the difference between the maximum possible revenue at instant t and the attainable revenue of each possible solution. When several solutions have equal Euclidean distance, only one of these solutions is randomly selected.

3.3.4   Lexicographic Order

Each objective function is given in an order of evaluation, similar to the ordering of letters in a dictionary. The objective functions can be arranged in several ways in order of priority. The work presented in [7] proposes two different lexicographic orders, representing the possible preferences associated to providers (provider preference) and quality of service (service preference). Logically, different orders of priority criteria may be considered depending on each specific context.

- **Provider preference order** (S4): The priority order is: (1) economical revenue, (2) power consumption, (3) inter-VM network traffic, (4) number of VM migrations and (5) network traffic overhead for VM migration.
- **Service preference order** (S5): The priority order is: (1) number of VM migrations, (2) network traffic overhead for VM, (3) inter-VM network traffic, (4) power consumption, and (5) economical revenue.

The work presented in [7] evaluates the above-mentioned selection strategies, where several experiments were performed. The following subsections summarize the experimental results.

Table 6 Hardware configuration of PM types considered in Experiment 4

PM type	Hardware configuration				Number of PMs	
	Hcpu [ECU]	Hram [GB]	Hhdd [GB]	pmax [W]	10 × 100.vmp	100 × 1000.vmp
h1.small	180	512	10,000	1,000	3	30
h1.medium	260	512	10,000	1,350	3	30
h1.large	350	1,024	10,000	1,800	3	30
h2.large	400	1,024	10,000	2,000	1	10
Total PMs					10	100

Table 7 Instance types of VMs considered in experiments. For notation see Eq. (20)

Instance type	Vcpu [ECU]	Vram [GB]	Vhdd [GB]	R [$]
t2.micro	1	1	0	9
t2.small	1	2	0	18
t2.medium	2	4	0	37
m3.medium	1	4	4	50
m3.large	2	8	32	100
m3. × large	4	15	80	201
m3.2 × large	8	30	160	403
c3.large	2	4	32	75
c3. × large	4	8	80	151
c3.2 × large	8	15	160	302
c3.4 × large	16	30	320	604
c3.8 × large	32	60	640	1209
r3.large	2	15	32	126
r3. × large	4	30	80	252
r3.2 × large	8	61	160	504
r3.4 × large	16	122	0	320
r3.8 × large	32	244	0	320

3.4 Experimental Environment

The Extended Memetic Algorithm presented in Sect. 3.2 was implemented using the ANSI C programming language (gcc). The source code is available online.[4]

The experimental scenarios included heterogeneous PMs with hardware configurations described in Table 6. Considered VMs were based on real instance types offered by Amazon Elastic Compute Cloud (EC2) [29] as presented in Table 7.

---

[4]https://github.com/dihara/MaVMP.

The experiments were performed considering two different experimental scenarios (a small and a medium sized datacenter infrastructure) simulating a theoretical day (i.e., 24 h) in a datacenter where VMs requests are received and processed hourly. In these experiments, the following configurations were considered:

- **10 × 100.vmp**: Problem instance with 10 PMs initially running 100 VMs.
- **100 × 1000.vmp**: Problem instance with 100 PMs initially running 1,000 VMs.

For simplicity, in what follows, the traffic between VMs was considered as constant, i.e., $T_{i,j}(t) = T_{i,j}$. The initial load for Experiment 4 represents 28% of CPU resources while in Experiment 5, it is 33% of CPU resources (see Table 9).

Experiments for each selection strategy were repeated 10 times, given the probabilistic nature of the Extended Memetic Algorithm. Results are analyzed in Sect. 3.5. The average number of non-dominated solutions found with each selection strategy is shown in Table 8. It can be seen that in both experiments, a similar average number of solutions and standard deviation were observed for all strategies.

Table 8 Number of non-dominated solutions per selection strategy

Selection strategy	10 × 100.vmp		100 × 1000.vmp	
	Average	Standard Dev.	Average	Standard Dev.
Random	25.2	8.6	36.2	11.3
Preferred solution	24.0	8.6	37.7	9.2
Distance to origin	21.4	8.7	30.8	10.1
Provider preference	20.8	9.9	24.0	8.7
Service preference	34.5	9.5	38.9	9.1

Table 9 Details of Experiment 4

Parameters	10 × 100.vmp	100 × 1000.vmp
# PM	10	100
Available CPU	2,770	27,700
Initial # VM	100	1,000
VMs with SLA 0	26	325
VMs with SLA 1	38	344
VMs with SLA 2	36	331
Initial CPU load	784 (28%)	9,023 (33%)
Initial revenue	33,973 US$	330,645 US$
Discrete time instants	24 h	24 h

Selection strategy	Objective functions averages					Dominance (row ≻ column) S1 S2 S3 S4 S5					Preference (row ≻$_p$ column) S1 S2 S3 S4 S5				
	$f_1(x)$	$f_2(x)$	$f_3(x)$	$f_4(x)$	$f_5(x)$	S1	S2	S3	S4	S5	S1	S2	S3	S4	S5
10x100.vmp															
S1	9,908	19,981	32,623	44	1,526	■					■				
S2	9,827	19,991	32,623	8	180		■				≻	■		≻	
S3	9,639	19,228	32,623	6	124	≻	≻	■			≻	≻	■	≻	≻
S4	8,543	21,038	32,623	19	520				■		≻			■	
S5	10,395	21,957	32,623	5	150					■					■
100x1000.vmp															
S1	104,559	371,664	325,217	650	26,886	■					■				
S2	104,835	373,467	325,217	37	1,204		■				≻	■		≻	
S3	104,378	370,489	325,217	26	804	≻	≻	■			≻	≻	■	≻	
S4	103,175	374,210	325,217	92	3,531				■		≻			■	
S5	104,860	373,230	325,217	20	618					■		≻		≻	■

Fig. 3 Selection Strategy Comparison. For selection strategy notation see Sect. 3.3

3.5 Experiment 4: Selection Strategy Evaluation

Figure 3 summarizes the results obtained in both experiments. As expected, when the lexicographic order is used, the most important objective function is the one with the best results, i.e., the S4 strategy (provider preference) obtains the best results in power consumption $f_1(x, t)$, with 20% less power consumption than the worst strategy in the 10×100.vmp instance and 2% less power consumption than the worst strategy in 100×1000.vmp. Analogously, when service perspective is prioritized (strategy S5), the objective functions $f_4(x, t)$ and $f_5(x, t)$ obtain the best results (Table 9).

However, as the focus of the work presented in [7] is the simultaneous optimization of all five objective functions with a multi-objective approach, a comparison is made considering the concept of Pareto dominance. As seen in Fig. 3 (dominance column), the S3 strategy dominates S2 and S1 in both experiments; however, it is non-comparable with respect to S4 and S5 in both tested problem instances.

Given that S3 cannot be declared as the best strategy considering exclusively Pareto dominance, a further comparison of selection strategies using the preference criteria (i.e., larger number of better objective functions) [5] is presented in the corresponding column of Fig. 3.

It may seem intuitive that the S2 strategy (that uses the preference criterion) should be the best; however, Table 3 shows that strategy S3 is preferred not only to S2 but also to S1 and to S4 in both tested problem instances. Additionally, it can be seen that S3 is preferred to S5 in problem instance 10×100.vmp while no strategy is preferred to S3, indicating that S3 (distance to origin) is the best strategy for solving the presented MaVMP problem formulation with reconfiguration of VMs.

As a consequence of the above results, for production cloud datacenters, instead of calculating all the Pareto set or a Pareto set approximation, the S3 strategy (distance to origin) could be used to combine all considered objective functions into only one objective function, therefore solving the studied problem considering a Multi-Objective solved as Mono-Objective (MAM) approach. It is important to mention that the obtained results are consistent with the selection strategy evaluation presented in [28] for solution of a traffic engineering problem in computer networks.

4   Open Research Problems: Many-Objective VMP for Cloud Computing Environments

After demonstrating the viability to formulate and solve MaVMP problems for initial placement of VMs and MaVMP problems with reconfiguration of VMs, this section presents relevant open research topics for the formulation and resolution of MaVMP problems for cloud computing environments.

4.1   IaaS Environments for VMP Problems

In real-world environments, IaaS providers dynamically receive requests for the placement of VMs with different characteristics according to different dynamic parameters. In this context, preliminary results of the authors identified that the most relevant dynamic parameters in the VMP literature are [30]: (1) resource capacities of VMs (associated to vertical elasticity) [31], (2) number of VMs of a cloud service (associated to horizontal elasticity) [32] and (3) utilization of resources of VMs (relevant for overbooking) [20]. Considering the mentioned dynamic parameters, environments for IaaS formulations of VMP problems could be classified by one or more of the following classification criteria: (1) service elasticity and (2) overbooking of physical resources [30].

In order to model these advanced IaaS environments, cloud services (i.e., a set of interrelated VMs) are considered instead of just VMs. A cloud service may represent cloud infrastructures for basic services such as Domain Name Service (DNS), web applications or even elastic applications such as MapReduce programs [30].

To the best of the authors' knowledge, there is no published work considering all these fundamental criteria, directly related to the most relevant dynamic parameters in the specialized literature [30]. CSPs efficiently solving formulations of the VMP problem in advanced IaaS environments considering service elasticity, including both vertical and horizontal scaling of cloud services, as well as overbooking of physical resources, including both server (CPU and RAM) and networking resources will represent a considerable advance on this research area and its cloud datacenters will be able to scale according to trending types of requirements with sufficient flexibility. A recommended path for future work is exploring and addressing challenges of particular environments identified in [30] as research opportunities before considering this advanced IaaS environment for solving VMP problems.

4.2 Uncertainty in VMP for Cloud Computing

Extensive research of uncertainty issues could be found in several fields such as: computational biology and decision-making in economics, just to cite a few. Particularly, studies of uncertainty for cloud computing are limited and uncertainty in resource allocation and service provisioning have not been adequately addressed, representing research challenges [33].

According to [33], uncertainties in cloud computing could be grouped into: (1) parametric and (2) system uncertainties. Parametric uncertainties may represent incomplete knowledge and variation of parameters, as presented in the considered VMP problem. The analysis of these uncertainties quantifies the effect of random input parameters on model outputs [33].

Research challenges in the context of VMP problems include designing novel resource management strategies to handle uncertainty in an effective way, as described by Tchernykh et al. in [33]. IaaS providers must satisfy requests for virtual resources in highly dynamic environments. Due to the randomness of customer requests, algorithms for solving VMP problems should be evaluated under uncertainty.

4.3 Two-Phase Optimization Schemes for VMP Problems

The VMP could be formulated as both online and offline optimization problems [2]. A VMP problem formulation is considered to be online when solution techniques (e.g., heuristics) makes decisions on-the-fly, without knowing upcoming VM requests [24]. On the other hand, if solution techniques have a complete knowledge of future VM requests of a problem instance, the VMP problem formulation is considered to be offline [11]. Considering the on-demand model of cloud computing with dynamic resource provisioning and dynamic workloads of cloud applications [34], the resolution of VMP problems should be performed as fast as possible in order to be able to support these dynamic requirements. In this context, the VMP problem for IaaS environments was mostly studied in the VMP literature considering online formulations, taking into consideration that VM requests are unknown a priori [2].

It is important to consider that online decisions made along the operation of a cloud computing infrastructure negatively affects the quality of obtained solutions of VMP problems when comparing to offline decisions [35]. Clearly, offline algorithms present a substantial advantage over online alternatives, when considering the quality of obtained solutions. This advantage is presented for the following two main reasons: (1) an offline algorithm has a complete knowledge of future VM requests of a VMP problem instance (which is impracticable on real-world IaaS environments because VM requests are uncertain) and (2) it considers migration of VMs between PMs, reconfiguring the placement when convenient.

To improve the quality of solutions obtained by online algorithms, the VMP problem could be formulated as a two-phase optimization problem, combining advantages of online and offline formulations for IaaS environments. In this context, VMP problems could be decomposed into two different subproblems: (1) incremental VMP (iVMP) and (2) VMP reconfiguration (VMPr) [36]. This two-phase optimization strategy combines both online (iVMP) and offline (VMPr) algorithms for solving each considered VMP subproblem.

The iVMP subproblem is considered for attending dynamic arriving requests where VMs should be created, modified and removed at runtime. Consequently, this subproblem should be formulated as an online problem and solved as fast as possible, where existing heuristics could be reasonably appropriate. Additionally, the VMPr subproblem is considered for improving the quality of solutions obtained by the iVMP, reconfiguring a current placement $P(t)$ through migration of VMs between PMs to an improved placement $P'(t)$. This VMPr subproblem could be formulated offline, where alternative solution techniques could result more suitable (e.g., metaheuristics).

The considered iVMP + VMPr optimization scheme has been briefly studied in the specialized literature. Consequently, several challenges for IaaS environments remain unaddressed or could be improved, considering that only basic methods have been proposed, specifically for VMPr Triggering and VMPr Recovering methods:

- **Research Question 1 (RQ1)**: when the VMPr problem should be triggered? (VMPr Triggering method).
- **Research Question 2 (RQ2)**: what should be done with cloud service requests arriving during the VMPr reconfiguration period? (VMPr Recovering method).

Research should advance by proposing more sophisticated VMPr Triggering methods, probably considering several different objective functions, as presented in this chapter for MaVMP problems. Additionally, most of the existing research works do not consider any VMPr Recovering method, when applicable. Only Calcavecchia et al. studied in [37] a very basic approach, canceling the VMPr whenever a new request is received. Consequently, the VMPr is only performed in periods with no requests that could result unrealistic for IaaS providers. Future works could be focused on proposing novel VMPr Recovering methods.

References

1. López-Pires, F., & Barán, B. (2015). Virtual machine placement literature review. http://arxiv.org/abs/1506.01509.
2. López-Pires, F., & Barán, B. (2015). A virtual machine placement taxonomy. In *Proceedings of the 2015 IEEE/ACM 15th International Symposium on Cluster, Cloud and Grid Computing*. IEEE Computer Society.
3. Cheng, J., Yen, G. G., & Zhang, G. (2014, October). A many-objective evolutionary algorithm based on directional diversity and favorable convergence. In *2014 IEEE International Conference on Systems, Man and Cybernetics (SMC)* (pp. 2415–2420).
4. Farina, M., & Amato, P. (2002). On the optimal solution definition for many-criteria optimization problems. In *Proceedings of the NAFIPS-FLINT International Conference* (pp. 233–238).

5. von Lücken, C., Barán, B., & Brizuela, C. (2014). A survey on multi-objective evolutionary algorithms for many-objective problems. *Computational Optimization and Applications*, 1–50.
6. Guzek, M., Bouvry, P., & Talbi, E.-G. (2015). A survey of evolutionary computation for resource management of processing in cloud computing. *Computational Intelligence Magazine, IEEE, 10*(2), 53–67.
7. Ihara, D., López-Pires, F., & Barán, B. (2015). Many-objective virtual machine placement for dynamic environments. In *Proceedings of the 2015 IEEE/ACM 8th International Conference on Utility and Cloud Computing*. IEEE Computer Society.
8. López-Pires, F., & Barán, B. (2015). A many-objective optimization framework for virtualized datacenters. In *Proceedings of the 2015 5th International Conference on Cloud Computing and Service Science* (pp. 439–450).
9. López-Pires, F., & Barán, B. (2017). Cloud computing resource allocation taxonomies. *International Journal of Cloud Computing* (To appear).
10. Gao, Y., Guan, H., Qi, Z., Hou, Y., & Liu, L. (2013). A multi-objective ant colony system algorithm for virtual machine placement in cloud computing. *Journal of Computer and System Sciences, 79*, 1230–1242.
11. López-Pires, F., & Barán, B. (2013). Multi-objective virtual machine placement with service level agreement: A memetic algorithm approach. In *Proceedings of the 2013 IEEE/ACM 6th International Conference on Utility and Cloud Computing* (pp. 203–210). IEEE Computer Society.
12. Tomás, L., & Tordsson, J. (2013). Improving cloud infrastructure utilization through overbooking. In *Proceedings of the 2013 ACM Cloud and Autonomic Computing Conference, CAC'13* (pp. 5:1–5:10). New York, NY, USA.
13. Beloglazov, A., Abawajy, J., & Buyya, R. (2012). Energy-aware resource allocation heuristics for efficient management of data centers for cloud computing. *Future Generation Computer Systems, 28*(5), 755–768.
14. Shrivastava, V., Zerfos, P., Lee, K.-W., Jamjoom, H., Liu, Y.-H., & Banerjee, S. (2011). Application-aware virtual machine migration in data centers. In *INFOCOM, 2011 Proceedings IEEE* (pp. 66–70). IEEE.
15. Donoso, Y., Fabregat, R., Solano, F., Marzo, J.-L., & Barán, B. (2005). Generalized multiobjective multitree model for dynamic multicast groups. In *2005 IEEE International Conference on Communications, 2005. ICC 2005* (Vol. 1, pp. 148–152). IEEE.
16. Báez, M., Zárate, D., & Barán, B. (2007). Adaptive memetic algorithms for multi-objective optimization. In *2007 XXXIII Latin American Computing Conference (CLEI)* (Vol. 2007).
17. Deb, K., Pratap, A., Agarwal, S., & Meyarivan, T. A. M. T. (2002). A fast and elitist multiobjective genetic algorithm: NSGA-II. *IEEE Transactions on Evolutionary Computation, 6*(2), 182–197.
18. Coello Coello, C., Lamont, G. B., & Van Veldhuizen, D. A. (2007). *Evolutionary algorithms for solving multi-objective problems*. Springer.
19. Sun, M., Gu, W., Zhang, X., Shi, H., & Zhang, W. (2013). A matrix transformation algorithm for virtual machine placement in cloud. In *2013 12th IEEE International Conference on Trust, Security and Privacy in Computing and Communications (TrustCom)* (pp. 1778–1783). IEEE.
20. Anand, A., Lakshmi, J., & Nandy, S. K. (2013). Virtual machine placement optimization supporting performance SLAs. In *2013 IEEE 5th International Conference on Cloud Computing Technology and Science (CloudCom)* (Vol. 1, pp. 298–305). IEEE.
21. Sato, K., Samejima, M., & Komoda, N. (2013). Dynamic optimization of virtual machine placement by resource usage prediction. In *2013 11th IEEE International Conference on Industrial Informatics (INDIN)* (pp. 86–91). IEEE.
22. Shi, L., Butler, B., Botvich, D., & Jennings, B. (2013). Provisioning of requests for virtual machine sets with placement constraints in iaas clouds. In *2013 IFIP/IEEE International Symposium on Integrated Network Management (IM 2013)* (pp. 499–505). IEEE.
23. Li, W., Tordsson, J., & Elmroth, E. (2011). Modeling for dynamic cloud scheduling via migration of virtual machines. In *2011 IEEE Third International Conference on Cloud Computing Technology and Science (CloudCom)* (pp. 163–171). IEEE.

24. Beloglazov, A., & Buyya, R. (2012). Optimal online deterministic algorithms and adaptive heuristics for energy and performance efficient dynamic consolidation of virtual machines in cloud data centers. *Concurrency and Computation: Practice and Experience, 24*(13), 1397–1420.

25. López-Pires, F., & Barán, B. (2017). Many-objective virtual machine placement. *Journal of Grid Computing* (In Review).

26. Tomás, L., & Tordsson, J. (2013). Improving cloud infrastructure utilization through over-booking. In *Proceedings of the 2013 ACM Cloud and Autonomic Computing Conference* (p. 5).

27. Svärd, P., Hudzia, B., Walsh, S., Tordsson, J., & Elmroth, E. (2015). Principles and performance characteristics of algorithms for live vm migration. *ACM SIGOPS Operating Systems Review, 49*(1), 142–155.

28. Talavera, F., Crichigno, J., & Barán, B. (2005). Policies for dynamical multiobjective environment of multicast traffic engineering. In *IEEE ICT*.

29. Amazon Web Services (2015, June). Amazon ec2 instances. http://aws.amazon.com/ec2/instance-types/.

30. Ortigoza, J., López-Pires, F., & Barán, B. (2016, April). A taxonomy on dynamic environments for provider-oriented virtual machine placement. In *2016 IEEE International Conference on Cloud Engineering (IC2E)* (pp. 214–215).

31. Li, K., Wu, J., & Blaisse, A. (2013). Elasticity-aware virtual machine placement for cloud datacenters. In *2013 IEEE 2nd International Conference on Cloud Networking (CloudNet)* (pp. 99–107). IEEE.

32. Wang, W., Chen, H., & Chen, X. (2012). An availability-aware virtual machine placement approach for dynamic scaling of cloud applications. In *2012 9th International Conference on Ubiquitous Intelligence & Computing and 9th International Conference on Autonomic & Trusted Computing (UIC/ATC)* (pp. 509–516). IEEE.

33. Tchernykh, A., Schwiegelsohn, U., Alexandrov, V., & Talbi, E.-G. (2015). Towards understanding uncertainty in cloud computing resource provisioning. *Procedia Computer Science, 51*, 1772–1781.

34. Mell, P., & Grance, T. (2009). The nist definition of cloud computing. *National Institute of Standards and Technology, 53*(6), 50.

35. López-Pires, F., Barán, B., Amarilla, A., Benítez, L., Ferreira, R., & Zalimben, S. (2016). An experimental comparison of algorithms for virtual machine placement considering many objectives. In *9th Latin America Networking Conference (LANC)* (pp. 75–79).

36. Zheng, Q., Li, R., Li, X., Shah, N., Zhang, J., Tian, F., et al. (2015). Virtual machine consolidated placement based on multi-objective biogeography-based optimization. *Future Generation Computer Systems*.

37. Calcavecchia, N. M., Biran, O., Hadad, E., & Moatti, Y. (2012). Vm placement strategies for cloud scenarios. In *2012 IEEE 5th International Conference on Cloud Computing (CLOUD)* (pp. 852–859). IEEE.

Performance Modeling and Optimization of Live Migration of Virtual Machines in Cloud Infrastructure

Minal Patel, Sanjay Chaudhary and Sanjay Garg

Abstract The cloud infrastructure is a base layer to support various types of computational and storage requirements of the users using Internet-based service provisioning. Virtualization enables cloud computing to compute different workloads using cloud service models. The performance of each cloud model depends on how effectively workloads are managed to give optimal performance. The process of workload management is obtained by migrating virtual machines using the pre-copy algorithm. In this chapter, we have improved pre-copy algorithm for virtual machine migration to calculate the optimal total migration time and the downtime using three proposed models: (i) compression model, (ii) prediction model, and (iii) performance model. The performance evaluation of different techniques using these three models is discussed in detail. Finally, we present open research problems in the field of resource utilization in cloud computing.

1 Introduction

This section presents the basics of cloud computing and virtualization. The technology of virtualization provides the ability to build a system which runs multiple operating systems simultaneously on the same physical machine. Due to this invention, virtualization provides various services that include migration, load balancing, debugging, and replication [1]. Virtualization is a program running on a virtual

M. Patel (✉)
Computer Engineering Department, A.D. Patel Institute of Technology,
Karamsad, Gujarat, India
e-mail: mppatel.adit@gmail.com

S. Chaudhary
School of Engineering and Applied Science, Ahmedabad University,
Ahmedabad, Gujarat, India
e-mail: sanjay.chaudhary@ahduni.edu.in

S. Garg
Institute of Technology, Nirma University, Ahmedabad, Gujarat, India
e-mail: gargsv@gmail.com

© Springer Nature Singapore Pte Ltd. 2017
S. Chaudhary et al. (eds.), *Research Advances in Cloud Computing*,
DOI 10.1007/978-981-10-5026-8_13

machine monitor (VMM) or a virtual set of hardware mapped to physical architecture. Virtualization provides a service that can be delivered anywhere and at anytime in cloud computing. Initially, the cloud was known as a computer network that could perform computer tasks effectively. The cloud is used to provide basic services for infrastructure, platform, and software. According to the definition of National Institute of Standards and Technology (NIST), cloud computing is the collection of three service models and four deployment models [2]. The cloud computing uses several utility-based applications such as server consolidation, data center management, high availability, automatic restart, disaster recovery, fault tolerance, test and development, etc.

The cloud manages following services as components: storage, communication and computing. Amazon is a well-known cloud computing company which provides cloud-based services. For example, Amazon S3 provides services for storage, Amazon EC2 provides communication and Amazon SQS provides network resources [2]. The main issue of handling virtualized resources is to balance workload in cloud computing. The computing service of a cloud requires load balancing between physical systems. The workload of running applications can be automatically balanced by migrating them to virtual machines [3, 4]. Live migration overcomes most difficulties of process migration used for transfer of ongoing processes. The OS migration has the following advantages compared to the process migration: (i) no residual dependencies (ii) automatic restarting mechanism and (iii) the ability to handle authentication issue. In residual dependencies, the host machine has to remain available to fulfill services of system calls in network-domain while VM migration process disconnects the host once the migration is completed. In virtualization, the user is not aware of an online game server or streaming media being migrated. The VM connects automatically without functioning like process migration to work with the kernel-state. During VM migration, operating system (OS) level issues for root access are not affected and the operator is not concerned about what is running on a virtual machine. The process migration has limitation over live migration to work with real-world applications of cloud computing [5].

In this chapter, following three models are developed: (i) compression model, (ii) prediction model and (iii) performance model. These models are evaluated to calculate downtime and total migration time of VM migration. The pre-copy technique has been selected and the same is modified for each model. The effectiveness of the above mentioned models is measured based on their ability to compress and predict dirty pages. Additionally, a dirty page rate model and a skip page rate model are also developed to improve the performance of VM migration.

1.1 Objectives and Scope

The data-centers in cloud computing provide services of infrastructure layer. The components of data-centers are mainly categorized into servers and networks, which are used for computation and storage, respectively. The primary objective of cloud-based infrastructure services is to provide efficient live migration of applications workload. The optimal computation of workloads depends on VM and its characteristics that can run cloud servers with load balancing, power management, fault tolerance and server consolidation activities. The migration of virtual machines that is the essential part of load balancing in the cloud which is focused in this chapter.

There are number of important issues raised for any live migration system: (i) criteria to select either pre-copy or post-copy technique (ii) selection of effective cloud platform for live migration (iii) selection of hypervisor under varying workloads (iv) issues of dirty rate as well as data rate parameters to manage (a) adaptive mechanism and (b) nonadaptive mechanism of live migration (v) selection of data set and dependency of parameters for live migration model.

The migration process has main three parameters to perform optimal migration: (i) VM size (ii) dirty rate and (iii) data rate (bandwidth). This chapter focuses on following tasks in order to develop live migration system:

- To Enhance pre-copy algorithm for live migration system to get optimal total migration time and downtime.
- To configure type-2 architecture using Xen and Ubuntu OS on DRBD storage.
- To propose combined approach of live migration to improve the performance.
- To design prediction model for live migration.
- To propose mathematical model to compute performance metrics on real dataset.

The scope of this chapter is addressed with following issues:

- In the proposed live migration system, the pre-copy algorithm [5–8] is chosen for development of cloud system and it is modified with three proposed models. The post-copy is not considered due to its limitation and it also gives poor performance on memory intensive pages.
- This proposed system is configured based on Xen [5, 6, 9] hypervisor and DRBD protocol. The type-2-based architecture has been configured with Xen on the top of Ubuntu OS. The experiments are tested on a real data set for both, prediction model and performance model.
- The system is tested on normal workloads (idle, kernel, and webserver) and complex workloads (RUBIS and OLTP) and finally, the results of proposed framework are compared to existing framework. Due to complex nature of workloads and their availability issues, this chapter is tested with chosen five workloads.

2 Migration in Cloud Computing

This section describes the model of live migration. It also presents two techniques: (i) pre-copy migration and (ii) post-copy migration.

2.1 Live Migration

The X86 architecture of Xen hypervisor [10, 11] is divided into rings, each ring has access to specific layer and privileges. User application has access to lower layer ring 3 and OS system has access to ring 0 which has full privilege to access hardware. The ring 1 and the ring 2 are not in use, so the application user cannot execute a system call or instruction which is reserved for OS access while residing over ring 3. Xen has a Xenmotion tool to migrate a VM. The Xenmotion can be operated on multiple hosts based on resource pool mechanism. Xen requires to run all hosts with same family and configuration. Live migration is performed based on two main configuration requirements: (i) gigabit ethernet and (ii) shared remote storage. The enterprise and platinum edition of Xenserver provide load balancing feature.

Live migration [12] refers to the process of transferring a running VM from host to destination. The simple live migration activity is shown in Fig. 1 with shared storage. A migration is called the seamless live migration, when downtime of a VM during a live migration is not noticeable. Live migration can be achieved based on pre-copy and post-copy approaches. The following are live memory migration types [5]: (a) stop and copy (b) demand migration (c) iterative pre-copy. The pre-copy retains an up-to-date state of the VM at the source during migration, whereas with post-copy, the VM's state is distributed over both source and destination. If the destination fails during migration, pre-copy can recover the VM, whereas post-copy cannot.

The advantages of live migration are as follows [13]:

- Reduces IT cost and provides flexibility for server consolidation
- Reduces downtime and increases reliability
- Improves energy efficiency by running less number of servers
- Load balancing (utilizing more processing power)
- Resource locality and resource sharing
- Fault resilience, simplified system administration, and mobile computing

Fig. 1 Live VM migration

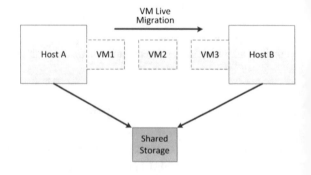

2.2 Pre-copy-Based Migration

The pre-copy technique is used to know running states of: the VM, storage or virtual disks, as well as existing client connections. In pre-copy model, few disk blocks are recopied if they are written during migration activity. While the stop-and-copy condition is raised, the hypervisor starts the final iteration and copies the remaining memory pages. Three major performance metrics of a live migration are: service downtime, total migration time, and total pages transferred [5].

Migration process between two hosts has following stages [5]:

Stage 0: Pre-migration stage—in this, destination host is to be preselected where resources are able to make guaranteed migration.

Stage 1: Reservation—resources are already registered on the destination for starting migration and even if, in case of a failure of VM, the host can be safe.

Stage 2: Iterative pre-copy—all memory pages are copied in the first iteration and subsequently modified pages are iteratively copied until the last iteration.

Stage 3: Stop-and-copy—makes a copy of fix dirty pages after stopping VM, so the host is no longer required and the destination machine becomes the main host.

Stage 4: Activation—the destination host is activated and it executes the post-migration activities.

Pre-copy algorithm is shown in Fig. 2 as a flowchart, where D represents dirty pages and W represents skip pages. Further, it presents mathematical model of the pre-copy algorithm when stop-and-copy condition is trigged.

Iterative process time is represented by the following equation [14]:

$$\textit{Time taken by iteration}(i-1) = \textit{pages dirtied in iteration}(i-1) \ / \textit{page dirtyrate}$$

$$(1)$$

Total migration time is represented by the following equation [14]:

$$\textit{Total migration time} = \textit{time taken by iterations} + \textit{service downtime} \quad (2)$$

In Eq. (1), it is assumed that pages are transferred at the maximum capacity. In nonadaptive migration, the dirty rate is able to take available bandwidth for transferring pages. The total migration time is shown in Eq. (2).

The working of pre-copy algorithm [5] is as follows:

The pre-copy algorithm is executed with the input of initial memory size and given transfer rate. Until the stop-and-copy condition is fired, the iterative process executes for each iteration and it calculates the pre-copy time for each iteration given by Eq. (1). When the pre-copy-based migration is reached to the stop-and-copy condition, total migration time is calculated by Eq. (2) and downtime is calculated based on the response time of last iteration.

Fig. 2 Flowchart of
Pre-copy algorithm

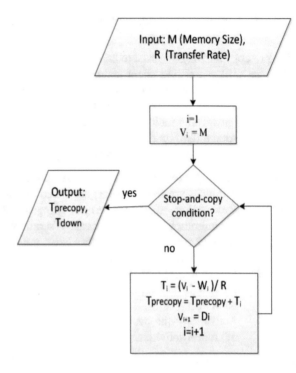

Figure 2 discusses stop-and-copy condition which is shown below [15]:

- The iterations have the maximum limit of 29.
- Limit on the maximum amount of data to be migrated is in the order of three times the size of RAM.
- The number of pages dirtied are 50, and it is considered a base threshold value at the time of current iteration.
- The rate of dirtying page of the last iteration is greater than the threshold (in Mbps).

This chapter is contributed on three aspects of live migration system using precopy algorithm. They are: (i) compression model for compressing pages during migration, (ii) prediction model for predicting dirty pages in advance, and (iii) performance model for analyzing dirty and skip pages during migration.

2.3 Post-copy-Based Migration

Post-copy sends each page exactly once over the network during a migration process. In contrast, pre-copy transfers the same page multiple times if the page is dirtied repeatedly at the source during migration.

Post-copy [16] includes the transfer of memory data after process state is transferred to destination. Memory faults in migration process are the demand-page over the network called self-ballooning and this mechanism is used to manage faults. There are four variants of post-copy: (i) demand paging, (ii) active push, (iii) pre-paging, and (iv) dynamic self-ballooning.

- Demand paging: When VM resumes target, page faults can be served over network for any page access. Network latency can be calculated which makes VM to be served at maximum cost.
- Active push: The source node can reduce the duration of residual dependencies to push the VM's pages when VM executes target. Demand paging handles most faults that are generated when active push avoids transferring pages in target VM. Demand paging or active push transfers each page.
- Pre-paging: It is used to hide the latency of page faults. It is used to predict future working set and loading of pages before accessing them.
- Dynamic self-ballooning: It refers to artificially making the request for memory within a guest OS and releasing that memory back to the hypervisor. The purpose of ballooning is used for memory resizing used in VMWare and Xen.

3 Compression Model

This section discusses logical flow of pre-copy algorithm. It also presents the algorithmic issues of live migration that are divided again into three categories. The evaluation of proposed compression model is briefly discussed at the end.

3.1 Logical Flow of Pre-copy Algorithm for Live Migration

The bitmap structure of Xen is used for iterative process of pre-copy algorithm. The Xen's pre-copy algorithm has three types of bitmap: (i) to_send, (ii) to_skip, and (iii) to_fix [5].

- to_send: This bitmap will send pages in the subsequent round, if pages have already been re-dirtied since last iteration and those pages are in non-dirty status.
- to_skip: If pages are dirty in current iteration, these pages are to be skipped in the next iteration.
- to_fix: To_fix bitmap considers those pages that gets modified frequently and they are sent to stop-and-copy phase during the last round.

Before starting VM migration process between two hosts, DRBD block is created on both hosts. Each virtual machine is installed on the DRBD resource which resides on the top of LVM. The logical flow of live migration will start to execute pre-copy after starting DRBD service on both hosts. The detailed steps for the working of pre-copy in Xen are given below [14, 17]:

Step 1: Initialization of pages

In this step, total number of guest pages and shadow pages are assigned using bitmap of Xen. The shadow pages are used in Xen for managing virtualization at the time of running VM to find updated pages. In Xen, guests and Dom0 are able to map available pages using pfn (physical frame number) and mfn (machine frame number) frame structures, respectively.

Step 2: Page fault mechanism

When a guest is trying to modify the page table, the page fault occurs. After that, this information is applied in shadow page table as well as log-dirty bitmap which is used for page transferring. The Xen uses the shadow page mechanism to transfer pages for the guest before migration process starts.

Step 3: Check the set bit in dirty bitmap iteratively

In the beginning, all the pages are transferred and are set to write the protected mode. The process of live migration identifies the set bit in the log-dirty bitmap for making the arrangement of pages to transfer between the source and the destination. Iterative process of migration uses two parameters XEN_DOMCTL_SHADOW_OP_PEEK and XEN_DOMCTL_SHADOW_OP_CLEAN, and the function xc_shadow_control is used during this process. If to_skip bitmap returns, dirty bitmap is scanned using PEEK parameter. The PEEK then will copy the dirty bitmap to to_skip bitmap and will update the WWS accordingly. If to_send bitmap returns, dirty bitmap is scanned using CLEAN parameter. This parameter will copy dirty bitmap to to_send and clears internal copy in the current iteration. If to_fix bitmap returns, the frequently modified pages are collected in WWS.

Step 4: Procedure for last iteration

This step is executed based on violation of condition in any of four parameters: (i) the number of maximum iteration, (ii) the maximum amount of data to be migrated, (iii) threshold value for minimum number of pages of last round, and (iv) threshold value of page dirty rate. All remaining pages are being transferred in the stop-and-copy phase. At the end, the shadow page table is destroyed and VM migration process will be terminated. VM can be migrated back to the source whenever the ongoing activity is completed.

3.2 Algorithmic Issues for Live VM Migration

Three basic types to deal with live migration of VM are: (i) basic techniques of live migration for reducing dirty pages and the same are also applied for process migration mechanism, (ii) compression techniques for migration, and (iii) other/advanced techniques for migration.

Live migration techniques can be classified into the following categories:

- Techniques for reducing dirty pages

  - Stunning rogue processes & freeing page cache pages [5]
  - CPU scheduling techniques [8, 18–20]

- Compression techniques

  - MEMCOM—memory compression-based VM migration [7]
  - Delta compression [21]
  - Other compression techniques—delta, LZ etc. [22–24]

- Other techniques-based on threshold, page-replacement, and combined algorithms

  - LRU-based technique [6, 9]
  - Matrix bitmap algorithm [25]
  - HCA Hierarchical copy algorithm [26]
  - Workload adaptive live migration [27]
  - Combined techniques [22, 25, 28, 29]

In [8, 18, 19], improved pre-copy algorithm is able to reduce dirty pages at the cost of reducing CPU cycles and this is one of the older approaches for live migration. Compression techniques [7, 21–24] and other general techniques [6, 9, 25–27] have also their limitation to improve the performance of migration system. The improved pre-copy algorithms given in [25, 28, 29] are able to produce effective performance based on the combination of two techniques. Hence, our mechanism has focused the novel approach in which LRU and compression-based two different methods are combined.

3.3 Proposed Compression Model: Improved Pre-copy Algorithm Using Combined Approach

This section discusses the proposed compression model with the help of pseudo-code. The compression model is combined into two parts: (i) LRU stack distance algorithm and (ii) delta compression.

In Xen's pre-copy algorithm, pages are likely to be sent by checking corresponding bit in the to_skip bitmap. In LRU stack distance algorithm, pages will be sent by considering two parameters: (i) checking corresponding bit in the to_skip bitmap and (ii) the distance between LRU stack and the dirty count.

The working of stack distance is based on two steps [14, 17]: (i) calculation of the reuse distance of VM's pages and (ii) retrieving the information about updated pages which have not been sent to the destination system in the current iteration. The algorithm also continuously checks the status of WWS. The main theme of this algorithm works to manage more pages in WWS for better prediction of dirty pages and sends fewer updated pages compared to the pre-copy algorithm during iterative process.

Table 1 Pseudo-code of combined approach

iterm:maximum iteration
p2m_size: size of memory pages or total number of guest pages
i,j, dirtypages_count, lru_update: temporary variables
bitmaps: to_send, to_fix, lru_stack
if(not last iteration)
for(i=0; i < p2m_size; i++)
if(page is not in to_send bitmap)
lru_stack[page] contains dirtypages_count
if(page is in lru_update)
to_send(page) to 1
else
lru_stack[page] contains distance between pages
if(page is to be compressed & page is in cache)
generate delta and update cache
if(page is to be uncompressed & page is in cache)
decode page using delta and save page
if(not first iteration)
for(j=0; j ≤ iterm; j++)
for(i=0; i < p2m_size; i++)
if(distance < dirtypages_count)
lru_update for particular page to 1
lru_stack(page)=0
if(page is to be compressed & page is in cache)
generate delta and update cache
if(page is to be uncompressed & page is in cache)
decode page using delta and save page
if(last iteration)
copy all remaining dirty pages of lru_stack and to_fix to destination

The delta compression [14, 17] is able to give optimal performance for heavy workload scenario of VM migration. It compresses pages which are strings of 0's and 1's. The compression is performed by XORing with current page to previous page and differences are being sent to destination. The decompression is performed by decoding the result between outcome and the content of the page. The pseudo-code of combined algorithm is given in Table 1.

3.4 Performance Evaluation

The framework is set up with Xen 4.2 on Intel core i3 CPU 550 @ 3.20 GHz, 3.19 GHz, and 3.80 GB of RAM with 100 MBPS Ethernet switch. Host OS and guest OS are Ubuntu 12.04 LTS [14].

The total migration time and service time are measured for comparative analysis in our modified pre-copy algorithm. The stop-and-copy phase is used to evaluate service time and the total migration time. The total migration time is calculated by merging the total time of two phases: (i) pre-migration and (ii) iterative phase. In Xen, XL migrate command is used for live migration operations.

The compression model is tested on three application scenarios called workloads: idle system, kernel compile, static web server [14].

1. **Idle system**: An idle Ubuntu OS without running any applications.

2. **Kernel compile**: This is considered a balanced workload which is able to test memory, CPU, and disk performance.

3. **Static web server** [30–32]: Apache web server is migrated in this workload with observing the changes of static content at the high rate. A single client is configured with 100 concurrent connections having a request of a file sized 512 KB.

The performance evaluation for idle system has been tested with 512 MB RAM and 1 VCPU. The service time and the total migration time have been tested with 1024 MB RAM and 1 VCPU. The evaluation process of service time and total migration time is discussed below:

Performance Evaluation for Idle System

The evaluation has following points to discuss:

• This experiment calculates the total migration time for an idle system using three types: (i) non-shared storage, (ii) NFS, and (iii) DRBD.

• The observation shows that DRBD storage is able to give optimal total migration time so it can work better compared to NFS and without shared storage options.

Performance Evaluation for Service Time and Total Migration Time

The following points are observed for this evaluation:

• When the VM is idle (or none application running), the performance of service time is approximately same for Xen's pre-copy and proposed compression model.

• When the VM is having workload, the proposed compression model is able to perform better for kernel compile and web server workloads.

• The performance of total migration time for idle system and kernel compile workload is approximately same for Xen's pre-copy and proposed compression model.

• When the VM is heavily loaded, the proposed compression model is able to perform better than Xen's pre-copy for web server workloads.

The combined approach of live VM migration is proposed here and following points are concluded:

• The proposed compression model is the combined model which merges an LRU stack distance and delta compression algorithm. The LRU stack distance algorithm manages frequently updated pages and the delta compression optimizes complexity for compressing updated pages. The overall performance is able to reduce approximately 10% of total migration time and 19% of downtime using improve pre-copy method.

• The proposed compression model is tested on three different workloads. The performance evaluation has also been discussed.

- In future work, delta compression is able to merge with other live migration techniques to improve pre-copy. Other compression methods can also be applied to LRU stack distance for combined approach of live migration.

4 Prediction Model

In this section, the overview of time series is discussed. The time series is used to generate data based on past observations. It also presents the statistical and regression models for prediction of virtual machine migration. The evaluation of prediction model is given at the end of this section.

4.1 Introduction

Time series has attracted a research community for several decades due to its dynamic nature into modeling of data. It collects data based on past observations, which is able to show the real-world working model of a series [33, 34]. The forecasting analysis is classified into three ways: short-term, medium-term, and long-term. The short-term forecasting is limited time period events (weeks or months), medium-term is represented as the period of one to two years, and long-term forecasting can be taken for many years. Qualitative prediction techniques are independent and these methods are analyzed based on experts opinion. On the other side, quantitative forecasting methods are based on historical data. It can be divided into three models: time-series models, smoothing models, and regression models.

The activities in the forecasting process are as follows:

- Problem definition
- Data collection
- Data analysis
- Model selection and fitting
- Model validation
- Forecasting model deployment
- Monitoring forecasting model performance

General model of time series

A stationary time series is considered as strictly stationary if its properties are not affected with time. If joint probability distribution of any two observations y_t and y_{t+k} is same then it is called stationary time series. A nonstationary time series is a series which exhibits a trend and it can be forecasted with proper modeling if the trend is eliminated. The regression model is the technique to work with nonstationary series. The general model of time series is written as follows [35]:

$$y_t = \phi_0 + \phi_1 x_{t1} + \phi_1 x_{t2} + \cdots + \varepsilon_t \tag{3}$$

where, $t = 1, 2, \ldots, N$

Here, x_t-based terms are called signal or trend, which is a deterministic function of time. A residual term ε_t, also called noise, which follows a probability law. Here, ϕ represents constant term, y_t is a time series used to build a forecasting model and N represents the most recent or last available observation.

Statistical Probability Model Versus Statistical Learning Model [36]

Two types of time-series model are discussed in this section: (i) statistical model and (ii) machine learning-based regression model. Hidden Markov and ARIMA models are common statistical models. These models are used to predict the accuracy of time-series models which are designed based on probability criteria. A hidden Markov model (HMM) uses a Markov process with unobserved states [37], while ARIMA model [33, 34] is generated from a modified version of an auto-regressive moving average (ARMA) model. This model is classified by ARIMA (p, d, q), where p states the auto-regressive components, d is known for integrated components, and q states moving average components. The working of ARIMA has accuracy and wide scope compared to HMM [37].

The learning-based regression model is classified into three categories: (i) linear discriminant analysis (LDA), (ii) neural networks (NNs), and (iii) support vector machine (SVM) [35]. LDA is used with classification for the applications of statistics, pattern recognition, and machine learning domain. NN is another model which works with classification and regression-based modeling. The third model is based on SVM which is a known technique for classification, regression, and outlier detection. The SVM is worked with new features and it has better performance compared to neural networks and LDA [37].

The ARIMA model and SVR model are discussed in next sections, respectively.

4.2 ARIMA Model

ARIMA model [36] can perform the series with stationary data and also forecast the training data. ARIMA has three phases [35]: (i) identification phase (ii) estimation and testing phase (iii) forecast phase. In identification phase, stationary series is identified first. The parameters of time series are estimated using the ARIMA (p, d, q) in the second phase of the model. Two functions are prepared using p, d, and q parameters: (i) ACF (Autocorrelation function) and (ii) PACF (Partial autocorrelation function).

The basic equations for ARIMA are as follows [35]:

$$AR(p) : x_t = a_0 + a_1 x_{t-1} + a_2 x_{t-2} + \cdots + a_p x_{t-p} + e_t \tag{4}$$

$$MA(q) : x_t - a_0 = e_t + b_1 e_{t-1} + b_2 e_{t-2} + \cdots + b_q e_{t-q} \tag{5}$$

Table 2 Algorithm for prediction of dirty pages using ARIMA model

Import following files: (i) forecast library, (ii) tseries library and (iii) real data set (.csv) file
Plot time series
Check the time series whether it is homogenous or not
Get the difference of non-homogenous time series
Apply AR term and MA term given in Eq. (1.4) and Eq. (1.5) respectively to plot ACF and PACF
Examine these plots
Design suitable ARIMA model by calculating AIC values
Forecast time-series for next data

The basic AR term of ARIMA model is given in Eqs. (4) and (5) presents computation of MA term.

4.2.1 Forecasting Analysis of ARIMA Model on Real Data Set

The algorithmic process of ARIMA model for forecasting is represented in this section. We have developed here ARIMA model on real data set of live migration system. On the other side, ARIMA could be developed for analysis of hypothetical data but it is not useful for practical purpose. In this chapter, the storage of real data is used in matrix of 2400 (pages) X 30 (iterations).

The algorithm for dirty pages prediction [36] is given here and it is developed in R language [34]. The input to the process is the time-series data of dirty pages and the output is evaluated based on accuracy. The algorithm for prediction of dirty pages using ARIMA model is given in Table 2.

4.3 SVR Model

This section presents SVM-based SVR model in detail. The SVR model is used for prediction of dirty pages for live migration of virtual machine. It is used to evaluate accuracy of real data set [38]. The lacking of ARIMA model is that it works on universal approximation and so, for complex models, ARIMA model is quite difficult to design.

4.3.1 Classification and Regression Analysis

The five parameters of SVM are [39, 40]: linearly separable data, linearly non-separable data, generalized optimal separating hyperplane, generalization in high dimensional space, and kernel functions. The mathematical model of SVM is based on $f(x) = \text{sign}(w^T x + b)$. The function $f(x)$ is divided into two classes: +1 and −1. The label +1 for all x above the boundary and the label −1 for all x below the boundary. The support vectors are generated based on keeping maximum boundaries between

Table 3 Algorithm for prediction of dirty pages using SVR model

Import following files:(i) e1071 library and (ii) real data set (.csv) file
Find the suitable SVM kernel
Decide the input and output series data
Find the best values of cost, gamma and epsilon using cross-validation
Apply SVM kernel (RBF is chosen here because of its wide scope)
Design suitable regression model of SVM based on above parameters
Forecast time-series for next data

two classes. The SVM is used to work with optimization of data for obtaining global solution. Here, C(cost) and γ parameters are used for cross-validation in kernel mechanism of SVM. These parameters are able to classify and predict data for SVR model.

4.3.2 Forecasting Analysis of SVR Model on Real Data Set

The algorithm for dirty pages prediction using SVR model [36] is given here. The proposed algorithm is developed in R language [34]. The input to the process is the same discussed in ARIMA model that is time-series data of dirty pages and the output is evaluated based on accuracy. The algorithm for prediction of dirty pages using SVR model is given in Table 3.

4.4 Performance Evaluation

The comparison of actual dirty pages and predicted dirty pages is performed for both models in this section.

Performance Evaluation of ARIMA Model

The performance evaluation of ARIMA model is calculated based on algorithm given above. ARIMA model can be estimated using p,d, and q parameters of ACF and PACF plots. The suitable ARIMA models are estimated and evaluation of accuracy is compared between them. The improved pre-copy algorithm using ARIMA is able to predict dirty pages with approximately 91% accuracy. This model has been designed with taking differences of real data (so the value of d is taken to 1). The p and q parameters are estimated to 5 and 1, respectively.

Performance Evaluation of SVR Model

The prediction of dirty pages is generated using support vector-based regression model. The RBF kernel has been applied on regression parameters in the SVR model. The accuracy of SVR model is approximately 95% which is more than the accuracy of ARIMA model. The confusion matrix is prepared based on 200 instances of test data set. This matrix is prepared based on predicted condition for: (i) condition positive and (ii) condition negative. The accurate data was predicted for 190 instances (either predicted condition positive or negative) and non-predicted instances were 10 (either predicted condition positive or negative).

The SVR model (95%) is compared with following models for accuracy: (i) Base Model [41] (81%) (ii) Simulation Model [42] (90%) (iii) Refined Model [41] (90.50%) (iv) our ARIMA model (91%)

Following points are concluded here:

- The ARIMA-based improved pre-copy algorithm is able to predict dirty pages with approximately 91% accuracy and the SVR-based improved pre-copy algorithm is able to predict dirty pages with approximately 95% accuracy on real data set.
- The confusion matrix was prepared based on 200 instances of test data set. This matrix is able to mitigate false prediction problem of ARIMA model which has its limitation to generate results based on an approximate model for given data. The following parameters are taken to find prediction of time-series data: (i) MSE, RMSE, Box & Jenkins test (for ARIMA model) and (ii) parameters are cost, γ, and epsilon values (for SVR model).
- In the future work, optimization of live migration can be extended with other regression techniques.

5 Performance Model: Dirty Page Rate and Skip Page Rate Models

This section presents the detailed analysis of performance models. It describes first the performance models of the dirty rate of memory pages using dirty rate model. This chapter also presents the performance models of skip rate of memory pages using skip rate model. The evaluation of dirty page rate and skip page rate models are shown at the end.

5.1 Introduction

Each iteration of pre-copy algorithm has a number of dirty pages during migration. If the dirty pages are tracked and managed properly then network traffic can be reduced and system performance can be improved. Whenever a page is being transferred in live migration, it has the following properties: (i) non-dirty page (ii) dirty page (iii) skip page. The dirty page rate model is generated by taking the product of iteration period and the page dirty rate. The page dirty rate is recognized as the number of pages dirtied in a second [41]. The dirty page rate model is used for identifying pages which are likely to be dirtied for the number of iterations. The skip page rate model is a special case of dirty page mechanism. Using this model subsequent iterations are able to avoid sending of dirty pages to current iteration based on the skip bitmap of Xen.

Dirty bitmap, provided by hypervisors, is used to compute the number of dirty pages in any iteration. There are a number of dirty models existed for the live migration system. These models are classified into three categories (i) average dirty page rate method (ii) exponential dirty page rate method (iii) probability dirty page rate method. The mathematical model-based performance modeling of dirty page rate model and skip page rate model are proposed here. The migration log-based dirty page model and hot pages-based dirty page model have been discussed with the proposed vMeasure approach. Existing skip page rate models are also discussed.

5.1.1 Migration Log-Based Dirty Page Rate Model

The migration log-based exponential average method [41] works using an exponential moving average instead of simple average. Parameters for this model are shown in Table 4. Total pages transferred called network traffic is given by Eq. (6):

$$V_{mi} = V_m (1 - \lambda^{n+1}) / (1 - \lambda) \qquad (6)$$

where, $\lambda = D/R$, the ratio between dirtying rate and transmission rate.
Total migration time is given by Eq. (7) as follows:

$$T_{mi} = V_m/R * (1 - \lambda^{n+1}) / (1 - \lambda) \qquad (7)$$

During the stop-and-copy phase, the time is spent on resuming VM on destination host compared to downtime. This time is denoted as T_{resume}, which is constant and set it to 20 ms. The downtime is given by Eq. (8) as follows:

$$T_{down} = T_n + T_{resume} \qquad (8)$$

The total number of iterations are $log_\lambda[V_{th}/V_m]$ and it fulfills the inequality $V_n \leq V_{th}$. In [41], the network traffic can be reduced if the smaller size of memory image and smaller λ are maintained. The value of γ is evaluated as per γ equation ($\gamma = aT_i + bD + c$ where a, b and c are constants). The values of constants are measured by taking multiple observations of model parameters.

Table 4 Parameters of migration log-based model

V_m	Memory size of VM
V_{mi}	Network traffic or total number of pages
T_{mi}	Total migration time
T_{down}	Downtime
R	Transmission rate of memory
D	Dirty rate of memory
V_{th}	Threshold value transferred at the last iteration
W_s	Writable working set (set of hot pages which are being written frequently)

5.1.2 Hot Pages-Based Dirty Page Rate Model

The two types of hot pages are [43]: (i) Type-1: in this type-1, all pages are migrated with hot pages (ii) Type-2: when the VM is down, at that time, hot pages are transferred. The hot pages are based on locality of reference. These pages have higher rate of dirtying compared to other pages. If number of pages are small they have higher chances of modification than the others. In [43], the analytic performance model is presented to perform better network utilization with proposing optimal α value. Hot pages are the pages which have a higher rate of dirtying than the other pages. The dirty rate of hot pages model is represented by Eq. (9).

$$S = S_c * (1 - \beta) + S_h * \beta \ [\beta < 1] \tag{9}$$

where, β: fraction of hot pages

S_c: dirtying rate of the non-hot pages and

S_h: dirtying rate of the hot pages. $S_h > S_c$

This model is useful for the follwoing three cases: (i) dirty rate with uniformity, (ii) hot pages transferring during the pre-copy phase, and (iii) hot pages transferring during downtime phase. The mechanism of this algorithm is based on a fraction of α of the pages transferred during migration. This phase will continue until such fraction of α of the pages completed. If the value of α increases then the downtime will also increase so the lower α is maintained in this model. This model is able to give more network utilization during migration process.

5.1.3 Skip Page Rate Models

This section discusses two types of skip page rate models.

Existing skip models are [44]: (i) Hot Skip Model [43] and (ii) Migration Log Record-based Model [41]

(i) Hot Skip Model

The model is presented by

$W_i = \beta M$

β represents fraction of VM's memory pages that is hot and M represents pages allocated to the VM

W_i represents skip pages

(ii) Migration Log Record-based Model

The model is presented by

$W_i = \gamma D_i$

γ and D_i is the ratio correlating with the memory dirtying rate and the duration of each iteration. In this model, three coefficients are learned as per dirty page rate model [41].

5.2   Proposed Dirty Page Rate Model

The proposed model is developed based on two methods: (i) average dirty page rate method and (ii) exponential dirty page rate method. This model is designed based on the criteria of checking linearity of dirty pages. If dirty rate is linear then it calculates the memory pages based on average dirty page rate. If the dirty rate is nonlinear then it calculates the memory pages with taking maximum size of WWS.

The proposed algorithm works based on either of two cognitions as given below:

- maximum of $((W_{i+1})_{max}, (W_{i+1})_{avg})$ is taken for high dirty rate pages
- minimum of $((W_{i+1})_{max}, (W_{i+1})_{avg})$ is taken for low dirty rate pages

It has been proved by proposed model that the optimal migration time will be $(W_i)max/R$ (for memory intensive pages) otherwise $(W_i)avg/R$.

5.3   Proposed Skip Page Rate Model

In this section, proposed skip page rate model is discussed. The model is based on the hypothetical analysis. The size of VM and memory intensive pages are focused to design this model.

The proposed model works with either of two conditions given below [44]:

- high dirty rate condition (1): $W_i = (\gamma D_i)_{max}$
- low dirty rate condition (2): $W_i = (\gamma D_i)_{avg}$

When VM is of larger size with the memory intensive application, it has more pages which are being skipped in the iterative process. It will consider condition (1) for evaluation. For the non-memory intensive application, it follows condition (2).

5.4   Performance Evaluation

In this section, proposed dirty page rate model and proposed skip page rate model are evaluated. These models are compared with existing dirty page models and skip page models.

5.4.1   Evaluation of Dirty Page Rate Models

The evaluation of dirty page model is based on three different workloads: (i) Kernel, (ii) RUBiS Database, and (iii) OLTP [38].

Following experiments are performed using different dirty rate models. The analysis of their performance on different workloads are also given as follows:

- Number of dirty pages: The hot pages model and modified log model have the optimal number of dirty pages than migration log model for kernel and OLTP workloads. The modified migration log has an optimal number of dirty pages than the other two models for RUBiS database workload.
- Downtime: The modified migration log model has optimal downtime than other two models for all three workloads.
- Total migration time: The modified migration log model has optimal total migration time than the other two models for all three workloads.
- R^2 value of workload: Except kernel workload for log-based model, all three models outperform optimal R^2 value for kernel, RUBiS, and OLTP workloads.

5.4.2 Evaluation of Skip Page Rate Models

The experiments are tested based on real data set [38] for the kernel workload. Following observations are given here as follows:

- The skip model outperforms over both hot pages model and migration log model.
- The R^2 value of this model is closer to 1 and the accuracy of this model is 91%.

The concluding remarks for the performance models are discussed below:

- Migration log-based dirty model is modified and this proposed model is able to give optimal total migration time and downtime. The R^2 value is also observed as the optimal with proposed dirty model for all workloads.
- The skip model is designed based on memory intensive applications for the evaluation of large VMs and it performs better than existing models.
- In future work, dynamic workloads can also be applied to evaluate different dirty and skip models. The same work can be tested on different hypervisors.

6   Open Research Problems

This section presents different three open research problems given below:

- Energy efficient resource management:
  The virtualization is the technology which can improve the efficiency of resources and so, reduce the consumption of power. It helps to manage resources due to the abstraction layer between OS and hardware. The following research issues are highlighted:

  - CPU can be turned to low power modes while other devices cannot work with this facility, so the use of virtualization mechanism (switching idle nodes to low power modes) can eliminate idle power consumption.

- Migrating VMs from under-utilized hosts to minimize active hosts and the same requires algorithmic process of (i) when to migrate VM (ii) which VMs to migrate (iii) where to migrate the VMs (iv) when and which physical nodes to switch on/off.
- Offloading VMs from hosts when those become overloaded to avoid performance degradation (violation of quality service SLA).
- Apply DVFS dynamic adjustment of volume and frequency for energy consumption versus application workload of CPU based on current resource demand.

- Resource utilization between cloud and mobile:
  The servers of public cloud are able to work distributed way in nature. In mobile cloud computing, efficient migration of VM is crucial requirement to fulfill the cloud-based mobile augmentation effectively. The issues of resource utilization related to mobile cloud computing is briefly given below:

  - The issue of latency and performance of application when the mobile user moves very far from the cloud server which has offloaded contents.
  - Effect of overhead of data in mobile cloud computing with low cost and low latency for resource management.

- Internet of Things (IoT) cloud and resource management:
  Live migration is very much essential to deal with cloud services effectively. The IoT-based cloud is the new platform which is used to mange IoT data. IoT cloud provides more flexibility to business without requiring the need of data analyst. Provisioning of cloud without IoT is based on device mobility and service requirements and IoT-based cloud can provide the way to manage resources that provide effective load balancing, minimization of infrastructure cost, and on-demand content delivery. Research issues for IoT cloud-based resource management are given below:

  - Hosting of resources to nearby public cloud is the challenging issue.
  - To develop the efficient mechanism in cloud networking (called fog computing) which can properly distribute data collected from different sensors.

7 Conclusion

In this chapter, we have improved the pre-copy algorithm for live migration system. The improved pre-copy algorithm is developed by three models: (i) compression model, (ii) prediction model, and (iii) performance model. Each model is used to evaluate downtime and total migration time of different workloads. In the first model, algorithmic issues for live migration is discussed and the proposed compression model is implemented. It performs migration of different sizes of VM with three workloads: (i) idle system, (ii) kernel compile, and (iii) static web server. These workloads are performed with nonadaptive dirty rate and nonadaptive data rate. It is observed that proposed compression model is able to perform better than existing framework of Xen. It is also observed that the nonadaptive data rate can allow maximum bandwidth and minimum dirty rate can allow efficient migration. The other models of live migration are prediction model and performance model. The prediction model is used to forecast data with time-series analysis. The general model of time series is discussed in this chapter. The prediction model is evaluated with proposed ARIMA model and proposed SVR model. This model works with adaptive dirty rate and adaptive data rate to evaluate complex workloads running in a VM. The performance model is used to find dirty pages using dirty page rate model. It also works with adaptive dirty rate and adaptive data rate for complex workloads. Two types of dirty page rate models are: (i) migration log-based dirty page rate model and (ii) hot pages-based dirty page rate model. These models are compared with proposed dirty page rate model. The skip page rate model is used to find skip pages during migration process. The evaluation of dirty page rate model and skip page rate model is discussed in detail. It is observed that both, prediction model and performance model are able to work efficiently than existing framework of Xen. We want to conclude that three proposed models are able to improve pre-copy and the results are tested for the same. In the future work, the different combined mechanisms for compression model are to be developed for live migration. The linear discriminant analysis (LDA) and neural networks (NNs) can be applied for prediction model. Both dirty page rate and skip page rate models are to be implemented using probability method.

References

1. Petrovi, D., & Schiper, A. (2012, March). Implementing virtual machine replication: A case study using xen and kvm. In *2012 IEEE 26th International Conference on Advanced Information Networking and Applications (AINA)* (pp. 73–80). IEEE.
2. Buyya, R., Vecchiola, C., & Selvi, S. T. (2013). *Mastering cloud computing: foundations and applications programming*. Newnes.
3. Vaquero, L. M., Rodero-Merino, L., Caceres, J., & Lindner, M. (2008). A break in the clouds: towards a cloud definition. *ACM SIGCOMM Computer Communication Review, 39*(1), 50–55.
4. Cherkasova, L., Gupta, D., & Vahdat, A. (2007). *When virtual is harder than real: Resource allocation challenges in virtual machine based it environments*. Technical Report, Hewlett Packard Laboratories, HPL-2007-25.
5. Clark, C., Fraser, K., Hand, S., Hansen, J. G., Jul, E., Limpach, C., et al. (2005, May). Live migration of virtual machines. In *Proceedings of the 2nd conference on Symposium on Networked Systems Design & Implementation-Volume 2* (pp. 273–286). USENIX Association.
6. Zaw, E. P., & Thein, N. L. (2012). Improved live VM migration using LRU and Splay tree algorithm. *International Journal of Computer Science and Telecommunications, 3*(3), 1–7.
7. Jin, H., Deng, L., Wu, S., Shi, X., & Pan, X. (2009, August). Live virtual machine migration with adaptive, memory compression. In *IEEE International Conference on Cluster Computing and Workshops, 2009. CLUSTER'09* (pp. 1–10). IEEE.
8. Jin, H., Gao, W., Wu, S., Shi, X., Wu, X., & Zhou, F. (2011). Optimizing the live migration of virtual machine by CPU scheduling. *Journal of Network and Computer Applications, 34*(4), 1088–1096.

9. Alamdari, J. F., & Zamanifar, K. (2012, December). A reuse distance based precopy approach to improve live migration of virtual machines. In *2012 2nd IEEE International Conference on Parallel Distributed and Grid Computing (PDGC)* (pp. 551–556). IEEE.
10. Chisnall, D. (2008). *The definitive guide to the xen hypervisor*. Pearson Education.
11. Lee, M., Krishnakumar, A. S., Krishnan, P., Singh, N., & Yajnik, S. (2010, March). Supporting soft real-time tasks in the xen hypervisor. In *ACM Sigplan Notices* (Vol. 45, No. 7, pp. 97–108). ACM.
12. Goldberg, R. P. (1974). Survey of virtual machine research. *Computer, 7*(6), 34–45.
13. Ahmad, R. W., Gani, A., Hamid, S. H. A., Shiraz, M., Xia, F., & Madani, S. A. (2015). Virtual machine migration in cloud data centers: a review, taxonomy, and open research issues. *The Journal of Supercomputing, 71*(7), 2473–2515.
14. Patel, M., Chaudhary, S. & Garg, S. (*in press*). Improved pre-copy algorithm using statistical prediction and compression model for efficient live memory migration. *International Journal of High Performance Computing and Networking, Inderscience*. http://www.inderscience.com/info/ingeneral/forthcoming.php?jcode=ijhpcn.
15. Nathan, S., Kulkarni, P., & Bellur, U. (2013, April). Resource availability based performance benchmarking of virtual machine migrations. In *Proceedings of the 4th ACM/SPEC International Conference on Performance Engineering* (pp. 387–398). ACM.
16. Shribman, A., Hudzia, B., & (2012, August). Pre-Copy and post-copy VM live migration for memory intensive applications. In *2012 Euro-Par Parallel Processing Workshops* (pp. 539–547). Heidelberg: Springer.
17. Patel, M., & Chaudhary, S. (2014, December). Survey on a combined approach using prediction and compression to improve pre-copy for efficient live memory migration on Xen. In *2014 International Conference on Parallel, Distributed and Grid Computing (PDGC)*, (pp. 445–450). IEEE.
18. Liu, Z., Qu, W., Liu, W., & Li, K. (2010, December). Xen live migration with slowdown scheduling algorithm. In *2010 International Conference on Parallel and Distributed Computing, Applications and Technologies (PDCAT)* (pp. 215–221). IEEE.
19. Liu, W., & Fan, T. (2011, August). Live migration of virtual machine based on recovering system and CPU scheduling. In *Information Technology and Artificial Intelligence Conference (ITAIC), 2011 6th IEEE Joint International* (Vol. 1, pp. 303–307). IEEE.
20. Stage, A., & Setzer, T. (2009, May). Network-aware migration control and scheduling of differentiated virtual machine workloads. In *Proceedings of the 2009 ICSE Workshop on Software Engineering Challenges of Cloud Computing* (pp. 9–14). IEEE Computer Society.
21. Svard, P., Hudzia, B., Tordsson, J., & Elmroth, E. (2011). Evaluation of delta compression techniques for efficient live migration of large virtual machines. *ACM Sigplan Notices, 46*(7), 111–120.
22. Zhang, Z., Xiao, L., Zhu, M., & Ruan, L. (2014). Mvmotion: a metadata based virtual machine migration in cloud. *Cluster Computing, 17*(2), 441–452.
23. Deng, L., Jin, H., Wu, S., Shi, X., & Zhou, J. (2011, December). Fast saving and restoring virtual machines with page compression. In *2011 International Conference on Cloud and Service Computing (CSC)* (pp. 150–157). IEEE.
24. Tafa, I., & Paci, H. (2011, September). The theoretical analysis of adaptive memory compression in Load Balancing page memory with Live-Migration approach. In Network-Based Information Systems (NBiS), 2011 14th International Conference on (pp. 450-455). IEEE.
25. Cui, W., & Song, M. (2010, August). Live memory migration with matrix bitmap algorithm. In *2010 IEEE 2nd Symposium on Web Society (SWS)* (pp. 277–281). IEEE.
26. Liu, Z., Qu, W., Yan, T., Li, H., & Li, K. (2010, October). Hierarchical copy algorithm for Xen live migration. In *2010 International Conference on Cyber-Enabled Distributed Computing and Knowledge Discovery (CyberC)* (pp. 361–364). IEEE.
27. Lu, P., Barbalace, A., Palmieri, R., & Ravindran, B. (2013, August). Adaptive live migration to improve load balancing in virtual machine environment. In *Euro-Par Workshops* (pp. 116–125).
28. Jing, Y. (2012, January). Key technologies and optimization for dynamic migration of virtual machines in cloud computing. In *2012 Second International Conference on Intelligent System Design and Engineering Application (ISDEA)* (pp. 643–647). IEEE.

29. Sun, G. F., Gu, J. H., Hu, J. H., & Zhao, T. H. (2011). Improvement of live memory migration mechanism for virtual machine based on pre-copy. *Computer Engineering, 37*(13).
30. Voorsluys, W., Broberg, J., Venugopal, S., & Buyya, R. (2009). Cost of virtual machine live migration in clouds: A performance evaluation. In *Cloud Computing* (pp. 254–265). Heidelberg: Springer.
31. Mosberger, D., & Jin, T. (1998). Httperfa tool for measuring web server performance. *ACM SIGMETRICS Performance Evaluation Review, 26*(3), 31–37.
32. Hu, Y., Nanda, A., & Yang, Q. (1999, February). Measurement, analysis and performance improvement of the Apache web server. In *Performance, Computing and Communications Conference, 1999 IEEE International* (pp. 261–267). IEEE.
33. Tabachnick, B. G., & Fidell, L. S. (2013). *Time-Series Analysis. Using Multivariate Statistics, CourseSmart eTextbook* (6th ed.). Pearson
34. Hyndman, R. J., & Khandakar, Y. (2007). Automatic time series for forecasting: the forecast package for R (No. 6/07). Monash University, Department of Econometrics and Business Statistics.
35. Montgomery, D. C., Jennings, C. L., & Kulahci, M. (2015). *Introduction to time series analysis and forecasting*. Wiley.
36. Patel, M., Chaudhary, S., & Garg, S. (2016). Machine learning based statistical prediction model for improving performance of live virtual machine migration. *Journal of Engineering, 2016.*
37. Adhikari, R., & Agrawal, R. K. (2013). An introductory study on time series modeling and forecasting. arXiv preprint arXiv:1302.6613.
38. Nathan, S., Bellur, U., & Kulkarni, P. (2015, August). Towards a comprehensive performance model of virtual machine live migration. In *Proceedings of the Sixth ACM Symposium on Cloud Computing* (pp. 288–301). ACM.
39. Hsu, C. W., Chang, C. C., & Lin, C. J. (2003). A practical guide to support vector classification.
40. Meyer, D. (2004). Support vector machines: The interface to libsvm in package e1071.
41. Liu, H., Jin, H., Xu, C. Z., & Liao, X. (2013). Performance and energy modeling for live migration of virtual machines. *Cluster Computing, 16*(2), 249–264.
42. Akoush, S., Sohan, R., Rice, A., Moore, A. W., & Hopper, A. (2010, August). Predicting the performance of virtual machine migration. In 2010 IEEE International Symposium on Modeling, Analysis & Simulation of Computer and Telecommunication Systems (MASCOTS) (pp. 37–46). IEEE.
43. Aldhalaan, A., & Menasc, D. A. (2013). Analytic performance modeling and optimization of live VM migration. In *Computer Performance Engineering* (pp. 28–42). Heidelberg: Springer.
44. Patel, M., Chaudhary, S., & Garg, S. (2016, April). Performance modeling of skip models for VM migration using Xen. In *2016 International Conference on Computing, Communication and Automation (ICCCA)* (pp. 1256–1261). IEEE.

Analysis of Security in Modern Container Platforms

Samuel Laurén, M. Reza Memarian, Mauro Conti and Ville Leppänen

Abstract Containers have quickly become a popular alternative to more traditional virtualization methods such as hypervisor-based virtualization. Residing at operating system level, containers offer a solution that is cheap in terms of resource usage and flexible in the way it can be applied. The purpose of this chapter is two-fold: first, we provide a brief overview of available container security solutions and how they operate, and second, we try to further elaborate and asses the security requirements for containers as proposed by Reshetova et al. We take a look at the current and past security threats and Common Vulnerabilities and Exposures (CVE) faced by container systems and see how attacks that exploit them violate the aforementioned requirements. Based on our analysis, we contribute by identifying more security requirements for container systems.

1 Introduction

The benefits of virtualization have long been understood. By loosening the coupling between operating systems and hardware, virtualization has enabled easier scaling and management of computational resources, lessened the burden of deployment and enabled better utilization of hardware resources.

Traditional virtualization methods work by providing guest operating systems with a complete set of virtualized hardware resources. The virtual machine monitor, or hypervisor, essentially divides the physical hardware resources into a set of virtual ones and then allocates them between the guests. This way of doing the virtualization of hardware level has many benefits, such as making the virtualization transparent to the guest operating system, and allowing unmodified versions of operating system to be run on top of the hypervisor.

S. Laurén · M. Reza Memarian (✉) · V. Leppänen
Department of Information Technology, University of Turku, Turku, Finland
e-mail: mohammad-reza.memarian@utu.fi

M. Conti
Department of Mathematics, University of Padua, Padua, Italy
e-mail: conti@math.unipd.it

© Springer Nature Singapore Pte Ltd. 2017
S. Chaudhary et al. (eds.), *Research Advances in Cloud Computing*,
DOI 10.1007/978-981-10-5026-8_14

The principal task of operating systems is to manage and share resources among applications. This is done through a set of useful abstractions such as processes, files and sockets. Collections of these resources form hierarchies and namespaces, such as process trees or sets of file descriptors. In turn, these collections of resources, along with the services provided by the operating system, define the operating environment for programs to run on. Traditionally, every process on a system shared the same operating environment: each process belonged to the same process hierarchy and had access to the same set of file systems and networks as every other process. In other words, there was just a single global namespace for these classes of resources.

Containers generalized this by dividing these previously global resources between different isolated entities, essentially creating multiple separate user spaces. This way, containers provide another form of virtualization by operating at a higher level of abstraction. Instead of managing virtualized, logical, hardware devices, container systems divide resource abstractions provided by the operating system. Where in the traditional hypervisor-based virtualization different guest operating systems share the same set of hardware, in the container-based approach the sharing is expanded to include the operating system kernel itself. In other words, all the containers on a system share the same kernel but are otherwise isolated from each other. In Sect. 2, we clarify the mentioned isolation.

Extending virtualization into kernel level (from the hardware level) has provided multiple benefits. The most obvious benefit of container-based systems is their efficiency in comparison to traditional virtualization methods, since the systems only require kernel to manage additional data structures instead of emulating the behavior of hardware devices. [1] found that the overhead introduced by containers was almost negligible. This is understandable since launching a container requires little more than creating a new process.

Another benefit of containers is compatibility. Where a hypervisor is often dependent on certain hardware features, such as Intel VT-x for efficient virtualization [2], containers have no such requirement and are able to run anywhere the kernel can run. There are exception to this, since certain security features (such as Seccomp filtering) are currently supported only on certain architectures [3].

However, the benefits of containers come at a cost. The shared kernel inevitably expands the attack surface in comparison to hypervisor-based virtualization. A great care needs to be taken to ensure that a process inside a container cannot affect other processes running inside different container's context in unexpected ways. For containers to be truly isolated, the entirety of the kernel's user space facing interface needs to be container aware. This is not a simple feature to retrofit into an existing operating system. The complexity of the task is manifested by the decade-long process of incorporating the required changes into the Linux kernel. Aside from security, another notable drawback is that shared-kernel architecture prevents running different operating systems on different containers.

In this chapter, we discuss the security properties of containers and help the readers to understand the benefits and costs associated with them. We base our analysis on the six requirements presented by [4]. As the presented requirements are rather abstract, and no grounds for their completeness is given in [4], we look at security threats of containers (classified by [5]) and security incidents (CVEs) reported on container systems and their underlying OS kernel. As a contribution, we compare those against the six requirements given in [4] in order to gain information on the coverage of the requirements and their possible practical relevance (concerning the reported incidents). Based on our analysis, we are able to complement the list of [4] by proposing three more security requirements for container systems. While container-like virtualization solutions exist for multiple operating systems, we concentrate only on container systems for Linux.

The rest of this chapter is organized as follows. In Sect. 2 we describe the main security requirements for containers. In Sect. 3, we present preliminary information about container technology's structure. In Sect. 4, we describe the main container platforms while, in Sect. 5, we discuss the main security threats to the containers. In Sect. 6, we analyze the security requirements for container with regard to previously discovered vulnerabilities. Finally in Sect. 7, we draw our conclusions and propose topics for future research.

2   Security Requirements for Containers

In their seminal work, [4] defined a set of requirements that any container system has to fulfill in order to be considered secure. The requirements deal with different types of operating systems' resources and interaction between different containers in relation to them. Surprisingly no real justification for the set of six requirements is given by [4]. Below, we provide a quick summary of the requirements:

R1—Isolation of processes: No process belonging to a container should be able to directly influence processes belonging to other containers. In other words, the operating system should only allow processes to access information about other processes within the boundaries of their own container. This also includes process control features such as signaling.

R2—Filesystem isolation: A process inside a container should not be able to (directly) affect filesystems that have not been allocated for it.

R3—Device isolation: Device drivers present a significant interface for potential attackers to exploit. A container system should adequately protect devices from containers.

R4—IPC isolation: Operating systems provide applications with various interprocess communication mechanisms. In a container-enabled system, these primitives should be restricted to operate only within the bounds of a single container. That is, no cross-container IPC should be allowed.

R5—Network isolation: Containers should not be able to eavesdrop or modify traffic originating from other containers.

R6—Resource management: A container system should be able to limit the resources used by containers. That is, it should be able to prevent individual containers from using up all the resources and, in effect, preventing other containers from running.

We note that R4 can be seen as a special case of R1.

3   Container Building Blocks

In this section, we take a look at the set of technologies that make containers possible. The road to containers on Linux has been a long one, supporting containers has required changes to many core parts of the operating system.

3.1   Namespaces

Namespaces [6] are the fundamental security related kernel feature enabling containers. In the introduction, we described containers as a way of partitioning operating system's resources into multiple isolated entities. Namespaces are the kernel feature making this possible.

Currently, Linux supports six distinct namespace categories for controlling different classes of resources. A process can move into a new namespace using the `unshare` system call [7] or alternatively, it can create a new child process that belongs to a namespace from the beginning using the `clone` system call [8]. Process can also join to an existing namespace using `setns` system call [9].

Processes inherit their namespace memberships to their children, that is, if a process creates a child, the child will share its parent's namespaces. The six namespace categories are the following (the actual names can vary):

Process Identifier (PID)   PID namespace controls the process ID numbers. Processes belonging to a different PID namespace can have the same process ID.

Mount   Mount namespace controls the list of mounted filesystems.

User   User namespaces control user and group identifiers along with other security-related information. User namespaces work by mapping IDs between namespaces. This has been particularly important in terms of container security, since it enables creation of unprivileged containers that do not have root access outside of their own namespace. The implications of user namespaces will be more widely discussed in Sect. 3.4.

Network   Network namespaces allow different namespaces to have different views of available network interfaces.

Interprocess Communications (IPC)   IPC namespace controls the access of processes to inter-process communication objects, such as POSIX message queues.

UTS   UTS namespace controls processes' host and domain name.

Each actual process belongs to one namespace in each of the six namespace categories. Thus, because the different resources can be separately controlled, we can achieve a great deal of flexibility in terms of isolation. This creates a whole spectrum of different containment solutions from sandboxes [10] targeting individual applications with limited isolation to full-featured container systems.

By combining these features, an individual process can be effectively isolated from the rest of the system. In this assessment, we will see how this isolation can fail and what problems there have been in real-world container implementations.

The six namespace categories are also connected to the six security requirements R1–R6. Obviously, R1 is strictly related to PID namespace but also to IPC namespace. R2 is related to Mount and User namespaces whereas R3 is slightly related to User namespace. R4 is linked to IPC namespace, and R5 is mostly related to Network and UTS namespaces. Requirement R6 is not really covered with namespaces as such but rather with the control group concept of the Sect. 3.2.

3.2   Control Groups

Control groups or `cgroups` are a feature of the Linux kernel that allows keeping track of groups of processes and assigning resource limits to them. In a way, they can be viewed as a greatly expanded and robust variant of `ulimits`, a traditional resource limiting facility that allowed to control individual processes' resource usage. Where *ulimit* fells short, is the ability to impose control over child processes. In contrast, `cgroups` membership is inherited to all the children in the process hierarchy.

Control groups are structured around multiple controllers. Individual controllers are responsible for managing certain classes of resources. For example, `memory` controller can be used to restrict processes' memory usage.

Because of their ability to limit resources used by containers, control groups are a key mechanism for preventing denial-of-service type attacks against containers.

At present, there are two orthogonal implementations of control groups, the original and the newer second generation "v2" design [11] that was published in Linux 4.5. In the original design different controllers could be individually mounted while the second version offers a single unified hierarchy where all the available controllers are automatically present.

On a practical level, control groups are managed through a special pseudo file system that is usually mounted in `/sys/fs/cgroup`. Through the use of this filesystem, control groups hierarchies can be constructed, controllers assigned to groups, processes placed inside them. Additionally, control groups can be nested in a way that each level of nesting can impose further restrictions while inheriting the limits of its parent.

3.3   Capabilities

Traditionally, UNIX allowed *root* to have unlimited power over the system. Capabilities [12] make program privileges more fine-grained by allowing processes to posses only a subset of the capabilities available to the root. For example, a program managing system time could just have cap_sys_time bit set in the binary, allowing it to modify system time settings. This can be contrasted with the traditional setuid-based approach where the binary would have gained full root privileges upon execution, making it a worthwhile target for attacks. Capabilities can be associated with threads and files and can be described in terms of bitmaps where each bit presents a capability. Each thread has four associated capability sets as follows:

Permitted   Permitted set represents the full set of capabilities that the thread can assume during its execution.

Inheritable   Inheritable set represents the set of capabilities that child processes can inherit.

Effective   Effective set represents the capabilities that the thread currently has. Kernel uses it to determine whether or not a privileged operation should be allowed. Thread's effective capabilities are always bounded by the capabilities in its Permitted set. The Effective set is useful as it provides for capability aware programs a way to temporarily lower permissions available for them.

Ambient   Ambient set is a newer addition to capabilities model. The Ambient set has been introduced to make it easier to keep capabilities after execve command. Before the Ambient set was introduced, losing capabilities due to empty file-level Inheritable set presented a problem.

Aside from threads, program binaries can also have associated capabilities. These capabilities are stored in files' extended attributes. Similar to the way thread capabilities work, file-level capabilities are defined in terms of sets as follows:

Permitted   In file-level capabilities, Permitted set defines the capabilities that threads will automatically have upon program execution. This is similar to the way setuid-binaries work.

Inheritable   For binaries, Inheritable set defines the bounding set of capabilities that the program can acquire through inheritance. When a thread execve's a binary, its Effective set of capabilities is AND'ed with its Inheritable set and then AND'ed with file's inheritable capabilities.

Effective   Aside from the two capability sets introduced above, files also have an associated effective bit. If the effective bit is set, the program threads will automatically receive all the permissions specified in the Permitted set upon execution. This allows programs that are unaware of the capability system be confined with it.

Capabilities are important security mechanism for containers since they allow limiting the program privileges to a minimum. What default capabilities the container platforms give out to the containers is one of the differentiating features worth assessing when comparing security of the systems.

3.4   Privileged and Unprivileged Containers

Ever since the dawn of UNIX, one of the things needing careful attention is the question of root. To be more specific, which components on the system are executing with the root privileges. Capabilities introduced a finer level of control over the privileges.

User namespaces are a relatively recent and large feature of the Linux kernel. Because of their significance to the security properties of the system, they are worthy of a more in-depth look. User namespaces allow mappings between user and group IDs, allowing *uid* within a namespace to correspond to a different *uid* outside. On a practical level, this mapping is implemented by shifting identifiers by a predetermined amount. For example, a process can execute with an *euid* of 0 within a namespace but have an *euid* of 10,000 outside of it. This allows processes to have the root privileges within a container but lack those on a system-wide scale.

Container security can greatly be enhanced by making use of this ability, by allowing containers to execute without root on the host. Privileged containers are those where the *uid* 0 within the container maps directly to the host's root, correspondingly, unprivileged containers are those where the two differ. Unprivileged containers can execute as a regular user on the host system and their access can be limited with traditional methods.

The difficulty of securing privileged containers is widely accepted, for example, the LXC documentation acknowledges the inherent riskiness of privileged containers [13]:

> As privileged containers are considered unsafe, we typically will not consider new container escape exploits to be security issues worthy of a CVE and quick fix.
>
> [...]
>
> LXC upstream's position is that those [privileged] containers aren't and cannot be root-safe.

3.5   Auxiliary Security Measures

The aforementioned techniques are roughly enough to achieve the baseline level of functionality required by containers. However, additional techniques can be deployed for more in-depth security. These additional measures are even more important in the case of privileged containers to restrict root within the containers.

Seccomp-BPF Filtering   Seccomp-BPF is a feature of the Linux kernel, which enables programs to perform a one-way transition into a more restricted state where all the system calls performed are passed through a program-defined filter. By default, Docker uses Seccomp-based system call blacklist with 52 potentially dangerous system calls [5]. However, it is worth noting that some of those calls could also be denied by the capabilities used.

Mandatory Access Control   Linux security modules (such as SELinux or AppArmor) that offer Mandatory Access Control style permission model are also valuable in further restricting containers against escapes.

4   Container Platforms

In this section we provide a brief overview of the dominant container platforms. We will focus on Docker [14] as we try to understand how modern container platforms employ the security mechanisms presented in Sect. 3. However, we will also look how other other popular platforms compare to it.

4.1   Docker

Docker is a popular container platform characterized by its encouragement for *ephemeral* and *immutable* single-application containers. Containers should be easy to create and destroy and all the mutable states should be stored separately from the container itself. This sets it further apart from more traditional virtual machine platforms.

From a security perspective, Docker's emphasis on single-application containers makes it arguably easier to secure than platforms offering a more traditional virtualization experience. A single application might not require all the privileges of a full-fledged system, enabling the use of more restrictive configurations, and reducing the attack surface.

Additionally, in search for even lighter containers, Docker recommends using smaller base images, which in turn reduces change of failure. Of course, having security-conscious best practices in place does not guarantee the security of any particular deployment. However, encouraging secure practices through default settings could increase the likelihood that containers will be properly configured.

In the previous sections, we highlighted the role of capabilities in securing containers. Linux supports around forty capabilities and by default Docker grants 14 of them to containers [15]. These are listed in Table 1. Aside from capabilities, Docker employs a default seccomp policy with a whitelist of allowed system calls [16].

Docker supports user namespaces, making it possible to map the root inside a container to an unprivileged user on the host. Unfortunately, this is not used by default and has to be manually enabled by the user [17].

Architecturally, Docker is composed of multiple components providing services at different levels of abstraction. From the user's point of view, the most visible component is the client, which can be invoked via the `docker` command. The client is used to communicate with the docker daemon. The docker daemon runs in the background and is responsible for managing containers. Communication between the client and the daemon happens over a UNIX socket or, alternatively, over TCP. Securing this communication channel is especially important since the Docker daemon often has considerable privileges on the host system [17].

The Docker daemon offers support for many high-level operations, such as downloading images from online sources. In turn, it outsources the lower level details of container management to another daemon, `containerd`, which is responsible for

Table 1 Docker's default capabilities [15]

SETPCAP	Remove capabilities or add them from thread's bounding set
MKNOD	Make block or character special files
AUDIT_WRITE	Write to audit log
CHOWN	Modify ownership information
NET_RAW	Use "raw" sockets
DAC_OVERRIDE	Bypass permission checks on file access
FOWNER	Bypass checks on certain file operations that require file owner ID to match the user ID
FSETID	Do not clear setuid and setgid flags after modifications
KILL	Send signals without regarding permissions
SETGID	Allow arbitrary setgid and setgroups operations
SETUID	Manipulate process UIDs
NET_BIND_SERVICE	Allows binding privileged ports
SYS_CHROOT	Change file system root
SETFCAP	Set file capabilities

Fig. 1 The runtime architecture of Docker

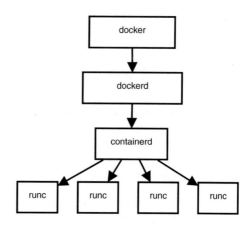

executing containers using a container runtime. By default, Docker utilizes the runc container runtime, which supports running Open Container Initiative compatible containers [18]. This multi-layered design makes it possible to swap out individual components (Fig. 1).

Docker makes use of *Dockerfiles* for specifying steps needed for building a container. These build specifications can be derived from other images allowing the reuse of common base images. For example, a Dockerfile can specify to inherit from a base image containing a particular Linux distribution. This inheritance can extend to multiple levels. For example, a Dockerfile for a particular application might inherit from an image for a particular application platform, which in turn might inherit from a distribution image.

4.2   Other Container Platforms

Linux Containers (LXC) [19] platform positions itself as a platform for running "system containers," containers which are more close to traditional virtual machines. From a deployment perspective, this is a major difference between LXC and Docker. Being oldest of the three covered alternatives, LXC has played a major role in the evolution of Linux-based containers. In its original formation, Docker used LXC as the backend.

One can view LXC's system containers approach to be a potential security issue, at least compared to single-application containers. Running a full-fledged general purpose system requires more capabilities than an individual application. From a security point of view, having more things in a container than is strictly necessary, increases the possible attack surface for an adversary to exploit. However, from a deployment point of view, LXC's system container approach might offer a simple migration path from the more traditional virtualization solutions.

CoreOS project's Rkt container system has many similarities with Docker in the sense that both projects encourage single-application containers [20]. Rkt differentiates itself by having no central daemon process. This makes integrating Rkt with other process supervisors like systemd supposedly simpler.

5   Container Threats

In their security analysis of Linux containers, [5] classified threats faced by containers into seven broad categories. There is some overlap between the categories and exploiting a weakness in one category may very well enable attacker to succeed in other categories as well. That is, an attack that enables the adversary to move from a container to the host will also likely enable them to perform cross-container attacks.

Kernel Threats   Since the defining features of container-based virtualization are the facts that container implementations need to trust on the security of underlying kernel and the different containers share the same underlying operating system kernel, attacks that exploit weaknesses in the kernel become especially important. Kernel provides an attacker with a huge potential attack surface and minimizing and hardening this should be a matter of utmost importance for anyone dealing with matters regarding container security.

Are these threats covered by security requirements R1–R6? Isolation-related requirements R1–R5 can be seen to partly cover the threats, especially when isolation is seen not only between containers but between a container and its underlying OS kernel. Mostly, the requirement descriptions isolate containers from each other (R3 is an exception). As the underlying kernel is in so much different role as the other containers, it would seem wise to form subclasses for each of the requirements R1–R5: e.g., R1.1 Isolation of processes between containers;

and R1.2 Isolation of processes between a container and the kernel.

However, the issue of container implementation based on some OS kernel still needs attention in the form of a security requirement. Although the container system implementation as such would meet all the security requirements R1–R6, it will not be enough if the underlying kernel is not trustworthy security-wise. It could be argued that the underlying kernel is part of the container system, but due to kernel's central role and the necessity of trust between underlying OS kernel and container system, we propose

R0—Security of underlying kernel: Container system's underlying OS kernel needs to be technically secure.

Inner-Container Threats   Attacks which only allow attacker to compromise an individual container's security. Insecure and unpatched applications can allow an attacker to take control over individual containers. Even when these problems do not allow the attacker to expand their control to other entities on the system.
These threats are not really covered by security requirements R1–R6. Yet, we do not consider this as a problem, since these threats can be seen as application-level security problems and are not related to the container system as such.

Cross-Container Threats   Attacks which allow an attacker to affect another container's state from within a container. A care should be taken when considering how the containers are connected to each other and what services are exposed, as usual the attack surface should be kept to the minimum.

We consider that the requirements R1–R5 are originally written for these threats and those are covered well.

Container-to-Host Threats   Attacks which allow an attacker to affect the host system from within a container. In other words, this class of threats includes the attacks that allow an attacker to escape the container. This could be considered to be the worst-case scenario since getting to the host system often allows an attacker to perform additional classes of attacks.

As already discussed in 'Kernel Threats' item, it would perhaps be wise to define a subclass for each of requirement R1–R5 considering these threats.

Container Manager Threats   Attacks that target the container manager itself. Container managers typically require considerable permissions on the host in order to work. For example, in the context of Docker, it is generally stated that being able to control the Docker daemon equals having root access to the machine since the daemon can be used to extensively control the host system.

We consider that this threat is not covered by R1–R6 and neither by R0. Thus, we propose a new security requirement as follows:

R7—Security of container manager: Container manager as a process needs to be technically secure.

Denial of Service Threats   A care should be taken to limit containers' resource usage so that no individual container can negatively affect other containers' performance by hogging all the resources.

We consider that requirement R6 covers these threats.

Threats introduced by new code   Arguably, the container technology is still in its infancy, at least compared to more traditional and well-understood hypervisor-based methods. To facilitate containerization, Linux kernel has introduced a number of major new features, such as user namespaces. As the general security wisdom goes, new code has, in general, a higher chance of containing bugs than code that has been well-tested and used in production for significant periods of time. As we shall see in Sect. 6, this wisdom seems to be empirically correct, since there has been a number of notable kernel bugs associated with these features.

We consider that this class of threats proposed by [5] is already covered by R0–R7.

6   Empirical Analysis

In this section, we take a look at some past security issues which have affected containers. This overview is not supposed to be systematic, that is, we do not try to cover everything since such endeavor would surely be outside the scope of a single chapter. Instead, the purpose of this overview is to offer a glimpse of the security landscape related to containers. Additionally, we try to view the exposed vulnerabilities through the lens of the requirements presented by [4] and its small elaboration by us in Sect. 5. What their analysis offers is a clear definition of isolation requirements. We have classified the attacks based on which of these requirements the attack allows adversary to violate. When classifying an attack into a single category is not meaningful, we have noted that in the attack description. In Sect. 6.7, we offer some discussion based on these findings.

In the following subsections we discuss on analysis of a set of 19 CVE (Common Vulnerabilities and Exposures) reports given in [8, 11, 12, 21–39] by MITRE (cve.mitre.org). The CVE database contains yearly some 10 reports explicitly related to containers, but due to their diverse nature (so many container systems), we mainly looked at Docker related issues yet extending the search to kernel issues. The 19 CVEs are claimed representative, yet those are just a tiny set of all CVEs.

6.1   Isolation of Processes

The first and, in some ways, the most fundamental requirement for containers that any implementation must fulfill, is the ability to partition processes into separate isolated hierarchies. Because PID namespaces are the enabling technology behind this partitioning, attacks against them have the potential to shake the very foundations of container security.

In CVE-*2009-1338*, kernel did not consider PID namespaces when executing KILL system call, allowing attacker to send arbitrary signals to every process on the system [21] (violating the requirements R0 and R1). This bug represents a typical namespace related vulnerability: a corner case where the namespace isolation was not properly enforced.

6.2 Filesystem Isolation

There have been numerous filesystem-related vulnerabilities in the Linux kernel that have allowed attackers to, among other things, escalate their privileges (CVE-*2016-2853*; [39]) or access files from containers in unintended ways. It is worth noting that many of the filesystem vulnerabilities are specific to some particular filesystem module.

Layered filesystems, that is filesystems that combine multiple underlying data sources to a single coherent view, are heavily relied on in many container platforms. For example, Docker makes use of them to support sharing and extension of system images. In Docker, the functionality is supported through multiple different backends, the generally recommended one being *overlayfs* which has the benefit of being in the mainline kernel and the older out-of-tree alternative *aufs*. Both of these filesystems have faced namespace related security vulnerabilities in the past. In CVE-*2016-2853* aufs incorrectly handled mount namespaces leading to a possible privilege escalation [39] (violating R0 and R2). CVE-*2016-1576* is a similar bug concerning overlayfs [38] (violating R0 and R2). In a similar vein, CVE-*2015-1328* exposed a flaw in overlayfs that could allow an attacker to escalate their privileges, because of the incorrect handling of user namespaces in overlayfs [32] (R0, R2). Even though the filesystem implementation is at fault here, the main result of the bug is not a filesystem isolation violation but privilege escalation.

Containers should only have access to the files and directories belonging to them. Unfortunately, there have been multiple vulnerabilities that, if exploited, would violate this requirement, allowing users within a container to traverse and access files outside of it. In CVE-*2014-9717*, an attacker was able to access filesystem locations beneath mount point by exploiting a vulnerability in the way kernel handled mount options [31] (violates R2). In CVE-*2015-4176*, a deletion of a file or directory could lead to unmounting of a filesystem and, subsequently, attacker gaining access to files beneath the mount point [34] (R2). In a similar vein, CVE-*2015-2925* described a scenario where an attacker could gain access to files outside bind mount by exploiting bugs related to renaming [33] (R0 and R2). Aside from accessing unintended files, vulnerabilities have also enabled attackers to write to filesystems that were intended to be immutable. CVE-*2014-5206* and CVE-*2013-1957* dealt with the way kernel handles read-only mount options in the presence of namespaces [24, 27] (R0, R2).

6.3 Device Isolation

When it comes to securing devices in containers, control groups' devices subsystem is a major mechanism. It offers the ability to restrict access to device nodes by defining whitelists. We were unable to find CVEs for this category.

6.4 IPC Isolation

One could argue that signals ought to fall into the IPC isolation category, since they are a primitive inter-process communication mechanism. This would indicate slight overlap between the IPC and process isolation categories as defined by [4]. If we decide to include signaling under the definition of IPC, CVE-*2009-1338* ([21]; violates R0 and R4) is also applicable here. One argument against including signaling under the requirement of IPC isolation, is that signaling can be restricted through the PID namespaces where other IPC mechanisms are governed by the IPC namespace. The IPC namespace is responsible for controlling System V objects and POSIX message queues.

6.5 Network Isolation

There have been some vulnerabilities directly related to network namespaces [37] (CVE-*2015-8543*), but they have not been about breaking network isolation guarantees. However, in the case of container systems, bad configuration presents a great risk to network isolation [5].

For example, in the case of Docker, all the containers are by default connected to the same virtual bridge interface, enabling them to communicate with each other [40]. If the containers using the bridge do not need the ability to communicate with each other, this represents an unnecessary capability with no benefits and potential security implications. If a container were to have a vulnerable service exposed to the bridge, this could lead to a cross-container attack.

6.6 Resource Management

Denial of service attacks against the kernel are not unheard of, after all, all that an attacker has to do to prevent a system from function is to make it crash. Such vulnerability was covered in CVE-*2015-4177*, where an attacker could leverage root inside user namespace to cause `collect_mounts` to make the system crash [35] (violates R6). Namespaced root was also utilized in CVE-*2015-4178* [36] (R6), where the system could crash after entering an inconsistent state. A more imaginative filesystem related denial of service attack was discovered in CVE-*2014-7970* [29] (R0 and R6) `pivot_root` system call's implementation did not correctly handle certain paths passed as an argument, which could lead kernel getting stuck in a loop [24]. In CVE-*2014-7975* (R0, R6), an attacker could prevent a system from writing to a filesystem by remounting it in read-only mode, this was allowed because the kernel did not require necessary capabilities from the user [30].

Networking related kernel sub-systems have also had their fair share of denial-of-service inducing vulnerabilities. CVE-*2015-8543* (R6) describes a situation enabling local users to cause system crash by providing a malformed protocol identifier which caused the kernel to dereference a NULL function pointer [37]. In CVE-*2009-1360* (R0, R6), remote attacker could crash the system by forcing the kernel to dereference a NULL pointer by utilizing the incorrect handling of IPv6 packets when the networking namespace support was enabled [22]. CVE-*2011-2189* (R0, R6) provided attackers with a way to corrupt kernel memory and crash the system by rapidly creating and cleaning up network namespaces [23].

6.7 Discussion and Some Other CVE Cases

The multitude of system calls and features provided by the kernel form an ample attack surface for potential attackers. Since container isolation is solely dependent upon the correctness of these interfaces, it has become important understanding how they have been vulnerable in the past and what kinds of security ramifications they have had. In the previous subsections, we reviewed relevant vulnerability reports mainly against R1–R6.

What is missing from the above analysis, however, are vulnerabilities that are not strictly about violating isolation and resource constraints. While analysis of this kind of course has its place, it leaves out many possible vectors of attack that a real-world deployment would have to take into account.

As an example, attacks that fall outside of the definition offered by [4] are attacks that target the container deployment process and the components responsible for it. For container deployment to be secure, the authenticity of deployed images should obviously be verified. In CVE-*2014-5277*, Docker used insecure HTTP connections as a fallback if the primary HTTPS connection to the container registry failed, this allowed potential attackers to facilitate downgrade attacks [28]. In a similar vein, CVE-*2014-0048* noted that Docker did some of its download over an insecure connection [25]. We propose one more security requirement:

R8—Security of deployment process: The container deployment process needs to be secure specifically in terms of integrity and confidentiality.

Table 2 Classification of container related vulnerabilities

	R0	R1	R2	R3	R4	R5	R6	R7	R8
CVE-2009-1338	✗	✗			✗				
CVE-2009-1360	✗						✗		
CVE-2011-2189	✗						✗		
CVE-2013-1957	✗		✗						
CVE-2014-0048									✗
CVE-2014-3499								✗	
CVE-2014-5206	✗		✗						
CVE-2014-5277									✗
CVE-2014-7970	✗						✗		
CVE-2014-7975	✗						✗		
CVE-2014-9717			✗						
CVE-2015-1328	✗		✗						
CVE-2015-2925	✗		✗						
CVE-2015-4176			✗						
CVE-2015-4177							✗		
CVE-2015-4178							✗		
CVE-2015-8543							✗		
CVE-2016-1576	✗		✗						
CVE-2016-2853	✗		✗						

Additionally, since the container engine typically wields considerable power in the host system, a care should be taken that only trusted users have the ability to control it. For example, in CVE-*2014-3499*, Docker's management socket did not have strict enough permissions specified, leading to possible security privilege escalation [26] (violates R7).

In Table 2, we have summarized the results of our vulnerability classification. Since containers are mainly an operating-system-level feature, that is, the kernel is responsible for providing most of the building blocks that enable containers, it is not surprising that R0 is well represented among the analyzed vulnerabilities. The security of the underlying kernel is paramount to the security of containers.

Arguably, a more informative view of the state of container security can be achieved through the more specific requirements. The fact that vulnerabilities touching upon file system isolation (R2) are so common highlights the need for robust and well-tested implementations in this space. Additionally, one might consider employing additional security measures such as mandatory access control systems to further harden file system containment.

Vulnerabilities dealing with resource management (R6) are also numerous in the data. These problems can potentially enable denial-of-service attacks against container systems. As a partial remedy, one might employ orchestration and monitoring services to make sure that the individual containers (and the hosts executing the containers) are responsive and automate steps to recover from resource exhaustion. Luckily, stateless containers are well suited for this sort of automated deployments.

7 Conclusions and Future Research

We believe that containers have already claimed their rightful place as a core piece in infrastructure deployment puzzle. Compared to traditional virtualization methods, they offer some similar features, mainly, the ability to create logically isolated environments for applications. Where traditional virtualization methods produced a jump in deployment flexibility by decoupling environments from hardware, container systems go even further by making this increasingly cheap in terms of resources.

However, the benefits come at a cost. Where individual physical servers offer better isolation compared to traditional virtualization methods, traditional virtualization methods offer arguably better isolation than containers. In this chapter, we have taken a look at the techniques behind Linux containers and highlighted some of the security concerns associated with them. We have introduced the core technological pieces that make containerization possible in Linux and discussed their security properties.

We presented the general security requirements, proposed by [4], that any container system has to uphold. We challenged this requirement list by considering it against a classification of container system related threats given by [5]. Moreover, we also analyzed a set of CVE reports to get more understanding on the coverage of previously proposed security requirements. As a contribution, we were able to propose three new security requirements for container systems and moreover there seems to be reported CVEs matching almost all the requirements. Some requirement (R0, R2, R6) violations would seem to be more common than the others, but our sample is small and thus such conclusion cannot be drawn.

As far as general security recommendations go, we emphasize the role of unprivileged containers for preventing container-to-host type vulnerabilities. Also, it should be noted that as far as default configurations go, existing container platforms try to accommodate a wide variety of use-cases, sometimes at the cost of granting more privileges to containers than what might be necessary for any specific application. This is why care should be taken to evaluate the privileges granted to containers. Good security principles like defence-in-depth should also be followed, this can mean restricting containers further by deploying mandatory access control policies on container hosts.

As further research we suggest making a systematic review on kernel and container related CVEs with respect to the formed requirements R0–R8. Moreover, one should aim at more precise definition for the requirements. We consider that each of R0–R8 should be elaborated more, especially thinking the container-to-host trust relation besides the inter-container isolation aspects.

References

1. Morabito, R., Kjallman, J., & Komu, M. (2015). Hypervisors vs. lightweight virtualization: a performance comparison. In *2015 IEEE International Conference on Cloud Engineering (IC2E)* (pp 386–393). IEEE.
2. Uhlig, R., Neiger, G., Rodgers, D., Santoni, A., Martins, F., Anderson, A., et al. (2005). Intel virtualization technology. *Computer, 38*(5), 48–56.
3. Wang, X., Lazar, D., Zeldovich, N., Chlipala, A., & Tatlock, Z. (2014). Jitk: A trustworthy in-kernel interpreter infrastructure. In *11th USENIX Symposium on Operating Systems Design and Implementation (OSDI 14), USENIX Association, Broomfield, CO* (pp. 33–47). Retrieved from https://www.usenix.org/conference/osdi14/technical-sessions/presentation/wang_xi.
4. Reshetova, E., Karhunen, J., Nyman, T., & Asokan, N. (2014). Security of OS-level virtualization technologies. In *Secure IT Systems* (pp. 77–93). Springer.
5. Grattafiori, A. (2016). *Understanding and hardening linux containers.* NCC Group: Whitepaper.
6. (2016) namespaces(7)—linux manual page. Retrieved from http://man7.org/linux/man-pages/man7/namespaces.7.html.
7. (2016) unshare(2)—linux manual page. Retrieved from http://man7.org/linux/man-pages/man2/unshare.2.html.
8. (2016) clone(2)—linux manual page. Retrieved from http://man7.org/linux/man-pages/man2/clone.2.html.
9. (2016) setns(2)—linux manual page. Retrieved from http://man7.org/linux/man-pages/man2/setns.2.html.
10. Potter, S., & Nieh, J. (2010). Apiary: Easy-to-use desktop application fault containment on commodity operating systems. In *ATC 2010: USENIX Annual Technical Conference.*
11. (2016) cgroups(7)—linux manual page. Retrieved from http://man7.org/linux/man-pages/man7/cgroups.7.html.
12. (2016) capabilities(7)—linux manual page. Retrieved from http://man7.org/linux/man-pages/man7/capabilities.7.html.
13. (2016b) Linux containers - lxc - security. Retrieved from https://linuxcontainers.org/lxc/security/.
14. (2016a) Docker—build, ship, and run any app, anywhere. Retrieved from https://www.docker.com.
15. (2016c) docker/defaults_linux.go at master docker/docker github. Retrieved from https://github.com/docker/docker/blob/master/oci/defaults_linux.go#L62-L77.
16. (2016d) Seccomp security profiles for docker-docker. Retrieved from https://docs.docker.com/engine/security/seccomp/.
17. (2016b) Docker security. Retrieved from https://docs.docker.com/engine/security/security/.
18. (2016) Open container project. Retrieved from https://runc.io.
19. (2016a) Linux containers. Retrieved from https://linuxcontainers.org.
20. (2016) rkt, a security-minded, standards-based container engine. Retrieved from https://coreos.com/rkt/.
21. (2009a) CVE-2009-1338. Available from MITRE, CVE-ID CVE-2009-1338. Retrieved from https://cve.mitre.org/cgi-bin/cvename.cgi?name=CVE-2009-1338.
22. (2009b) CVE-2009-1360. Available from MITRE, CVE-ID CVE-2009-1360. Retrieved from https://cve.mitre.org/cgi-bin/cvename.cgi?name=CVE-2009-1360.
23. (2011) CVE-2011-2189. Available from MITRE, CVE-ID CVE-2011-2189. Retrieved from https://cve.mitre.org/cgi-bin/cvename.cgi?name=CVE-2011-2189.
24. (2013) CVE-2013-1957. Available from MITRE, CVE-ID CVE-2013-1957. Retrieved from https://cve.mitre.org/cgi-bin/cvename.cgi?name=CVE-2013-1957.
25. (2014a) CVE-2014-0048. Available from MITRE, CVE-ID CVE-2014-0048. Retrieved from https://cve.mitre.org/cgi-bin/cvename.cgi?name=CVE-2014-0048.
26. (2014b) CVE-2014-3499. Available from MITRE, CVE-ID CVE-2014-3499. Retrieved from https://cve.mitre.org/cgi-bin/cvename.cgi?name=CVE-2014-3499.

27. (2014c) CVE-2014-5206. Available from MITRE, CVE-ID CVE-2014-5206. Retrieved from https://cve.mitre.org/cgi-bin/cvename.cgi?name=CVE-2014-5206.

28. (2014d) CVE-2014-5277. Available from MITRE, CVE-ID CVE-2014-5277. Retrieved from https://cve.mitre.org/cgi-bin/cvename.cgi?name=CVE-2014-5277.

29. (2014e) CVE-2014-7970. Available from MITRE, CVE-ID CVE-2014-7970. Retrieved from https://cve.mitre.org/cgi-bin/cvename.cgi?name=CVE-2014-7970.

30. (2014f) CVE-2014-7975. Available from MITRE, CVE-ID CVE-2014-7975. Retrieved from https://cve.mitre.org/cgi-bin/cvename.cgi?name=CVE-2014-7975.

31. (2014g) CVE-2014-9717. Available from MITRE, CVE-ID CVE-2014-9717. Retrieved from https://cve.mitre.org/cgi-bin/cvename.cgi?name=CVE-2014-9717.

32. (2015a) CVE-2015-1328. Available from MITRE, CVE-ID CVE-2015-1328. Retrieved from https://cve.mitre.org/cgi-bin/cvename.cgi?name=CVE-2015-1328.

33. (2015b) CVE-2015-2925. Available from MITRE, CVE-ID CVE-2015-2925. Retrieved from https://cve.mitre.org/cgi-bin/cvename.cgi?name=CVE-2015-2925.

34. (2015c) CVE-2015-4176. Available from MITRE, CVE-ID CVE-2015-4176. Retrieved from https://cve.mitre.org/cgi-bin/cvename.cgi?name=CVE-2015-4176.

35. (2015d) CVE-2015-4177. Available from MITRE, CVE-ID CVE-2015-4177. Retrieved from https://cve.mitre.org/cgi-bin/cvename.cgi?name=CVE-2015-4177.

36. (2015e) CVE-2015-4178. Available from MITRE, CVE-ID CVE-2015-4178. Retrieved from https://cve.mitre.org/cgi-bin/cvename.cgi?name=CVE-2015-4178.

37. (2015f) CVE-2015-8543. Available from MITRE, CVE-ID CVE-2015-8543. Retrieved from https://cve.mitre.org/cgi-bin/cvename.cgi?name=CVE-2015-8543.

38. (2016a) CVE-2016-1576. Available from MITRE, CVE-ID CVE-2016-1576. Retrieved from https://cve.mitre.org/cgi-bin/cvename.cgi?name=CVE-2016-1576.

39. (2016b) CVE-2016-2853. Available from MITRE, CVE-ID CVE-2016-2853. Retrieved from https://cve.mitre.org/cgi-bin/cvename.cgi?name=CVE-2016-2853.

40. (2016e) Understand docker container networks. Retrieved from https://docs.docker.com/v1.10/engine/userguide/networking/dockernetworks/.

Identifying Evidence for Cloud Forensic Analysis

Changwei Liu, Anoop Singhal and Duminda Wijesekera

Abstract Cloud computing provides increased flexibility, scalability, failure tolerance and reduced cost to customers. However, like any computing infrastructure, cloud systems are subjected to cyber-attacks. Post-attack investigations of such attacks present unusual challenges including the dependence of forensically valuable data on the deployment model, multiple virtual machines running on a single physical machine and multi-tenancy of clients. In this chapter, we use our own attack samples to show that, in the attacked cloud, evidence from three different sources can be used to reconstruct attack scenarios. They are (1) IDS and application software logging, (2) cloud service API calls and (3) system calls from VMs. Based on our example attack results, we present the potential design and implementation of a forensic analysis framework for clouds, which includes logging all the activities from both the application layer and lower layers. We show how a Prolog based forensic analysis tool can automate the process of correlating evidence from both the clients and the cloud service provider to reconstruct attack scenarios for cloud forensic analysis.

1 Introduction

Digital forensics applies scientific techniques to the identification, collection, examination, and analysis of data while preserving information integrity and maintaining a strict chain of custody for the data during post-incident examinations [1]. Being a

C. Liu (✉) · D. Wijesekera
Department of Computer Science, George Mason University,
Fairfax, VA 22030, USA
e-mail: cliu6@gmu.edu

D. Wijesekera
e-mail: dwijesek@gmu.edu

A. Singhal · D. Wijesekera
National Institute of Standards and Technology, 100 Bureau Drive,
Gaithersburg, MD 20899, USA
e-mail: anoop.singhal@nist.gov

© Springer Nature Singapore Pte Ltd. 2017
S. Chaudhary et al. (eds.), *Research Advances in Cloud Computing*,
DOI 10.1007/978-981-10-5026-8_15

component of digital forensics, network forensics analyzes network traffic in order to gather information from intrusion detection systems or logs to constitute legal evidence [2]. Considered as an emerging branch of forensics that combines network and system forensics, cloud forensics addresses post-incident analysis of systems with the complexities of distributed processing, multi-tenancy, virtualization and mobility of computations that have challenges in identifying and preserving digital evidence, including [3]:

1. Dependence of forensically valuable data on the deployment model and methods.
2. Large volume in content and proprietary formats of data logs.
3. The diversity and the number of simultaneously operating virtual machine instances of a single physical machine isolated by using virtualization and weak registries used in cloud frameworks. Consequently, extra efforts are needed in segregating resources without breaching user confidentiality and analyzing traces.
4. Instances of servers running on virtual machines in the cloud monitored by hypervisors lack of warnings, procedures and tools for forensic investigation.

Although much research is available in digital forensics, methods used in traditional digital forensics are inadequate for forensic investigation in clouds, as clouds have not been designed for evidence retention and integrity. Recently, National Institute of Standards and Technology (NIST) and other researchers have published papers in cloud governance, security and risk assessment [4], and proposed implementing forensic-enabled clouds. For example, Dykstra et al. proposed implementing cloud to collect forensic data from system level that is below the virtual machines [5], and Zawod et al. provided a complete, trustworthy and forensic-enabled cloud architecture to collect logs for forensic analysis [6]. However, these implementations only focus on evidence acquaintance on Infrastructure as a Service (IaaS) cloud deployment model. To the best of our knowledge, reconstructing attack scenarios by using the evidence collected in a virtualized cloud environment has not been addressed. In this chapter, using some example attacks in a private cloud, we show what evidence can be used to reconstruct corresponding attack scenarios in the cloud, and discuss how we may implement and automate the forensic analysis in the cloud with the objective of saving forensic investigators' time and effort in cloud forensic analysis [7].

The rest of the chapter is organized as follows. Section 2 provides background and related work. Section 3 describes a Prolog based tool used to automate the process of reconstructing attack scenarios. Section 4 shows our experimental attacks in the cloud, and how we identify the evidence from the cloud to reconstruct attack scenarios by using the Prolog based tool. Section 5 shows how we use system call sequences to reconstruct attack steps when other evidence is unavailable. Section 6 describes the open research problems in cloud forensics. We conclude the chapter by discussing how we may implement and automate the cloud forensic analysis in Sect. 7.

2 Background and Related Work

We present the background and research related to digital and cloud forensics in this section.

2.1 Digital Forensics

Digital forensics utilizes scientifically accepted methods to collect, validate and preserve digital evidence derived from digital sources for reconstructing events found to be criminally motivated or support unauthorized actions that disrupt planned operations [8]. Digital forensic investigators seek to extract evidence of attacks from computers and networks by using so-called imaging tools. Typically, imaging tools extract data from the physical memory or disk sectors of computers to a file, and then investigators feed the extracted file into tools to perform live or dead forensic analysis [9]. To obtain network evidence, forensic investigators analyze network traffic and gather information from intrusion detection systems or logs to construct legal evidence of attacks.

2.2 Cloud Forensics

NIST-defined cloud model uses three service deployment models: Software as a Service (SaaS), Platform as a Service (PaaS) and Infrastructure as a Service (IaaS) [10]. SaaS allows customers to use the provider's applications running on the cloud infrastructure. PaaS allows customers to deploy customer-created/acquired applications on the cloud by using programming languages, libraries, services and tools supported by the provider. IaaS provides customers with the capability of provisioning processing, storage, networks, and other fundamental computing resources, so that customers can deploy and run arbitrary software including operating systems and applications on this cloud model [10, 11].

According to Ruan et al., cloud forensics is a subset of network forensics that follows the main phases of network forensics with techniques tailored to cloud computing environments [3]. For example, data acquisition is different in SaaS and IaaS, because the investigator must solely depend on cloud service providers in SaaS. In IaaS, investigators can get virtual machine images from customers.

2.3 Related Work

Data acquisition is a main issue confronting cloud forensics because of resource sharing, geographical distribution, decoupling of cloud-username and physical users, data preservation/integrity, timelines and correlation [12]. Many methods have been proposed to collect evidence from clouds, including remote data acquisition, live forensics, analysis on management plane and snapshot images [13].

Forensic tools can be used to retrieve data from the cloud. For example, by using Guidance EnCase and Access Data FTK, Dykstra et al. successfully retrieved volatile and nonvolatile data from Amazon EC2 cloud user instance [13, 14]. However, those tools do not validate data integrity. To obtain evidence with validated integrity, researchers recommended and developed some toolkits to collect related logs from cloud infrastructure while preserving their integrity. Assuming the cloud provider is trustworthy, Dykstra et al. developed the FROST toolkit that can be integrated to OpenStack [15] to collect logs from the operating system level that supports the virtual machines [5]. To address the trustworthiness, Zawod et al. designed a complete, trustworthy and forensic-enabled cloud [6]. Hay et al. proposed live digital forensic analysis on clouds using virtual introspection to observe the state of a virtual machine (VM) from either the hypervisor (VMM) or some other VM, and presented a suite of virtual introspection tools developed for Xen (VIX tools) [16]. Management plane, also called management console, is the web interface that interfaces with the cloud infrastructure including cloud provider's underlying filesystem, hypervisor, firewalls and VMs. Cloud customers including forensic investigators could download log files, disk images and packet captures from the management plane for forensic analysis. However, this solution requires trust in the management plane, which is a potential vulnerability that does not exist in non-virtualized physical computers [13, 14]. Snapshot technologies enable customers to store a specific state of VM that can be restored by being loaded to a target VM later for forensic analysis [17]. By using snapshots, investigators can gain information on the previous running state of a VM that is supported by hypervisor vendors, including Xen, VMWare, ESX, Hyper-V, and cloud providers that support snapshot features [13].

Forensic tools like Encase, the Sleuth Kit, Snort, Wireshark can collect digital evidence from computers and networks, which provide important information for forensic analysis. In order to reconstruct potential attack scenarios by using the evidence obtained from these tools, researchers have proposed aggregating redundant alerts by similarities and correlating them by using pre-defined attack scenarios to determine multi-step, multi-stage attacks [18, 19]. Currently, this method is non-automated and rather ad-hoc. In order to reduce the investigators' time and effort in reconstructing attack steps, other researchers proposed using rules to automate the process of correlating evidence by finding the causality between items of evidence [20, 21]. Liu et al. implemented a Prolog based tool with two databases, including a vulnerability database and an anti-forensic database, to ascertain the admissibility of evidence and explain missing evidence that is removed by the attacker [21]. These rule-based forensic analysis frameworks have been used for network forensics, but not for cloud forensics.

3 A Prolog-Based Tool for Attack Scenario Reconstruction

In [21, 22], we described an application of MulVAL [23], which uses rules representing generic attack techniques to ascertain the causality between different items of evidence collected from an attacked network to reconstruct attack steps. Created using expert knowledge, these rules are used as investigators' hypotheses to link chains of evidence that are written in the form of Prolog predicates to form attack steps. This system reconstructs attack scenarios in the form of acyclic graphs, defined as follows (this definition and the corresponding example are from our previous work [22]).

Definition 1 (*Logical Evidence Graph-LEG*) A LEG=(N_r, N_f, N_c, E, L, G) is said to be a logical evidence graph (LEG), where N_f, N_r and N_c are three sets of disjoint nodes in the graph (they are called fact, rule, and consequence fact nodes respectively), E $\subseteq$ (($N_f \cup N_c$) × N_r) $\cup$ (N_r × N_c), L is the mapping from a node to its labels, and G$\subseteq N_c$ are the observed attack events. Every rule node has a consequence fact node as its single child and one or more fact or consequence fact nodes from prior attack steps as its parents. Node labels consist of instantiations of rules or sets of predicates specified as follows:

1. A node in N_f is an instantiation of predicates that codify system states including access privileges, network topology consisting of interconnectivity information, or known vulnerabilities associated with host computers in the system. We use the following predicates:

a. "hasAccount(_principal, _host, _account)", "canAccessFile(_host, _user, _access, _path)" and etc. to model access privileges.

b. "attackerLocated(_host)" and "hacl(_src, _dst, _prot, _port)" to model network topology, namely, the attacker's location and network reachability information.

c. "vulExists(_host, _vulID, _program)" and "vulProperty(_vulID, _range, _consequence)" to model vulnerabilities exhibited by nodes.

2. A node in N_c represents the predicate that codifies the post attack state as the consequence of an attack step. We use predicates "execCode(_host, _user)" and "netAccess(_machine, _protocol, _port)" to model the attacker's capability after an attack step. Valid instantiations of these predicates after an attack will update valid instantiations of the predicates listed in (1).

3. A node in N_r consists of a single rule in the form $p \leftarrow p_1 \wedge p_2, \cdots, \wedge p_n$, where p as the child node of N_r is an instantiation of predicates from N_c, and all p_i for $i \in \{1 \ldots n\}$ as the parent nodes of N_r are the collection of all predicate instantiations of N_f from the current step and N_c from prior attack steps.

Figure 1 is an example LEG. The notation of all nodes, which is in the form of instantiated rules or predicates as defined in Definition 1, is listed in Table 1 (Due to layout issues, the notation is in a separate table). In Fig. 1, fact, rule and consequence fact nodes are represented as boxes, ellipses, and diamonds respectively. Consequence fact nodes (Node 1 and 3) codify attack status obtainable from event logs or other forensic tools recording the post-conditions of attack steps. Fact nodes

Table 1 The notation of nodes in Fig. 1

Node	Notation	Source
1	execCode (workStation1, user)	Evidence obtained from event log
2	THROUGH 3 (remote exploit of a server program)	Rule 1 (hypothesis 1)
3	netAccess (workStation1, tcp, 4040)	Evidence obtained from event log
4	THROUGH 8 (direct network access)	Rule 2 (hypothesis 2)
5	hacl (internet, workStation1, tcp, 4040)	Network setup
6	attackerLocated (internet)	Evidence obtained from log
7	networkServiceInfo (workStation1, httpd, tcp, 4040, user)	Computer setup
8	vulExists (workStation1, 'CVE-2009-1918', httpd, remoteExploit, privEscalation)	Exploited vulnerability obtained from IDS Alert

Fig. 1 An example logical evidence graph

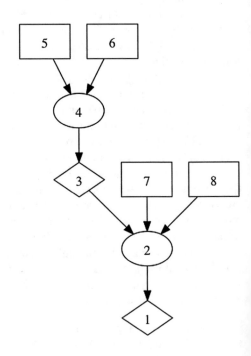

(Nodes 5, 6, 7 and 8) include network topology of a network (Nodes 5 and 6), computer configuration (Node 7) and the software vulnerability (Node 8) extracted from a forensic tool by analyzing captured evidence. Rule nodes (Nodes 4 and 2) represent specific rules that change the attack status based on attack steps.

To illustrate how rules are used to correlate corresponding items of evidence in this Prolog based tool, we list two rules between Line 9 and Line 17 in Fig. 2, which correspond to Rule 1 and Rule 2 mentioned in the third column of Table 1. Rules use the Prolog notation ": -" to separate the head (consequence) and the body (facts). In Fig. 2, Line 1 to Line 8 identifies fact and consequence predicates of the two rules. Rule 1 between Line 9 to Line 12 represents an attack step that states: if (1) the attacker is located in a "Zone" such as "Internet" (Line 10- attackerLocated(Zone)), and (2) if a host computer "H" can be accessed from the "Zone" by using "Protocol" at "Port" (Line 11-hacl(Zone, H, Protocol, Port)), then (3) the host "H" can be accessed from the "Zone" by using "Protocol" at "Port" (Line 9- netAccess(H, Protocol, Port)) by using (4) "direct network access" (Line 12–the description of the rule). Rule 2 between Line 13 to 17 states: (1) if a host computer "H" has software vulnerability that can be remotely exploited (Line 14- vulExists(H, _, Software, remoteExploit, privEscalation)), (2) "H" can be reached by using "Protocol" at "Port" with privilege

//Rule Head–post attack status as derived fact obtained from forensic analysis on evidence
1. Consequence: execCode(_host, _user).
2. Consequence: netAccess(_machine, _protocol, _port).
// Rule body–access priviledge
3. Fact: hacl(_src, _dst, _prot, _port).
//Rule body–software vulnerability obtained from forensic tool
4. Fact: vulExists(_host, _vulID, _program).
5. Fact: vulProperty(_vulID, _range, _consequence).
//Rule body–network topology
6. Fact: hacl(_src, _dst, _prot, _port).
7. Fact: attackerLocated(_host).
//Rule body–computer configuration
8. Fact: hasAccount(_principal, _host, _account).

Rule 1:
9. (netAccess(H, Protocol, Port) :-
10. attackerLocated(Zone),
11. hacl(Zone, H, Protocol, Port)),
12. rule_desc('direct network access', 1.0).

Rule 2:
13. (execCode(H, Perm) :-
14. vulExists(H, _, Software, remoteExploit, privEscalation),
15. networkServiceInfo(H, Software, Protocol, Port, Perm),
16. netAccess(H, Protocol, Port)),
17. rule_desc('remote exploit of a server program', 1.0).

Fig. 2 The example rules representing attack techniques

"Perm" (Line 15- networkServiceInfo(H, Software, Protocol, Port, Perm)), and (3) the attacker can access "H" by "Protocol" and "Port" (Line 16-netAccess(H, Protocol, Port)), then the attacker can remotely exploit the host computer "H" and obtain the privilege "Perm"(Line 13- execCode(H, Perm)) by using "remote exploit of a server program" technique (Line 17).

Evidence collected from attacks instantiates the corresponding predicates. Items between lines 1 to 8 in Fig. 2 show an example of such instantiation.

4   Using Alerts and Logs to Reconstruct Attack Scenario

In this section, we describe three experimental attacks we launched on a private cloud and how we reconstruct the attack scenarios by using the evidence we obtained from the cloud.

4.1   Experimental Environment Setup

OpenStack is a collection of python-based software projects that manage access to pooled storage, computing and network resources that reside in one or multiple machines of a cloud. This collection has six core projects: Neutron (Networking), Nova (Compute), Glance (Image Management), Swift (Object Storage), Cinder (Block Storage) and Keystone (Authorization and Authentication) [15]. OpenStack can be used to deploy any of the three service models–SaaS, PaaS and IaaS, but is mostly deployed as IaaS.

"DevStack" is a series of extensible scripts that can invoke an OpenStack environment quickly. By using "DevStack", we deployed a private IaaS cloud with the version of "Juno" on an Ubuntu 14.04 Desktop (with IP address 172.16.168.100). Authenticated users can manage OpenStack services by tying IP address 172.16.168.100 on their browsers to access the cloud's control dashboard "Horizon" as shown in Fig. 3.

We deployed two VMs (also called running instances), a webserver (named "WebServer" associated with the IP address 172.16.168.226) and a fileserver (named "FileServer" associated with the IP address 172.16.168.229), under the authenticated user "Admin" in our OpenStack cloud. In the "WebServer", we deployed an Apache web server and a MySQL database, allowing users to query their data using the web server. Authenticated users can access the "FileServer" by remotely using "ssh". In order to launch an attack, we also installed Kali (the penetration testing and ethical hacking Linux distribution tool [24]) in the same network (with the IP address 172.16.168.173).

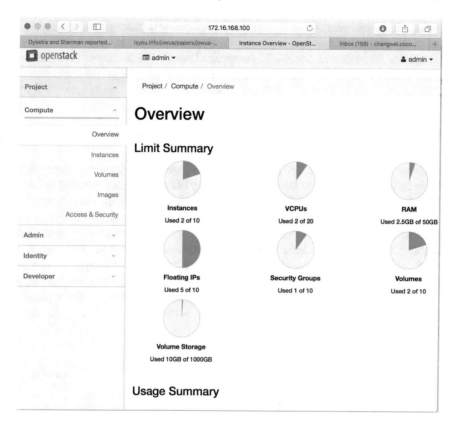

Fig. 3 OpenStack web user interface–Horizon

4.2 Example Attacks

We launched three attacks, including a SQL injection attack, a DDoS attack and a DoS attack towards the two VMs in our IaaS cloud.

Our SQL injection attack exploits un-sanitized user inputs (CWE89) in the "Web-Server". Our DDoS attack known as "TCP connection flood" used "nping" in Kali to flood the "FileServer" in order to prevent legitimate requests. While SQL injection and DDoS attacks can happen to any network including a cloud that has corresponding vulnerabilities, only IaaS privileged users can resize and delete a VM by launching DoS attacks that exploit the vulnerability "CVE-2015-3241" [25]. According to [25], the vulnerability "CVE-2015–3241" that is in OpenStack Compute (Nova) versions 2015.1 through 2015.1.1, 2014.2.3 and earlier allows authenticated users to cause Denial of Services(DoS) by resizing and then deleting an instance (VM). The process of resizing and deleting an instance in this way is also called instance migration. With "CVE-2015-3241", the migration process does not terminate when an instance is deleted, so an authenticated user could bypass user quota enforcement to deplete all available disk space by repeatedly performing instance migration. Figure 4 shows the process of our resizing the file server from "ds512M" to "ds1G", where we can see the instances' availability zone was "nova". We continued to resize and delete instances until Nova was so depleted that it could not accept any new instance.

4.3 Identifying Evidence to Reconstruct Attack Scenarios

To obtain evidence for forensic analysis, we configured the web server and the SQL database in "WebServer" to log access and query history. We also installed Snort in "WebServer" and "FileServer" VMs and deployed Wireshark in the host Ubuntu OS to monitor the network traffic. Snort captured the SQL injection attack and generated alerts with appropriate rules. Also, Wireshark captured packets that formed the DDoS attack. Figure 5 lists some Snort alerts and MySQL query logs of the SQL injection attack, which shows the attack was done by using "or '1'='1' " to bypass the SQL query syntax check. The snapshot of packets captured by Wireshark is listed in Fig. 6, where we can see Kali Linux at 172.16.168.173 sent out numerous SYN packets to "FileServer" at 172.16.168.229, and the "FileServer" sent numerous SYN-ACK packets back to Kali Linux.

	Instance Name	Image Name	IP Address	Size	Key Pair	Status	Availability Zone
☐	FileServer	-	10.0.0.13 Floating IPs: 172.16.168.229	ds1G	default	Confirm or Revert Resize/Migrate	nova
☐	WebServer	-	10.0.0.5 Floating IPs: 172.16.168.226	m1.small	default	Active	nova

Fig. 4 Resizing "FileServer"

```
[**] SQL Injection Attempt --1=1 [**]
08/16-14:37:27.818279 172.16.168.173:1715 -> 172.16.168.226:80
TCP TTL:128 TOS:0x0 ID:380 IpLen:20 DgmLen:48 DF
******S* Seq: 0xDEDBEABF Ack: 0x0 Win: 0xFFFF TcpLen: 28
TCP Options (4) => MSS: 1460 NOP NOP SackOK


160813 14:37:29 40 Connect
...
40 QuerySET GLOBAL general_log = 'ON' 40 Queryselect * from profiles where
name='Alice' AND password='alice' or '1'='1'
Gen_log 2: 130813 14:39:56
...
```

Fig. 5 The SNORT alert and the MySQL database log

No.	Time	Source	Destination	Protocol	Length	Info
217	10.405625326	172.16.168.173	172.16.168.229	TCP	74	34818 → 80 [SYN] Seq=0 Win=2920...
218	10.405682554	172.16.168.173	172.16.168.229	TCP	74	44208 → 80 [SYN] Seq=0 Win=2920...
219	10.405746104	172.16.168.173	172.16.168.229	TCP	74	38032 → 80 [SYN] Seq=0 Win=2920...
220	10.408041819	172.16.168.173	172.16.168.229	TCP	74	34348 → 80 [SYN] Seq=0 Win=2920...
221	10.408111539	172.16.168.173	172.16.168.229	TCP	74	38769 → 80 [SYN] Seq=0 Win=2920...
222	10.408205849	172.16.168.173	172.16.168.229	TCP	74	36846 → 80 [SYN] Seq=0 Win=2920...
223	10.408275950	172.16.168.173	172.16.168.229	TCP	74	35307 → 80 [SYN] Seq=0 Win=2920...
224	10.408329211	172.16.168.229	172.16.168.173	TCP	60	80 → 41930 [RST, ACK] Seq=1 Ack...
225	10.408355690	172.16.168.229	172.16.168.173	TCP	60	80 → 44471 [RST, ACK] Seq=1 Ack...
226	10.408388686	172.16.168.173	172.16.168.229	TCP	74	35276 → 80 [SYN] Seq=0 Win=2920...
227	10.408430802	172.16.168.229	172.16.168.173	TCP	60	80 → 45714 [RST, ACK] Seq=1 Ack...
228	10.408465024	172.16.168.229	172.16.168.173	TCP	60	80 → 35431 [RST, ACK] Seq=1 Ack...
229	10.408494300	172.16.168.173	172.16.168.229	TCP	74	45076 → 80 [SYN] Seq=0 Win=2920...
230	10.408557887	172.16.168.229	172.16.168.173	TCP	60	80 → 35247 [RST, ACK] Seq=1 Ack...
231	10.408583684	172.16.168.229	172.16.168.173	TCP	60	80 → 36321 [RST, ACK] Seq=1 Ack...
232	10.408616274	172.16.168.173	172.16.168.229	TCP	74	35152 → 80 [SYN] Seq=0 Win=2920...

Fig. 6 A snippet of packets caught by wireshark

Fig. 7 Prolog predicates for SQL injection and DDoS evidence

//The initial attack status and final attack status
attackerLocated(internet).
attackGoal(serviceDown(fileServer,user)).
attackGoal(execCode(database,user)).

//The network topology and computer configuration
//"_" means any port
hacl(internet, webServer, tcp, 80).
hacl(internet, fileServer, tcp, _).
directAccess(webServer,database,modify,user).

//The evidence found in webServer
vulExists(webServer, 'SQLInjection', httpd).
vulProperty('SQLInjection', remoteExploit, privEscalation).
networkServiceInfo(webServer , httpd, tcp , 80 , user).

//The evidence captured by WireShark
vulExists(fileServer,'DDoS', httpd).
vulProperty('DDoS', remoteExploit, privEscalation).
networkServiceInfo(fileServer, httpd, tcp, _, user).

We used our Prolog based tool to automate the process of correlating items of evidence to reconstruct potential attack scenarios. In order to do so, we converted the available evidence and the cloud configuration to corresponding Prolog predicates, forming an input file as shown in Fig. 7. The reconstructed attack paths are shown in Fig. 8, with the notation of all nodes listed separately in Table 2. In Fig. 8, the left path ([7, 8] → 6 → [5, 9, 10] → 4 → [3, 11] → 2 → 1) represents the SQL injection attack that used the web server vulnerability to maliciously obtain the information from the MySQL database, and the right path ([8, 16] → 15 → [14, 17, 18] → 13 → 12) represents the DDoS attack that brought down the "FileServer".

Snort and Wireshark failed in capturing our DoS attack on the "FileServer" that exploited the "CVE-2015-3241" vulnerability on OpenStack Nova service. Because the logs of OpenStack service Application Programming Interface (API) provide information about user operations on the running instances, we used the OpenStack service API logs as evidence. Figure 9 lists a snippet of Nova API logs that are

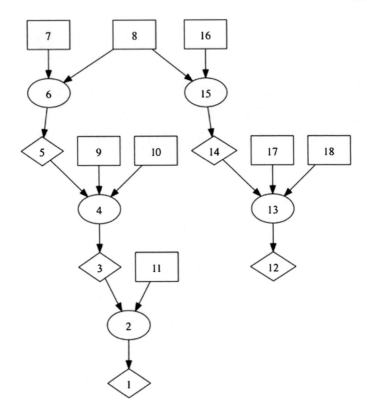

Fig. 8 Attack path reconstructed for SQL injection and DDoS

related to our instance migration of the DoS attack, where the commands in bold font show the instance "bd1dac18-1ce2-44b5-93ee-967fec640ff3" representing the "FileServer" VM (as shown in Table 3, which was obtained by running "nova list" in the Ubuntu host system) has been resized using commands "mv" (move) and "mkdir" (create new directory) operated by the user "admin". Combining with the corresponding attack status and the system configuration, we aggregated the related Nova API calls as evidence and encoded them to the corresponding evidence predicates, which formed the input file as shown in Fig. 10. By running our Prolog based tool on the input file, we obtained the attack scenario in the same graphical form as Fig. 1, but with different notation of all nodes in Table 4. The attack scenario shows the attack path that used the control dashboard "Horizon" exploiting the "CVE-2015-3241" vulnerability.

Because of the location difference of attackers, Fig. 8 representing the SQL injection and DDoS attacks and Fig. 1 representing the DoS attack cannot be grouped together. In addition, in Fig. 1, the attack happened in the cloud compute service instead of a VM, although the attacker launched the attack from a VM. This is because all VMs share the same compute service in our cloud.

Table 2 The notation of nodes in Fig. 8

Node	Notation
1	execCode (database, user)
2	THROUGH 7 (Attack by compromised computer)
3	execCode (webServer, user)
4	THROUGH 3 (remote exploit of a server program)
5	netAccess (webServer, tcp, 80)
6	THROUGH 9 (direct network access)
7	hacl (internet, webServer, tcp, 80)
8	attackerLocated (internet)
9	networkServiceInfo (webServer, httpd, tcp, 80, user)
10	vulExists (webServer, 'SQLInjection', httpd, remoteExploit, privEscalation)
11	directAccess (webServer, database, modify, user)
12	execCode (fileServer, user)
13	THROUGH 3 (remote exploit of a server program)
14	netAccess (fileServer, tcp, _)
15	THROUGH 9 (direct network access)
16	hacl (internet, fileServer, tcp, _)
17	networkServiceInfo (fileServer, httpd, tcp,_, user)
18	vulExists (fileServer, 'DDoS', httpd, remoteExploit, privEscalation)

2016-09-18 07:52:00.237 DEBUG oslo_concurrency.processutils [req-f79c7911-04ed-4a0c-adbe-0ae0a487c0f7 admin admin] Running cmd (subprocess): **mv /opt/stack/data/nova/instances/bd1dac18-1c e2-44b5-93ee-967fec640ff3= /opt/stack/data/nova/instances/bd1dac18-1ce2-44b5-93ee-967fec640ff3_resize from (pid=41737)** execute /usr/local/lib/python2.7/dist-packages/oslo_concurrency/processutils.py:344

2016-09-18 07:52:00.253 DEBUG oslo_concurrency.processutils [req-f79c7911-04ed-4a0c-adbe-0ae0a487c0f7 admin admin] CMD **"mv /opt/stack/data/nova/instances/bd1dac18-1ce2-44b5-93ee-967fec640ff3 /opt/stack/data/nova/instances/bd1dac18-1ce2-44b5-93ee-967fec640ff3_resize"** returned: 0 in 0.016s from (pid=41737) execute /usr/local/lib/python2.7/dist-packages/oslo_concurrency/processutils.py:374

2016-09-18 07:52:00.254 DEBUG oslo_concurrency.processutils [req-f79c7911-04ed-4a0c-adbe-0ae0a487c0f7 admin admin] Running cmd (subprocess): **mkdir p /opt/stack/data/nova/instances/bd1dac18-1ce2-44b5-93ee-967fec640ff3 from (pid=41737)** execute /usr/local/lib/python2.7/dist-packages/oslo_concurrency/processutils.py:344

2016-09-18 07:52:00.271 DEBUG oslo_concurrency.processutils [req-f79c7911-04ed-4a0c-adbe-0ae0a487c0f7 admin admin] CMD **"mkdir p /opt/stack/data/nova/instances/bd1dac18-1ce2-44b5-93ee-967fec640ff3"** returned: 0 in 0.017s from (pid=41737) execute /usr/local/lib/python2.7/dist-packages/oslo_concurrency/processutils.py:374

Fig. 9 Nova API Call logs

Table 3 The VM instance IDs, names and IPs

ID	Name	Networks
bd1dac18-1ce2-44b5-93ee-967fec640ff3	FileServer	private = 10.0.0.13, 172.16.168.229
c01d5e66-c20d-4544-867b-d3e2b70bfc60	WebServer	private = 10.0.0.5, 172.16.168.226

```
//the initial and final attack status
attackerLocated(controlDashboard).
attackGoal(execCode(nova,admin)).

//the fileserver VM could be reached from control dashboard
hacl(controlDashboard, fileServer, http, _).

//the evidence of attack using 'CVE-2015-3241' that uses RESTful service
vulExists(nova,'CVE-2015-3241', 'REST').
vulProperty('CVE-2015-3241', remoteExploit, privEscalation).
networkServiceInfo(nova, 'REST', http, _, admin).
```

Fig. 10 The input file for attack using "CVE-2015-3241"

Table 4 The notation of nodes for DoS attack

Node	Notation
1	execCode (nova, admin)
2	THROUGH 3 (remote exploit of a server program)
3	netAccess (nova, http, _)
4	THROUGH 9 (direct network access)
5	hacl (controlDashboard, nova, http, _)
6	attackerLocated (controlDashboard)
7	networkServiceInfo (nova, 'REST', http, _, admin)
8	vulExists (nova, 'CVE-2015-3241', 'REST', remoteExploit, privEscalation)

5 Using System Call Invocations for Evidence Analysis

Because system calls allow user level processes to request kernel level services including access to storage operations, memory or network access and process management, system call sequences are often used for intrusion detection and forensic analysis [26]. When evidence or expert knowledge is unavailable to recognize the interaction between user level processes to kernel level services as a known attack, forensic investigators analyze the system calls to ascertain program behaviors. According to [27], it is rare or unlikely to have an attack path, in which every attack step is a zero-day attack. As such, we use system calls to reconstruct the missing attack steps only when other evidence is unavailable.

There are many mechanisms to trace the system calls in a cloud based VM: (1) use "ptrace" command to set up system call interception and modification by modifying a software application, (2) use "strace" command to log system calls and signals, (3) use auditing facilities within the kernel, (4) modify the system call table and write system call wrappers to log the corresponding system calls, (5) intercept the system call within the hypervisor [28]. Because OpenStack supports different hypervisors, including Xen, QEMU, KVM, LXC, Hyper-V and UML, there isn't a generic solution to intercept system calls within a hypervisor. Thus, we use methods 2 and 4 to log relevant system calls.

Now we show how to use system call sequences to reconstruct an attack step by using an attack example. In this experimental attack launched from our Kali Linux, we, as the attacker, used ssh to log into "FileServer" by using stolen credentials from a legitimate user named "coco". In order to simulate the stealthy attack without triggering IDS alerts, we assumed that the attacker could use social engineering attacks, such as shoulder surfing, to obtain the legitimate user's (username, password) credentials. The corresponding sshd log from "/var/log/auth.log" in "FileServer" is listed in Fig. 11, where the user "coco" was listed to log into "FileServer" from "172.16.168.173" that actually belonged to the attacker, which indicates that the attacker stole this user's credentials.

A process is typically composed of many system calls, of which only some of them are important to ascertain a process' behavior (we use the ones presented in [27]. These system calls are listed in the second column of Table 5). Figure 12 is a snippet of important system calls captured from the attack of using coco's stolen credentials to modify a file in "FileServer" (due to space limitations, we list a part of captured system calls). By analyzing these system calls, we noticed that the "write/read" system calls (in bold font) indicated that the attacker used "vi test.txt" ("vi" is a text editor) command to modify "test.txt" file. In the "write/read" system call, the first argument is the file descriptor where the process reads or writes, the second argument represents the content in the buffer, the third argument represents how many bytes the system call will write/read, and "= 1/ <any number greater than 1>" indicates that the system call executed successfully.

We encoded the program behavior, the attacker's opening and modifying a legitimate user's file, to the Prolog Predicate "canAccessFile(fileServer, user, modify,_)" (This predicate means that the attacker as the user can modify the file located at "_"

Sep 25 00:15:49 FileServer sshd[829]: Server listening on 0.0.0.0 port 22.
Sep 25 00:15:49 FileServer sshd[829]: Server listening on :: port 22.
Sep 25 00:28:15 FileServer sshd[1162]: Accepted password for coco from 172.16.168.173 port 44842 ssh2
Sep 25 00:28:16 FileServer sshd[1162]: pam_unix(sshd:session): session opened for user coco by (uid=0)

Fig. 11 The authentication log for sshd

Table 5 Important system calls

Tasks	System calls
Process modifies file	write, pwrite64, rename, mkdir, linkat, link, symlinkat, symlink, fchmodat, fchmod, chmod, fchownat, mount
Process uses but does not modify file	stat64, lstat6e, fsat64, open, read, pread64, execve, mmap2, mprotect, linkat, link, symlinkat, symlink
Process uses and modifies file	open, rename, mount, mmap2, mprotect
Process creation or termination	vfork, fork, kill
Process creation	Clone

write(9, "v", 1) = 1
read(11, "v", 16384) = 1
write(3, "\0\0\0\20\331\255\275\264c\2173)z2j\32\255n\2007d\366m\21\316\2648\240\207\31\211"..., 36) = 36
read(3,"\0\0\0\20\240\253\341\227\321xU\305\347\226\246\361\316\242S   =
\30\341QT\231\n\343\314\343\307\f\361"..., 16384) = 36
write(9, "i", 1) = 1
read(11, "i", 16384) = 1
write(3,"\0\0\0\20\177\352\313\332\373yjM\3416l\230\215\10\220p\252g\375\365\1\f\335\361\r\273\374\357"..., 36) = 36
read(3,"\0\0\0\20\27\334?\201x\300\16\356\346,\0379\32\220{\372)\366\4\v\1   =
\347\263\311\250k\353"..., 16384) = 36
write(9, " ", 1) = 1
read(11, " ", 16384) = 1
write(3,"\0\0\0\20ti\321\344\220\313\322\254S\252o\201\225;6v\243\205\10gs\253\237\325\375\332v"..., 36) = 36
read(3,   "\0\0\0\20\5\27k;\254\301\24\n\\ZN\267\260\336\323t\323\32\345\2b\226 −
\271|[B\21"..., 16384) = 36
write(9, "t", 1) = 1
read(11, "t", 16384) = 1
read(3,"\0\0\0\20\325\261\7\254\211(\201\331\272\344[\355\200\\u4\357G\347\232\276:
\201\376\342\202\201."..., 16384) = 36
write(3,"\0\0\0\20\320\254\#\312\211_\3022\n\227u\16l\372\202\347\37\252T\257\220\210E\343\222\342\24S"..., 36) = 36
write(9, "e", 1) = 1
read(11, "e", 16384) = 1
write(3,   "\0\0\0\20\334n}4\375Q\212o\353\375\262\342\316\334w   −
F\213\303\277t\312\245\16\266\255B|"..., 36) = 36
read(3,   "\0\0\0\20\274\376\7J\214L\314OL\1c\22\364   −
gvJ\%\21\344J¡,h\363\261\36\10"..., 16384) = 36
write(9, "\t", 1) = 1
read(11, "st.txt ", 16384) = 7
...

Fig. 12 Traces of "Read" and "Write" system calls

//The initial attack status
attackerLocated(internet).
// the attacker was able to log into "FileServer" by using stolen credentials
attackGoal(logInService(fileserver, tcp,22)
attackGoal(princinpalCompromised(user))
//InCompetent user
InCompetent(user).

//The attack status obtained from analyzing system call sequence
attackGoal(canAccessFile(fileServer,user,modify,_)).
//The user could login fileserver by using ssh protocol
networkServiceInfo(fileServer , sshd, tcp, 22, _).
//the user who has the account on "FileServer" has the privilege to modify a file
localFileProtection(fileServer,user,modify,_).

Fig. 13 Input file for modifying a file with stolen credentials

representing the home directory of the user). With the evidence obtained from the
log shown in Fig. 11 showing that the attacker with stolen credentials (represented
by predicates "attackGoal (princinpalCompromised (user))", "InCompetent (user)"
and "attackerLocated (internet)") logged into the "FileServer" by using ssh (represented by Predicate "attackGoal (logInService (fileserver, tcp,22))") and the fact user
"coco", who had an account on "FileServer", had the privilege to modify files (the
corresponding predicate is "localFileProtection (fileServer, user, modify ,_)"), we
formed the input file as illustrated in Fig. 13 to use our Prolog based tool. The reconstructed attack path is shown in Fig. 14, and the notation of all nodes is in Table 6.
In Fig. 14, the attack step [3, 4, 7] → 2→1 has two pre-conditions represented by
Node 4 and Node 7. Node 4 is obtained from the fact that the "FileServer" can be
accessed by using ssh with Protocol tcp from Port 22. Node 7 is obtained from ssh
authentication log in Fig. 11 that indicates the user's credentials were stolen by the
attacker. Without the evidence obtained from the system call sequence (Node 1), the
attack step [3, 4, 7] → 2→1 would not have been reconstructed.

Notice the two rule nodes (Node 5 and Node 2) in Fig. 14 do not have any rule
description because of the obvious correlation between Node 6 and Node 4 (if the
network provides the service of using ssh to log into a file server by using tcp at
Port 22, the user including the attacker could log into the file server with stolen
credentials), nodes [3,4,7] and Node 1 (if a user is allowed to have the privilege of
modifying a file in the file server, the attacker with stolen credentials from the user
could access the file and modify it).

Fig. 14 The attack step
reconstructed by using
evidence obtained from
system calls

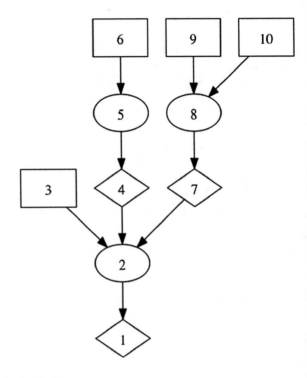

Table 6 The notation of all nodes in Fig. 14

Node	Notation
1	canAccessFile (fileserver, user, modify, _)
2	THROUGH 23()
3	localFileProtection (fileserver, user, modify, _)
4	logInService (fileserver, tcp, 22)
5	THROUGH 18 ()
6	networkServiceInfo (fileserver, sshd, tcp, 22, user)
7	princinpal Compromised (user)
8	THROUGH 16 (password sniffing)
9	inCompetent (user)
10	attacker Located (internet)

6 Open Research Problems

The properties of cloud computing, including multi-tenancy, customers' lack of controlling their data and high degree of virtualization, bring challenges to cloud forensics. Two major issues are the inaccessibility of forensically valuable data and loss of governance [13].

Many digital artifacts created for cloud services can be used as evidence for cloud forensics. These artifacts include cloud service logs, software application logs, database access logs, etc. [13]. However, in a virtualized cloud environment, the physical inaccessibility to underlying hardware and data being located across multiple locations makes evidence collection, identification, separation more challenging. Even though the data location is known, due to multi-tenancy, acquiring the data could breach other customers' data confidentiality. In clouds, customers cede service governance to the cloud providers, which makes the control of evidence depends on what cloud service providers are willing to provide to customers. In the three cloud models–IaaS, PaaS and SaaS, as the control of functionality and services decreases, less forensic data is available to cloud customers [13].

Researchers have proposed to use cryptography and store data hashes to resolve the two major issues [5, 6]. However, in a cloud environment where the hypervisors that monitor the VMs lack warning, procedures and tools for forensic investigation, and VMs can dynamically migrate from one location to another, the above research that only focuses on data is not enough. It is critical to build trustworthy mechanisms at every architectural layer including the hardware layer and the virtualization platform. Besides, extra effort should be taken to deal with the large volume in content and proprietary formats of data and segregating resources without breaching user confidentiality and analyzing traces.

7 Conclusion and Future Work

Cloud computing can increase the flexibility and efficiency of organizations or enterprises. However, clouds present significant challenges to forensics, including customers' lack of control of the physical locations of their data, the large volume of data logs and the prevalence of proprietary formats [3]. To solve the above problems, we explored what evidence could be useful for cloud forensic analysis.

Our example attacks show evidence from three sources can be used to reconstruct attack scenarios: (1) IDS and application software logging, (2) cloud service API calls, and (3) system calls from VMs. To extract evidence from the three sources, the forensic-enabled cloud needs three extensions, which can (1) retrieve IDS and software service logging; (2) store and secure OpenStack service API call logs, firewall logs and snapshots for running instances; (3) obtain system calls when the evidence from (1) and (2) is missing. We are in the process of implementing forensic-enabled clouds with the above extensions, resolving the data integrity issue, reducing the large volume and abstracting the proprietary nature of cloud forensic data.

Disclamier

This chapter is subject to the approval from the National Institute of Standards and Technology, United States.

References

1. Kent, K., Chevalier, S., Grance, T., & Dang, H. (2006). Guide to integrating forensic techniques into incident response. p. 800 e86. NIST Special Publication.
2. Palmer, G. (2001). A road map for digital forensic research. Report from DFRWS 2001, First Digital Forensic Research Workshop, Utica, New York, August 7–8, pp. 27–30.
3. Ruan, K., Carthy, J., Kechadi, T. & Crosbie, M. (2011). Cloud forensics. In *IFIP International Conference on Digital Forensics*, pp. 35–46. Springer, Heidelberg.
4. Hogan, M., Liu, F., Sokol, A., & Tong, J. (2011). NIST cloud computing standards roadmap. NIST Special Publication 35.
5. Dykstra, J., & Sherman, A. (2013). Design and implementation of FROST: Digital forensic tools for the OpenStack cloud computing platform. *Digital Investigation, 10*(Supplement), S87–S95.
6. Zawoad, S., & Hasan, R. (2015). FECloud: A trustworthy forensics-enabled cloud architecture. In *Proceedings 11th International Federation for Information Processing WG 11.9 International Conference Digital Forensics*, pp. 271–285.
7. Liu, C., Singhal, A., & Wijesekera, D. (2017). *Identifying evidence for implementing a cloud forensic analysis framework*. Orlando, Florida: Accepted by IFIP International Conference Digital Forensics.
8. Jaquith, A. (2007). Security Metrics: Replacing Fear, Uncertainty, and Doubt. Addison Wesley, Mar 26, 2007.
9. Liu, C., Singhal, A., & Wijesekera, D. (2012). Mapping evidence graphs to attack graphs. In *2012 IEEE International Workshop on Information Forensics and Security (WIFS)*, (pp. 121–126). IEEE.
10. Mell, P., & Grance, T. (2009). NIST definition of cloud computing. National Institute of Standards and Technology. October 7, 2009.
11. Tribunella, T., & Tribunella, H. (2016). Twenty questions on the sharing economy and mobile accounting apps. CPA Journal. May 2016; 32. Available from: Associates Programs Source, Ipswich, MA.
12. Spyridopoulos, T., & Katos, V. (2013). Data Recovery Strategies for Cloud Environments.
13. Pichan, A., Lazarescu, M., & Soh, S. T. (2015). Cloud forensics: technical challenges, solutions and comparative analysis. *Digital Investigation, 13*, 38–57.
14. Dykstra, J., & Sherman, A. T. (2012). Acquiring forensic evidence from infrastructure-as-a-service cloud computing: Exploring and evaluating tools, trust, and techniques. In *Proceedings of the 12th Annual Digital Forensics Research Conference (DFRWS12), Washington, DC, USA, Digital Investigation*, vol. 9, August 2012, pp. 90–98.
15. OpenStack Open Source Cloud Computing Software. Retrieved from https://www.openstack.org.
16. Hay, B., & Nance, K. (2008). Forensics examination of volatile system data using virtual introspection. *ACM SIGOPS Operating Systems Review, 42*(3), 74–82.
17. Birk, D., & Wegener, C. (2011). Technical issues of forensic investigations in cloud computing environments. In *6th International Workshop on Systematic Approaches to Digital Forensic Engineering-IEEE/SADFE*, pp. 1–10. Oakland, CA. USA.
18. Dain, O., & Cunningham, R. (2001). Building scenarios from a heterogeneous alert stream. In *Proceedings of the 2001 IEEE Workshop on Information Assurance and Security*, pp. 231–235, June 2001.

19. Debar, H., & Wespi, A. (2001). Aggregation and correlation of intrusion detection alerts. In *Recent Advances in Intrusion Detection 2001, LNCS 2212*, pp. 85–103.
20. Wang, W., & Thomas, E. D. (2008). A graph based approach toward network forensics analysis. ACM Transactions on Information and Systems Security *12* (1).
21. Liu, C., Singhal, A., & Wijesekera, D. (2015). A Logic Based Network Forensics Model for Evidence Analysis. In *IFIP International Conference on Digital Forensics, Orlando, Florida*, January 24–26 2015.
22. Liu, C., Singhal, A., & Wijesekera, D. A probabilistic network forensic model for evidence analysis. In *IFIP International Conference on Digital Forensics* (pp. 189–210). Springer International Publishing.
23. Ou, X., Govindavajhala, S., & Appel, A. W. (2005). MulVAL: A logic-based network security analyzer. In *USENIX security*.
24. Kali Linux–Penetration Testing and Ethical Hacking Linux Distribution. Retrieved from https://www.kali.org.
25. MITRE Common Vulnerabilities and Exposures List. Available from http://cve.mitre.org.
26. Hofmeyr, S. A., Forrest, S., & Somayaji, A. (1998). Intrusion detection using sequences of system calls. *Journal of computer security, 6*(3), 151–180.
27. Sun, X., Dai, J., Singhal, A., Liu, P. & Yen, J. (2016). Towards probabilistic identification of zero-day attack paths. In *Accepted for IEEE Conference on Communication and Network Security, Philadelphia, October 17th 19th, 2016*.
28. Beck, F., & Festor, O. (2009). Syscall interception in xen hypervisor. 19.
29. Zhang, Q., Cheng, L., & Boutaba, R. (2010). Cloud computing: state-of-the-art and research challenges. *Journal of internet services and applications, 1*(1), 7–18.

An Access Control Framework for Secure and Interoperable Cloud Computing Applied to the Healthcare Domain

Mohammed S. Baihan and Steven A. Demurjian

Abstract The healthcare domain is an emergent application for cloud computing, in which the Meaningful Use Stage 3 guidelines recommend health information technology (HIT) systems to provide cloud services that enable health-related data owners to access, modify, and exchange data. This requires mobile and desktop applications for patients and medical providers to obtain healthcare data from multiple HITs, which may be operating with different paradigms (e.g., cloud services, programming services, web services), use different cloud service providers, and employ different security/access control techniques. To address these issues, this chapter introduces and discusses an *Access Control Framework for Secure and Interoperable Cloud Computing (FSICC)* that provides a mechanism for multiple HITs to register cloud, programming, and web services and security requirements for use by applications. FSICC supports a global security policy and enforcement mechanism for cloud services with role-based (RBAC), discretionary (DAC), and mandatory (MAC) access controls. The Fast Healthcare Interoperability Resources (FHIR) standard models healthcare data using a set of 93 resources to track a patient's clinical findings, problems, etc. For each resource, an FHIR Application Program Interface (API) is defined to share data in a common format for each HIT that can be accessed by mobile applications. Thus, there is a need to support with a heterogeneous set of information sources and differing security protocols (i.e., RBAC, DAC, and MAC). To demonstrate the realization of FSICC, we apply the framework to the integration of the Connecticut Concussion Tracker (CT^2) mHealth application with the OpenEMR electronic medical record utilizing FHIR.

M.S. Baihan (✉) · S.A. Demurjian
Department of Computer Science & Engineering, University of Connecticut,
371 Fairfield Way, Storrs, CT 06269-4155, USA
e-mail: mohammed.baihan@uconn.edu

S.A. Demurjian
e-mail: steven.demurjian@uconn.edu

© Springer Nature Singapore Pte Ltd. 2017
S. Chaudhary et al. (eds.), *Research Advances in Cloud Computing*,
DOI 10.1007/978-981-10-5026-8_16

1 Introduction

Cloud computing has emerged as a de facto approach throughout society, commercial and government sectors, and research/academic communities. The Gartner group forecasts cloud computing will represent the majority of IT funding by 2016 [44]. The International Data Corporation [24] reports that organizations and enterprises around the world spent approximately $70 billion to adopt cloud computing services in 2015 with the number of cloud-based services expected to triple by 2020. Cloud computing is provided by major corporations (e.g., Amazon [5], AT&T [6], Dell [11], etc.). The wide usage of mobile devices means that average users understand the storage and synching of photos, videos, email, contacts, files, etc., in the cloud. Security breaches have come to the forefront [27] especially in personal cloud storage [52]. Outsourced data and services are located on servers that belong to security domains which are different from an organization's security domain, raising numerous security and privacy issues [46]. Other efforts have included a survey of the different data/network security, authentication, authorization, and confidentiality issues that impact cloud computing [45]; a review of the available cloud computing advances in concepts, functionalities, unique features, and technologies [51]; and the characterization of cloud computing as the likely dominant technology for computing on the Internet [40].

One emergent application for cloud computing is health care where in the United States, the Center of Medicare and Medicaid Services released the Meaningful Use Stage 3 [23] guidelines that require all health information technology (HIT) systems to have cloud services to access, modify, and exchange health-related data. HIT systems include electronic health records (EHR) and personal health records (PHR). In support of the interoperability and exchange of healthcare data, the international Health Level 7 (HL7) [19] organization has taken a leadership role for standards to allow the integration, sharing, and exchange of electronical healthcare data, specifically HL7 Version 2 [20], HL7 Version 3 [21], the Clinical Document Architecture (CDA) [16], and HL7 Fast Healthcare Interoperability Resources (HL7 FHIR) [17]. Fast Healthcare Interoperability Resources (FHIR) provides a RESTful Application Program Interface (API) to share data in a common format. FHIR conceptualizes and abstracts information for HL7 into 93 Resources that effectively decompose HL7 into logical components to track a patient's clinical findings, problems, allergies, adverse events, history, suggested physician orders, care planning, etc. The intent is to allow a unified access to FHIR's RESTful health-related data sharing APIs so that applications can be easily built to uniformly utilize multiple HIT systems. Concurrent with these activities has been an explosion of mobile health (mHealth) applications for both patients and medical providers [1]. These mHealth applications also require access to health data via cloud services from multiple HIT systems to ensure that all of the necessary information is collected for patient care. Each of these HIT systems may operate with different paradigms (e.g., cloud, API, web services) and employ different security/access control techniques. Thus, mHealth applications would need to work with a heterogeneous collection of paradigms and security protocols, with the strong likelihood that set of information sources may grow or shrink over time. This makes it problematic to develop mHealth applications that are easily maintained and evolved.

The main issue for health care is to ensure that the available services of these HIT systems are carefully authorized to control which mHealth application can utilize which service at which time; this is specifically what FHIR has been defined to provide. For example, an HIT system for a pharmacy would have cloud services for the following: a physician to submit a prescription (R_x) electronically to the pharmacy; a pharmacist to be able to fill the R_x and reduce the number of refills; notification via text/phone to the patient that the R_x is available; the insurance company to access the information on the R_x for approval and payment; the physician to have the R_x inserted into his/her EHR; the patient to access medications in the PHR; and so on. Access control for cloud services of an HIT system can ensure that the mHealth application and its authorized user are restricted to particular services. The problem is that there is currently no solution that allows cloud services to be controlled on this basis, complicated by the fact that cloud services are available from different cloud suppliers that may not be compatible with one another.

To address the aforementioned issues, this chapter introduces an *Access Control Framework for Secure and Interoperable Cloud Computing (FSICC)* applied to the healthcare domain in Fig. 1 that provides a mechanism for multiple sources (bottom of Fig. 1) to register their services and security requirements for use by mobile, web, and desktop applications (top of Fig. 1). More specifically, the framework allows any system to register its local services (bottom of Fig. 1), which can be cloud, web, or traditional programmable APIs. Such different services are converted into a unified

Fig. 1 An access control framework for secure and interoperable cloud computing (FSICC) applied to the healthcare domain

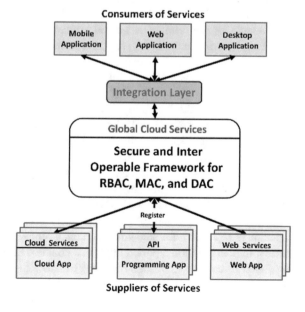

set of global cloud RESTful services, using an integration layer as shown in Fig. 1, which is available for mobile, web, and desktop applications to call. The integration layer is where technologies exist to facilitate the bidirectional mapping and exchange of information. Representative technologies to support the implementation of FSICC would include the aforementioned FHIR standard; the DIRECT project [47] that allows the sharing of information with best practices that have trust and privacy considerations; and the HEART WG project [39] that provides privacy and security specifications for authorization and access to health-related RESTful APIs.

The intent of the *Access Control Framework for Secure and Interoperable Cloud Computing* (FSICC) is to provide one-stop shopping to the application side with a set of global cloud services that transparently connect to the services from multiple diverse sources. In health care, an mHealth application would utilize a set of global cloud services via the integration layer (e.g., via FHIR, DIRECT, etc.) that provides a common means to interact with multiple HIT systems and their specific cloud, API, or web services. The resulting FSICC provides a global policy authorization and enforcement mechanism for a wide range of sources that collects cloud services, APIs, and web services from multiple sources to offer one combined cloud service collection to applications. FSICC should be able to support varied and multiple access control models such as Role-based Access Control (RBAC) [13], Discretionary Access Control (DAC) [12], Mandatory Access Control (MAC) [9], Usage Control (UCON) [42], Attribute-Based Access Control (ABAC) [53], etc. FSICC is intended to organize the cloud services, APIs, and web services from multiple suppliers so that they can be globally managed, discovered, and utilized by different applications. FSICC can be customized to utilize the aforementioned collection of standards and emergent technologies for easing the access of healthcare data by mHealth applications, specifically, FHIR which conceptualizes and abstracts information for HL7 into Resources that effectively decompose HL7 into logical components for information usage and exchange. The twofold focus of this chapter is to: first, describe in detail the proposed secure interoperable framework for access control as given in Fig. 1 focusing on its requirements, capabilities, and a detailed example in health care; and second, apply FSICC to an actual mobile health (mHealth) application.

To demonstrate the feasibility of our work, the chapter utilizes the Connecticut Concussion Tracker (CT^2) mHealth application that has been developed as a joint effort between the Departments of Physiology and Neurobiology, and Computer Science & Engineering at the University of Connecticut, in collaboration with faculty in the Schools of Nursing and Medicine. CT^2 was developed in support of a newly passed law to track concussions for school children (kindergarten through high school) in Connecticut [43]. The CT^2 mHealth application has been linked to a back-end repository that includes the OpenEMR [37] HIT systems to represent the clinical repository for students with concussions. To illustrate, Fig. 2 details our current implementation reported in [7] that contains the integration layer from Fig. 1 expanded to capture the usage of FHIR to allow the CT^2 mHealth application to access OpenEMR via FHIR. In Fig. 2, each of the two resources (CT^2 Database and OpenEMR,) has an FHIR interface. For OpenEMR, their APIs extract information

Fig. 2 The integration layer with FHIR for CT^2

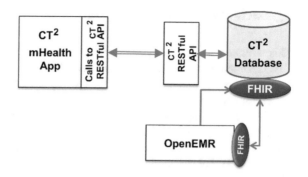

that is then converted into the aforementioned FHIR resources to be available for use by the CT^2 mHealth application. The CT^2 database also has an FHIR layer that maps the MySQL database tables into the same set of FHIR resources. The end result is an easy exchange of information between these three resources without the need to modify the CT^2 mHealth application or its RESTful API. This overall process is part of the proposed secure and interoperable framework and represents the realization of the integration layer from Fig. 1 via FHIR and its RESTful APIs to enable the two HIT systems (CT^2 Database and OpenEMR) to register their services to allow the CT^2 mHealth application to discover and utilize such RESTful API services and to define their security requirements to restrict the access of CT^2 mHealth application to their services.

The remainder of this chapter has six sections. Section 2 presents background on cloud computing, access control models, and FHIR. Section 3 introduces a health-care scenario that serves as the generalized example for the FSICC in Fig. 1 with multiple HIT sources. Section 4 is organized in four parts. Part one proposes five critical requirements for the FSICC: numerous and varied access control models, different categories of cloud services, control access to cloud services using RBAC, support delegation of cloud services using DAC, and control access to cloud services using MAC. Part two details three capabilities with associated components of the FSICC: local service registration and mapping to global services; local security policies registration to yield global security policy; and global registration, authentication, authorization, and service discover for consumers. Part three discusses the security risks of adopting the FSICC with possible mitigations. Part four reviews related work in cloud computing as compared to FSICC. Section 5 presents a proof-of-concept prototype utilizing the CT^2 mHealth concussion app and fully illustrates the development processes of the FSICC utilizing FHIR that reformulates the architecture given in Fig. 2 using the FSICC as shown in Fig. 1 to illustrate the way that the FSICC can improve the interconnection of the CT^2 mHealth application with the CT^2 Database and OpenEMR. Section 6 reviews select open research problems. Finally, Sect. 7 concludes and discusses ongoing work.

2 Background and Motivation

This section provides background on cloud computing, access control models, and Fast Healthcare Interoperability Resources (FHIR) standard. To begin, the National Institute of Standards and Technology (NIST) [31] defines "Cloud computing is a model for enabling convenient, on-demand network access to a shared pool of configurable computing resources (e.g., networks, servers, storage, applications, and services) that can be rapidly provisioned and released with minimal management effort or service provider interaction." Cloud computing emerged from existing technologies [54] that are combined in a certain way to provide a new business model. These technologies include grid computing [14], utility computing [41], autonomic computing [28], service-oriented architecture [35], and virtualization [8] to name a few.

Service-oriented architecture (SOA) is a model for designing systems in which the focus is around offering services for different consumers. SOA implementation, such as the web services standard, adopts the eXtensible Markup Language (XML) which enables systems to provide and consume services in a common manner without the need to use a specific programming language or operating system. This facilitates services integration. Service suppliers define and publish services for use by consumers. Cloud services are provided and delivered based on the cloud service model [32] by leveraging concepts from SOA. In cloud computing, there are three main components: Cloud Service Supplier, Cloud Service Consumer, and Cloud Service Registry. The *Cloud Service Supplier* component publishes services to the Cloud Service Registry. The *Cloud Service Consumer* component discovers services from Cloud Service Registry and consumes them. The *Cloud Service Registry* component maintains information about available cloud services. Cloud services are the APIs that define the way that cloud consumers can access and utilize cloud computing resources such as software. These cloud services can be designed using web services such as Representational State Transfer (REST), Simple Object Access Protocol (SOAP), etc. Any API designed based on REST is called a RESTful API which utilizes Hypertext Transfer Protocol (HTTP) requests to interact with the data of a resource. RESTful requests are frequently referred to as CRUD to create, read, update, and delete functions. CRUD operations from an HTTP perspective are typically defined as GET to retrieve data; PUT or POST to insert data; POST, PUT, or PATCH to update data; and DELETE to remove data. RESTful APIs have become a dominant choice for designing and implementing cloud APIs or services.

Access control models have gained wide acceptance in computing as represented by the three classic approaches: role-based access control (RBAC) [13], discretionary access control (DAC) [12], and mandatory access control (MAC) [9]. The RBAC model consists of three main components: *elements* that describe the different components, *relations* that exist between the various elements, and *constraints* that can be defined on the elements. There are five main elements in RBAC: *objects* that represent functionality for an application, *operations* that are defined on objects, *permissions* that are the allowed operations on the different objects, *roles* that represent a set of responsibilities for a user of the application to capture the defined permissions, and *users* assigned a role during a session of an application. RBAC elements can be organized into relations: a *role-user relation* to assign users to roles, a *role-permission relation* to assign permissions to roles, a *role-session relation* to assign sessions to roles, a *user-session relation* to assign users to sessions, and an *operation-object relation* to assign objects to operations. Finally, RBAC supports a number of constraints that can be defined to restrict a user playing a specific role with further constraints.

DAC utilizes the concept of delegation to pass privileges among users to delegate both authority and permissions to another user. For example, in health care, a physician Charles that is leaving the office for the weekend would delegate his responsibilities (e.g., patients) to the on-call physician Lois that will be covering any queries from patients. Charles can delegate all of his permissions and also the ability to further delegate those permissions beyond the original scope. For example, if the on-call physician Lois has to attend an emergency, she could then employ user-directed delegation to delegate the permissions passed to her by Charles to another user Thomas. Administrative-directed delegation has a security officer to control delegation.

In MAC, sensitivity levels are assigned to subjects (clearance) and objects (classification) with the permissions for the subject to read and/or write an object dependent on the relationship between clearance (assigned to users) and classifications (assigned to objects). MAC typically is modeling using four sensitivity levels which are hierarchically ordered from most to least secure: top secret (TS) < secret (S) < confidential (C) < unclassified (U); this is referred to as the multilevel security model (MLS). These terms are defined in the U.S. classification of information systems in a Presidential Executive Order [34]:

"(1) "Top Secret" shall be applied to information, the unauthorized disclosure of which reasonably could be expected to cause exceptionally grave damage to the national security.

(2) "Secret" shall be applied to information, the unauthorized disclosure of which reasonably could be expected to cause serious damage to the national security.

(3) "Confidential" shall be applied to information, the unauthorized disclosure of which reasonably could be expected to cause damage to the national security."

In MAC, the central authority maintains a classification for each resource and a clearance for each user in the system. Suppose that there is resource R1 with a confidential classification, resource R2 with a top secret classification, user U1 with a top secret clearance, and user U2 with a secret clearance. In this setting, U1 can access R1 and R2, while U2 can only access R1. Traditionally, RBAC, DAC, and MAC models define permissions over objects and operations of a system. However, in the case of cloud services, RBAC, DAC, and MAC models need to be modified so that permissions can be with this change; it is then possible to specify which role can access which cloud service, define a classification of each cloud service, and delegate a cloud service from one user to another user. This allows the FSICC to authorize a mobile, web, and desktop applications, by roles, to access cloud services.

The FHIR standard is primarily structured around the concept of FHIR resources [17] which are the data elements and associated RESTful application programmer interfaces (APIs) that can be leveraged for exchanging healthcare information, particularly between mobile applications and HIT systems. FHIR resources, the main building block in FHIR, can hold any type of information that FHIR deals with to be exchanged from one health information technology system to another via RESTful API services that utilize with an XML or JSON format. Resources are broadly classified into Clinical Findings; Patient Problems, Allergies, and Adverse Events; Patient History; Suggested Physician Orders; and Interdisciplinary Care Planning. To illustrate, sample FHIR resources from the 93 currently defined are the practitioner resource to track medical providers (physicians, nurses, office staff, etc.); the Patient resource can track demographic data on patients; the RelatedPerson resource to track parents/guardians; the FamilyMemberHistory for basic information on a family medical history; the Condition resource to track the relevant medical conditions; the Observations resource to track symptoms, and other medical observations; and the Encounter/EpisodeOfCare resources to track the different times that changes to patient data occur based on a visit (Encounter) or action at the visit (Episodeof-Care). One popular server is the HAPI FHIR [49] open-source implementation of the FHIR server in Java. FHIR resources can be utilized by HIT systems and mHealth applications for different purposes. For example, an mHealth application may use the Patient resource to store and exchange information about patients back and forth with different HIT systems. All FHIR resources have five main properties in common: a unique URL for identification purposes, common metadata, a human readable section, a number of predefined data elements, and an extension element that enables a system to add new data elements. FHIR provides three equivalent representation formats: UML for a diagrammatic representation of the resource, XML that is subset of the HL7 schema for the resource, and JSON to facilitate a programmatic exchange via a RESTful API. FHIR supports a number of REST API services to enable a system to retrieve and modify data in the resources. The main five services are *Create* to add a new instance of a resource, *Read* to retrieve an existing instance of a resource, *Update* to manipulate data in an existing instance of a resource, *Delete* to remove an existing instance of a resource, and *Search* to retrieve all existing instances of a resource.

3   A Healthcare Scenario

To assist in the explanation process in Sect. 4 of this chapter, a detailed scenario in health care is provided to support FSICC as given in Fig. 1. To begin, the first column of Table 1 contains four different HIT systems: a Pharmacy HIT system (PharmHIT), an Insurance Company HIT system (ICHIT), an electronic health record (EHR) HIT system (EHRHIT), and a personal health record (PHR) HIT system (PHRHIT). Briefly, PharmHIT is used by pharmacist at pharmacies for filling and processing prescriptions (R_x) that have been submitted electronically by medical

Table 1 HIT systems, services, and explanations

HIT(local)	LSid	Service name	Explanation
PharmHIT	Rx1	PUT /PharmHIT/NewRx/Patient/id newprescriptioninfo	Submit a prescription (Rx) to the pharmacy
	Rx2	GET /PharmHIT/AllRx/Patient/id	Retrieve all Rx prescribed for a patient
	Rx3	GET /PharmHIT/CanRefill/Patient/id	Retrieve all Rx eligible for refill for a patient
	Rx4	PUT /PharmHIT/FillNewRx/Patient/id newprescription	Fill new Rx
	Rx5	PUT /PharmHIT/RefillRx/Patient/id existingprescription	Refill existing Rx which reduce refill number
	Rx6	GET /PharmHIT/AllInteractions medicationlist	Check a list of medications for interactions
	Rx7	GET /PharmHIT/GernicList/Patient/id drugname	Find all generics drug to a brand name drug
	Rx8	PUT /PharmHIT/RequestRefillRx/Patient/id existingprescription	Submit a Rx refill request
ICHIT	IC1	PUT /ICHIT/NewRxPaymentApproval/Patient/ id newprescriptioninfo	Get payment approval for a new Rx for a patient
	IC2	PUT /ICHIT/ExistingRxRefillApproval/Patient/ id existingprescriptioninfo	Get payment approval for a patient's refill on Rx
	IC3	PUT /ICHIT/VisitApproval/Patient/id typeofvisit	Get payment approval for a visit for a patient
	IC4	PUT /ICHIT/ScanApproval/Patient/id typeofscan	Get preapproval for a medical scan for a patient
EHRHIT	E1	public void addRx(patientID, physicianID)	Insert a Rx into the EHR for a patient
	E2	public void addVisitSummary(patientID, physicianID)	Insert a new visit summary of for a patient
	E3	public void apprPatientAppoin(patientID, appointmentID, physicianID)	Get approval for a patient appointment request
	E4	public void addAppointment(patientID, physicianID)	Request an appointment for a patient

(continued)

Table 1 (continued)

HIT(local)	LSid	Service name	Explanation
	E5	public List<String> getAllAllergies(patientID)	Retrieve the list of all allergies list for a patient
	E6	public List<Object> getUpcomingAppointment (patientID, physicianID)	Retrieve upcoming appointments for a patient
	E7	public List<String> getMentalHistory(patientID)	Get mental history for a patient
PHRHIT	P1	GET /PHRHIT/AllMedsandSupplements/ Patient/id	Retrieve a patient's medications & supplements
	P2	PUT /PHRHIT/NewDemoProfile/Patient/id newdemoprofileinfo	Create a demographic profile for a patient
	P3	PUT /PHRHIT/NewEmergencyProfile/Patient/id newemergencyprofileinfo	Create an emergency profile for a patient
	P4	PUT /PHRHIT /NewRx/Patient/id newprescriptioninfo	Insert an Rx from EHR for a patient
	P5	PUT /PHRHIT /NewAppt/Patient/id newapptinfo	Insert an upcoming appointment for a patient

providers; ICHIT is used by insurance companies to process approvals and payments for medications and visits to medical providers; EHRHIT is utilized by medical providers in the treatment of patients; and PHRHIT is used by patients to manage their own health and fitness data. These systems all interact with one another and are utilized by different stakeholders (e.g., patients, physicians, pharmacists, insurance company representatives, etc.). The services of each HIT system are labeled using unique local service ID (LSid) in column 2 so that they can be referred to in the scenarios. Each service is presented, in column 3 of Table 1 using four main parts: a CRUD method such as GET, a base URI such as /PharmHIT, an endpoint such as /GernicList/Patient/id, and an input variable such as drug name, if there is one. Finally, column 4 of Table 1 has a brief description of each service.

PharmHIT cloud services are a physician submitting prescription (R_x) electronically (Rx1), filling a new (Rx4) or refilling (Rx5) a Rx by a pharmacist, checking for medication interactions (Rx6), a patient submitting a Rx refill request (Rx8), and retrieving all Rx prescribed for a particular patient (Rx2). ICHIT cloud services are approving payment for a new Rx (IC1) or refill (IC2), approving payment for a patient visit (IC3), and approving a medical scan (IC4). EHRHIT Java API methods are adding a new Rx (E1) or visit (E2) for a patient, dealing with appointments (E3, E4, and E6), and listing allergies (E5) or mental health history (E7). PHRHIT web services are retrieving all of a patient's medications and supplements (P1), entering information (P2, P3), and inserting a new Rx (P4) or appointment (P5).

These four HIT applications are directly and indirectly accessed by stakeholders. For example, a physician directly uses the EHRHIT and submits an electronic prescription (R_x) via the EHRHIT that in turn accesses the PharmHIT system (and its services). A pharmacist utilizes a desktop application at the pharmacy that interacts with appropriate PharmHIT services which in turn utilizes services from ICHIT. A patient utilizes either an mHealth app that utilizes GET services from PharmHIT or EHRHIT or a web-based personal health record (e.g., Microsoft HealthVault, WebMD, etc.) that utilizes the PHRHIT services which in turn may call the EHRHIT services. For the information given in Table 1, the physician, pharmacist, and patient have access to different services from the four HITs via their end-user application. Specifically, the physician utilizes services Rx1, Rx2, Rx3, E1, E2, and E3; the pharmacist utilizes services Rx2, Rx3, Rx4, Rx5, and Rx7; and the patient utilizes services Rx2, Rx3, Rx8, E4, E5, E6, P1, P2, and P3. These stakeholders via end-user applications are authorized to different services so as to control access of who can use which services of different HIT systems. To summarize, Table 2 contains the local security policies for PharmHIT, ICHIT, EHRHIT, and PHRHIT, listing the roles (pharmacist, physician, and patient) as well as the other HIT systems that utilize the services. For example, in Table 2a, the PharmHIT services are used by the physician, pharmacist, and patient as described previously, along with the use of services by both the PHRHIT (Table 2d) and the EHRHIT (Table 2b). Note that the ICHIT services are only used by the PharmHIT and EHRHIT systems and not by any user by role directly (see Table 2c).

Table 2 Local policies of PharmHIT, EHRHIT, ICHIT, and PHRHIT

(a)

Role	PharmHIT services by ID
Physician	Rx1, Rx2, Rx3
Pharmacist	Rx2, Rx3, Rx4, Rx5, Rx7
Patient	Rx2, Rx3, Rx8
PHRHIT system	Rx2, Rx3
EHRHIT system	Rx6

(b)

Role	EHRHIT services by ID
Physician	E1, E2, E3
Patient	E4, E5, E6
EHRHIT system	E7

(c)

Role	ICHIT services by ID
PharmHIT system	IC1, IC2
EHRHIT system	IC3, IC4

(d)

Role	PHRHIT services by ID
Paitent	P1, P2, P3
EHRHIT system	P1, P4, P5

The secure and interoperable FSICC as given in Fig. 1 allows the four HIT systems to register their services as defined in Table 1 along with basic access control in terms of the allowable roles. For simplifying the discussion, we assume that there are three roles (physician, pharmacist, and patient) that are registered by most of the systems. In addition, each HIT system registers the services and API calls given in Table 1. The FSICC combines that information to present a set of global services that unify the available services as shown in Table 3. A unique global service ID (GSid) is assigned to each service, as the first column of Table 3 shows, and the third column of Table 3 contains an explanation of the effective or pass-through call that must be made from the global service to the underlying HIT's local service/API call. Notice that the global services are now all RESTful—the API calls of EHRHIT have been replaced with RESTful equivalents. This results in a common global RESTful interface presented to the mobile, web, and desktop apps, greatly simplifying the programming complexity and removing the need for end-user apps to utilize multiple heterogeneous platforms.

Table 3 Global services of the FSICC

GSid	Service name	LS Call
GS1	PUT /SIF/NewRx/Patient/id newprescriptioninfo	Rx1
GS2	GET /SIF/AllRx/Patient/id	Rx2
GS3	GET /SIF/CanRefill/Patient/id	Rx3
GS4	PUT /SIF/FillNewRx/Patient/id newprescription	Rx4
GS5	PUT /SIF/RefillRx/Patient/id existingprescription	Rx5
GS6	GET /SIF/AllInteractions medicationlist	Rx6
GS7	GET /SIF/GernicList/Patient/id drugname	Rx7
GS8	PUT /SIF/RequestRefillRx/Patient/id existingprescription	Rx8
GS9	PUT /SIF/NewRxPaymentApproval/Patient/id newprescriptioninfo	IC1
GS10	PUT /SIF/ExistingRxRefillApproval/Patient/id existingprescriptioninfo	IC2
GS11	PUT /SIF/VisitApproval/Patient/id typeofvisit	IC3
GS12	PUT /SIF/ScanApproval/Patient/id typeofscan	IC4
GS13	PUT /SIF/AddRx/Patient/id prescriptioninfo	E1
GS14	PUT /SIF/AddVisitSummary/Patient/id visitsummaryinfo	E2
GS15	PUT /SIF/ApprPatientAppoin/Patient/id visitsummaryinfo	E3
GS16	PUT /SIF/AddAppointment/Patient/id appointmentinfo	E4
GS17	GET /SIF/AllAllergies/Patient/id	E5
GS18	GET /SIF/UpcomingAppointment/Patient/id upcomingappointmentinfo	E6
GS19	GET /SIF/MentalHistory/Patient/id	E7
GS20	GET /SIF/AllMedsandSupplements/Patient/id	P1
GS21	PUT /SIF/NewDemoProfile/Patient/id newdemoprofileinfo	P2
GS22	PUT /SIF/NewEmergencyProfile/Patient/id newemergencyprofileinfo	P3
GS23	PUT /SIF/NewRx/Patient/id newprescriptioninfo	P4
GS24	PUT /SIF/NewAppt/Patient/id newapptinfo	P5

The end result is that the applications (mobile, web, desktop) can discover and utilize a unified set of global cloud services that based on differing security policies (RBAC, MAC, DAC, etc.) at different times which are made available via a set of global cloud services that have combined the constituent cloud, API, and web services into a common global cloud-based API.

4 FSICC Requirements and Capabilities

The *Access Control Framework for Secure and Interoperable Cloud Computing, FSICC,* as given in Fig. 1, as applied to the healthcare domain, is an infrastructure for cloud computing that provides a global policy authorization and enforcement mechanism and is capable of supporting different access control models (e.g., RBAC, DAC, MAC, UCON, and ABAC). FSICC organizes and globally manages the local cloud services, APIs, and web services from multiple service suppliers into a set of global services so that applications can easily discover and utilize them in order to interact with multiple constituent systems with a common interface. This was illustrated in Sect. 3, where the local services of the four systems (i.e., PharmHIT, ICHIT, EHRHIT and PHRHIT) in Table 1 were unified into a set of global services in Table 3. The presentation in the remainder of this section is in four parts. First, Sect. 4.1 defines five critical requirements for FSICC: numerous and varied access control models, different categories of cloud services, control access to cloud services using RBAC, support delegation of cloud services using DAC, and control access to cloud services using MAC. Second, Sect. 4.2 details three capabilities with associated components of the FSICC: local service registration and mapping to global services, local security policies registration to yield global security policy, and global registration, authentication, authorization, and service discover for consumers. Third, Sect. 4.3 presents the security risks of adopting FSICC. Finally, Sect. 4.4 discusses research in cloud computing as compared with FSICC.

4.1 FSICC Requirements

This section discusses five requirements for FSICC. To accompany this discussion, there must be a shift in focus on the concept of RBAC, DAC, and MAC permissions from objects and operations to one that assigns permissions to individual cloud services. For RBAC, this corresponds to the global services in Table 3 being assigned to different users by role. For MAC, global services in Table 3 are assigned classifications (T, S, C, U) with a user having a clearance and performing domination checks on classification versus clearance for every service invocation. For DAC, this corresponds to the ability to delegate services from user to user by role and potentially limited by classification/clearance checks if MAC has defined. The remainder of this section presents and discusses the five requirements: *Numerous and Varied*

Access Control Models, Different Categories of Cloud Services, Control Access to Cloud Services Using RBAC, Support Delegation of Cloud Services Using DAC, and *Control Access to Cloud Services Using MAC.*

Requirement 1: Numerous and Varied Access Control Models. The first requirement acknowledges that the constituent systems (i.e., service suppliers) that wish to publish access to cloud, API, or web services may have access control and security protocols that are varied. Thus, FSICC must be capable of supporting a wide range of access control models including RBAC [13], DAC [12], MAC [9], UCON [42], or ABAC [53]. In the scenario of Sect. 3, we assumed that each HIT supported RBAC as illustrated in Table 2. We can extend this assumption so that the EHRHIT system also supports DAC to allow permissions (services) to be delegated from a physician Charles to the on-call physician Lois after hours and weekends. FSICC of Fig. 1 must integrate these local security policies (as shown for PharmHIT, ICHIT, EHRHIT, and PHRHIT in Table 2) into a global security policy as shown in Table 4. Specifically, Table 4 defines, for each role (physician, pharmacist, and patient) and the three HITs (PharmHIT, EHRHIT, and PHRHIT), the global services are from Table 3 assigned by role. For the model level, this was accomplished as discussed by mapping permissions to call local services (cloud, web, and API) from Table 2 into permissions to call global cloud services in Table 3.

Requirement 2: Different Categories of Cloud Services. Services, in general, are developed and published for different purposes and for different sets of users. This means services can be categorized as private, partner, community, or public. A *private service* is utilized by a developer of services for a supplier to implement core and sensitive services. For example, applications such as iCloud would have private services that are utilized by Apple developers in designing other partners, community, or public services. While there are no private services shown in Table 1 for the healthcare scenario, one could have a private service on EHRHIT that would be able to mark a portion of the patient record as "invalid". In health care, and in an EHR, information in a medical record is never deleted. However, if it is the case that an incorrect entry is entered for a patient such as the wrong laboratory test result, then such a result is marked as "invalid" but never deleted. A *partner service* is utilized by a partner developer, in which the partner organization has a relationship with the service supplier, to enhance some core services of the service supplier.

Table 4 Global policy (RBAC) of FSICC

Role	FSICC services by GSid
GPhysician	GS1, GS2, GS3, GS13, GS14, GS15
GPharmacist	GS2, GS3, GS4, GS5, GS7
GPatient	GS2, GS3, GS8, GS16, GS17, GS18, GS20, GS21, GS22
GPHRHIT system	GS2, GS3
GPharmHIT system	GS9, GS10
GEHRHIT system	GS6, GS11, GS12, GS19, GS20, GS23, GS24

In Table 1, IC1, IC2, IC3, and IC4 are *partner* services since they need to interact with both PharmHIT and EHRHIT in order to be able to successfully approve new prescriptions and refills, visits, and scans. The partner developer may need to have access to certain private services in order to use partner services. A *community service* is utilized by a general developer to add new functionalities to an application of the service supplier. In Table 1, all services of PharmHIT other than Rx6 are community services, as all are services of EHRHIT and PHRHIT. These are the services that are to be authorized by RBAC by role which is then enforced within the application that a stakeholder is utilizing. Community services contain sensitive information which must be controlled by users. A *public service* is available to any application and is directly called as a result of a user's action in an application. In Table 1, Rx6 is a *public* service that retrieves mediation interactions when given a list of medications; such a list can be independent of any identification of the patient—hence it is more public oriented.

Requirement 3: Control Access to Cloud Services Using RBAC. Since services are published in a cloud environment, the number of consumers of such services is expected to be high. Thus, global cloud services of all categories, as described in Requirement 2, need to be controlled based on roles, in which each role can be assigned on a consumer-by-consumer basis. To support RBAC in FSICC, global services as defined in Table 3 can be assigned by role in the healthcare scenario. To illustrate, Table 4 defines six main global roles: GPhysician (global physician), GPharmacist (global pharmacist), and GPatient (global patient) would be assigned to individuals that are utilizing applications, while GPHRHIT (global PHRHIT), GPharmHIT (global PharmHIT), and GEHRHIT (global EHRHIT) represent the roles of the systems that may need to utilize services. The GPhysician role is used by a doctor to access his/her patients' electric information and to provide better healthcare services for his/her patients. The GPharmacist role is used by a pharmacist to fill and refill drugs for patients and to deal with other related tasks. The GPatient role is used by a patient to access his/her digital information and to request different healthcare services. The GPHRHIT system role is used by a PHR system to gather a patient's related medical information from other systems and call services of other HITs. The GPharmHIT system role is used by a pharmacy system to gather information related to patients' medication bills and call services of other HITs. The GEHRHIT system role is used by an EHR system to gather medical information of physician's patients and to call services of other HITs. The list of global services for each of the six global roles is given in Table 4. In addition, we are currently working on the ability to constrain the invocation of a service based on values.

Requirement 4: Support Delegation of Cloud Services Using DAC. Users of applications, which consume services, may need to collaborate with other users to accomplish a better job; and/or to have other users to perform some of their tasks on behalf of them in case of emergency. To enable this, FSICC supports the ability to delegate cloud services from one user to another. For example, consider a user Charles with a GPhysician role is leaving the office for the day or the weekend and is interested in delegating his/her authority to access the services for his patient to the on-call physician Lois who will be covering night and weekend inquiries from patients. In this case, Lois will then be utilizing a mobile application to access patient data that is available via EHRHIT cloud services. Charles could delegate all or some of his EHRHIT services to Lois. For example, Charles may delegate GS13 and GS14 that involve patient data but not delegate GS15 that involves appointments. If the delegation for Charles to Lois is during the week (Monday to Thursday), it could go into effect at 5 pm (close of business) and be revoked at 9 am (start of business). For weekend calls, the delegation would go from Friday at 5 pm to Monday at 1 am.

Requirement 5: Control Access to Cloud Services Using MAC. Many services may access very sensitive information, e.g., patient data, that needs to be more strongly controlled than other parts of the patient data. For example, mental health data is limited to a psychiatrist or psychologist and not available to a family medical provider. Mandatory access control (MAC) and its usage of classifications (for services) and clearances (for users) may be very useful for controlling access to a service and the data passed by a service. Thus, to further restrict access to cloud services, FSICC supports MAC in addition to RBAC and DAC. That is, all of the global services as given in Table 3 may be labeled with classification levels, and all roles and users may be labeled with clearance levels. Specifically, each of the global cloud services in FSICC can all be labeled with a classification level (i.e.,Top Secret, Secret, Confidential, or Unclassified) as shown in Table 5. There is a single Top Secret service, EHRHIT GS19 which involves the very sensitive mental health data on a patient. All of the services related to prescriptions are Secret including GS1, GS2, and GS4 of PharmHIT; GS13 and GS14 of EHRHIT; and GS23 of PHRHIT. Services with confidential classifications involve regular patient data that doesn't rise to the level of secret including of the allergies (GS3 & GS17), requesting refills (GS8), approving medications/refills, scans, and visits (GS9-GS12) of ICHIT, etc. Finally, unclassified services including services for medication interactions (GS6) and generic equivalents (GS7), appointments (GS15, GS16, GS18, & GS24), and emergency contact (GS22).

4.2 FSICC Capabilities

The set of five requirements in Sect. 4.1 leads to the definitions of a set of three FSICC capabilities for Fig. 1 that brings together all of the concepts and focuses on the process and components of FSICC. Capability 1, *Local Service Registration and Mapping to Global Services,* is for systems to register local services where mapped to a global set. Capability 2, *Local Security Policies Registration to Yield Global Security Policy,* is for systems to register their local security policy to generate a global security policy. Capability 3, *Global registration, authentication, authorization, and service discover for Consumers,* is to support the process of a consumer (mobile, web, or desktop app) registration to discover and be authenticated and then authorized to utilize services by role. The remainder of this section discusses these three capabilities using the healthcare scenario of Sect. 3.

Table 5 Global policy (MAC) of FSICC

GSid	Classification	Service name
GS1	Secret	PUT/SIF/NewRx/Patient/id newpresb criptioninfo
GS2	Secret	GET/SIF/AllRx/Patient/id
GS3	Confidential	GET /SIF/CanRefill/Patient/id
GS4	Secret	PUT/SIF/FillNewRx/Patient/id newprescription
GS5	Secret	PUT/SIF/RefillRx/Patient/id existingprescription
GS6	Unclassified	GET/SIF/AllInteractions medicationlist
GS7	Unclassified	GET/SIF/GenericList/Patient/id drugname
GS8	Confidential	PUT/SIF/RequestRefillRx/Patient/id existingprescription
GS9	Confidential	PUT/SIF/NewRxPaymentApproval/Patient/id newprescriptioninfo
GS10	Confidential	PUT/SIF/ExistingRxRefillApproval/Patient/id existingprescriptioninfo
GS11	Confidential	PUT/SIF/VisitApproval/Patient/id typeofvisit
GS12	Confidential	PUT/SIF/ScanApproval/Patient/id typeofscan
GS13	Secret	PUT/SIF/AddRx/Patient/id prescriptioninfo
GS14	Secret	PUT/SIF/AddVisitSummary/Patient/id visitsummaryinfo
GS15	Unclassified	PUT/SIF/ApprPatientAppoin/Patient/id visitsummaryinfo
GS16	Unclassified	PUT/SIF/AddAppointment/Patient/id appointmentinfo
GS17	Confidential	GET/SIF/AllAllergies/Patient/id
GS18	Unclassified	GET/SIF/UpcomingAppointment/Patient/id upcomingappointmentinfo
GS19	Top Secret	GET/SIF/MentalHistory/Patient/id
GS20	Confidential	GET/SIF/AllMedsandSupplements/Patient/id
GS21	Confidential	PUT/SIF/NewDemoProfile/Patient/id newdemoprofileinfo
GS22	Unclassified	PUT/SIF/NewEmergencyProfile/Patient/id newemergencyprofileinfo
GS23	Secret	PUT/SIF/NewRx/Patient/id newprescriptioninfo
GS24	Unclassified	PUT/SIF/NewAppt/Patient/id newapptinfo

Capability 1: Local Service Registration and Mapping to Global Services. This capability enables a service supplier to register its cloud, programming, and/or web services as indicated by the blue (right) arrows in Fig. 3. Referring to column 3 in Table 1, PharmHIT registers the cloud services Rx1 to Rx8; ICHIT registers the cloud services IC1 to IC4; EHRHIT registers the Java API methods E1 to E7; and PHRHIT registers the web services P1 to P5. For example, PharmHIT registers Rx1 with name PharmHIT, URI (/PharmHIT/NewRx/Patient/id), PUT CRUD method, and input variable newprescriptioninfo; ICHIT registers IC1 with name ICHIT, service's URI (/ICHIT/NewRxPaymentApproval/Patient/id), PUT CRUD method, and input variable newprescriptioninfo; EHRHIT registers E1 with name EHRHIT, method name addRx, parameters patientID, physicianID, and a void return type; and, PHRHIT registers P1 with name PHRHIT, URI (/PHRHIT/AllMedsandSupplements/Patient/id),

Fig. 3 The components of FSICC

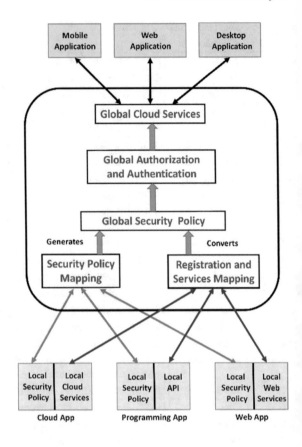

and GET CRUD method. Each registered local service needs to be assigned to one of the four service categories: private, partner, community, or public.

The end result of the registration is that all of the local cloud services, API calls, and web services of Table 1 are transitioned to a set of equivalent global services in Table 3, where each new global service has a unique identifier (column 1), global service name (column 2), and the pass-through call to the corresponding local service (column 3). For each local cloud, API, or web services, a global cloud service is created with appropriate components that mirror the signature of the local service named as a new global cloud service. The cloud service Rx1 PUT PharmHIT/NewRx/Patient/id newprescriptioninfo: is mapped to GS1 as given in Table 3 where the SIF has replaced PharmHIT and GS1 now calls Rx1. Note that the existence of Rx1 is no longer visible to the mobile, cloud or web application; this is true for all of the converted services/API calls. Cloud services of ICHIT are similarly created. The Java API method E1 public void addRx(patientID, physicianID) is mapped to GS13 in Table 3 which now calls E1 of EHRHIT. The web services for PHRHIT are converted in a similar manner to the cloud services. The end result is a unified set of global cloud services to be presented to the mobile, web, or desktop applications as supported by the *Registration and Services Mapping* component, which maintains a mapping list of local to global cloud services.

Capability 2: Local Security Policies Registration to Yield Global Security Policy. This capability allows HIT systems to register their local security policies (roles and permissions to APIs) that can then be combined to yield a global security policy. The local policy registration process of this capability enables a service supplier to specify the security requirements or policy to access its local services (cloud, web, and API) as indicated by the green (left) arrows in Fig. 3. After the service suppliers register the local services, as given in Table 1, they can then register the local security policies that are available in their system as given in Table 2. This includes for a particular HIT system: the defined roles, the permissions that are defined on each local service, the permissions authorized to each role, the classifications for each role and service, allowable delegations, etc.

As local security policies are registered over time, a security administrator or policy officer is responsible to design and evolve an appropriate global security policy that would encompass all of the local requirements (from all different access control models) and provide a unified view for the applications. This is represented as the Security Policy Mapping (box in lower left side of Fig. 3). The security officer defines a global security policy over global cloud services based on defined local roles and associated permissions (bottom of Fig. 3) to define a set of global roles and their permissions. This is accomplished by defining global roles, assigning global permissions to global cloud services, authorizing global roles to global permissions, and defining constraints over these assignments. In the healthcare scenario, the global roles can be defined and evolved over time by considering and unifying all of the particular roles of the originally registered HIT systems (PharmHIT, ICHIT, EMHIT, and PHRHIT) and new systems that are added over time. These new global roles are realized within the *Global Security Policy* component that also maintains all of the information related to the global security policy of FSICC in the middle of Fig. 3.

Specifically, for the healthcare scenario, the RBAC permissions as given by the roles and local API services in Table 2 are mapped to a global set of roles and the global API services in Table 3. For example, for the patient role, the permissions to the local services Rx2, Rx3, and Rx8 of PharmHIT are mapped into the permissions to the global cloud services GS2, GS3, and GS8 and the permissions to the local services P1, P2, and P3 of PHRHIT are mapped into the permissions to the global cloud services GS20, GS21, and GS22. Essentially, at a high level the authorized permissions to the local role patient of PharmHIT and the local role patient of PHRHIT are mapped into a new *GPatient* (global patient) role. The security officer needs to make similar mapping and define new global roles (GPharmacist, GPhysician) for the other local roles and the other systems that are also functioning as roles (GEHRHIT and GPHRHIT). These processes are supported by the *Security Policy Mapping* component of FSICC as shown in Fig. 3. A mapping list of local to global policies is maintained by the *Global Security Policy* component of FSICC. This information is captured in Tables 4 and 5.

Capability 3: Global registration, authentication, authorization, and service discover for Consumers. This capability enables services consumers (mobile, web, or desktop app) to register themselves, which then allows application users to discover and be authenticated and then authorized to utilize services by role. The intent is to provide access for application users to the global roles and the authorized global services. All of the activities associated with Capability 3 are supported by the *Global Authorization and Authentication* component in the middle of Fig. 3. This component maintains a list of consumers' identification information, and a list of consumers and their authorized roles. Note that we distinguish between consumers that are designing and deploying new mobile, web, or desktop applications vs. ones that are retrofitting an existing mobile, web, or desktop application that may have its own access control (RBAC, DAC, and/or MAC) and cloud/web/programming APIs.

For consumers designing and deploying a new application, we extend the healthcare scenario of Sect. 3 with a mobile application for the patient, a web application for the pharmacy technician, and a desktop EHR application for the physician; all of these applications have been developed using the global cloud services from Table 3. To accomplish this development, each application must register with FSICC in order to gain the relevant global roles to be authorized to each application user. A user of the mobile application for the patient would be authorized to the GPatient global role and limited to the services authorized to GPatient as shown in Table 4: GS2, GS3, GS8, GS16, GS17, GS18, GS20, GS21, and GS22. The pharmacy technician utilizing the web application that allows dispensing medications would be authorized to the GPharmacist global role and limited to the services authorized to GPharmacist as shown in Table 4: GS2, GS3, GS4, GS5, and GS7. The physician using the EHR desktop application would be authorized to the GPhysician global role and limited to the services authorized to GPhysician as shown in Table 4: GS1, GS2, GS3, GS13, GS14, and GS15. For the HIT systems, PHRHIT would have the GPHRHIT global role with services GS2 and GS3; PharmHIT would have the GPharmHIT global role with services GS9 and GS10; and EHRHIT would have the GEHRHIT global role with services GS6, GS11, GS12, GS19, GS20, GS23, and GS24.

Capability 3 is also utilized to allow a consumer of a new application to discover global cloud services, from Table 3, for example, for the healthcare scenario. This is accomplished by utilizing a service discovery request to the Global Cloud Services component. The discovery request returns a list of all available services by GSid, name, a category, and description. Discovery is supported by the *Global Cloud Services* component in Fig. 3 which maintains a list of global cloud services. Upon successful discovery, the service consumer (application) can then submit a request to utilize one or more discovered services. The application can send a list of the global services requested and its identification information to the Global Authorization and Authentication component which authenticates the application, authorizes the appropriate global user role associated with the requested services, and then forward the service access request along with the application's global role to the Global Security Policy component. The Global Policy component then authorizes the requested global services only if the application's global role is authorized to access such a service. As a result of calling a global cloud service, the mapped local service or API call of a local HIT system is invoked. Note that the local HIT system allows the call only as long as the application's global role is mapped to an equivalent local role that is authorized to access such a local service. For example, suppose that the web application utilized by the pharmacy technician sends a service discovery request to the Global Cloud Services component to find a service to return all of the prescriptions (Rx) for a patient. The discovery sends back the GS2 service from Table 3: GSid (GS2), name (GET /SIF/AllRx/Patient/id), category (community), and description (calls the Rx2 of the PharmHIT system). Based on this, the pharmacy web application can send a GS2 service access request along with the application identification information to the Global Authorization and Authentication component. This component can then authorize the application to utilize the GPharmacist role and forward the GS2 service access request along with the GPharmacist role to the Global Security Policy component. The Global Security Policy component also authorizes the pharmacy web application to access the GS2 global service, since the GPharmacist global role can access GS2. Then, the Global Security Policy component retrieves the Pharmacist local role, of PharmHIT system, which is mapped to the GPharmacist global role. As a result of calling the GS2 global service, an access request to the mapped local service Rx2 along with the Pharmacist local role is sent to the PharmHIT system. The PharmHIT local system allows the application to access the local service Rx2 since the Pharmacist local role is authorized to access Rx2.

For consumers retrofitting an existing mobile, web, or desktop application, there is an extra layer of functionality that must be considered. Suppose that there is an existing mHealth concussion reporting app that is utilized by parents, coaches, athletic trainers, and school nurses to report concussions on students in kindergarten through high school with its own API to access the database of concussion data that has been collected. The consumer that owns the mHealth concussion reporting app wants to expand its capabilities in order to gather information on medications (from PharmHIT) and from the medical provider (from EHRHIT) so that information on medications and a student's medical conditions, allergies, etc., are available. Suppose also that the mHealth concussion reporting app already has defined roles for parents, coaches, athletic trainers, and school nurses that impact the way that the app works for different users in terms of the concussion data collected can be entered, viewed, and/or edited. In order to make use of the global roles and services of FSICC, the existing mHealth concussion reporting app needs to be able to map its own app roles to appropriate global roles, and programmatically link its API so that it will be able to call the appropriate global services of PharmHIT and EHRHIT. In order to support this programmatic link, the mHealth concussion reporting app may also operate in the role of a provider per capability 1 to define and register a new set of services for the mHealth app that link its current API services to the global services. This requires a similar process as described above to map from the local mHealth roles to the global roles.

4.3 Security Risks

Global services and APIs, in general, are created and published to make such services available and accessible by different types of applications to support software reusability. While FSICC does not retain sensitive data that belongs to service providers such as patient records in the healthcare scenario of Sect. 3, the global services and global policies that FSICC provides functions as a conduit to pass information to/from local service providers that have the responsibility for protecting their own sensitive data. FSICC's role as a global conduit that allows service consumers to securely interact with multiple service providers can give rise to a variety of security risks such as unauthenticated access to global services, unauthorized access to global services, malicious input to global services, and confidentiality. These risks are discussed in this section along with possible countermeasures.

From a security perspective, *unauthenticated access to global services* must be meticulously controlled for two main reasons: to limit the services that are accessible to the intended applications; and to trace actions of applications, and applications users as the services are utilized, in case of a security breach or attack. From the service consumer side, each consumer is assigned a unique ID and an associated key or token, which may access such services, and all interactions of global services by consumers are logged so that they could be audited in the future. Every time a consumer needs to access a service, the associated credentials must be provided and the access is logged. In FSICC, we have achieved this capability via the Global registration, authentication, authorization, and service discover for Consumers capability, as discussed in Sect. 4.2. For example, a mobile application needs to register itself into FSICC, in which FSICC assigns an ID and a token (i.e., credentials) to the mobile application, then the mobile application is only allowed to access the global services of FSICC after providing such credentials.

Authenticating the identity of an application should not allow the application to access all available global services in FSICC, requiring a monitoring of *unauthorized access to global services* by consumers. For example, in Sect. 4.2, a user of a mobile application for a patient should not be able to access the GS23 global service, which is designed to be only accessed by an EHR system. To mitigate this issue, security policies must be enforced to restrict the access to each global service in FSICC by utilizing access control systems such as RBAC and MAC, in which each consumer is assigned to a global role, or a global clearance level, that is authorized to a set of global services. Another approach could develop a disallowed list of services for each consumer that is prohibited from access. In FSICC, we have partially obtained such a solution through the Global registration, authentication, authorization, and service discover for Consumers capability, as discussed in Sect. 4.2. That is, the user of the mobile application for the patient would be authorized to the GPatient global role and will be limited to access the services authorized to GPatient global role as shown in Table 4 in Sect. 4.1. Extending the global policy for RBAC in Table 4 could in the future include a list of the explicit disallowed services, as they are implicit in the table (since they are not assigned).

Authorizing an application to a set of global services does not necessarily mean an application would behave as expected which means that one needs to be concerned with *malicious input to global services*. That is, a consumer invoking a global service may attempt an SQL injection attack by sending a carefully crafted malicious input to an authorized global service that will forward such an input to the associated local service in which the malicious input may force the local service to retrieve/modify any item in the local database of the local system that was not permitted. For example, in Sect. 4.2, a user of a mobile application for a patient, who is assigned to the GPatient global role, can send a carefully crafted malicious input to the authorized GS2 global service, which in turn forward such a malicious input to the associated local service Rx2 of the local system PharmHIT. In this case, instead of retrieving a list of patient prescriptions, the Rx2 local service may be forced to submit a new prescription or to delete other aspects of a patient's data. To mitigate this issue, each global service of the FSICC could be designed in the future to intercept all service calls in order to sanitize as need before passing the call to the associated local service.

The process of calling global and local services involves the transmission of data initiated by the consumer to/from multiple services providers via a series of invocations between local and global services; in this situation, *confidentiality* is paramount. Data passed between consumer and service providers may contain sensitive data such as patient personal information. However, this may lead to confidentiality issues, since an attacker can intercept these calls to access the sensitive data. To reduce the impact of such an attack, our approach in FSICC is to recommend that the local service providers encrypt all data sent to/from global services of the FSICC by using standard encryption algorithms in which consumer applications will decrypt such data upon its receipt. This is particularly relevant for the healthcare domain, where organizations predominately encrypt PHI and PII before transmission or exchange.

4.4 Related Work in Cloud Computing

In this section, we present a number of related efforts in cloud computing, from both academic and industrial communities, that are solving similar problems to FSICC, comparing and contrasting their work to FSICC. The first effort [10] proposed a framework named InterCloud for federating cloud services to manage the services of multiple cloud service providers in which the framework allocates cloud services to the cloud consumers based on quality of service (QoS) needs of the consumer. To accomplish this, the Cloud Broker, which is a component of the framework, determines the most suitable cloud service provider based on the cloud services preferences through the Cloud Exchange, which is another component of InterCloud. Our use of global services in FSICC provides a one-stop shopping location for consumers, but our work utilizes the global roles (and their assigned services by RBAC and MAC) in order to control which services each consumer is allowed to perform.

A second effort [33] introduced a framework design for cloud services that support features including data confidentiality and integrity for cloud service consumers, enable cloud service providers to publish cloud services that are unified to the cloud service consumers and manage the published cloud services. Their framework allows the cloud service providers to receive access requests from the framework without the knowledge of the actual service consumer requesting such an access, and enforces access control over the published cloud services. Their approach contrasts with our approach, particularly for the healthcare domain, where the knowing the identity of the consumer by the provider is vital to restrict access to protected health information (PHI).

A third effort in [48] proposed a cloud broker that enables a heterogeneous set of cloud service providers, in which each provider may require a different infrastructure to operate, to integrate with the cloud broker. Such a cloud broker is capable of optimizing placement of virtual infrastructures across variant clouds and hiding the processes of deploying and managing the cloud services of the cloud providers. The proposed broker utilizes a scheduling algorithm that manages the processes of cloud services deployment. Our work on FSICC is similar to their effort, since our global roles and services effectively hide the location of the local services providers.

The fourth effort [50], the Vordel Cloud Service Broker, supports integrating local on-site applications with offsite cloud services in a secure manner. Vordel also provides monitoring, management, and policy enforcement services. Vordel is located between the cloud service providers and the cloud consumers referred to as organizations. An organization may utilize Vordel broker to introduce a level of trust within the cloud application of such an organization. Work on Vordel is similar to our efforts in FSICC that map local roles/services to global roles/services that offer RBAC, DAC, and MAC security.

A fifth effort [25], the JamCracker platform, unifies the processes of cloud management and governance. Specifically, JamCracker provides a number of services including risk and policy compliance management, operation management, and create, deliver, and multi-cloud services management. JamCracker also allows cloud service providers to unify delivery and management of private and public cloud application/services and distribute them to cloud service consumers. The work of JamCraker is similar to our categorization of cloud services as private, partner, community, or public in Requirement 2 (see Sect. 4.1).

A final effort [4] proposed a cloud broker that acts as a component that manages the use, performance, and delivery of cloud services; and mediates the process of enabling cloud service consumers to access cloud services of service providers. This is achieved by the proposed cloud broker utilizing an agent that dynamically identifies a set of cloud services from various providers based on the service consumer requirements. The architecture of the cloud broker agent [4] is presented along with its implementation in [3]. Their management and mediation of cloud services are similar to our management of global services in FSICC. The major difference of the aforementioned efforts [3, 4, 10, 25, 33, 48, 50] is that their focus is on solving portions of the problems that we are attempting to address in FSICC; none of these efforts provides a comprehensive solution for the problem of securing and integrating cloud and none-cloud services provided from different service providers.

5 Prototyping the FSICC in FHIR

This section presents a proof-of-concept prototype that demonstrates the usage of FSICC with the Connecticut Concussion Tracker (CT^2) mHealth as the service consumer, the electronic health record OpenEMR [37], and HAPI FHIR [49] as global services. CT^2 has been developed as a joint effort between the Departments of Physiology and Neurobiology, and Computer Science & Engineering at the University of Connecticut, in collaboration with faculty in the Schools of Nursing and Medicine and allows the user to report and manage the concussion incidents of students from kindergarten through high school. In the process, we fully illustrate FSICC from Sect. 4 utilizing FHIR that reformulates the architecture given in Fig. 2 (see also [7]) to align to FSICC in Fig. 3 which illustrates the way that FSICC can improve the interconnection of the CT^2 mHealth application with the CT^2 Database and OpenEMR. For supporting FSICC, one of two-third party libraries can be utilized: the HL7 Application Programming Interface (HAPI) FHIR library developed by the HAPI community [15], and the FHIR reference implementation [18] which is built directly from the FHIR specification [26]. The HAPI FHIR library was selected for the demonstration effort, based on the fact that the HAPI implementation is already accepted by HL7 that is used by many organizations in the health informatics community.

To explain the customization of FSICC utilizing HAPI, Fig. 4 updates Fig. 3 so that CT^2, OpenEMR, and HAPI FHIR are represented, which enables the CT^2 mHealth application to utilize HAPI FHIR global services to take advantage of the OpenEMR services without the need to have a direct access to OpenEMR. Note that each of the OpenEMR system and the CT^2 mHealth application has HAPI FHIR services in front of their local services that enable these systems to interact with the HAPI FHIR global services. In Fig. 4, the OpenEMR system starts the process by registering its HAPI FHIR services and local policy into FSICC using the components from Sect. 4.2: Registration and Services Mapping, and Security Policy Mapping, respectively. After that, FSICC generates equivalent HAPI FHIR global services along with global security policy that restricts access to such global services based on the provided local services and security policy. In fact, CT^2 mirrors the discussion of the mHealth concussion reporting app for Capability 3 in Sect. 4.3. As a result, as part of the Security Policy Mapping process, once the global roles are created, they are mapped to/from the OpenEMR local roles and also the CT^2 local roles. In addition, the CT^2 mHealth application will need to develop a set of local CT^2 HAPI FHIR services that link the API of CT^2 and provide the ability to call the HAPI FHIR global services.

The remainder of this section is organized into three subsections. In Sect. 5.1, we briefly review the CT^2 mHealth application from a user/functionality perspective,

Fig. 4 FSICC from Fig. 3
customized to CT^2,
OpenEMR, and HAPI FHIR

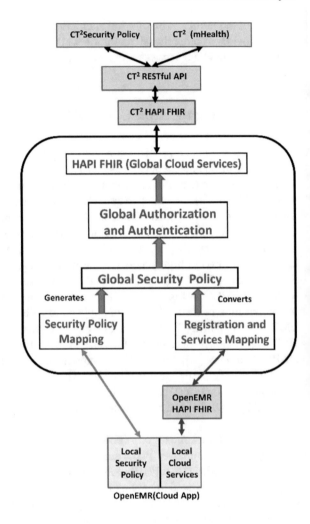

the CT^2 API as a consumer in FSICC, and the CT^2 local roles. Note that the CT^2 app as defined includes four different roles. In Sect. 5.2, we briefly introduce OpenEMR as a local provider, the OpenEMR local API, and the OpenEMR local roles. Finally, in Sect. 5.3, we explore the mapping process that creates the Global roles and Global API as a bridge to/from the CT^2 local roles to the OpenEMR local roles.

5.1 The CT^2 mHealth Application

The CT^2 mHealth App (both Android and iOS versions) have seven screens: the 'Home' screen allows the user to enter a concussion, to retrieve an open case, or to find a student by name; the 'List' screen which contains the list of students the user has permission to view and, for each student gives him/her the option to add a concussion or edit an existing one; the 'Student' screen allows the user to input the student's general information (e.g., name, birthdate, school, and the date of concussion); the 'Cause' screen allows the user to specify how and where the concussion occurred; the 'Symptoms' screen allows users to record the symptoms the student had within 48 hours and other pertinent data; the 'Follow-up' screen allows users to record the status of the student over time; and the 'Return' screen allows users to specify when the student can return to various activities at school. There are four types of users that can interact with the app to report and manage concussion incidents for students. A *School Nurse* user has access to all seven screens to manage a student's concussion incident from its occurrence to its resolution. An *Athletic Trainer* (*AT*) user has access to home, list, student, cause, and symptoms screens to do a limited preliminary assessment if a concussion incident occurs at the event. A *Coach* user has access to home, list, student, and cause screens to report a concussion incident at an athletic event with very limited information on the student. A *Parent/Guardian* user has access to home, list, student, cause, and symptoms screens to both report a concussion incident on his/her child while attending the athletic event or to track the current status of his/her children that have ongoing concussions.

The CT^2 mHealth application for Android and iOS shares the CT^2 API in order to manage its data. The CT^2 API consists of eight services CT1 to CT8 (note that CT^2 API has more than eight services, we selected eight services, however, for the demonstration purposes) as shown in Table 6. These services are presented using the same structure that we used to present the local services of HIT systems (see Table 1 in Sect. 3), i.e., column 1 provides a system name, column 2 contains a service ID, column 3 has a service name, and column 4 explains a service. Services CT1 and CT2 enable CT^2 mHealth application to add/modify a status of a concussion of a certain student, and retrieve information about such a status, respectively. The CT^2 mHealth application utilizes services CT3 and CT4 to query the database about a student information and create/update new student information, respectively. Services CT5 and CT6 provide ways for the CT^2 mHealth application to create/update a student follow-up summary and retrieve information about such a follow-up, respectively. Finally, by calling services CT7 and CT8 the CT^2 mHealth application can query the database about concussion information of a certain student and add/modify new concussion information of a certain student, respectively.

As mentioned above, there are four application roles, and for the purposes of the chapter, we just focus on three of the roles in Table 7: Coach, Nurse, and Parent. The API service calls listed for each role are the ones authorized to the role which in turn dictate the behavior of the mHealth application. In Table 7, for all three roles, all of the GET service calls are listed (CT2, CT3, CT6, CT7), and they all get two PUT service calls (CT4, CT8); Parent has an additional PUT (CT5) while Nurse has access to all PUTs.

Table 6 CT^2 API services

Consumer	Sid	Service name	Explanation
CT^2	CT1	PUT /CT2/concussion/status statusINFO	Add/modify a status of a student
	CT2	GET /CT2/concussion/status statusID	Query the system for a student status
	CT3	GET /CT2/student studentID	Retrieve a student information
	CT4	PUT /CT2/students/add studentINFO	Add/modify a student information
	CT5	PUT /CT2/followup/add followupINFO	Add/modify a summary of a student follow-up
	CT6	GET /CT2/followups followupID	Query the system for a student follow-up
	CT7	GET /CT2/concussion/student studentID	Retrieve a student concussion
	CT8	PUT /CT2/concussions/add concussionINFO	Add/modify a student concussion

Table 7 Local roles for CT^2

Service	Coach	Nurse	Parent
GET	CT2, CT3, CT6, CT7	CT2, CT3, CT6, CT7	CT2, CT3, CT6, CT7
PUT	CT4, CT8	CT1, CT4, CT5, CT8	CT4, CT5, CT8

5.2 The OpenEMR Local Provider

OpenEMR [37] is an open-source Electronic Health Record (EHR) system and medical practice management application that can be utilized by any health/medical organization around the world, that is Meaningful Use Stage 2 [22] and is expected to be a Meaningful Use Stage 3 EHR certified soon [23]. In addition to a web-based interface, OpenEMR has a RESTful API in PHP from which we have selected eight PUT and GET services as shown in Table 8. These services are examples of local services (Table 1 in Sect. 3) of local HIT systems. The OpenEMR services are presented with the following: column 1 provides a system name, column 2 contains a service ID, column 3 breaks down a service name, and column 4 explains a service. Services EMR1 and EMR2 enable an external application to add/update a note about a patient and retrieve information about such a note, respectively. The external application utilizes services EMR3 and EMR4 to query the database about a patient information and create/update new patient information, respectively. Services EMR5 and EMR6 provide ways for the external application to create/update a patient follow-up summary and retrieve information about such a follow-up, respectively. Finally, by calling services EMR7 and EMR8 the external application can query the database about a condition information of a certain patient and add/modify new condition information

Table 8 The OpenEMR local services

HIT(local)	LSid	Service name	Explanation
OpenEMR	EMR1	PUT/OpenEMR/updatepatientnotes noteINFO	Add/modify a note about a patient
	EMR2	GET /OpenEMR/getnotes noteID	Query the system for a patient note
	EMR3	GET /OpenEMR/getallpatients patientID	Retrieve patient information
	EMR4	PUT /OpenEMR/addpatient patientINFO	Add/modify patient information
	EMR5	PUT /OpenEMR/addvisit visitID	Add/modify a summary of a patient visit
	EMR6	GET /OpenEMR/getvisits visitINFO	Query the system for a patient visit
	EMR7	GET /OpenEMR/getlist conditionID	Retrieve a patient condition
	EMR8	PUT /OpenEMR/addlist conditionINFO	Add/modify a patient condition

Table 9 Local roles for OpenEMR

Service	L_Coach	L_Nurse	L_Parent
GET	EMR2, EMR3, EMR6, EMR7	EMR2, EMR3, EMR6, EMR7	EMR2, EMR3, EMR6, EMR7
PUT	EMR4, EMR8	EMR1, EMR4, EMR5, EMR8	EMR4, EMR5, EMR8

of a certain patient, respectively. All of the OpenEMR services fall in the community category, since these services are designed to be utilized by the OpenEMR's stakeholders, as we explained in Sect. 4.1.

In this prototype, the OpenEMR system has a local policy that should be enforced to control access to its local services through RBAC by using three local roles: L_Coach, L_Nurse, and L_Parent as given in Table 9. This local policy is an example of local policies (Table 2 in Sect. 3) of local HIT systems. In Table 9, for all three roles, all of the GET service calls are listed (EMR2, EMR3, EMR6, EMR7), and they all get two PUT service calls (EMR4, EMR8); Parent has an additional PUT (EMR5,) while Nurse has access to all PUTs.

5.3 Mapping to Global Roles and Global Services

In this section, we mirror the discussion in Sect. 4.2 to map the OpenEMR local services (EMR1 to EMR8 in Table 8) to corresponding FHIR global services that external applications, such as CT^2 mHealth application, may indirectly utilize the

OpenEMR local services. This includes mapping the local security policy of Open-EMR to the global security policy in order to restrict access to these FHIR global services. For this demonstration, as previously mentioned, we utilize the HAPI FHIR library which supports all of the 93 resources, as Java classes, that are suggested by the FHIR specification including Patient, Encounter, Condition, and Observation. The HAPI FHIR library also provides an Interceptor feature which is a Java class that can be used to intercept any request to access a HAPI FHIR resource and allow/deny request based on any requirement such as security policies.

In order for OpenEMR to registrar its local services (EMR1 to EMR8) in FSICC, OpenEMR needs to have HAPI FHIR services (as described in Sect. 4), which convert data to/from HAPI FHIR format into OpenEMR format, in front of OpenEMR local services to enable the HAPI FHIR global services to access OpenEMR local services as shown in Table 10. In Table 10, each OpenEMR service EMRi has corresponding FHIR HAPI service, EMR.FHIRi. Basically, for each HAPI FHIR global service, e.g., SIF.FHIR1, an equivalent OpenEMR HAPI FHIR local service, e.g., EMR.FHIR1, is created in front of a corresponding OpenEMR local service EMR1. Specifically, SIF.FHIR1 calls EMR.FHIR1 which in turn calls EMR1. These OpenEMR HAPI FHIR local services are calling the OpenEMR local services from Table 8.

OpenEMR can register the eight HAPI FHIR local services (EMR.FHIR1 to EMR.FHIR8 in Table 10) as indicated by the blue (right) arrow in Fig. 4 and the local security policy (security roles in Table 9) as indicated by the orange (left) arrow in Fig. 4, into FSICC through Capabilities 1 and 2, respectively, as described earlier in Sect. 4.2. Using the Local Service Registration and Mapping to Global Services capability, OpenEMR registers EMR.FHIR1 with name OpenEMR, URI (/EMR/Observation), UPDATE CRUD method, and input variable obsINFO. EMR.FHIR2 to EMR.FHIR8 services can be registered in a similar way. These registered services (Table 10) are transitioned to a set of equivalent HAPI FHIR global cloud services SIF.FHIR1 to SIF.FHIR8 as shown in Table 11, where each new global service has a unique identifier (column 1), global service name (column 2), and the pass-through call to the corresponding local OpenEMR HAPI FHIR service (column 3). These services are examples of global services similar to Table 3 in Sect. 4.2.

Table 10 OpenEMR services, OpenEMR HAPI FHIR, and HAPI FHIR global services

Call from	Sid	Service name	Call to GS
EMR1	EMR.FHIR1	UPDATE /EMR/Observation obsINFO	SIF.FHIR1
EMR2	EMR.FHIR2	READ /EMR/Observation obsID	SIF.FHIR2
EMR3	EMR.FHIR3	READ /EMR/Patient patientID	SIF.FHIR3
EMR4	EMR.FHIR4	UPDATE /EMR/Patient patientINFO	SIF.FHIR4
EMR5	EMR.FHIR5	UPDATE /EMR/Encounter encID	SIF.FHIR5
EMR6	EMR.FHIR6	READ /EMR/Encounter encINFO	SIF.FHIR6
EMR7	EMR.FHIR7	READ /EMR/Condition conditionID	SIF.FHIR7
EMR8	EMR.FHIR8	UPDATE /EMR/Condition conditionINFO	SIF.FHIR8

Table 11 OpenEMR local services mapped to global services

GSid	Service name	LS call
SIF.FHIR1	UPDATE /SIF/S1/Observation obsINFO	EMR.FHIR1
SIF.FHIR2	READ /SIF/S1/Observation obsID	EMR.FHIR2
SIF.FHIR3	READ /SIF/S1/Patient patientID	EMR.FHIR3
SIF.FHIR4	UPDATE /SIF/S1/Patient patientINFO	EMR.FHIR4
SIF.FHIR5	UPDATE /SIF/S1/Encounter encID	EMR.FHIR5
SIF.FHIR6	READ /SIF/S1/Encounter encINFO	EMR.FHIR6
SIF.FHIR7	READ /SIF/S1/Condition conditionID	EMR.FHIR7
SIF.FHIR8	UPDATE /SIF/S1/Condition conditionINFO	EMR.FHIR8

For each local OpenEMR HAPI FHIR service, a global cloud service is created with appropriate components that mirror the signature of the local OpenEMR HAPI FHIR service named as a new global cloud service. That is, EMR.FHIR1 UPDATE EMR/Observation obsINFO becomes SIF.FHIR1 as given in Table 11 where the SIF/S1 has replaced OpenEMR and SIF.FHIR1 now calls EMR.FHIR1. Note that the existence of EMR.FHIR1 is not visible to the CT^2 mHealth application; this is true for all of the converted OpenEMR HAPI FHIR services calls. All HAPI FHIR services of OpenEMR are community services.

In the next step of the process, the Local Security Policies Registration to Yield Global Security Policy capability is utilized in order to allow OpenEMR to register its security policy including roles to OpenEMR services as shown in Table 9. Note that each role that authorized to an OpenEMR local service is also authorized to the corresponding OpenEMR HAPI FHIR local service, for example, the local role L_Parent is authorized to both EMR1 and EMR.FHIR1 local services. Registering the OpenEMR security policy includes the defined roles (L_Coach, L_Nurse, and L_Parent), the permissions that are defined on each local service (PUT/GET methods), and the permissions authorized to each role (PUT/GET methods). After registering such local security policy, the security officer, who is in charge of maintaining FSICC, defines a global security policy over global cloud services based on defined local roles and associated permissions to define a set of global roles and their permissions (as Table 12 shows). This process includes defining global roles (G_Coach, G_Nurse, and G_Parent), assigning global permissions to global cloud services (UPDATE/READ methods), and authorizing global roles to global permissions (UPDATE/READ methods). This global policy is an example of global policies (Table 4) of FSICC as mentioned in Sect. 4 of this chapter. In Table 12, the G_Coach global role is authorized to call all global services except SIF.FHIR1 and SIF.FHIR5 services. Moreover, the G_Parent global role is restricted to only access SIF.FHIR1, SIF.FHIR2, SIF.FHIR3, SIF.FHIR4, SIF.FHIR6, SIF.FHIR7, and SIF.FHIR8. Finally, all global services SIF.FHIR1 to SIF.FHIR8 are authorized to the G_Nurse global role. Moreover, the security officer will map the global policy with the OpenEMR local policy. That is, each global role will be mapped to the

Table 12 Global security policy (roles)

Service	G_Coach	G_Nurse	G_Parent
READ	SIF.FHIR2, SIF.FHIR3, SIF.FHIR6, SIF.FHIR7	SIF.FHIR2, SIF.FHIR3, SIF.FHIR6, SIF.FHIR7	SIF.FHIR2, SIF.FHIR3, SIF.FHIR6, SIF.FHIR7
UPDATE	SIF.FHIR4, SIF.FHIR8	SIF.FHIR1, SIF.FHIR4, SIF.FHIR5, SIF.FHIR8	SIF.FHIR1, SIF.FHIR4, SIF.FHIR8

corresponding OpenEMR local role: L_Coach is mapped to G_Coach, L_Nurse is mapped to G_Nurse, and L_Parent is mapped to G_Parent. A list of mapped Open-EMR local roles–FSICC global roles is maintained by the Global Security Policy component of FSICC.

Once the HAPI FHIR global services and global security policies have been created (Tables 11 and 12) and mapped to OpenEMR local services and security policies, they become available for usage by mHealth applications. To accomplish this, there is a mapping process from the local roles of the CT^2 mHealth application to the global roles as given in Table 4, as well as the process that is needed to transition from the CT^2 API service calls to FHIR calls. Specifically, the CT^2 application must have HAPI FHIR services defined which convert data to/from HAPI FHIR format into the CT^2 application format, in front of the CT^2 API to enable calls to the HAPI FHIR global services. In Table 13, each HAPI FHIR global service, e.g., SIF.FHIR1, is mapped to an equivalent CT^2 HAPI FHIR local service, e.g., CT.FHIR1, positioned in front of a corresponding CT^2 local service CT1. In Table 13, CT1 calls CT.FHIR1 which in turn calls SIF.FHIR1. These CT^2 HAPI FHIR local services are used to provide a link from the CT^2 API to the global services. In addition, there is also a similar mapping process from the Coach, Nurse, and Parent local roles of CT^2 to the global roles G_Coach, G_Nurse, and G_Parent, respectively. A list of mapped CT^2 local roles–FSICC global roles is maintained by the Global Security Policy component of FSICC.

Once Table 13 has been defined and the roles have been mapped, the CT^2 mHealth application can use the Global registration, authentication, authorization, and service discover for Consumers capability, to register itself and its local users into FSICC in which the FSICC security officer will assign each CT^2 local user with one global role based on each user' local role. That is, G_Coach is assigned to a local user with a Coach local role, G_Nurse is assigned to a local user with a Nurse local role, and G_Parent is assigned to a local user with a Parent local role. A list of CT^2 local users and their assigned global roles is maintained by the Global Security Policy component of FSICC. Moreover, the CT^2 application needs to be modified such that each CT^2 local service such as CT1 calls a corresponding CT^2 HAPI FHIR local service such as CT.FHIR1 which is conFig.d to call the equivalent HAPI FHIR global service such as SIF.FHIR1 (see Table 13). Now, when each CT^2 local user requests an access to any global service, FSICC first queries the Global Security Policy component to retrieve the assigned global role. Then, FSICC will allow the CT^2 local user to access the requested global service only if the assigned global role

Table 13 CT^2 API services, CT^2 HAPI FHIR, and HAPI FHIR global services

Call from	Sid	Service name	Call to GS
CT1	CT.FHIR1	UPDATE /CT2/Observation obsINFO	SIF.FHIR1
CT2	CT.FHIR2	READ /CT2/Observation obsID	SIF.FHIR2
CT3	CT.FHIR3	READ /CT2/Patient patientID	SIF.FHIR3
CT4	CT.FHIR4	UPDATE /CT2/Patient patientINFO	SIF.FHIR4
CT5	CT.FHIR5	UPDATE /CT2/Encounter encID	SIF.FHIR5
CT6	CT.FHIR6	READ /CT2/Encounter encINFO	SIF.FHIR6
CT7	CT.FHIR7	READ /CT2/Condition conditionID	SIF.FHIR7
CT8	CT.FHIR8	UPDATE /CT2/Condition conditionINFO	SIF.FHIR8

is authorized to the requested global service. That is, a user of the CT^2 application who has authorized to the CT^2 Parent local role, which is mapped to the G_Parent global role, is allowed to access all HAPI FHIR global services except SIF.FHIR5 in Table 12. Moreover, a user that is authorized the CT^2Nurse local role, which is mapped to the G_Nurse global role, can access all of the HAPI FHIR global services from SIF.FHIR1 to SIF.FHIR8 in Table 12. Finally, a user who has authorized to the CT^2Coach local role, which is mapped to G_Coach role, cannot access the HAPI FHIR global services from SIF.FHIR1 to SIF.FHIR5 in Table 12.

6 Open Research Problems

This section reviews open research problems related to our work on FSICC. The discussion is focused on emerging efforts in FHIR, specifically SMART on FHIR, SMART on FHIR Genomics, and HEART profile for FHIR. The Substitutable Medical Apps and Reusable Technology (SMART) project was initiated by Harvard Medical School and Boston Children's Hospital with an aim to enable interoperability between medical applications by providing a specification to enable developers in the health informatics community to create medical applications once and deploy them across different HIT systems without rewriting the application code for each HIT system [30]. SMART on FHIR [29] is a recently released version of SMART that adopts numerous FHIR features, including FHIR data models, data formats, and API; authorization using OAuth2 [36]; authentication utilizing OpenID connect [38]; SMART profiles that integrate with FHIR profiles; and EHR user interface integration. Additionally, the SMART on FHIR reference platform has been implemented with three main servers: an API server that provides create, read, update, and delete services for all FHIR resources with an implementation of the FHIR search service; an authorization server which is a modified implementation of an open-source OAuth2 and OpenID servers; and an application server that uses an EHR-like framework for developers to retrieve a list of patient data. By providing this reference platform,

SMART on FHIR is a cloud solution that enables flexibility and innovations, and enables systems to grow quickly as user needs change.

SMART on FHIR Genomics [2] is a specification that adds genomic capabilities to FHIR with the intent to integrate genomic and clinical data in the cloud. The work proposes three new FHIR resource and extension definitions: a Sequence resource for capturing a patient's genetic data, a SequencingLab extension to capture the specific sequencing technique which is utilized to generate sequences, and a GeneticObservation extension to associate a phenotype to variant data. SMART on FHIR Genomics extends the SMART on FHIR platform by adding features that enable developers to bridge between the genomics and clinical communities via one integrated platform that operates in the cloud, thereby supporting the combination of genomic information and electronic health record clinical data. The end result of such a combination is the ability to develop new types of medical and healthcare applications in the cloud that can be utilized for precision and personalized medicine.

The HEART Working Group [39] was formed to develop a unified set of privacy and security specifications that would be able to control authorization to RESTful APIs in a cloud computing setting. As part of this effort, a HEART profile is proposed that is capable of interacting with various authentication protocols and tools, including OAuth 2.0, OpenID Connect, FHIR OAuth 2.0 Scopes, and User-Managed Access. The addition of the OAuth 2.0 protocol to the FHIR standard to prevent privacy and security issues that a FHIR implementation may face would be an important extension to FHIR that further enhances the interoperability of FHIR thereby providing critical cloud security capabilities. The intent is to allow customized access to a set of RESTful health-related data sharing (API) that would be capable of controlling access to different portions of the API on a user/role and/or application basis. This extends OAuth 2.0 from a typical focus on the access of a client to a system to a more fine-grained security access to control who can utilize which services of an API. To achieve this, the HEART profile for FHIR introduces the concept of scopes to restrict access to different parts of an API. For example, scopes can be utilized to restrict: the type of resource (e.g., Patient, Observation, etc.) to be protected; the type of access to a requested resource (e.g., read, create, and delete) which is essentially the CRUD services that can be invoked; and the exact part of a resource to be accessed (e.g., user ID and resource ID). A scope value is a composite text that contains the type of permission, the type of resource, and the type of access to that resource being requested. The HEART working group will provide important security capabilities for cloud computing platforms.

7 Conclusion

In this chapter, we introduced a unifying Access Control Framework for Secure and Interoperable Cloud Computing, FSICC (see Fig. 1), applied to the healthcare domain, which provided a mechanism for multiple sources to register their services and security requirements for use by applications. The presentation included a review of cloud computing, access control models, and the FHIR standard in Sect. 2 followed by the introduction of a healthcare scenario to facilitate discussion in the chapter in Sect. 3. Using this as basis, Sect. 4.1 detailed five requirements for the FSICC: Numerous and Varied Access Control Models, Different Categories of Cloud Services, Control Access to Cloud Services Using RBAC, Support Delegation of Cloud Services Using DAC, and Control Access to Cloud Services Using MAC. Based on these requirements, three capabilities were presented in Sect. 4.2 accompanied by a detailed view of FSICC's components (see Fig. 3), namely Local Service Registration and Mapping to Global Services; Local Security Policies Registration to Yield Global Security Policy; and Global registration, authentication, authorization, and service discover for Consumers. Security and risks of adopting FSICC with possible mitigations were discussed in Sect. 4.3. Section 4.4 discussed research in cloud computing as compared with FSICC. In Sect. 5, we provided a proof-of-concept prototype utilizing the CT^2 mHealth concussion app and fully illustrates the development processes of FSICC utilizing FHIR by adapting Figs. 3 and 4. To complete the presentation, Sect. 6 reviewed open research problems on improved access to data in EHRs via SMART on FHIR, integration of genomic and clinical data in EHRs via SMART on FHIR Genomics, and improved security and authorization for cloud computing to apply to FHIR via the HEEART Working Group. Overall, we believe that FSICC is an important first step in instituting a higher level of organization of cloud computing to allow for multiple systems to securely interact with one another with access control on cloud services.

References

1. Aitken, M. (2013). Patient apps for improved healthcare: From novelty to mainstream. Retrieved May 9, 2016, from http://www.imshealth.com/en/thought-leadership/ims-institute/reports/patient-apps-for-improved-healthcare.
2. Alterovitz, G., Warner, J., Zhang, P., Chen, Y., Ullman-Cullere, M., Kreda, D., & Kohane, S. (2015). SMART on FHIR genomics: Facilitating standardized clinico-genomic apps. *Journal of the American Medical Informatics Association*, 1–6.
3. Amato, A., & Venticinque, S. (2013). Multi-objective decision support for brokering of cloud SLA. In *27th International Conference on Advanced Information Networking and Applications Workshops (WAINA)* (pp. 1241–1246).
4. Amato, A., Di Martino, B., & Venticinque, S. (2012). Evaluation and brokering of service level agreements for negotiation of cloud infrastructures. In *International Conference on Internet Technology and Secured Transactions* (pp. 144–149).
5. Amazon.com. (2016). Cloud products. Retrieved May 24, 2016, from https://aws.amazon.com/products/?nc1=f_cc.
6. AT&T. (2016). Cloud services. Retrieved May 23, 2016, from http://www.business.att.com/enterprise/Portfolio/cloud/#fbid=FlPXyoa3SmP.
7. Baihan, M., Rivera Sánchez, Y., Shao, X., Gilman, C., Demurjian, S., & Agresta, T. (2017). A blueprint for designing and developing an mHealth application for diverse stakeholders utilizing fast healthcare interoperability resources. In R. Rajkumar (Ed.), *Contemporary Applications of Mobile Computing in Healthcare Settings*. IGI Global.
8. Barham, P., Dragovic, B., Fraser, K., Hand, S., Harris, T., Ho, A., et al. (2003). Xen and the art of virtualization. *ACM SIGOPS Operating Systems Review, 37*(5), 164–177.

9. Bell, D., LaPadula, L., Ben-Ari, M., et al. (1988). Secure computer system unified exposition and multics interpretation. *Communications of the ACM, 1,* 271–280.
10. Buyya, R., Ranjan, R., & Calheiros, R. (2010). Intercloud: Utility-oriented federation of cloud computing environments for scaling of application services. In *International Conference on Algorithms and Architectures for Parallel Processing* (pp. 13–31).
11. Dell.com. (2016). Cloud computing. Retrieved May 20, 2016, from http://www.dell.com/en-us/work/learn/dell-cloud-computing.
12. Dittrich, K., Härtig, M., & Pfefferle, H. (1988). Discretionary access control in structurally object-oriented database systems. In *DBSec* (pp. 105–121).
13. Ferraiolo, D., Sandhu, R., Gavrila, S., Kuhn, D., & Chandramouli, R. (2001). Proposed NIST standard for role-based access control. *ACM Transactions on Information and System Security (TISSEC), 4*(3), 224–274.
14. Foster, I. (2002). What is the grid? A three point checklist. Retrieved May 4, 2016, from http://www.mcs.anl.gov/~itf/Articles/WhatIsTheGrid.pdf.
15. HAPI Community. (2016). About HAPI. Retrieved March 23, 2016, from http://hl7api.sourceforge.net/.
16. Health Level 7. (2016). Clinical document architecture. Retrieved March 15, 2016, from http://www.hl7.org/implement/standards/product_brief.cfm?product_id=7.
17. Health Level 7. (2016). FHIR overview. Retrieved June 16, 2016, from http://hl7.org/fhir/overview.html.
18. Health Level 7. (2016). Health intersections FHIR server. Retrieved March 8, 2016, from http://fhir2.healthintersections.com.au/open.
19. Health Level 7. (2016). Health level seven international. Retrieved June 11, 2016, from http://www.hl7.org/index.cfm?ref=nav.
20. Health Level 7. (2016). HL7 Version 2. Retrieved March 14, 2016, from http://www.hl7.org/implement/standards/product_brief.cfm?product_id=185.
21. Health Level 7. (2016). HL7 Version 3. Retrieved March 14, 2016, from https://www.hl7.org/implement/standards/product_brief.cfm?product_id=186.
22. Himss.org. (2012). Meaningful use stage 2 overview. Retrieved April 17, 2016, from https://www.cms.gov/regulations-and-guidance/legislation/ehrincentiveprograms/downloads/stage2overview_tipsheet.pdf.
23. Himss.org. (2015). Meaningful use stage 3 final rule. Retrieved May 11, 2016, from http://www.himss.org/ResourceLibrary/genResourceDetailPDF.aspx?ItemNumber=44987.
24. Idc.com. (2015). Public cloud computing to reach nearly $70 billion in 2015 worldwide. Retrieved May 11, 2016, from https://www.idc.com/getdoc.jsp?containerId=prUS25797415.
25. Jamcracker. (2016). Jamcracker platform. Retrieved May 12, 2016, from http://www.jamcracker.com/.
26. Kasthurirathne, N., Mamlin, B., Kumara, H., Grieve, G., & Biondich, P. (2015). Enabling better interoperability for healthcare: Lessons in developing a standards based application programing interface for electronic medical record systems. *Journal of Medical Systems, 39*(11), 1–8.
27. Kelion, L. (2014). Apple toughens iCloud security after celebrity breach. Retrieved May 17, 2016, from http://www.bbc.com/news/technology-29237469.
28. Kephart, J., & Chess, D. (2003). The vision of autonomic computing. *Computer, 36*(1), 41–50.
29. Mandel, C., Kreda, A., Mandl, D., Kohane, S., & Ramoni, B. (2016). SMART on FHIR: A standards-based, interoperable apps platform for electronic health records. *Journal of the American Medical Informatics Association, 23,* 899–908.
30. Mandl, D., Mandel, C., Murphy, N., Bernstam, V., Ramoni, L., Kreda, A., & Kohane, S. (2012). The SMART platform: Early experience enabling substitutable applications for electronic health records. *Journal of the American Medical Informatics Association,* 597–603.
31. Mell, P., & Grance, T. (2011). The NIST definition of cloud computing. Retrieved May 2, 2016, from http://faculty.winthrop.edu/domanm/csci411/Handouts/NIST.pdf.
32. Microsoft.com. (2016). Service oriented architecture. Retrieved May 7, 2016, from https://msdn.microsoft.com/en-us/library/bb833022.aspx.

33. Nair, S., Porwal, S., Dimitrakos, T., Ferrer, A., Tordsson, J., Sharif, T., et al. (2010). Towards secure cloud bursting, brokerage and aggregation. In *IEEE 8th European Conference on Web services (ECOWS)* (pp. 189–196).
34. National Archives. (2016). Executive orders. Retrieved April 21, 2016, from https://www.archives.gov/federal-register/codification/executive-order/12356.html.
35. Newcomer, E., & Lomow, G. (2005). *Understanding SOA with Web services*. New Jersey: Addison-Wesley.
36. OAuth. (2016). About OAuth 2.0. Retrieved March 06, 2016, from https://oauth.net/2/.
37. OpenEMR. (2016). What is OpenEMR. Retrieved April 12, 2015, from http://www.open-emr.org/.
38. OpenID. (2016). About OpenID connect. Retrieved March 24, 2016, from http://openid.net/connect/.
39. OpenID. (2016). What is HEART WG. Retrieved June 7, 2016, from http://openid.net/wg/heart.
40. Pallis, G. (2010). Cloud computing: The new frontier of internet computing. *IEEE Internet Computing, 5,* 70–73.
41. Rappa, M. (2004). The utility business model and the future of computing services. *IBM Systems Journal, 43*(1), 32–42.
42. Sandhu, R., & Park, J. (2003). Usage control: A vision for next generation access control. *Computer network security* (pp. 17–31). Berlin, Heidelberg: Springer.
43. Senate and House of Representatives in General. (2014). An act concerning youth athletics and concussions. Retrieved April 12, 2016, from http://www.cga.ct.gov/2014/act/pa/pdf/2014PA-00066-R00HB-05113-PA.pdf.
44. Shetty, S. (2013). Gartner says cloud computing will become the bulk of new IT spend by 2016. Retrieved May 10, 2016, from http://www.gartner.com/newsroom/id/2613015.
45. Subashini, S., & Kavitha, V. (2011). A survey on security issues in service delivery models of cloud computing. *Journal of Network and Computer Applications, 34*(1), 1–11.
46. Takabi, H., Joshi, J., & Ahn, G. (2010). Security and privacy challenges in cloud computing environments. *IEEE Security & Privacy, 6,* 24–31.
47. The Direct Project. (2016). Direct project overview. Retrieved April 18, 2016, from http://directproject.org/content.php?key=overview.
48. Tordsson, J., Montero, R., Moreno-Vozmediano, R., & Llorente, I. (2012). Cloud brokering mechanisms for optimized placement of virtual machines across multiple providers. *Future Generation Computer Systems, 28*(2), 358–367.
49. University Health Network. (2016). HAPI-FHIR. Retrieved May 29, 2016, from http://hapifhir.io.
50. Vordel. (2016). Vordel products. Retrieved May 12, 2016, from http://www.vordel.com/solutions/cloud-servicebroker.html.
51. Wang, L., Von Laszewski, G., Younge, A., He, X., Kunze, M., Tao, J., et al. (2010). Cloud computing: A perspective study. *New Generation Computing, 28*(2), 137–146.
52. Wingfield, E. (2015). Personal cloud will be a $90 billion a year business by 2020. Retrieved May 12, 2016, from http://www.cloudwedge.com/personal-cloud-will-be-a-90-billion-a-year-business-by-2020/.
53. Yuan, E., & Tong, J. (2005). Attributed based access control (ABAC) for web services. In *IEEE International Conference on in Web Services (ICWS'05)* (pp. 569–577).
54. Zhang, Q., Cheng, L., & Boutaba, R. (2010). Cloud computing: State-of-the-art and research challenges. *Journal of Internet Services and Applications, 1*(1), 7–18.

Security and Privacy Issues in Outsourced Personal Health Record

Naveen Kumar and Anish Mathuria

E-health effectively uses information and communications technology to support health-related services for its users. The primary objective of an e-health system is to manage e-health information of individuals and provide them better health services. In recent time, personal health record evolves as the most accepted patient-centric model for e-health system. It is a collection of private health-related information of an individual. A record management system for personal health records is called personal health record management system (PHRMS). A cloud-based PHRMS allows a user with limited configured device to store, share, and update her personal health record in a cloud, and access medical services online anytime and from anywhere. Although it provides many essential features, security, and privacy of personal health record are the major concerns for its owner due to the presence of untrusted cloud service provider. In this chapter, we give a detailed survey on existing PHRMSs with respect to the security and privacy features they are providing.

1 Introduction

In the present era of the digital world, the information-rich industries are moving toward digitization process of their vast information so that it will be efficiently available and communicated over the Internet. Today's health industry is one of the information-rich enterprises that require efficient electronic health data communi-

N. Kumar (✉)
IIIT Vadodara, Gandhinagar, India
e-mail: naveen_kumar@iiitvadodara.ac.in

A. Mathuria
DA-IICT Gandhinagar, Gandhinagar, India
e-mail: anish_mathuria@daiict.ac.in

© Springer Nature Singapore Pte Ltd. 2017
S. Chaudhary et al. (eds.), *Research Advances in Cloud Computing*,
DOI 10.1007/978-981-10-5026-8_17

cation between different departments (such as medical consultation room, medical laboratories, pharmacy, etc.) working together to provide fast and accurate service to the patients. In the past, individual's electronic health information was adopted as Electronic Health Record (EHR [1]) by different private and public health organizations. EHR information is expected to be available anywhere and anytime so that it can be efficiently used when needed by the patient. However, the EHRs are created and maintained by one or more healthcare providers to facilitate their own internal operations and are not necessarily accessible to patients. The patient's EHR information can be distributed to more than one healthcare provider with different access policies. The patients have no control over their EHR.

In contrast to the EHR, Personal Health Record (PHR) with a similar set of information is patient-centric in nature and are recently gaining more attention. Kaelber et al. [2] define the PHR as *"a set of computer-based tools that allow people to access and coordinate their lifelong health information and make appropriate parts of it available to those who need it."* A PHR is access controlled and managed entirely by an individual. It contains medical prescriptions, progressive notes, lab reports, allergic information, emergency contacts, etc. A PHR helps in managing the health of an individual in many ways such as viewing their medical history, review prescription or laboratory test results, and providing accurate medical practices [3].

There are three types of approaches to building PHRs [4]: Standalone systems, Tethered systems, and Networked systems. In the first type, an individual may create his/her PHR on standalone systems that do not tie up with any healthcare system. For example, Google Health [5] and Microsoft's Health Vault [6]. Tethered systems are tied into a healthcare system of a particular organization who maintains the data. For example, My HealtheVet PHR from U.S. Department of Veterans Affairs. A networked (or untethered) system does not connect to any healthcare system and all information are entered and controlled by the individual. However, the PHR information is stored on a website owned by a service provider. Networked PHRs will allow the transfer of information between multiple systems such as service providers, insurance agencies, and pharmacies. As information is now integrated with other electronic health record systems, it provides more benefits than a standalone system for users [7].

There is three type of e-health record management systems: hospital-centric Electronic Health Record Management System (EHRMS), Partial patient-centric and patient-centric PHRMS. EHRMS is maintained by healthcare service providers (for example, hospitals) that can have undesirable overall access to the patient's personal data. Partial patient-centric are smart card-based system where health record is stored in a card kept with the patient. For processing any information from the card, a card reader is needed which is kept with the healthcare service providers. This requires the presence of both the patient (with its secret PIN or password) and the service provider's card reader. The Third type PHRMS is solely managed by patient itself and is ideal for controlling access to patient's secret health data. Such a system permits a user to manage her record efficiently and securely.

With the emergence of cloud computing, small-scale health-care organizations get motivated to outsource their PHRMS service to connect more users globally and give

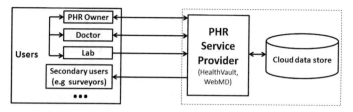

Fig. 1 The PHRMS reference model

better health care facilities to the end users. The service provider is now responsible for providing PHR accessibility to the authorized users from any place and at any time. We assume that the data availability and scalability are the responsibilities of cloud service provider and are not in the scope of this chapter. In this chapter, we are focusing on security and privacy aspects of patient-centric PHRMS for a cloud.

1.1 Reference Model

The data access control policy is solely enforced by the PHR owner itself. A PHR owner is assumed to be equipped with a personal digital assistant device for storage and computations. An outline model of the proposed PHRMS is shown in Fig. 1. The model comprises of three major entities.

1. Users: a user is either primary or secondary. A primary user is actively involved with a PHR such as creating or maintaining it. A secondary user can only use it. Examples of primary users are a PHR owner, a doctor, a medical laboratory, an insurance company, etc., and of secondary users are researchers and surveyors. A short description of some of these users is as follows.

   (a) A PHR owner is a user (or patient) who creates and maintains his PHR in a cloud in association with the cloud service provider. The patient receives medical consultation from doctors, request for medical laboratory reports, gets insurance, etc.
   (b) A doctor is responsible for generating medical prescriptions and progressive notes for a PHR owner whenever asked.
   (c) A medical laboratory (or Lab) is responsible for generating patient's medical laboratory report whenever asked by a PHR owner.
   (d) An insurance company registers and insure a PHR owner whenever it is requested.
   (e) Researchers and surveyors are the secondary users. Such users are the essential part of the PHRMS who indirectly support the society from their study and research results.

2. PHR service provider (PHRSP): It is the central core of a PHRMS. Their responsibilities are: registering users, maintaining system data including each (registered) patient's PHR information, and to fulfill the read and write access requests
   from the authorized users. PHRSP stores the system data at the cloud data store,
   maintained by the cloud service provider itself. PHRSP is assumed to be honest-
   but-curious (also called semi-trusted), i.e., it is curious about knowing the PHR
   information but correctly follows the given service level agreement.

1.2   Use Cases

Here, we discuss two use cases that help in understanding the working of a hospital
scenario and related issues.

Case 1: Non-trivial Access to PHR Documents

In general, a doctor can access all historical documents related to her specialty class.
As a non-trivial case, a doctor may require access to one or more specific documents
belongs to other specialty classes. For example, a physician requires access to an
ongoing medication (or prescription) related to an ENT (Ears, Nose, and Throat)
class. In this case, the PHR owner needs to delegate the specific document's access
to the doctor ensuring that it will not affect the accessibility to rest of the documents
in that specialty class. Another possibility is that the PHR owner will download the
required document and send it to the Doctor through a secure channel.

Case 2: Treatment to Minors

A PHR is required to be created for a minor, immediately after she takes birth.
However, the minor cannot be able to handle her PHR for her initial years. She
will use to go with their parents to the Doctor, for consultation. Therefore, a secure
mechanism is needed to access a minor's PHR in her initial years and later the PHR
is securely handed over to the candidate. The age of handover of a PHR to its owner
can differ in different states/countries as per their local laws. It is assumed that the
parents securely manage the minor's PHR until they handed it back to him or her.
After getting custody of the PHR, the owner may need to restrict her parent's access
to his or her PHR. This may require the owner generates new keys and re-encrypts
all the PHR documents with the new keys. Now, without knowing the new secret
keys the owner's parents cannot access his or her PHR.

Discussion on Hospital Scenario

Consider an example scenario where a patient approaches a specialty department in a hospital that may have more than one doctor in the panel. At a time, only one doctor from the panel may present for consultation. To handle such situation, an extra communication is required prior to the start of consultation process so that the patient knows which doctor is in the consulting room. The patient may request for a specific doctor for consultation in the concerned department of the hospital. In this case, the hospital may return the doctor's credentials (such as the public key of the doctor) so that the patient can use it to send consulting information request to that specific doctor. Also, the hospital may regret the request and send the credentials of an available doctor in the consulting room.

A hospital generally has junior doctors and nurses associated with each specialty department. The junior doctor(s) can receive the patient request, assign it a case ID (internal to the hospital), maintains it and finally uploads it to the server on behalf of the senior consulting doctor. Since they are doctors, the PHR owner or the consulting doctor can trust them and may give the access credential to them. However, the PHR owner may sometimes do not allow his or her PHR data access to the junior doctors. Therefore, it requires a mechanism in a PHRMS to restrict such unwanted access.

Other important entities in the hospital are the nurses. The nurses may require writing notes on the current prescription for example patient temperature, weight, medication with time, etc. It requires that the nurses will be authorized for a limited access to a patient PHR. For example, any old PHR information will be restricted from the nurses. However, they can write notes to the current patient's prescription.

In what follows, Sect. 2 discusses different security and privacy requirements for a cloud-based PHRMS. Section 3 gives a brief survey of existing mechanisms used for handling these requirements. Section 4 concludes this chapter.

2 Security and Privacy Requirements

Essential security and privacy properties required with a PHR are as follows.

- Confidentiality of patient's PHR: This ensures that only authorized users can access to the PHR information. Confidentiality is an obvious security requirement with sensitive PHR data [8]. It is desired that no unauthorized user can access any PHR information until authorized by the PHR owner. Usually, a doctor should only need access to the patient health information specific to the doctor's medical specialty. Therefore, the PHR data can be divided according to the doctors' specialty classes for access control [9]. To cryptographically handle access control in such classification, each class of information can be encrypted with distinct keys and the appropriate keys can be given to the consulting doctor at the time of consultation.

- Patient's control: This ensures that only a patient can authorize an entity to access her health information. It is desired that a patient can hide certain health information from a medical practitioner who has already have access to her PHR.
- Forward secrecy: This ensures that a doctor in the consultation is restricted from accessing any future PHR document using any of his old access authorization [10].
- Data integrity: This ensures that an unauthorized user cannot tamper the outsourced PHR data. The data storage must be protected from unauthorized tampering. A doctor may require access to the old PHR documents of his patient in consultation. However, access to future PHR information by the doctor using old authorization secrets must be restricted (forward secrecy). This is because the patient may change her doctor at any time. If forward secrecy is not provided, an unauthorized doctor can see the patient's future consultation information, such as to whom she is consulting and what prescriptions she is getting. A solution to handle this is to encrypt each new class document with a fresh secret key whenever the patient will consult a new doctor.
- Authentication: This ensures that an authorized entity such as the PHR owner can authenticate the sender or creator of the PHR document. This is an important property because an authorized entity always interested in knowing the other communicating party.
- Non-repudiation: This ensures that a PHR document writer (a Doctor or Lab) cannot deny later that the document was written by them. It may happen that the doctor or Lab may deny their report in case some misdiagnosis happens. This property defends the patient as well as the document writer at the time of dispute between them.
- Data unlinkability: This ensures that no unauthorized user including the PHRSP can identify a linkage between a PHR owner and her PHR information. In other words, the information gained from linking different communications of PHR data should be insufficient to establish a link between the patient and its data [11]. A stronger property named unobservability ensures that no unauthorized user can observe a communication between the users over Internet. It is to be noted that unlinkability does not imply unobservability, whereas the converse is true [12]. This is because using network traffic analysis one can identify who communicates with whom.
- Secure access right revocation: This ensures that the PHR owner can revoke access rights for her PHR at any instant of time. This is an important property because the PHR owner can change her doctor at any point in time. In such case, she may immediately want to revoke access rights of her old doctor.
- Secure data access by the secondary users: Efficient and secure data access by the secondary users such as medical researchers and surveyors [13] is another important requirement for PHRMS. For example, surveyors studying the malaria cases in a city must be able to access all the related reports created by the Laboratories (Labs) present in that city. If the Lab reports are stored in encrypted form, then providing access to researchers and surveyors requires either giving them the corresponding decryption keys or, somebody on PHR owner's behalf to decrypt the

documents and send to them. As researchers or surveyors are not trusted by a PHR owner, giving them access to Lab reports may leak data confidentiality.

- Emergency access to PHR: In the case of emergency, it is desired that the patient's PHR information will be disclosed to the doctor in consultation. The patient is not necessarily in a position to hand over the access credentials during an emergency. Thus, we require a break glass mechanism [14] so that the patients' secret access credentials will be accessed by the medical service providers to give emergency aid immediately to the patient. There are two possible measures discussed in the literature. First, secret PHR credentials will be given to some family member and the name is disclosed to a central authority. The family member can be approached in the case of emergency by the central authority. Second, the secret PHR credentials are deposited to a trusted central office which discloses this information directly to the hospital in case of emergency.
- Information accountability in PHR sharing: This ensures how PHR information is reached to a certain PHRMS entity, who was involved in its sharing and transfer. This property is important since most of the privacy threats arise due to the involvement of insiders of healthcare organization, either accidentally or intentionally [15]. This property put accountability on intermediators in case information privacy is leaked.

3 Survey of Existing PHRMS

Several incidents in the past explain why healthcare users are concerned about the security and privacy of their personal health information. In a report by Markle Foundation [16], 91% of people report that they are "very concerned" about the security and privacy of their personal health information. Patient's greatest concern about electronic PHR stored with an untrusted service provider is the potential misuse of health record data.

In 1996, the Health Insurance Portability and Accountability Act (HIPAA) [17] outlined legal security and privacy protection for PHR. The HIPAA privacy rule first time standardized the privacy of PHR held by "covered entities" (i.e., health insurance agents/employer, and medical service providers engaged in different transactions). However, it does not sufficiently address all the issues involved, for example, it does not usually include cloud providers. Primary cloud platform providers for PHR services are Google (Google Health [5]), Microsoft (Microsoft Health Vault [6]), and Dossia. Therefore, a user PHR system's security and privacy currently have no legal protection.

3.1 Security Mechanisms

As best of our knowledge, initial PHRMS was introduced by Szolovits et al. [18] and was followed by the PHRMS system named Indivo [19]. In [19], PHR data is stored in encrypted and it uses a trusted Indivo server which can access data encryption keys and decrypt the data before sending it to the users. Systems like Google Health [5] and Microsoft Health Vault [6] allows storing individual's e-health information on a central server. Data is encrypted at the server and encryption keys are stored with the service providers. Such systems provide server-side security (such as access control) and require user's trust on the system.

Many other proposals [20–25] require dedicated hardware devices such as smart cards where data will be processed (encrypted or decrypted) only if the patient's smart card and the medical reader device are present along with their secrets (such as secret pin or passwords). Hu et al. [21] propose a hybrid solution uses public key infrastructure for mutual authentication and data communication, while data is encrypted with symmetric keys. A medical smart card is given to each patient to store her public-private key pair with other information. User's PHR is entirely stored with service providers. Yu and Chekhanovoskiy [25] proposes symmetric key-based patient-centric system with the use of smart card device. W B Lee and C D Lee [23] proposed another solution based on smart card technology. Another work that uses smart card devices are proposed by Chen et al. [20] and Huang et al. [22] using Elliptic Curve Cryptography (ECC). Odelu et al. [26] claim that symmetric key-based schemes are efficiently utilized in medical systems as compared to ECC-based systems. Also in [26], service provider manages all the keys and is considered to be trusted. However, it was noticed that since the smart card is read by a dedicated reader device present with the health providers, they can disclose an individual's PHR information for the treatment purposes. Therefore, we believe that use of smart card devices and dedicated hardware like temper-resistance devices must be carefully used in such applications. Keoh et al. [27] pointed out related threats such as denial-of-service, card theft and misuse of break glass when using card-based systems.

Ming Li et al. [9] proposed a framework for PHRMS using attribute-based encryption (ABE). The framework allows user's access right revocation. However, the collision of a fixed number of attribute authorities can break the security of the system. A user needs to manage multiple keys. Narayan et al. [28] proposed another ABE scheme combine with public key encryption. Due to the use of public keys, decryption cost of a data file increases. Also, re-encryption of data files are required by the PHR owner whenever access policies are changed. Lee et al. [24] recently proposed a PHRMS allowing add or revoke user authorization. However, it is smart card-based key management solution based on Taiwan's health care administration infrastructure. We note that ABE-based schemes require a trusted third party (TTP) to provide attribute-level access control. The advantage of using ABE is that it allows server-side encryption, thereby reducing the encryption cost at data owner. However, using TTP to enforce access control limits the data owner's control over her data. Also, these schemes require a significant number of keys with each user, one corresponding to each attribute of the authorized data files. Benaloh et al. [29] proposed a patient-centric system using hierarchical identity-based encryption. However, a patient needs to create, manage a large number of keys and verify healthcare provider's credentials.

Chen et al. [30] scheme for PHR uses a Lagrange interpolation function for access control. Users are grouped into classes, creates a partially ordered hierarchy. However, the order of interpolation function depends on a number of data files and classes in the system. The function is needed to be updated as a data file is added or removed, or there is a change in the relationship between user classes. Thilakanathan et al. [31] recently proposed a PHRMS that uses secret sharing. Implementation of secret sharing also requires a TTP for data sharing service and a number of proxy services to store secret keys and encrypted data pieces. However, such secure proxy services are difficult to implement on the cloud. Dekker et al. [32] give a framework using audit-based mechanism for posterior access control where security decisions are taken after the security lapse happens. Kumar et al. [10] first time introduces the forward secrecy requirement in PHRMS and implements it using symmetric key cryptography. It will be beneficial for patient's data security. They show that the forward secrecy property can be achieved using one-way hash chains in a PHR.

3.2 Privacy Mechanisms

Privacy is an underlying requirement in a healthcare system. It is the desire of an individual to control the disclosure of her personal health information. Not all access users need to know everything about a patient's PHR. A patient needs to share her related private PHR information to the physicians to get a better diagnosis. However, the patient will hesitate to share some of the private information to the physicians like mental health diagnosis information such as depression or alcoholism, HIV report [33], psychiatric behavior [8], teenagers [34], battered women [35], that may lead to her social discrimination [36, 37].

To protect the privacy of PHR documents, we require the property called "unlinkability". Unlinkability is defined by Pfitzmann and Hansen [12] as "within the system, the attacker cannot sufficiently distinguish whether given item of interests (e.g., messages, subjects, …) are related or not. " In our PHR system, we require that a PHR document's information must be unlinkable with its owner. In follows, we discuss the existing schemes used for unlinkability in PHR system.

Sweeney [38] proposed a model for protecting privacy called *k-anonymity* where the data is released in groups and within a group, a person's identifier cannot be distinguished from at least k individuals. Concept is extended in *l-diversity* [39] and *t-closeness* [40] to further reduce identification probability. However, the privacy of these methods are limited to the value of k, l and t respectively, and therefore they require trusted servers. Also, anonymity here is irreversible, i.e., one cannot link the data back to the owner. This makes them suitable for secondary users such as research and survey purposes only [41]. A healthcare system requires reversible anonymity so that a medical care provider (or doctor) can link a document with the patient while viewing her medical history.

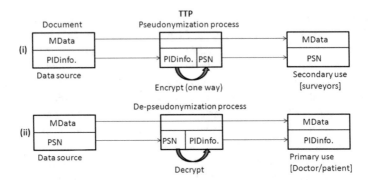

Fig. 2 Pseudonymization and de-pseudonymization process

3.2.1 Pseudonymization-Based Techniques

The known reversible techniques are using pseudonymisation [41] where the identity of a data file is replaced by an encrypted identifier called pseudonym. Pseudonymization process is shown in Fig. 2 (i). In the figure, *MData* represents medical data, *PIDinfo.* is patient's identity information and *PSN* is pseudonym. Pseudonyms are generally used as secret links between the users and their PHR documents. A user capable of decrypting the pseudonym (called de-pseudonymisation) can only able to find a link between the document and the patient. De-pseudonymization process is shown in Fig. 2 (ii). Since in PHR systems, the doctor in consultation needs to decrypt patient's PHR, the process of de-pseudonymization and pseudonymization must be separated. This separation commonly implemented using asymmetric keys and the presence of a TTP for de-pseudonymization process. Thus, do allow a separation but with a significant computation cost [42]. A detailed study of existing schemes using pseudonymization is given in [42].

Pseudonymization-based techniques work well as reversible anonymity and for secondary users but are secure as long as the communication architecture is intact. An adversary can link a document with its owner while observing the real-time communication between the entities especially when the same pseudonym is used more than once [12]. As each PHR document is having a single fixed pseudonym in a PHR system, the linkability with its owner can be observable. Thus, it requires the use of distinct pseudonym each time a PHR document is accessed, which is difficult to achieve in healthcare systems where documents may be stored on third party servers. Therefore, a secure communication healthcare architecture is needed where data access patterns are unobservable by an adversary who can sniff the communication traffic, even when the service provider (or server) is untrusted.

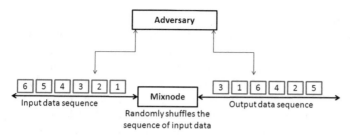

Fig. 3 Function of mix node

3.2.2 Use of Mix Node

As network traffic analysis can be used to identify who communicates with whom, the unlinkability property is not sufficient in the presence of untrusted service provider. Therefore, the unobservability property is an essential requirement. For unobservability between the users in communication, [10] uses the concept of mix node [43]. The mix node function is shown in Fig. 3. It randomly shuffles the input sequence of packets so that no unauthorized user including the cloud service provider can find a link between input and output packets. Although the process provides unobservability between the PHR owner and its PHR data, it adds a delay in data communication. However, the communication delay will be significantly less than the document generation time.

Modeling Unobservability Using ProVerif

To model the unobservability property in PHR document publishing protocol, consider two documents $R1$ and $R2$ generated by a lab (or a doctor) for two users $U1$ and $U2$, respectively. The unobservability property is specified in terms of observational equivalence between two variants of the document publishing protocol. Say, two variants are observational equivalent if an attacker cannot distinguish between the two variants by interacting with either of them. The unobservability can be specified by the following observational equivalence:

$$X\{R1/U1\}\{R2/U2\} \sim X\{R1/U2\}\{R2/U1\}$$

where process $X\{R1/U1\}\{R2/U2\}$ represents that the document $R1$ is for user $U1$ and $R2$ is for user $U2$, respectively. Similarly in process $X\{R2/U1\}\{R1/U2\}$, $R2$ is for user $U1$ and $R1$ is for user $U2$, respectively. To further simplify the above equivalence, consider that the first document published is R for the two input requests from the patients $U1$ and $U2$. The observational equivalence can be now relaxed to $X\{R/U1\} \sim X\{R/U2\}$ where, $R \in \{R1, R2\}$.

We model the four communicating parties *Patient*, *Mix Node*, *Lab* (or *Doctor*), and *PHRSP* as processes written in ProVerif calculus [44] with corresponding public ids P, Mx, L, and SP, respectively. *Mix Node* process work as a mix node. It randomly chooses a document request out of two input users requests and forwards it to the receiver (a *Lab* or a *Doctor*). The main *process* shown below defines the parallel execution of above processes including two patients processes, one for each $U1$ and $U2$. Let $r1$ and $r2$ are two random numbers used for message synchronization and, $k1$ and $k2$ are two random keys, used by $U1$ and $U2$, respectively. Let, $kU1M$ is the session key between $U1$ and Mx. Similarly, $kU2M$ is between $U2$ and Mx, kMx is between Mx and L, and $kLSP$ is between L and SP. $prkL$ and $pbkL$ are the private and public keys of L.

```
(** main process **)
process
new r1:RandNum; new r2:RandNum;
new kMx:Key; new kLSP:Key; new k1:Key;
new k2:Key;
new prkL:prkey; let pbkL=pk(prkL)
in out(c3,pbkL);
out(c3,kLSP);
!((let U=U1 in let r=r1 in let k=k1 in
let kU1M = Sessk(U1) in Patient(kU1M)) |
(let U=U2 in let r=r2 in let k=k2 in
let kU2M = Sessk(U2) in Patient(kU2M)) |
MixNode(Sessk(U1),Sessk(U2),kMx) |
Lab(kMx,kLSP,prkL) |
PHRSP(kLSP) )
```

The main process shown above verifies the equivalence between at least two runs wherein the first run, *Lab* handles request from one user and in the second run, from another user. Equivalence between these two processes implies that an adversary (including the PHRSP) who can listen from the communicating channel cannot distinguish whether the published report (R) request comes from user $U1$ or $U2$.

3.3 Comparison

A comparison of existing PHRMSs is shown in Table 1. The comparison is done on the basis of following properties: whether the scheme requires any special hardware, uses symmetric or asymmetric encryption method, whether access right revocation is addressed, uses hierarchical access control (HAC) or not, and whether forward secrecy property is addressed. From the comparison table, we can see that a number of schemes [20–25] are hardware-based. Some of the schemes [22, 24, 28] use

Table 1 Coarse level comparison of PHRMS schemes

Scheme	Special h/w required	Encryption	Access right revocation	HAC based	Forward secrecy
Huang et al. [22], Chen et al. [20]	Yes	Symmetric	No	No	No
Lee et al. [24]	Yes	Asymmetric	Yes	No	No
Narayan et al. [28]	No	Asymmetric	Yes	No	No
Odelu et al. [26], Liu et al. [30]	No	Symmetric	No	Yes	No
Li et al. [9]	No	Symmetric	Yes	Yes	No
Thilakanathan et al. [31]	No	Symmetric	Yes	No	No
Kumar et al. [10]	No	Symmetric	Yes	No	Yes

Table 2 Comparison of anonymity related issues in PHRMS schemes

Scheme	Method	Remark
Thilakanathan et al. [31]	Secret sharing	
Neubauer et al. [45]	Pseudonymization	Not patient-centric
Benaloh et al. [29]	Searchable encryption	HAC based, required significant number of keys
Moor et al. [46]	Pseudonymization	Uses pseudonymization
Aamot et al. [42]	Pseudonymization	Use asymmetric encryption
Kumar et al. [10]	Mix node	Introduce communication delay

asymmetric key cryptosystem. Cheng et al., Li et al., and Odelu et al. [9, 26, 30] use hierarchical access control. These schemes require a significant amount of system public storage for storing the key derivation hierarchy and key derivation information. Also, the key derivation cost for accessing PHR document varies with the height of the hierarchy. Thilakanathan et al. [31] is secret sharing-based scheme thus require trusted proxy servers for secret computation. Kumar et al. [10] first time introduce forward secrecy requirement using symmetric keys. In addition, we have discussed earlier that [9, 28] require a variable number of secret keys with each system user. Also, [30] is not scalable with add or delete file operation or change in the relationship between user classes.

Table 2 compares the existing schemes with respect to privacy requirement in PHRMS. All of them uses a TTP in their implementation. Thilakanathan et al. [31] uses secret sharing mechanism and requires a TTP for data sharing service. Neubauer and Heurix [45] is not patient-centric. The solution in [29] needs to create and manage multiple keys by users and service providers. Pommerening et al. [47] uses 2 TTP's one for each pseudonymization and de-pseudonymization process. Meyer et al. [46] uses a separate data provider rather than another TTP to perform the pre-pseudonymization process. Aamot et al. [42] use asymmetric cryptosystem for pseudonymization method. As compare to pseudonymization-based anonymity, [10] uses mix node to provide unobservable communication.

4 Conclusions and Open Problems

In this chapter, we give a survey on security and privacy requirements of cloud-based PHRMS. We conclude that it will be a wise decision to classify PHR data according to the specialty classes of doctors. This is because a doctor generally interested in viewing the PHR data belongs to their specialty class only.

As an important privacy requirement, PHR data must be stored anonymously with its owner. Two recent mechanisms for implementing the anonymous requirement in a PHRMS are by using pseudonymization or mix node. However, both of them have their advantages and disadvantages. Pseudonymization does not provide unobservability while data communication through an open channel using mix node adds communication delay to the data access mechanism. Therefore, we believe that there is a significant scope in this area of research to find an efficient mechanism that achieves data unobservability. Also, the existing solutions enable the presence of a trusted third party. It will be a challenge to efficiently achieve unobservability property in a PHRMS without using any trusted party.

For efficiency and privacy reasons, it is desired that a medical document is outsourced by its generator directly to the cloud without communicated it through the PHR owner. However, since the service provider is untrusted, the PHR owner requires a posterior mechanism such as "auditing" so that it can verify its outsourced PHR content and take appropriate action in case any unauthorized update happens to the outsourced PHR. We realize that this area can be further explored to get an efficient and secure auditing mechanism by the PHR owner for its outsourced secret content.

PHR information accountability is another important area of research when PHR data is communicated over the open environment and through untrusted entities such as cloud service provider. Secure PHR data is traveling through various PHRMS entities which indirectly handle the data and are not trivially trusted by a PHR owner. Therefore, making each intermediate communication entity accountable to the system is another important requirement in a PHRMS.

Irrespective of huge benefits of using PHRs, the "digital divide" [48], i.e., the users with low computer and health literacy [49] are still having problem that affects the usage of PHRs. The studies in [50–52] report the effect of illiteracy in the expansion of PHR. Therefore, we believe that even though the PHR has great health benefits, it will be a challenge to adopt it globally.

References

1. Gunter, T. D., & Terry, N. P. (2005). The emergence of national electronic health record architectures in the united states and australia: Models, costs, and questions. *Journal of Medical Internet Research, 7*, 1.
2. Kaelber, D. C., Jha, A. K., Johnston, D., Middleton, B., & Bates, D. W. (2008). A research agenda for personal health records (phrs). *JAMIA, 15*(6), 729–736.
3. Liu, L. S., Shih, P. C., & Hayes, G. R. (2011). Barriers to the adoption and use of personal health record systems. In *Proceedings of the 2011 iConference*, iConference '11 (pp. 363–370), New York, NY, USA, 2011. ACM.
4. Tang, P. C., & Lansky, D. (2005). The missing link: Bridging the patient?provider health information gap. *Health Aff (Millwood), 24*(5), 1290–1295.
5. Health, G. Retrieved from http://www.healthvault.com/personal/index.html.
6. Health Vault, M. Retrieved from http://www.google.com/intl/en-US/health/about/index.html.
7. Tang, P. C., Ash, J. S., Bates, D. W., Overhage, J. M., & Sands, D. Z. (2006). Personal health records: Definitions, benefits, and strategies for overcoming barriers to adoption. *JAMIA, 13*(2), 121–126.
8. Lindenthal, J. J., & Thomas, C. S. (1982). Psychiatrists, the public, and confidentiality. *The Journal of Nervous and Mental Disease, 170*(6), 319–23.
9. Li, M., Yu, S., Lou, W., & Ren, K. (2010). Securing personal health records in cloud computing: Patient-centric and fine-grained data access control in multi-owner settings. In *SecureComm* (pp. 89–106).
10. Kumar, N., Mathuria, A., & Das, M. L. (2015). Achieving forward secrecy and unlinkability in cloud-based personal health record system. In *2015 IEEE TrustCom/BigDataSE/ISPA, Helsinki, Finland, 20–22 Aug. 2015* (Vol. 1, pp. 1249–1254).
11. Haas, S., Wohlgemuth, S., Echizen, I., Sonehara, N., & Müller, G. (2011). Aspects of privacy for electronic health records. *International Journal of Medical Informatics, 80*(2), e26–e31.
12. Pfitzmann, A., & Hansen, M. (2010). A terminology for talking about privacy by data minimization: Anonymity, unlinkability, undetectability, unobservability, pseudonymity, and identity management. Retrieved Aug. 2010 from http://dud.inf.tu-dresden.de/literatur/Anon_Terminology_v0.34.pdf. v0.34.
13. Safran, C., Bloomrosen, M., Hammond, W. E., Labkoff, S. E., Markel-Fox, S., Tang, P. C., et al. (2007). White paper: Toward a national framework for the secondary use of health data: An american medical informatics association white paper. *JAMIA, 14*(1), 1–9.
14. Break-glass—An approach to granting access to healthcare systems. Joint security and privacy committee nema/cocir/jira, international medical informatics. Retrieved from http://www.nema.org/prod/med/security/upload/break-glass_-_emergency_access_to_healthcare_systems.pdf.
15. Mashima, D., & Ahamad, M. (2012). Enabling robust information accountability in e-healthcare systems. In *3rd USENIX Workshop on Health Security and Privacy, HealthSec'12, Bellevue, WA, USA, 6–7 Aug 2012*.
16. Foundation, M. Connecting for health. The personal health working group final report.
17. Law, U. P. (1996). Health insurance portability and accountability act of 1996. In *104th Congress* (pp. 104–191).
18. Szolovits, P., Doyle, J., Long, W. J., Kohane, I., & Pauker, S. G. (1994). *Guardian angel: Patient-centered health information systems*, Technical report, Cambridge, MA, USA.
19. Mandl, K. D., Simons, W. W., Crawford, W. C. R., & Abbett, J. M. (2007). Indivo: a personally controlled health record for health information exchange and communication. *BMC Medical Informatics and Decision Making, 7*, 25.
20. Chen, Y.-Y., Lu, J.-C., & ke Jan, J. (2012). A secure EHR system based on hybrid clouds. *Journal of Medical Systems 36*(5), 3375–3384.
21. Hu, J., Chen, H.-H., & Hou, T.-W. (2010). A hybrid public key infrastructure solution (HPKI) for HIPAA privacy/security regulations. *Computer Standards and Interfaces, 32*(5–6), 274–280.

22. Huang, H.-F., & Liu, K.-C. (2011). Efficient key management for preserving HIPAA regulations. *Journal of Systems and Software, 84*(1), 113–119.
23. Lee, W.-B., & Lee, C.-D. (2008). A cryptographic key management solution for HIPAA privacy/security regulations. *IEEE Transactions on Information Technology in Biomedicine, 12*(1), 34–41.
24. Lee, W.-B., Lee, C.-D., & Ho, K. I.-J. (2014). A HIPAA-compliant key management scheme with revocation of authorization. *Computer Methods and Programs in Biomedicine, 113*(3), 809–814.
25. Yu, W. D., & Chekhanovskiy, M. A. (2007). An electronic health record content protection system using smartcard and PMR. In *e-Health Networking: Application and Services* (pp. 11–18).
26. Odelu, V., Das, A. K., & Goswami, A. (2013). An effective and secure key-management scheme for hierarchical access control in e-medicine system. *Journal of Medical Systems, 37*, 2.
27. Keoh, S. L., Asim, M., Kumar, S. S., & Lenoir, P. (2011). Secure spontaneous emergency access to personal health record. In *3rd International Workshop on Security and Privacy in Spontaneous Interaction and Mobile Phone Use*.
28. Narayan, S., Gagné, M., & Safavi-Naini, R. (2010). Privacy preserving EHR system using attribute-based infrastructure. In *CCSW* (pp. 47–52).
29. Benaloh, J., Chase, M., Horvitz, E., & Lauter, K. (2009). Patient controlled encryption: Ensuring privacy of electronic medical records. In *CCSW* (pp. 103–114).
30. Liu, C.-H., Chen, T.-S., Chen, T.-L., Chen, C.-S., Bau, J.-G., & Lin, T.-C. (2012). Secure dynamic access control scheme of PHR in cloud computing. *Journal of Medical Systems 36*(6), 4005–4020.
31. Thilakanathan, D., Chen, S., Nepal, S., Calvo, R., & Alem, L. (2014). A platform for secure monitoring and sharing of generic health data in the cloud. *Future Generation Computer Systems, 35*, 102–113.
32. Dekker, M. A. C., & Etalle, S. (2007). Audit-based access control for electronic health records. *Electronic Notes in Theoretical Computer Science, 168*, 221–236.
33. Beedham, H., & Wilson-Barnett, J. (1995). Hiv and aids care: Consumers' views on needs and services. *Journal of Advanced Nursing, 22*(4), 677–86.
34. Ford, C. A., Millstein, S. G., Halpern-Felsher, B. L., & Irwin Jr, C. E. (1997). Influence of physician confidentiality assurances on adolescents' willingness to disclose information and seek future health care. A randomized controlled trial. *JAMA, 278*(12), 1029–1034.
35. Rodriguez, M. A., Craig, A. M., Mooney, D. R., & Bauer, H. M. (1998). Patient attitudes about mandatory reporting of domestic violence. implications for health care professionals. *Western Journal of Medicine, 169*(6), 337–341.
36. Applebaum, P. S. (2002). Privacy in psychiatric treatment: Threats and response. *American Journal of Psychiatry, 159*.
37. Bass, A. (1995). Hmo puts confidential records on-line: Critics say computer file-keeping breaches privacy of mental health patients. *Boston Globe*.
38. Sweeney, L. (2002). k-anonymity: A model for protecting privacy. *International Journal of Uncertainty, Fuzziness and Knowledge-Based Systems, 10*(5), 557–570.
39. Machanavajjhala, A., Kifer, D., Gehrke, J., & Venkitasubramaniam, M. (2007). L-diversity: Privacy beyond k-anonymity. *TKDD, 1*, 1.
40. Li, N., Li, T., & Venkatasubramanian, S. (2007). t-closeness: Privacy beyond k-anonymity and l-diversity. In *ICDE* (pp. 106–115).
41. Heurix, J., Karlinger, M., Schrefl, M., & Neubauer, T. (2011). A hybrid approach integrating encryption and pseudonymization for protecting electronic health records. In *Proceedings of the Eighth IASTED International Conference on Biomedical Engineering* (2011).
42. Aamot, H., Kohl, C. D., Richter, D., & Knaup-Gregori, P. (2013). Pseudonymization of patient identifiers for translational research. *BMC Medical Informatics and Decision Making, 13*, 75.
43. Chaum, D. (1981). Untraceable electronic mail, return addresses, and digital pseudonyms. *Communications of the ACM, 24*(2), 84–88.

44. Blanchet, B. (2001). An, & efficient cryptographic protocol verifier based on prolog rules. In *14th IEEE Computer Security Foundations Workshop (CSFW-14)* (pp. 82–96), 11–13 June 2001. Cape Breton, Nova Scotia, Canada.
45. Neubauer, T., & Heurix, J. (2011). A methodology for the pseudonymization of medical data. *International Journal of Medical Informatics, 80*(3), 190–204.
46. Meyer, F. D., Moor, G. D., & Fourquet, R. (2008). Privacy protection through pseudonymisation in eHealth. *Studies in Health Technology and Informatics, 141*, 111–118.
47. Pommerening, K. et al. (2006). Pseudonymization service and data custodians in medical research networks and biobanks. In *GI Jahrestagung (1)* (pp. 715–721).
48. Kim, E., Mayani, A., Modi, S., Kim, Y., & Soh, C. (2005). Evaluation of patient-centered electronic health record to overcome digital divide. In *Annual International Conference of the IEEE Engineering in Medicine and Biology Society* (Vol. 2), pp. 1091–1094.
49. Archer, N., Fevrier-Thomas, U., Lokker, C., McKibbon, K. A., & Straus, S. E. (2011). Personal health records: A scoping review. *JAMIA, 18*(4), 515–522.
50. Kim, E. H., Stolyar, A., Lober, W. B., Herbaugh, A. L., Shinstrom, S. E., Zierler, B. K., et al. (2009). Challenges to using an electronic personal health record by a low-income elderly population. *JMIR, 11*, 4.
51. Lober, W. B., Zierler, B., Herbaugh, A., Shinstrom, S. E., Stolyar, A., Kim, E. H., & Kim, Y. (2006). Barriers to the use of a personal health record by an elderly population. In *AMIA Annual Symposium Proceedings/AMIA Symposium.*
52. Yamin, C. K., Emani, S., Williams, D. H., Lipsitz, S. R., Karson, A. S., Wald, J. S., et al. (2011). The digital divide in adoption and use of a personal health record. *Archives of Internal Medicine, 171*(6), 568–574.

Applications of Trusted Computing in Cloud Context

Mohammad Reza Memarian, Diogo Fernandes, Pedro Inácio,
Ville Leppänen and Mauro Conti

Abstract Trusted computing is a technology that enables computer systems to behave in a given expected way. Achieving that goal happens by arming an isolated piece of hardware with embedded processing, cryptographic capabilities such as encryption key that is kept safe from software layer attacks. The mentioned module is accessible to the rest of the computer system via a well-defined and tested application programming interface. Trusted computing protects the system against external attackers and even against the owner of the system. Cloud computing enables users to have access to vast amounts of computational resources remotely, in a seamless and ubiquitous manner. However, in some cloud deployment models, such as public cloud computing, the users have very little control over how their own data is remotely handled and are not able to assure that their data is securely processed and stored. Cloud administrators and other parties can be considered threats in such cases. Given the ground that cloud has been gaining and the rate at which data is generated, transmitted, processed, and stored remotely, it is vital to protect it using means that address the ubiquitous nature of the cloud, including trusted computing. This chapter investigates applications of trusted computing in cloud computing areas where security threats exist, namely in live virtual machine migration.

M. Reza Memarian · V. Leppänen (✉)
Department of Information Technology, University of Turku, Turku, Finland
e-mail: Ville.Leppanen@utu.fi

M. Reza Memarian
e-mail: mohammad-reza.memarian@utu.fi

D. Fernandes
PepsiCo, Michrów, Poland

P. Inácio
Computer Science, University of Beira Interior, Covilhã, Portugal

M. Conti
Department of Mathematics, University of Padua, Padua, Italy
e-mail: conti@math.unipd.it

S. Chaudhary et al. (eds.), *Research Advances in Cloud Computing*,
DOI 10.1007/978-981-10-5026-8_18

1 Introduction

In computing, the term *trust* refers to establishing a high degree of confidence in the behavior of a system, provided that particular inputs are expected to render certain outputs. Trust is knowledge of the user on the precise functioning of the system. Due to the diversity of computing systems, this matter can not be addressed in a straight-forward manner. The state in which a single computing system can be is determined by running a set of configurations with varying dimensionality that can be reshuf-fled and recombined in a multitude of ways. That set changes as the system is used throughout time due to installation, upgrade or removal of software and replace-ment of hardware. For example, the Linux kernel subsystem implements an Integrity Measurement Architecture (IMA) that can be explored for integrity attestation pur-poses [7]. Hence, identifying the entire state set of a system can be an unfeasible task. Smaller subsets of well-known configurations are more manageable, but that does not satisfy the diversity of the computing systems. Frequently, trust assurance is achieved using cryptographic proofs that testify reliability of a system, regardless of the adjacent conditions and inputs at the cost of some overhead. Other approaches consist of formally proving that software works according to requirements.

Despite concerns over the security of cloud environments [16], cloud computing has been developing and maturing. This technology enables the envisioned comput-ing as a utility, essentially by eliminating the hassle of establishing on-site Infor-mation Technology (IT) infrastructures. It is capable of allocating, on-demand and off-site, fine-grained resources with minimal cost, by leveraging economy of scale. However, outsourcing private data and storage to providers with multi-tenant environ-ments raises security concerns. Trusted computing is, therefore, an essential com-ponent to cloud environments that can alleviate some of those security concerns. Nevertheless, the setup of cloud infrastructures under the service delivery models translates into an interplay of different hardware, virtualization and software tech-nologies at multiple layers. That interplay, in turn, creates computing diversity that poses as a difficulty in achieving trusted remote computing in a holistic manner.

In the light of the benefits of trusted computing to cloud environment, it is impor-tant to study current applications of one to the other, taking into consideration the challenges and requirements of cloud computing. This chapter makes that discus-sion by analyzing the security requirements in terms of trust to cloud services and by studying the applicability of trusted solutions to such requirements. Therefore, the contributions of this chapter are twofold. First, cloud computing is described with a focus on its trust requirements. Second, current applications of trusted computing are enumerated and weighted according to different criteria within the cloud security requirements.

Next, Sect. 2 gives an introductory overview of the cloud computing deploy-ment models and subsequently focuses on cloud services and security requirements. Section 3 describes trusted computing and enumerates applications of that technology to cloud computing environments. Section 4 summarizes the discussion and points out open issues. Finally, Sect. 5 concludes the chapter.

2 Cloud Computing

Computing in the *cloud* emerged several years ago as a means to describe computing as a *utility* off-site. This computing model not only offloads some storage and computing responsibilities to a cloud provider, but also the burden of managing IT infrastructures and security duties. For providers, services wrap well-defined resources from elastic pools that are measured and allocated as needed to users. In turn, consumers of the services are charged per subscription, which can significantly decrease costs for all kinds of small to large businesses.

The National Institute of Standards and Technology (NIST) adds the notions of ubiquitous access, monitored, on-demand, and shift provision of resources with minimal management burden to the definition of cloud computing [28]. This computing paradigm consists of three main service delivery models, Software-as-a-Service (SaaS), Platform-as-a-Service (PaaS), and Infrastructure-as-a-Service (IaaS), that can be set up in four deployment modes: private, public, community, and hybrid.

2.1 Cloud Services

Initially, cloud services were largely discussed according to three delivery models (as described in other chapters of this book) that illustrate the different layers of the cloud stack: IaaS, PaaS, and SaaS. Concerning trust and applications in the cloud context, the layers SaaS and IaaS are the most interesting, as those primarily provide the end-user applications and raw computing and storage resources, respectively. The description of services, however, is now often particularized under Anything-as-a-Service (XaaS), conveying the meaning that cloud services can deliver anything in the form of services. In fact, new service definitions have been made in an arbitrary way throughout time, resulting in a lack of a unified XaaS scheme [13], a view that was foreseen several years ago by Armbrust et al. [3].

The virtualization layer underpinning IaaS infrastructures brings many benefits, despite the implied overhead. A Virtual Machine Monitor (VMM) can handle several Virtual Machines (VMs), each one possibly encapsulating a different Operating System (OS) (a guest) with distinct settings. Access to the hardware is regulated by the manager according to a scheduling algorithm. This setup has noticeable advantages in terms of security by design, such as controlled isolation of the environment, regardless of vulnerabilities, and close monitoring of resource usage and communications. With the dependency between guest and native OSs removed, VMs can be rolled back to previously saved states (i.e., snapshots) or be moved around, in a process termed *migration*. This VM independence implies that, within IaaS infrastructures, data can be in one of three postures at a given time: at *transport* (data-in-motion), at *rest* (data-in-rest), and at *runtime* (data-in-processing). Migration of data between VMs or live VM migration is central to achieve energy-efficient consolidated workloads in clouds by minimizing the number of servers that are underutilized or idle [11].

2.2 Security Issues

Assuring security in all aspects of systems and end-to-end communications constitutes often a burden, because it is not granted by design. Unfortunately, security issues are likely prone to appear as a consequence. This principle holds true for cloud environments, as they are built on top of current networks and web technologies. Apart from mentioned technologies, virtualization is a vital component of cloud computing structure. OS-level virtualization provides the building blocks for running multiple OSs while sharing hardware resources, and effectively enhances isolation by means of sandboxing. Nonetheless, the virtualization technology may not be completely free of vulnerabilities, allowing adversaries to escape the controlled environment, a process known as VM *escape*. A prime real-world example of VM escape is the VENOM [9] vulnerability, identified by CVE-2015-3456. This vulnerability allows an attacker to run any code in the hypervisor process context by exploiting a buffer overflow in the Floppy Disk Controller (FDC) of the Quick Emulator (QEMU) hypervisor used by Xen and Kernel-based Virtual Machine (KVM) platforms.

Migration of VMs can always expose data as it is in motion. In the process of migration, VMMs copy memory pages of the VM to be migrated from source host to destination host seamlessly, while guest VMs are still running. This opens opportunities for attackers (especially malicious insiders) to access raw memory data of migrating VM. A myriad of information lies in the memory as everything in the OS traverses through the Random Access Memory (RAM), including passwords and cryptographic keys. In 2011, researchers employed simple forensics techniques to recover sensitive information from Xen VM snapshots, which contain copies of memory from a certain point in time in [32, 33].

Needless to say that snapshots at rest comprise tempting targets too, in case the storage media is accessible. Beyond the sensitive data they may hold, a compromised snapshot or image can be used to spread malware within the cloud environment if used as a golden image to boot up VMs.

To better arrange the discussion below, the threats and security requirements to cloud computing are discussed against the three postures the data can have in the cloud. We assume that the attacker is either an individual inside the infrastructure or has equivalent access. The threats with regard to data postures are as follows:

- When *at transport*, data potentially moves from a given (physical) system to another. As such, vulnerabilities related with networking technologies also play an additional role in such a scenario. The potential insecure communication channel is part of the attack model. If the data is moving between data centers, in an ecosystem known as *intercloud*, threats such as data leakage or modification are more prominent. Examples include the modification of VM's image during migration, namely to inject malicious software during the procedure. In this case, the data may be accessed or modified along the path from the source to the destination, which may render the intrusion or leakage more difficult to detect or account for.
- Within the context of cloud, data *at rest* may concern files and database instances of SaaS, PaaS applications or IaaS VM images. Clouds are also commonly used

to store backups of entire remote systems on demand or on a regular basis. If the data is stored in plaintext, or with insecure schemes (e.g., data may be encrypted with keys generated in the cloud itself), then it is susceptible to eavesdropping, data modification or leakage (the attacker may copy the data elsewhere). Eavesdropping may lead to compromise of private or confidential data, namely of industrial secrets, causing monetary harms. Modification of VM images may be performed with the goal of injecting malware, while eavesdropping has the intention of accessing confidential data. Modification of data at rest from PaaS or SaaS applications may be performed to induce a different behavior on the development environment or applications.

- The cloud is an ecosystem for very diverse runtime environments, and gives rise to very specific scenarios. In this case, data may leak from one execution environment to another or be injected between allegedly isolated sandboxes. Specific threats include cross-VM and container attacks [44], and malicious software installed at the hypervisor layer reading the contents of the memory from a running VM. Multi-tenancy is a core technology for the cloud, but brought its new set of security issues, especially in public clouds [27]. In such multi-tenancy scenario, two customers may be sharing the same technology, libraries, global variables and storage, which need to be adequately provisioned. At the *runtime* posture, threats are mainly coming from co-resident systems or applications [37].

2.3 Security Requirements

Two of the main security requirements of users in any secure environment are data confidentiality and integrity. It is vital for users to make sure that those properties of their data are preserved and guaranteed at any stage of operation. In addition to the mentioned requirements, trust is another factor which is more desired in the cloud than in other environments. There should be mechanisms in place to assure users that the trusted party transports and processes their data securely. In this section, we discuss security requirements for user data in the cloud with respect to cloud services mentioned in the previous section.

In most cases, confidentiality is the most important security requirement for user's data in cloud computing. It applies to any of the previously identified postures that data can be in. Privacy is also becoming more important in an age where ubiquity is increasing. Moreover, integrity of the user data is the other vital security requirement that shall be preserved in all the mentioned states, along with data authentication during transmission. At the transport state, adequate controls shall be implemented in place in order to provide a secure transport channel. Encryption mechanisms and Message Authentication Codes (MACs) are typically employed to provide a confidential and authenticated channel between cloud instances. Nonetheless, the aforementioned security mechanisms have an impact on the performance of the systems, which may hinder full deployment on every communication. Furthermore, usage of controls such as Network Intrusion Detection System (NIDS) can help to detect network level attacks and suspicious activities.

In addition to the transport and at rest states, data can be at the processing state. While users offload their heavy computational activities on cloud resources, they need trustworthy computational activity by the service provider. Parties with adequate privileges or via exploitation of vulnerabilities can access, modify or delete other users data. As such, confidentiality and integrity of data should be preserved at storage and computation time too [42]. However, the typical ciphers and integrity mechanisms cannot be used to protect data in the processing state. Data would have to be loaded in plaintext to the memory [34] to be processed. All the mentioned concerns arise from the fact that users do not have physical access to their data and applications. Recent research lines on homomorphic encryption schemes are motivated by the mentioned scenarios.

As pointed out earlier, main security properties that shall be preserved in any secure computing environment are confidentiality, integrity, and availability which are referred to as the CIA triangle. Trusted Computing (TC) can contribute to preservation of confidentiality and integrity of the data while availability is not directly achieved by implementation of TC. Starting from the described requirements and postures, it is now possible to investigate how TC can be used to provide assurance of the properties to the user.

3   Contribution of Trusted Computing to Cloud Security

The trust issue is best put into perspective when considering the evolution of IT infrastructures throughout time. Amoroso [2] accurately described, a few years ago in the context of modern enterprise infrastructures, a decisive point in time where the transition of IT infrastructures to the cloud was accelerating. The early IT model of the 1990s considered assets to be on-site, enclosed by a well-defined and controlled perimeter. Evolving business and communication needs, however, required to open network ports into the environment. Such is the case with Virtual Private Networks (VPNs), websites and email, all still in use today, and Internet access. Email, for instance, has been and still is one of the most concerning open channels into the network as it is heavily explored by attackers to deploy malware. Eventually, this drop in trust leads to a multitude of network and host-based monitoring and detection technology.

Fast forward to the current day, with cloud computing booming, the scope of the trust issue enlarges and worsens, leapfrogging from on-site IT infrastructures into off-site cloud environments. Trusted computing technology, however, helps alleviating the problem. The first part of this section describes TC, while the remaining parts point out deployments of that technology addressing the specific security issues of cloud environments discussed before.

3.1   Definition of Trusted Computing

TC refers to a set of software-based and hardware-based definitions and technologies that enable computer systems to behave in a desired and expected way. In the TC design, systems are less dependent on their owners while, even to some extent, are protected against them. TC requires a set of public and private key pairs to be generated and fixed on the hardware at the manufacturing time. The key pair is referred to as Endorsement Key (EK). Using the hard coded EK, platforms can authenticate each other and applications running on a platform can assure other applications on other platforms about their origin platform. TC also enables running of a particular desired software only and various desired restriction can be imposed on runtime behavior of applications.

TC is specifically applicable to distributed applications in environments such as cloud computing. In such environments, applications can make sure that the other applications or platforms are the correct ones. One of the key concepts in TC design is remote attestation. Remote attestation enables authorized parties to detect unwanted changes to the computing system. It is applicable in various areas of computing such as detection of unwanted change in the licensed software and verifying the platform that an application is executing on it.

Trusted Platform Module (TPM) is a standard for a piece of hardware (microprocessor) that acts as an enabler of TC. Using TPM, a user can ensure that the application is running on the specific hardware and OS. This secure cryptographic module delivers a hardware-based method to handle authentication of user, data protection, and network access, and brings out the matter of security from the software layer only. Hardware-based TPMs are bound to a single standalone device by design. The origin of trust is therefore limited in scope, which turns out to be unsuitable for applications where sharing is desired or for cross-device scenarios. An extension of the version 2.0 of the TPM specification is presented in [8] in order to address multi-device scenarios. The extension for TPM v2.0 actually trusts and relies on the cloud to share an additional key, though it does not address any particular cloud security issue.

3.2   Trusted Cloud Computational Security

One of the critical postures that user data can be at is the processing state (while using the cloud services). At that state, data require substantial protection in order to ban privileged insiders to interfere with the user computational processes. The processing state refers to the execution of internal processes for computing over user data. It encompasses various types of calculation, simulation, data processing, and program execution. Hence, clients shall have methods in hand to verify integrity and confidentiality of their data at computation time on the cloud. That concern enforces limitations of using cloud for security-critical computations such as confidential simulations.

   While the data of a user can be at processing state at any service level, the case of IaaS is the most relevant for this study. At the IaaS level, users have more control over the underlying infrastructure of the service, when compared to other service layers. That enables users to have a more deterministic role in determining the security level of their service at IaaS level while in other service levels, the providers get that role. On the other hand, applying trusted computing techniques to the PaaS and SaaS levels but not to the IaaS level would be unnatural, since trust building is transitive and one should start it from the lowest levels. Having trusted computational security for the IaaS level can be seen to implicitly provide it also for the PaaS and SaaS levels. Hence, it is no surprise that applications of TC are mostly proposed for the IaaS level. However, some papers propose additional trusted computing solutions for the PaaS and SaaS layers.

   In the following, we survey some works having focus in computational issues of trusted cloud. Many of these works are actually wide in scope—describing overall trusted cloud solution with computational capabilities. The papers are summarized in Table 1.

   At the IaaS level, services are provided in the form of VM. Those VMs are started based on some images. The user can either purchase the image from the image repository of the service provider or the user can upload an arbitrary image to be used for the user's VM. To verify the integrity of the started system, the user shall make sure that the started VM booted an expected image. Incorporation of TC into cloud computing platforms is an effort in that regard. Wallom et al. [41] proposed myTrustedCloud which incorporated TC into the Eucalyptus cloud platform. Trusted computing enables users of the cloud to be assured about the integrity of the VM itself and the underlying VMM. Each VM executes the desired applications on top of a commodity OS. That condition simulates a form of the open-box system. On the other hand, users can modify the settings of an OS in order to satisfy the security requirements of their applications and diminish the unrequited services from a large OS. That simulates a form of closed-box system. The closed-box setting creates an execution environment that disables malicious insiders from accidentally or

Table 1 Overview of trusted cloud papers having focus in computational issues

Paper	Layer	Overview
[41]	IaaS	An outline of trusted cloud for security-critical computation.
[17]	IaaS	Early (2003) constructive work on Terra system for trusted general-purpose computing
[22]	IaaS	Introduces open source cloud computing framework Eucalyptus.
[40]	PaaS	Trusted computing based solution for Java environment. The solution is applicable to cloud context
[6]	PaaS/SaaS	Efficient and Secure Educational Platform (ESEP) for cloud computing based on TPMs
[30]	SaaS	Provides trusted SLA (service level agreement) monitoring services as part of a cloud based billing system

intentionally accessing and tampering the user data at processing time [34]. The requirement for that is to have a VMM that supports trusted computing.

Garfinkel et al. [17] proposed Terra, a Trusted Virtual Machine Monitor (TVMM) architecture that is able to simultaneously run VMs in both open and closed-box settings. That allows each application to run on a specifically modified version of an OS. Furthermore, the architecture of Terra allows the TVMM to apply TC requirements such as remote attestation of the applications for each VM. Hence, it is effective for implementation of distributed applications in cloud environments. Using trusted computing, the user can verify the integrity of the VM itself, the Node Controller (NC) and the Elastic Block Store (EBS). In order to verify integrity of the VM, the integrity of all three mentioned elements should be verified, which is called iterative attestation. That verifies the operation of the trustworthy VM on a trusted platform [22].

As opposed to Terra, which is suitable for operation on a single platform, Trusted Cloud Computing Platform (TCCP) [34] operates on multiple platforms (data center wide) enabling VMs to move around and use the live migration feature. As such, the attestation encompasses the entire service ensuring the customer about the security of each platform that computation is taking place on. Important components of TCCP are TVMM and a third-party trusted coordinator. Nodes shall go through a secure boot process in order to install the TVMM. That trusted coordinator keeps a list of trusted nodes that the user can have for user's own VM to securely operate on. To be trusted a node shall run a TVMM and be in the secure perimeter. One of the important points here is that the VM's launch time is a critical moment requiring protection and other operations such as suspend and resume [34].

While attestation is a useful mechanism for remote verification of trust, it has two shortcomings. By attestation, some private information of the service provider such as details about the platform and the internal structure of internal systems can be uncovered. Potential malicious users can benefit from that information to form attacks. Secondly, if third parties handle the attestation [22], they become the single point of failure [41].

Even though cryptography can contribute to preserve confidentiality and integrity of data at transport and storage states, it is currently ineffective during computation time [34], as data shall be loaded in plaintext to memory. Fully Homomorphic Cryptography (FHC) allows a set of limited operations on the encrypted data, but the performance of FHC is not at a level to be operational in practice. This problem is more severe in the cloud because it has a multi-tenant environment and the infrastructure is not under control of the data owner. Cloud employees either accidental or maliciously might tamper or access data, causing violation of confidentiality and integrity. At situations where user data is unprotected in the memory for processing, anyone with privileged access level can have access to the data. A preliminary countermeasure is to limit the physical access to the hardware and servers. However, limiting the physical access only thwarts a small portion of the attacks as various other attacks take place with remote access, and existing solutions are not fully effective in mitigating attacks in that field [32].

One can also find PaaS level solutions of trusted computing. One such is trusted computing implementation for platform-independent Java environment by Toegl et al. [40]. To be precise, the paper only sees cloud computing as one possible context for their technical solution, and thus this work is only indirectly cloud related.

SaaS level solutions do also exist. In such cases, the SaaS solution has some specific data and functionality that is secured with trusted computing techniques. Brohi et al. [6] describe a secure cloud infrastructure for an Efficient and Secure Educational Platform (ESEP)—it can be seen either as a SaaS or a PaaS level solution. The actual solution also contains elements from the IaaS level. A different kind SaaS level trusted service is provided from the THEMIS system by Park et al. [30]. The THEMIS system is a billing system implemented for a cloud computing environment, but the system provides monitoring of service level agreement (SLA) properties by implementing that functionality based on TPM modules. In fact, there are several other papers that provide similar SLA related functionality based on trusted computing techniques in cloud computing contexts.

3.3 Trusted Cloud Transport Security

The attestation process can be the target of network layer attacks. Two of the related attacks in that layer are reply attacks and Man-in-the-Middle (MitM). In order to prevent reply attacks, a cryptographic nonce, which is generated by the user shall be used for the attestation session. In order to tackle the MitM, the NC shall make sure that the VM requesting attestation is running and is connected to that NC itself [41].

At the VM transport time, user data can be the target of leakage and tampering attempts [34]. In live migration, the states of a VM are transferred between two nodes, which both need to be trusted.

We have looked at papers focusing on transport security in trusted cloud context. In the following, we survey some recent such papers and summarize the results as Table 2. Almost all such papers deal with VM migration at IaaS level—such constructions are also surveyed recently in [1, 25]. This is quite natural, as considering the SaaS level, the mechanisms to securely transmit SaaS application data from one (cloud) system to another are already well understood and solved even outside the cloud context. On the other hand, sharing SaaS level data is an elementary part of

Table 2 Overview of trusted cloud papers having focus in migration issues

Paper	Layer	Overview
[10]	IaaS	Virtual TPM-based solution for VM migration in private clouds
[4]	IaaS	VM migration solution focusing on developing trust token-based protocol
[15]	IaaS	Further developed VM-vTPM solution where the focus is in TLS channel
[19]	PaaS/IaaS	Virtual TPM-based solution enabling container migration
[38]	IaaS	An OpenStack and TPM-based solution for VM migration

the whole idea of cloud computing. Migrating applications from a cloud system to another neither seems to be a popular topic in the literature. The reason perhaps is that a cloud application corresponds to a service and instead of moving services from one place to another, one can replicate the same service in several places (and then moving corresponds to setting a service up in one place and closing it down in another place—not necessarily moving any data related to the service). There is however one seemingly growing exception to this PaaS level activity—the container technology is gaining more popularity and one can think of moving a container (typically made just for one application) as a PaaS level migration activity. A virtual TPM-based such framework is described in [19].

In Danev et al. [10], three security requirements are enumerated for secure migration of VMs based on Trusted Platform Modules (vTPMs), namely VM-vTPM confidentiality and integrity, initiation authenticity (of the migration requester), and preservation of the trust chain. The last one is of particular importance when considering the different elements of the cloud stack and trust transitivity, as well as the strong association between hardware TPMs and vTPMs. To cope with these requirements, Danev et al. [10] described a protocol where migration of VM-vTPM pairs is made possible between attested nodes by introducing an additional key layer between TPMs and vTPMs, at the cost of some overhead. Moreover, Aslam et al. [4] add as a requirement that the destination of a migration should be trustworthy too. To cope with that, and other cloud requirements like scheduling, transparency, and scalability, a token-based trust scheme is described to attest that the same software state trusted by the user is found on platforms where the VM are migrated to. This scheme relies on a TPM-based communication protocol between the source and destination systems, as well as on trust tokens pre-generated by the cloud provider in a segregated network.

Another constructive solution for VM migration is given by Fan et al. [15]—their work especially focuses on development of TLS-based migration protocol. VM migration is studied in several contexts. Syed et al. [38] study the issue in OpenStack context applying TPM, libvirt, and QEMU.

3.4 Trusted Cloud Storage Security

Cloud storage is used for file, system and image backups. Guaranteeing security against confidentiality and integrity breaking attempts means usually to encrypt and authenticate the data. Depending on the usage and type of data, TPM may be used as a means to derive encryption keys, perform encryption and decryption of data, and testify the integrity of the data during retrieval.

In the case of remote storage of files and system backups (e.g., Dropbox), data should already be in an encrypted format when it reaches the cloud, though this does not always happen nowadays. If special functions over the data, such as search, are required, TPM may be used to perform them in a safe environment, returning sanitized values. In the case of image storage, TPM is particularly useful for attestation purposes.

Table 3 Overview of trusted cloud papers having focus in storage issues

Paper	Layer	Overview
[35]	IaaS	Technical solution for server and client side focusing on handling and sharing of encryption keys
[36]	IaaS	A general encryption and trusted computing based solution for cloud data
[20]	SaaS	Specific solution for trustworthy flow cytometry data analyses
[5]	SaaS	Provenance-based trusted solution for access control and provenance information provision for the users
[39]	PaaS	Provenance solution for forensics needs based on trusted computing
[43]	IaaS	An OpenStack-based cloud solution for forensics-enabled investigations
[21]	IaaS	A trust-based solution in hybrid cloud setting for geographically fenced data
[31]	IaaS	TGVisor: A storage solution for controlling geolocation of data with trusted computing and supporting especially mobile clients
[26]	IaaS	SecLoc: A solution for supporting location sensitivity of cloud data storage with trusted computing

In the following, we review a small set of rather recent works that focus on providing storage security in the trusted cloud context. Often the papers also deal with other issues besides the storage security. The papers are summarized in Table 3.

Shin et al. [35] consider the access control mechanism provided for typical cloud storage to require improvement. They propose a technical solution called DFCloud for an improved TPM-based solution of managing encryption keys and overall key sharing between dynamically defined legal users. Special focus is given for mobile devices as means to access such cloud storage. On the client side, DFCloud is based on using ARM's TrustZone technology. From the cloud point of view, the DFCloud works at IaaS level.

There are several general solutions proposed for securing cloud data using trusted computing technologies. Singh et al. [36] describe a TPM-based solution, NUYA, using Kerberos for generally securing data in the cloud context. As opposed to generic solutions, there exist also some rather specific application related data that are secured with trusted computing based techniques in the cloud context. Javanmard et al. [20] give such a solution for the medical field, specifically for flow cytometry analyses to support disease diagnosis activities. As specific solutions are more like applications, the TSC (Trustworthy and Scalable Cytometry) solution of [20] can be seen to be made for the SaaS layer.

Concerning cloud storage, there is occasionally a clear need to be able to track the usage and origins of data. *Provenance* on data is information of actions that are taken on it since the creation of data (including creation). Many cloud systems support data provenance as a feature, but technical solutions for guaranteeing trusted provenance-based access and information are also presented in the literature. A survey of provenance solutions is given in [24]. Bates et al. [5] present a trusted computing based provenance solution for access control but also provide the provenance data as a SaaS-like service for the user. Progger (Provenance Logger) is another technical solution by Ko and Will [23] for provenance information but unlike [5] it is not really based on trusted computing but on a kernel-space solution. In many works, provenance-based solutions are developed towards auditing and forensics needs. One such paper is by Taha et al. [39], where that kind of trusted computing based solution is given. The solution is made for a set of applications and thus it can be considered as a PaaS/SaaS level solution. Another OpenStack-based solution is given by Zawoad and Hasan [43]. They describe a construction named FECloud to support forensics-enabled investigations concerning data provenance. Their solution is indirectly based on trusted computing.

One rather recent challenge for cloud computing systems has been the (often law-based) requirement to enforce governmental data privacy regulations and to ensure that data (and computations on the data) do not cross some specific geographic boundaries. There are several specific trusted computing based technical solutions provided for securing location sensitivity of the data in a cloud system. In general, the idea of such trustworthy geographically fenced hybrid clouds (TGHC) is described by Jayaram et al. [21]. TGVisor, by Park et al. [31], represents a more detailed technical IaaS solution for more or less the same problem but also supporting mobile clients. Another related solution is SecLoc by Li et al. [26]. SecLoc is specifically made for needs raising from Canadian law—to provide a location-sensitive cloud storage for example, storing health records.

4 Discussion and Open Challenges

Despite the research advancements in this field, one of the fundamental issues of trust remains open. That issue is the one revolving around the perception of trust, specifically what different individuals and groups make of it both in concept and in relation to technology. This is especially relevant to cloud environments, such as the project described in [14], which aimed at identifying issues in a pilot High-Performance Computing Cluster (HPCC) in the cloud for several stakeholders of the petrochemical industry. Their main finding is the one described as a clash between organizational behavior, a *political cloud* so to speak. Moreover, in [29], trust relates to reputation and not as in mathematical attestations using a hardware module, further highlighting the point of awareness. How TPMs and vTPMs come to address this multi-tenant scenario where users have distinct understanding of the underlying concepts is still unknown. Nevertheless, it is foreseeable that the technological solutions based on encryption will continue to be developed, not only to cope with the security, privacy, and trust needs, but also to provide a seamless cloud experience.

Another important challenge in trusted cloud computing is trust transitivity and zoning. This is well illustrated when considering the complex interaction of trust from the bare metal to the hypervisor and to the interface, in view of the IaaS hybrid interplay of multiple software instances and devices, whether virtual or physical. Here, zoning refers to the secure isolation of trust zones for and between tenants. This calls for trust assessment models such as the one described in [18], which considers different scenarios with and without TPM availability for the processor and Basic Input/Output System (BIOS) or hypervisor signing. Furthermore, trust is an issue of source and destination, such as the works done upon live VM migration. The transitivity and zoning also encompass all that is in between, so a network building trust path [12] is needed too for intra-cloud and intercloud migrations.

5 Conclusions

Cloud computing and trusted computing are increasingly the focus on several studies to address the security issues posed by the former. Virtualization is advantageous from the computing and cost-efficiency points of view, allowing to create multi-tenant infrastructures running co-resident operating systems. Pre-packaged software development environments in the cloud are also useful centralized repositories to save time when setting up dependencies, libraries, and tools, which allow devising cloud applications. Nevertheless, a lack of trust in computing, storage, and transport is evident when considering the offload of IT responsibilities to third-party cloud providers.

A number of security requirements from the trust standpoint were discussed in this chapter. These security requirements highlight that cloud environments need improvement at several levels so that the trust chain of the cloud stack holds throughout the several heterogeneous cloud systems, such as live VM migration from one cloud platform to another. Multiple works describe ways to enhance trust attestation in certain points, but may be limited in scope and do so not without introducing additional complexity and cryptographic and communication overhead or a third-party entity. That establishes that realizing fully trusted cloud environments to users is not yet within grasp. Achieving this ideal setup would require to mimic the same levels of trust as users have with their own on-site systems.

References

1. Ahmad, R. W., Gani, A., Hamid, S. H. A., Shiraz, M., Xia, F., & Madani, S. A. (2015). Virtual machine migration in cloud data centers: a review, taxonomy, and open research issues. *The Journal of Supercomputing, 71*(7), 2473–2515.
2. Amoroso, E. G. (2013). From the enterprise perimeter to a mobility-enabled secure cloud. *IEEE Secur Privacy, 11*(1), 23–31.
3. Armbrust, M., Fox, A., Griffith, R., Joseph, A. D., Katz, R., Konwinski, A., et al. (2010). A view of cloud computing. *Commun ACM, 53*(4), 50–58.
4. Aslam, M., Gehrmann, C., & Björkman, M. (2012). Security and Trust Preserving VM Migrations in Public Clouds. *IEEE 11th International Conference on Trust, Security and Privacy in Computing and Communications (TrustCom)* (pp. 869–876).
5. Bates, A., Mood, B., Valafar, M., & Butler, K. (2013). Towards secure provenance-based access control in cloud environments. In *Proceedings of the Third ACM Conference on Data and Application Security and Privacy* (pp. 277–284). ACM.

6. Brohi, S. N., Bamiah, M. A., Chuprat, S., Ab Manan, J. L. (2012). Towards an efficient and secure educational platform on cloud infrastructure. In *2012 International Conference on Cloud Computing Technologies, Applications and Management (ICCCTAM)* (pp. 145–150). IEEE.
7. Cesena, E., Ramunno, G., Sassu, R., Vernizzi, D., & Lioy, A. (2011). On Scalability of remote attestation. In *Proceedings of the 6th ACM Workshop on Scalable Trusted Computing (STC)* (pp. 25–30). New York, NY, USA: ACM
8. Chen, C., Raj, H., Saroiu, S., & Wolman, A. (2014). cTPM: A cloud tpm for cross-device trusted applications. In: *Proceedings of the 11th USENIX Conference on Networked Systems Design and Implementation (NSDI), USENIX Association, Berkeley, CA, USA* (pp. 187–201).
9. CrowdStrike. (2015). VENOM Vulnerability. Retrieved May 2016, from http://venom.crowdstrike.com/.
10. Danev, B., Masti, R. J., Karame, G. O., & Capkun, S. (2011). Enabling secure VM-vTPM migration in private clouds. In *Proceedings of the 27th Annual Computer Security Applications Conference (ASAC)* (pp. 187–196). New York, NY, USA: ACM
11. Dargie, W. (2014). Estimation of the cost of VM migration. In *23rd International Conference on Computer Communication and Networks (ICCCN)* pp. 1–8.
12. Divakarla, U., & Chandrasekaran, K. (2016). Trusted path between two entities in Cloud. In *6th International Conference on Cloud System and Big Data Engineering (Confluence)* pp. 157–162.
13. Duan, Y., Fu, G., Zhou, N., Sun, X., Narendra, N. C, & Hu, B. (2015). Everything as a service (XaaS) on the cloud: origins, current and future trends. In *IEEE 8th International Conference on Cloud Computing* pp. 621–628.
14. Eldred, M., Adams, C., & Good, A. (2014) Trust challenges in a high performance cloud computing project. In *IEEE 6th International Conference on Cloud Computing Technology and Science (CloudCom)* (pp. 1045–1050).
15. Fan, P., Zhao, B., Shi, Y., Chen, Z., & Ni, M. (2015). An improved vTPM-VM live migration protocol. *Wuhan University Journal of Natural Sciences, 20*(6), 512–520.
16. Fernandes, D. A. B., Soares, L. F. B., Gomes, J. V., Freire, M. M., & Inácio, P. R. M. (2014). Security Issues in Cloud Environments—A Survey. *International Journal of Information Security (IJIS): Special Issue Named Security in Cloud Computing, 13*(2), 113–170.
17. Garfinkel, T., Pfaff, B., Chow, J., Rosenblum, M., & Boneh, D. (2003). Terra: A virtual machine-based platform for trusted computing. In *Proceedings of the Nineteenth ACM Symposium on Operating Systems Principles, SOSP '03* (pp 193–206). ACM.
18. Gonzales, D., Kaplan, J., Saltzman, E., Winkelman, Z., & Woods, D. (2015). Cloud-trust—A security assessment model for infrastructure as a service (IaaS) clouds. *IEEE Transactions on Cloud Computing PP*(99), 1–14.
19. Hosseinzadeh, S., Laurén, S., & Leppänen, V. (2016). Security in container-based virtualization through vTPM. In *Proceedings of the 9th International Conference on Utility and Cloud Computing* pp. 214–219. ACM.
20. Javanmard, M., Salehi, M. A, & Zonouz, S. (2015). TSC: Trustworthy and scalable cytometry. In 2015 IEEE 17th International Conference on High Performance Computing and Communications (HPCC), 2015 IEEE 7th International Symposium on Cyberspace Safety and Security (CSS), 2015 IEEE 12th International Conferen on Embedded Software and Systems (ICESS) (pp. 1356–1360). IEEE.
21. Jayaram, K., Safford, D., Sharma, U., Naik, V., Pendarakis, D., & Tao, S. (2014). Trustworthy geographically fenced hybrid clouds. In *Proceedings of the 15th International Middleware Conference* (pp. 37–48). ACM.
22. Khan, I., Rehman, H., & Anwar, Z. (2011). Design and deployment of a trusted eucalyptus cloud. In *2011 IEEE International Conference on Cloud Computing (CLOUD)* (pp. 380–387). IEEE.
23. Ko, R. K., & Will, M. A. (2014). Progger: An efficient, Tamper-evident Kernel-space logger for cloud data provenance tracking. In *2014 IEEE 7th International Conference on Cloud Computing (CLOUD)* (pp. 881–889). IEEE.

24. Lee, B., Awad, A., & Awad, M. (2015). Towards secure provenance in the cloud: A survey. In *2015 IEEE/ACM 8th International Conference on Utility and Cloud Computing (UCC)* (pp. 577–582). IEEE.

25. Leelipushpam, P. G. J, & Sharmila, J. (2013). Live VM migration techniques in cloud environment a survey. In 2013 IEEE Conference on Information & Communication Technologies (ICT), (pp. 408–413). IEEE.

26. Li, J., Squicciarini, A., Lin, D., Liang, S., & Jia, C. (2015). SecLoc: Securing location-sensitive storage in the cloud. In *Proceedings of the 20th ACM Symposium on Access Control Models and Technologies* (pp. 51–61). ACM.

27. Memarian, M. R., Conti, M., & Leppänen, V. (2015). EyeCloud: A Botcloud Detection System. In *2015 IEEE Trustcom/BigDataSE/ISPA* (Vol. 1, pp. 1067–1072).

28. NIST. (2011). The NIST definition of cloud computing. Retrieved June 2016, from http://nvlpubs.nist.gov/nistpubs/Legacy/SP/nistspecialpublication800-145.pdf.

29. Noor, T. H., Sheng, Q. Z., Yao, L., Dustdar, S., & Ngu, A. H. H. (2016). CloudArmor: Supporting reputation-based trust management for cloud services. *IEEE Transactions on Parallel and Distributed Systems, 27*(2), 367–380.

30. Park, K. W., Han, J., Chung, J., & Park, K. H. (2013). THEMIS: A Mutually verifiable billing system for the cloud computing environment. *IEEE Transactions on Services Computing, 6*(3), 300–313.

31. Park, S., Yoon, J. N., Kang, C., Kim, K. H., & Han, T. (2015). TGVisor: A tiny hypervisor-based trusted geolocation framework for mobile cloud clients. In *2015 3rd IEEE International Conference on Mobile Cloud Computing, Services, and Engineering (MobileCloud)* (pp. 99–108). IEEE.

32. Rocha, F., & Correia, M. (2011). Lucy in the sky without diamonds: Stealing confidential data in the cloud. In *IEEE/IFIP 41st International Conference on Dependable Systems and Networks Workshops (DSN-W)* (pp. 129–134).

33. Rocha, F., Abreu, S., & Correia, M. (2011). The Final Frontier: Confidentiality and Privacy in the Cloud. *Computer, 44*(9), 44–50.

34. Santos, N., Gummadi, K. P., & Rodrigues, R. (2009). Towards trusted cloud computing. In *Proceedings of the 2009 Conference on Hot Topics in Cloud Computing, USENIX Association, Berkeley, CA, USA, HotCloud'09.*

35. Shin, J., Kim, Y., Park, W., & Park, C. (2012). DFCloud: A TPM-based secure data access control method of cloud storage in mobile devices. In *2012 IEEE 4th International Conference on Cloud Computing Technology and Science (CloudCom)* (pp. 551–556). IEEE.

36. Singh, N. K., Patel, Y. S., Das, U., & Chatterjee, A. (2014). NUYA: An encrypted mechanism for securing cloud data from data mining attacks. In *2014 International Conference on Data Mining and Intelligent Computing (ICDMIC)* (pp. 1–6). IEEE.

37. Somani, G., Gaur, M. S., Sanghi, D., & Conti, M. (2016) DDoS attacks in cloud computing: Collateral damage to non-targets. *Computer Networks.*

38. Syed, T. A., Musa, S., Rahman, A., & Jan, S. (2015). Towards secure instance migration in the cloud. In *2015 International Conference on Cloud Computing (ICCC)* (pp. 1–6). IEEE.

39. Taha, M. M. B., Chaisiri, S., Ko, R. K. (2015). Trusted tamper-evident data provenance. In *2015 IEEE Trustcom/BigDataSE/ISPA* (Vol. 1, pp. 646–653). IEEE.

40. Toegl, R., Winkler, T., Nauman, M., & Hong, T. (2009). Towards platform-independent trusted computing. In *Proceedings Of The 2009 Acm Workshop On Scalable Trusted Computing* (pp. 61–66). ACM.

41. Wallom, D., Turilli, M., Martin, A., Raun, A., Taylor, G., Hargreaves, N., et al. (2011). myTrustedCloud: Trusted cloud infrastructure for security-critical computation and data management. In *IEEE Third International Conference on Cloud Computing Technology and Science (CloudCom).* (pp. 247–254).

42. Wei, L., Zhu, H., Cao, Z., Jia, W., & Vasilakos, A. V. (2010). SecCloud: Bridging secure storage and computation in cloud. In *IEEE 30th International Conference on Distributed Computing Systems Workshops* (pp. 52–61).

43. Zawoad, S., & Hasan, R. (2015) FECloud: A trustworthy forensics-enabled cloud architecture. In *Proceedings of 11th Annual International Federation for Information Processing WG 11.9 International Conference on Digital Forensics* (pp. 271–285).
44. Zhang, R., Su, X., Wang, J., Wang, C., Liu, W., & Lau, R. W. H. (2015). On Mitigating the Risk of Cross-VM Covert Channels in a Public Cloud. *IEEE Transactions on Parallel and Distributed Systems, 26*(8), 2327–2339.

Printed in the United States
By Bookmasters